You know when you think about writing a book, you think it is overwhelming. But, actually, you break it down into tiny little tasks any moron could do.
ANNIE DILLARD

I have rewritten—often several times—every word I have ever published. My pencils outlast their erasers.   VLADIMIR NABOKOV

Writing for me is a very happy activity—I actually enjoy the time of writing more than publication day.   EDWARD HOAGLAND

A writer is a person for whom writing is more difficult than it is for other people.   THOMAS MANN

I am never as clear about any matter as when I have just finished writing about it.   JAMES VAN ALLEN

A note: despair at the badness of the book: can't think how I ever could write such stuff—and with such excitement: that's yesterday: today I think it good again. A note, by way of advising other Virginias with other books that this is the way of the thing: up down up down—and Lord know the truth.
VIRGINIA WOOLF

The St. Martin's Guide to Writing

Short Edition

THE ST. MARTIN'S

RISE B. AXELROD

University of California, Riverside

CHARLES R. COOPER

University of California, San Diego

GUIDE TO WRITING

SHORT EDITION

ST. MARTIN'S PRESS
New York

Design by Betty Binns Graphics/Betty Binns

ACKNOWLEDGMENTS

Agee, James. "The Treasure of the Sierra Madre." Reprinted by permission of Grosset & Dunlap from AGEE ON FILM, Vol. 1, copyright © 1958 by The James Agee Trust.

Angelou, Maya. "The Store," From I KNOW WHY THE CAGED BIRD SINGS, by Maya Angelou. Copyright © 1969 by Maya Angelou. Reprinted by permission of Random House, Inc.

Attenborough, David. Excerpted from LIFE ON EARTH by David Attenborough. Copyright © 1979 by David Attenborough Productions, Ltd. By permission of Little, Brown and Company and by permission of Wm. Collins and Sons Co., Ltd.

Baker, Russell. From GROWING UP by Russell Baker. Copyright © 1982 by Russell Baker. Reprinted by permission of Congdon & Weed, Inc., New York.

Baraka, Amiri. Excerpted from THE AUTOBIOGRAPHY OF LEROI JONES/AMIRI BARAKA. Copyright © Imamu Amiri Baraka 1984. Freundlich Books, New York. Used by permission.

Bly, Carol. Pages 59–63 from LETTERS FROM THE COUNTRY by Carol Bly. Copyright © 1977 by Carol Bly. Reprinted by permission of Harper & Row, Publishers, Inc.

Didion, Joan. "Holy Water." From THE WHITE ALBUM by Joan Didion. Copyright © 1979 by Joan Didion. Reprinted by permission of Simon & Schuster, Inc.

Dillard, Annie. Specified excerpts (approximately 500 words in toto) from TEACHING A STONE TO TALK: Expeditions and Encounters by Annie Dillard. Copyright © 1982 by Annie Dillard. Reprinted by permission of Harper & Row, Publishers, Inc.

Fuchs, Victor. Excerpt reprinted by permission of the publishers from HOW WE LIVE by Victor R. Fuchs, Cambridge, Mass.: Harvard University Press, Copyright © 1983 by the President and Fellows of Harvard College.

Acknowledgments and copyrights continue at the back of the book on pages 562–563, which constitute an extension of the copyright page.

To the Instructor

Our goal in this book is to help students discover and develop ideas. We aim to teach them to manage the writing process, to think critically and use evidence wisely. The *St. Martin's Guide to Writing* continues a centuries-old tradition that treats rhetoric very seriously indeed, not just as a matter of producing correct prose but as one of thinking, reading, and writing intelligently. To the best insights from that tradition, we have added what we believe to be the most promising developments in the "New Rhetoric" that has emerged in this country since the 1960s.

A comprehensive rhetoric with readings, the *St. Martin's Guide to Writing,* Short Edition, introduces students to the major forms of nonfiction writing: personal sketches, reports, proposals, evaluations, explanations, literary interpretations, and profiles. Part One provides several models of each kind of writing (both professional and student) along with detailed commentary and carefully structured guides to help students understand the constraints and possibilities of each kind of writing they attempt. The guides include specially designed invention activities as well as advice for drafting, critiquing a draft, revising, and editing. Each chapter ends with a section called "A Writer at Work," which shows one stage of the writing process from a student essay in that chapter.

Part Two looks at the basic strategies, or modes, of writing; at logic and reasoning; at paragraphing and coherence; and at purpose, audience, voice, and style. Examples and exercises are almost all taken from contemporary nonfiction, and many exercises deal with selections appearing in Part One. This cross-referencing will, we hope, facilitate teaching writing strategies together with the model readings.

Part Three covers research and invention strategies. The chapter on invention and inquiry catalogues various mapping, writing, and reading activities students can use to generate and organize material for their writing. These general invention heuristics can be used independently or to supplement the more particularized invention strategies in Part One. The research chapters discuss both field and library research and include thorough guidelines for using and documenting sources, with detailed examples of the two prominent documentation styles, those of the Modern Language Association and the American Psychological Association. The part concludes with a sample student research paper.

Part Four treats a special kind of academic writing: essay examinations. Here we show students how to analyze different kinds of exam questions and offer strategies for writing answers. The chapter is illustrated with actual questions from courses throughout the disciplines, plus two sample student essays.

The *St. Martin's Guide to Writing* contains much that is familiar in current college rhetorics as well as much that is new. Among the noteworthy new features we would like to point out are the practical guides to writing, the particularization of invention, the integration of modes and aims, and the articulation between critical reading and writing.

Practical Guides to Writing. We do not merely talk about the composing process; rather, we offer practical, flexible guides that will lead students through the entire process, from invention to final revision and self-evaluation. Thus, the book is more than just a rhetoric that students will refer to occasionally. It is a guidebook that will actually help students learn to write. Because these writing guides are commonsensical and easy to follow, students quickly internalize their lessons. They learn how to assess the rhetorical situation, how to identify the kinds of information they will need, how to ask probing questions and find answers, and how to organize their writing to achieve their purpose most effectively.

Particularization of Invention. Like most other current rhetorics, we offer a full catalogue of general invention heuristics. But because we recognize how hard it is for students to know when and how to use these tools, we have designed specific invention strategies for each writing guide in Part One. By particularizing invention, the *St. Martin's Guide* helps students discover the pertinent questions to ask in any writing situation. Consequently, students learn the general heuristics the old-fashioned way— by generalizing from their own experience. Moreover, our treatment of invention promotes a certain recursiveness in the composing process by encouraging students to continue generating and testing their ideas as well as analyzing and synthesizing information at all stages of planning, drafting, and revising. That is, we teach students to put off closure until they have explored the full possibilities of their topic.

Integration of Modes and Aims. The *St. Martin's Guide* treats the traditional modes of writing—describing, narrating, defining, classifying, and so forth—from two perspectives: as forms to be mastered, and as writing strategies to be used to achieve particular purposes. Unlike many current rhetorics and readers, we do not distinguish writing by its modes but rather by its aims. Hence, while we focus on craft in our discussion of the modes in Part Two, we emphasize the integration of modes with aims through exercises analyzing how the modes are used strategically in the essays in Part One.

Articulation between Critical Reading and Writing. Not only do we have hundreds of selections (including thirty-eight complete essays) for students to analyze, but we treat readings somewhat differently than other rhetorics or readers. Because we see a close relationship between the abilities to read critically and to write intelligently, the *St. Martin's Guide* combines reading instruction with writing instruction. The questions for analysis following the readings make students aware of how they as readers respond to a text and at the same time help them understand the decisions writers make. Students are challenged to apply these insights to their own writing as they imagine their prospective readers, set goals, and write and revise their drafts.

As a rhetoric and reader, the *St. Martin's Guide* may be used in courses with diverse emphases. Courses focusing on the writing process, for example, might rely most heavily on the writing guides and the "Writer at Work" sections of Part One, whereas writing workshops might be centered on the guides' invention activities and shared critical readings of student drafts. For courses based on the traditional modes of writing, this book has a chapter on each one. Such courses might emphasize the chapters on modes in Part Two, with selected readings assigned from Part One. Courses in writing centered in readings, on the other hand, have nearly forty complete pieces and more than a hundred passages to consider.

Detailed course plans for these and other courses, as well as commentary and teaching suggestions for every chapter in the book, can be found in the Instructor's Manual that accompanies both this short edition and the longer edition with handbook. Whatever approach is taken, we hope our book will provide an exciting and innovative course of study for your students.

ACKNOWLEDGMENTS

We owe a great deal to others. The history of rhetoric reaches back to Greece in the fifth century B.C., and among our predecessors are teachers and scholars—Aristotle, Quintilian, and Cicero in classical times; Erasmus from the early Renaissance; the eighteenth-century Scotsmen George Campbell and Hugh Blair; and Henry Day, the author of the most distinguished American rhetoric of the nineteenth century—who believed that rhetoric instruction was of great intellectual, social, and ethical importance. They considered rhetoric to be a study of thinking, speaking, and writing intelligently and responsibly, not a matter of memorizing rules and producing correct prose. From this humanistic tradition comes our belief that students must learn to write well to realize their potential as thinkers, and as citizens.

And we owe a great deal to our contemporaries. Any list of debts will necessarily be incomplete, but we would be remiss in failing to acknowledge how much we have learned from Arthur Applebee, Walter Beale, Mary Beaven, Rexford Brown, Kenneth Burke, James Britton, Wallace Chafe, Francis Christensen, Robert Connors, Robert de Beaugrande, Gabriel Della-Piana, Peter Elbow, Janet Emig, Jeanne Fahnestock, Linda Flower, Toby Fulwiler, Sidney Greenbaum, Joseph Grimes, Anne Gere, M.A.K. Halliday, Ruqnia Hasan, Thom Hawkins, John Hayes, George Hillocks, David Holbrook, James Kinneavy, William Labov, Richard Larson, Richard Lloyd-Jones, Elaine Maimon, Ann Matsuhashi, John Mellon, James Moffett, Ina Mullis, Donald Murray, Lee Odell, Anthony Petrosky, Ira Progoff, Sir Randolph Quirk, Tristine Rainer, Richard Rieke, D. Gordon Rohman, Mike Rose, John Schultz, Marie Secor, Mina Shaughnessy, Malcolm Sillars, Frank Smith, William Strong, Barbara Tomlinson, Stephen Toulmin, Tuen van Dijk, P. C. Wasan, John Warnock, Eliot Wigginton, Joseph Williams, Ross Winterowd, Richard Young, and Robert Zoellner.

We must also acknowledge immeasurable lessons learned from all the writers, professional and student alike, whose works we read in search of selections and examples for this text. The clarity and grace found in much current nonfiction prose have repeatedly astounded us. To all the writers represented in this text we owe a great debt—together, they have set a high standard indeed for all writers. Our aim has been not to contradict their practice by anything we recommend to students in this book.

We are especially indebted to the staff, instructors, and students in the Third College Composition Program at the University of California at San Diego. Since 1979, this book has been developed very gradually in courses there, with instructors and students helping us to discover what worked and what did not. We appreciate their candor and support. Of about forty instructors who used drafts of the book, a few have provided exceptionally helpful criticism and advice: Richard Boyd, Sheryl Fontaine, Kate Gardner, Keith Grant-Davie, Tom Larson, Carol Mavor, Cezar Ornatowski, Kathryn Shevelow, Judith Shushan, Peggy Stamon, Erika Suderburg, Dawn Tebor, Carol Vernallis, and Barbara Wrasidlo. Betty Cain offered astute criticism and steady encouragement, and Barbara Tomlinson contributed insight and kind support. Had Phyllis Campbell not managed the program's daily affairs so well, no one would have had time to write or try out—new teaching materials. We owe an enormous debt to Rebekah Kessab, who did a superlative job of typing and producing for classroom use the steadily changing early versions of many of the chapters in this book. We would like to express special thanks to our students, for generous and willing feedback and for the student essays in this book.

Colleagues at the University of California at Riverside also contributed mightily. We especially wish to thank Steven Axelrod, David Bender, John Briggs, Gladys Craig, Gretchen Davidson, Linda Halisky, Melinda Rosenthal, Kris Scarano, and Aliessa Zoecklin.

Writing instructors across the country have contributed their time and expertise to helping us make this a better book. We could not have done without the generous and valuable criticism of Lucien Agosta, Kansas State University; Harry Brent, Bernard Baruch College, CUNY; Ruth Clogston, University of New Hampshire; Robert Connors, University of New Hampshire; Rick Eden, University of New Mexico–Albuquerque; Lester Faigley, University of Texas–Austin; David Kaufer, Carnegie-Mellon University; Barry Kroll, Indiana University–Bloomington; Susan Landstrom, University of North Carolina–Chapel Hill; Ben McClelland, Rhode Island College; George and Stephanie McCulley, Michigan Technological University; Donald Murray, University of New Hampshire; and Michael Vivion, University of Missouri–Kansas City. We want especially to thank Richard Larson, Herbert H. Lehman College, CUNY, and Nancy Sommers, Rutgers University.

To the staff at St. Martin's Press we cannot begin to express our thanks: Tom Broadbent, who had the foresight and generosity to sign us; Marilyn Moller, who edited the manuscript with great skill and sensitivity; Mark Gallaher and Andrea Guidoboni, who undertook tasks large and small with energy and efficiency; and most of all our editor, Nancy Perry, who was with us at the start, stuck with us through the hard times, and will, we hope, stay with us for many years to come.

Finally, we want to thank our families: Rise Axelrod's husband, Steven; son, Jeremiah; and parents, Edna and Alexander Borenstein; and Charles Cooper's wife, Mary Anne; daughters, Susanna and Laura; and son, Vincent.

Contents

GUIDE TO WRITING

A WRITER AT WORK

5

Reporting Information   128

GUIDE TO WRITING

6

READINGS

10 *Profiling People and Places* 304

The St. Martin's Guide to Writing

Short Edition

Introduction

Why is writing important? Is good writing worth the required effort, or has advanced technology reduced the importance of writing? Are words now processed, rather than written? If you have just opened this book and are about to begin a writing course, you may be asking yourself questions like these. If so, read on. This book has some of the answers.

Writing makes a special contribution to the way people think. When we write, we compose meanings. We put together facts and ideas and make something new, whether in a letter home, in a college essay, or in a memo to the boss. When we write, we create a complex web of meaning in which sentences have different relationships to each other. Some sentences are general and some specific; some expand a point and others qualify it; some define and others illustrate. These sentences, moreover, are connected in a still larger set of relationships, with every sentence related in some way to every other. Controlling the complex process is one of the challenges of writing.

Writing also contributes uniquely to the way we learn. When we take notes during lectures or as we read, writing enables us to store new information in memory. Taking notes permits us later to review for tests or to find information for an essay. When we outline or summarize new information, writing provides an overview of a subject and fosters close analysis of it. Note taking is almost a form of conversation—even debate—with the author. Thus, writing makes us more active, critical readers.

But writing makes another important contribution to learning. Because it is always a composing of new meaning, writing enables us to find and establish our own connections and networks of information and ideas. It allows us to bring together and connect new and old ideas. Writing enables us to clarify and deepen our understanding of a new concept and to find ways to connect it to other ideas within a discipline. Thus, writing tests, clarifies, and extends understanding.

Writing does still more: it contributes to personal development. As we write we become more potent thinkers and active learners, and we come eventually to a better understanding of ourselves through the recording, clarifying, and organizing of our personal experiences and our innermost thoughts.

By now it should be obvious to you that writing helps fulfill our need to communicate. The impulse to write can be as urgent as the need to

1

converse with someone sitting across the table in a restaurant or to respond to a provocative comment in a classroom discussion. Sometimes we want readers to know what we know; we want to share something new. Sometimes we want to influence our readers' decisions, actions, or beliefs. We may even want to irritate or outrage readers. Or we may want to amuse or flatter them. Writing allows us to communicate in all of these ways.

Good writing also contributes to success in college and on the job. Students who write well will most likely learn more and earn better grades, for a student's writing is often the only basis an instructor has for an evaluation. Your first job may not require you to write, but later advancement often depends on skill in writing letters, memos, reports, and proposals. The United States in the 1980s has become an "information" society, one in which the ability to organize and synthesize information and to write intelligently and effectively will be even more important than it was in the past. Computers do not compose. They store information composed by people. The ability to write will continue to be a decisive factor in the careers of larger and larger numbers of people every year. But for many college students, writing is more of an obstacle than an opportunity. Because writing seems difficult and threatening, they approach it reluctantly, even with fear. Knowing *how* writing works, however, can dispel the mystery and reduce the threat.

HOW WRITING WORKS

What is the nature of the writing process? From research and published interviews with writers as well as our own experience as writers, we know certain well-established features of the process.

Perhaps the most important point to remember is this: writing is not a mystery, something that can be accomplished by only a few. To be sure, writing is a complex process and, as such, contains elements of mystery and surprise. But we know and believe that writing is a skill that anyone can learn to manage. Greatness as a writer requires talent, a certain kind of experience and training, and, above all, an early commitment and de-

3

termination. Only a few of us will pursue that dream. But we can all learn to write well enough to feel confident that we can handle any writing situation we encounter in college or on the job.

Writing is a process of discovery. Experienced writers rarely gather and understand immediately all the information they need. They collect miscellaneous facts and concepts, start writing, and then let the writing lead them to understanding. They know they will be making significant discoveries as they write.

> I don't see writing as a communication of something already discovered, as "truths" already known. Rather, I see writing as a job of experiment. It's like any discovery job; you don't know what's going to happen until you try it.   William Stafford

Even if the process seems messy and meandering, writers tend to trust it.

> I don't believe a writer should know too much where he's going.
> James Thurber

In fact, writers are likely to trust the power of language to lead them to new ideas and plans.

> The language leads, and we continue to follow where it leads.
> Wright Morris

Writing gives form to thought. When we write something down, we can examine it from one angle and then another, studying its many facets as we would a diamond. Many writers claim they write to discover what they think.

> I write entirely to find out what I'm thinking, what I'm looking at, what I see and what it means.   Joan Didion
> How do I know what I think until I see what I say.   E. M. Forster

Even when they are away from their desks, writers are always alert for ideas. They keep journals and notebooks. Always they are ready for new thoughts and discoveries.

> I never quite know when I'm not writing.   James Thurber

Experienced writers accept the fact that writing takes time and hard work.

> I believe in miracles in every area of life *except* writing. Experience has shown me that there are no miracles in writing. The only thing that produces good writing is hard work.   Isaac Bashevis Singer

The hard work in writing comes in thinking things out on paper, in keeping journals, filing notes, and being alert for new ideas.

> You have to work problems out for yourself, on paper. Put the stuff down and read it—to see if it works.   Joyce Cary

Sometimes the hardest part of writing is getting started, just writing that first sentence. You will be reassured to know what agony this first sentence sometimes causes published writers:

> I suffer always from fear of putting down that first line. It is amazing the terrors, the magics, the prayers, the straightening shyness that assails one. John Steinbeck

Most writers know they will solve problems if they can just get started and keep on going. Consequently, they have all kinds of strategies to keep the writing flowing, particularly during early drafting. Since almost all writers revise their first drafts, they need not worry about getting it right the first time. They know that agonizing indecision is unproductive.

> There may be some reason to question the whole idea of fineness and care in writing. Maybe something can get into sloppy writing that would elude careful writing. I'm not terribly careful myself, actually. I write fairly rapidly if I get going. . . . In trying to treat words as chisel strokes, you run the risk of losing the quality of utterance, the rhythm of utterance, the happiness.   John Updike

Experienced writers know that strong writing does not always emerge in a first draft. Writers are revisers. "Writing *is* rewriting," Donald Murray insists. Writers approach revising as an opportunity to gain an entirely new perspective on a topic. They may move paragraphs around, rewrite whole sections, or add substantial new material. They may even throw out the whole draft and start over.

> What makes me happy is rewriting. . . . It's like cleaning house, getting rid of all the junk, getting things in the right order, tightening things up. Ellen Goodman

> I have never thought of myself as a good writer. Anyone who wants reassurance of that should read one of my first drafts. But I'm one of the world's great revisers.   James Michener

For most writers frustration in the early period of drafting is natural. So they establish routines and rituals to make the process familiar and comfortable. They set a time to write and find a quiet place away from interruptions.

In spite of the time it takes, the inevitable delays, and the hard work, writers persist because of the great personal fulfillment and pride that writing often brings. Many writers write in order to earn a living, but it is not true that they live lives of unrelenting torment. They struggle, but they also celebrate, and they find great satisfaction in the process of writing.

Well, it's a beautiful feeling, even if it's hard work.   Anne Sexton

There is much more to say about how writing works. Although it requires commitment and hard work, it is something you can learn to do. You can learn more about your own way of managing the writing process and develop new skills to make the process even easier to control. You can accept the fact that writing usually requires rewriting and give yourself the time you need to draft and revise your essays. You can expand the number of writing strategies you use and learn the special requirements of the particular kinds of writing you need to master. This book will help you develop these skills and understand the writing process. Using it will give you confidence that you can make the writing process work for you.

ABOUT THIS BOOK

This book is divided into two major sections:

Part I, Chapters 2 through 10, will guide you in composing several important kinds of nonfiction prose: stories about remembered events, sketches of people and places, reports, proposals, evaluations, explanations, literary interpretations, and profiles. Each chapter invites you to read carefully the work of published writers and college students and then to write an essay of your own.

Parts II through IV, Chapters 11 through 22, illustrate basic writing and research strategies. They also provide guidelines for writing research papers and essay exams, and for using sources.

As you work on the essays in Part I, you will be engaged in a writing process of inventing, drafting, and revising. Each chapter in Part I is designed to support your efforts in all of these stages of the writing process.

Invention and research   The Guide to Writing in each essay assignment chapter in Part I begins with invention activities designed to help you

- ☐ find a topic
- ☐ discover what you already know about it
- ☐ research it further
- ☐ test your ideas in writing
- ☐ analyze your readers

These activities engage you in the thinking, planning, problem solving, and writing required for a full exploration of your topic and a promising first draft. Invention—gathering information, searching your memory, generating ideas, making decisions—is the basic ongoing preoccupation of writers. Invention is necessary to produce any writing of any type or length. Writers cannot choose *whether* to invent. They can only decide *how* to invent. Systematic invention in writing can be especially productive if carried out intensely before you begin drafting.

The invention activities at the beginning of each Guide to Writing ask you to think and write about your topic in systematic ways. They may result in quite a bit of writing. The activities include timed exploratory writing, the making of lists and charts, and the stating and clarifying of your focus or thesis. You may choose to complete all the invention activities, or you may select only a few that seem especially appropriate to your topic. Even if you do all of the activities, you will usually not need more than two hours to complete them. The easiest and most productive way to complete the invention activities is to do only one or two each day for several days, thus allowing your mind the longest possible time to do its work on your topic. Completing all the activities gives you the advantage of fully exploring your topic before you attempt a draft.

But there are other ways to use the invention activities. You might feel so confident about your topic and so certain about what you want to achieve that you will attempt a complete draft immediately. During or after the completion of the draft, you might become aware of problems, which the invention activities could help you solve. Even if you do not see problems in your first draft, reviewing the invention activities would help you see possibilities you have overlooked.

The invention activities may also be useful when you revise. As a result of your own evaluation of your draft or comments from your instructor or classmates, you may discover problems that must be corrected. The invention activities will help you to correct the problems in your draft. They can help you make small changes or major reorganizations; they can even be useful for drafting entirely new sections.

The invention activities, then, may help you at several stages in the writing of an essay: during initial exploration, while drafting, and during revising. The special advantage of the invention activities in each essay assignment chapter is that they let you go right to work inventing solutions to the problems of a particular kind of writing. Whatever your topic may be, the activities will help ensure full, rich, focused invention.

The catalog of strategies in Chapter 18: Invention and Inquiry complements the invention activities for each essay assignment. You may explore your topic with one or more of these general invention activities. Unlike the focused invention activities in the essay assignment chapters, each activity in the invention catalog may be used to explore or plan many kinds of writing. Because the catalog activities are so adaptable, they are valuable to know. You may need to practice an activity two or three times before you feel confident using it on your own.

Planning and drafting

Once a period of intense invention is completed, you should review what you have learned about your topic and start to plan your essay. After thinking about your goals and making a tentative outline, you will be ready to draft. Drafting challenges you to put your ideas in order. Invention does not cease with drafting, but it does become less free; instead of thinking of new ideas and gathering information, your task is to forge new and meaningful relations among your ideas and information. The Guide to Writing in each chapter offers specific as well as general advice on drafting an essay.

Drafting gives you a chance to bring all your information together into a readable essay. This draft is usually called a first draft—the initial effort to find out what you have to say but surely not the only draft you will need. Some call it a rough draft, indicating an essay that is not yet polished or smooth, while others call it a discovery draft, meaning that you are still trying to discover what you want to say and how to say it. It has even been called a zero draft, that is, a draft that does not count yet.

Although a draft is rough, quick, and full of discoveries, it should be as complete as you can make it. Unless you are writing under the most extreme time pressure, with no chance to make any changes, you should expect to revise this draft, possibly changing it substantially, maybe even throwing it out and starting over. As you begin your first draft, you should try to keep in mind a number of helpful and practical points, many of which have assisted professional writers as they begin drafting:

Choose the best time and place. You can write a draft any time and any place, as you probably already know. You can write in the bathtub or in a restaurant. You can add a sentence while waiting for the bus. Writing gets done under the most surprising conditions. However, drafting is likely to go smoothly if you choose a time and place ideally suited for sustained and thoughtful work. The experience of writers (reported mainly in interviews) suggests you need a place where you can concentrate for a few hours without repeated interruptions. Writers usually find one place where they write best, and they return to that place whenever they have to write. Try to find such a place for yourself. On a college campus, you may discover the quietest corner of the quietest floor of the library. Or you and your roommate may work out a schedule of quiet times for writing. And—of equal importance—arrange to write at your own best time of day, when you are most relaxed, creative, and productive.

Have your tools at hand. If you are well-supplied, you will not have to interrupt your drafting to search for an eraser or a piece of paper. If you draft by hand, have plenty of paper and pencils or pens within sight. Be generous in supplying yourself with tools. Have a big stack of paper. Have a dozen sharpened pencils, an eraser, and a good pencil sharpener close by. If you type, have plenty of typing paper and at least one extra ribbon. Later, for rearranging a draft you will need scissors and tape (or paste or a stapler). For revision, you will also need a dictionary and a thesaurus.

The word processor is an increasingly common tool for composing in writing. If you own one, be sure you have a spare disk or two. If you have your own printer, keep a generous amount of paper on hand. Have a spare printing wheel to ensure dark, readable printing. Since you can only see about twenty lines of type at one time on the screen, you may want to print out your invention writing or research notes before you plan your draft. That way, you can spread out for inspection everything you have turned up.

Make revision easy. Write on only one side of the page. Leave wide margins. Write on every other line or triple-space your typing. Laying your draft out on the page this way invites changes, additions, and cutting and taping when you revise.

Set reasonable goals. Set yourself the goal of writing one page or paragraph at a time. A goal of completing an entire essay may be so intimidating that it keeps you from starting. Just aim for a small part of the essay at a time.

Lower your expectations. Be satisfied with less than perfect writing. Remember, you are working on a draft you will be able to revise. Approach the draft as an experiment or an exercise, and do not take it too seriously. Try things out. Follow diversions. You can always go back and cross out a sentence or a section.

Write any sentence first. Do not agonize over the first sentence. Just write. Do not try to write a perfect first sentence or a perfect opening paragraph of your revised essay.

Do the easy parts first. If you have trouble with the introduction, write an anecdote or example or argument first, if that seems easier. If you have a lot of information, start with the part you understand best. If you get stuck at a difficult spot, skip over it and go on to an easier part. If you cannot think of just the right word, or if you have forgotten an important fact, just keep on drafting. You can search out the fact or find the elusive word later.

Write quickly. If you have reasonable goals, have not set your expectations too high, and are doing the easy parts first, then you should be able to draft quickly. Now and then, of course, you will want to reread what you have written, but do not reread obsessively. Return to drafting new material as soon as possible. Avoid too much editing or revising. You need not have everything exactly right in the draft. Say what you want to say as well as you can and move on. Review your notes, make a plan, and then put your notes aside. You can always return to them later or refer to them if you need an exact quote or fact. Over-reliance on notes may get in the way of smooth drafting. If you want to delete a phrase or sentence, draw a line through it rather than erasing. Perhaps you will want to use the phrase or sentence later. Add copy above the line or in the margins, but *not* on the back.

Take short breaks—and reward yourself! Drafting can be hard work. You may find a need for a short break to refresh yourself. But be careful not to wander off for too long or you may lose momentum! Set small goals and reward yourself regularly. That makes it easier to stay at the task of drafting.

Revising   To read a draft critically, you need to be both positive and skeptical—positive in that you are trying to create an essay that is as good as it possibly can be, skeptical in that you are questioning every assumption and decision that has been made. Writers naturally read and reread as they write, just as they keep refocusing their thoughts as they plan. Rereading should be a constructive process. When the draft is completed, a good critical reading should help the writer re-envision the essay and could very well lead to substantial rewriting.

The Guide to Writing in each chapter in Part I includes a section on reading a draft with a critical eye, which you or others may use to analyze your draft to see how it might be improved with revision. The Guide offers specific advice for revising the particular kind of writing you are working on.

In addition to the specific advice on revising in each chapter, we offer here some general advice on revising.

Seek advice. Response from readers is critically important for revising. Get some if you possibly can. Ask readers to talk to you about all aspects of your paper, not just spelling and punctuation. Ask them about your beginning and ending, focus and pacing, information and ideas. Ask them where they were bored, surprised, confused, whether they wanted to know more or less about your topic.

Listen objectively to everything readers have to say, and try not to be irritated or defensive. Accept advice judiciously. Some, but not all, advice is likely to be helpful.

Refocus on readers and purpose. If you can, put the draft aside for a day or two. When you read it again, you will be able to see it much more objectively. Before you read a draft in order to revise it, refocus on your readers and purpose. Ask yourself: how can I improve this draft to make it more readable and memorable for my readers? How can I change it in order to more fully realize my purpose in writing?

Take action. Read to take action, to make changes, even big changes. Be prepared to write more, to cut, to simplify, to keep the good parts. Be prepared even to start over.

Read first for an overall impression. On first reading, do not be distracted by errors of spelling, punctuation, or word choice. Look at big issues. Look for clear focus, strong direction of movement, forecast and follow-through, framing, consistent tone, novelty, quality of ideas. Try to imagine that someone else wrote the draft. Stepping outside may make it easier for you to decide to make major revisions.

Read again for the development of parts or features. Read again, slowly this time, evaluating individual parts of the essay. Read the beginning and ending, looking for coherence and development of paragraphs, adequacy of illustration and information. If your revision has been extensive, you may need to cut the draft apart to rearrange the parts, discard some material, and add new material.

Word processors are designed to make the process of major revision easy. They let you move parts around with the touch of a button. As a precaution against accidental erasure in the word processor, however, you may want to have a printout of a draft before you start revising it. In revising a long paper you may need a printout as well, to overcome the limitations of seeing only a small portion of the essay on the screen.

Editing Once you have finished revising, you will then want to edit carefully to ensure that every word, phrase, and sentence is clear and correct. Using language and punctuation correctly is an essential part of good writing. Errors will distract readers and lessen your credibility as a writer.

The essay assignment chapters are designed to encourage you to turn your attention to editing only *after* you have planned and worked out a revision. Too much editing too early in the writing process can limit, even block, invention and drafting. The writing you do for the predrafting invention exercises and the first draft itself should be quick and exploratory. Your main goal is to discover ways to put information together and to find out what you have to say. Worrying obsessively about spelling, punctuation, or precisely the right word at the beginning of the writing process would be the wrong use of your attention and energy.

Learning from writing   The final activity in each chapter in Part I gives you an opportunity to reflect on what you learned from the process of writing the essay. You can reread everything you have written from beginning to end and reflect on discoveries you made and problems you solved. You can analyze changes you made when you revised the draft and explain how those changes strengthened the revision. You can decide what was hardest and what was easiest about this particular kind of writing. You can compare your writing process in this essay to the process you used in writing another.

These and other reflections can lead you to a deeper understanding of how writing works and why writing is important. They can be a valuable record of what you are learning in this course.

EXERCISE 1.1

Make a list of the uses you have made of writing *outside* school in the last four weeks. Include everything from lists, notes, and letters to applications, essays, and sonatas.

What can you conclude about the recent uses you have made of writing? Summarize your conclusions for your instructor.

EXERCISE 1.2

William Styron said that "writing is hell." What metaphor might you use to describe writing? Try then to elaborate on your statement. Consider your own writing habits. How do you go about writing in the classroom, library, or study hall? What conditions make it easy or hard for you to write? How do you plan and organize? Do you write first drafts slowly or quickly? Do you revise on your own or only at the request of your teacher? What kind of revisions do you usually make?

Do you do things differently when you write at home? Where do you write at home? At what time of day or night? With music? TV? Food? With a pencil or at a typewriter? What is required for you to get started? To sustain the writing until you finish?

Do you regularly involve anyone else in your teacher-assigned writing? Do you discuss it with friends or parents?

EXERCISE 1.3

Look at what you wrote in Exercises 1.1 and 1.2, and write a brief account of your strengths and weaknesses as a writer. Now explain your goals in this course. What improvements do you hope to make in your writing?

Writing Activities

Remembering Events

☐ A scientist writes a book about a discovery she and several colleagues made, one that revolutionized scientific knowledge in her field. In the chapter about how the discovery was made, she tells the dramatic story of the race between her research team and a rival group at another university. Her team had nearly solved the problem when they heard a rumor that the other researchers had made a breakthrough. She confesses that she actually broke down and cried, imagining the Nobel Prize being awarded to her rivals. The rumor turned out to be false, and her team did indeed get credit for the discovery. She admits how jealous she was, though she writes about the incident with humor and detachment.

☐ In her autobiography, a black writer recalls her high school graduation from an all-black school in rural Arkansas in 1940. She writes about how very proud she felt until a white superintendent of schools made a condescending and insulting speech. Describing his speech and the self-hatred it inspired in her, she remembers thinking that she alone was suffering until she heard the restrained applause and recognized the proud defiance in everyone's eyes. Thus the incident, in many ways so grim, actually renewed her sense of racial pride.

☐ As part of his counseling program, a troubled man keeps a diary of his feelings and insights. In this diary he finds himself returning again and again to events just before his divorce. One particular event turns up several times in his writing—the time that he terrified his family by driving recklessly because he was angry. He writes about what he did, what his wife said, how he responded, what caused him to do it, and how he felt afterward. Writing about the incident helps him realize how desperate and destructive he had been.

☐ For her freshman English class, a student writes about some surprising events that occurred when she was preparing to send her high school newspaper to the printer. She and other staff writers had been working late for two consecutive nights. When the editor expressed irritation at how slowly she was working, she became furious with him. Then when she got home and tried to fall asleep, she had hallucinations that he was actually trying to harm her, that he was in her room approaching her bed. She writes about how astounded she was to realize later that she had hallucinated. In her paper she reflects on the way this experience gave her some understanding about uncontrollable mental events and how it increased her sympathy for other people who experience them.

☐ A student in a sociology class studying friendship patterns writes a personal essay about the time in junior high when a girls' gang tried to enlist her. Though she didn't know any of the gang members, she guessed they wanted her because they heard she was taking karate lessons. She describes how frightened she was when they demanded to meet with her after school and then how relieved she felt after they decided she wasn't tough enough. As she writes about this incident, she is able to chuckle at her actions and feelings at the time.

As these writing situations illustrate, people of all ages write about events in their lives for many different reasons: to tell a story, to discover something about themselves, to share the story and discovery with particular readers. The goal of autobiography is to present yourself, to tell a story that will disclose something significant about your life. The way you tell the story allows your readers to learn a little about you as a person.

The event can be any single experience in your past. It may be a brief incident that lasted only a few minutes, or it may be a phase in your life that extended over several months. Usually, you will describe the place where the event occurred, and often you will mention other people involved. But the focus will be on you and on your account of what happened.

The story may be about an ordinary event or a bizarre one. You may tell it seriously or humorously. But you must tell it honestly. When you write about an event from your past, you must be willing to delve into its significance in your own life and to discuss this significance in writing.

In writing about significant remembered events in your life, you need not be limited to documenting the past. Your goal is not historical research; rather, it is to make an artistic statement from an event in your life. The truth about the event comes from your effort to present the mood and to discuss the importance of what happened. For you as a writer, this effort can lead to new insights into the event and to a clarification of your own experience.

Autobiography has always been a popular genre of writing, perhaps because it leads readers to reflect on their own lives. We are all interested in other people's lives, in what they have learned from their experiences, in how they have made their way in the world. When you write well about events in your life, you will be providing readers this unusual pleasure. As you read the selections that follow and later read the autobiographical essays of other students, you will see the pleasures of reading autobiography.

The following selections illustrate many possibilities for writing about remembered events. As you read them and consider the questions that follow each selection, you may get ideas for your own writing.

READINGS

The first essay is from Kate Simon's autobiography *Bronx Primitive*. Simon came to America from Poland with her family when she was four years old, just after World War I. The event described in this essay took place when she was about ten years old. The time was the 1920s; the place was the Bronx, the neighborhood in New York City where she grew up. As you read, ask yourself what Simon seems to be telling us about herself.

JIMMY AND DEATH
KATE SIMON

Jimmy Petrides, my brother's best friend from the time we moved to Lafontaine Avenue when both boys were about five, was lank and had a neat face, as if someone had made a careful drawing of it before he was born; the lines of his thin eyebrows and thin nose straight, the lower line of his eyes straight, and the arches above as complete and round as the pretty hollow at the back of his neck. Like all the other boys he leaped and bellowed in the street but he was quiet and shy when he came to our house on rainy or cold days to make trains of boxes or spools and to match baseball cards with my brother. Although they lived in our house, two stories below us, we knew very little of his family. His father was one of the many anonymous men in caps with paper bags under their arms who rushed to the El in the morning and came back more slowly at night. Jimmy had a younger sister whom he began to take to school when he was about eight, a dark-gold little girl who clutched his hand and wouldn't talk to anyone else. Once home from school, she stayed in her house; we rarely saw her on the street even as she grew older. Mrs. Petrides was also rarely visible and wonderful when she was, a silent solitary thing like a tree alone in a field. There may have been other Greek families on the block but not in our immediate houses, and she had very few English words to exchange with her neighbors. Nevertheless, families in immigrant neighborhoods being inevitably interdependent, for shopping advice, for medical information, for the care of each other's children and the exchange of kitchen delicacies, Mrs. Petrides was offered strudel by Mrs. Nagy, the *Ungarische dripke* who was the best baker on the block. Big, clumsy Mrs. Kaplan, the loudest behemoth of the house, took her a length of *kishka* (stuffed intestine), her specialty, which Jimmy told us they couldn't eat; all that rubbery stuff. My mother's contribution was to ask Jimmy if his mother would like to go to the English classes with her, explaining that they were held during afternoon school hours and she would be back before three o'clock. He said, "She won't, she's too ashamed," the word for embarrassed or shy. There must have been a number of women like Mrs. Petrides on the block, who had no one to speak with when the husband and children were away, no one to ask where she could buy feta cheese or Greek oil. Tall and slender, with Jimmy's long eyebrows and straight nose, her sandy hair in a long full knot at the back of her head, her high-arched eyes fixed straight ahead, she looked like a lady on the front of a storybook ship, as strong and as lonely.

My mother and the other women said that if Mrs. Petrides had taken 2 them into her house to see Jimmy when he got sick—it didn't need words— or had asked the De Santis boys to take him to Fordham Hospital, Jimmy might not have died. We never found out the cause of his death; children were told about the deaths of the old but never of children, a knowledge too dreadful to speak. The first intimations of Jimmy's illness came from my brother, who was hanging around one rainy October day being mean and restless. He got in my mother's way as she was trying to boil diapers in the steaming cauldron on the stove; he woke our little sister, who had been sick and was napping; he hid my brand-new pencil with the removable cap eraser. My mother suggested he go down to play in Jimmy's house or ask him to come up. He said Jimmy was sick, he hadn't gone to school that day. The next day and the next when he was asked if Jimmy had been in school he again answered, "No," and although the weather had cleared, he refused to go down into the street. He pushed spools and boxes around for a while, read for a while, colored a picture with the baby for a while, but mostly he hung around, like a tired little old man.

The whole house was quiet. The women didn't talk much; only Tobie 3 Herman clattered noisily up and down the stairs. My mother must have known that Jimmy was dying, but I knew nothing until my brother burst into the house crying as neither my father with his beatings nor I with my fierce teasing could make him cry. His face was broken, tears pouring down his sweater, his fists clenched and shaking as if he were fighting, his feet stamping. When we calmed him a little, though he still shuddered and wept, he told us that Mr. Petrides, home from the factory that day, came over to him and said that Jimmy was dead, that we would never see him again. "What does he mean, *never*? That I won't ever see Jimmy again? What does he mean?" and his heels stamped the floor and his fist punched the air again and the terrible crying started again. I wanted to console him, not quite knowing what to say, saying something while my mother held him on her lap, a big boy of nine who allowed the indignity because he was in terrible trouble.

That evening when my father came home he was still shuddering, lying 4 on our bed with the baby, who offered him her doll and conversation. He didn't respond, which made her cry. That night he didn't eat, and he slept deeply, shuddering every once in a while. Like the street, school was hushed the next morning. The news of Jimmy's death, carried in whispers through the auditorium, in the playground, on the stairs, in toilets, was a funerary garland that wrapped itself around the whole red brick building. Street life stopped: no ball, no marbles, no ropes lashing at the sidewalk, no stickball, no fights, no singing on the stoop. The day of the funeral must have been

Saturday, there was no school. We returned books to the library and picked out others early and quickly, then went home to clean up and wait, not knowing quite what we were waiting for. We had seen funerals in the movies, in the news, but they were of grand and old people, not of a boy, not on our street. It was a cool sunny day, the big garbage cans and the metal roof of the De Santis garage shining bright and hard. As we sat on the stoop we heard stirrings on the inside stairs. The inner door opened and two men came down into the small hall where the letter boxes were, carrying a long black box. My brother gasped and I dragged him down the block, looking back to see what was happening. After the box came Mr. Petrides in a black coat and Mrs. Petrides with a black veil over her head and falling down her black coat. Behind them a few more people in black, one of the women holding by the hand the little Petrides girl whose head, too, was covered with a black scarf. The box was carried slowly down the stoop stairs, into the gutter, and then, followed by the family, headed toward 180th Street. Telling my brother that funerals were quiet so he shouldn't make noise, I ran ahead to look at Mrs. Petrides from the sidewalk. She wasn't crying; she had died, too, with only the clear drawing of her features left on dull white paper.

As the family walked slowly, following the black box, held high by the 5 four black arms like burned tree branches, the children began to trail after, led off by the two youngest De Santis boys, both in their early teens, and then the other Italian children, who seemed to know about funerals: Maria Silvestri and her brother Louis, Caroline and Petey Santini, the Bianchi kids. My brother ran into the gutter to join Petey, and I followed him, hesitating for a moment, to walk with Caroline. Awkwardly, hesitantly, the Jewish kids watching from the sidewalk began to walk with us, some of them kids who might later be hit for joining a *goyish* funeral. The two Ruthies came and Helen, Rachel, and Hannah, Sidney and Milton, the Sammies, the Izzys. My brother began to cry, quietly, and I went to him while Caroline took Petey, whose face had begun to quiver. More crying around me, behind me, growing louder and louder, coming out of twisted eyes, leaking into open mouths. (Those weeping faces combine inextricably in my memory with the image of the mourning cherubim of Giotto, wailing as they hover over the body of Christ.)

I couldn't understand why they were all crying. My brother, yes, Jimmy 6 had always been his very best friend and he liked him more than anyone else in the world, more than our mother. The other boys had liked him too, an easy, gentle boy who yielded to them rather than fight. But why were the girls crying over a Greek boy they had hardly ever played with? What did they know about death that I didn't? What were they seeing? What were they feeling? Like them, I knew dead people were put in a hole in the ground and covered with earth. Were they crying because the earth might choke him, because he might open his eyes in the dark, alone, screaming, and no one to hear him? Maybe then he would really, truly die. Was that what they meant by "frightened to death"? As a Christian boy he should become an angel. Was there a saw in the coffin to cut through the black wood and a shovel to dig away the dirt? And once out, how long would he have to stand in the dark alone before God sent the blond lady with the naked baby down through the windy night clouds to carry him back up with her?

Seeing sick Jimmy standing alone, waiting—for how long?—to be rescued 7 from the dark made me cry as fully, with my whole body, as I couldn't on Third Avenue in the dark, when I was five. Maybe my brother was crying the same memory: in a dark, unknown place, lost, unprotected. We were crying for the same reason that we hid our heads in the movies when a child wandered alone, that we quickly skipped pages when a book threatened to tell about an abandoned child. (Maybe we were also crying, like the women who went to the movies "to enjoy a good cry," for the relief not too often permitted us.)

By the time we reached 180th Street, my mother had caught up with us. 8 Taking us each by the hand, she said she didn't think they would let us into the Greek church and certainly not into the cemetery; come home, stop crying. We ate, we slept, we went to school, we asked no questions. One of the block chroniclers said the Petrides family had gone back to Greece, another said they moved downtown near cousins who had a stable. We were no longer interested in the family—the godlike child's gesture of quickly dissolving away anything that wasn't immediately attached to our ears, our eyes, our greeds, our envies. Our fears hung on for a while. No one mentioned Jimmy. His name was a blank, a black omen, a sign that children could die, and as fast as we could, we obliterated his name, too.

Questions for analysis

1. In paragraphs 6 and 7, Simon tries to remember what questions children have about death. How successful do you think she is? What other questions might you have included?

2. What question about death in paragraph 6 makes Simon cry with her "whole body"? Why do you think that question—and the visual image it produces in paragraph 7—upsets her so?

3. What autobiographical significance does Jimmy's death seem to hold for Simon?

4. How does Simon's story of this important event in her life lead you to reflect on your life? What memories and feelings come to mind?

5. In paragraph 3, how does Simon use dialogue and specific physical action to express her brother's grief?

6. How does Simon present the scene for the funeral in paragraphs 4 and 5? What neighborhood features, objects, people, physical actions, and visual details does she include? What do these choices disclose about Simon herself?

7. Would you be willing to write about some personal fear, grief, or confusion from your past? Think of a particular event. How would you

present it? How might you use the event to tell readers something about yourself?

Simon writes about a bewildering, painful, even terrifying event in her childhood. Notice that she does not directly interpret the incident from her adult perspective. Instead, she tries to remember the confusions, questions, and fears at the time. She tries to imagine the way everyone looked, what they said, how they moved. See how she recalls scenes of Jimmy and her brother playing together, of her brother's expression of bewilderment and grief when he realized that Jimmy was dead, of the funeral procession. Because she shows us so clearly what took place, we can infer what people were feeling at the time. Her description of one particular death and several different reactions to it allows us to participate fully in a universal experience—children's bewilderment about death and their fear of it.

By showing instead of telling and by being particular instead of general, autobiographers reveal something about themselves and at the same time lead us to reflect on our own experience. In writing about remembered events, you will be able to achieve the same result by specifically naming features or objects at the scene of the event; by describing features, objects, and people; and by showing people moving, talking, and interacting. Storytellers succeed by being specific.

Simon's essay raises a very important question about the emotional distance necessary for writing about events. She says that she and the other children "obliterated," or wiped out, Jimmy's name as fast as they could after his death. Yet, writing decades later in her sixties, she is still able to recall many specific actions and feelings. How is it that events so firmly forgotten can be remembered so fully years later? We can explain by considering the notion of emotional distance. As a child, Simon could forget Jimmy's death because she had to in order to get on with her own life without terrible fear and anxiety. As an adult, she is able to remember it fully because she no longer needs to protect herself from it emotionally. Time has given her the emotional distance to see what happened and to understand why it was important in her life.

Emotional distance comes with distance in time. For some events, just a few days are required; for others, emotional distance may not exist even after many years. When you select an event to write about, consider carefully your emotional distance from it. It may be risky to try to write about an event from which you have no emotional distance. Not only might you have difficulty bringing it into focus, but also you may not be able to understand fully its autobiographical significance. Emotional distance lets you write about events in your life with a perspective and tone readers trust—reflective, insightful, balanced, sometimes even humorous or ironic.

Whatever else she does in this piece, Simon tells a good story. She writes a straightforward narrative, recounting what happened first, then what happened next, and so on until the action of the story is complete. In the first paragraph she introduces Jimmy and his family. Her story actually begins in the second paragraph, when her brother announces that Jimmy is ill. The pace of the narrative moves slowly because the story line itself is so simple and because Simon provides so much information about scenes and feelings. Notice, for example, how the movement of the story stops for paragraphs 6 and 7 and then picks up again abruptly in paragraph 8. (For a more detailed discussion of pace in narrative, see Chapter 13: Narrating.)

The author of this next selection discloses not bewilderment or fear but pride, pride in his own physical coordination and courage—passing his acrobatics test as a Navy flight student. And the voice we hear in the writing is different. Whereas Kate Simon is unrelentingly serious, Russell Baker is consistently humorous and self-deprecating.

Baker is a nationally syndicated columnist for the *New York Times*; in this selection from *Growing Up*, his Pulitzer Prize-winning autobiography, he writes of an event toward the end of World War II, when he was in his early twenties. As you read, notice the kinds of things that he is willing to disclose about himself.

SMOOTH AND EASY
RUSSELL BAKER

For the longest time . . . I flew and flew without ever being in control of any airplane. It was a constant struggle for power between the plane and me, and the plane usually won. I approached every flight like a tenderfoot sent to tame a wild horse. By the time I arrived at the Naval Air Station at Memphis, where Navy pilots took over the instruction, it was obvious my flying career would be soon ended. We flew open-cockpit biplanes—"Yellow Perils," the Navy called them—which forgave almost any mistake. Instructors sat in the front cockpit, students behind. But here the instructors did not ride the controls. These were courageous men. Many were back from the Pacific, and they put their destinies in my hands high over the Mississippi River and came back shaking their heads in sorrow. [1]

"It's just like driving a car, Baker," a young ensign told me the day I nearly killed him trying to sideslip into a farm field where he wanted to land and take a smoke. "You know how it is when you let in the clutch? Real smooth and easy." [2]

I knew nothing about letting in the clutch, but didn't dare say so. "Right," I said. "Smooth and easy." [3]

I got as far as the acrobatic stage. Rolls, loops, Immelman turns. Clouds spinning zanily beneath me, earth and river whirling above. An earnest young Marine pilot took me aside after a typical day of disaster in the sky. "Baker," he said, "it's just like handling a girl's breast. You've got to be gentle." [4]

I didn't dare tell him I'd never handled a girl's breast, either. [5]

The inevitable catastrophe came on my check flight at the end of the 6
acrobatic stage. It was supposed to last an hour, but after twenty minutes in
the sky the check pilot said, "All right, let's go in," and gave me a "down,"
which meant "unfit to fly." I was doomed. I knew it, my buddies knew it.
The Navy would forgive a "down" only if you could fly two successful check
flights back-to-back with different check pilots. If you couldn't you were out.

I hadn't a prayer of surviving. On Saturday, looking at Monday's flight 7
schedule, I saw that I was posted to fly the fatal reexamination with a grizzled
pilot named T. L. Smith. It was like reading my own obituary. T. L. Smith was
a celebrated perfectionist famous for washing out cadets for the slightest
error in the air. His initials, T. L., were said to stand for "Total Loss," which
was all anyone who had to fly for him could expect. Friends stopped by my
bunk at the barracks to commiserate and tell me it wasn't so bad being
kicked out of flying. I'd probably get soft desk duty in some nice Navy town
where you could shack up a lot and sleep all day. Two of my best friends,
wanting to cheer me up, took me to go into Memphis for a farewell weekend
together. Well, it beat sitting on the base all weekend thinking about my
Monday rendezvous with Total Loss. Why not a last binge for the condemned?

We took a room at the Peabody Hotel and bought three bottles of bour- 8
bon. I'd tasted whiskey only two or three times before and didn't much like
it; but now in my gloom it brought a comfort I'd never known. I wanted
more of that comfort. My dream was dying. I would plumb the depths of
vice in these final hours. The weekend quickly turned into an incoherent
jumble of dreamlike episodes. Afterwards I vaguely remembered threatening
to punch a fat man in a restaurant, but couldn't remember why. At some
point I was among a gang of sailors in a hotel corridor, and I was telling
them to stop spraying the hallway with a fire hose. At another I was sitting
fully dressed on what seemed to be a piano bench in a hotel room—not at
the Peabody—and a strange woman was smiling at me and taking off her
brassiere.

This was startling, because no woman had ever taken her brassiere off in 9
front of me before. But where had she come from? What were we doing in
this alien room? "I'll bet I know what you want," she said.

"What?" 10

"This," she said, and stepped out of her panties and stretched out flat 11
on her back on the bed. She beckoned. I stood up, then thought better of
it and settled to the floor like a collapsing column of sand. I awoke hours
later on the floor. She'd gone.

With the hangover I took back to the base Sunday night, I would have 12
welcomed instant execution at the hands of Total Loss Smith, but when I
awoke Monday morning the physical agony was over. In its place had come
an unnatural, disembodied sensation of great calm. The world was moving
much more slowly than its normal pace. In this eerie state of relaxation nothing seemed to matter much, not the terrible Total Loss Smith, not even the
end of my flying days.

When we met at the flight line, Total Loss looked just as grim as everybody 13
said he would. It was bitterly cold. We both wore heavy leather flight suits
lined with wool, and his face looked tougher than the leather. He seemed
old enough to be my father. Wrinkles creased around eyes that had never
smiled. Lips as thin as a movie killer's. I introduced myself. His greeting was
what I'd expected. "Let's get this over with," he said.

We walked down the flight line, parachutes bouncing against our rumps, 14
not a word said. In the plane—Total Loss in the front seat, me in the back—
I connected the speaking tube which enabled him to talk to me but didn't
allow me to speak back. Still not a word while I taxied out to the mat, ran
through the cockpit checks, and finished by testing the magnetos. If he was
trying to petrify me before we got started he was wasting his efforts. In this
new state of peace I didn't give a damn whether he talked to me or not.

"Take me up to 5,000 feet and show me some rolls," he growled as I 15
started the takeoff.

The wheels were hardly off the mat before I experienced another eerie 16
sensation. It was a feeling of power. For the first time since first stepping into
an airplane I felt in complete mastery of the thing. I'd noticed it on takeoff.
It had been an excellent takeoff. Without thinking about it, I'd automatically
corrected a slight swerve just before becoming airborne. Now as we climbed
I was flooded with a sense of confidence. The hangover's residue of relaxation
had freed me of the tensions that had always defeated me before. Before,
the plane had had a will of its own; now the plane seemed to be part of
me, an extension of my hands and feet, obedient to my slightest whim. I
leveled it at exactly 5,000 feet and started a slow roll. First, a shallow dive to
gain velocity, then push the stick slowly, firmly, all the way over against the
thigh, simultaneously putting in hard rudder, and there we are, hanging
upside down over the earth and now—keeping it rolling, don't let the nose
drop—reverse the controls and feel it roll all the way through until—coming
back to straight-and-level now—catch it, wings level with the horizon, and
touch the throttle to maintain altitude precisely at 5,000 feet.

"Perfect," said Total Loss. "Do me another one." 17

It hadn't been a fluke. Somewhere between the weekend's bourbon and 18
my arrival at the flight line that morning, I had become a flyer. The second
slow roll was as good as the first.

"Show me your snap rolls," Total Loss said. 19

I showed him snap rolls as fine as any instructor had ever shown me. 20

"All right, give me a loop and then a split-S and recover your altitude and 21
show me an Immelman."

I looped him through a big graceful arc, leveled out and rolled into the 22
split-S, came out of it climbing, hit the altitude dead on at 5,000 feet, and
showed him an Immelman that Eddie Rickenbacker would have envied.

"What the hell did you do wrong on your check last week?" he asked. 23
Since I couldn't answer, I shrugged so he could see me in his rearview mirror.

"Let me see you try a falling leaf," he said. 24

Even some instructors had trouble doing a falling leaf. The plane had to 25 be brought precisely to its stalling point, then dropped in a series of sickening sideways skids, first to one side, then to the other, like a leaf falling in a breeze, by delicate simultaneous manipulations of stick, rudder pedals, and throttle. I seemed to have done falling leaves all my life.

"All right, this is a waste of my time," Total Loss growled. "Let's go in." 26

Back at the flight line, when I'd cut the ignition, he climbed out and 27 tramped back toward the ready room while I waited to sign the plane in. When I got there he was standing at a distance talking to my regular instructor. His talk was being illustrated with hand movements, as pilots' conversations always were, hands executing little loops and rolls in the air. After he did the falling-leaf motion with his hands, he pointed a finger at my instructor's chest, said something I couldn't hear, and trudged off. My instructor, who had flown only with the pre-hangover Baker, was slackjawed when he approached me. _to walk_ ← _laboriously or wearily_

"Smith just said you gave him the best check flight he's ever had in his 28 life," he said. "What the hell did you do to him up there?"

"I guess I just suddenly learned to fly," I said. I didn't mention the hang- 29 over. I didn't want him to know that bourbon was a better teacher than he was. After that I saw T. L. Smith coming and going frequently through the ready room and thought him the finest, most manly looking fellow in the entire corps of instructors, as well as the wisest.

Questions for analysis

1. This piece includes several surprising personal disclosures. What exactly does Baker tell us about himself? What impression do we get of him from these disclosures?

2. In what ways does Baker's story of his triumph as a student pilot cause you to reflect on your own life? What memories and feelings return?

3. Paragraphs 1,2, and 4 contain three images of flying, based on wild horses, cars, and women. What do these suggest that Baker must learn in order to pass the acrobatics test? Now review all of his activities on the drunken weekend in Memphis before taking the test (paragraphs 8 and 9). What exactly does he report doing? Does he learn anything demanded by the earlier images?

4. Baker does not tell us the consequences of his success. In fact, he never even mentions his feelings on realizing that he passed the test. Why do you think he omits this information? In paragraphs 27–29, what does he do instead?

5. This story relies heavily on dialogue. As a reader, how do you respond to the dialogue? How does it seem to contribute to the story Baker wants to tell? Why do you suppose he uses so much dialogue, rather than just summarizing what people said?

6. Would you be willing to write about a moment of triumph or success in your own life? Think of a particular moment. How would you

wish to write about it? In addition to telling your story, what would you choose to reveal about yourself?

Baker tells a straightforward, fast-moving story with autobiographical significance. There are many people in the story, but only Total Loss is described, and he only very briefly. The flight instructors, Baker's buddies, and the woman in the hotel room are just mentioned, not described. Baker provides very little description of the various scenes. By contrast, Simon gives many details of people and scenes, and as a result her narrative has a slower pace. Only when we reach the crucial moment in the cockpit of the test plane does Baker slow his narrative to tell us about each of his movements and of the plane's reactions.

One notable feature of Baker's piece is that he takes neither his failure nor his success very seriously. Though he may have been upset to flunk his acrobatics test, he certainly has it in perspective as he writes about it. He sees and appreciates the humor in each incident. Not only does he feel sorry for instructors he endangered, but he can even laugh at himself for passing out in the hotel room. In telling his story, he is able to maintain a good distance from the actual incidents.

Baker's distance from these incidents is literally one of time—about forty years. Certainly it is an emotional distance as well. Most autobiographers try to establish some distance from the significant events they describe. Like Baker, they may do it with humor. Painful or embarrassing events can often be approached only in this way. Also, readers tend to trust autobiographers who can write about themselves with humor or irony.

In this next selection the British writer George Orwell describes an event few people have ever witnessed—death of a man by hanging. Writing in 1931, Orwell recalls this incident from his years in the 1920s as a government official in British colonial Burma. Not only does he present this horrifying event in dramatic detail, Orwell gives us many details of the scene and describes several of the people. As you read, ask yourself what his reflections on the hanging tell us about him.

A HANGING
GEORGE ORWELL

It was in Burma, a sodden morning of the rains. A sickly light, like yellow tinfoil, was slanting over the high walls into the jail yard. We were waiting outside the condemned cells, a row of sheds fronted with double bars, like small animal cages. Each cell measured about ten feet by ten and was quite bare within except for a plank bed and a pot for drinking water. In some of them brown, silent men were squatting at the inner bars, with their blankets draped round them. These were the condemned men, due to be hanged within the next week or two.

One prisoner had been brought out of his cell. He was a Hindu, a puny 2
wisp of a man, with a shaven head and vague liquid eyes. He had a thick,
sprouting moustache, absurdly too big for his body, rather like the moustache
of a comic man on the films. Six tall Indian warders were guarding him and
getting him ready for the gallows. Two of them stood by with rifles and fixed
bayonets, while the others handcuffed him, passed a chain through his handcuffs and fixed it to their belts, and lashed his arms tight to his sides. They
crowded very close about him, with their hands always on him in a careful,
caressing grip, as though all the while feeling him to make sure he was there.
It was like men handling a fish which is still alive and may jump back into
the water. But he stood quite unresisting, yielding his arms limply to the
ropes, as though he hardly noticed what was happening.

Eight o'clock struck and a bugle call, desolately thin in the wet air, floated 3
from the distant barracks. The superintendent of the jail, who was standing
apart from the rest of us, moodily prodding the gravel with his stick, raised
his head at the sound. He was an army doctor, with a grey toothbrush
moustache and a gruff voice. "For God's sake hurry up, Francis," he said
irritably. "The man ought to have been dead by this time. Aren't you ready
yet?"

Francis, the head jailer, a fat Dravidian in a white drill suit and gold 4
spectacles, waved his black hand. "Yes sir, yes sir," he bubbled. "All iss
satisfactorily prepared. The hangman iss waiting. We shall proceed."

"Well, quick march, then. The prisoners can't get their breakfast till this 5
job's over."

We set out for the gallows. Two warders marched on either side of the 6
prisoner, with their rifles at the slope; two others marched close against him,
gripping him by arm and shoulder, as though at once pushing and supporting
him. The rest of us, magistrates and the like, followed behind. Suddenly,
when we had gone ten yards, the procession stopped short without any order
or warning. A dreadful thing had happened—a dog, come goodness knows
whence, had appeared in the yard. It came bounding among us with a loud
volley of barks, and leapt round us wagging its whole body, wild with glee
at finding so many human beings together. It was a large woolly dog, half
Airedale, half pariah. For a moment it pranced round us, and then, before
anyone could stop it, it had made a dash for the prisoner and jumping up
tried to lick his face. Everyone stood aghast, too taken aback even to grab
at the dog.

"Who let that bloody brute in here?" said the superintendent angrily. 7
"Catch it, someone!"

A warder detached from the escort, charged clumsily after the dog, but 8
it danced and gambolled just out of his reach, taking everything as part of
the game. A young Eurasian jailer picked up a handful of gravel and tried to
stone the dog away, but it dodged the stones and came after us again. Its
yaps echoed from the jail walls. The prisoner, in the grasp of the two warders,
looked on incuriously, as though this was another formality of the hanging.

It was several minutes before someone managed to catch the dog. Then we put my handkerchief through its collar and moved off once more, with the dog still straining and whimpering.

It was about forty yards to the gallows. I watched the bare brown back 9 of the prisoner marching in front of me. He walked clumsily with his bound arms, but quite steadily, with that bobbing gait of the Indian who never straightens his knees. At each step his muscles slid neatly into place, the lock of hair on his scalp danced up and down, his feet printed themselves on the wet gravel. And once, in spite of the men who gripped him by each shoulder, he stepped slightly aside to avoid a puddle on the path.

It is curious, but till that moment I had never realized what it means to 10 destroy a healthy, conscious man. When I saw the prisoner step aside to avoid the puddle I saw the mystery, the unspeakable wrongness, of cutting a life short when it is in full tide. This man was not dying, he was alive just as we are alive. All the organs of his body were working—bowels digesting food, skin renewing itself, nails growing, tissues forming—all toiling away in solemn foolery. His nails would still be growing when he stood on the drop, when he was falling through the air with a tenth-of-a-second to live. His eyes saw the yellow gravel and the grey walls, and his brain still remembered, foresaw, reasoned—reasoned even about puddles. He and we were a party of men walking together, seeing, hearing, feeling, understanding the same world; and in two minutes, with a sudden snap, one of us would be gone—one mind less, one world less.

The gallows stood in a small yard, separate from the main grounds of the 11 prison, and overgrown with tall prickly weeds. It was a brick erection like three sides of a shed, with planking on top, and above that two beams and a crossbar with the rope dangling. The hangman, a grey-haired convict in the white uniform of the prison, was waiting beside his machine. He greeted us with a servile crouch as we entered. At a word from Francis the two warders, gripping the prisoner more closely than ever, half led half pushed him to the gallows and helped him clumsily up the ladder. Then the hangman climbed up and fixed the rope around the prisoner's neck.

We stood waiting, five yards away. The warders had formed in a rough 12 circle round the gallows. And then, when the noose was fixed, the prisoner began crying out to his god. It was a high, reiterated cry of ''Ram! Ram! Ram! Ram!'' not urgent and fearful like a prayer or cry for help, but steady, rhythmical, almost like the tolling of a bell. The dog answered the sound with a whine. The hangman, still standing on the gallows, produced a small white cotton bag like a flour bag and drew it down over the prisoner's face. But the sound, muffled by the cloth, still persisted, over and over again: ''Ram! Ram! Ram! Ram! Ram!''

The hangman climbed down and stood ready, holding the lever. Minutes 13 seemed to pass. The steady, muffled crying from the prisoner went on and on, ''Ram! Ram! Ram!'' never faltering for an instant. The superintendent, his head on his chest, was slowly poking the ground with his stick; perhaps he was counting the cries, allowing the prisoner a fixed number—fifty, per- haps, or a hundred. Everyone had changed colour. The Indians had gone grey like bad coffee, and one or two of the bayonets were wavering. We looked at the lashed, hooded man on the drop, and listened to his cries—each cry another second of life; the same thought was in all our minds: oh, kill him quickly, get it over, stop that abominable noise!

Suddenly the superintendent made up his mind. Throwing up his head 14 he made a swift motion with his stick. "Chalo!" he shouted almost fiercely.

There was a shaking noise, and then dead silence. The prisoner had van- 15 ished, and the rope was twisting on itself. I let go of the dog, and it galloped immediately to the back of the gallows; but when it got there it stopped short, barked, and then retreated into a corner of the yard, where it stood among the weeds, looking timorously out at us. We went round the gallows to inspect the prisoner's body. He was dangling with his toes pointed straight downwards, very slowly revolving, as dead as a stone.

The superintendent reached out with his stick and poked the bare brown 16 body; it oscillated slightly. "*He's* all right," said the superintendent. He backed out from under the gallows, and blew out a deep breath. The moody look had gone out of his face quite suddenly. He glanced at his wrist-watch. "Eight minutes past eight. Well, that's all for this morning, thank God."

The warders unfixed bayonets and marched away. The dog, sobered and 17 conscious of having misbehaved itself, slipped after them. We walked out of the gallows yard, past the condemned cells with their waiting prisoners, into the big central yard of the prison. The convicts, under the command of warders armed with lathis, were already receiving their breakfast. They squat- ted in long rows, each man holding a tin pannikin, while two warders with buckets marched round ladling out rice; it seemed quite a homely, jolly scene, after the hanging. An enormous relief had come upon us now that the job was done. One felt an impulse to sing, to break into a run, to snigger. All at once everyone began chattering gaily.

The Eurasian boy walking beside me nodded towards the way we had 18 come, with a knowing smile: "Do you know, sir, our friend (he meant the dead man) when he heard his appeal had been dismissed, he pissed on the floor of his cell. From fright. Kindly take one of my cigarettes, sir. Do you not admire my new silver case, sir? From the boxwallah, two rupees eight annas. Classy European style."

Several people laughed—at what, nobody seemed certain. 19

Francis was walking by the superintendent, talking garrulously: "Well, sir, 20 all hass passed off with the utmost satisfactoriness. It was all finished—flick! like that. It iss not always so—oah, no! I have known cases where the doctor wass obliged to go beneath the gallows and pull the prissoner's legs to ensure decease. Most disagreeable!"

"Wriggling about, eh? That's bad," said the superintendent. 21

"Ach, sir, it iss worse when they become refractory! One man, I recall, 22 clung to the bars of hiss cage when we went to take him out. You will scarcely credit, sir, that it took six warders to dislodge him, three pulling at each leg. We reasoned with him. 'My dear fellow,' we said, 'think of all of the pain and trouble you are causing to us!' But no, he would not listen! Ach, he wass very troublesome!"

I found that I was laughing quite loudly. Everyone was laughing. Even the 23 superintendent grinned in a tolerant way. "You'd better all come out and have a drink," he said quite genially. "I've got a bottle of whiskey in the car. We could do with it."

We went through the big double gates of the prison into the road. "Pull- 24 ing at his legs!" exclaimed a Burmese magistrate suddenly, and burst into a loud chuckling. We all began laughing again. At that moment Francis' anecdote seemed extraordinarily funny. We all had a drink together, native and European alike, quite amicably. The dead man was a hundred yards away.

Questions for analysis

1. Beginning with paragraph 16 the mood of the guards and officials changes. Did this change take you by surprise? Why, or why not?

2. Except for the reflection in paragraph 10, Orwell tells us about himself mainly by reporting the words and actions of the group he is a part of. What do we learn about Orwell in this essay? What sort of man is he? What are his moral and political views?

3. The event seems to be presented in great detail, yet we can assume that Orwell left out much that he remembered. He might also have omitted any mention of the dog: it is easy to imagine the story without it. Why do you think Orwell included the dog and gave it such a prominent place in the story?

4. Beginning at paragraph 18, the essay is largely dialogue. Look again at the dialogue in paragraphs 18–24. What does it tell us? How does Orwell use this dialogue to disclose the significance of the event?

5. Look again at paragraphs 2, 6, 8, and 9 to see how Orwell describes the prisoner and his treatment by the guards. What specific actions and details are described, and what impression do they give of the prisoner? How do they make you feel about him?

6. Have you ever been party to an action that you later regretted? Or have you ever seen or participated in a particularly shocking event? Under what conditions would you be willing to write about such an event? Think about a particular event of this sort. How would you present it? How might you disclose something about yourself in your description of the event?

Like Kate Simon and Russell Baker, Orwell writes about an event that occurred years earlier. All three writers have considerable distance in time from the events they write about—and they have emotional distance as well. Notice how Orwell is able to acknowledge that he participated fully in the event, though we can assume it gives him no pleasure to do so. He remembers thinking how wrong it was to destroy a life, and yet he did not hesitate in carrying out his assigned role as one of the destroyers.

Orwell tells a compelling story. Though his story has a fast, direct narrative pace, he does give us a much fuller description of both the scene and the people than does Baker. Through Orwell's description of the prison, the gallows, the prisoner, and the dog, we can understand the significance the event had for him personally.

This next essay was written by Jean Brandt, a college freshman. She tells us of an unexpected event on a Christmas shopping trip. As you read, ask yourself what the writer discloses about herself as a person in this story.

CALLING HOME
JEAN BRANDT

As we all piled into the car, I knew it was going to be a fabulous day. 1 My grandmother was visiting for the holidays; and she and I, along with my older brother and sister, Louis and Susan, were setting off for a day of last-minute Christmas shopping. On the way to the mall we sang Christmas carols, chattered, and laughed. With Christmas only two days away, we were caught up with holiday spirit. I felt light-headed and full of joy. I loved shopping—especially at Christmas.

The shopping center was swarming with frantic last-minute shoppers like 2 ourselves. We went first to the General Store, my favorite. It carried mostly knickknacks and other useless items which nobody needs but buys anyway. I was thirteen years old at the time, and things like buttons and calendars and posters would catch my fancy. This day was no different. The object of my desire was a 75-cent Snoopy button. Snoopy was the latest. If you owned anything with the Peanuts on it, you were "in." But since I was supposed to be shopping for gifts for other people and not myself, I couldn't decide what to do. I went in search of my sister for her opinion. I pushed my way through throngs of people to the back of the store where I found Susan. I asked her if she thought I should buy the button. She said it was cute and if I wanted it to go ahead and buy it.

When I got back to the Snoopy section, I took one look at the lines at 3 the cashiers and knew I didn't want to wait thirty minutes to buy an item worth less than one dollar. I walked back to the basket where I found the button and was about to drop it when suddenly, instead, I took a quick glance around, assured myself no one could see, and slipped the button into the pocket of my sweatshirt. I hesitated for a moment, but once the item was in my pocket, there was no turning back. I had never before stolen anything, but what was done was done. A few seconds later my sister appeared and asked, "So, did you decide to buy the button?"

"No, I guess not." I hoped my voice didn't quaver. As we headed for the 4 entrance, my heart began to race. I just had to get out of that store. Only a few more yards to go and I'd be safe. As we crossed the threshold, I heaved a sigh of relief. I was home free. I thought about how sly I had been and I felt proud of my accomplishment.

An unexpected tap on my shoulder startled me. I whirled around to find 5 a middle-aged man, dressed in street clothes, flashing some type of badge and politely asking me to empty my pockets. Where did this man come from? How did he know? I was so sure that no one had seen me! On the verge of panicking, I told myself that all I had to do was give this man his button back, say I was sorry, and go on my way. After all, it was only a 75-cent item.

Next thing I knew he was talking about calling the police and having me 6 arrested and thrown in jail, as if he had just nabbed a professional thief instead of a terrified kid. I couldn't believe what he was saying.

"Jean, what's going on?" 7

The sound of my sister's voice eased the pressure a bit. She always man- 8 aged to get me out of trouble. She would come through this time too.

"Excuse me. Are you a relative of this young girl?" 9

"Yes, I'm her sister. What's the problem?" 10

"Well, I just caught her shoplifting and I'm afraid I'll have to call the 11 police."

"What did she take?" 12

"This button." 13

"A button? You are having a thirteen-year-old arrested for stealing a 14 button?"

"I'm sorry, but she broke the law." 15

The man led us through the store and into an office, where we waited 16 for the police officers to arrive. Susan had found my grandmother and brother who, still shocked, didn't say a word. The thought of going to jail terrified me, not because of jail itself, but because of the encounter with my parents afterward. Not more than ten minutes later two officers arrived and placed me under arrest. They said that I was to be taken to the station alone. Then they handcuffed me and led me out of the store. I felt alone and scared. I had counted on my sister being with me, but now I had to muster up the courage to face this ordeal all by myself.

As the officers led me through the mall, I sensed a hundred pairs of eyes 17 staring at me. My face flushed and I broke out in a sweat. Now everyone knew I was a criminal. In their eyes I was a juvenile delinquent, and thank God the cops were getting me off the streets. The worse part was thinking my grandmother might be having the same thoughts. The humiliation at that moment was overwhelming. I felt like Hester Prynne being put on public display for everyone to ridicule.

That short walk through the mall seemed to take hours. But once we 18 reached the squad car, time raced by. I was read my rights and questioned. We were at the police station within minutes. Everything happened so fast I didn't have a chance to feel remorse for my crime. Instead, I viewed what was happening to me as if it were a movie. Being searched, although em- barrassing, somehow seemed to be exciting. All the movies and television programs I had seen were actually coming to life. This is what it was really like. But why were criminals always portrayed as frightened and regretful? I was having fun. I thought I had nothing to fear—until I was allowed my one phone call. I was trembling as I dialed home. I didn't know what I was going to say to my parents, especially my mother.

"Hi, Dad, this is Jean." 19

"We've been waiting for you to call." 20

"Did Susie tell you what happened?" 21

"Yeah, but we haven't told your mother. I think you should tell her what 22 you did and where you are."

"You mean she doesn't even know where I am?" 23

"No, I want you to explain it to her." 24

There was a pause as he called my mother to the phone. For the first 25 time that night I was close to tears. I wished I had never stolen that stupid pin. I wanted to give the phone to one of the officers because I was too ashamed to tell my mother the truth, but I had no choice.

"Jean, where are you?" 26

"I'm, umm, in jail." 27

"Why? What for?" 28

"Shoplifting." 29

"Oh no, Jean. Why? Why did you do it?" 30

"I don't know. No reason. I just did it." 31

"I don't understand. What did you take? Why did you do it? You had 32 plenty of money with you."

"I know but I just did it. I can't explain why. Mom, I'm sorry." 33

"I'm afraid sorry isn't enough. I'm horribly disappointed in you." 34

Long after we got off the phone, while I sat in an empty jail cell, waiting 35 for my parents to pick me up, I could still distinctly hear the disappointment and hurt in my mother's voice. I cried. The tears weren't for me but for her and the pain I had put her through. I felt like a terrible human being. I would rather have stayed in jail than confront my mom right then. I dreaded each passing minute that brought our encounter closer. When the officer came to release me, I hesitated, actually not wanting to leave. We went to the front desk, where I had to sign a form to retrieve my belongings. I saw my parents a few yards away and my heart raced. A large knot formed in my stomach. I fought back the tears.

Not a word was spoken as we walked to the car. Slowly I sank into the 36 back seat anticipating the scolding. Expecting harsh tones, I was relieved to hear almost the opposite from my father.

"I'm not going to punish you and I'll tell you why. Although I think what 37 you did was wrong, I think what the police did was more wrong. There's no excuse for locking a thirteen-year-old behind bars. That doesn't mean I con-done what you did, but I think you've been punished enough already."

As I looked from my father's eyes to my mother's, I knew this ordeal was 38 over. Although it would never be forgotten, the incident was not mentioned again.

Questions for analysis   1. Brandt ends her essay with the comment that the incident was never mentioned again. Why do you think she chose to resurrect it for a college essay, particularly since it was both embarrassing and painful?

2. Brandt writes about an experience that occurred when she was thirteen. How much emotional distance does she seem to have? How does she convey that distance in the story?

3. How does this story cause you to reflect on events or people in your own life?

4. What part does dialogue play in Brandt's story? At what points does she use it? Does all of the dialogue seem realistic to you? If not, where does it seem unrealistic?

5. Brandt does not describe any of the other people in the story. Why do you think she chose not to tell us more about them?

6. The story begins and ends in a car. How is the situation different in each car? What role do the two car situations play in the narrative?

7. Where does the pace of the story seem fast to you? Where does it seem slow? What is going on in the story at these fast and slow spots? What can you conclude about pace in stories?

8. Is there an embarrassing event in your past you would be willing to write about? How would you present this event? How would you indicate the autobiographical significance of this event?

Brandt's story, like Russell Baker's, is told mainly through action and dialogue. Also like Baker, she keeps the focus narrowly on herself throughout the story. By contrast, Kate Simon gives Jimmy and her brother a prominent place in her story and George Orwell gives the doomed Hindu prisoner a prominent place in his.

Brandt tells us something important about herself, choosing a significant event and telling her story in a way that seems honest and revealing. She seems interested more in getting at the autobiographical significance of the event than in making herself look good.

BASIC FEATURES OF ESSAYS ABOUT REMEMBERED EVENTS

Essays about remembered events share certain basic features: a well-told story, a detailed presentation of scenes and people, and a clear indication of autobiographical significance.

A well-told story   Writing about events means first of all telling a good story. Whatever else the writer may attempt to do, he or she must tell a readable, memorable story.

Events which make good stories have some tension or suspense. We may expect a surprise or sense disaster. We could shudder in anticipation of a troubling personal disclosure. We might look forward to a humorous turn of events. The important point is that the writer makes us want to know what will happen. We want to know what will happen to Jimmy in Kate Simon's story, and how everyone will react to his death. We really wonder whether Russell Baker will pass his flight test. George Orwell makes us curious about how the hanging will be carried out. We are anxious to hear what Jean Brandt's parents will say to her.

Nearly always autobiographers adopt the first person point of view, telling the story as "I" or "we." All the readings in this chapter are told from this point of view.

They may tell the story as a straightforward chronological narrative—presenting events in just the order in which they occurred—or they may flash back or flash forward to events which occurred at other times. All the writers in this chapter follow a regular narrative sequence.

Good writers manage pace carefully. They may follow an even pace, or they may alternate pace, speeding up to give an account of some activities or slowing down to describe a scene, a person, a critical moment or to relate some dialogue. We have already noticed how Simon's pace seems slow because she gives us so many visual details, whereas Baker's seems fast because he presents so many activities so quickly. However, Baker slows the pace abruptly when he describes the actual test flight. Brandt's story comes to a halt during the dialogues with the detective and her parents. Narration accelerates the pace of a story; description and dialogue slow it down. (All of these strategies for presenting a well-told story are presented in Chapter 13: Narrating.)

A detailed presentation of significant scenes and people

Essays about remembered events include specific details from the scene of the event. Writers deliberately move in close and show specific objects: prison cells, handcuffs, bugle call, dog, cigarette case, and whiskey in Orwell; the strudel, doll, garbage cans, and coffin in Simon. They also give details of these objects, as Orwell does in presenting the prison cells as "the condemned cells, a row of sheds fronted with double bars, like small animal cages" and the dog as "a large woolly dog, half Airedale, half pariah."

Writers can choose from a variety of strategies for presenting the important people in the events, including physical description, action, or dialogue. They can give details of the person's appearance, as Baker does for Total Loss: ". . . his face looked tougher than the leather [of his flight suit]. He seemed old enough to be my father. Wrinkles creased around eyes that had never smiled. Lips as thin as a movie killer's." Another example is Simon's description of Mrs. Petrides: "Tall and slender, with

Jimmy's long eyebrows and straight nose, her sandy hair in a long full knot at the back of her head, her high-arched eyes fixed straight ahead, she looked like a lady on the front of a storybook ship, as strong and as lonely." Both of these writers give us carefully chosen visual details of the person—size, physical features, dress. Notice also how they use imagery to bring the people to life: "lips as thin as a movie killer's," lonely as a "storybook ship" lady.

Writers also show people in action. Not only does Orwell describe his condemned man, but he shows him walking: "He walked clumsily with his bound arms, but quite steadily, with that bobbing gait of the Indian who never straightens his knees. At each step his muscles slid neatly into place, the lock of hair on his scalp danced up and down, his feet printed themselves on the wet gravel."

Writers can also present people through dialogue, letting us infer what they are like from what they say. All the readings in this chapter include dialogue. In Simon's essay it is a minor feature. In Orwell's essay, however, the participants' attitudes toward the hanging are revealed in part by what they say. (The strategies for presenting scenes and people are discussed in detail in Chapter 12: Describing.)

Instead of generalizing and paraphrasing, skillful writers take us to the actual scene and let us hear the people. By very carefully selecting what to show us, they can demonstrate the significance the event has held in their lives.

A clear indication of the event's significance In essays about remembered events we expect a well-told story with vivid details of the scenes and the people. But we expect more: since these essays are autobiographical, we expect to find some kind of self-disclosure, a statement about the significance the event holds in the writer's life. In casual relationships we concentrate on making ourselves look as good as possible. We never admit anything that would make us look bad. By contrast, in autobiographical writing just about our only chance to look good is to satisfy the reader that we really are willing to admit just about anything about ourselves. There is no way to fake this honesty. Readers know an honest voice, and they applaud it—perhaps because it is an opportunity to reflect on their own lives and on the human condition in general. Autobiographical writers must be willing to admit shame, embarrassment, panic, failure, joy, success. We all know these feelings, of course, which is why we are curious about how others experience them.

One way writers manage the self-disclosure in autobiography is by deliberately distancing themselves emotionally from the events, usually choosing an event which occurred many years earlier. Moreover, their disclosures are in voices of serious detachment, wise reflection, humor. Most important, they disclose the autobiographical significance of the events by showing us why they were important, instead of by telling us directly, as in a moral at the end of a fable. They invest the event with significance, rather than moralizing about it. None of the readings in this chapter ends with the writer summarizing for us just what the event meant; and yet in each case we are able to see the autobiographical significance.

GUIDE TO WRITING

THE WRITING TASK

Write an essay about a significant event in your life. Choose an event which will be engaging for readers and which will, at the same time, tell them something about you.

INVENTION

Before drafting an essay about a remembered event you need to remember what happened and to explore its significance. Only then can you write confidently and will your draft be full and rich. Invention is designed to help you do this—to help you choose an appropriate event, define its autobiographical significance, recall important details, and organize the story you want to tell.

Choosing an event to write about   You may already have an event in mind. Even so, you may want to consider several events in order to make the best possible choice. If you are decided upon an event, however, turn now to Testing Your Choice on the facing page.

Listing events. List several events you might write about. Make the list as long as you can. Include all different kinds of events: common and unusual, brief ones and longer ones, events close and distant emotionally, events recent and distant in time. The following categories of significant personal events may give you some ideas for your list:

☐ Any incident charged with strong emotions such as fear, anger, jealousy, embarrassment, sadness, guilt, frustration, hurt, pride, happiness, joy

☐ Any turning point in your life when the way you feel, think, or act was challenged or changed

☐ Any "first" such as when you first realized you had a special skill, ambition, or problem; when you first felt rejected or needed; when you first became aware of injustice

☐ Any critical moment when you were forced to examine your basic values, attitudes, beliefs, assumptions

☐ Any occasion when things did not turn out the way you expected they would: when you expected to be praised and were criticized, when you were convinced you would fail but succeeded

☐ Any memorably difficult situation: when you had to play an unfamiliar or uncomfortable role, when someone you admired let you down (or you let someone down who was depending on you), when you had to make a tough choice

☐ Any event which shaped you in a particular way, making you perhaps independent, proud, insecure, fearful, courageous, ambitious

Choosing a significant event. Look closely at your list and choose one event to write about. Select one which will make a good story and disclose something significant about you.

You might find just the right event immediately. Most writers, however, need time to weigh the advantages and disadvantages of several equally attractive possibilities. As you work your way through the writing process, you may well find yourself repeatedly testing your choice and defining its significance.

For now, it will be helpful to stop and focus your thoughts. In a sentence or two, try to state why this event is significant to you.

Testing your choice Next you should examine your choice to see whether it is worth writing about and to be sure you will be able to do so. Do this by asking yourself these questions:

☐ As a fragment of my life story, does this event say anything important about me or my life?

☐ Will I be able to communicate to readers the significance the event holds in my life?

☐ Will this event produce a compelling, memorable story?

☐ Do I remember enough specific details of the scene or people to write well about the event?

These questions will help you test your choice as you write your essay, and you may want to consider them again and again. If at any point—inventing, drafting, revising—you decide that you cannot answer these questions affirmatively and confidently, you may want to consider writing about a different event.

Defining the event's autobiographical significance

The invention activities that follow can help you discover and understand what the event discloses about your life.

Recalling first reactions. Try to remember your first response to the event: what were your feelings as it was happening and immediately thereafter? Spend around ten minutes jotting down notes about this response, using these questions to stimulate your memory:

☐ What was my first response to the event? What did I think? How did I feel? What did I do?

☐ How did I show my feelings?

☐ What did I want those present to think of me and why?

☐ What did I think of myself at the time?

☐ Did I talk to anyone just after the event? What did I say?

☐ How long did these first feelings last?

☐ What were the immediate consequences of the event for me personally?

Stop a moment to focus your thoughts. In two or three sentences try to articulate what your first responses to the event seem to disclose about you as a person.

Exploring your present perspective. Now think about your present perspective on the event—your current feelings as well as any reflections or insights you may have had. Write for ten minutes about your present perspective, using these questions to get you started:

☐ How do I now feel about the way I acted at the time of the event? Was my response appropriate? Why, or why not?

☐ Looking back, how do I feel about this event? Do I understand it differently now?

☐ What do my actions at the time of the event say about the kind of person I was then? In what ways am I different now? How would I respond to the same event if it occurred today?

☐ How would I summarize my current feelings?

☐ What is my emotional distance from the event?

☐ Are my feelings settled, or do they still seem to be changing? Am I sure of myself or ambivalent?

Now you should focus your thoughts on your current reaction. In two or three sentences say what your present perspective on the event seems to reveal about you.

Redefining the event's autobiographical significance. Once you have explored both your first response and your present perspective, write a sentence or two restating the significance of the event in your life. Just how is the event important to you? What exactly can you say about yourself by writing about this event?

Recalling specific sensory details

Sensory details are the specific sights, sounds, and smells of the story you want to tell. The following activities will help you recall physical features of the scene and precise sensory details of these features.

Listing important features. Pretend that you are once again at the scene of the event. Make a list of any significant features or objects that you remember. (Exclude people from this list.) If you were planning to write about a water-skiing incident, for example, you might list the skis, rope, boat, plumes of water thrown up by your skis, lake, mountain, other boats, dock, and so on.

Describing important features. Choose at least three items from your list, and write for around five minutes on each one. Try to remember and record specific sensory details: size, shape, color, texture; side view, back view, top view, view from a distance and from up close; sounds and smells. Does it remind you of something else? Would you compare it with anything else?

Recalling other people

These activities will help you remember all the significant people in the event—what they looked like, what they did, what you might have said to them.

Listing significant people. List all the people who played more than a casual role in the event. You may have only one or two people to list, or you may have several.

Describing significant people. Choose one or more persons from your list who played a central role in the event. You should select those who may help you to make clear what this event taught you about yourself. Write about each person for around five minutes, describing the person's appearance and actions and stating his or her significance in the event.

Re-creating conversations. Try to reconstruct a conversation between one or more of these persons and yourself. Set it up as a dialogue, as Jean Brandt does on pages 51–52.

You may not remember exactly what was said, but you can compose a dialogue which will probably reflect accurately your relationship with that person. Try for a conversational dialogue—no speeches, just a quick, informal exchange of comments. Make an effort to extend the conversation to around ten comments by each person.

Here you should try to focus your thoughts about the other people. Reread your descriptions of them and of the conversations you had with them. Write a sentence or two about what your relationship with these people says about you.

Organizing the narrative   An autobiographical essay about a remembered event should be first of all a good story. The way you organize this story will depend on what happened, what significance it had for you, who your readers will be, and what impression you want to give them. As you draft and revise, you will discover the most appropriate narrative line for your story. For now, you can begin thinking about this narrative line by listing the main incidents in the event. List them in the order in which you think they should be presented in your story. (See Chapter 13: Narrating for a full discussion of narrative strategies.)

PLANNING AND DRAFTING

These next activities are designed to help you to use your invention writing, to set goals for drafting the essay, and to discover the possibilities of your story in a first draft.

Seeing what you have   You have now done a lot of thinking and writing about elements basic to an essay about a remembered event: your feelings, the autobiographical significance, specific sensory details, dialogue, a basic story line. Before you do any further invention or begin planning and drafting, you should reread everything you've written to see what you have. As you read through your invention writings, be on the lookout for surprising details or new insights. Watch for meaningful patterns and relationships. Highlight any such promising material with underscoring or notes in the margin. Guided by the questions that follow, you should now be able to decide whether you have enough material for a successful essay and whether you understand the autobiographical possibilities well enough to proceed.

☐ Do I understand the autobiographical significance of the event? Have I been able to state and restate it clearly?

☐ Will I be able to make any significant statements about myself? What will they be? Can I find them in the invention writing?

☐ Does my tentative narrative line indicate that I can tell a dramatic and compelling story?

☐ Do I have enough sensory details to be sure that my memory of the event is still sharp? Do any of the details look promising?

If you do not see interesting details, connections, and patterns in your invention writing, you may want to write about a different event. An impoverished invention sequence is not likely to yield a good draft. Starting over is no fun, but there is no sense in starting to draft a composition if you do not feel confident about your topic.

If your invention writing looks thin but promising, there are several ways you may be able to fill it out. You might try revising or extending the narrative line, composing other conversations, recalling additional sensory details, thinking more about your own reactions to the event, elaborating on significant people, describing other people who were involved.

Setting goals Before starting to draft, you should set goals to guide further invention and planning. Some of these goals concern the piece as a whole, like holding readers' interest with a compelling story, satisfying their curiosity with meaningful self-disclosure, maintaining a good pace in the narrative, or framing the story in a satisfying way. Other goals have to do with smaller issues, like including memorable sensory details, creating vivid images, or making each dialogue sound like real conversation. You will be making dozens of decisions—and solving dozens of problems—as you work your way into a draft; these decisions and solutions are determined by the goals you set.

Following are some questions that can help you set such goals as you plan and draft. Consider all of them thoughtfully before you start drafting. You may also want to return to them as you work, to help keep your main goals in focus.

Your readers

☐ Will the event be familiar to my readers? How much can I assume they will know about such events? If they know little about such an event, can I expect them to understand what happened? How can I help them to do so?

☐ How can I help readers to see the significance the event has for me?

☐ How can I get readers to recognize the shared human experience of my story and to reflect on their own lives?

The beginning

- [ ] How shall I begin? What can I do in my very first sentence that will capture my readers' interest? Shall I begin with a mystery, as Baker does? ("For the longest time . . . I flew and flew without ever being in control of any airplane.") Shall I try a "once upon a time" beginning, like Orwell's? ("It was in Burma, a sodden morning of the rains.") Or shall I begin by having someone say something, or with someone doing something?
- [ ] What information should I give first? Should I begin with the main event, integrating essential background information as I tell the story? Should I establish the setting and situation right away, as Orwell and Brandt do? Should I first present myself, as Baker does? Or should I provide the complete context for the event, as Simon does?

Telling the story

- [ ] What is the most appropriate pace for my story?
- [ ] How can I integrate details of the scene, objects, and people smoothly into the narrative?
- [ ] How can I let actions and conversations carry part of the narrative?

The autobiographical statement

- [ ] Shall I discuss the personal significance of my story in direct commentary, as Simon and Brandt do? Or shall I present it more indirectly, as is done by Orwell and Baker?
- [ ] How can I be sure to satisfy readers that I have told them something significant about myself? How can I persuade them that I am honest?
- [ ] What sort of person do I want to present? What kind of voice will readers hear in my essay?

The ending

- [ ] How should the essay end? Should I continue the narrative to the end, as Baker and Orwell do? Or should I end as Simon does, summarizing the immediate consequences of the event?
- [ ] What do I want the ending to accomplish? Do I want to frame the essay by referring to the beginning? Would it be good to jolt the reader with something unexpected?
- [ ] Do I need to finish up the action of the story? Or should I reflect on the autobiographical significance?

Drafting the essay   Before you begin drafting an essay about an event, you may want to review the general advice on drafting in Chapter 1. As you write, try to maintain a focus on what took place in the event you are recounting. Probably you will be telling about the incident chronologically—that is, in the order that everything took place. Remember that you must strive to paint a realistic and memorable picture of the scene of the event and of any important people involved. Try also to describe the event in such a way as to say something about yourself. If you feel stuck at any point in drafting the essay, try returning to the writing activities in the Invention section of this chapter. Whereas drafting requires a certain focus, these activities are designed to free you to write without too much focus.

READING A DRAFT WITH A CRITICAL EYE

The next step is to read over the draft. Whether you are reading your own draft or that of another student, you should make an effort to focus your reading, to read with a critical eye. The commentary that follows offers advice on reading someone else's draft; however, it should be as useful for reading your own draft.

First general impression   First read the draft straight through to get a quick general impression. Read to enjoy the story and to get a sense of the autobiographical significance of the event. Try to overlook any errors in spelling, punctuation, or usage. After finishing this first reading, tell the writer what you learned about him or her from the draft. What sort of voice do you hear? What does the story tell you about the writer? How would you summarize the autobiographical significance of the essay?

Pointings   One good way to maintain a critical focus as you read the essay is to highlight noteworthy features of the writing with *pointings*. A simple system of lines and brackets, these pointings are quick and easy to do, and they can provide a lot of helpful information for revision. Use pointings in the following way:

☐ Draw a straight line under any words or images that impress you as especially effective: strong verbs, specific details, memorable phrases, striking images.

☐ Draw a wavy line under any words or images that seem flat, stale, or vague. Also put a wavy line under any words or phrases that you consider unnecessary or repetitious.

☐ Look for pairs or groups of sentences that you think should be combined. Put brackets [ ] around these sentences.

☐ Look for sentences that are garbled, overloaded, or awkward. Put parentheses ( ) around these sentences. Put them around any sentence which seems even slightly questionable; don't worry now about whether or not you're certain about your judgment. The writer needs to know that you, as one reader, had even the slightest hesitation about understanding a sentence.

Analysis   To see the possibilities for revision, a writer needs a comprehensive analysis of the main parts and features of the draft—beginning, ending, narrative, scenes and people, action and dialogue, autobiographical disclosure. Following is a list of things to consider in analyzing a draft.

1. Evaluate the beginning. Say whether or not the first sentence captured your interest and whether or not the first paragraph made you want to read the essay. Consider whether some other part of the draft might make a better beginning.

2. Evaluate the ending. See if there is any way to improve the ending. Is it too obvious? Does it frame the essay by making some connection with the beginning? (Framing is not a requirement, but it can be a nice touch.) Consider whether the essay might end well at some earlier point.

3. Consider the completeness of the story. Point out any places where you have questions about what happened, where you need or would like more information, where you see gaps in the story.

4. Evaluate the pace. Try to point out sections which seem too slow or too fast.

5. Say whether you want to know more about the scene or the people . . . or whether you would be happy to know less because the detail seems unnecessary. Point out any memorable scenes and people.

6. Look for unnecessary commentary. Strong writing about events *shows* people in action, rather than telling what they are doing by editorializing. Point out places where you need to see people in action as well as places where this is shown effectively.

7. Dialogue is an effective way of presenting people, of showing what they are like by the way they talk. It is a good way to disclose autobiographical significance as well, because it can show the writer interacting with others. Review the dialogue, pointing out effective passages and suggesting ways to improve any weak passages. Look for places where new dialogue might improve the draft, where you would like to hear people talking to each other.

8. Now that you have analyzed the draft closely, consider the autobiographical disclosure again. Does it seem honest and full? Were you surprised by any of it? Can you see any way to make the disclosure more significant?

9. Consider how the essay caused you to reflect on your own life. Was it important to you personally? If so, how? If not, how might it be made more so?

REVISING AND EDITING

Revising may involve strengthening particular sections of your draft, or it may produce a completely rewritten and quite different essay. This section provides guidance in planning your revision.

Revising an essay about an event

Once you have had time to reflect on your draft and perhaps gotten comments from other students or your instructor, you are ready to revise. Before considering the following specific guidelines for revising an event essay, you may want to review the general advice about revision in Chapter 1. To solve certain revision problems you may want to return to the invention activities in this chapter or to have a look at some of the invention activities in Chapter 18: Invention and Inquiry.

Revising for autobiographical significance

☐ Reconsider the autobiographical significance of the event.

☐ Reconsider your tone of voice and emotional distance from the event.

☐ Eliminate any incidents, dialogue, or detail which do not contribute to a focus on autobiographical significance.

Revising for readability

☐ Reconsider your beginning. Decide whether there is a better way to open your essay.

☐ Improve pacing and flow by strengthening connections between sentences and paragraphs.

☐ Reconsider your ending. Decide whether you can end more effectively.

☐ Re-evaluate the whole essay in terms of your readers' needs and interests. Decide whether you've told readers everything they need to know or whether you've given them more than they need to know.

Revising for particularity

☐ Eliminate all unnecessary commentary. Check to see that readers discover the scene and the people through action and dialogue.

☐ Decide whether you need to describe the scene or people more fully.

Editing and proofreading

As you revise a draft for the final time, you need to edit it closely. Though you probably corrected obvious errors in the drafting stage, usage and style were not your first priority. Now, however, you must find and correct any errors of mechanics, usage, punctuation, or style.

When you've edited the draft and produced the final copy, you must proofread carefully before turning your essay in.

LEARNING FROM YOUR OWN WRITING PROCESS

Your instructor may ask you to evaluate what you have learned in writing this autobiographical essay. If so, begin by reviewing quickly the writings and notes you produced during invention and planning. How successful was this part of your writing process? What major discoveries did you make during invention? Were there obstacles in drafting that your invention writings did not help you overcome?

Next, reread your draft, any written analysis of it, and your revision. What did you discover about the event as you were drafting? How did other readers' comments help you improve the draft? What changes did you make between draft and revision? If you had more time, is there anything you would still like to improve? What are you most pleased with in your revision?

A WRITER AT WORK

FROM INVENTION TO DRAFT TO REVISION

Here we will look at the writing process that Jean Brandt followed in composing her essay "Calling Home." You will see some of her invention writing and her complete first draft, which you can then compare to the final draft, printed on pages 32–34.

Invention

Brandt's invention produced about nine handwritten pages, but it took her only two hours, spread out over four days. Here is a selection of her invention writings, showing her first attempts to bring the autobiographical significance of the event into focus as she explores her remembered feelings and present perspective. She begins by listing eight possible events to write about. After some reflection, she chooses to write about the time she was arrested for shoplifting. Then she attempts to focus her thoughts about the significance of the event:

> Being arrested for shoplifting was significant because it changed some of my basic attitudes. Since that night I've never again considered stealing anything. This event would reveal how my attitude toward the law and other people has changed from disrespectful to very respectful.

Brandt begins by stating tentatively that the importance of the event was the lesson it taught her. Reading this statement might lead us to expect a moralistic story of how someone learned something the hard way. As we look at the subsequent invention activities and watch the draft develop, however, we will see how her memories of her relations with other people in the incident considerably change this potentially simplistic beginning.

Recalling the first reactions

> I was scared, humiliated, and confused. I was terrified when I realized what was happening. I can still see the manager and his badge and remember what I felt when I knew who he was. I just couldn't believe it. I didn't want to run. I felt there wasn't anything I could do—I was afraid, embarrassed, worried, mad that it happened. I didn't show my feelings at all. I tried to look very calm on the outside, but inside I was extremely nervous. The nervousness might have come through in my voice a little. I wanted the people around me to think I was tough and that I could handle the situation. I was really disappointed with myself. Getting arrested made me realize how wrong my actions were. I felt very ashamed. Afterward I had to talk to my father about it. I didn't say much of anything except that I was wrong and I was sorry. The immediate consequence was being taken to jail and then later having to call my parents and tell them what happened. I hated to call my parents. That was the hardest part. I remember how much I dreaded that. My mom was really hurt.

Brandt's exploration of her first reaction is quite successful. Naming specific feelings, she focuses on the difference between what she felt and how she acted. She remembers her humiliation at being arrested as well as the terrible moment when she had to tell her parents. As we will see, this concern with her parents' reaction, more than her own humiliation, becomes the most important theme in her essay.

In exploring her first response to the event, Brandt writes quickly, noting down memories as they come to mind. Next, she rereads this first exploration and attempts to state briefly what the incident really reveals about her:

I think it reveals that I was not a hard-core criminal. I was trying to live up to Robin Files' (supposedly my best girlfriend) expectations, even though I actually knew that what I was doing was wrong.

After longer pieces of exploratory writing, stopping to focus her thoughts like this helps Brandt see the point of what she has just written. Specifically, it helps her to connect diverse invention writings to her main concern: discovering the autobiographical significance of the event. Thus does she reflect on what her remembered feelings of the event reveal about the kind of person she was at the time: not a hard-core criminal. She identifies a friend, who will disappear from the writing after one brief mention. Next she looks at her present perspective on the event.

Exploring your present perspective

At first I was ashamed to tell anyone that I had been arrested. It was as if I couldn't admit it myself. Now I'm glad it happened, because who knows where I'd be now if I hadn't been caught. I still don't tell many people about it. Never before have I written about it. I think my response was appropriate. If I'd broken down and cried, it wouldn't have helped me any, so it's better that I reacted calmly. My actions and responses show that I was trying to be tough. I thought that that was the way to gain respectability. If I were to get arrested now (of course it wouldn't be for shoplifting) for something, I think I'd react the same way because it doesn't do any good to get emotional. My current feelings are ones of appreciation. I feel lucky because I was set straight early. Now I can look back on it and laugh, but at the same time know how serious it was. I am emotionally distant now because I can view the event objectively rather than subjectively. My feelings are very settled now. I don't get upset when I think about it. I don't feel angry at the manager or the police. I think I was more upset about my parents than about what was happening to me. After the first part of it was over I mainly worried about what my parents would think.

Writing about her present perspective confirms that Brandt has emotional distance from the event. She finds that she can laugh about it even after probing her feelings seriously. Reassessing her reaction at the time, she decides she acted reasonably. She is obviously pleased to recall that she did not lose control. Then, once again, Brandt tries to summarize the autobiographical disclosures she makes about herself in exploring her present perspective on the event.

My present perspective shows that I'm a reasonable person. I can admit when I'm wrong and accept the punishment that was due me. I find that I can be concerned about others even when I'm in trouble.

Finally, at the end of this first set of invention activities, Brandt reflects on what she has written in order to articulate the autobiographical significance of the event.

Redefining the event's autobiographical significance

> The event was important because it entirely changed one aspect of my character. I will be disclosing that I was once a thief, and I think many of my readers will be able to identify with my story, even though they won't admit it.

After this first set of invention activities, completed in about forty-five minutes on two separate days, Brandt is confident she has chosen an event with personal significance. She knows what she will be disclosing about herself and feels comfortable doing it—now that she knows she has sufficient emotional distance. In her brief focusing statements she begins by moralizing ("my attitude . . . changed") and blaming others (Robin Files) but concludes by acknowledging what she did. She is now prepared to disclose it to readers ("I was once a thief"). Also, she has begun to consider her readers: she thinks they will like her story because she suspects many of them will recall doing something illegal and feeling guilty about it, even if they never got caught.

Brandt is now ready to try to recall specific details from the scene of the event and about the other people involved. She writes two dialogues, one with her sister Sue and the other with her father. We include here the dialogue with her sister.

Re-creating conversations

SUE: Jean, why did you do it?

ME: I don't know. I guess I didn't want to wait in that long line. Sue, what am I going to tell Mom and Dad?

SUE: Don't worry about that yet, the detective might not really call the police.

ME: I can't believe I was stupid enough to take it.

SUE: I know. I've been there before. Now when he comes back try crying and act like you're really upset. Tell him how sorry you are and that it was the first time you ever stole something but make sure you cry. It got me off the hook once.

ME: I don't think I can force myself to cry. I'm not really that upset. I don't think the shock's worn off. I'm more worried about Mom.

SUE: Who knows? Maybe she won't have to find out.

ME: God, I hope not. Hey, where's Louie and Grandma? Grandma doesn't know about this, does she?

SUE: No, I sort of told Lou what was going on so he's just taking Grandma around shopping.

ME: Isn't she wondering where we are?

SUE: I told him to tell her we would meet them in an hour at the fountain.

ME: Jesus, how am I ever going to face her? Mom and Dad might possibly understand or at least get over it, but Grandma? This is gonna kill her.

SUE: Don't worry about that right now. Here comes the detective. Now try to look like you're sorry. Try to cry.

This dialogue helps Brandt recall an important conversation with her sister. Dialogues are an especially useful form of invention for Brandt because people and conversations played such an important part of the event she wishes to write about. Dialogue and action will therefore be prominent in her essay.

Brandt writes this dialogue quickly, trying to capture the language of excited talk, keeping the exchanges brief. She includes a version of this dialogue in her second draft but excludes it from her revision. The dialogue with her father does not appear in any of her drafts. Even though she eventually decides to feature other completely different conversations, these invention dialogues enable her to evaluate how various conversations would work in her essay.

The first draft   The day after completing the invention writing, Brandt writes her first draft. It takes her about an hour.

Her draft is handwritten and contains few erasures or other changes, and so we know that she writes steadily, probably letting the writing lead her where it will. She knows this will not be her only draft.

Before you read the first draft, reread the final draft, "Calling Home," printed on pages 32–34. Then as you read the first draft, consider what part it was to play in the total writing process.

It was two days before Christmas and my older sister and brother, my grandmother, and I were rushing around doing last minute shopping. After going to a few stores we decided to go to Lakewood Center shopping mall. It was packed with other frantic shoppers like ourselves from one end to the other. The first store we went to (the first and last for me) was the General Store. The General Store is your typical gift shop. They mainly have the cutesy knick-knacks, posters, frames and that sort. The store is decorated to resemble an old-time western general store but the appearance doesn't quite come off. 1

We were all browsing around and I saw a basket of buttons so I went to see what the different ones were. One of the first ones I noticed was a Snoopy button. I'm not sure what it said on it, something funny I'm sure and besides I was in love with anything Snoopy when I was 13. I took it out of the basket and 2 showed it to my sister and she said "Why don't you buy it?" I thought about it but the lines at the cashiers were outrageous and I didn't think it was worth it for a 75 cent item. Instead I figured just take it and I did. I thought I was so sly about it. I casually slipped it into my jacket pocket and assumed I was home free because no one pounced on me. Everyone was ready to leave this shop so we made our way through the crowds to the entrance.

My grandmother and sister were ahead of my brother and I. They were al- 3 most to the entrance of May Co. and we were about 5 to 10 yards behind when I felt this tap on my shoulder. I turned around, already terror struck, and this man was flashing some kind of badge in my face. It happened so fast I didn't know what was going on. Louie finally noticed I wasn't with him and came back for me. Jack explained I was being arrested for shoplifting and if my parents were here then Louie should go find them. Louie ran to get Susie and told her about it but kept it from Grandma. By the time Sue got back to the General Store I was in the back office and Jack was calling the police. I was a little scared but not really. It was sort of exciting. My sister was telling me to try and cry but I couldn't. About 20 minutes later two cops came and handcuffed me, led me through the mall outside to the police car. I was kind of embarrassed when they took me through the mall in front of all those people.

When they got me in the car they began questioning me, while driving me 4 to the police station. Questions just to fill out the report—age, sex, address, color of eyes, etc.

Then when they were finished they began talking about Jack and what a 5 nuisance he was. I gathered that Jack had every single person who shoplifted, no matter what their age, arrested. The police were getting really fed up with it because it was a nuisance for them to have to come way out to the mall for something as petty as that. To hear the police talk about my "crime" that way felt good because it was like what I did wasn't really so bad. It made me feel a bit relieved. When we walked into the station I remember the desk sergeant joking with the arresting officers about "well we got another one of Jack's hardened criminals." Again, I felt my crime lacked any seriousness at all. Next they handcuffed me to a table and questioned me further and then I had to phone my mom. That was the worst. I never was so humiliated in my life. Hearing the disappointment in her voice was worse punishment than the cops could ever give me.

This first draft establishes the main narrative line of events. About a third of it is devoted to the store manager, an emphasis which disappears by the final draft. What is to have prominence in the final draft—Brandt's feelings about telling her parents and her conversations with them—appears here only in a few lines at the very end. But its mention suggests its eventual importance, and we are reminded of its prominence in Brandt's invention writing.

Brandt writes a second draft for another student to read critically. In this draft, she includes dialogues with her sister and with the policemen. She also provides more information about her actions as she considered buying the Snoopy button and then decided to steal it instead. She includes visual details of the manager's office. This second draft is not essentially different in emphasis from the first draft, however, still ending with a long section about the policemen and the police station. The parents are mentioned briefly only at the very end.

The student reader tells Brandt how much he likes her story and admires her autobiographical disclosure. However, he does not encourage her to develop the dramatic possibilities in calling her parents and meeting them afterward. In fact, he encourages her to keep the dialogue with the policemen about the manager and to include what the manager said to the police on the phone in his office.

Brandt's revision shows that she does not take her reader's advice. She reduces the role of the police officers, eliminating any dialogue with them. She greatly expands the role of her parents: the last third of the paper is now focused on her remembered feelings about calling them and seeing them afterward. In dramatic importance the phone call home now equals the arrest. Remembering Brandt's earliest invention writings, we can see that she was headed toward this conclusion all along . . . but she needed invention, three drafts, a critical reading, and about a week to get there.

Remembering People

☐ In an article for a sports magazine about the person who most influenced him, a professional football player writes about his high school football coach. In the essay, he admits that his coach held such a powerful influence that he still finds himself doing things to win his approval and admiration, even though he never was able to please him in high school. He relates several anecdotes to show how the coach deliberately tried to humiliate him: challenging him to an arm-wrestling match and laughing at him when he lost, or making him do so many pushups and run so many laps that he actually collapsed in exhaustion.

☐ A novelist writes in her autobiography about an aunt who was notorious for lying. She describes some of her aunt's most fantastic lies and the hilarious trouble they caused. Most members of the family found the woman's behavior annoying and embarrassing, but the writer acknowledges having secretly sympathized with her. As she describes her aunt, the writer points out the resemblance between them: not only does she look like her aunt, but she too has a vivid imagination and likes to embellish reality.

☐ For his political science class, a college junior writes a term paper about his internship as a campaign worker for an unsuccessful candidate. In one part of the paper he focuses on the candidate, whom he came to know well and to admire. He describes the woman's energy and ambition, her broad understanding of issues and attention to detail. The student writes about the anger and bitterness he felt when she lost and his amazement that the candidate seemed genuinely philosophical about her defeat.

☐ Upon learning that her former law professor is to be honored for his service to the community, an attorney decides to write an article about him for her law school alumni magazine. She criticizes him for the hard time he gave her, the first black woman to attend the school, illustrating her point with a few anecdotes. But she also admits that she now realizes that although he often seemed unfair, he prepared her for the competitive world of law better than any of her other teachers did.

3

□ For a composition class, a student writes about an old friend who had once been like a sister to her. Along with anecdotes demonstrating how very close they were, she composes a dialogue of a conversation they had that she's never forgotten. In it they talked about their hopes for the future, specifically about going away to college together and eventually opening a small business. But the friend got married instead and they have since grown apart. Reflecting on her friend and on what happened to their friendship, the writer describes the feelings of anger and betrayal she has harbored but realizes that they really are unfair. The friendship just took its natural course.

As these examples suggest, there may be many occasions when writing about a person you have known seems appropriate. Whatever the reason, your writing must bring the person to life. The person should be carefully described, with distinct physical features and mannerisms, with his or her own characteristic way of thinking and talking, and with a recognizable personal style and sense of values.

Whenever you write about someone else, you also make clear your own feelings and attitudes. In expressing your view of another person, you reveal the values and character traits you admire. In this sense, all biographical writing is to some extent autobiographical. And when you write about a person who has been significant in your life—as you will be asked to do in this chapter—your writing becomes even more personal and autobiographical.

As in the examples that begin this chapter, your aim will be not only to portray the person as an individual but also to indicate how the person has been significant in your life. You may, like the football player and the attorney, decide to write about someone who was once in a position of authority over you. Or you may, like the composition student, choose to describe a peer. The person you select may have been a passing acquaintance, like the unsuccessful candidate, or someone you knew for a long time, like the overly imaginative aunt. The possibilities are endless.

Readers enjoy biography for the same reason they enjoy autobiography: It leads them to reflect on their own lives and on the human condition in general. We are all curious about other people. We want to know what they are like, how they lead their lives, how they relate to others, how they feel. Biography taps this natural curiosity. It can help us know ourselves better and lead us to empathize with others. As you read the selections that follow, think about what they show you about how people behave, think, and interrelate.

READINGS

We begin with a selection from *The Autobiography of Leroi Jones*. The author, Amiri Baraka, is a well-known writer who has published poems, novels, plays, and works of nonfiction under the name of Leroi Jones. He is probably best known for his play *Dutchman* and for his study of jazz, *Blues People: Negro Music in White America*.

Here Baraka writes about his grandmother, Nana. He portrays her as a special individual with her own unique characteristics and values, letting us see that she is not just another grandmother. As you read, pay attention to the way he manages to make her so distinct.

NANA

AMIRI BARAKA

1   Now my grandmother was my heart and soul. She carried sunshine around with her, almost in her smile. She'd have some little hat cocked to one side and she strutted when she walked. Rocked when she was a little weary. But full of fun, her eyes sparkled. You cross her, you were gonna get at least pinched. Like mess up in church, be talking, or fidgeting, she'd cop your flesh between her fingers and rival the Inquisition with their more complicated shit. And she had to do that to me quite often in church because I would go completely out, like some kind of menace. A little big-eyed monster, yapping, running up and down stairs, giggling and laughing. One time I turned off the electricity down in the basement for the whole church and the organist (another Miss Ada) was pushing on the keys and people rushed to her thinking she was having another stroke. They caught me just as I came up out of the basement. Even the special policeman, Mr. Butler, wanted to smash me. But I got ate up when I got home.

2   My grandmother was deeply and completely religious. Her life was defined by Jesus and the Holy Ghost. Every aspect of her life either had God in it or she hooked him up some way. And the church was her world. She was head of the Ladies' Aid Society, an usherette, and a teacher in the Sunday School. And now and again she'd get "happy" in church and start fanning and weeping, rocking back and forth, but most times she'd just sing and listen and amen, under her little flat-top hat trying to see God from behind her rimless glasses.

3   It was my grandmother who most times fed us and kept us, and her spirit is always with us as a part of our own personalities (I hope). I loved my grandmother so much because she was Good. If that had any meaning in the world. She'd tell you, "Do unto others as you'd have them do unto you," and you knew that's what she believed and that's what she practiced. She'd tell me when I was doing something she approved of, "Practice makes per-

fect!'' Maybe it was being polite, emptying the garbage like I was supposed to, or having shined shoes, or even getting good grades in grammar school. ''Practice makes perfect.''

And she was funny, really. Like all those various ''teams'' on radio and 4 later television whose names she'd turn around. I'm not sure why—was it intentional or why she had to twist it up, but it always cracked my sister and me up. Like she'd talk about Abner and Lum or Costello and Abbott. And when she came out with Andy and Amos I thought she was putting us on, but she would pull it with a straight sincere look and it cracked us up.

And she dug *The Road of Life, Life Can Be Beautiful, Ma Perkins, Young* 5 *Widder Brown, Our Gal Sunday, Stella Dallas, Lorenzo Jones* (and his wife, Belle). She'd be listening when we came in and then the kid adventure stuff would come on and she'd fade to do her dinner, preparing stuff, though sometimes she listened with me. Hop Harrigan, Jack Armstrong, Captainnnnnnn Midnight, Tom Mix (and Wash White). And then later she'd be into Beulah, Andy and Amos, and them. When I was sick and had to stay in bed I heard all those soaps along with her while I sprawled. All had organ music and a voice-over telling you what was up. It was a crazy world of villains in civilian clothes.

Plus when my grandmother was working up at those Fortes' house and 6 the other rich white folks', when she'd come back, jim, she'd have a bundle of goodies. Clothes, books, I got the collected works of Dickens, H. Rider Haggard, and random books of the Pooh bear, Sherlock Holmes, and even an almost whole set of Rudyard Kipling, if you can get to that! They were gifts, is what she told us. The white folks was just giving stuff away. I guess they had better stuff, or they needed room. Some of the stuff she brought my sister would have ''Anna Marie Forte'' sewn on labels in the collars. I always wondered about those goddamn Fortes, how they could have all that stuff up there in Essex Fells, how they looked and what they had to say. But I never found out.

My grandmother also had gone to Poro beauty school and she talked 7 about that. She was a hairdresser. The shop she worked in in Newark still sits there on Norfolk Street. So sometimes Elaine and I would be out in front of the beauty parlor, weekends, running around, but connected to the hot curling irons and pressing combs of Ora's beauty parlor and our grandmother sitting there talking and straightening hair with that hunk of grease on the back of her hand.

If I have ever thought seriously about ''heaven'' it was when my grand- 8 mother died, because I wanted her to have that since she believed so strongly. I wrote a poem saying that. I'd been writing for a while when she died. Mostly poems in magazines, and I always regretted that she never got to see a book of mine. I had the dust jacket of *Blues People* in my hand around the time she died, a few weeks later it came out. And I wanted her to see that all the dreams and words she'd known me by had some reality, but it was too late. She'd already gone.

I wrote a story about my grandfather in a magazine my first wife and I 9
published called *Zazen*. It was called "Suppose Sorrow Was a Time Machine?"
She'd seen that and my mother told me she'd liked it. But it wasn't a book.
I wanted my Nana to see that I'd learned "Practice Makes Perfect." But she
was gone.

Questions for analysis   1. Baraka begins by showing us how rebellious he was in church.
What does this anecdote suggest about his attitude toward religion? Compare his religious views to his grandmother's.

2. Baraka clearly loves and admires his grandmother, but what do you
suppose he means when he says in the opening sentence, "my grandmother was my heart and soul"?

3. In paragraphs 4–7 he recalls some things his grandmother used to
do. How do these anecdotes help us to know his grandmother and to
understand her significance in his life?

4. Baraka writes here in an informal, conversational style. Look again
at the writing for specific instances of this and cite two or three examples.
What do these examples suggest about the way Baraka wishes to present
himself to his readers?

5. How does Baraka's portrait of his grandmother lead you to reflect
on your own life or on other people's lives?

6. Imagine yourself writing about someone as important to you as
Baraka's grandmother was to him. Think of a particular person. How
would you describe this person? How would you disclose this person's
significance in your life?

This essay shows us the two features most important to a biographical
essay: a vivid image of the person and a strong sense of his or her significance to the writer. Baraka presents his grandmother by describing her
and telling us about her.

He describes her with a few choice images, leaving out many of the
details you might expect to find in a biographical essay. For instance,
instead of mentioning her height and physique, he characterizes the way
she "strutted" with "her hat cocked to one side," thereby revealing more
of what she was like than he would have by giving facts about her height
and weight.

He tells us about her through direct statements saying she was "funny"
and "full of fun," and showing ways she used to make him laugh. He
explains that she was "deeply and completely religious," that she practiced
what she preached, and that she expected him to do the same. He tells
us when she would praise him—for being polite, for emptying the garbage, for getting good grades—and when she would punish him—for
talking or fidgeting in church.

Baraka explicitly announces, in the very first sentence, how significant his grandmother was in his life. He tells us in the third paragraph that he loved her very much and why: she was not only a companion and caretaker, but a spiritual guide who nurtured his highest values and personal aspirations. Yet his portrait is not all adoration. Like the other portrait writers you will read, Baraka avoids sentimentalizing about his grandmother. The feelings he expresses are not excessive. They are either stated directly and simply ("I loved my grandmother so much") or understated (". . . it was too late. She'd already gone.") Moreover, he allows that he was sometimes rebellious and that his grandmother was quick to punish him when he misbehaved. We infer that he has forgiven her, but that he does not enjoy the memory of it. By showing us such conflicts and by admitting to some mixed feelings about her, Baraka makes his portrait credible.

The next portrait is by Mary McCarthy, a writer whose works include critical essays on social and political issues as well as novels noted for incisive analysis and satiric wit. The selection here comes from an autobiographical work, *Memoirs of a Catholic Girlhood*. In it McCarthy focuses on her paternal grandmother, who nursed her and her family when they were taken ill—and who, after the death of her parents, placed her and her brothers in the custody of their ogreish Uncle Myers and Aunt Margaret.

Whereas Amiri Baraka describes his grandmother as his "heart and soul," McCarthy openly criticizes, even satirizes, hers. Her criticism is so severe, in fact, that readers may well wonder how she can even claim any bond of affection existed between herself and her grandmother. As you will see, she manages to reconcile her mixed feelings in this portrait.

GRANDMOTHER McCARTHY
MARY McCARTHY

White hair, glasses, soft skin, wrinkles, needlework—all the paraphernalia 1
of motherliness were hers; yet it was a cold, grudging, disputatious old woman who sat all day in her sunroom making tapestries from a pattern, scanning religious periodicals, and setting her iron jaw against any infraction of her ways.

Combativeness was, I suppose, the dominant trait in my grandmother's 2
nature. An aggressive churchgoer, she was quite without Christian feeling; the mercy of the Lord Jesus had never entered her heart. Her piety was an act of war against the Protestant ascendancy. The religious magazines on her table furnished her not with food for meditation but with fresh pretexts for anger; articles attacking birth control, divorce, mixed marriages, Darwin, and secular education were her favorite reading. The teachings of the Church did not interest her, except as they were a rebuke to others; "Honor thy father and thy mother," a commandment she was no longer called upon to practice,

was the one most frequently on her lips. The extermination of Protestantism, rather than spiritual perfection, was the boon she prayed for. Her mind was preoccupied with conversion; the capture of a soul for God much diverted her fancy—it made one less Protestant in the world. Foreign missions, with their overtones of good will and social service, appealed to her less strongly; it was not a *harvest* of souls that my grandmother had in mind.

This pugnacity of my grandmother's did not confine itself to sectarian 3 enthusiasm. There was the defense of her furniture and her house against the imagined encroachments of visitors. With her, this was not the gentle and tremulous protectiveness endemic in old ladies, who fear for the safety of their possessions with a truly touching anxiety, inferring the fragility of all things from the brittleness of their old bones and hearing the crash of mortality in the perilous tinkling of a tea cup. My grandmother's sentiment was more autocratic: she hated having her chairs sat in or her lawns stepped on or the water turned on in her basins, for no reason at all except pure officiousness; she even grudged the mailman his daily promenade up her sidewalk. Her home was a center of power, and she would not allow it to be derogated by easy or democratic usage. Under her jealous eye, its social properties had atrophied, and it functioned in the family structure simply as a political headquarters. Family conferences were held there, consultations with the doctor and the clergy; refractory children were brought there for a lecture or an interval of thought-taking; wills were read and loans negotiated and emissaries from the Protestant faction on state occasions received. The family had no friends, and entertaining was held to be a foolish and unnecessary courtesy as between blood relations. Holiday dinners fell, as a duty, on the lesser members of the organization: the daughters and daughters-in-law (converts from the false religion) offered up Baked Alaska on a platter, like the head of John the Baptist, while the old people sat enthroned at the table, and only their digestive processes acknowledged, with rumbling, enigmatic salvos, the festal day.

Yet on one terrible occasion my grandmother had kept open house. She 4 had accommodated us all during those fatal weeks of the influenza epidemic, when no hospital beds were to be had and people went about with masks or stayed shut up in their houses, and the awful fear of contagion paralyzed all services and made each man an enemy to his neighbor. One by one, we had been carried off the train which had brought us from distant Puget Sound to make a new home in Minneapolis.

We awoke to reality in the sewing room several weeks later, to an at- 5 mosphere of castor oil, rectal thermometers, cross nurses, and efficiency, and though we were shut out from the knowledge of what had happened so close to us, just out of our hearing—a scandal of the gravest character, a coming and going of priests and undertakers and coffins (Mama and Daddy, they assured us, had gone to get well in the hospital)—we became aware, even as we woke from our fevers, that everything, including ourselves, was different. We had shrunk, as it were, and faded, like the flannel pajamas we wore, which during these few weeks had grown, doubtless from the disinfectant they were washed in, wretchedly thin and shabby. The behavior of the people around us, abrupt, careless, and preoccupied, apprised us without any ceremony of our diminished importance. Our value had paled, and a new image of ourselves—the image, if we had guessed it, of the orphan—was already forming in our minds. We had not known we were spoiled, but now this word, entering our vocabulary for the first time, served to define the change for us and to herald the new order. Before we got sick, we were spoiled; that was what was the matter now, and everything we could not understand, everything unfamiliar and displeasing, took on a certain plausibility when related to this fresh concept. We had not known what it was to have trays dumped summarily on our beds and no sugar and cream for our cereal, to take medicine in a gulp because someone could not be bothered to wait for us, to have our arms jerked into our sleeves and a comb ripped through our hair, to be bathed impatiently, to be told to sit up or lie down quick and no nonsense about it, to find our questions unanswered and our requests unheeded, to lie for hours alone and wait for the doctor's visit, but this, so it seemed, was an oversight in our training, and my grandmother and her household applied themselves with a will to remedying the deficiency.

Their motives were, no doubt, good; it was time indeed that we learned 6 that the world was no longer our oyster. The happy life we had had—the May baskets and the valentines, the picnics in the yard, and the elaborate snowman—was a poor preparation, in truth, for the future that now opened up to us. Our new instructors could hardly be blamed for a certain impatience with our parents, who had been so lacking in foresight. It was to everyone's interest, decidedly, that we should forget the past—the quicker, the better— and a steady disparagement of our habits ("Tea and chocolate, can you imagine, and all those frosted cakes—no wonder poor Tess was always after the doctor") and praise that was rigorously comparative ("You have absolutely no idea of the improvement in those children") flattered the feelings of the speakers and prepared us to accept a loss that was, in any case, irreparable. Like all children, we wished to conform, and the notion that our former ways had been somehow ridiculous and unsuitable made the memory of them falter a little, like a child's recitation to strangers. We no longer demanded our due, and the wish to see our parents insensibly weakened. Soon we ceased to speak of it, and thus, without tears or tantrums, we came to know they were dead.

Why no one, least of all our grandmother, to whose repertory the subject 7 seems so congenial, took the trouble to tell us, it is impossible now to know. It is easy to imagine her "breaking" the news to those of us who were old enough to listen in one of those official interviews in which her nature periodically tumefied, becoming heavy and turgid, like her portentous bosom, like peonies, her favorite flower, or like the dressmaker's dummy, that bombastic image of herself that, half swathed in a sheet for decorum's sake, lent a museumlike solemnity to the sewing room and aroused our first sexual curiosity. The mind's ear frames her sentences, but in reality she did not speak, whether from a hygienic motive (keep the mind ignorant and the bowels open), or from a mistaken kindness, it is difficult to guess. Perhaps really she feared our tears, which might rain on her like reproaches, since the family policy at the time was predicated on the axiom of our virtual insentience, an assumption that allowed them to proceed with us as if with pieces of furniture.

For my grandmother, the recollection of the dead became a mode of 8 civility that she thought proper to exercise toward us whenever, for any reason, one of us came to stay at her house. The reason was almost always the same. We (that is, my brother Kevin or I) had run away from home. . . . The family would not acknowledge error, but it conceded a certain mismanagement on Myers' and Margaret's part. Clearly, we might become altogether intractable if our homecoming on these occasions were not mitigated with leniency. Consequently, my grandmother kept us in a kind of neutral detention. She declined to be aware of our grievance and offered no words of comfort, but the comforts of her household acted upon us soothingly, like an automatic mother's hand. We ate and drank contentedly; with all her harsh views, my grandmother was a practical woman and would not have thought it worthwhile to unsettle her whole schedule, teach her cook to make a lumpy mush and watery boiled potatoes, and market for turnips and parsnips and all the other vegetables we hated, in order to approximate the conditions she considered suitable for our characters. Humble pie could be costly, especially when cooked to order.

Doubtless she did not guess how delightful these visits seemed to us once 9 the fear of punishment had abated. Her knowledge of our own way of living was luxuriously remote. She did not visit our ménage or inquire into its practices, and though hypersensitive to a squint or a dental irregularity (for she was liberal indeed with glasses and braces for the teeth, disfiguring appliances that remained the sole token of our bourgeois origin and set us off from our parochial-school mates like the caste marks of some primitive tribe), she appeared not to notice the darns and patches of our clothing, our raw hands and scarecrow arms, our silence and our elderly faces. She imagined us as surrounded by certain playthings she had once bestowed on us—a sandbox, a wooden swing, a wagon, an ambulance, a toy fire engine. In my grandmother's consciousness, these objects remained always in pristine condition; years after the sand had spilled out of it and the roof had rotted away, she continued to ask tenderly after our lovely sand pile and to manifest displeasure if we declined to join in its praises. Like many egoistic people (I have noticed this trait in myself), she was capable of making a handsome outlay, but the act affected her so powerfully that her generosity was still lively in her memory when its practical effects had long vanished. In the case of a brown beaver hat, which she watched me wear for four years, she was clearly blinded to its matted nap, its shapeless brim, and ragged ribbon by the vision of the price tag it had worn when new. Yet, however her mind embroidered the bare tapestry of our lives, she could not fail to perceive that we felt, during these short stays with her, *some* difference between the two establishments, and to take our wonder and pleasure as a compliment to herself.

She smiled on us quite kindly when we exclaimed over the food and the 10 nice, warm bathrooms, with their rugs and electric heaters. What funny little creatures, to be so impressed by things that were, after all, only the ordinary amenities of life! Seeing us content in her house, her emulative spirit warmed slowly to our admiration: she compared herself to our guardians, and though for expedient reasons she could not afford to deprecate them ("You children have been very ungrateful for all Myers and Margaret have done for you"), a sense of her own finer magnanimity disposed her subtly in our favor. In the flush of these emotions, a tenderness sprang up between us. She seemed half reluctant to part with whichever of us she had in her custody, almost as if she were experiencing a genuine pang of conscience. "Try and be good," she would advise us when the moment for leave-taking came, "and don't provoke your aunt and uncle. We might have made different arrangements if there had been only one of you to consider." These manifestations of concern, these tacit admissions of our true situation, did not make us, as one might have thought, bitter against our grandparents, for whom ignorance of the facts might have served as a justification, but, on the contrary, filled us with love for them and even a kind of sympathy—our sufferings were less terrible if someone acknowledged their existence, if someone were suffering for us, for whom we, in our turn, could suffer, and thereby absolve of guilt.

During these respites, the recollection of our parents formed a bond be- 11 tween us and our grandmother that deepened our mutual regard. Unlike our guardians or the whispering ladies who sometimes came to call on us, inspired, it seemed, by a pornographic curiosity as to the exact details of our feelings ("Do you suppose they remember their parents?" "Do they ever *say* anything?"), our grandmother was quite uninterested in arousing an emotion of grief in us. "She doesn't feel it at all," I used to hear her confide, of me, to visitors, but contentedly, without censure, as if I had been a spayed cat that, in her superior foresight, she had had "attended to." For my grandmother, the death of my parents had become, in retrospect, an eventful occasion upon which she looked back with pleasure and a certain self-satisfaction. Whenever we stayed with her, we were allowed, as a special treat, to look into the rooms they had died in, for the fact that, as she phrased it, "they died in separate rooms" had for her a significance both romantic and somehow self-gratulatory, as though the separation in death of two who had loved each other in life were beautiful in itself and also reflected credit on the chatelaine of the house, who had been able to furnish two master bedrooms for the emergency. The housekeeping details of the tragedy, in fact, were to her of paramount interest. "I turned my house into a hospital," she used to say, particularly when visitors were present. "Nurses were as scarce as hen's teeth, and *high*—you can hardly imagine what those girls were charging an hour." The trays and the special cooking, the laundry and the disinfectants recalled themselves fondly to her thoughts, like items on the menu of some long-ago ball-supper, the memory of which recurred to her with a strong, possessive nostalgia.

My parents had, it seemed, by dying on her premises, become in a lively 12 sense her property, and she dispensed them to us now, little by little, with a genuine sense of bounty, just as, later on, when I returned to her a grown-up young lady, she conceded me a diamond lavaliere of my mother's as if the trinket were an inheritance to which she had the prior claim. But her generosity with her memories appeared to us, as children, an act of the greatest indulgence. We begged her for more of these mortuary reminiscences as we might have begged for candy, and since ordinarily we not only had no candy but were permitted no friendships, no movies, and little reading beyond what our teachers prescribed for us, and were kept in quarantine, like carriers of social contagion, among the rhubarb plants of our neglected yard, these memories doled out by our grandmother became our secret treasures; we never spoke of them to each other but hoarded them, each against the rest, in the miserly fastnesses of our hearts. We returned, therefore, from our grandparents' house replenished in all our faculties; these crumbs from the rich man's table were a banquet indeed to us. We did not even mind going back to our guardians, for we now felt superior to them, and besides, as we well knew, we had no choice. It was only by accepting our situation as a just and unalterable arrangement that we could be allowed to transcend it and feel ourselves united to our grandparents in a love that was the more miraculous for breeding no practical results.

Questions for analysis

1. McCarthy uses many words her readers may not know—*pugnacity, refractory, tumefied*, among others. Why do you suppose McCarthy might deliberately use words such as these? What impression of her do they give? In answering this question, it might be helpful to consider one or two paragraphs of her writing and try substituting words that are more common. How does the essay change?

2. In focusing on a significant childhood relationship, McCarthy is able to look at her own life with some emotional distance. In what ways is this distance clear in her writing?

3. Consider the following sentence from paragraph 3: "Holiday dinners fell, as a duty, on the lesser members of the organization: the daughters and daughters-in-law (converts from the false religion) offered up Baked Alaska on a platter, like the head of John the Baptist, while the old people sat enthroned at the table, and only their digestive processes acknowledged, with rumbling, enigmatic salvos, the festal day." Do you find this description witty, and if so, why? Do you find it odd that McCarthy would try to treat such traumatic experiences with humor? Do you consider it an effective strategy?

4. McCarthy directly states her grandmother's dominant character traits. Reread the selection, jotting down the qualities—good and bad—she attributes to her grandmother. Then, consider whether McCarthy's analysis of her grandmother's character seems fair. Why, or why not?

5. Contrast the image that McCarthy gives of her grandmother in paragraph 1 with the image she offers of herself in paragraph 5. What do these two images tell us about the two women and about the bond that formed between them?

6. Even readers who have never had to endure experiences like those McCarthy describes may be able to gain some insight into their own lives or into human life generally from this memoir. What thoughts crossed your mind as you read about McCarthy's portrait?

7. If you were asked to write a portrait of someone from your past whom you recall with mixed feelings, whom would it be? How would you go about describing this person and characterizing your relationship? How would you convey your mixed feelings?

This piece lets us see that autobiographers and biographers are really interpreters and not just reporters of human behavior. McCarthy does not withhold judgment; she announces in the very first sentence that her grandmother was a "cold, grudging, disputatious old woman." Nor does she expect readers to accept her judgment without evidence, illustrating her character analysis with specific anecdotes and other examples that are intended to be representative of her grandmother's behavior and attitudes.

Because she is *so* critical, McCarthy runs the risk of alienating readers by seeming mean-spirited herself. She overcomes this problem in at least two ways: by showing some affection for her grandmother, and by acknowledging some of her kindnesses. She describes both with irony, calling her love for her grandmother "miraculous" and saying of her generosity that "she was liberal indeed with glasses and braces for the teeth." Yet, McCarthy wins some sympathy by using the same ironic tone to describe herself and her brother, telling how they treasured the "memories doled out by our grandmother" and not only "begged for more" but then "hoarded them" from each other!

Probably the greatest challenge McCarthy faced was finding a way to write about someone she so closely associates with the loss of her parents. Yet, it is also possible that writing about her grandmother actually enabled her to come to terms with their death. Perhaps her emotional distance from her grandmother—due to time as well as to her own ambivalence—allowed her to disclose deeply personal and painful feelings.

In the next selection, you will see how a thirty-year relationship can be condensed to fit into a brief essay. The essay was written by one famous writer, the playwright Lillian Hellman, about another, the novelist Dashiell Hammett. Hellman's work includes the plays *The Children's Hour* and *The Little Foxes* and a series of memoirs. This selection is taken from *An Unfinished Woman,* the first of her memoirs.

Commenting on the difficulty of writing a coherent essay about a man she knew for thirty years, Hellman writes, "the memories skip about and make no pattern." As you read the essay, try to identify the pattern Hellman imposed on her memories.

DASHIELL HAMMETT
LILLIAN HELLMAN

He did not wish to die and I like to think he didn't know he was dying. 1
But I keep from myself even now the possible meaning of a night, very late, a short time before his death. I came into his room, and for the only time in the years I knew him there were tears in his eyes and the book was lying unread. I sat down beside him and waited a long time before I could say, "Do you want to talk about it?"

He said, almost with anger, "No. My only chance is not to talk about it." 2

And he never did. He had patience, courage, dignity in those last, awful 3
months. It was as if all that makes a man's life had come together to prove itself: suffering was a private matter and there was to be no invasion of it. He would seldom even ask for anything he needed, and so the most we did—my secretary and Helen, who were devoted to him, as most women always had been—was to carry up the meals he barely touched, the books he now could hardly read, the afternoon coffee, and the martini that I insisted upon before the dinner that wasn't eaten.

One night of that last year, a bad night, I said, "Have another martini. It 4
will make you feel better."

"No," he said, "I don't want it." 5

I said, "O.K., but I bet you never thought I'd urge you to have another 6
drink."

He laughed for the first time that day. "Nope. And I never thought I'd 7
turn it down."

Because on the night we had first met he was getting over a five-day 8
drunk and he was to drink very heavily for the next eighteen years, and then one day, warned by a doctor, he said he would never have another drink and he kept his word except for the last year of the one martini, and that was my idea.

We met when I was twenty-four years old and he was thirty-six in a 9
restaurant in Hollywood. The five-day drunk had left the wonderful face looking rumpled, and the very tall thin figure was tired and sagged. We talked of T.S. Eliot, although I no longer remember what we said, and then went and sat in his car and talked at each other and over each other until it was daylight. We were to meet again a few weeks later and, after that, on and sometimes off again for the rest of his life and thirty years of mine.

Thirty years is a long time, I guess, and yet as I come now to write about 10
them the memories skip about and make no pattern and I know only certain
of them are to be trusted. I know about the first meeting and the next, and
there are many other pictures, and sounds, but they are out of order and out
of time, and I don't seem to want to put them into place. I ask myself now
if it can mean much to anybody but me that my second sharpest memory is
of a day when we were living on a small island off the coast of Connecticut.
It was six years after we had first met: six full, happy, unhappy years. . . . I
was returning from the mainland in a catboat filled with marketing and
Hammett had come down to the dock to tie me up. He had been sick that
summer—the first of the sicknesses—and he was even thinner than usual.
The white hair, the white pants, the white shirt made a straight, flat surface
in the late sun. I thought: Maybe that's the handsomest sight I ever saw,
that line of a man, the knife for a nose, and the sheet went out of my hand
and the wind went out of the sail. Hammett laughed as I struggled to get
back the sail. I don't know why, but I yelled angrily, "So you're a Dostoevsky
sinner-saint. So you are." The laughter stopped, and when I finally came in
to the dock we didn't speak as we carried up the packages and didn't speak
through dinner.

Later that night, he said, "What did you say that for? What does it mean?" 11
I said I didn't know why I had said it and I didn't know what it meant.   12
Years later, when his life had changed, I did know what I had meant that 13
day: I had seen the sinner—whatever is a sinner—and sensed the change
before it came. When I told him that, Hammett said he didn't know what I
was talking about, it was all too religious for him. But he did know what I
was talking about and he was pleased.

But the fat, loose, wild years were over by the time we talked that way. 14
When I first met Dash he had written four of the five novels and was the
hottest thing in Hollywood and New York. . . . In his case it was of extra
interest to those who collect people that the ex-detective who had bad cuts
on his legs and an indentation in his head from being scrappy with criminals
was gentle in manner, well educated, elegant to look at, born of early settlers,
was eccentric, witty, and spent so much money on women that they would
have liked him even if he had been none of these things. But as the years
passed from 1930 to 1948, he wrote only one novel and a few short stories.
By 1945, the drinking was no longer gay, the drinking bouts were longer
and the moods darker. I was there off and on for most of those years, but
in 1948 I didn't want to see the drinking anymore. I hadn't seen or spoken
to Hammett for two months until the day when his devoted cleaning lady
called to say she thought I had better come down to his apartment. I said I
wouldn't, and then I did. She and I dressed a man who could barely lift an
arm or a leg and brought him to my house, and that night I watched delirium
tremens, although I didn't know what I was watching until the doctor told
me the next day at the hospital. The doctor was an old friend. He said, "I'm
going to tell Hammett that if he goes on drinking he'll be dead in a few

months. It's my duty to say it, but it won't do any good." In a few minutes he came out of Dash's room and said, "I told him. Dash said O.K., he'd go on the wagon forever, but he can't and he won't."

But he could and he did. Five or six years later, I told Hammett that the 15 doctor said he wouldn't stay on the wagon.

Dash looked puzzled. "But I gave my word that day." 16

I said, "Have you always kept your word?" 17

"Most of the time," he said, "maybe because I've so seldom given it." 18

He had made up honor early in his life and stuck with his rules, fierce in 19 the protection of them. In 1951 he went to jail because he and two other trustees of the bail bond fund of the Civil Rights Congress refused to reveal the names of contributors to the fund. The truth was that Hammett had never been in the office of the Congress, did not know the name of a single contributor.

The night before he was to appear in court, I said, "Why don't you say 20 that you don't know the names?"

"No," he said, "I can't say that." 21

"Why?" 22

"I don't know why. I guess it has something to do with keeping my word, 23 but I don't want to talk about that. Nothing much will happen, although I think we'll go to jail for a while, but you're not to worry because"—and then suddenly I couldn't understand him because the voice had dropped and the words were coming in a most untypical nervous rush. I said I couldn't hear him, and he raised his voice and dropped his head. "I hate this damn kind of talk, but maybe I better tell you that if it were more than jail, if it were my life, I would give it for what I think democracy is, and I don't let cops or judges tell me what I think democracy is." Then he went home to bed and the next day he went to jail.

Questions for analysis

1. Hellman calls Hammett a "Dostoevsky sinner-saint." How does she present him as both a sinner and a saint?

2. How do Hellman's descriptions of Hammett reinforce this image of him as a sinner and a saint?

3. Hammett created a new kind of hero in his fiction: the tough loner who lives by his own code of honor, a figure epitomized by Humphrey Bogart in the film version of Hammett's novel *The Maltese Falcon*. To what extent does Hellman make Hammett seem like the fictional hero he created?

4. As a playwright, Hellman is expert at using dialogue to reveal people and their relationships. Look, for example, at the first conversation she reconstructs (paragraphs 1 and 2). What does this dialogue suggest about the kind of person Hammett was and Hellman's relationship with him?

5. Reread the passage in which Hellman tells of Hammett's delirium tremens (paragraph 14). She must have strong memories of the incident, yet she does not describe it in vivid detail. Why not?

6. How does Hellman engage us as readers, making us want to learn about Dashiell Hammett and her relationship with him?

7. How does Hellman's essay about this important person in her life lead you to reflect on your own life? What memories and feelings does this essay call up?

8. If you were to write about someone you knew for a long time, whom would you choose? Think of a particular person. How might you organize your memories of this person?

Although Hellman says her "memories skip about and make no pattern," there is nothing random about this essay. It is organized chronologically, beginning with a flashforward to Hammett dying. But Hellman does not simply string a series of incidents along a time line. Through anecdote and dialogue, she shows us incidents which form a pattern, a pattern defined by the central, unifying image of Hammett as a "sinner-saint."

In presenting Hammett as a "sinner-saint," Hellman makes him appear larger than life. His alcoholism seems as extreme as his quitting cold turkey. Weak and purposeless on one hand, he possesses enormous moral strength and courage on the other. His tendency to destroy himself is overshadowed by his willingness to sacrifice himself for what he believes. Everything Hammett does—good or bad—is on a grand scale.

By making him seem larger than life, Hellman gives Hammett heroic stature and distances herself from the actual man she knew. Still, in writing about her "closest" and "most beloved friend," it is impossible for Hellman not to disclose some of her feelings. Reading the dialogues and anecdotes, we sense the stresses in their relationship and her feelings of annoyance, frustration, admiration, and sadness. Hellman tells us directly that Hammett's alcoholism tore them apart, and by scarcely describing them, she reveals the horror of his delirium tremens. Through dialogue, she suggests another, subtler strain on their relationship—Hammett's reticence. In writing about his death, however, Hellman is as tight-lipped as Hammett. It is as if she, too, decided that her "only chance is not to talk about it"—at least not directly.

In our next selection, a daughter portrays her father, a man for whom she feels strong ambivalence. The essay was written by Jan Gray, a college freshman. Notice, as you read this piece, how Gray uses description to convey her feelings about her father.

FATHER

JAN GRAY

My father's hands are grotesque. He suffers from psoriasis, a chronic skin 1
disease that covers his massive, thick hands with scaly, reddish patches that
periodically flake off, sending tiny pieces of dead skin sailing to the ground.
In addition, his fingers are permanently stained a dull yellow from years of
chain smoking. The thought of those swollen, discolored, scaly hands touching me, whether it be out of love or anger, sends chills up my spine.

By nature, he is a disorderly, unkempt person. The numerous cigarette 2
burns, food stains, and ashes on his clothes show how little he cares about
his appearance. He has a dreadful habit of running his hands through his
greasy hair and scratching his scalp, causing dandruff to drift downward onto
his bulky shoulders. He is grossly overweight, and his pullover shirts never
quite cover his protruding paunch. When he eats, he shovels the food into
his mouth as if he hasn't eaten for days, bread crumbs and food scraps
settling in his untrimmed beard.

Last year, he abruptly left town. Naturally, his apartment was a shambles, 3
and I offered to clean it so that my mother wouldn't have to pay the cleaning
fee. I arrived early in the morning anticipating a couple hours of vacuuming
and dusting and scrubbing. The minute I opened the door, however, I realized
my task was monumental: Old yellowed newspapers and magazines were
strewn throughout the living room; moldy and rotten food covered the kitchen
counter; cigarette butts and ashes were everywhere. The pungent aroma of
stale beer seemed to fill the entire apartment.

As I made my way through the debris toward the bedroom, I tried to 4
deny that the man who lived here was my father. The bedroom was even
worse than the front rooms, with cigarette burns in the carpet and empty
bottles, dirty dishes, and smelly laundry scattered everywhere. Looking around
his bedroom, I recalled an incident that had occurred only a few months
before in my bedroom.

I was calling home to tell my mother I would be eating dinner at a girl- 5
friend's house. To my surprise, my father answered the phone. I was taken
aback to hear his voice because my parents had been divorced for some time
and he was seldom at our house. In fact, I didn't even see him very often.

"Hello?" he answered in his deep, scratchy voice. 6

"Oh, umm, hi Dad. Is Mom home?" 7

"What can I do for you?" he asked, sounding a bit too cheerful. 8

"Well, I just wanted to ask Mom if I could stay for dinner here." 9

"I don't think that's a very good idea, dear." I could sense an abrupt 10
change in the tone of his voice. "Your room is a mess, and if you're not
home in ten minutes to straighten it up, I'll really give you something to
clean." Click.

Pedalling home as fast as I could, I had a distinct image of my enraged 11
father. I could see his face redden, his body begin to tremble slightly, and
his hands gesture nervously in the air. Though he was not prone to physical
violence and always appeared calm on the outside, I knew he was really

seething inside. The incessant motion of those hands was all too vivid to me as I neared home.

My heart was racing as I turned the knob to the front door and headed 12 for my bedroom. When I opened my bedroom door, I stopped in horror. The dresser drawers were pulled out, and clothes were scattered across the floor. Everything on top of the dresser—a perfume tray, a couple of baskets of hair clips and earrings, and an assortment of pictures—had been strewn about. The dresser itself was tilted on its side, supported by the bed frame. As I stepped in and closed the door behind me, tears welled up in my eyes. I hated my father so much at that moment. Who the hell did he think he was to waltz into my life every few months like this?

I was slowly piecing my room together when he knocked on the door. I 13 choked back the tears, wanting to show as little emotion as possible, and quietly murmured, "Come in." He stood in the doorway, one arm leaning against the door jamb, a cigarette dangling from the other, flicking ashes on the carpet, very smug in his handling of the situation.

"I want you to know I did this for your own good. I think it's time you 14 started taking a little responsibility around this house. Now, to show you there are no hard feelings, I'll help you set the dresser back up."

"No thank you," I said quietly, on the verge of tears again. "I'd rather 15 do it myself. Please, just leave me alone!"

He gave me one last look that seemed to say, "I offered. I'm the good 16 guy. If you refuse, that's your problem." Then he turned and walked away. I was stunned at how he could be so violent one moment and so nonchalant the next.

As I sat in his bedroom reflecting on what he had done to my room, I 17 felt the utmost disgust for this man. There seemed to be no hope he would break his filthy habits. I could come in and clean his room, but only he could clean up the mess he had made of his life. But I felt pity for him, too. After all, he is my father—am I not supposed to feel some responsibility for him and to love and honor him?

Questions for analysis   1. Gray opens the essay by describing her father's hands as "grotesque." Why do you think she focuses on his hands? What impression does this opening have on you as a reader?

2. What does the anecdote in paragraphs 5–16 tell us about her father and their relationship?

3. How does Gray use dialogue to reveal her father's character? Notice her father's choice of words and her description of his tone and posture.

4. Notice the parallel between Gray cleaning up her father's apartment and him tearing apart her room. What does this parallel suggest about their relationship?

5. Look again at the descriptions of the disorder in her father's apartment and her own room (paragraphs 3, 4, and 12). How does Gray make these scenes so vivid?

6. How does this essay lead you to reflect on your own experience? What feelings and memories come to mind?

7. Imagine writing about someone with whom you had a serious conflict. Whom would you write about? How would you present this person? What overall impression of this person would you like your readers to get from your essay?

Although description of place often plays a minimal role in essays about remembered people, it can be an important feature, as it is in this essay. Gray needs to describe her room and her father's apartment to show how destructive her father could be and how out of control his life was. Gray compiles long lists of things she sees, using specific names and sensory details to describe them vividly. She uses a stationary vantage point to orient her readers as she describes the rooms.

The last essay was also written by a college freshman, Chris Stirrat. This selection presents C.J., a man Stirrat knew for a brief time but with whom he developed a complicated relationship. As you read the essay, think about how Stirrat helps you appreciate C.J.'s significance in his life.

C.J.
CHRIS STIRRAT

"Hey you!" 1

"Yah?" I answered, used to the informal no-name ways of the place. 2

"We got a welder for you to work with." 3

I was excited, figuring that helping a welder had to be more interesting 4 than my current job of chipping foam insulation off pipe. Also, I wanted to learn how to use a sub-arc welding machine.

The foreman took me over and introduced me to the welder. C.J. stood 5 an intimidating six-foot-three or so and looked about fifty. Except for some pudginess around the middle, he had the strong, muscular build of someone who had been an athlete when he was younger. His large head was shaped almost exactly like an egg, with grey stubble on the dome and large ears sticking out prominently at the sides. His face seemed soft and flabby.

He was wearing standard welder's glasses and attire. Over his jeans and 6 flannel shirt, he had on brown Carharts, ugly overalls with pockets everywhere, and a leather welding coat. He also wore a train engineer's hat in a patchwork of bright colors. Apart from the hat, the only thing that revealed his personality were his cowboy boots. C.J. was a "good ol' boy" from Louisiana. I figured we'd get along just fine.

Soon after I started working with him, though, I began to have doubts. 7 Once, he was putting in short welds to hold two pieces of pipe together and

I was grinding down the edges of his welds. This is dangerous work because the grinding wheel can get stuck in the gap between the two pieces of pipe and make the grinder jump back—at about sixty miles an hour. I was grinding the top of the pipe, so I was able to keep an eye on the gap pretty well. When I was done with the top, I asked C.J. to rotate the pipe on its roller.

He refused, insisting that I do the grinding on the bottom in order to 8 learn how to do it that way. I knew that grinding on the bottom was more dangerous because it's harder to see the gap. C.J. knew it too. He told me to be careful, saying he once saw a helper get his face cut in half when a grinder jumped back at him. It was as if he was taunting me, testing to see if I had the nerve to do the job. Even though I was scared, I felt I had to show him I could do it.

I crouched down and started grinding. Almost instantly the grinder jumped 9 back and hit me in the head. It gouged my arm (I still have a beautiful scar) and then flew about ten feet behind me. After I recovered enough to speak, I asked C.J. to roll the pipe so I could grind it from the top. Absolutely furious, he yelled back, "Get back under there and try again, only this time ask Jesus Christ for the strength and courage to do it."

Ten seconds after I started grinding, the wheel jumped again, this time 10 getting my leg. The foreman came over and told C.J. to roll the pipe before I killed myself. He rolled it, but he told me over and over again how disappointed he was in me and how badly I was starting out.

From the first, C.J. seemed to expect me to know everything. He would 11 be surprised whenever I asked for help and always refused to show me ahead of time how to do things. Afterwards, he'd say, "Son, what's wrong with you?" and yell at me for screwing things up. I remember one time when he deliberately humiliated me in front of a group of workers, screaming, "Boy! Where the hell is your brain? You ruined that whole pipe!"

After these outbursts, though, he would say something like, "You're doing 12 just fine; you're still just learning. We'll go a long way together. You'll see." I never knew what to say to him. I would be mad at him for yelling at me and mad at myself for doing such a lousy job. He said he was only trying to help me learn, that he hoped he wasn't too hard on me. And he'd ask me over and over, "What are you gonna tell your dad about me? Tell him good things." I still don't know why he wouldn't explain things to me more or show me how to do something before I screwed it up.

Most of the time he acted fatherly towards me. He would tell me what I 13 should and shouldn't do: when to go to bed, what to eat, what movies to see. He said that I shouldn't drink or swear or gamble. One time when I was drinking a beer with the boys after work, he came over and grabbed the bottle out of my hands just like he was my dad. He was a born-again Christian and kept trying to talk me into going to church. But when I finally went one Sunday, he wasn't there.

When I got my lay-off notice, he seemed genuinely sad to see me go. 14 Though I was actually relieved to be getting away from him, I didn't let on. I think he really liked me. I guess I was the son he never had.

Questions for analysis

1. Stirrat says C.J. acted fatherly toward him. How is their relationship like that of a father and son?

2. How would you characterize Stirrat's first impression of C.J.? What do you think was his attitude toward C.J. at the time he wrote this essay?

3. In paragraphs 9, 11, and 12, Stirrat lets us hear the way C.J. used to talk to him. What do C.J.'s words say about him as a person?

4. What does Stirrat disclose about himself in this essay?

5. How does Stirrat's story cause you to reflect on your own life? What does it make you think about human nature in general?

6. Would you consider writing an essay about someone you knew for a short time? Think of a particular person. How would you present this person? What significance did this person hold for you?

Anecdotes figure in all these readings about remembered people, but Stirrat puts an anecdote right at the center of his essay. In showing what happened when C.J. refused to rotate the pipe for him, Stirrat dramatizes their relationship, letting us see C.J. exercising and abusing his authority.

Another key element in this story is its suspense. From the outset, we do not know what will happen. The tension mounts as Stirrat repeatedly tries to resist C.J.'s will, and it does not fall until the intervention of the foreman—C.J.'s authority.

BASIC FEATURES OF ESSAYS ABOUT REMEMBERED PEOPLE

Successful essays about remembered people share certain basic ingredients: they paint a vivid portrait of their subject, they give detailed presentations of any important scenes and incidents, and they indicate the person's significance to the writer.

A vivid portrait

Writing about people might be seen as painting a portrait with words. The writer's foremost goal must be to present a vivid picture of an actual person he or she has known firsthand. A good portrait produces a distinct impression of the subject; never is it vague or generalized.

Some writers sketch the portrait in a few broad strokes—Amiri Baraka shows us his grandmother's strut, her little hat cocked to one side, her sparkling eyes. Others cover the canvas with images—Mary McCarthy gives us her grandmother's iron jaw, her aggressive piety, her portentous bosom. But all writers provide some visual description, images to help readers picture the person.

Portrait writers use the full range of description strategies—naming, detailing, and comparing—to bring their subjects to life. We can see these strategies at work in the readings in this chapter. They are also fully discussed in Chapter 12: Describing.

In describing a person, most writers focus in on him or her by naming particular physical features and objects they associate with the person. Chris Stirrat focuses on C.J.'s head, Carharts, engineer's hat, cowboy boots; McCarthy describes her grandmother's white hair, iron jaw, and needlework.

To these features or objects can be added specific visual details. Stirrat does this in depicting C.J. as wearing "jeans and flannel shirt . . . brown Carharts, ugly overalls with pockets everywhere, and a leather welding coat."

In addition to naming and detailing, writers describe people with comparisons. These comparisons take the form of similes and metaphors: Stirrat says C.J.'s head was "shaped almost exactly like an egg," and McCarthy describes her grandmother's nature as "heavy and turgid, like her portentous bosom, like peonies, her favorite flower, or like the dressmaker's dummy, that bombastic image of herself that, half swathed in a sheet for decorum's sake, lent a museumlike solemnity to the sewing room and aroused our first sexual curiosity."

Combined, these description strategies—naming, detailing, and comparing—produce a vivid image of the subject. In addition, writers select descriptive language that will reinforce the overall impression of the person. McCarthy does this when she describes her grandmother as a "cold, grudging, disputatious old woman who sat all day in her sunroom . . . setting her iron jaw against any infraction of her ways." Lillian Hellman does the same in picturing Hammett as saintlike and spectral, "the white hair, the white pants, the white shirt [making] a straight, flat surface in the late sun."

Portrait writers also tell us about the person through direct statements. McCarthy says her grandmother was cold, grudging, combative, self-satisfied; Hellman calls Hammett patient, courageous, dignified, elegant, eccentric, honorable; Gray tells us her father was disorderly, smug, nonchalant. Each of these statements identify personal qualities, values, character traits. As generalizations based on close observation of the person's habitual conduct, they represent the writer's analysis and judgment of the person.

In addition to helping readers understand the person, direct statements provide insight into his or her significance for the writer. Because they are generalizations, however, such statements need to be made specific through examples. For this reason, writers generally illustrate direct statements with anecdotes and dialogue.

A detailed presentation of important incidents and scenes

Essays about remembered people show us people in action. Writers generally present key incidents as anecdotes—short, pointed stories—to reveal the person's character and to dramatize their own relationship with him or her.

Portrait writers use many different narrating strategies. They choose an appropriate point of view: third person ("he" or "she") when referring to their subject's actions and first person ("I") for their own. In organizing their portraits, they may use narrative, like Hellman and Stirrat, to review the most memorable and revealing incidents in the relationship. Or, like Baraka, they may use narrative primarily to illustrate their analysis of the person. As they narrate, writers vary the pace of the action, quickening it to emphasize critical moments and heighten the drama. Notice how Gray intensifies the pace when she describes her rush to get home and how Stirrat builds tension by dramatizing his confrontation with C.J. over rotating the pipe. (See Chapter 13: Narrating for a complete discussion of all the various narration strategies.)

One strategy used extensively in portrait writing is dialogue. All the readings in this chapter include some dialogue. In letting readers infer what people are like from their own words, dialogue is especially appropriate to essays about people. When we hear Baraka's grandmother saying things like "Do unto others as you'd have them do unto you" and "Practice makes perfect" we get a sense of her simple values. In the same way, Gray's conversations with her father let us see how very manipulative and threatening he was. People's attitudes, values, and character can often be inferred from what they say and the way they say it.

Dialogue can also allow writers to dramatize the significance of the relationship between themselves and their subject. The opening dialogue in Hellman's essay reveals her intimacy with Hammett while at the same time suggesting how hard it was for them to talk about their feelings. The bits of dialogue in Stirrat's essay show us C.J.'s contradictory behavior—critical and humiliating one moment, reassuring and fatherly the next.

Sometimes writers describe places they associate with the person. In this chapter Gray includes important scenes, describing in detail her father's apartment and her bedroom. In these descriptions she uses many strategies often used to present places. She establishes her vantage point on the scene—from the threshold as she enters the room—and describes what she saw—yellowed newspapers and magazines, cigarette butts, moldy food—and what she smelled—stale beer. Besides providing a vivid image of the scene, these sensory descriptions reinforce our impression of her father's character, his disorderliness and potential for violence.

A clear indication of the person's significance

Because essays about remembered people are autobiographical as well as biographical, we expect writers not only to tell us about their subject but also to tell us something about themselves and their relationship with their subject. Portrait writers choose to write about people they consider significant—those who have influenced them, those whom they have loved or feared, those they've tried to impress or who have impressed them— and they must make clear exactly what that significance is.

Some writers do this by stating directly their feelings about the person, as Baraka does when he tells us he loved his grandmother. But all writers convey their feelings indirectly by letting us see what the relationship was like. They dramatize the relationship, revealing the stresses and the harmonies, the conflicts and the intimacies.

Good writers avoid sentimentalizing the relationship by neither damning nor idealizing the person. Though Baraka loved his grandmother, his portrait is not all adoration, showing both his rebelliousness and her sometimes harsh punishment of him. Even if she is angry at her grandmother, McCarthy can still express affection toward her. Gray criticizes her father's faults but admits to certain feelings of filial responsibility toward him. Writers of essays about remembered people acknowledge any mixed or ambivalent feelings, for they know significant relationships are not simple, but complex. As they probe this complexity in their writing, they tell us something about themselves.

Yet portrait writers, like autobiographers, must distance themselves emotionally from their subject. They distance themselves in time by choosing to write about people with whose memory they've made peace. And they distance themselves in the process of writing by analyzing the person and exploring their relationship with him or her. They also distance themselves with humor and self-irony. Like autobiographers, they disclose their feelings, but they often do so subtly, giving us but a glimpse of themselves as they focus our attention on their subject. Thus, we get to know something about Hellman through her analysis of Hammett and dramatization of their relationship. In the same way, we gain insight into Gray by seeing her father and her ambivalence toward him and get some understanding of Stirrat by recognizing his confusion over the mixed signals C.J. sends him.

Inevitably, portrait writers reveal their own values when they describe other people, as when Baraka admires his grandmother's goodness and her lack of hypocrisy. They also admit personal fears and insecurities, as Stirrat does in disclosing his fear of failure. By admitting to such emotions as fear, disappointment, love, admiration, inadequacy, they appeal to their readers' curiosity about how other people cope with such feelings, and ultimately gain their empathy and understanding.

GUIDE TO WRITING

THE WRITING TASK

Write an essay about a person important in your life, someone with whom you have had a significant relationship. Strive to present a vivid image of this person, one that will let your readers see his or her character and personal significance to you.

INVENTION

Invention means searching your memory and discovering the possibilities of your subject. The following activities will help you choose a subject for your portrait, describe the person, define his or her significance for you, and characterize your relationship.

Choosing a person to write about   You may already have a person in mind. If so, turn to Testing Your Choice (page 81). Even if you do have someone in mind, however, you may first want to consider other people in order to choose the best possible subject for your portrait.

Listing people. Make a list of people you could write about. Make your list as complete as you can, including people you knew for a long time and those you knew briefly, people you knew long ago and those you knew recently, people you knew well and those you knew superficially, people you liked and those you disliked. Following are some categories of significant people that may give you ideas for your list:

- ☐ Anyone who was in a position of authority over you or for whom you felt responsible
- ☐ Anyone who helped you through a hard time or made life difficult for you
- ☐ Anyone whose advice or actions influenced you
- ☐ Anyone who taught you something important about yourself
- ☐ Anyone who ever inspired strong emotions in you—admiration, envy, disapproval, fascination
- ☐ Anyone whose behavior or values led you to question your own behavior or values
- ☐ Anyone who really surprised or disappointed you

Choosing a significant person. Select someone you can describe vividly and whose significance you will be willing and able to disclose.

Before making a choice, ask the following questions about each person on your list: how well do I remember this person? Can I portray this person vividly? How has this person been significant in my life? Will I feel comfortable disclosing this significance to my readers?

These questions are something of a first step. In working your way through the various steps of the writing process, you will dig back deeper into your memory and probably find many other ways to present this person. In so doing, you will be testing and retesting your choice and refining your own understanding of the person's significance.

Stop now to focus your thoughts. In a sentence or two, state your tentative understanding of why this person is significant to you.

Testing your choice   After selecting a subject, ask yourself the following questions to determine whether you have chosen someone you will be able to write about vividly and incisively:

☐ Will I be able to help readers visualize and understand this person?
☐ Will I be able to convey the significance this person holds in my life?
☐ Will my portrait of this person lead readers to reflect on their own experience or on human experience generally?

These questions can serve as touchstones for you to consider as you plan and write this essay. If you decide at any point that you cannot answer them affirmatively, you should reconsider your choice.

Describing the person   Here are two invention activities that should help you recall specific information you can use to describe the person.

Describing the person's appearance. List everything you remember about the person's appearance: distinctive physical features, dress, posture, mannerisms, way of talking, any objects you associate with him or her. The list should be as extensive as possible; make no effort to limit it.

Reread your list and add specific details to particularize the items in your list—color, shape, size, texture, value—anything that might help readers visualize the person. As you think and write more about this person, additional images may come to mind. Simply add them to this list.

Making general statements about the person's character. Reflect on what you know about this person: analyze, judge, explain, evaluate. Try to make some generalizations about him or her.

Put down as many statements as you can about the person's character: values, attitudes, personality, conduct. Include anything you think might help readers understand him or her as a person.

Defining the persons's significance

Now you should consider what significance the person has had in your life. The following activities can help you discover this significance and find a way to share it with your readers.

Recalling first impressions. Call to mind your earliest memories of the person. Take about ten minutes to put your thoughts in writing, using the following questions to stimulate your memory:

- [ ] What do I remember about our first meeting—place, time, occasion, particular incidents, other people, words exchanged?
- [ ] What did I expect him or her to be like?
- [ ] What was my initial impression?
- [ ] How did I act? What kind of impression was I trying to make?
- [ ] Did I talk about the person to anyone? What did I say?

Now stop to focus your thoughts. In a couple of sentences, indicate how important the person was to you early in your relationship.

Exploring your present perspective. Think about how you feel now in reflecting on your relationship with this person. Try to articulate your insights about his or her importance in your life. Take about ten minutes to put your thoughts on paper, using these questions as a guide:

- [ ] Would I have wanted the person to behave any differently toward me? How?
- [ ] How do I feel about the way I acted? Would I have behaved any differently had I known then what I know now? What might I have done differently?
- [ ] Looking back at our relationship, do I understand it any differently now than I did at the time?
- [ ] What did I want out of the relationship? What were my needs and expectations? How well were these needs satisfied?
- [ ] Were my feelings toward the person ambivalent? How? Do I still feel the same way? How would I describe my current feelings? Do I have enough emotional distance to write about this person and our relationship?

Now focus your thoughts about your present perspective. In two or three sentences describe your present perspective on the person.

Defining your relationship with the person. People often play roles with one another, acting variously as helper, judge, teacher, servant, parent, sister, friend, foe. They may play a supportive role one moment, a destructive one the next. Think about what roles you and your subject played for each other. Describe the roles, recalling specific occasions when you played each role. Write no more than ten minutes.

Once again take time to focus your thoughts. In two or three sentences, say what the roles you have just described tell you about the person's significance in your life.

Redefining the person's significance. Now that you have explored your first impressions and your present perspective and examined the dynamics of your relationship, write a sentence or two restating the person's significance. What will you be saying about the person—and about yourself—in your essay?

Recalling key incidents and conversations

You should now try to recollect important incidents and conversations that took place with the person. Putting these in the form of anecdotes and dialogues can help both to reveal the person's character and to dramatize the relationship.

Listing incidents. List any incidents you might use in presenting the person. Include incidents which show what the person was like as well as ones which suggest what your relationship was like. Make no effort to limit your list at this point—include little things and major events, things that happened often and those that occurred one time only.

Developing an anecdote. Choose one incident from the list that you might use in the essay. Writing for no more than ten minutes, tell what happened. Give as much detail as you can remember. Make it dramatic. Tell the story in such a way as to illuminate the person's character and make clear his or her significance to you. Be careful, however, not to explain explicitly what the anecdote shows. Let it speak for itself.

Re-creating conversations. Try to reconstruct one or more conversations you had with the person. Choose significant conversations, ones that reveal something important about the person or the way you spoke to each other. Do more than just write, "John said. . . ." Describe John as he spoke—the tone of his voice, his facial expressions, any gestures or body language. Your goal is to let readers hear what was said *and* see how it was said.

Here, stop to focus your thoughts. Explain in a few sentences what the anecdote and dialogues disclose. Consider what exactly you want them to illustrate about the person. What do you want them to say about you?

PLANNING AND DRAFTING

This section serves as a bridge between invention and drafting. It can help you see what you have and determine what you need to explore more fully as well as guiding you in establishing goals and planning your essay.

Seeing what you have   You have now produced a lot of writing focused on the basic features of a portrait: descriptions of the person's appearance and character, disclosure of his or her significance to you, anecdote, dialogue. Before going on to plan and draft your essay, go back and reread what you have already written.

Look for patterns as you read, evidence of growth or deterioration, harmony or tension, consistency or contradiction in the person or in the relationship. See if you make any new discoveries or gain fresh insight. Jot down your ideas in the margins, and underline or star any promising material.

Guided by the following questions, you should now be able to decide whether you have enough material and whether you understand the person's significance well enough.

☐ Do I remember specific details about the person? Will I be able to describe him or her vividly?

☐ Do I understand how the person was significant to me? Have I been able to state it clearly?

☐ Do my anecdotes and dialogues capture the person's character or portray our relationship effectively?

☐ Will I be able to disclose my feelings about this person?

If your invention writing is not full of detail, if it seems superficial, if it has not led you to a clear understanding of the significance the person holds in your life, then you may well have difficulty writing a coherent, developed draft. It may be that the person you have chosen is not a good subject after all. The person may not really be important enough to you personally; conversely, you may not yet have enough emotional distance to write about him or her. As frustrating as it is to start over, it is far better to do so now than later.

If your invention writing looks thin but promising, you may be able to fill it out easily with brief additional writings by returning to the appropriate pages in the guide. You might try thinking more about your relationship with the person, elaborating on your analysis, adding descriptive details, recalling other important events, reconstructing additional conversations, probing your feelings more deeply. (You can also use one of the all-purpose invention activities from the catalogue in Chapter 18: Invention and Inquiry.)

Setting goals   Before actually beginning to draft, most writers set goals for themselves—things to consider and problems to solve. These can include goals for the whole piece, like keeping readers' interest alive, satisfying any curiosity about the person's significance, creating a vivid portrait of that person. Other goals involve smaller issues, like selecting rich visual details, creating realistic dialogue, finding fresh images, connecting paragraphs to one another. All these goals—large and small—require you to make decisions.

Already you have made some decisions, and you will be making more as you draft. When you reach the revision stage, you will probably find yourself reconsidering some of these decisions. Following are some questions that should help you in making further decisions and setting goals for your essay. These questions relate to your goals for anticipating and satisfying your readers' expectations, beginning and ending your essay effectively, presenting the person vividly, and relating his or her significance.

Your readers

☐ Are my readers likely to know someone like this person? If so, how can I help them imagine this particular person?

☐ Will my readers be surprised by this person or by our relationship? Might they disapprove? If so, how can I break through their prejudices to get them to see the person as I do?

☐ How can I help readers see the significance this person has for me?

☐ How can I get readers to empathize with the person I am portraying? How can I lead them to reflect on their own lives and our common human experience?

The beginning

☐ How can the first sentence capture my readers' attention? I could begin as Gray does, with a startling announcement and vivid image ("My father's hands are grotesque."), or as Stirrat does, with someone saying something ("Hey you!"). Or should I open as does Baraka, with a direct disclosure of the person's significance ("Now my grandmother was my heart and soul."), or as does Hellman, sharing a confidence ("He did not wish to die. . . .")?

☐ On what note should I open? Should I first present myself, or should I focus immediately on my subject? How should I modulate my voice—should it sound casual, distant, confiding, coy, mournful, angry, sarcastic?

☐ Should I provide a context, as Gray does, or jump right into the action, as Stirrat does? Should I let readers *see* the person right away? Or should I *tell* them about the person first?

Presenting the person: showing and telling

☐ Which descriptive details best present the person?

☐ What direct statements should I make to characterize the person? What values, attitudes, conduct, character traits should I emphasize?

☐ If I want my readers to understand my relationship with this person, what can I show them in our conversations and experience together?

☐ What insights or feelings do I need to discuss explicitly so my readers will see the person's significance in my life?

☐ What image would best symbolize this person or our relationship?

The ending

☐ What do I want the ending to accomplish? Should it sum things up? Fix an image in readers' minds? Give readers a sense of completion? Open up new possibilities?

☐ How shall I end? With reflection? With a statement of the person's significance? With mention of my own feelings, as does Gray, or speculation about my subject's feelings, as does Stirrat? With an image of the person? With the person's words? With an anecdote?

☐ Shall I frame the essay by having the ending echo the beginning? (Hellman does this, opening with Hammett's death and ending with his departure for jail, as does Baraka, recalling his grandmother's words "Practice makes perfect.")

Drafting the essay   After setting some goals for yourself, make a tentative outline of the points you will cover as you draft. (See Chapter 18: Invention and Inquiry if you need any help outlining.) Then review the advice on drafting in Chapter 1. Do not be alarmed if you find yourself diverging from your outline as you draft. You may well be discovering a more natural way of arranging your points. If you get stuck while drafting, try exploring the problem in writing. You may simply need to recall more details, or you could be on the verge of an important discovery.

READING A DRAFT WITH A CRITICAL EYE

At this point you will want to read over the draft. Whether you are reading your own draft or that of another student, you should read it closely, with a critical eye. The following guidelines will help you analyze the particular features of portrait writing. Before beginning actual analysis, however, you will be asked to give your first general impression of the draft.

First general impression   Read the draft straight through before making any response. Read for enjoyment, ignoring spelling, punctuation, and usage errors for now. Try to imagine the person. Think about his or her significance for the writer. From the essay try to reflect on your own experience or on human nature generally.

   When you have finished this first quick reading, tell the writer what overall impression you got of the person from the essay. Summarize the person's significance as you understand it. If you have any insights about the person or the relationship, share your thoughts.

Pointings   One method of maintaining a critical focus as you read the essay is to highlight noteworthy features of the writing with *pointings*. This simple system of marking a draft with underlining and brackets is quick and easy to do and provides a lot of helpful information about revising the draft. Use pointings in the following way:

☐ Draw a straight line under any words or images that seem especially effective: strong verbs, descriptive details, memorable phrases, striking images.

☐ Draw a wavy line under any words or images that impress you as flat, stale, or vague. Also put a wavy line under any words or phrases that seem unnecessary or repetitious.

☐ Look for pairs or groups of sentences that you think should be combined. Put brackets [ ] around these sentences.

☐ Look for sentences that are garbled, overloaded, or awkward. Put parentheses ( ) around these sentences. Parenthesize any sentence which seems even slightly questionable; don't worry now about whether or not it is actually incorrect. The writer needs to know that you, as one reader, had even the slightest difficulty understanding a sentence.

Analysis   Following are the major points to consider when analyzing a draft of an essay about a remembered person.

1. Strong descriptive writing must be specific and detailed. Note any places where you would like greater specificity or more detail. One way to make the writer see what more you would like to know is by asking questions that seem unanswered. Point out any descriptions which are particularly effective as well as any which seem to contradict the overall impression the rest of the essay gives about the person.

2. Writers often analyze and judge a person's character and conduct by making general statements. Look for vague or unnecessary statements as well as for those which need illustration. Point out any particularly revealing statements, ones which help you understand the person's character or significance. Indicate any statements which seem to be contradicted by the overall impression created by the anecdotes and dialogues.

3. Review the anecdotes, alerting the writer to any that seem pointless, unnecessary, or contradictory. Say if there is anything else you think might be well illustrated by anecdote. Evaluate each anecdote: is it gripping, dramatic, fast-paced?

4. Review the dialogues. Point out any particularly effective dialogue, for instance, any that helps you to understand the person and to get a feeling for his or her importance to the writer. Indicate also those you find inferior, ones which sound artificial or stilted, which move too slowly, or which seem pointless or undramatic.

5. Look again at the beginning. Now that you have thought some about the essay, do you consider the beginning effective? Did it capture your interest and set up the right expectations? Point out any other passages in the essay that you think would make a better beginning, and explain why.

6. Look again at the ending. Is it satisfying? Does it repeat what you already know? Does it oversimplify? If you think the essay could end at an earlier point, indicate where. If you can imagine a better ending—a way to frame the portrait or bring the writer's feelings into perspective—say what it is.

7. Consider again the person's significance. Does the writer sentimentalize the person or the relationship? Is the person's significance stated directly or indirectly? How is it shown? What advice can you give the writer for strengthening this disclosure?

8. Tell the writer what effect this essay had on you personally. How did it lead you to reflect on your own life or on human nature generally?

REVISING AND EDITING

With the insight gained from a critical reading of your draft, you are now ready to revise and edit it. The following advice will help you identify and solve specific problems.

Revising a portrait   Once you have reread your draft and reflected on any comments from other students or your instructor, you can begin to revise it. Before you consider the specific advice for revising a portrait, you may want to review the general advice on revising in Chapter 1. To resolve certain revision problems pointed out in the critical reading, you may want to return to specific invention activities in this chapter or try out the all-purpose invention activities in the catalogue in Chapter 18: Invention and Inquiry.

Revising to clarify the person's significance

☐ Reconsider the person's significance, and strengthen the overall impression you give about it, if necessary.

☐ Eliminate or recast any description, statements, or dialogue that contradict the overall impression about the person's significance. Refocus the essay if necessary.

☐ Reconsider your tone of voice and your emotional distance from the person.

Revising for readability

☐ Look closely at your use of transitional devices. Strengthen any that seem weak; add any that are missing.

☐ Reread any anecdotes for dramatic effect. Try varying the pace if they seem dull.

☐ Reconsider your beginning. Ask yourself whether you could improve it with a better anecdote, image, statement, or dialogue.

☐ Reconsider your ending, making sure it accomplishes what you want it to.

Revising for particularity

☐ Eliminate any statements which tell what you can better show.

☐ Be sure you have enough specific descriptive detail.

☐ Reread dialogues to be sure they show people as they really talk. Eliminate any dialogue that slows the pace or that does not in some way disclose the significance of your subject.

Editing and proofreading   As you revise a draft for the last time, you need to edit it closely. Though you no doubt corrected obvious errors of usage and style in the drafting stage, it was not your first priority. Now, however, you must find and correct any errors of mechanics, usage, punctuation, or style.

When you've edited the draft and produced the final copy you must proofread it for any careless mistakes.

LEARNING FROM YOUR OWN WRITING PROCESS

If you are asked to write about your experience composing this essay, begin by reviewing everything you have written. Look especially closely at the exploration of the person's significance you did in your invention writing and at any difficulties you encountered finding adequate emotional distance.

Next, discuss the changes you made from draft to revision. What seemed to work in the draft and what needed revising? How did others' analysis of the draft help you to see its problems? What other changes would you make if you had the opportunity? What pleases you most about your essay?

A WRITER AT WORK

REVISING A DRAFT AFTER A CRITICAL READING

In this section we will look at the way Jan Gray's essay about her father evolved from draft to revision. Included here are her first draft and a written critique of it done by one of her classmates. Read them, and then turn back to reread her final draft, "Father," printed on pages 72–73 in this chapter.

The first draft   Gray drafted her essay after spending a couple of hours on the invention and planning activities. She had no difficulty choosing a subject, since she had such strong feelings and vivid memories of her father. She wrote the draft in one sitting and did so quickly, not worrying about punctuation or usage. Though she wrote in pencil, Gray's draft appears here typed with numbered paragraphs and marked up with the pointings from the critical reading.

My father is a large intelligent, overpowering man. He's well-respected in the food-processing trade for his clever but shrewd business tactics but I find his manipulative qualities a reflection of the maturity that he lacks (For as long as I can remember he's always had to be in control, decision-maker of the family and what he said was law.) There was no compromising with this man and for that reason I've always feared him.

When I was little and he used to still live with us, everytime he came home from work I avoided him as best I could. If he came in the kitchen I went in the livingroom and if he came in the livingroom I went upstairs to my bedroom just to avoid any confrontation.

Family trips were the worst. (There was nowhere to go, I was locked up with him in a camper or motel for 1 week, 2 weeks or however long the vacation lasted.) I remember one trip in particular. It was the summer after my 12th Birthday and the whole family (5 kids, 2 adults and one dog) were going to go "out west" for a month. (We travelled through Wyoming, North and South Dakota, Colorado and other neighboring states were on the agenda.) My father is the type who thinks he enjoys these family outings because as a loyal husband and father that's what he should do. Going to the state parks and the wilderness was more like a business trip than a vacation. He had made the agenda so no matter what we were to stick to it. That meant at every road sign like Yellowstone Nat'l Park we had to stop, one or more of the kids would get out stand by the sign and he'd take a picture just so he could say we've been there. Get in and get out as quick as possible was his motto to cover as much ground in as little time as he could. I hated having to take those pictures because it seemed so senseless—who cares about the dumb signs anyway? But dad is a very impatient man and any sign of non conformity was sure to put him in a rage. Not a physical violence, no, my father never did get violent but you always knew when he was boiling up inside. I could sense it in the tone of his voice and the reddish glaze that would cover his eyes. He would always stay very calm yet he was ready to explode. He never physically hurt anyone of us kids—sure we've all been spanked before but only when we were younger. Although he constrained himself from inflicting harm on people he didn't hold back from damaging objects.

I remember one time I was calling my mother from a girlfriend's house to ask if I could stay over for dinner when my father unexpectedly answered the phone. "Hello?" he said, in his usually gruffy manner.

"Oh, hi dad. Is Mom around?"

"What can I do for you?"

"Well, I just wanted to ask her if I could eat dinner over here at Shana's."

"I don't think that's a very good idea. Your room is a shambles and if your not home in 10 minutes I'm really going to make a mess for you to clean up." Click.

I was in shock. I hadn't expected him to be there because at this time my   9
parents were divorced but I knew he was serious so I jumped on my bike and
pedalled home as fast as I could. I know I was there within ten minutes but
apparently he didn't think so. I walked in the front door and headed straight
for my room. When I opened my bedroom door I couldn't believe what I saw.
<u>My dresser drawers were all pulled out and clothes strewn about the room,</u> the
dresser was lying on its side and everything on top of the dresser had been cast
aside in a fit of anger. <u>I closed my door and tears began to well up in my eyes.</u> <u>I
hated him so much at the moment.</u> All those years of fear suddenly turned to
anger and resentment. <u>Who the hell was this man to do this when he didn't
even live in the house anymore?</u> I was slowly piecing my room back together
when he knocked on the door. <u>I choked back the tears</u> because I didn't want
him to know that his little outrage had gotten to me and quietly said, "Come
in."

He opened the door and <u>stood in the doorway one arm leaning on the door   10
jamb and a cigarette with ashes falling on the carpet dangling from his other
hand.</u>

"I want you to know I did this for your own good" He said. "I think its time   11
you started taking a little responsibility around this house. Now let me help
you put the dresser back up."

"No thanks. I'd rather do it myself."   12

"Aw, come on. Let's not have any hard feelings now."   13

"Please, I said. I'd rather do it myself so would you please leave me alone."   14
By this time I was shaking and on the verge of breaking out in tears. He gave
me <u>one last look that seemed to say, "I offered, I did the right thing, I'm the
good guy and she refused me so now it's her problem"</u> and he walked out.

I was so upset that he could be so violent one moment and then turn   15
around and patronize me by offering to help clean up what he had done. That
one incident revealed his whole character to me.

<u>My father is a spiteful, manipulative, condescending, malicious man and   16
from that day on I knew I would never understand him or want to.</u>

Gray opens her draft by telling about her father, making a series of direct
statements describing his character. She explicitly states her feelings about
him. The second paragraph illustrates what we were told in the first.
Paragraph 3 also serves as illustration, showing his domination over the
family and concluding with a physical description and a suggestion of his
potential for violence.

In paragraphs 4 to 15, Gray relates an anecdote. Though long, it is
fast paced and dramatic. She uses dialogue to show us her father's character and description to let us visualize the damage he did to her room.
The essay ends as it began—with a series of statements and explicit disclosure of the writer's feelings.

A critical reading   A classmate named Tom Schwartz read Gray's draft. He first read the draft once and quickly wrote down his general impression. Following the critical reading guide, Schwartz then reread the draft to analyze its features closely. It took him a little more than half an hour to complete a full written critique of Gray's draft. Following is Schwartz's critique. Each numbered point corresponds to the same step in the guide to critical reading on pages 87–88.

FIRST GENERAL IMPRESSION: Your dad sure seems crazy. I can see how he's impossible to live with. Because he's your dad he's naturally significant. You say you hate him and you call him a lot of names. But you also say he thought of himself as a loyal father. Was there anytime he was ok?

1. I can't picture him. What did he look like? I like the description of your messed up room. I'd like even more detail, like what clothes were thrown around and where. Did he break anything when he tipped the dresser? Was the whole room a wreck or just the dresser? Oh yeah, the detail of his cigarette ashes falling on the carpet is great. He's the one who's making the mess, not you.

2. You make a lot of statements. Most need illustration. I don't get it about there being no compromising with him. What do you expect him to do? My dad is pretty strict too. But he doesn't wreck my room. I like his being impatient and violent.

3. I don't get the vacation. Was it a birthday trip? Didn't you go to Yellowstone? Or did you just take pictures of signs? Sounds weird. The room anecdote is the best. It's really dramatic. The dialogue works as a frame I think. He had some nerve offering to help pick up the dresser. How smug and self-satisfied. Patronizing is right. Great anecdote.

4. I already talked about the dialogue. It could use description.

5. The beginning doesn't lead one to expect the room anecdote. The stuff about his business seems out of place. You're writing about your relationship with him not about his business. I don't have any suggestions.

6. The ending may be going too far now that I think of it. Also, even though you say you don't want to understand him, here you are writing about him. Maybe there's more to it than you're admitting. You could end with the paragraph before. The incident sure does reveal his character.

7. I just said you might have more feelings than you're admitting. You certainly have every reason to hate him. You say he never really hit you. But he certainly was violent, like you said.

8. I guess it makes me feel lucky my dad and I get along. I don't know what I'd do if he was like your dad. I still wonder if your dad was all that bad. He must have some good sides.

Gray found Schwartz's critique extremely helpful in revising her draft. Reread her revision now to see what she changed; as you will see, many of her changes were suggested by Schwartz.

In writing about what she learned from writing this essay, Gray remarked: "Tom's criticism helped me a lot. He warned me against making too many statements without illustrating them. He said I needed more showing and less telling. He also questioned the vacation anecdote. I guess it didn't have much of a point. And the incident with my room seemed to work so well I decided to add the part about my dad's apartment."

Gray realized that the heart of her essay was in the anecdote about her room. She also saw, from Schwartz's comments, that the opening paragraphs weren't working. Responding to his request for more physical description of her father, Gray returned to the invention activity in which she listed important details about the person's appearance. From this exploration, she came up with the detailed description of her father that now opens the essay. As she was describing her father, she remembered the incident of cleaning his apartment and decided to use the description of his filthy apartment to frame the description of her own ransacked room.

Perhaps Schwartz's greatest contribution, however, was in helping Gray re-examine the real significance her father held in her life. Specifically, Schwartz made her realize that her feelings were more complicated than she let on in her first draft. In writing about what she learned, Gray concluded, "The feelings I wanted to express didn't come across. I had a hard time writing the paper because I held back on a lot of things. I'm pretty ambivalent in my feelings toward my father right now." Gray discovered she could distance herself emotionally and at the same time disclose her feelings by showing her father, his room, and the confrontation over her room. Gray's portrait of her father turned out to be somewhat more sympathetic than her comments about him. She can express her ambivalence—her fury as well as her pity.

Remembering Places

☐ A retired Mexican-American lawyer opens his autobiography with a description of the barrio where he grew up. He describes his family's small stucco house and the others like it on a street lined with palm trees and crowded with parked cars in various states of repair. He sketches portraits of neighborhood people: old women with their gossip and young ones with their children; men of all ages—some retired and aimless, others exhausted from hard work; teenage gangs with time to kill. Reflecting on his old neighborhood, he feels a mixture of relief at having gotten out and nostalgia for the joys of a simple life.

☐ In a proposal to improve safety in city parks, an urban planner describes the park where she played as a child. The playground still exists, unchanged. She describes its rusty old swings, its cement pavement littered with broken glass and beer cans, its drug dealers. She recalls the bruises and cuts small children routinely suffered from falling on the hard surface and the occasional more serious accidents, pointing out one time when a three-year-old child nearly died from injuries suffered when he was thrown from a broken teeter-totter. She uses this personal reminiscence to give substance to her plea for funding for better maintenance and safety precautions for neighborhood playgrounds.

☐ For his freshman English class, a student writes about his grandparents' house, where he spent summer vacations as a child. He describes the basement workshop: hobby magazines piled high, paint and wood-working paraphenalia cluttering the shelves, dusty model ships and planes sus-pended from the ceiling. These were all projects he and his grandfather labored on during summer evenings, the ball game blaring on the radio. When he was a teenager, he had given up all these projects as kid stuff, but writing about them now makes the student see how important they were.

☐ A businesswoman about to have her first child is considering leaving the city and returning to the small town where she grew up. In an effort to sort out her feelings, she begins to keep a diary. She finds herself contrasting her own small-town childhood to what she expects her child would experience in the city. She recalls the tidy green lawns and towering oak trees, the front porch with its creaking swing and chirping cricket, the lemonade stand she and her friend Ellen set up each summer. With this picture, she contrasts the city's drive and bustle, the skyscrapers and theatres and museums, the sometimes unsafe public parks. On reflection, however, she admits her tendency to sentimentalize about her hometown and to exaggerate the city's dangers.

☐ In an article for the Sunday news magazine, a writer describes the town dump where he and his friends spent much of their time as teenagers. They would spend hours rummaging through cracked dishes, broken toys, warped furniture, occasionally finding things of some interest—a rusty knife, an unbroken picture frame, a Kennedy-Johnson campaign button, a slew of old *National Geographic*s. Once he found a whole set of Shakespeare. He concludes that exploring the dump was not only fun, but also educational. It gave him something his school books never did: a palpable sense of the past.

People often write about remembered places. They do so for many different reasons: to evaluate places they have visited, to report on their travels, to provide a setting for stories, to reminisce. The selections about remembered places in this chapter—those you will read as well as the essay you will write—are all primarily autobiographical. That is, they present a place that was once significant in the writer's life, and it is this significance, along with a vivid image of the place, that the writer is trying to convey to readers.

Writing about the significance of a place, as of an event or a person, involves some degree of self-disclosure. Inevitably, writers reveal both memories and feelings in discussing important places in their lives. They may even make new discoveries, resolve old problems, or recognize hidden feelings. For readers, autobiography not only satisfies curiosity about how others live, it also leads to personal reflection. Reading about places from other people's memories can give us all insights about ourselves and about others, insights which help us recognize what is universal about human experience. As you read the selections in this chapter, make an effort to reflect on what they suggest about the writer as well as about human experience in general.

READINGS

The first selection comes from Maya Angelou's autobiography *I Know Why the Caged Bird Sings*. Author and poet, Angelou was raised in Stamps, Arkansas, by her grandmother. Along with her brother Bailey and their crippled Uncle Willie, she lived in the back of her grandmother's country store. In this selection, Angelou writes about this store, which she tells us was her "favorite place to be." As you read, ask yourself how Angelou helps you understand what makes this store so special to her.

THE STORE
MAYA ANGELOU

Weighing the half-pounds of flour, excluding the scoop, and depositing 1
them dust-free into the thin paper sacks held a simple kind of adventure for
me. I developed an eye for measuring how full a silver-looking ladle of flour,
mash, meal, sugar or corn had to be to push the scale indicator over to eight
ounces or one pound. When I was absolutely accurate our appreciative customers used to admire: "Sister Henderson* sure got some smart grandchil-
drens." If I was off in the Store's favor, the eagle-eyed women would say,
"Put some more in that sack, child. Don't you try to make your profit offa
me."

Then I would quietly but persistently punish myself. For every bad judg- 2
ment, the fine was no silver-wrapped Kisses, the sweet chocolate drops that
I loved more than anything in the world, except Bailey. And maybe canned
pineapples. My obsession with pineapples nearly drove me mad. I dreamt of
the days when I would be grown and able to buy a whole carton for myself
alone.

Although the syrupy golden rings sat in their exotic cans on our shelves 3
year round, we only tasted them during Christmas. Momma used the juice
to make almost-black fruit cakes. Then she lined heavy soot-encrusted iron
skillets with the pineapple rings for rich upside-down cakes. Bailey and I
received one slice each, and I carried mine around for hours, shredding off
the fruit until nothing was left except the perfume on my fingers. I'd like to
think that my desire for pineapples was so sacred that I wouldn't allow myself
to steal a can (which was possible) and eat it alone out in the garden, but
I'm certain that I must have weighed the possibility of the scent exposing me
and didn't have the nerve to attempt it.

Until I was thirteen and left Arkansas for good, the Store was my favorite 4
place to be. Alone and empty in the mornings, it looked like an unopened
present from a stranger. Opening the front doors was pulling the ribbon off
the unexpected gift. The light would come in softly (we faced north), easing
itself over the shelves of mackerel, salmon, tobacco, thread. It fell flat on the
big vat of lard and by noontime during the summer the grease had softened
to a thick soup. Whenever I walked into the Store in the afternoon, I sensed
that it was tired. I alone could hear the slow pulse of its job half done. But
just before bedtime, after numerous people had walked in and out, had
argued over their bills, or joked about their neighbors, or just dropped in "to
give Sister Henderson a 'Hi y'all,' " the promise of magic mornings returned
to the Store and spread itself over the family in washed life waves.

Momma opened boxes of crispy crackers and we sat around the meat 5
block at the rear of the Store. I sliced onions, and Bailey opened two or even
three cans of sardines and allowed their juice of oil and fishing boats to ooze
down and around the sides. That was supper. In the evening, when we were

---

* Sister Henderson is the name Angelou's grandmother is known as to friends and neighbors. Angelou herself calls her Momma.

REMEMBERING PLACES 99

alone like that, Uncle Willie didn't stutter or shake or give an indication that he had an "affliction." It seemed that the peace of a day's ending was an assurance that the covenant God made with children, Negroes and the crippled was still in effect.

Questions for analysis

1. In the first half of the piece, Angelou writes about working in the store and about her obsession with pineapples. What do these anecdotes tell you about her—the kind of child she was, her attitudes, values, and needs?

2. Notice the many references to food. We naturally expect some mention of food in a description of a country store, but Angelou gives food an unusually prominent place here. Why? What are her personal associations with food? How was food important to her? Do you have any special memories of food also?

3. In the last sentence, Angelou refers to a "covenant" with God. A covenant is a promise or pledge. Why do you think she brings this idea of a covenant into her piece? How does it concern her grandmother's store?

4. In paragraph 4 Angelou describes the store. How does she organize this description? What is the effect of organizing it this way? How else might a description of a store be organized?

5. Even if your childhood experience differs from Angelou's, reading her essay probably reminded you of something in your own experience. How did this essay lead you to reflect on your own life?

6. Imagine writing about a favorite remembered place. What place would you choose to write about? How would you convey its special quality to readers?

Angelou presents the store by showing us what she used to do there and what the place looked like. She re-creates a series of specific memories—weighing flour for customers, carrying around the Christmas pineapple slice, watching the sun soften the big vat of lard, eating supper around the meat block at the back of the store.

To present a vivid image of the store, Angelou uses the full repertoire of description strategies, naming particular objects and characterizing them with sensory details. She uses images evoking the sense of sight ("a silver-looking ladle"), taste ("sweet chocolate drops"), smell (the "perfume" of pineapple), and touch ("heavy soot-encrusted iron skillets"). To evoke the sense of hearing, she uses metaphor (the sound of the store's "slow pulse"). She also uses simile (the store in the morning seeming "like an unopened present").

Even though she writes about this place as an adult, Angelou does not give her present perspective, describing it instead as she knew it when she was a child. She infuses her description with strong feelings and memories, creating in a few simple images a powerful evocation of the place. In this way, she gives readers an intimate glimpse into her past.

Writers follow the same basic strategies to present a remembered place as they use to present remembered people and events. They describe places and people, re-create dialogue, and tell stories. The autobiographical significance of the place, person, or event is disclosed explicitly through direct statement and implicitly with anecdote and imagery.

The next selection, excerpted from Mark Twain's autobiography, presents his uncle's farm, a place he visited every summer as a youth. Twain is of course one of America's greatest writers, best known for *The Adventures of Huckleberry Finn*. He grew up in Missouri in the mid-1800s and so had firsthand knowledge of slavery, knowledge he used in his writing to expose the hypocrisy of a God-fearing yet slaveholding society.

As you read this selection, notice how Twain brings his feelings about slavery into this piece. Ask yourself how these references to slavery affect your overall impression of his uncle's farm.

UNCLE JOHN'S FARM
MARK TWAIN

It was a heavenly place for a boy, that farm of my uncle John's. The house 1 was a double log one, with a spacious floor (roofed in) connecting it with the kitchen. In the summer the table was set in the middle of that shady and breezy floor, and the sumptuous meals—well, it makes me cry to think of them. Fried chicken, roast pig; wild and tame turkeys, ducks and geese; venison just killed; squirrels, rabbits, pheasants, partridges, prairie-chickens; biscuits, hot batter cakes, hot buckwheat cakes, hot "wheat bread," hot rolls, hot corn pone; fresh corn boiled on the ear, succotash, butter beans, string beans, tomatoes, peas, Irish potatoes, sweet potatoes; buttermilk, sweet milk, "clabber"; watermelons, muskmelons, cantaloupes—all fresh from the garden; apple pie, peach pie, pumpkin pie, apple dumplings, peach cobbler—I can't remember the rest. . . .

The farmhouse stood in the middle of a very large yard and the yard was 2 fenced on three sides with rails and on the rear side with high palings; against these stood the smokehouse; beyond the palings was the orchard; beyond the orchard were the Negro quarters and the tobacco fields. The front yard was entered over a stile made of sawed-off logs of graduated heights; I do not remember any gate. In a corner of the front yard were a dozen lofty hickory trees and a dozen black walnuts, and in the nutting season riches were to be gathered there.

Down a piece, abreast the house, stood a little log cabin against the rail 3 fence; and there the woody hill fell sharply away, past the barns, the corncrib, the stables and the tobacco-curing house, to a limpid brook which sang along

despite
frolic

over its gravelly bed and curved and frisked in and out and here and there
and yonder in the deep shade of overhanging foliage and vines—a divine
place for wading, and it had swimming pools, too, which were forbidden to
us and therefore much frequented by us. For we were little Christian children
and had early been taught the value of forbidden fruit. . . .

All the Negroes were friends of ours, and with those of our own age we 4
were in effect comrades. I say in effect, using the phrase as a modification.
We were comrades and yet not comrades; color and condition interposed a
subtle line which both parties were conscious of and which rendered complete fusion impossible. . . .

to write   *to dislike*   *to accuse*

In my schoolboy days I had no aversion to slavery. I was not aware that 5
there was anything wrong about it. No one arraigned it in my hearing; the
local papers said nothing against it; the local pulpit taught us that God
approved it, that it was a holy thing and that the doubter need only look in
the Bible if he wished to settle his mind—and then the texts were read aloud
to us to make the matter sure; if the slaves themselves had an aversion to
slavery they were wise and said nothing. In Hannibal we seldom saw a slave
misused; on the farm never.

There was, however, one small incident of my boyhood days which touched 6
this matter, and it must have meant a good deal to me or it would not have
stayed in my memory, clear and sharp, vivid and shadowless, all these slow-
drifting years. We had a little slave boy whom we had hired from someone,
there in Hannibal. He was from the eastern shore of Maryland and had been
brought away from his family and his friends halfway across the American
continent and sold. He was a cheery spirit, innocent and gentle, and the
noisiest creature that ever was, perhaps. All day long he was singing, whis-
tling, yelling, whooping, laughing—it was maddening, devastasting, unen-
durable. At last, one day, I lost all my temper and went raging to my mother
and said Sandy had been singing for an hour without a single break and I
couldn't stand it and *wouldn't* she please shut him up. The tears came into
her eyes and her lip trembled and she said something like this:

"Poor thing, when he sings it shows that he is not remembering and that 7
comforts me; but when he is still I am afraid he is thinking and I cannot bear
it. He will never see his mother again; if he can sing I must not hinder it, but
be thankful for it. If you were older you would understand me; then that
friendless child's noise would make you glad."

It was a simple speech and made up of small words but it went home, 8
and Sandy's noise was not a trouble to me any more. She never used large
words but she had a natural gift for making small ones do effective work. . . .

I can see the farm yet, with perfect clearness. I can see all its belongings, 9
all its details; the family room of the house, with a "trundle" bed in one
corner and a spinning wheel in another—a wheel whose rising and falling
wail, heard from a distance, was the mournfulest of all sounds to me and
made me homesick and low spirited and filled my atmosphere with the wandering spirits of the dead; the vast fireplace, piled high on winter nights with

low bed usually under another not in use.

flaming hickory logs from whose ends a sugary sap bubbled out but did not go to waste, for we scraped it off and ate it; the lazy cat spread out on the rough hearthstones; the drowsy dogs braced against the jambs and blinking; my aunt in one chimney corner, knitting; my uncle in the other, smoking his corncob pipe; the slick and carpetless oak floor faintly mirroring the dancing flame tongues and freckled with black indentations where fire coals had popped out and died a leisurely death; half a dozen children romping in the background twilight; "split"-bottomed chairs here and there, some with rockers; a cradle—out of service but waiting with confidence; in the early cold mornings a snuggle of children in shirts and chemises, occupying the hearthstone and procrastinating—they could not bear to leave that comfortable place and go out on the wind-swept floor space between the house and kitchen where the general tin basin stood, and wash.

Along outside of the front fence ran the country road, dusty in the sum- 10 mertime and a good place for snakes—they liked to lie in it and sun themselves; when they were rattlesnakes or puff adders we killed them; when they were black snakes or racers or belonged to the fabled "hoop" breed we fled without shame; when they were "house snakes" or "garters" we carried them home and put them in Aunt Patsy's work basket for a surprise; for she was prejudiced against snakes, and always when she took the basket in her lap and they began to climb out of it, it disordered her mind. . . .

I spent some part of every year at the farm until I was twelve or thirteen 11 years old. The life which I led there with my cousins was full of charm, and so is the memory of it yet. I can call back the solemn twilight and mystery of the deep woods, the earthy smells, the faint odors of the wild flowers, the sheen of rain-washed foliage, the rattling clatter of drops when the wind shook the trees, the far-off hammering of woodpeckers and the muffled drumming of wood pheasants in the remoteness of the forest, the snapshot glimpses of disturbed wild creatures scurrying through the grass—I can call it all back and make it as real as it ever was, and as blessed. . . .

Questions for analysis

1. In the opening sentence Twain calls his uncle's farm "a heavenly place." What language and imagery does he use throughout the piece to associate the farm with paradise?

2. When one thinks of an earthly paradise, one naturally thinks of the Garden of Eden. What parallels do you find between that garden and Uncle John's farm?

3. Twain describes the farm in remarkable detail, yet his attention seems to swerve away from the actual farm in paragraphs 4 through 8. Why do you think he gives this long digression such prominence?

4. In paragraph 3 Twain suggests that all Christian children are taught the value of forbidden fruit. How is this an ironic statement?

5. Autobiographers often contrast their past, or childish, point of

view with their present, adult perspective. Do you think Twain makes this contrast? If so, where and why?

6. In the opening paragraph Twain gives a long list of "sumptuous" dishes. As a strategy, did this engage your attention, or did you find yourself skipping over it? All the readings in this chapter include lists. Why would listing be such a common strategy for describing places?

7. Did this essay cause you to reflect on your own life or on human experience in general? How? Specify any memories or feelings that came to mind as you were reading.

8. Imagine writing about a place you once visited regularly. Think of a particular place. How do you think you would present this place? How might you make clear its personal significance?

Twain presents his uncle's farm vividly, bombarding readers with descriptive detail. He relies primarily on visual images but appeals to all the senses (the mournful wail of the spinning wheel, sugary sap of the hickory log, the warmth of the fireplace on cold mornings, the faint odors of wild flowers). In addition, he identifies and gives details of every imaginable object and feature of the farm: foods (the fried chicken, hot corn pone, apple dumplings); buildings (the farmhouse, log cabin, barn, stables); possessions (the spinning wheel, trundle bed, split-bottomed chairs).

We can see in this piece some of the strategies writers use to organize descriptions and orient readers. Notice how Twain presents some things in long lists, catalogues that lend his description fullness and specificity. Other things he presents topographically, just as they are arranged in space. For instance, he describes the farm's layout by depicting one part in relation to the other parts. To show the relation of those parts, he relies on transitions or connectives: the farmhouse *in the middle of* the yard; the smokehouse *against* the palings *at the rear of* the house.

In describing the farm's layout, Twain takes a distant vantage point, giving a panoramic view. By contrast, he moves in close to present the family room in detail, showing us the way the oak floor mirrors the fire's flames and the sap bubbles out the ends of hickory logs. Sometimes, he scans the scene from a fixed vantage point (describing the family room with a trundle bed in one corner, a spinning wheel in another); other times, he uses a moving vantage point (guiding us down the hill past the barns to the brook).

The next selection comes from *A Walker in the City,* an autobiographical work by the literary critic Alfred Kazin. The son of Russian Jewish immigrants, Kazin grew up in the 1930s in Brownsville, a poor section of Brooklyn, New York. The selection printed here focuses on his memories of his family's kitchen.

Although he views the kitchen primarily from his present, adult perspective, Kazin also recalls his feelings as a child. Notice how these remembered feelings are disclosed through imagery—images of fire and machines in particular.

THE KITCHEN
ALFRED KAZIN

In Brownsville tenements the kitchen is always the largest room and the 1 center of the household. As a child I felt that we lived in a kitchen to which four other rooms were annexed. My mother, a "home" dressmaker, had her workshop in the kitchen. . . . Our apartment was always full of women in their housedresses sitting around the kitchen table waiting for a fitting. My little bedroom next to the kitchen was the fitting room. The sewing machine, an old nut-brown Singer with golden scrolls painted along the black arm and engraved along the two tiers of little drawers massed with needles and thread on each side of the treadle, stood next to the window and the great coal-black stove which up to my last year in college was our main source of heat. By December the two outer bedrooms were closed off, and used to chill bottles of milk and cream, cold borscht and jellied calves' feet.

The kitchen held our lives together. My mother worked in it all day long, 2 we ate in it almost all meals except the Passover *seder,* I did my homework and first writing at the kitchen table, and in winter I often had a bed made up for me on three kitchen chairs near the stove. On the wall just over the table hung a long horizontal mirror that sloped to a ship's prow at each end and was lined in cherry wood. It took up the whole wall, and drew every object in the kitchen to itself. The walls were a fiercely stippled whitewash, so often rewhitened by my father in slack seasons that the paint looked as if it had been squeezed and cracked into the walls. A large electric bulb hung down the center of the kitchen at the end of a chain that had been hooked into the ceiling; the old gas ring and key still jutted out of the wall like antlers. In the corner next to the toilet was the sink at which we washed, and the square tub in which my mother did our clothes. Above it, tacked to the shelf on which were pleasantly ranged square, blue-bordered white sugar and spice jars, hung calendars from the Public National Bank on Pitkin Avenue and the Minsker Progressive Branch of the Workman's Circle; receipts for the payment of insurance premiums, and household bills on a spindle; two little boxes engraved with Hebrew letters. One of these was for the poor, the other to buy back the Land of Israel. . . .

The kitchen gave a special character to our lives; my mother's character. 3 All my memories of that kitchen are dominated by the nearness of my mother sitting all day long at her sewing machine, by the clacking of the treadle against the linoleum floor, by the patient twist of her right shoulder as she automatically pushed at the wheel with one hand or lifted the foot to free the needle where it had got stuck in a thick piece of material. The kitchen was her life. Year by year, as I began to take in her fantastic capacity for labor and her anxious zeal, I realized it was ourselves she kept stitched together. I can never remember a time when she was not working. She worked because the law of her life was work, work and anxiety; she worked because she would have found life meaningless without work. . . . When I awoke in the morning she was already at her machine, or in the great morning crowd of housewives at the grocery getting fresh rolls for breakfast. When I returned from school she was at her machine, or conferring over *McCall's* with some neighborhood woman who had come in pointing hopefully to an illustration—"Mrs. Kazin! Mrs. Kazin! Make me a dress like it shows here in the picture!" When my father came home from work she had somehow mysteriously interrupted herself to make supper for us, and the dishes cleared and washed, was back at her machine. When I went to bed at night, often she was still there, pounding away at the treadle, hunched over the wheel, her hands steering a piece of gauze under the needle with a finesse that always contrasted sharply with her swollen hands and broken nails. . . .

The kitchen was the great machine that set our lives running; it whirred 4 down a little only on Saturdays and holy days. From my mother's kitchen I gained my first picture of life as a white, overheated, starkly lit workshop redolent with Jewish cooking, crowded with women in housedresses, strewn with fashion magazines, patterns, dress material, spools of thread—and at whose center, so lashed to her machine that bolts of energy seemed to dance out of her hands and feet as she worked, my mother stamped the treadle hard against the floor, hard, hard, and silently, grimly at war, beat out the first rhythm of the world for me. . . .

At night the kitchen contracted around the blaze of light on the cloth, 5 the patterns, the ironing board where the iron had burned a black border around the tear in the muslin cover; the finished dresses looked so frilly as they jostled on their wire hangers after all the work my mother had put into them. And then I would get that strangely ominous smell of tension from the dress fabrics and the burn in the cover of the ironing board—as if each piece of cloth and paper crushed with light under the naked bulb might suddenly go up in flames. Whenever I pass some small tailoring shop still lit up at night and see the owner hunched over his steam press; whenever in some poorer neighborhood of the city I see through a window some small crowded kitchen naked under the harsh light glittering in the ceiling, I still smell that fiery breath, that warning of imminent fire. I was always holding my breath. What I must have felt most about ourselves, I see now, was that we ourselves were like kindling—that all the hard-pressed pieces of ourselves and all the hard-used objects in that kitchen were like so many slivers of wood that might go up in flames if we came too near the white-blazing filaments in that naked bulb. Our tension itself was fire, we ourselves were forever burning—to live, to get down the foreboding in our souls, to make good.

Questions for analysis   1. Sensory images are to be expected in writing about remembered places, but the memory of particular sounds and smells seems unusually strong for Kazin. Find places in the selection where he evokes particular sounds and smells. How do these sensory details help you understand his feelings about this place?

2. In paragraph 4 Kazin describes his mother as "so lashed to her machine that bolts of energy seemed to dance out of her hands and feet." Why do you think he describes her this way? What does this image suggest to you about his feelings toward his mother and their home?

3. Kazin closes paragraph 3 with a remarkable series of parallel sentences:

When I awoke . . . she was. . . .
When I returned . . . she was. . . .
When my father came home . . . she had. . . .
When I went to bed . . . she was. . . .

Though he could have varied his sentence structure, he deliberately repeated the same sentence pattern. Why do you think he chose to do this?

4. Look again at the description of the kitchen in paragraph 2. What organizing strategies does Kazin use? Does he take a moving or a fixed vantage point? Does he move in close or give a panoramic view? Does he use listing?

5. Some readers have noticed that Kazin's voice changes in the last part of the piece: his attitude toward the subject seems to intensify, and therefore his tone of voice changes. Skim the essay, looking for such a shift in tone or intensity. Describe what you find.

6. How does Kazin's description of his family's kitchen lead you to reflect on important places in your own life?

7. Can you identify one room that has been important to you? What room would you choose to write about? Think of a particular room: how would you present it? How might you describe the room so that it says something meaningful about you?

In addition to bringing the place to life, writers of essays about places need to find a way to disclose the place's significance. They could do this with a simple statement—"This place was important to me because . . ."— but that would not allow readers to share their experience. They would simply be telling what their experience was, not re-creating it for readers. If you want readers to know what you know and feel what you feel, you have to show them what the experience was like as well as tell them about it.

Kazin shows as well as tells. He tells us that his memories of the kitchen are wound up with memories of his mother, that his mother worked very hard, and that her work kept the family together. He also tells us what he remembers feeling as a child: that their orderly life was uncertain, that the threat of failure was always with them, that their very existence was precarious.

He shows us what his life was like by presenting the kitchen in full detail and by describing his mother's endless labor there. By identifying his mother with the sewing machine—both as a prisoner lashed to the machine and as an automatonlike extension of it— he conveys the horror of his memory of her: "silently, grimly at war." He ends the essay with images of fire, suggesting the intensity and fragility of their life together.

In addition to helping us to understand Kazin's feelings, showing allows him to express those feelings. By showing rather than telling, he is able to resurrect some powerful memories and to share these memories with us. His writing is charged with emotional energy, feelings derived not only from his memories but also from the experience of writing about them.

Herein lies the satisfaction of autobiographical writing. Discovering feelings, reaching new insights, imposing order on a jumble of ideas and memories, distancing yourself from these memories while acknowledging their significance—and finding words to convey all of this—requires tremendous work. But the rewards can be great—for reader and writer alike.

Whereas the first three readings all focus on places the writers knew intimately as children, our last selection presents a place the writer visited only once. The essay was written by a student named Sarah Schoolcraft. Though she spent but a short time at the place, it left a profound impression on her. As you read her essay, ask yourself why this place was so significant for Schoolcraft.

THE OLD PLANTATION
SARAH SCHOOLCRAFT

My mother is yelling at me and my brother. We're on our way to visit an old plantation in my mother's hometown in Virginia, and she has discovered the orange we were playing catch with is now a permanent part of the rent-a-car's carpeting. Because I am ten, I blame it on my brother. Because my brother is thirteen, he's laughing hysterically on the seat next to me.

My mother decides it can be cleaned up later, and my dad continues coaxing the dust-covered car down the deeply rutted dirt path, past the twisting, fragile dogwood limbs stretching across the road. The smell of damp leaves and blossoms fills the car. After a while, the car kicks up one last burst of dust as it pulls out of the woods and into a gradually sloped field. Tall, pale yellow grass covers the field, bending in the breeze under its own weight. We pull up to a wooden farm gate. My mother climbs out of the car and with a flick of her wrist and a push swings open the squeaking gate. Back in the car, she begins describing the house we're going to see. She describes its Jeffersonian columns, its balconies with carved railings, its great hallways with rosewood floors, and its gracious front porch. She tells us about the garden that sat nestled among oak trees behind the house. In the spring time, the three elderly ladies who lived there would pay her a quarter for tending the vegetables. As she describes the smell of the sweet peas, she cranes her head forward so she can see the house the moment it appears. It's been fifteen years since she last visited the house, and as we drive along, I find myself leaning forward in my seat, so I can also see the house as soon as it appears.

We round a final bend in the road, and my father brings the car to an abrupt halt. Ahead of us stands a hill dotted only by a few trees and covered with dried up wild grass and weeds. At the top of the hill sits the house— paint peeling, windows broken, balconies collapsed. The tall columns framing the great porch sag under the weight of the two floors above. With boards covering the bay windows, the house appears as if it were shutting its eyes in shame. 3

After a moment my father turns off the ignition, climbs out of the car, and begins making his way through the dried grass towards the house. The rest of us follow silently. The only sounds are those of seatbelts retracting, car-door buzzers going off, doors slamming, and sneakers shuffling through the dirt and weeds. 4

My brother scuffs noisily behind me and starts humming the theme from "Twilight Zone." Swinging around quickly my mother tells him to be quiet, her voice unusually high and warbling. 5

We climb up the side of the hill, past gopher holes and rusted tins of cat food. Halfway up the hill, I turn around to look at the view. Beneath me lie barren fields where before the Civil War acres of cotton covered the earth like a giant cloud. I go up to the front of the house, where my father is gingerly making his way across the rain-warped porch to the front door. All of the wood stain and polish has long since eroded away, revealing pale, sun-bleached wood. With each step my father takes, the boards wobble, an occasional loose end rising into the air. I make my way around the house, pausing occasionally to pull off a loose slat from the siding. 6

While exploring the outside of the house, I have a little luck and stumble across a window that has not been boarded up. I peer inside, being careful of the dusty, jagged edges of glass. Unable to see much because of the bright sun, I feel as if the house does not want me looking through its eyes to its heart. This house seems so strange to me. I try to picture the people who had lived in it during the past hundred and thirty years, people who loved this house, fought for it, and gave it a life of its own. Sitting on the trampled grass, I think of all the nights I have been allowed to stay up late while my mother tells us Indian legends and folktales and family tales. I know that not twenty miles from here, one of my ancestors lost a leg in battle. Yet it all seems so distant, so foreign to me. 7

Looking up, I see my brother kicking something about. Every so often he chips it up into the air, and I see a flash of white. Getting up and walking closer, I realize it is the skull of a cat. Then I notice at least half a dozen cat skeletons. I do the only rational thing: I run screaming to my mother. I find her sitting on the edge of the garden. When she was my age, she was picking kale and turnips from this garden. Now she sits laboriously tugging at two-foot-tall weeds. An old wrinkled oak, its arms withered, strains to hold up its leaves, dropping many of them to the ground. I sit down on a patch of grass and begin picking the foxtails and burrs out of my ankle socks and green toughskins. My mom stops her work to help, and as she does, she apologizes for the condition of the house. For the first time I notice the skin around her eyes is beginning to tug, forming tiny wrinkles. 8

She had hoped that on this trip my brother and I would learn who we are and take pride in our past. But all that is left for us to see is a house, neglected and no longer important to society. She retells a few of the stories about our ancestors, and then after pulling the last foxtail out of my shoelace, we go back to the car and leave. No one took any photographs; no one made any journal entries. 9

Questions for analysis

1. Do you think Schoolcraft learned what her mother wanted her to? Did she learn anything else?

2. At the end of paragraph 7, Schoolcraft says she could not find any connection with the people who lived in this place. What kind of connection does she eventually make with this place? How is it significant for her?

3. Schoolcraft uses a child's point of view during much of the essay, yet she also manages to convey her mature insights and feelings. How does she combine these two perspectives?

4. What description strategies does Schoolcraft use? What senses do her descriptions appeal to? Does she use a moving or a fixed vantage point, or both?

5. Look again at the way this essay opens. Notice that we're not brought face to face with the plantation until the third paragraph. Why the delay? What do the opening paragraphs accomplish?

6. What thoughts and feelings did you have as you read this essay? Does it lead you in any way to reflect on your own experience or on human experience generally?

7. Can you think of a place you visited only once that you would like to write about? Think of a particular place. How would you make your readers see its significance to you?

This essay seems simple enough: it is about a place Schoolcraft visited once when she was ten. But, it is also about Schoolcraft's mother's visit to a place that had been significant to her as a child. In fact, the significance of this place for Schoolcraft derives from its significance for her mother.

Since she visited the plantation only once, Schoolcraft decides to present it by telling what happened during her visit. She begins her story before they arrive there, setting up her readers' expectations by suggesting her mother's and her own expectations. By using the present tense to write about this past experience, she heightens the immediacy and drama of her narrative.

BASIC FEATURES OF ESSAYS ABOUT REMEMBERED PLACES

Essays about remembered places typically share the following basic features: a vivid scene, a detailed presentation of significant people and incidents, and a clear indication of the place's significance.

A vivid scene   Just as writing about events means telling a story and writing about people means painting a portrait, so writing about places means describing a scene. Whatever other purpose the writer may have, he or she must evoke for readers a striking image of the remembered place.

Scenes in such essays cannot be vague or generalized. Rather, they must be distinctly drawn and particular. Maya Angelou's store is not just any store. It is not even a small country store like the one she knew as a child. Angelou describes one particular small country store—the one her grandmother owned in Stamps, Arkansas. Moreover, she does not present this store as an objective observer might have known it. Instead, she re-creates for us—and for herself—images of the store as she remembers knowing it as a child. Her description is subjective, overflowing with personal memories, associations, and feelings. The store we see is the one she cherishes in her memory.

Writers can make scenes come alive for us by using the three basic description strategies: naming, detailing, and comparing. They name important objects and features of the scene: chocolate kisses, a vat of lard, a can of sardines. To particularize these items, they add specific details, creating images which appeal to our senses: the kisses are "silver-wrapped," the lard is a "thick soup," the sardine juice oozes "down and around the sides" of the cans. To enrich the naming and detailing, they add figurative language, comparisons which evoke special associations and feelings. Look at the similes and metaphors Angelou uses to describe the store: in the morning, it looked "like an unopened present from a stranger"; in the afternoon, it seemed tired, "the slow pulse of its job half done"; before bedtime, "the promise of magic mornings returned . . . and spread itself over the family in washed life waves."

Visual images predominate in scene descriptions, for readers need first of all to visualize the place. Writers rely on visual imagery to identify objects and features as well as to note their details. By specifying such characteristics as size, shape, color, design, and location, a writer can sketch the scene with graphic, realistic detail. Alfred Kazin thus pictures his mother's sewing machine as "an old nut-brown Singer with golden scrolls painted along the black arm and engraved along the two tiers of little drawers massed with needles and thread on each side of the treadle." Visual images are also used to show the state or condition of something; Sarah Schoolcraft, for example, describes rusted tins of cat food, a warped wooden porch, peeling paint, broken windows.

Writers can give a visual description from different vantage points. They may describe a place from a stationary vantage point, as it appears to a stationary observer scanning the scene. Kazin, for example, surveys the various objects around the kitchen: the mirror over the table on one wall, a large electric bulb hanging in the center of the room, the toilet and wash tub in the corner. Or they may describe it from a moving vantage point, as it appears to an observer moving through the scene. Schoolcraft takes us in the car down the dirt path and out of the woods and into a field. Sometimes, writers identify their position in the scene, as Schoolcraft does when she announces, "Halfway up the hill, I turn around to look at the view." More often, however, their position is only implied.

Although scene writers rely most heavily on the sense of sight, they often use the other senses as well. Taste, touch, smell, and hearing can be used to suggest immediacy. Taste and touch convey immediacy because of the physical proximity required. Smell and hearing can also be used to suggest distance and detachment. Mark Twain does this when he evokes the far-off sound of woodpeckers hammering and the faint odors of wildflowers carried in the wind; Kazin evokes the more immediate whirring of a sewing machine and smell of ironed fabric. Visual imagery can also convey a sense of distance. Schoolcraft uses visual imagery to give us a wide panoramic view from the top of a hill, while Kazin moves us in close enough to see "the fiercely stippled whitewash" on kitchen walls.

A detailed presentation of significant people and incidents

Writers of essays about remembered places often inhabit their scenes with people. Sometimes their memories center on certain special people. Kazin's mother, for instance, dominates his memory of the family kitchen. These people may be described in detail, but they are more often presented with a few well-chosen images. Kazin does this when he sketches out images of his mother "pounding away at the treadle, hunched over the wheel . . . swollen hands and broken nails."

Writers also use anecdotes to illustrate key occurrences, be they typical or exceptional. Angelou tells about typical everyday events at her grandmother's store: waiting on customers, eating supper at the end of the day. Twain tells about something less everyday in his anecdote about the slave-child Sandy. Notice that although this incident did not even occur at his uncle's farm, he associates it with the farm because of the presence of slaves there. Twain uses the anecdote to suggest a flaw in this otherwise idyllic place.

A clear indication of the place's significance

Probably the hardest part of writing about remembered places is thinking of places as significant. It is relatively easy to consider certain events significant. Events may be remembered as turning points in our lives, moments of joy or disappointment, revelations inspiring strong feelings. It is also likely that certain people will be especially important in our lives—those we have loved, hated, feared, admired. But places somehow seem more abstract and impersonal than events and people.

The writers considered in this chapter all chose places that are really rather ordinary—a family store, an uncle's farm, a kitchen, an old house and garden. These places are neither exotic nor unique. The only thing special about them is that they call up strong personal feelings, memories, and associations for the writers.

Autobiographers discover the significance of their past experience by exploring their memories and associations. Scene writers disclose the significance in their essays much as they would if they were writing about events or people: they show, and they tell. Angelou tells us directly that her grandmother's store was her favorite place to be, but she also shows through imagery and anecdote that she associates the place with the simple pleasures and joys of childhood.

Carefully chosen, meaningful descriptive details can also give a sense of a place's significance. The long list of foods that opens Twain's essay suggests abundance and contentment, making the farm seem Edenic. Other details also contribute to this impression. Snakes not only fit in the scene but also add to the idea that the farm is a sort of Garden of Eden. These details not only help us picture the scene, they evoke the mood and suggest the place's significance. Twain tells us the farm was "a heavenly place"; these details show us that this was the case.

GUIDE TO WRITING

THE WRITING TASK

Write an essay in which you describe a place you remember very well, a place rich in remembered feelings and personal significance. In presenting this place, let your readers understand how it was significant in your life.

INVENTION

The following invention activities can help you choose a significant place you can write about confidently, recall details about the place, and explore its significance.

Choosing a place to write about

You may already have a place in mind. If so, turn now to Testing Your Choice. But even if you do have a place in mind, you may want to consider several other possibilities before deciding on your essay topic.

Listing places. List all the places you could write about. Make this list as extensive as possible, including places you would like to write about and those you think you would be able to write about. Try to include all different kinds of places: small and large, public and solitary, places from the distant past and also from the more recent past, places you visited only briefly and places you knew intimately over a long period. Some of the most promising places may be those that have not crossed your mind for years. Consider the following suggestions as you compile your list:

- ☐ Any place that haunts your memory or your dreams
- ☐ Any place where something especially joyful or traumatic took place
- ☐ Any place you loved, hated, or reacted to with strong feelings
- ☐ Any place where you learned something important
- ☐ Any place that either did not live up to your expectations or exceeded them
- ☐ Any place that has changed in an important way or that you associate with a major change in you

Choosing a significant place. Choose a place you remember well, one you think has significance you could share with your readers. You may make up your mind immediately. Most writers, however, find it helpful—and sometimes imperative—to weigh the advantages of several possibilities. Even if you decide upon your original choice, the process of comparing it to other attractive possibilities can be a valuable way of identifying its strengths and weaknesses. This will not be the last time to scrutinize your topic: as you work your way through this writing guide, you will be repeatedly testing your choice.

Take time now to focus your thoughts. In a sentence or two, try to state the reason this place was significant in your life.

Testing your choice

Now ask yourself these questions to examine more closely whether you will be able to compose a descriptive and meaningful essay about the place you have selected:

☐ Do I remember the place well enough to present a clear and sharp image of it to readers?

☐ Will I be willing—and able—to disclose the place's significance in my life?

☐ Will my essay lead readers to reflect on their own experience and on human experience generally?

These questions may prove helpful at later stages of writing. If at any point—planning, drafting, or revising—you find yourself unable to answer these questions positively, you should probably consider writing about a different place.

Defining the place's significance

One of the most difficult aspects of writing about a place from your past is figuring out why the place seems important. The invention activities that follow will help you discover how the place is significant to you.

Recalling first impressions. Try to recall your very earliest memories of the place or the first time you were there. Write for around ten minutes, using the following questions as a starting point:

☐ What was the place like when I first knew it? How can I re-create its mood and atmosphere for my readers?

☐ How important did it seem at the time? What about it was important to me?

☐ What were my expectations of the place? Were they satisfied? Was my first experience there at all surprising? How?

☐ Do I associate any people with the place? Who? What comes to mind when I picture them there?

☐ What took place there? What were my feelings about events or activities there?

After writing down something about your early memories of the place, take time once again to focus your thoughts. Indicate in a sentence or two what your first impressions suggest about the place's significance in your life.

Exploring your present perspective. How do you now feel about the place as you reflect on your memories of it? Why do you think it was important to you? What was its significance? Take ten minutes to write about your current understanding of its significance in your life. Think about these questions as you reflect:

☐ What do my memories of this place suggest about my state of mind, my needs and fears, values and attitudes at the time?

☐ As I reflect on the people and events there, what feelings and insights do I have?

☐ Does this place's significance seem universal, or does it seem unique? What other places might have similar significance? Do I know of anyone who has found similar significance in a place?

Focusing your thoughts once again, write a few sentences describing your present perspective on this place's significance in your life.

Using simile and metaphor to discover a place's significance. Sometimes it is easier to express feelings indirectly through simile and metaphor than to state them directly. Try stating your personal impressions and associations in terms of similes and metaphors. These figures of speech can get you thinking in new, exciting ways, and you may be able to use some of them in your essay. Here are several examples from Angelou and Kazin:

☐ "Alone and empty in the mornings [the store] looked like an unopened present from a stranger. Opening the front doors was pulling the ribbon off the unexpected gift."

☐ "The kitchen held our lives together. . . . [It] was the great machine that set our lives running; it whirred down a little on Saturdays and holy days. . . . I still smell that fiery breath. . . . we ourselves were like kindling. . . ."

Recalling specific sensory impressions To sketch a vivid picture of the scene, you will need to probe your memory for lasting impressions, to identify prominent objects and features of the scene, and to characterize some of these objects with specific detail.

Probing your memory. Write for no more than five minutes, noting random images that come to mind. Think about particular sights, sounds, smells, tastes, and textures you associate with the place.

Listing objects. Pretend you are there now. What do you see? If the place is small (a room, a backyard, one end of a street) you might imagine yourself standing in one spot to look it over. If it is large (a park, a neighborhood, a farm) you might imagine yourself walking through it. From whichever vantage point you choose—stationary or moving—list any distinguishing features and notable objects you see. (For now, exclude people from your list.)

Detailing objects. Choose at least three of the most characteristic objects or features from your list. Take five minutes to write about each one, attempting to remember specific sensory details: size, shape, color, condition, odor, taste, texture, sound. Picture each item from different angles—from the side, from behind, from above; from a distance, from close up.

Recalling key events and people

Places frequently take on significance because of specific activities or people. Think about whether this might be the case with the place you have chosen to write about.

Listing events. List any special events or incidents you remember there. List any events you associate with the place whether or not they actually happened there. Include everyday events and unusual ones, good as well as bad, important and trivial.

Exploring one event. Choose the single most significant event from your list, one which seems likely to reveal why the place is important to you. Write for no more than ten minutes, describing what happened and stating why it is significant.

Listing people. List any people you associate with the place. Include acquaintances and close friends, family members and strangers—anyone who comes to mind when you remember this particular place.

Considering one person. Choose one special person from your list, someone you associate strongly with the place. Write for around ten minutes, stating the person's connection with the place, indicating what was special about him or her, and describing your relationship.

Redefining the place's significance

Now that you have probed your memory—recalled your first impressions, explored your present perspective, written several similes and metaphors, resurrected specific sense impressions, thought about key events and people—write a couple of sentences restating the place's significance in your life.

PLANNING AND DRAFTING

This section can help you prepare to write your first draft by reviewing what you discovered in doing the invention activities, outlining the scene, and setting goals for drafting the essay.

Seeing what you have

By now you have probably written several pages and accumulated many ideas and details. Before you begin drafting, you should reread these notes thoughtfully. As you read, reflect on what you have discovered about the place's significance. Look for patterns—repeated ideas or images, for example. Look also for any contradictions in what you have written—good and bad feelings about the place, signs of harmony as well as conflict. Exploring such patterns and contradictions can help you to see and understand the place's significance. Annotate your invention writing with any thoughts or questions, and underline or star promising material.

Consider now the following questions to decide whether you have enough material for a draft:

☐ Do I remember specific sensory impressions of the place? Can I describe any features or objects in detail? Will I be able to portray the scene graphically and memorably?

☐ Do I understand how the place was significant in my life? Have I been able to state the significance clearly? Have I found a way to show it through imagery, simile, metaphor, and anecdote?

If you cannot respond to the preceding questions affirmatively, you may have difficulty writing a focused, detailed draft. The place you have chosen may not really be important enough for you to remember much about it. Another problem might be that you are still too emotionally involved to write about it. In either case, you should consider starting over with a different subject.

If your materials look thin but promising, you can try doing some of the activities again—examining further your first and current impressions, writing other similes and metaphors, recalling additional sensory impressions, and so on.

Outlining the scene   Writing about remembered places may be organized in many ways. Think now about how you might want to organize your essay.

If, like Angelou and Kazin, your memories of the place are connected by a single, common thread, you could try organizing your reflections around a central idea, mood, or person. Clustering (see Chapter 18) provides a simple way of organizing material in this way.

If, like Twain, you want to give readers a graphic picture of the place, you might actually find it useful to sketch a map of the scene. Or, you might list the important features of the scene in the order you intend to present them, starring those you will describe in greater detail.

If, like Schoolcraft, your experience of the place can be conveyed through narrative, you might try constructing a time line of the incidents you associate with the place.

Setting goals   Another helpful step to take before actually drafting is to establish goals for your essay. Some goals will involve large issues like creating a faithful and lively image of the place and making clear its meaning in your life.

Others will be smaller—selecting strong sensory images and characteristic things or features, adopting an appropriate point of view, organizing the descriptive details, finding the right word or phrase. Large or small, all of these goals require decisions.

Following are some questions that can help you set goals for drafting an essay on a remembered place. The questions are designed to guide you in such specific concerns as your readers, and your essay's beginning, ending, descriptions, and disclosures. As you draft, you will want to keep these goals in mind.

Your readers

☐ Are my readers likely to know this place? If so, how can I get them to see it as I do? What is special about the way I remember the place? Might they be at all surprised about my view? How?

☐ Are my readers likely to be familiar with places like this one? If so, how can I use their knowledge of similar places to help them imagine this particular place? What can I assume they will know?

☐ If my readers are totally unfamiliar with such a place, how much information will they need to visualize it? How can I draw on their experience to help them imagine a place like this?

☐ How can I help readers understand how this place is significant in my life? What common experiences are we likely to share? How can I tap any such experiences to help my readers understand the place's significance?

☐ How can my essay lead readers to reflect on their own experience or on human nature in general?

The beginning

☐ How can I capture my readers' attention in the very first sentence? I could begin as Angelou does, indicating what I typically do at the place: "Weighing the half-pounds of flour . . . held a simple kind of adventure for me." Like Twain, I could simply announce that the place is special: "It was a heavenly place for a boy." Or I might open by generalizing about the place's usual prominence, as Kazin does: "In Brownsville tenements the kitchen is always the largest room and the center of the household." Or should I begin with action as Schoolcraft does: "My mother is yelling at me and my brother"? Other ways to begin might be with dialogue, image, metaphor, or simile.

☐ How should I present myself? Should my voice be warm and friendly or cool and detached? Should my writing be formal or informal?

Describing the place

☐ Should I bombard my readers with details as does Twain or use just a few as does Angelou?

☐ Should I appeal to all five senses? Which one is the most important for describing this place?

☐ Should I list things, as Twain and Kazin do?

☐ What vantage point best fits my subject? Should I take a fixed or a moving vantage point, or should I alternate between the two? Should I move in close or give a panoramic view of the scene? Should I announce my position or simply imply it?

Disclosing its personal significance: showing or telling

☐ Which descriptive images best characterize the place? Do any images symbolize the place for me?

☐ What metaphors and similes might disclose my feelings to readers?

☐ What should I tell readers directly about my feelings toward this place?

☐ What anecdotes would help to convey the significance the place has for me?

☐ How much do I need to explain about myself for readers to understand the place's importance to me?

The ending

☐ What should my ending accomplish? Should it fix an image in readers' minds? State the place's significance? Give them insight into my feelings?

☐ How shall I end? With more details, as does Twain? With a new idea, as does Angelou? With reflection on my discovery, as does Kazin? With a telling comment, as does Schoolcraft?

Drafting the essay Before you begin to draft, reread what you have already written and review the advice on drafting in Chapter 1. Concentrate, as you draft, on drawing a clear and lively picture of the place and on helping readers appreciate how and why the place was significant for you. Use your outline, but go with the flow. If your writing takes you into uncharted territory, go with it and see what you discover. You can always return to your outlined plan if you reach a dead end.

READING A DRAFT WITH A CRITICAL EYE

Once you have a complete draft, you need to go over it carefully, reading with a critical eye. Whether you are reading your own draft or one written by another student, the aim is the same: to discover what works and what does not work and to find ways of improvement.

First general impression   Read the draft straight through, reading primarily for enjoyment and ignoring any errors. Try to visualize the place, and think about its importance to you. Reflect on what your essay says about your own experience and suggests about human experience generally.

When you have finished this quick, first reading, tell the writer what impression you have of the place from reading the essay. State your understanding of the place's significance to the writer. What have you learned about him or her from the essay?

Pointings   It is important to maintain a critical focus as you read the essay now; one way to do this is by highlighting notable features of the writing with *pointings*. A simple system of marking a draft with underlining and brackets, these pointings are quick and easy to do and provide a lot of helpful information for revising the draft. Use pointings in the following way:

☐ Draw a straight line under any words or images that impress you as especially effective: strong verbs, precise descriptive details, memorable phrases, striking images.

☐ Draw a wavy line under any words or images that seem flat, stale, or vague. Also put a wavy line under any words or phrases that seem unnecessary or repetitious.

☐ Look for pairs or groups of sentences that you think should be combined. Put brackets [ ] around these sentences.

☐ Look for sentences that are garbled, overloaded, or awkward. Put parentheses ( ) around these sentences. Parenthesize any sentence which seems even slightly questionable; don't spend time worrying about whether it actually is incorrect. The writer needs to know that someone had even the slightest difficulty understanding a sentence.

Analysis   In analyzing a draft of a place essay, you should consider the following points.

1. Good description is particular and vivid. Look closely at how the writer presents objects and features of the scene, and point out any places where you would suggest greater specificity or more detail. One way of

helping the writer to see what more you would like to know is by asking questions that seem unanswered. Note also any especially good description.

2. Look closely at the sensory images. Does the writer evoke any sense other than sight? Point out each sensory image, noting which senses it appeals to. If you can, suggest ways of bringing in any of the other senses.

3. Similes and metaphors liven the language and convey feelings especially well, but they must be fresh and striking. Let the writer know how effective his or her similes and metaphors are.

4. Consider the vantage point the writer uses in this essay—is it moving or fixed, close up or distant? If there is more than one vantage point, are the shifts disruptive or confusing? Does the writer announce the vantage point or simply imply it?

5. If any person has a strong presence in the essay, tell the writer what you understand that person's role to be.

6. Evaluate any anecdotes, indicating how they contribute to your understanding of the place's significance.

7. Look again at the beginning of the essay. Now that you have thought some about the essay, do you consider its beginning effective? Did it capture your interest and set up fair expectations? Point out any other passages in the essay that might serve as a better beginning, and explain why.

8. Evaluate the ending. Does it give you a sense of completion, or does it leave you hanging? Suggest an alternative ending, if you can.

9. Consider the place's significance. Does it strike you as really important for the writer? Where in the essay does the writer best convey the significance?

10. Tell the writer how this essay helped you to reflect on your own experience or on human experience in general.

REVISING AND EDITING

This stage involves re-evaluating and fixing up your draft. It is an opportunity to reflect on what you have written and what you have discovered as you were writing. Take this opportunity to clarify your thoughts as well as to polish your prose.

Revising an essay about a place   Now it is time to revise your draft in light of what you learned from the critical reading. If you have had the benefit of someone else's analysis, carefully consider his or her responses. Even if you do not agree with any specific advice, be alert to the fact that your draft may have problems that need addressing.

Before you consider the specific advice for revising a place essay, you may want to review the general advice on revising in Chapter 1. To resolve certain revision problems pointed out in the critical reading, you may find it useful to return to specific invention activities in this chapter or to try one of the general activities in Chapter 18: Invention and Inquiry.

Revising to clarify the place's significance

☐ Reconsider the place's significance. If necessary, strengthen the overall impression you give readers about it.

☐ Eliminate or recast any description, anecdotes, or statements that contradict the overall impression of the place's significance. Refocus the essay if necessary.

☐ Reconsider your tone of voice and your emotional distance from the subject.

Revising for readability

☐ Look at your use of transitions and connectives, strengthening any that seem feeble and adding any that seem necessary. Pay special attention to seeing that spatial relationships are clear.

☐ Consider the flow of the prose. Combine short sentences to reduce choppiness, or vary the lengths of your sentences to add variety and rhythm to your prose.

☐ Reconsider your beginning. Consider different images, anecdotes, or general statements that might be other ways to open your essay. Would they catch readers' interest better than your present beginning does?

☐ Reconsider your ending. Do you need to develop the ending so as to help readers understand the place's significance? Should you conclude with one memorable image of the scene? Would a metaphor or simile sum up your essay nicely?

Revising for particularity

☐ Make sure you have provided adequate descriptive detail. Do you want to give a fuller description? Should you name more material objects, features, or people?

☐ Consider whether you want to enlarge the range of sensory details and images.

☐ Look over all anecdotes—could they be more specific?

☐ Doublecheck to see that the description of the scene evokes the impression you want. Eliminate any unnecessary or contradictory details.

Editing and proofreading When you are ready to revise a draft for the final time, you must sit down and edit it carefully. When you were drafting your essay, your main focus was on figuring out what you wished to say; usage and style, therefore, were justifiably ignored. Now, however, you must take the time to find and correct any errors of mechanics, usage, punctuation, or style.

After editing the draft and typing or writing out your final copy, you must then proofread closely before submitting your essay to your instructor.

LEARNING FROM YOUR OWN WRITING PROCESS

If you are asked to write about your experience writing this essay, begin by reviewing the work you did inventing and planning. Look closely at your exploration of the place's significance: how did thinking about both your first impression and present perspective help you to define the place's significance? Discuss any difficulties you had recalling specific sensory details and developing a plan for your essay.

Next, discuss the changes you made from draft to revision. What seemed to work in the first draft and what needed revising? How did others' analysis of the draft help you to see its strengths and weaknesses? What further changes would you make if you had the time? What pleases you about your essay?

A WRITER AT WORK

SOME TYPES OF REVISION

In this section we will look at several ways writers revise their work. Specifically, we will focus on Sarah Schoolcraft's essay "The Old Plantation." The final version of this essay is printed on page 107, but here we will look only at the second paragraph. By studying the paragraph in its first and second drafts and then rereading the final draft, we will be able to see the process of writing, reading, and revising that Schoolcraft followed.

The first draft Schoolcraft's first draft shows changes made in the process of initially composing the paragraph. Like all writers, she pauses occasionally to read what she has just written. She may stop and read after a few words or sentences, or after several paragraphs, mainly to see that she is on the right track and that her ideas are coming across clearly.

My mother decides it can be cleaned up later, and my dad continues ~~driving~~ *coaxing*
the dust covered car ~~along~~ the ~~dirt road through~~ *down* *deeply rutted dirt path past* the ~~groves of~~ twisting ,
~~branches of the dogwood trees that~~ *fragile dogwood limbs* stretch *ing* their fingers across the dirt road.
After a while, we reach a *wooden* farm gate. My mother ~~opens the door~~ *gets out* of the car and

with a flick of her wrist and a push swings open the gate. Back in the car, de-

scribing the house we're going to see. She describes it's wide, polished porch so

shiny there's a reflection, it's Jeffersonian columns, it's balconies and great

hallways. As she talks, she cranes her head forward so she can see the house

the moment it appears. It's been fifteen years since she had seen the house, and

it's what she remembers most of her childhood.

Some of her changes are stylistic, intended to make the writing more graceful and flowing. For example, the change from "the twisting, fragile limbs of the dogwood trees" to "the twisting, fragile dogwood limbs" enables her to eliminate a prepositional phrase in a sentence overloaded with prepositional phrases.

Other revisions make the writing more specific and detailed. Notice, for instance, the change from the general word *driving* to the more specific and descriptive word *coaxing*. We can also see this movement from general to particular in the change Schoolcraft made from "along the dirt road" to "down the deeply rutted dirt path."

When asked about these revisions, she said she was trying to be as specific as possible and to use lots of sensory details in her description. She also remarked that she had trouble getting started. Indeed, we can see that she made fewer changes after the first few sentences. Once she focused on her main goal of being specific and found strategies to attain her goal, the writing became easier and better.

Notice that Schoolcraft was not overly concerned with usage, punctuation, or spelling errors when she was revising this first draft. She knew she would have plenty of opportunity to edit her writing and also that she might change it substantially before she was ready to hand it in.

The second draft   A couple of days after writing the first draft, Schoolcraft wrote a second draft. The first thing you will notice about the second draft is that it is basically a revision of the first draft. Although it shows many changes and additions, Schoolcraft did not abandon the first version and start over again.

> My mother decides it can be cleaned up later, and my dad continues coaxing
>
> the dust covered car down the deeply rutted dirt path past the twisting, fragile
>
> dogwood limbs stretching across the road. ~~Soon after,~~ ṫhe smell of damp leaves _pulls out_
> _one last burst of_
> and blossoms fills the car. After a while, the car kicks up ~~more~~ dust as it ~~trav-~~ ~~enters a~~
> _of_ ~~cleaning in~~ _gradually sloped field_ _covers the field,_
> ~~els through~~ the woods and into a ~~clearing~~. Tall, pale yellow grass ~~that spurts~~
> _bending in the breeze_
> ~~up to waist height and then bends~~ under it's own weight ~~covers the field~~. We
>   M
> pull up to a wooden farm gate ~~and my~~ mother climbs out of the car and with a
>
> flick of her wrist and a push swings open the squeeking gate. Back in the car,
>
> she begins describing the house we're going to see. She describes it's Jefferson-
>   _it's_
> ian columns, it's balconies with carved railings, ~~the~~ great hallways with rose-
>   _gracious_   _she tells us about the_
> wood floors, and it's ~~wide~~ front porch. ~~In the back of the house was a~~ garden
>   _behind the house._
> that sat nestled among oak trees, In the spring time, the three elderly ladies
>
> that lived there would pay her a quarter for tending the vegetables. As she de-
>
> scribes the smell of sweet peas, she cranes her head forward so she can see the
>   _as soon as_
> house ~~the moment~~ it appears. It's been fifteen years since she last visited the
>
> house, and as we drive along, I find myself leaning forward in my seat, so I can
>
> also see the house as soon as it appears.

This draft is substantially longer than the first version, nearly doubled in length. Apart from a few words made more specific, Schoolcraft made only one notable change from the first draft: She corrected the unintentional fragment ("Back in the car, describing the house . . . .").

However, she made many additions to the first version. Schoolcraft reported that her goal of making her writing as descriptive as possible influenced many of her decisions. We can certainly see this effort to add description in the long, detailed sentence describing the path the car took.

She added description elsewhere as well, but in those instances her decisions were guided by her other primary goal of revealing the place's significance. Her description of the garden her mother used to tend gives us a sense of the place's importance for her mother. In the last sentence, when she shows herself leaning forward like her mother to get a glimpse of the house, Schoolcraft lets us see how much she identified with her mother and thus how significant the place was becoming for her too.

For the final revision of this paragraph (pages 107–108), she made no major revisions. All she did was edit her writing. She inserted a hyphen between the compound modifiers *dust-covered* and corrected two spelling errors, removing the apostrophe from the possessive *its* and correcting the misspelled *squeeked*. She also made two separate sentences of the run-on sentence beginning "We pull up to a wooden farm gate," fixed an incorrect verb tense, and replaced the pronoun *that* with *who* because it refers to people.

Looking at the first two drafts and then reading the final draft, we see that Schoolcraft's essay is essentially the same in all three versions. Once she determined her major goals, however, the focus of her essay seemed to sharpen with each revision. By adding more and more detail—and by choosing carefully which elements to describe closely and which ones to skip over—she paints a colorful scene and lets us see what importance it had in her life.

Reporting Information

For distribution to the media, a staff member at the U.S. Bureau of the Census writes a report explaining state-by-state population changes between 1970 and 1980. The report centers on a large table which contains 1970 and 1980 population figures for all fifty states. In his report the writer explains how the table is organized and what it reveals about population changes.

A new edition of *Jane's Fighting Ships,* the British publication which is the standard reference on the world's navies, includes an article about a new Swedish antisubmarine cruiser. The article contains technical information along with drawings and photographs. In focusing on the innovative features of this new ship, the writer compares it to several antisubmarine ships in other national navies.

Two authors noted for their research on cats write an article for a popular magazine on the history of the cat. The article explains the religious and economic importance cats held in ancient Egypt, China, Greece, and Rome and then shows how they spread throughout Europe during the period of the Roman Empire.

On an in-class final exam in an introductory sociology class, a college freshman answers a question about eighteenth- and nineteenth-century American minority groups with unconventional life styles. She focuses specifically on the Amish and the Shakers, comparing and contrasting their religious, educational, and economic systems.

A take-home final essay exam in a linguistics course asks students to trace children's syntactic development from the earliest two-word sentences through all basic sentence patterns. After reviewing his textbook and lecture notes, one student divides the information into stages of development and describes what children do within each stage. He includes several sentences to illustrate each of the stages and documents his discussion with reference to specific researchers and research findings. Because he is writing for a reader—his instructor—who is knowledgeable about the topic, he does not have to define any of the special linguistic terms necessary to such a discussion.

☐ For an American history term paper a student decides to write about Susan B. Anthony. Her specific focus is on Anthony's contributions to the women's suffrage movement. The student lists these contributions and discusses the importance of each one as well as reporting several historians' assessments of them.

All writing reports information. There is written information in autobiographies, legal briefs, advertisements, novels, poems, and post cards. But each of the situations listed at the start of this chapter calls for a special type of writing—one where the writer's main purpose is to organize and report information clearly in order to make a point that readers will find interesting and informative.

Organizing and reporting information may seem like an easy kind of writing. Most writers, however, find it quite challenging, mainly because of the need to decide on a point, or thesis, and to organize the information to demonstrate the point. It is also a challenge to assess accurately how much readers already know about a subject so that the writer includes information that suits their knowledge and interests and also tells them something new.

Reporting information is a familiar writing situation to college students. On essays, reports, and term papers you will need to organize and report information learned from books and lectures.

The readings to follow are all examples of how professional and student writers report information. Each reading is followed by questions, which will direct you to the central issues and possibilities in this kind of writing. These readings will also give you many ideas for essays you yourself might write. As you read, note down any thoughts you might have for an essay reporting information.

READINGS

This first reading comes from *Taking the Quantum Leap,* a book introducing modern theoretical physics (quantum mechanics) to nonscientists. The writer, Fred Wolf, is a physicist, teacher, and author. As you read, notice the various ways Wolf presents information about Galileo, the sixteenth-century scientist whom he considers the first experimental physicist.

**GALILEO:
THE FIRST ACTIVE
OBSERVER**

FRED WOLF

Galileo is the prime example of the modern physicist. He devised methods 1
of observation, description, and analysis that today we take as the basis for
all physics. His essential contribution to the eventual discovery of quantum
mechanics was the replacement of the passive observer with the active observer.

Passive observation was any observation that the observer wished to per- 2
form that left the observed undisturbed by the observer. In other words,
passive observation required that the presence of the observer have no effect
on the outcome of whatever was observed. For example, the sun rises whether
or not we look at it. Our observations have no effect upon the movement
responsible for that observation, which we now recognize is the rotation of
the earth about its axis. There is little if anything we can do to stop the earth
from spinning. We take this for granted.

Until Galileo's time, little had been done to attempt to discover reasons 3
for motion other than those offered by Aristotle. Experimentation or actual
analysis of motion was difficult and was not even attempted. But Galileo was
part of the new breed. When he was barely seventeen years old, he made a
passive observation of a chandelier swinging like a pendulum in the church
at Pisa where he grew up. He noticed that it swung in the gentle breeze
coming through the half-opened church door. Bored with the sermon, he
watched the chandelier carefully, then placed his fingertips on his wrist, and
felt his pulse. He noticed an amazing thing: the pendulum-chandelier made
the same number of swings every sixty pulse beats.

"How could this be so?" he asked himself. "The wind coming through 4
the door changes the swing at random. Sometimes the chandelier swings
widely and sometimes it hardly swings at all. Yet it always swings at the same
rate." Persisting in his passive observation of the chandelier, he had discovered the principle of the first mechanical clock. The movement of a pendulum
could be relied on to measure time.

Later he would remember this experiment. Time would provide the nec- 5
essary background for the measurement of all motion, not just the years it
takes to observe the movements of planets, but also the seconds it takes to
observe motions nearer to the earth. . . . Galileo was bringing observation
down to earth. Not satisfied with just looking, he had to bring instruments
into the play of science.

In a popular story, Galileo stands before his inquisitors, begging them to 6
peek through his telescope and observe mountains and craters on the moon.
No, they say. The instrument cannot be trusted to give a true view. It is not
worth their while to look into it. "What we would see is produced by the
telescope and does not exist objectively and independent from it," they claim.
Galileo points out the features of the lunar surface. But even when one of
the inquisitors finally peers into the instrument, he does not see anything
that resembles what Galileo had described. "The craters are in your mind,"
the antagonist cries. "No," Galileo insists, "they are really there. Why can't
you see them?"

In another story, Galileo appears before the Medici, a wealthy ruling family 7
in medieval Italy. He has set up an inclined plane, a plank with one end
elevated above the other, and proceeds to roll various objects down the plank.
He has devised this experiment to demonstrate that objects accelerate as they
roll down the incline, that they do not move with constant speed as Aristotle
predicted. Even more surprising, all the rolling objects, whether light or heavy,
accelerate at the same rate and all reach the bottom at the same time. This
is definitely not according to Aristotle, who said that the heavier objects
would roll faster and reach the bottom of the inclined plane ahead of the
lighter objects.

The Medici are unimpressed. Indeed, they suspect that Galileo has pro- 8
vided nothing more than a good magic show. "How can we trust your pres-
tidigitations, Galileo? Clearly, you must be pulling a fast one. For nothing you
have shown us makes any sense according to Aquinas and Aristotle. Do not
mistake us for fools. We, too, are distinguished philosophers and observers.
But we wouldn't presume to equate the tricks of such primitive playthings
with God's true motions. Such activities on the part of any observer must be
discouraged. You, Galileo, are responsible for these observations, not natural
law." Their words echo in Galileo's ears.

In both of these stories, Galileo brought before his skeptics a new way 9
of science. It was the *doing* of science, the active participation of the observer
with the observed. Yet, in the first story involving Galileo's telescope, the
skeptical inquisitors cannot see the moon's craters. They do not trust the
instrument, and their minds cannot accept that Galileo's creation can make
visible what their eyes alone cannot see. It is beyond "reason" that such
should be true. In the second story, Galileo's attempts to demonstrate natural
law are ridiculed because his methods are too gross. His detractors are of-
fended that nature's continuous movements should be disrupted by Galileo's
rude interventions.

But Galileo understood that such experiments were only approximate 10
indications of the true nature of motion. He agreed that his methods were
crude. He didn't agree, however, that he was disrupting nature. Instead, he
was attempting to reveal the natural laws of motion by *removing* those dis-
ruptions that keep us from seeing the truth. Through careful analysis, he was
able to pierce all the extraneous influences that otherwise cloud our observations. In Galileo's mind, analysis meant simplification and discovery of God's
laws. By reaching out and touching the universe, Galileo had set the prece-
dent of modern experimental physics.

Questions for analysis   1. What do you find most informative about this reading? What do
you think you will most likely remember from it?

2. Wolf illustrates his points about Galileo mainly with anecdote. Review the three stories in paragraphs 3–4, 6, and 7–8. What is the point
of each story? How does Wolf help you to see the story's point? How do
the stories all illustrate the author's main point?

3. How does paragraph 9 relate to paragraphs 7 and 8? How does it relate to paragraphs 1 and 5? Did you find paragraph 9 helpful for understanding Wolf's main point? If so, what exactly makes it helpful?

4. How does Wolf begin? Look closely at each of the sentences in paragraph 1. What function does each have in the piece as a whole?

5. How does Wolf end? Does the ending frame the composition by repeating some key term or main point in both the beginning and ending sections? If so, how does it help you to understand and remember the information?

6. Because clarity is so crucial when reporting information, writers are careful to impose clear and obvious patterns and to use transitional phrases or sentences as signals to readers. Often these signals are found at the beginnings of paragraphs. Identify the transitional signals in this piece. Do they provide sufficient guidance to follow the information easily? If not, can you suggest any way to improve them?

7. If you were asked to write about some great historical figure, whom would you choose, and for what audience? How might you write about the person so as to interest your readers? On what would you focus?

Wolf does not expect any of his readers to challenge his main point: he has no reason to think anyone would question the assertion that Galileo was the first to establish the usefulness of active observation. In general, this reading deals with well-established facts.

This selection may make reporting information seem easy, but in fact it requires extraordinarily careful, sentence-by-sentence decisions about what information to include and how to present it. The writer must have a very strong sense of the readers' knowledge and experience in order to decide what definitions are necessary and what kinds of illustrations will be the most helpful.

Wolf, for example, writes for nonscientists. He thus begins by defining "passive observation" (paragraph 2), a concept essential for readers to understand how Galileo could be said to be the "first active observer." Later in the same paragraph he illustrates this definition with an example about the sun rising. In later paragraphs (3,4,6,7,8) he offers more illustrations of Galileo's "active observation" with stories about his methods of observation and others' reactions to his methods.

This essay shows an issue that is important to all types of writing, but is absolutely vital to writing that reports information: the relation of generalizations, which state the main points, to definitions and illustrations, which develop or elaborate these main points. Naturally, all generalizations must be clear and straightforward. Often they are stated several times in different ways.

Most reports have very few generalizations and a great many illustrations. Assuming the composition is well-focused and that its main point is clear and worth discussing, then good writing can be defined mainly by the quantity and quality of its illustrations. Unless readers have facts, particulars, details, examples, or stories, they lose interest, just as they would if they were listening to a dull and abstract lecture. In Wolf's piece the generalizations are concentrated in paragraphs 1, 5, 9, and 10. The rest is illustrations, with an occasional generalization about a particular illustration.

This reading shows three features basic to all essays reporting information: a general subject, a specific subject, and a thesis. Wolf's general subject is Galileo. His specific subject is Galileo's contribution to science and particularly to modern physics. His thesis, or main point, is that Galileo was the first active observer and the first to develop methods for active observation. These distinctions—general subject, specific subject, thesis—show how a writer focuses on a specific or limited subject within a larger subject and then devises a thesis for that specific subject. In essays presenting information, the thesis is the assertion that engages, holds, and focuses a reader's attention. It is the main point and thus determines how the information must be organized.

The thesis is generally stated concisely in one or two sentences, but it may be presented more indirectly as part of a larger discussion. Whether stated or implied, a thesis usually mentions or forecasts other key points of the essay as well as giving some indication of the overall plan.

This next reading is from *Life on Earth,* a natural history of the earth written by the British naturalist David Attenborough. As you will see, it was written for a general readership; notice what devices Attenborough uses to engage your interest in the information he reports.

THE EXTERNAL SKELETON OF THE INSECT
DAVID ATTENBOROUGH

By any standards, the insect body must be reckoned the most successful 1 of all the solutions to the problems of living on the surface of the earth. Insects swarm in deserts as well as forests; they swim below water and crawl in deep caves in perpetual darkness. They fly over the high peaks of the Himalayas and exist in surprising numbers on the permanent ice caps of the Poles. One fly makes its home in pools of crude oil welling up from the ground; another lives in steaming hot volcanic springs. Some deliberately seek high concentrations of brine and others regularly withstand being frozen solid. They excavate homes for themselves in the skins of animals and burrow long winding tunnels within the thickness of a leaf. The number of individual insects in the world seems beyond any computation, but someone has made the attempt and concluded that at any one time, there must be something of the order of one thousand million thousand million. Put another way, for every human being alive, there are about a million insects—and together these insects would weigh about twelve times as much as he does.

There are thought to be about three times as many species of insect as 2 of all other kinds of animal put together. So far, man has described and named about 700,000 of them and there are certainly three or four times as many still unnamed, awaiting the attentions of anyone who has the time, patience and knowledge to sit down and make a systematic review of them.

Yet all these different forms are variations of one basic anatomical pat- 3 tern: a body divided into three distinct parts—a head bearing the mouth and most of the sense organs; a thorax filled almost entirely with muscles to operate the three pairs of legs beneath and, usually, one or two pairs of wings above; and an abdomen carrying the organs needed for digestion and reproduction. All three sections are enclosed within an external skeleton made, primarily, of chitin. This brown fibrous material was first developed over 550 million years ago by the early segmented creatures, the trilobites and crustaceans. Chemically, it is similar to cellulose and in its pure form it is flexible and permeable. The insects, however, cover it with a protein called sclerotin that makes it become very hard. This produces the heavy inflexible armour of the beetles, and mouthparts sharp and tough enough to gnaw through timber and even cut metals like copper and silver.

The chitinous external skeleton seems to be particularly responsive to the 4 demands of evolution. Its surface can be sculpted without affecting the anatomy beneath. Its proportions can be varied to take on new shapes. Thus the chewing mouthparts possessed by the early cockroach-like insects have been turned by their descendants into siphons and stilettos, saws, chisels, and probes that when unreeled are as long as the whole body. Legs have become elongated into catapults that can propel an insect two hundred times its own body length, broad oars to row it through water or thin hairtipped stilts with a wide stride that enables their owners to walk on the surface of pools. Many limbs carry special tools moulded from the chitin—pouches for holding pollen, combs for cleaning a compound eye, spikes to act as grappling irons and notches with which to fiddle a song.

An external skeleton, however, is also an unexpandable prison. The tri- 5 lobites in the ancient seas escaped its restrictions by moulting. That is still the insects' solution. The process may sound wasteful, but they conduct it with great economy. A new chitinous shell, much folded and compressed, forms beneath the old one. A layer of liquid separates the two and this absorbs the chitin from the old skeleton, leaving the hard sclerotinised parts connected by the thinnest of tissues. The chitin-rich liquid is then absorbed through the still permeable new skeleton back into the insect's body. The old plates split apart, usually along a line running down the back, and the insect hauls itself out. As it does so, its liberated body begins to swell, filling out the folds in the new skin. In a short time, the chitin hardens and becomes strengthened by new deposits of sclerotin.

Questions for analysis   1. What information in this reading was completely new to you? What surprised you? Is there anything you think you are unlikely to forget? What?

2. Attenborough manages to engage our interest in his subject from the very first sentence and to capture our attention with the entire first paragraph. Look carefully at this paragraph to see if you can analyze how he does this. What particular strategy does he use?

3. Attenborough writes for a general readership. How much does he seem to assume they know about insects? What would he do differently if he were writing for entomologists? How would his thesis be different?

4. The general subject of this reading is insects. What is the more specific subject? What is the thesis, or main point, that Attenborough advances?

5. How would you describe the voice in this reading? Does it seem formal or informal, serious or playful? What is there about Attenborough's language that creates this voice? How is it an appropriate voice for the intended readers?

6. If you were assigned to write about an unusual aspect of natural history, what topic would you choose? What sort of readers would you want to address? How would you go about engaging their interest in your subject?

Attenborough seems eager to share what he knows about insects and goes to great lengths to amaze us with little-known facts about their anatomy. He probably starts out very deliberately with this barrage of surprising details in order to entice us to read what he wants to say about insects' external skeletons.

Attenborough does not try to tell us everything about insects in this short reading (actually the opening paragraphs of a chapter). Rather, he takes just one aspect of a huge subject and holds it in focus long enough for us to learn something new. He selects facts and examples carefully to support his thesis, including just enough information to make the point.

He also limits his definitions very distinctly. Though he defines *chitin* and *sclerotin,* he gives enough detail only for nonspecialists to understand his main point. He does not define *thorax* or *cellulose* at all, though he is careful to use them in a context that allows us to understand those terms well enough to keep reading and see the point.

Although Attenborough includes many specific facts from natural history and biology, he does not document any of them—that is, he does not refer to any other sources where he found these facts. In the preceding selection about Galileo, Fred Wolf also offers no documentation. Very often when writers use widely recognized information they simply summarize what specialists have already established. If they are using commonly accepted information, they need not document their sources.

Writers do document their facts when they are reporting new findings or when they quote another person, however. The amount of documentation can depend on the authority of the source and on the expertise of the readers. In much college writing, you may be expected to document your facts in order to identify the sources you used. In reporting research to an audience of experts, you may want to document facts to show that you have followed other authorities' work closely.

Whether or not you provide documentation will depend on your subject and readers. If you take information from other reports or quote other writers, you will need to document your sources. The last reading in this chapter, "Everything Is Theater," by Scott Sumner, shows some example documentation, and Chapter 21: Using and Acknowledging Sources outlines accepted procedures for documentation.

In this next reading we hear the familiar impersonal voice of textbooks and scholarly journals. First published in *Scientific American*, the essay synthesizes information from many published sources on an event of great historical importance—the Black Death, the plague that overtook Europe in the fourteenth century. Notice the wide range of information the author, William Langer, presents about the Black Death.

THE BLACK DEATH
WILLIAM LANGER

In the three years from 1348 through 1350 the pandemic of plague 1 known as the Black Death, or, as the Germans called it, the Great Dying, killed at least a fourth of the population of Europe. It was undoubtedly the worst disaster that has ever befallen mankind. Today we can have no real conception of the terror under which people lived in the shadow of the plague. For more than two centuries plague has not been a serious threat to mankind in the large, although it is still a grisly presence in parts of the Far East and Africa. Scholars continue to study the Great Dying, however, as a historic example of human behavior under the stress of universal catastrophe. In these days when the threat of plague has been replaced by the threat of mass human extermination by even more rapid means, there has been a sharp renewal of interest in the history of the 14th-century calamity. With new perspective, students are investigating its manifold effects: demographic, economic, psychological, moral and religious.

Plague is now recognized as a well-marked disease caused by a specific 2 organism (*Bacillus pestis*). It is known in three forms, all highly fatal: pneumonic (attacking primarily the lungs), bubonic (producing buboes, or swellings, of the lymph glands) and septicemic (killing the victim rapidly by poisoning of the blood). The disease is transmitted to man by fleas, mainly from black rats and certain other rodents, including ground squirrels. It produces high fever, agonizing pain and prostration, and it is usually fatal within five or six days. The Black Death got its name from dark blotches produced by hemorrhages in the skin.

There had been outbreaks of plague in the Roman Empire in the sixth 3 century and in North Africa earlier, but for some reason epidemics of the disease in Europe were comparatively rare after that until the 14th century. Some historians have suggested that the black rat was first brought to western Europe during the Crusades by expeditions returning from the Middle East. This seems unlikely: remains of the rat have been found in prehistoric sites in Switzerland, and in all probability the houses of Europe were infested with rats throughout the Middle Ages.

In any event, the 14th-century pandemic clearly began in 1348 in the 4 ports of Italy, apparently brought in by merchant ships from Black Sea ports. It gradually spread through Italy and in the next two years swept across Spain, France, England, central Europe and Scandinavia. It advanced slowly but pitilessly, striking with deadliest effect in the crowded, unsanitary towns. Each

Approximate chronology of the Black Death's rapid sweep through Europe in the middle of the 14th century is indicated on this map, which shows the political divisions as they existed at the time. The plague, which was apparently brought from Asia by ships, obtained a European foothold in the Mediterranean in 1347; during the succeeding three years only a few small areas escaped.

year the epidemic rose to a peak in the late summer, when the fleas were most abundant, and subsided during the winter, only to break out anew in the spring.

The pandemic of 1348–1350 was followed by a long series of recurrent 5 outbreaks all over Europe, coming at intervals of 10 years or less. In London there were at least 20 attacks of plague in the 15th century, and in Venice the Black Death struck 23 times between 1348 and 1576. The plague epidemics were frequently accompanied by severe outbreaks of typhus, syphilis and "English sweat"—apparently a deadly form of influenza that repeatedly afflicted not only England but also continental Europe in the first half of the 16th century.

From the 13th to the late 17th century Europe was disease-ridden as 6 never before or since. In England the long affliction came to a climax with an epidemic of bubonic plague in 1665 that killed nearly a tenth of London's estimated population of 460,000, two-thirds of whom fled the city during the outbreak. Thereafter in western and central Europe the plague rapidly died away as mysteriously as it had come. The theories advanced to explain its subsidence are as unconvincing as those given for its rise. It was long supposed, for instance, that an invasion of Europe early in the 18th century by brown rats, which killed off the smaller black rats, was responsible for the decline of the disease. This can hardly be the reason; the plague had begun to subside decades before, and the brown rat did not by any means exterminate the black rat. More probably the answer must be sought in something that happened to the flea, the bacillus or the living conditions of the human host.

This article, however, is concerned not with the medical but with the 7 social aspects of the Black Death. Let us begin by examining the dimensions of the catastrophe in terms of the death toll.

As reported by chroniclers of the time, the mortality figures were so 8 incredibly high that modern scholars long regarded them with skepticism. Recent detailed and rigorously conducted analyses indicate, however, that many of the reports were substantially correct. It is now generally accepted that at least a quarter of the European population was wiped out in the first epidemic of 1348 through 1350, and that in the next 50 years the total mortality rose to more than a third of the population. The incidence of the disease and the mortality rate varied, of course, from place to place. Florence was reduced in population from 90,000 to 45,000, Siena from 42,000 to 15,000; Hamburg apparently lost almost two-thirds of its inhabitants. These estimates are borne out by accurate records that were kept in later epidemics. In Venice, for example, the Magistrato della Sanità (board of health) kept a meticulous count of the victims of a severe plague attack in 1576 and 1577; the deaths totaled 46,721 in a total estimated population of about 160,000. In 1720 Marseilles lost 40,000 of a population of 90,000, and in Messina about half of the inhabitants died in 1743.

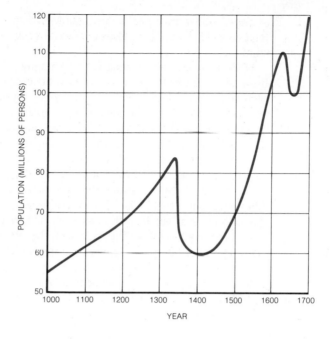

Impact on population from recurrent plagues in Europe is indicated. For more than 300 years after 1347 the plagues checked the normal rise in population; sometimes, as in the 14th and 17th centuries, they resulted in sharp reductions. The figures shown on this chart derive from estimates by students of population; actual data for the period are scarce.

It is now estimated that the total population of England fell from about 3.8 million to 2.1 million in the period from 1348 to 1374. In France, where the loss of life was increased by the Hundred Years' War, the fall in population was even more precipitate. In western and central Europe as a whole the mortality was so great that it took nearly two centuries for the population level of 1348 to be regained. 9

The Black Death was a scourge such as man had never known. Eighty per cent or more of those who came down with the plague died within two or three days, usually in agonizing pain. No one knew the cause of or any preventive or cure for the disease. The medical profession was all but helpless, and the desperate measures taken by town authorities proved largely futile. It is difficult to imagine the growing terror with which the people must have watched the inexorable advance of the disease on their community. 10

They responded in various ways. Almost everyone, in that medieval time, interpreted the plague as a punishment by God for human sins, but there were arguments whether the Deity was sending retribution through the poisoned arrows of evil angels, "venomous moleculae" or earthquake-induced or comet-borne miasmas. Many blamed the Jews, accusing them of poisoning the wells or otherwise acting as agents of Satan. People crowded into the churches, appealing for protection to the Virgin, to St. Sebastian, to St. Roch or to any of 60 other saints believed to have special influence against the disease. In the streets half-naked flagellants, members of the century-old cult 11 of flagellantism, marched in processions whipping each other and warning the people to purge themselves of their sins before the coming day of atonement. . . .

The sufferings and reactions of humanity when the plague came have 12 been depicted vividly by writers such as Boccaccio, Daniel Defoe, Alessandro Manzoni and the late Albert Camus (in his novel *The Plague*) and by artists from Raphael and Holbein to Delacroix. Boccaccio's *Decameron,* an account of a group of well-to-do cavaliers and maidens who shut themselves up in a country house during the Black Death in Florence and sought to distract themselves with revelry and spicy stories, illustrates one of the characteristic responses of mankind to fear and impending disaster. . . .

Many people of all classes gave themselves up to carousing and ribaldry. 13 The Reformation theologian John Wycliffe, who survived the Black Death of the 14th century, wrote with dismay of the lawlessness and depravity of the time. Everywhere, wrote chroniclers of the epidemics in London then and later, there was "drinking, roaring and surfeiting. . . . In one house you might hear them roaring under the pangs of death, in the next tippling, whoring and belching out blasphemies against God." Even the sober Samuel Pepys admitted to his diary that he had made merry in the shadow of death, indulging himself and his wife in a "great store of dancings." The university town of Oxford, like London, also was the scene of much "lewd and dissolute behavior."

The outbreak of an epidemic of plague was almost invariably the signal 14 for a wave of crime and violence. As Boccaccio wrote, "the reverend authority of the laws, both human and divine, was all in a manner dissolved and fallen into decay, for lack of the ministers and executors thereof." In the midst of death, looting and robbery flourished. Burial gangs looted the houses of the dead and stripped the corpses of anything of value before throwing them into the pits. On occasion they even murdered the sick.

Just as desperation drove some to a complete abandonment of morality, 15 it drove others, perhaps the majority, to pathetic extravagances of religiosity or superstition. The poet George Wither noted this contrast in the London epidemic of 1625:

Some streets had Churches full of people, weeping;
Some others, Tavernes had, rude-revell keeping;
Within some houses Psalmes and Hymnes were sung;
With raylings and loud scouldings others rung.

Many people threw themselves on God's mercy, showered the church 16 with gifts and made extravagant vows for the future. Others hunted down Jews and witches as the originators of the plague. The Black Death generated a startling spread of belief in witchcraft. Even as learned a scholar and theologian as John Calvin was convinced that a group of male and female witches, acting as agents of Satan, had brought the plague to Geneva. In the cult of Satanism, as in that of flagellantism, there was a strong strain of sexuality. It was believed that the women accused of being witches had intercourse with the Devil and could strike men with sexual impotence. From the psychoanalytic point of view this belief may have stemmed from an unconscious reaction to the tremendous shrinkage of the population.

Jews and witches were not the only victims of the general panic. The 17 wrath of the people also fell on physicians. They were accused of encouraging or helping the spread of the plague instead of checking it. Paré tells us that some of them were stoned in the streets in France. (In the 19th century physicians were similarly made scapegoats during epidemics of cholera. Some people accused them of poisoning public water supplies, at the behest of the rich, in order to kill off the excessive numbers of the poor.)

Although we have fairly accurate knowledge of the immediate effects of 18 the great plagues in Europe—they were fully and circumstantially chronicled by many contemporary writers—it is not so easy to specify the long-term effects of the plagues. Many other factors entered into the shaping of Europe's history during and after the period of the plague epidemics. Nevertheless, there can be no doubt that the Great Dying had a profound and lasting influence on that history.

In its economic life Europe suffered a sudden and drastic change. Before 19 the Black Death of 1348–1350 the Continent had enjoyed a period of rather rapid population growth, territorial expansion and general prosperity. After the pandemic Europe sank into a long depression: a century or more of economic stagnation and decline. The most serious disruption took place in agriculture.

For a short time the towns and cities experienced a flush of apparent 20 prosperity. Many survivors of the epidemic had suddenly inherited substantial amounts of property and money from the wholesale departure of their relatives. They built elegant houses and went on a buying spree that made work (and high prices) for the manufacturing artisans. The churches and other public institutions, sharing in the wealth of the new rich, also built imposing and expensive structures.

The rural areas, on the other hand, virtually collapsed. With fewer people 21 to feed in the towns and cities, the farmers lost a large part of the market for their crops. Grain prices fell precipitately. So did the farm population. Already sadly depleted by the ravages of the plague, it was now further reduced by a movement to the towns, which offered the impoverished farmers work as artisans. In spite of strenuous efforts by landlords and lords of the manor to keep the peasants on the land by law and sometimes by force, the rural population fled to the cities en masse. Thousands of farms and villages were deserted. In central Germany some 70 per cent of all the farm settlements were abandoned in the period following the Black Death. (Many of these "lost" farms and villages, long overgrown, have recently been located by aerial photography.)

Farms became wilderness or pasture. Rents and land values disappeared. 22
The minor land-owning gentry sank into poverty. In the words of the 14th-century poet Petrarch, "a vast and dreadful solitude" settled over the land. And of course in the long run the depression of agriculture engulfed the cities in depression as well.

Some authorities believe that Europe had begun to fall into a period of 23
economic decay before the Black Death and that the epidemics only accentuated this trend. The question is certainly a complicated one. Wars and other economic forces no doubt played their part in Europe's long recession. It seems probable, however, that the decisive factor was the repeated onslaught of epidemics that depleted and weakened the population. The present consensus on the subject is that population change is a main cause of economic change rather than vice versa. Surely it must be considered significant that Europe's economic revival in the 17th and 18th centuries coincided with the disappearance of the plague and a burst of rapid population growth. . . .

The psychological effects of the ordeal of the plague are at least as im- 24
pressive as the economic ones. For a long time it held all of Europe in an apocalyptic mood, which the Dutch historian Johan Huizinga analyzed brilliantly a generation ago in his study *The Waning of the Middle Ages.* As Arturo Castiglioni, the eminent Yale University historian of medicine, has written: "Fear was the sovereign ruler of this epoch." Men lived and worked in constant dread of disease and imminent death. "No thought is born in me that has not 'Death' engraved upon it," wrote Michelangelo.

Much of the art of the time reflected a macabre interest in graves and 25
an almost pathological predilection for the manifestations of disease and putrefaction. Countless painters treated with almost loving detail the sufferings of Christ, the terrors of the Last Judgment and the tortures of Hell. Woodcuts and paintings depicting the dance of death, inspired directly by the Black Death, enjoyed a morbid popularity. With pitiless realism these paintings portrayed Death as a horridly grinning skeleton that seized, without warning, the prince and the peasant, the young and the old, the lovely maiden and the hardened villain, the innocent babe and the decrepit dotard.

Along with the mood of despair there was a marked tendency toward 26
wild defiance—loose living and immoralities that were no doubt a desperate kind of reassertion of life in the presence of death. Yet the dominant feature of the time was not its licentiousness but its overpowering feelings of guilt, which arose from the conviction that God had visited the plague on man as retribution for his sins. Boccaccio, a few years after writing his *Decameron,* was overcome by repentance and a sense of guilt verging on panic. Martin Luther suffered acutely from guilt and fear of death, and Calvin, terror-stricken by the plague, fled from each epidemic. Indeed, entire communities were afflicted with what Freud called the primordial sense of guilt, and they engaged in penitential processions, pilgrimages and passionate mass preaching.

Some 70 years ago the English Catholic prelate and historian (later car- 27 dinal) Francis Gasquet, in a study entitled *The Great Pestilence,* tried to demonstrate that the Black Death set the stage for the Protestant Reformation by killing off the clergy and upsetting the entire religious life of Europe. This no doubt is too simple a theory. On the other hand, it is hard to deny that the catastrophic epidemics at the close of the Middle Ages must have been a powerful force for religious revolution. The failure of the Church and of prayer to ward off the pandemic, the flight of priests who deserted their parishes in the face of danger and the shortage of religious leaders after the Great Dying left the people eager for new kinds of leadership. And it is worth noting that most if not all of the Reformation leaders—Wycliffe, Zwingli, Luther, Calvin and others—were men who sought a more intimate relation of man to God because they were deeply affected by mankind's unprecedented ordeal by disease.

This is not to say that the epidemics of the late Middle Ages suffice to 28 explain the Reformation but simply that the profound disturbance of men's minds by the universal, chronic grief and by the immediacy of death brought fundamental and long-lasting changes in religious outlook. In the moral and religious life of Europe, as well as in the economic sphere, the forces that make for change were undoubtedly strengthened and given added impetus by the Black Death.

Bibliography

The Black Death G. G. Coulton. Ernest Benn Limited, 1929.

The Black Death Philip Ziegler. John Day, 1969.

The Black Death: A Chronicle of the Plague Compiled by Johannes Nohl. George Allen and Unwin Ltd., 1926.

The Blight of Pestilence on Early Modern Civilization Lynn Thorndike in *The American Historical Review,* Vol. 32, No. 3, pages 455–474; April, 1927.

The Bubonic Plague and England Charles F. Mullett. University of Kentucky Press, 1956.

A History of Bubonic Plague in the British Isles J. F. D. Shrewsbury. Cambridge University Press, 1970.

Introduction à la Demographie Historique des Villes d'Europe Roger Mols. University of Louvain, 1956, 3 vols. Vol. 2, pages 426–441.

Plague and Pestilence in Literature and Art Raymond Crawfurd. Oxford University Press, 1914.

Questions for analysis

1. How informative did you find this essay? What do you think you will remember from it?

2. The general subject of this piece is of course the Black Death. What is the specific subject? More particularly, what is the writer's thesis, or main point? A thesis may be stated directly or just implied. How is it given here?

3. Imagine Langer asking this question as he wrote each sentence in the first paragraph: "How can I make my subject seem significant and interesting, so that readers will continue reading?" Consider each sentence in the paragraph and point to things he might have done in response to such a question.

4. How does Langer end his essay? Before answering this question, you might want to compare the last paragraph to the last sentence in paragraph 1. What are some advantages of Langer's ending? Can you name any disadvantages?

5. Explicit transitions are essential to informative writing, particularly to an essay as long as Langer's. Paragraph 7, for example, contains three transitional cues to the reader: the word *not* refers back to the preceding paragraph, *but* signals the next topic, and the phrase "let us begin by . . ." introduces the discussion to follow. Look now at paragraphs 11, 15, 17, 21, and 26, and identify the transitions in each one. Then choose one paragraph and analyze the way the transitions help the reader.

6. Graphs, charts, and tables can be very useful for presenting information. What kind of information does Langer present graphically? Do the chart on chronology and the graph on population repeat information from the text or offer new information? How do they help you understand the essay?

7. If you were to write about an event of great historical significance, which event would you choose? What readership would you address, and how would you limit or focus your essay? What would you do to capture your readers' interest in the subject?

In this essay we recognize all of the essential features of reporting information. The writer engages our interest by telling us something new. Within a huge subject covering decades of European history, he finds a smaller subject and keeps it in focus throughout the piece. Though the essay is packed with facts, anecdotes, and examples—enough to make us feel we have received a complete and comprehensive presentation of the subject—the writer forecasts his plan and keeps us on track with brief summaries and transitions.

Forecasting—announcing or suggesting to readers what you intend to say and how you will go about saying it—is an important strategy in reports. In his first paragraph Langer forecasts what exactly he will discuss about the Black Death: the demographic, economic, psychological, moral, and religious effects. Because his discussion follows the order of the list, his forecast helps the reader anticipate the plan of the essay.

A forecast basically tells the reader how information is being classified. One of the greatest tasks of reporting information is to organize facts and examples in a way that will make a particular point about a subject. This point is the thesis. (See Chapter 15: Classifying for a more detailed discussion of this writing strategy.)

To develop his thesis about the profound long-term effects of the Black Death, Langer divides the historical information into five groups, naming each group concisely at the end of paragraph 1:

Division	Paragraphs
demographic	8–18
economic	19–23
psychological	24–25
moral	26
religious	27

Notice also the brief summary at paragraph 18 of this essay. Internal summaries can be very helpful in longer reports, providing a break in the flow of new information as well as a chance to review what has been covered and to see what remains to be discussed.

Like Fred Wolf and David Attenborough, Langer does not document his sources with footnotes. Even though he quotes others, he indicates his sources only by mentioning them within the article. He does include a bibliography listing his major sources (which also serves the very useful purpose of referring readers to the most authoritative books on the topic). There are two reasons for not having more thorough documentation. For one thing, he reports information that is well-known among historians; he does not claim it to be his own. Second, the essay was written for *Scientific American,* whose policy is to include only a bibliography.

Next is an essay written by a college freshman, Eric Marcusson. Asked to explain a scientific principle to other students in his composition class, he chose to write about photosynthesis. Though very few of his readers planned to major in biology, all had taken a biology course in high school. As you read, see if you can recognize what Marcusson assumed about his readers' knowledge of photosynthesis.

PHOTOSYNTHESIS
ERIC MARCUSSON

If it were not for photosynthesis, life as we know it could not exist. If the process of photosynthesis were to stop today, all higher animals, human beings included, would die within twenty-five years. [1]

Despite the fact that photosynthesis is such a critical process, it is still not fully understood. A simplified explanation of what is known about photosynthesis follows. A pigment called chlorophyll, which is responsible for the green color of plants, absorbs some of the energy of light. When this happens, the chlorophyll molecule is said to be in an excited state, which means that it has [2] more energy than usual. This excited chlorophyll molecule is then returned to its original energy level over several steps. As this happens, energy is slowly released. If this release were to occur all at once, most of the energy would be given off as heat and would not be useable. As it is, the plant uses the energy it gains from this process to synthesize glucose (a form of sugar) from carbon dioxide (a gas) and water. Plants use this glucose in two ways. First, they use it to create their own structure. The main constituent of plants is a substance called cellulose. This cellulose is made of hundreds of glucose molecules strung together by chemical bonds. Second, plants use glucose to obtain the energy they need by burning it to synthesize other organic molecules.

Although photosynthesis is generally thought to affect only plants, it plays 3 a major role in animal nutrition. Living organisms are thermodynamically unstable: they require a constant input of energy. In the case of animals, this energy comes in the form of food. Two of the most commonly eaten classes of food are carbohydrates and starches. Both of these classes of food are synthesized from glucose molecules. These foods are burned to carbon dioxide in order to obtain the energy needed by animals. Photosynthesis is the only way to regenerate glucose from carbon dioxide. If it were not for photosynthesis, then, animals would not be able to obtain the energy they need to run the processes of life.

Photosynthesis also plays an important role in maintaining the correct 4 balance of gases in the atmosphere. There is a remarkable reciprocity in the processes of plants and animals. In photosynthesis, carbon dioxide is used and oxygen is given off as a waste product. Animals need to use the oxygen given off by photosynthesis in the process of respiration, which gives off carbon dioxide as its waste product. If it were not for photosynthesis, this system would be thrown off balance, and all animals would die of asphyxiation.

Photosynthesis is thus a major contributor to the processes by which 5 organisms live. It is one of the most important pathways in biology. Through the energy of the sun, it provides most of the energy needed by the living world. It also helps to maintain the delicate balance of gases needed in the environment. If it were not for photosynthesis, life as we know it would not have been able to evolve to its present state.

Questions for analysis   1. What did you find informative in this essay? What do you think you will remember from it?

2. The general subject of this report is photosynthesis. What specific subject does the writer focus on? What is his thesis?

3. How does Marcusson go about defining photosynthesis in paragraph 2? Do you find such a definition clear or troublesome? Explain.

4. Read over the first and last paragraphs once again. How do they function together in this report? How successful do you find them?

5. Throughout his essay, Marcusson offers cues to orient readers and keep them on track. Identify these cues.

6. How would you characterize the voice in this essay—personal or impersonal? casual or businesslike? In your response, cite specific words and phrases that contribute to that voice. Can you suggest a different voice that would be more appropriate?

7. If you were asked to write about an important principle in the natural or social sciences, which principle would you choose? Assume you were writing for readers who had no knowledge of the topic. How would you get them interested in your subject?

Marcusson makes one important point and organizes his information carefully to develop that point. There is no irrelevant information. The information is unified and focused precisely on the point, like a hot spot of sunlight focused through a magnifying glass. After defining his central concept, he divides the information into two parts: the role of photosynthesis in animal nutrition and in maintaining the correct balance of gases in the atmosphere.

The final essay, written by college freshman Scott Sumner, reports on the American composer John Cage. Sumner had some knowledge about Cage, but did some further research for his report. Though it is not a full-length research paper, his essay illustrates how a small amount of research can enrich a composition.

EVERYTHING IS THEATER
SCOTT SUMNER

In 1953 the American composer John Cage wrote *Imaginary Landscape No. 4*, a musical composition scored for twelve radios tuned in randomly. Fifteen years later he gave the world *Reunion*, a symphony of chess pieces moving across an electrified board. These are two altogether typical examples of Cage's many contributions to modern music. Cage's innovations over the past forty years have done no less than break down musical boundaries in place for centuries. 1

Morton Feldman, an associate of Cage, explained his importance in the following way: "You have to remember how straight-laced everything had always been in music. Just to change one thing in music was a life's work. But John changed everything."[1] Before Cage, the dominance of the classical harmonic structure, where composition is based on harmony, had all but deadened Western music. As a student of Arnold Schoenberg, who had totally abandoned tonality and Western harmony, Cage was introduced to atonality. Following Schoenberg's teachings to a logical conclusion, he eventually came to regard all sounds, noises, and even silences as equal—that is, "no matter what kind of sound it is, it can become musical by taking its place in a piece of music."[2] 2

In 1938 Cage was asked to write a score for Syvilla Fort's *Bacchanale*. It 3
was to be performed in a very small theater, which frustrated Cage's plans
for an extensive percussion section. His solution was nothing less than the
development of an entirely new instrument, the prepared piano. By inserting
bolts, rubber, wood, glass, and other materials between the piano strings,
Cage made a piano that was in effect "a percussion orchestra under the
control of a single player."[3] Offering an entirely new range of sounds, the
prepared piano helped Cage to realize a whole new kind of music, percussion
music. Based on time, rather than harmony, this became Cage's alternative
to classical music. In percussion, structure is implicit still, but tonality is no
longer the necessary means by which structure is created. Rather, Cage "in-
vestigated time-lengths as a more comprehensive means."[4]

In 1943 Cage gave a series of concerts in New York. Beginning with a 4
recital at the Museum of Modern Art, these concerts quickly established his
reputation in the art community. Virgil Thompson, music critic for the *Herald
Tribune*, wrote, "Mr. Cage has . . . develop[ed] the rhythmic element of composition . . . to a point of sophistication unmatched in the technique of any
living composer."[5] Cage had already pushed beyond classical harmonic structure, but also now he had even surpassed Schoenbergian atonality. And his
most important development, indeterminacy, was still seven years away.

In the spring of 1950, while working on a score for Merce Cunningham's 5
Sixteen Dances, Cage came upon a totally new approach to composition:
chance. He had drawn up a series of charts to plot rhythmic structure and
came to see that he "could compose according to moves on these charts
instead of according to [his] own tastes."[6] This new method led Cage to what
Calvin Tomkins described as "a music that went beyond chance, into what
is now called indeterminacy—music whose sounds cannot be foreseen."[7]
Unlike determinacy, which is characterized by a direct, determined relationship among the parts, indeterminacy may (or may not) be random. Graphisms
and theatrical, or "causal," notations are used to indicate *actions to be made,*
rather than notes to be played. The notations for *Water Walk,* for example,
consist of two pages: "Properties and Instruments Used," which include a
stop-watch, a bathtub three-quarters full, a toy fish, a grand piano, a whistle,
an iron pipe; and the score itself, "Notes Regarding Some of the Actions to
be Made in the Order of Occurance," which specify actions to be made with,
upon, or around the "properties and instruments." The result is structure that
is free of all content. As Eric Forsythe was to say, "What saves . . . [a] piece
from chaos or whim (the enemies of indeterminacy) is the performer's awareness of pure structure."[8]

During the early 1950s Cage went through two more major develop- 6
ments. The first occurred when, in a sound-proof chamber at Harvard, he
actually heard his own blood circulating, his own nervous-system operating.
This led him to conclude that there was no such thing as true silence in
nature. The second was his move toward theater, which he defined as follows: "theater takes place all the time wherever one is and art simply facili-

tates persuading one this is the case.''[9] Combining his discovery in the sound-proof chamber with the concept of ever-present theater, Cage arrived at his most famous composition, *4'3."* Four minutes, three seconds in length, it was divided into three parts and was first performed by pianist David Tudor. The beginning of each movement was marked by closing the piano cover; the end came at the specified time by opening the cover again. No actual notes were played. Tomkins described the premier performance as follows: ''In the Woodstock hall, which was wide open to the woods at the back, attentive listeners could hear during the first movement the sound of wind in the trees; during the second, there was a patter of raindrops on the roof; during the third, the audience took over and added its own perplexed mutterings to the other 'sounds not intended' by the composer.''[10] These ''sounds not intended'' (as Cage was to refer to these musical silences) *were* the composition.

Since his original break with classical structure and his later departure 7 from Schoenbergian atonality, Cage's investigations and experiments (electronics, silences, indeterminacy) have always been directed toward an attempt to create art beyond individual self-expression. He delights in seeing ''the performer . . . and the listener too . . . *discovering* the nature of the structure.''[11] Forsythe's review of a performance of Cage's *Theater Piece* discussed its success in terms of what usually transpires *after* a Cage performance: the audience mingles, ''a party begins: some dancing, more questions. Another theatre piece, this one not structured by Cage, is beginning. And everyone is aware of it.''[12]

In Cage's terms, this is art succeeding in its ultimate purpose—to imitate 8 nature. Through imitation of nature (which Cage views as indeterminate and without design), art should wake the audience up to the life they themselves are living.

Notes

[1]Calvin Tomkins, *The Bride and the Bachelors* (Virginia: R. R. Donnelley and Sons Co., 1962), p. 109.

[2]Tomkins, p. 87.

[3]Tomkins, p. 90.

[4]John Cage, *Empty Words* (Middletown, Connecticut: Wesleyan University Press, 1979), p. 178.

[5]Tomkins, pp. 96–97.

[6]Tomkins, p. 108.

[7]Tomkins, p. 108.

[8]Eric Forsythe, ''Theatre Piece. By John Cage,'' *Educational Theatre Journal,* 29 (Dec. 1977), p. 561.

[9]Tomkins, p. 118.

[10]Tomkins, p. 119.

[11]''John Cage and Roger Reynolds: A Conversation,'' *The Music Quarterly,* Oct. 1979, p. 582.

[12]Forsythe, p . 562.

Questions for analysis   1. What did you learn about John Cage from Sumner's essay? What do you think you will remember?

2. Sumner uses several words—*atonality, indeterminacy, graphisms*—likely to be unfamiliar to many readers. How does he help these readers to understand this technical terminology? What else might he do?

3. How does Sumner organize his information? Outline the essay briefly.

4. How exactly does Sumner begin his essay? Can you suggest a better way?

5. Sumner cites many sources in his essay. How effectively does he integrate these materials into the essay?

Sumner's essay shows all of the key features of reporting information. He chooses a general subject, narrows it to a more manageable specific subject, and then focuses it further with a thesis. He attempts to engage readers' interest and make the thesis seem significant in his opening two sentences. A report on the musical theories of John Cage is potentially very abstract and difficult, so Sumner wisely opens by describing two of Cage's most amusing compositions. He develops his thesis about Cage's innovativeness with examples of his achievements as well as quotations from critics. His essay is organized chronologically, with the important events in Cage's career mostly presented in order. Musical terms that may be unfamiliar to readers are defined.

In addition, he documents all his sources. He uses four sources, two books and two journal articles, and follows the old Modern Language Association style of documentation (Chapter 21: Using and Acknowledging Sources gives full detail about MLA style).

BASIC FEATURES OF ESSAYS REPORTING INFORMATION

From your analysis of the readings, you know that essays reporting information display certain basic features. This section summarizes those features.

A subject and a thesis   At the basis of every report are a subject and a thesis. The subject may be selected by the writer, or it may be assigned by someone else. Once the general subject is determined, the writer must narrow the topic somewhat by deciding on a specific subject. Finally, within this specific subject, the writer must develop a thesis, which is the main point of the report. Consider as an example the subject and thesis of the last reading in this chapter, Scott Sumner's essay on John Cage:

General Subject: John Cage
Specific Subject: Cage's experiments and innovations
Thesis: "Cage's innovations over the past forty years have done no less than break down musical boundaries in place for centuries."

The thesis is the assertion the writer wishes to make about the specific subject. As such, it controls the entire essay, determining what information is included and how it is organized.

An appeal to readers' interests

In reporting information, good writers try to make a direct appeal to their readers' interests. If they have selected the topic, they make some effort to declare the significance of their subject. They try to capture their readers' interest with an engaging beginning. Attenborough, Langer, and Marcusson all begin with an arresting fact, for example:

> By any standards, the insect body must be reckoned the most successful of all the solutions to the problems of living on the surface of the earth. David Attenborough

> In three years from 1348 through 1350 the pandemic of plague known as the Black Death, or, as the Germans called it, the Great Dying, killed at least a fourth of the population of Europe.   William Langer

> If it were not for photosynthesis, life as we know it could not exist. Eric Marcusson

Clear definitions

Essays reporting information depend on clear definitions. In order to relate information clearly, a writer has to be sensitive to the readers' knowledge; any terms that are likely to be misunderstood must be explicitly defined. Marcusson gives an extended definition of photosynthesis, for example, assuming his readers know little or nothing about the process. Following are some examples of sentence definitions from other readings in this chapter:

> Passive observation was any observation that the observer wished to perform that left the observed undisturbed by the observer.   Fred Wolf

> This brown fibrous material [chitin] was first developed over 550 million years ago. . . . Chemically, it is similar to cellulose and in its pure form it is flexible and permeable.   David Attenborough

> It [plague] is known in three forms, all highly fatal: pneumonic (attacking primarily the lungs), bubonic (producing buboes, or swellings, of the lymph glands) and septicemic (killing the victim rapidly by poisoning of the blood). William Langer

Many more examples of definitions are discussed in Chapter 14: Defining.

A logical plan   Reports must follow a clear path to keep readers on track. For organizing reports and cueing readers, writers rely on many strategies. They divide the information in such a way that supports the thesis and then alert readers to these divisions with forecasting statements and transitions. They try to frame the essay for readers by relating the ending to the beginning. Langer, for example, organizes his essay around five effects of the plague, forecasting this organization in the first paragraph and cueing the reader with transitional phrases and sentences as the essay moves along. He frames the essay by identifying the five effects in both the first and final paragraphs. We have seen these features repeatedly in the readings in this chapter. (See Chapter 15: Classifying for a detailed discussion of dividing and Chapter 11: Cueing the Reader for more details about that strategy.)

Good writers never forget that readers need many signals. Because a writer knows the information so well and is aware of how it is organized, it is difficult to see it the way someone reading the essay for the first time would. That is precisely what must be done, however, to be sure that the essay includes all the signals the reader will need to stay on track in a first reading. In long essays especially, readers may welcome a pause for a brief summary or a forecast of what follows. In paragraph 18 of his essay, Langer provides such a summary.

Appropriate writing   Writers have available many strategies for presenting information. The
strategies   strategies they use are determined by the point they want to make and the kind of information they have to work with. Following are some of the writing strategies that are particularly useful in reports.

Classification. Our minds work naturally to classify experience and information. Writers of reports use classification in several ways. First, they use it to find a significant focus for a jumble of information. Once they have an idea of their focus, or thesis, they must search out information to support it, classifying as they go. As we have seen in several of this chapter's readings (Langer's is the best example), the writer's way of classifying information to support the thesis also produces a plan for the essay. Writers classify on a smaller scale as well, usually as part of defining: Langer does this when he classifies types of the plague (paragraph 2); Attenborough does the same when he classifies and names the parts of an insect's anatomy (paragraph 3).

Narration. Writers may present information as anecdotes or as step-by-step narratives. Wolf's primary way of informing us about Galileo is to tell us anecdotes about him. These stories dramatize the way that Galileo challenged the accepted wisdom of his time. Paragraphs 3 through 6 of Langer's essay are narrative, telling something of the history of the

Black Death in order to provide a historical context for the subsequent discussion of its effects. Marcusson also uses narration, as he tells about the process photosynthesis follows. (Narrative strategies are analyzed and illustrated in more detail in Chapter 13: Narrating.)

Illustration. Two good ways of supporting a thesis are developed examples and lists of facts. Attenborough, for example, opens with a list of amazing facts about insects. Later he gives examples to illustrate two generalizations about insects: that their skeleton has undergone evolutionary change (paragraph 4) and that the skeleton is "an unexpandable prison" (paragraph 5). Langer gives many, many examples of the effects of the Black Death. (These and other forms of illustration are discussed in Chapter 16: Illustrating.)

Comparison and contrast. This strategy is especially useful in presenting information because it helps readers to understand something new by showing how it is similar to or different from things they already know. Attenborough does this when he compares the number of insects to the number of humans. To help readers recognize the extreme reactions to the Black Death, Langer compares criminals and revelers to religious fanatics. In the same way, Sumner contrasts music before and after John Cage in order to show Cage's significance. (See Chapter 17: Comparing and Contrasting for a more detailed discussion of this writing strategy.)

GUIDE TO WRITING

THE WRITING TASK

Write an essay that reports information. Choose a subject which you can write about with confidence and some authority; if necessary, do research to get more information. Before you begin, decide who your readers will be; then, focus the thesis so as to engage their interest and inform them about the topic.

INVENTION AND RESEARCH

The following activities are designed to help you to write a focused, developed, interesting report. They will help you to find a subject and a thesis, scrutinize your choice of subject, analyze your readers, figure out what you know about the topic and what you need to learn. Together, these invention and research activities will produce most of the material necessary for an essay that reports information.

Finding a subject   You may already have a topic in mind. From work, recreation, travels, and reading, you probably have several things you might write about. As you consider any such topic, ask yourself whether or not you know enough about it to share with others. The following listing activities can help you. Even if you already have a subject in mind, you might want to complete these activities in order to be certain yours is the best possible choice.

If you are absolutely certain about your topic, however, you may turn now to Probing your Subject on the facing page.

Listing subjects. The possibilities may seem limitless. Remember, however, that some subjects—war, politics, and religion, for example— are so general that they would be extraordinarily difficult to discuss in a short essay. Other subjects may be inappropriate because you would not have sufficient time to find out enough about them.

Consider each of the categories that follow, listing as many subjects as you can under each one. The longer your list, the more likely you are to find just the right subject for your essay. And, should your first choice not work out, you will have a ready list of alternatives.

Include topics you already know something about as well as some you know only slightly and would like to research further. If any of the following examples of subjects interest you, add them to your list.

☐ An important academic breakthrough: Newton's law of gravity, Darwin's theory of evolution, Leeuwenhoek's microscope, DNA, Einstein's theory of relativity, Freud's theory of the unconscious, Marx's analysis of class conflict

☐ A significant academic principle or theory: *cohort size* in economics, the *uncertainty principle* in physics, *invention* in composition, *irony* in literature, *existentialism* in philosophy, *osmosis* in biology, *I.Q.* in psychology, *phonology* in linguistics, *ionic bonds* in chemistry, *socialization* in sociology

☐ Any ordinary event you might like to know more about: sunsets, cloud formations, potholes, jet lag, sneezing, yawning

☐ A current danger to public health, the environment, or the social order: acid rain, high-fat diets, inflation, malnutrition, oil spills, car accidents, rape, child abuse

☐ A common object you would like to know something about: baseballs, pianos, fingernail clippers, microwave ovens, microprocessors, automatic bank tellers

☐ The historical context for some current issue: handgun control, capital punishment, abortion, government subsidies for private schools, social security, federal price supports for agricultural products, congressional filibusters

☐ A landmark or historic site: the Mississippi River, Mount Rushmore, Lincoln Memorial, the Watts Towers, the Brooklyn Bridge, the Alamo, Gettysburg, Alcatraz

☐ An influential nonfiction book or article that you could summarize

☐ An important current issue or problem, one which is a topic of published research studies

☐ A topic you are currently studying (or reporting on) for another course

Choosing a subject. Now look over your list and select one subject to explore. Pick a subject that interests you a lot and that might interest others. Write a few sentences about the subject: say what it is, describe how you first learned about it, explain why you remain interested in it.

Probing your subject To find out whether this is a good subject for an essay, invest a few minutes to explore it in writing, using the next three activities as guides.

Finding out what you already know. Take around ten minutes to jot down everything you know about this subject. Write quickly, putting down your thoughts just as they occur. You may fill in any details later. Feel free to write in sentences, or phrases, or lists. Make drawings or charts. The goal is to get everything you know about this subject down on paper.

Writing generalizations. Review what you have written, and reflect further on your subject. Now write a few very general statements about it: define it, describe it, sum up its importance, note anything unusual about it. Making such statements may help you to narrow the subject and find a thesis.

Asking questions. List any questions you have about your subject. Next, try to imagine what questions readers might have. Which of these questions would your essay attempt to answer? These questions may help you focus the subject and ultimately may suggest a thesis.

Selecting a thesis Review your general statements and questions thoughtfully to find the thesis, or main point, you wish to write about. The thesis must interest you and should be manageable in a brief essay. It ought to be an assertion that you will be able to illustrate. Write down this thesis, and then state in writing why you consider it a good choice.

Testing your choice   Now stop to examine your topic to see whether it is worth reporting on and whether you will be able to do so. The following questions can help you to test your choice.

☐ Do I have a strong personal interest in this thesis?
☐ Are my readers likely to be interested in this thesis?
☐ Do I know enough about it already, or can I find out what I need to know about it within the time available?
☐ Can I discuss this specific subject well in a short essay?

You may want to reconsider these questions later, as you invent and plan and draft. If at any point you feel unable to answer the questions affirmatively, you should consider finding a different specific subject and thesis, or even a whole new general subject.

Analyzing your readers   Decide who your readers will be, and think carefully about the interests, knowledge, and expectations they will bring to your essay. Your readers are a very important consideration, one that will help determine what information you include and that will influence the way you pace the information. Even if you are writing only for your instructor, you must be aware of his or her knowledge of your subject.

Write for at least ten minutes describing your readers. Consider the following questions as you write:

☐ Who are my readers? Are they all similar, or are they a diverse group?
☐ How much are they likely to know about this subject? What assumptions might they have about the subject?
☐ Why might they want to read about this subject?
☐ How can I hold their interest?
☐ Are there any aspects of my subject that may surprise my readers?

Finding out more about your subject   Thus far you have taken account of what you already know about your subject and thought about what your readers are likely to know. Now you should turn your attention to finding out additional information. Look at your thesis statement: what facts or examples or details do you need to support that thesis? To find such information, you will probably need to do some research at the library or perhaps even to seek help or advice from an expert on the topic.

Finding information at the library. The best place to start your research is your college library. Figure out the subject headings that you should consult for information on your topic, and then look in the card catalog, in encyclopedias (both general and specialized), in bibliographies, and in periodical indexes. If your library has open stacks, you can probably find a lot of information just by finding the right area and browsing. Chapter 20: Library Research will provide detailed guidance for finding information at a library.

One thing you should look for in your research is authoritative opinions and information. Once you have identified the experts on your topic, look for articles, books, and interviews by and with them. Find out their opinions, and see if anything they have said would help to support your thesis. You can quote them directly, or you can summarize or paraphrase their words (see Chapter 21: The Research Paper for discussion of quoting, summarizing, and paraphrasing).

Consulting an expert. Is there someone very knowledgeable about your subject who might be helpful? If you are writing about a subject from another college course, for example, the teaching assistant or professor might be someone to consult. Not only could such a person answer questions, but also he or she might direct you to important or influential articles or books. At the very least, he or she could advise you on who the preeminent people in the field are. See Chapter 19: Field Research for specific advice on interviewing.

Refocusing your thesis statement

You have already written at least a tentative thesis statement. Now you should look at it closely to see that it does indeed say something significant about your information.

Look at what you wrote about your readers. Now think about any additional information you have found about your subject. Does your original thesis still ring true, or does it seem weak? If you are not satisfied, try to determine what is wrong—is it too general? too bland? too reckless? too hard to illustrate? If need be, compose a whole new thesis. Remember that it is the thesis that provides the focus of the report; it must be as good as you can make it.

Defining key terms

Make a list of the key terms your readers need to understand. These terms might refer to general concepts, steps in a process, parts of an object, or important people. Then decide which terms may be unfamiliar to your readers.

Write definitions of those terms. Consider what kinds of definitions are necessary—a simple synonym, a single sentence, an example, or an extended definition. (Strategies for writing definitions are presented in Chapter 14: Defining.)

PLANNING AND DRAFTING

Here are some activities that should help you to get the most out of your invention writing, to decide on some specific goals for your report, and to write a first draft.

Seeing what you have   Reread everything you have written so far. This is a critically important time for reflection and evaluation. Before beginning the actual draft, you must decide whether your subject is worthwhile and whether you have sufficient information for a successful essay.

These questions may be useful to consider as you reflect on your notes:

- ☐ Is my subject suitable for a brief report?
- ☐ Do I have enough information to present this subject comprehensively?
- ☐ Do I have a clear thesis for this subject?
- ☐ Have I found information that readers will find interesting?

It may help as you read to annotate your invention writings. Look for details that will support your thesis and appeal to your readers. Underline or circle key words, phrases, or sentences; make marginal notes. Your goal here is to identify the important elements in what you have written so far.

Be realistic. If at this point your notes do not look promising, you may want to select a different general subject or specific subject to write about. If your notes seem thin but promising, you should probably do further research to find more information before continuing.

Outlining the report   Now you should give some thought to organization. Many writers find it helpful to outline their material before actually beginning to write. Whatever organizing you do before you begin drafting, consider it only tentative. Never be a slave to an outline. As you draft, you will usually see some ways to improve on your original plan. Be ready to revise your outline, to shift parts around, to drop or add parts. Chapter 18: Invention and Inquiry includes a thorough discussion of outlining.

Consider the following questions as you plan:

- ☐ How should I divide the information? (See Chapter 15: Classifying.)
- ☐ What order will best serve my thesis?
- ☐ Where should the thesis go?
- ☐ Will I need brief summaries at any point in the essay?
- ☐ What kinds of transitions will I need between the main parts of my

essay? (See Chapter 11: Cueing the Reader, for a discussion of transitions.)

Setting goals Successful writers are always looking beyond the next sentence to larger goals. Indeed, the next sentence is easier to write if you keep larger goals in mind. The following questions can help you set these goals. Consider each one now and then return to them as necessary while you write.

Your readers

☐ How much are my readers likely to know about this subject? How can I build on their knowledge?

☐ What new information can I present to them?

☐ How much information will be enough and how much will be too much?

☐ How can I organize my essay so that my readers will be able to follow it easily?

☐ What voice would be most appropriate?

The beginning

☐ How shall I begin? Should I open with a surprising fact, as Attenborough and Langer do? Should I begin with an anecdote? a quotation? a question? What kind of opening would be most likely to capture my readers' attention?

☐ Should I assert my thesis immediately, as Marcusson does? Or should I first set the context?

☐ How can I best forecast the plan my report will follow? Should I offer a detailed forecast as Langer does? Or is a brief description sufficient?

The ending

☐ How shall I end? Should I restate my thesis, as Marcusson and Langer do?

☐ Should I relate the ending to the beginning, so as to frame the essay?

Special writing strategies

☐ How much do I need to define my terms? Can I rely on brief sentence definitions or will I need to write extended definitions?

☐ Should I include any tables, charts, or graphs?

☐ Do I need to include any particular examples?

☐ Would comparison or contrast help readers to understand the information?

☐ Should I include any anecdotes, as Wolf does?

☐ Do I need to tell about any processes, as Marcusson does? Or describe any historical events, as Langer does?

Drafting the report   Before you begin drafting your report, take time to review the general advice about drafting in Chapter 1. As you write, keep your mind on your thesis statement. Remember that this assertion is the reason for your report; everything you include must in some way support the thesis. Remember also the needs and expectations of your readers; organize and define and explain with them in mind.

READING A DRAFT WITH A CRITICAL EYE

Now read over the draft. Whether you are reading your own work or that of another student, you should keep in mind the following basic question: how can this draft be improved so that it will be as readable, engaging, and memorable as possible?

The tasks that follow can help you answer that challenging question.

First general impression   Read the essay straight through to get a quick general impression. Write down your reactions in a few sentences. Is the report readable? Is it informative? Did it hold your interest? Did anything surprise you? What do you like best about it? Does anything seem weak? This reading should not be for detailed analysis, but rather to express your first reaction.

Pointings   One good way to maintain a critical focus as you read the report is to highlight noteworthy features of the writing with *pointings*. A simple system of lines and brackets, these pointings are quick and easy to do, and they can provide a lot of helpful information for revision. Use pointings in the following way:

☐ Draw a straight line under any words or images that seem especially effective: strong verbs, specific details, memorable phrases, striking images.

☐ Draw a wavy line under any words or images that seem flat, stale, or vague.

☐ Also put the wavy line under any words or phrases that you consider unnecessary or repetitious.

☐ Look for pairs or groups of sentences that you think should be combined into one sentence. Put brackets [ ] around these sentences.

☐ Look for sentences that are garbled, overloaded, or awkward. Put parentheses ( ) around these sentences. Put them around any sentence which seems even slightly questionable; don't worry now about whether or not you are sure of your impression. The writer needs to know that you, as one reader, had even the slightest hestitation about understanding a sentence.

Analysis   Now make a more thorough analysis of the draft. As you read, consider the following things.

1. Describe the subject in your own words. Is it too big? too small? Can you think of ways to refocus the subject that might make the essay more successful?

2. Identify the thesis. What is the main point? Is it stated directly or just implied? If it is implied, state in your own words what you understand the thesis to be. If you recognize no thesis (stated or implied), suggest one.

3. Look at the way the report is organized. Is the information logically divided? Can you suggest another way to organize it? Consider also the order—can you suggest a better way of sequencing the information?

4. Describe the voice you hear in the report. Is it appropriate for the intended readers? Do you hear the same voice throughout the report?

5. Evaluate the beginning. Does it pull you into the essay and make you want to continue? Does it adequately forecast the direction of the essay? You may be able to suggest alternative beginnings to the writer.

6. Find the obvious transitions and internal summaries in the draft. Are they helpful? If not, can you improve any of them? Can you see any places where additional transitions or summaries would be helpful?

7. Consider the use of facts and examples. Is the draft too factual? too general? Point out any places where more facts or examples are needed. Look also at any anecdotes—are they interesting? Do they contribute to the overall report, or do they stray from the point?

8. Think about the draft's content. Does it seem complete? Does it tell you all that you want to know right now about this subject? Specify any additional information you think should be included. Is there any information you consider superfluous? If it describes a process, are all important steps included?

9. Examine the definitions. Are they clear? Is everything defined that needs to be?

10. Evaluate the ending. Is is effective? Does it frame the report? Should it? Can you suggest any alternative endings?

11. Now imagine someone with limited time reading this essay. This reader wants—and needs—to proceed at an even, quick pace, with as little effort as possible. Where might this draft slow a reader down?

REVISING AND EDITING

The next step is to revise your draft. First, however, be sure to review the general advice on revising in Chapter 1.

Revising a report

After you have studied, reread, and reflected on your draft and perhaps gotten some reactions and comments from other students or your instructor, you can start your final revision. Following are some particular guidelines for revising a report.

Revising to sharpen the focus

☐ Reconsider your thesis. Make sure that it focuses on the right point and that it is neither overstated nor understated.

☐ Remove any information which is not directly relevant to your thesis. Unrelated details, no matter how fascinating, merely detract from the main point.

Revising to clarify the organization

☐ Look once more at the way you divided your information. Be sure the divisions are parallel and do not overlap.

☐ Reconsider the sequence of information. Be sure that the most important information receives the proper emphasis—should it be placed first or last? Is there any information that must be presented first?

Revising to enrich the content

☐ Reconsider the total content to be sure nothing seems vague or unexplained. If necessary, do additional reading or other research.

☐ Evaluate the information your report gives. Consider whether it is too familiar; if so, try to replace some unsurprising facts with new or unexpected information.

Revising for readability

☐ Consider other beginnings to be sure that you forecast your plan and engage your readers' interest as well as possible.

☐ Look over all the cues you provide readers to be sure they are sufficient and helpful.

☐ Reconsider your conclusion; does it frame the report? If not, should it?

☐ Scrutinize each sentence. Does it repeat the previous sentence? Does it say exactly what you want it to say? Does it have clear connections to the sentences around it? Should it be broken into two sentences or combined with another sentence?

Editing and proofreading
Once you revise a draft for the last time, you must edit it closely. As you were drafting, you surely corrected obvious errors of usage and style, but correctness probably was not your first priority. Now, though, you must look at your draft critically and objectively in order to find and correct any errors of mechanics, usage, punctuation, or style.

After you have edited the draft and produced your final copy, proofread your report to be certain that it contains no mistakes.

LEARNING FROM YOUR OWN WRITING PROCESS

Your instructor may ask you to think or write about the process you followed in producing this essay. If so, begin by skimming your invention writing and then reread your draft and revision. Look at specific changes you made between draft and revision, and explain why you made them. Think about any problems you encountered choosing a subject and gathering information. Decide what pleases you the most about your final draft and what you would try to improve if you had more time. What did you learn about writing to report information?

A WRITER AT WORK

FINDING A PLAN

This section presents the plan Scott Sumner followed in the first draft of his essay "Everything Is Theater." The final draft is printed in this chapter on pages 147–149.

Even before he began researching his subject, John Cage, Sumner knew that he wanted to write about Cage's special contributions to music. He had first learned about Cage in a music-history course and knew he would find interesting material about Cage's innovations. Thus, he had his thesis; next, he began to read and take notes.

Once he had enough material, Sumner had to decide how to organize his essay. Though he could have organized it around Cage's innovations, he decided that because they appeared over a period of twenty years, it would be better to organize the report chronologically. He said he thought a chronological plan might be easier for readers to follow and remember.

Sumner then had to find out whether his chronological plan would work—would it organize the important information about Cage's innovations? Would it be appropriate for his thesis? Would it lead to a plan readers could easily follow? He attempted a scratch outline, covering the main information he would include under each major date in Cage's career. Here is that outline:

1938: *Bacchanale*—prepared piano, led to percussion music.

1939: *Imaginary Landscape No. 5*—first piece of tape music.

1943: Museum of Modern Art concerts in NYC.

Spring of 1950: *Sixteen Dances*—charts of actions to be made, rather than notes to be played. *Water Walk.* Graphisms. Indeterminacy.

1950s: Sound-proof chamber experience at Harvard, interest in theater.

4' 3"—silent piano composition.

1953: *Imaginary Landscape No. 4*

1968: *Reunion*

If you compare this outline to the final revised essay, you will see how well it predicts the final plan. Paragraphs 1, 3, 4, 5, and 6 all begin with dates. Notice that it does *not* suggest the amount of space Sumner will devote to each time period, however. Notice also that he decided to put 1953 and 1968 events ahead of the 1938 event, saying that the later two compositions seemed like a better way to engage readers' attention.

Making Proposals

☐ After their team loses an NFL play-off game as a result of a very questionable pass-interference call, the owner and coach together develop a proposal arguing that officials should view instant TV replays on all close or critical calls. In their proposal to the football commissioner, they concentrate on demonstrating that such replays are technically feasible without being terribly costly. They conclude by suggesting that the National Football League might field-test their plan for one year in one stadium.

☐ The business manager of a large hospital writes a proposal to the board of directors requesting the purchase of a new word-processing and billing system that she recently saw demonstrated at a convention. She argues that the new system would both improve efficiency and save money. In support of her proposal she reminds them of the limitations of the present system and points out the advantages of the new one.

☐ Researchers at an oceanographic institute write a proposal to the National Science Foundation for funding to study the effects of ocean temperatures on weather patterns. To convince the foundation that their research should have priority over other proposed projects, they argue that the world economy is being adversely affected by erratic weather conditions. They discuss in detail the case of the El Niño phenomenon of 1983, with its extreme temperatures and severe storms, as evidence of the catastrophic effects changes in ocean temperature can have.

☐ The Women's Center at a small private college is losing support, both from campus administration and students. Not only has it sponsored fewer activities, but students are much less aware of its existence. One student who values the center decides that it really needs one full-time coordinator to organize and publicize its programs. With two friends she writes a proposal to the associated students board, which funds student activities. She describes in detail the current problems and potential consequences, trying to show how a rejuvenated Women's Center can benefit everyone on campus.

☐ Several students in the predentistry program at a large state university realize how uncertain they are about requirements, procedures, and strategies for applying to dental school. One of them writes a proposal to the head of the program suggesting the need for some sort of a handbook for predentistry students. To dramatize that a problem exists and is considered serious by students, he points out their students' declining rates of admission to dental schools and includes an informal survey of students presently in the program. He also mentions several other programs that offer this kind of pamphlet for their students. Realizing that few faculty members would take time for such a project, he proposes that students would do the actual writing as well as handling the printing and distribution; two faculty members would simply serve as advisers. He asks that the publication costs be borne by the predentistry program, pointing out, however, that students would donate their time.

☐ A college student who works part-time at a pizzeria near campus notices certain problems created by high turnover of employees. Newcomers often misplace things, forget procedures for cleaning up, and interrupt other employees to ask for help operating the espresso machine. Since the company offers cash awards for innovative ideas for improving procedures or service, the student writes a proposal suggesting ways to reduce these problems. Knowing that high turnover is inevitable in such a job, she concentrates on procedures for orienting and training new employees.

Writers of proposals identify a problem, offer a solution, and attempt to convince their readers to accept the proposed solution. Usually they describe the problem in some detail, giving information about its causes and history; often they will also outline how their solution can be implemented. In addition, they may anticipate and directly address potential doubts and questions readers might have about their proposed solution; sometimes they will even discuss the pros and cons of solutions others have proposed. Proposals thus are an especially challenging form of argumentative writing, demanding the most painstaking problem-analysis reasoning. They also require an acute sensitivity to readers. The proposal writer's purpose, after all, is to convince readers to take action.

People write proposals every day in government, business, education, and the professions. They are a basic ingredient of the world's work. Proposals are written for readers who can be expected to be aware of a problem, or for those who must first be convinced that a problem exists. Sometimes a writer's proposed solution is the only one ever suggested and is thus likely to win readers' applause and support; at other times it must compete with other proposed solutions. The stakes can be great: proposals often involve large expenditures or affect many people.

Proposals also serve everyday, though no less urgent, purposes. Some problems are just argued about and solved in committee meetings, but very often they are also written out for circulation among committee members or for publication in a newsletter. For example, a student may propose a way to improve teaching evaluations or a tenant may propose to other tenants in a large apartment building a plan for forcing the landlord to make needed repairs; in either case, a written proposal introduces the suggested plan of action.

The reading selections that follow illustrate many of the strategies proposal writers use to analyze a problem and persuade readers to accept their solution. You will find that all the writers in this chapter address fairly well-defined audiences. Knowing what your readers know, what their assumptions and biases are, what kinds of arguments will be appealing to them is a central part of proposal writing, indeed of all good writing. You will be asked to direct your own proposal essay in this chapter to specific readers who want to think seriously about the problem or find a solution to it in their own lives. As you read the following pieces, you may see strategies you find effective and wish to use in your own writing.

READINGS

This first proposal offers a solution to the problem of what last name to record for children of marriages where both the husband and wife keep their own family names. Written by Jeanette Germain, a professional writer, this selection was first published in 1982 in *CoEvolution Quarterly*, a magazine concerned with environmental and social issues.

As is evident from her opening paragraph and title, Germain assumes her readers—mostly women—will regard her proposal sympathetically even if they do not recognize the existence of the problem she is addressing. Although it is risky to generalize about readers, it is fair to assume that anyone reading this magazine would be unlikely to find Germain's proposal absurd.

As you read, notice how long we must wait to learn Germain's proposed solution. What does she tell us before actually announcing her solution?

WHAT TO NAME THE CHILDREN WHEN HE'S KEPT HIS NAME AND YOU'VE KEPT YOURS
JEANETTE GERMAIN

No one questions the fact that many women now keep their last names 1 when they marry. We all recognize that women shouldn't automatically give up a piece of their identity in order to express a commitment to a long-term relationship. Most couples now discuss the issue before they marry. Some women keep their names. Some prefer their husband's name. Some husbands even prefer their wife's name.

But few couples, as far as I can tell, ever talk about the last names their 2 children will carry. A mother may choose to keep her name separate. But the children, it is assumed, need *one* family name. And that family name is usually the father's.

Why don't couples consider other alternatives? Why isn't this topic as 3 burning an issue today as maiden and married names were a decade ago?

I asked these questions at a family wedding about five years ago. One of 4 my female cousins had just married and had decided to keep her maiden name. Most family members thought that was a sensible choice. After all, she was already known in her profession by her maiden name.

But in the next breath, my uncles began talking about who would pass 5 down the family name. They began urging my male cousins to take action on this important matter.

I wondered why none of my female cousins were being included in the 6
conversation. Why shouldn't women be able to pass down a family name, I
asked.

Nobody had an answer for me. My customarily gabby family couldn't 7
even talk about the subject. Everyone was so dumbfounded by my suggestion
that they forgot to ask how I proposed to carry it out.

I wasn't sure myself at the time. 8

I like my name and don't want to change it. But until that wedding five 9
years ago, I hadn't really thought about the children I hope to have. I wouldn't
want them to automatically have their father's last name. They will be my
children, too. But I can't name them after me, either, without substituting a
one-sided maternal society for the one-sided paternal society I'm rejecting.

So what are the alternatives? I considered Latin, English, Icelandic, and 10
even science-fiction solutions before finding my answer.

Jones Germain

I had studied Spanish, so I knew something about Latin names. I knew 11
that in many Spanish-speaking countries a person's full name includes a sur-
name followed by the mother's name. So if I marry a Mr. Jones, our children
could be named Jones Germain. The drawback is that the mother's name
often isn't used familiarly in those countries. Multiple names are shortened
and the woman's name is dropped. The same thing would probably happen
here.

The mother's last name is her father's anyway. So double Latin names 12
are still patriarchal and not too successful.

Germain-Jones

In this country and in England, there is a tradition of hyphenated or double 13
last names. When the Mountbatten-Windsors first joined their names that
way, the partnership of two aristocratic families was enhanced. Adela Rogers
St. Johns decided early in her journalistic career to use both her maiden and
married name because her readers already knew her as Adela Rogers. Now
television stars (Farrah Fawcett-Majors) and many of my friends are using the
same solution.

But I'd like to see both the father's and mother's name carried down 14
through the generations. Hyphenated or double last names are uncomfort-
ably long for most of us, even in the first generation. By the second and third
generations, they would get ridiculous. What if my friends Kent and Karen
had hyphenated their last name to Little-Pressman, and their child used that
full last name? Their child might then marry my child, and their child would
be a Germain-Jones-Little-Pressman. Forget that approach.

Germones, Jomain

Innovative couples, I learned, have attempted to simplify matters with 15
hybrid names. Germain-Jones, for example, could become Germones or Jo-
main. But that sounds silly to me, and the combinations down through the

generations might get worse. All those changes would dilute the personal and family identity that I value.

Hybrid names would also bring me back to changing my own last name. I don't want to do that. 16

Pat or Chris or Randy

I could give my child only one name, I considered, eliminating the last 17 name altogether.

That extreme solution was suggested by Ursula K. LeGuin in her science- 18 fiction novel *The Dispossessed*. . . . In this utopian nonsexist book, the people of the planet Anarres have only one name each. It is selected by computer at birth so that no two individuals will share a name. The names are unique and also genderless. Because a name indicates no gender or family heritage, it discourages discrimination on either basis. You can't tell from an Anarres name the sex or parents of an individual.

The idea interests me, but it goes too far. I look forward to picking out 19 masculine or feminine names for my children. I think they will be identity assets for both the boys and the girls. I would also be uneasy about subjecting my children to the confusion of having no last name in a "last name, first name, middle initial" culture.

Jeanettesdottir

Iceland finally brought me to the verge of a solution. Everyone is identified 20 primarily by the first name in Iceland, but everyone also has a last name. For men it works this way: Magnus has a son named Einar whose full name is Einar Magnusson (son of Magnus). Einar then has a son he names Johann, who becomes Johann Einarsson. Johann fathers a son, Sigurd, who is Sigurd Johannsson.

I thought that Icelandic girls might be named in the same manner—as 21 daughters of their mothers. So Gudrun would have a daughter Anna and would call her Anna Gudrunsdottir (Gudrun's daughter). But it doesn't work that way. Gudrun is Olavsdottir (her father's daughter). If Gudrun marries Kristin Gudmundsson, she does not take her husband's last name. But her daughter takes the father's name and becomes Kristinsdottir.

The Answer

Iceland nevertheless brought me to an answer. I was certain by then that 22 I wanted both matriarchal and patriarchal names for my children. It doesn't matter to me that men have lineage expressed directly by their name—if women have the same thing.

It's really very simple. *Daughters should have their mother's last name.* 23 *Sons should have their father's.*

The family heritage that I value so strongly wouldn't be diluted by the 24 change. Men would continue to see their names passed down through their sons as they have always been. The change would make little difference for the men, because their daughters might not keep their fathers' names in marriage anyway.

And for the women, I see the gains as important. For the first time in 25 recent western history, daughters and granddaughters could have a visible lineage of their own. They could have a clear identity and heritage as women. They could have *one* last name.

My only hesitation would be in beginning with a patriarchal last name— 26 my last name is my father's. But tracing my female ancestors back even four generations was very difficult. Each generation has maiden and married names. I would probably have to trace back to prehistory to find a matriarchal name, if I were able to find one at all. I finally settled on "Germain" as a good last name to begin with. It was originally the name I wanted to keep anyway.

The little research I did into the names of my female ancestors also re- 27 vealed a female lineage carried through first and middle names. I was named after my grandmother, who was named after her grandmother. My mother was named after her grandmother.

I'm very pleased with that discovery, but it took me 26 years to find. If 28 the women in my family had all kept one last name, I would have known my maternal heritage sooner.

Now I look forward to having a daughter of my own. I want to name her 29 after her grandmother and after me. I hope to find a partner who will be amenable. This approach to naming children seems reasonable to me.

Does anyone else agree? 30

Questions for analysis

1. Even though Germain assumes a sympathetic audience, she cannot be sure they either recognize the existence or seriousness of the problem she is addressing. How does she establish, in paragraphs 1–9, that the problem exists and is serious enough to need solving?

2. Paragraphs 4–8 contain an autobiographical anecdote. Is it surprising to find such an anecdote in a problem-solving essay? Why do you think Germain brings her personal experience into the essay?

3. How many alternative solutions does Germain consider before announcing her own? Review each one and notice just how she argues against it. For what reasons does she finally reject each one? Are you convinced that the alternatives are all unacceptable?

4. At least half the essay is devoted to rejecting alternative solutions. Why do you think Germain gives such prominence to "bad" alternatives?

5. Germain's solution is unmistakable: she announces it in italics in paragraph 23. How does she argue the advantages her solution would have for both men and women?

6. Do you think her proposed solution really solves the problem? She makes it seem easy to implement. Is it really that easy? Can you suggest any problems with her solution?

7. Germain seems to assume that men are more likely than women to oppose her solution. At several points in her essay she specifically anticipates men's reservations and tries to reassure them. Cite two or three places where she does this. How effective do you think her reassurances are?

8. Would you be willing to write a proposal to solve a personal problem? Think of difficulties that come up between people, for example. Consider the different kinds of relationships you have with others—as a friend, a brother or sister, a parent or spouse, a student, patient, or employee. Identify a problem in one of these relationships. How would you establish that a problem exists and that people should be concerned about it? What solution would you propose? How would you convince people to accept your solution?

This essay illustrates all the basic features of proposal writing: a well-defined problem, a proposed solution, and arguments supporting the solution. Germain uses three basic strategies to support her proposal: she considers and rejects other possible solutions, gives reasons why her own solution is preferable, and addresses possible objections or counterarguments to her proposal.

Just as the thesis of a report states the main point, so the thesis of a proposal states the writer's solution to a problem. It is the author's forum for telling readers, "This is the way I think we should solve the problem." Germain's thesis appears in paragraph 23: "Daughters should have their mother's last name. Sons should have their father's." Sometimes the thesis of a proposal includes an explanation of how the proposed solution would be implemented. Other times, writers add to this main assertion a statement forecasting why they think their solution is the best one possible.

In addition to stating her own solution, Germain evaluates several alternative solutions—ones used in Spanish-speaking countries and in England, for example. These other solutions may come from actual proposals written by others or may simply be ideas Germain came up with while thinking about the problem. Presenting other possible solutions, considering their feasibility, and rejecting them in favor of her own proposed solution constitute part of her argument.

Another important part of a writer's argument is to deal with potential counterarguments, objections, or criticisms. Specifically, a writer very often tries to anticipate any such counterarguments and to refute, or argue against, them. Germain, for example, anticipates the counterargument that family heritage would be "diluted" if children were named as she proposes. She refutes this counterargument directly, arguing in paragraphs 24 and 25 that the change "would make little difference for the men" and would in fact only strengthen feelings of family heritage among women.

Before proposing her solution, rejecting alternative solutions, and refuting possible counterarguments, Germain defines the problem, stating it directly in her title. She then goes on to develop the definition—establishing its existence and importance—in the first nine paragraphs. All writers devote part of their proposal to defining the problem, though some problems require more elaboration than others. Problem definition is so important to proposal writing that it is considered a secondary thesis.

Throughout the essay we see evidence of Germain's careful attention to her readers, both men and women. She wants us to agree that her proposal is workable, and so she is careful to anticipate any objections we may have and to refute any alternatives we may think of. She presents herself as someone we can trust. We see that she has researched the problem thoroughly, that she knows more about it than we do, and that she discusses it in a reasonable way. She does everything she can to keep the attention of readers who are likely to oppose her proposal.

The next selection was written by Carol Bly, a writer who lives in rural Minnesota. Her essay, which originally appeared in *Minnesota Monthly*, proposes the institution of a special high school class for farming communities. She addresses her proposal to parents, trying to draw their attention to a problem she considers serious and at the same time to offer a possible solution.

As you read, pay attention to the way that Bly makes a case for her proposal. Does she claim her solution will eliminate the problem altogether or that it will be a positive first step in that direction?

TO UNTEACH GREED
CAROL BLY

For the moment, at least, we are stuck with advising high schoolers that they must expect to take jobs they don't look forward to, because the interesting ones are too rare. In my hometown, for example, six or seven of each high school class express an interest in forestry, parks, and similar outdoor work, but the vocational school that trains for those jobs, Brainerd, has only thirteen openings a year. Girls want to be dental assistants, but St. Cloud, which has the appropriate program, gets three hundred applications for its forty places. Minnesota city dwellers may find it odd but it is nonetheless true that to get into farming—and I use the term here to mean just to get a job as a hand—you have to "know somebody." The good jobs, which by their nature are satisfying to sense and sensibility, are cruelly hard to land.

Therefore, a realistic high school counselor teaches kids to get ready for disappointment. He or she may seem a villain in steering young people to the 600,000 clerk-typist openings when they want forestry, or in not making a whole lot out of the Phillips (Andover, Massachusetts) Academy's imaginative Short Term Institutes—six weeks' programs for high school kids from around the country, designed to give them the idea of knowledge-for-the-joy-of-it before they get washed into the Vo-Tech stream of cost/benefit thinking. It seems tough to advise kids that someone must work in the deafening assembly lines; why not advise them someone must staff the top offices everywhere, and raise their expectations to that?

The counselors are being realistic, and their advice isn't cruel. What *is* cruel is that we do not teach a decent philosophical way to look at life; so that those in our countryside who work with hands or head are misled, and waste years finding their inner life. People are taught to be drones. 3

Only once in a public information meeting in my part of the country have I heard the farm populace approached as if they were people with anything but money making in their heads. In countless Countryside Council meetings, countless Democratic party meetings, countless senior citizens' group meetings (which I went to when working on a minibus task force) and nearly always in Lutheran Church meetings—where the ministers are constantly saying, "We think too much of money," as if money consciousness were a uniform, requisite sin—in all these public meetings the audience was regarded as people wanting profit or high income only. The schools assume that even the children will be interested only in profit and high income. Once I saw a sixth-grade movie against shoplifting in which the two motives provided for not shoplifting were 4

1. you might be caught, and if you have a police record it will be hard to get a job;
2. shoplifting indirectly raises prices so you eventually will have to pay more for things;

both reasons being self-interest. Nowhere did the movie say,

1. it is mean to shoplift;
2. you do not want to be an unkind person.

The single occasion on which I heard an adult group out here addressed as if they had any moral nature or philosophical nature at all was April 2, 1977, at a 208 Water Quality meeting arranged by the 6-W Regional Development Commission. The speaker, Judge Miles Lord, said, "You farmers can act on motivations beyond greed . . . you can think of natural resources in terms of sharing what we all have, not just in terms of exploitation." 5

It was rather a surprising address. One farmer, a panelist, was querulous because a Minnesota law made it illegal for us to dye our potatoes with that poisonous red dye but Missouri farmers could still dye theirs, so it was hard for a Minnesota potato producer and shipper to compete with the Missouri people (housewives still being ignorant enough of the chemical danger to buy potatoes because of the handsome color). The speaker's reply to this was "There speaks the voice of greed!" The audience was a little surprised. It was refreshing to hear the word aloud—*greed*—and to be expected to do better. 6

How refreshing it is to get to think about the moral aspect of things! 7
How immensely boring our countryside life in Minnesota is, despite its beauty,
for the simple reason we never get to consider the morals of things—together, publicly.

I have a practical suggestion to make to raise the moral consciousness 8
out here. I suggest we keep or make English required of our juniors and
seniors but with the following two strict conditions:

1. That *no techniques* of literature be taught or discussed ever. All approaches to stories being read must be to what they show of life—
   inner life, feelings, public life, morals.
2. And that we teach courses with a rural-literature emphasis.

Technique is the enemy of philosophy and goodness. The "technique or 9
form creates content" attitude of the 1940s New Criticism makes for cold
treatment of stories, deliberate mental superiority over literature—as if literature were something to be seen through. You see it in the frosty way English
departments of universities and colleges, still stuck with that interest in technique, handle their freshman curricula. Tolstoy has a terrific passage in *Anna
Karenina* against technique. Some art "appreciators" are in a painter's studio,
looking at a picture he has just passionately finished in which Christ is one
of the figures.

"Yes—there's a wonderful mastery!" said Vronsky. . . . "There you have technique." . . . The sentence about technique had sent a pang through Mihailov's
[the painter's] heart, and looking angrily at Vronsky he suddenly scowled. He
had often heard this word technique, and was utterly unable to understand . . . a mechanical facility for painting or drawing, entirely apart from its
subject.

Here is a tentative format for an Ag Lit course:

Akenfield, especially the chapters about Muck Hill Farm and the Young
Farmers' League, and the one about the old Scot who couldn't adjust to
the new gardening ways

"How Much Land Does a Man Need?" from Tolstoy's *Russian Stones and
Legends*

Growing Up in Minnesota, especially Robert Bly's strange chapter about
the sheriff railroading a farmhand to jail in Madison, Minnesota

All Things Bright and Beautiful and *All Creatures Great and Small*

"To a Mouse" by Burns

"Home Burial" and "The Hill Wife" by Frost

Furrow's End, edited by D. B. Greenberg, especially the story of the young
sheepherder and his girl from squatter background—one of the most
terrific young-love stories with a farming scene

Winesburg, Ohio

My Antonia

String Too Short to Be Saved, Donald Hall's autobiography, with a terrific chapter on a hired hand whose sole passion in life was Mounds bars.

These stories and poems should be read by people who are going to live 10 in Minnesota small towns and on farms if they're lucky; and if the stories and verse are studied in the spirit in which they were written, instead of in the spirit of methodology, the young people may come to like English, and enjoy seeing what people think about life.

We especially need to do this if we can't have the jobs we want. If the 11 competitive profit-making part of our lives is going to fall short, and it will for most, then the reflective, intuitive part of life had better be more rewarding than it is. A very nice by-product of an Ag Lit course would be something for men and women to talk about besides Starsky and Hutch. We need a thousand more things to ruminate about together out here. We need conversations that take in the moral aspect of things as well as their money-making aspect. It will bring to the countryside a sorely needed gentleness.

Questions for analysis

1. What is the problem for which Bly is proposing a solution?

2. Why do you think she begins the essay by talking about the lack of "interesting" jobs? What does this problem have to do with her proposal?

3. Bly seems to be referring to her readers when she speaks of people being "taught to be drones" (paragraph 3) and caring only about "profit or high income" (paragraph 4). What is her strategy here? Why does she talk about her readers this way?

4. What kind of person does Bly seem to be? What kind of voice do you hear in this essay? Cite some specific examples in support of your answer.

5. In paragraph 8, Bly announces a "practical suggestion" to solve the problem. Just how practical does her suggestion seem to you? Why do you suppose she calls it practical? How specific is she on how her proposal might be implemented?

6. Writers sometimes conclude an essay with a rhetorical device known as *framing*, returning to something mentioned in the beginning of the essay. How does Bly frame her essay? Why do you think framing is an especially effective way to end a proposal?

7. Does Bly digress in paragraphs 8–9 when she criticizes the teaching of "technique" in literature classes? Why do you think she brings in this issue? How does it pertain to her proposal?

8. Can you think of a practical proposal to solve an important cultural or moral problem? Name a particular problem. What might you propose to solve this problem? How could your proposal be put into practice? How exactly would it help to solve the problem?

Whereas Jeanette Germain devotes most of her essay to alternative solutions, Bly does not so much as mention any other possible solution. Instead, she spends most of her discussion (paragraphs 1–8) trying to define the problem and make her readers recognize its existence. It is an especially difficult problem to define because it is so abstract. She speaks about the lack of "interesting" jobs and about how most high school graduates have to settle for relatively boring jobs, but her real concern is stated in the title—greed. The problem she addresses is a moral one: that all action is motivated by the desire for profit and self-interest.

Although this problem is a universal one, Bly keeps her focus local, addressing her proposal to a group of which she is a member. Rather than attempting to reform all of society, she offers what she calls a "practical" suggestion to solve the local, immediate problem. The difficulty in this proposal as in any is whether or not the suggested solution will in fact solve the problem. This is especially true with a problem as deeply rooted in the value system of an entire community or culture as this one is. Bly's proposal has the advantage of practicality: she offers some specific changes in the school curriculum that may well enhance the "reflective, intuitive part of life," and thereby enrich people's own lives.

In the next selection, a college student proposes changes in the operation of a research project. She addresses her proposal to the research group leader—that is, to the very person who can implement her suggestions. Unfortunately, this group leader is the person most directly responsible for the problem this proposal sets out to correct.

Wendy Jo Niwa, the writer, is therefore faced with an awkward rhetorical situation: how to convince her reader of the seriousness of the problem without making him feel he is being criticized? As you read, notice the ways that Niwa handles this delicate writing problem.

A PROPOSAL TO STRENGTHEN THE LANGUAGE ACQUISITION PROJECT
WENDY JO NIWA

Our present research project involving content analysis of mother-and-child conversations has exciting possibilities. The data we have gathered thus far promise conclusions about some perplexing questions about language acquisition. However, we do not yet have an efficient system of analyzing the data and our progress is therefore quite slow. Many mistakes and inconsistencies occur because we lack specific criteria for counting mean length of utterances or for verifying or coding the transcripts. Too often, we decide how to do something only *after* the task has been completed. Consequently, we have to take time to recheck the transcripts once again, thus spending twice the time necessary on the task. Not only does this kind of disorganization jeopardize the validity and reliability of the study, but also it lowers the morale of everyone working on it. Students become frustrated, you have more to worry about, and everything takes more time than it might. Whereas students suffer simply because our work on the project is less than satisfying, you have a lot to lose, as the disorganization could affect the quality of your dissertation. This is most unfortunate, for we students have so much to learn from working with you . . . just as you have something to gain from any help we can give to your project.

One of the main causes of these problems is a lack of communication 2 among group members. Information and decisions concerning the transcripts are not always passed along, which results in disruptive and confusing inconsistency. Because we do not keep a record of important decisions, they are often forgotten. Confusion results. Without specific guidelines, we often find ourselves merely guessing, and individual biases are introduced into your work.

Some blame must be placed on the independent study program itself. 3 Unfortunately, the Psychology Department has offered little guidance to any of us. Your focus is understandably on your project, and students' needs must come second. If we could get the Psychology Department to assume some oversight responsibility, students' educational needs could be better balanced with the project's needs. Perhaps they would show more interest in the program if they realized that our dissatisfaction may deter other students from participating in future research projects.

If these problems continue to be ignored, the result could be lower quality 4 work. Misleading conclusions may be drawn from the study, or significant findings may fail to surface due to the inconsistency among student assistants. Should the findings become too inconsistent, they may not serve to support a conclusion. The research would then have failed.

Since you are the researcher and are the one most likely to be hurt by 5 these problems, I am directing this proposal to you. I see several ways of improving the quality and effectiveness of our research program, ways that I feel sure would be beneficial to us all. I propose that we meet at least once a week for around an hour. At the meetings we could discuss any problems or questions we may have involving the transcripts and doublecheck procedures followed. Such meetings should promote much greater consistency and enable us to monitor progress and plan for the next stage in the research. If there were no problems or business involving the project to discuss, we could use the time as a workshop to discuss relevant topics in the field. In this way, we students would learn from your experience and expertise in developmental psychology.

To find a time when we could all attend such a meeting, we would each 6 submit our class schedules and preferred meeting times. A meeting time convenient for everyone could then be chosen. In addition, a sign-up sheet could be posted in the lab for workshop presentations. Each student would be responsible for one workshop a month when he or she would summarize background reading on a chosen topic and prepare a short presentation on the topic. These topics would either concern our specific research project or developmental psychology in general.

We would keep a record of all plans and decisions made at the meetings. 7 Responsibility for keeping this record would rotate. This record would be typed and made available to everyone in the lab. Surely such a record would be useful to you when you later must describe research procedures in your final paper.

There are several reasons why you should find my proposal valuable. First, 8 these weekly meetings would only help eliminate any major inconsistencies and prevent other problems from occurring which might require us to go back and review the transcripts. Thus, time would be saved and the study would progress at a much faster pace. Second, the workshops should help to increase student enthusiasm for the project and therefore improve everyone's work. Third, keeping a record of all decisions made would ensure that we all follow the same criteria rather than our own individual criteria, thus improving the reliability of your research. Also, putting the plans in print would help since all of us have a tendency to forget things when they are not written down. Best of all, this solution would be easy to implement.

You may be concerned that the meetings would interfere with our work 9 on the transcripts. I feel sure that the meetings would take less time than is used presently in going back over finished transcripts several times. Not only would our work be much more efficient if we discussed problems and issues together, but also we could get through many more transcripts if we were clearer on what we were doing. We could, however, meet outside of the ten hours we are required to work on the project.

You might think that we should have the meetings but not the work- 10 shops, or that we should meet only to deal with the research and that if there are no problems, there should be no meetings. If all we do is work on transcripts, however, the independent study program will not be as valuable a learning experience as it might be. One of the purposes of the program is to give undergraduates a chance to learn from others who have more education, experience, and expertise. It is of course true that we could meet individually with you without having to organize a group. That would obviously require more time on your part, however, and would not solve the inconsistency problem in your project. Also, individual meetings may not be as productive as group meetings, since individuals tend to be stimulated by the exchange of ideas.

My proposal to have a group meeting once a week is the best way to 11 solve all of our problems at once. Besides being the most efficient and fair way, it would be easy to implement: All we need is an hour each week. The most important reason to accept this proposal, however, is that the final results of your study would be obtained sooner and the quality of your research would improve. The meetings would enhance group cohesiveness, which would facilitate communication among members. Morale would be lifted and interest heightened as a result of the privileged attention received in the workshops.

Questions for analysis   1. Why do you think Niwa spends one third of the proposal (paragraphs 1–4) defining the problem? How exactly does she avoid blaming her reader and forge an alliance of common interests? Cite specific passages as examples.

2. Why do you suppose Niwa mentions the independent study program (paragraph 3)?

3. Niwa does not mention consulting with any other student assistants about either the problem or her proposed solution. How could this lapse affect the chances of her proposal being accepted? Suppose she had discussed her proposal with her colleagues: how could she have best made this known in the essay? Add a few sentences of your own mentioning consultation with the others.

4. What objections or counterarguments does she anticipate? How does she handle them?

5. What alternative solutions does she discuss? What reasons does she give for rejecting them? Does she present any evidence in support of these reasons?

6. How does Niwa present herself in this essay? What kind of voice do you hear? How important do you consider self-presentation or voice in a proposal?

7. How does Niwa conclude her proposal? How does she avoid repeating herself?

8. Have you ever had occasion to write a proposal to solve a problem at school—in one of your classes, in your department, in your high school or college, in a lab, library, or other facility? Think of a particular problem you might propose a solution for. How would you go about trying to convince others of the importance of the problem? Would you address your proposal to the person able to resolve it (as Niwa does) or to those affected by the problem (as Carol Bly does in the preceding selection)?

Niwa does what all proposal writers must do: she builds a bridge of shared concerns between herself and her reader. This is essential if she has any hope of solving the problem. If she were to blame or even criticize the research group leader in any way, he would be unlikely to respond positively to her proposal.

One obvious way Niwa forges an alliance between herself and the reader is by using the pronoun *we*. Instead of establishing an adversary *us* (the student assistants) against *you* (the group leader) relationship, she shows from the first sentence that she considers herself a partner with her reader, working together on an important research project.

She also shows her respect for her reader by indicating that she values the project. It is, after all, his dissertation project. Niwa makes it clear in the first paragraph that the problem she is writing about threatens the success of a project both she and her reader care a great deal about. Furthermore, she makes it seem that she regards him highly when she says that weekly workshops would be valuable because students could "learn from your experience and expertise" (paragraph 5).

The last selection was also written by a student, Jim Chow. It deals with a problem in Moraga, California, Chow's hometown. Chow originally wrote the proposal for his composition class, but did in fact later send it to the editor of the local newspaper. As a letter to the editor, this proposal is, like Carol Bly's magazine article, an open letter to community members. Whereas these readers cannot act directly to solve the problem, they can get action through their civic leaders. Chow's purpose in writing is to mobilize community support for his proposal. As you read, notice how he informs readers about a problem they are most likely already familiar with.

THE DEER PROBLEM OF MORAGA
JIM CHOW

It was a cold winter night when a friend and I were driving home from a midnight movie. The headlights arced out a narrow path in front of the car. All of a sudden, a deer bolted onto the road. Swerving to avoid hitting the animal, we scraped a car parked on the side of the road. Total damages amounted to more than three hundred dollars. The troublesome deer of Moraga had struck again. 1

All of us in Moraga are familiar with this problem. Many have not escaped as cheaply as we did from encounters with the deer. Winter nights can be especially treacherous when the weather worsens and the deer come to town in search of food. They leave their natural habitat in the canyons when the vegetation becomes scarce and come to dine on the proudly tended gardens and parks in town. Local gardeners rank deer as their most destructive pest, worse even than gophers and caterpillars. In addition to being a nuisance, deer are a health risk, since they carry diseases communicable to humans. 2

In fact, the deer problem is potentially lethal to us and to them. Nocturnal creatures, the deer invade our town at night. Traveling along the sides of our winding roads, they add to the danger of driving at night. Occasionally, for 3 example, a deer will be frightened by the headlights of a car, and, in a moment of panic, run onto the road. It is all too often that the deer gets hit, the car is damaged, or both.

The question is, what can we do about the deer? The most cost-effective 4 method of solving the problem is to allow hunters to shoot them. In fact, I have heard this suggestion offered several times, though I can't tell if those proposing it are serious. We must reject this proposal. For one thing, the possibility of a stray shot hitting a bystander is too great. Second, animal lovers would surely protest the inhumanity and cruelty of such a policy. Furthermore, this proposal would not even solve the problem, since it wouldn't prevent the surviving deer from coming to Moraga in search of food. We would have to shoot a good many deer in the area to solve this problem completely.

Another possible solution that has been suggested is to capture the deer 5 and relocate them to a national park or some other protected area. Although this is a more humane proposal, it is no more workable: Finding, capturing, and relocating enough deer to solve the problem would be extraordinarily expensive. It has been estimated that this effort would cost our town over two hundred and fifty thousand dollars. The damage caused by the deer does not even approach that much money, so spending so much could not be justified. But even if we found the money, there is another reason why this proposed solution is not feasible. You see, we here in Moraga have a double standard: we want to keep the deer out of town, but we like having them in the canyon because it adds to the secluded, natural environment that helps to make Moraga special.

I would like to propose a solution that is both economical and practical: 6 during the winter when their natural food supply is low, we should feed the deer, regularly, in the woods. Before the cold season starts, we should stock about a hundred food stations in the woods, located in areas known to have high concentration of deer. These spots can be found by trial and error: if we discover a station is not being used extensively, then we can find another location that is more popular. Once winter hits the area, volunteers can regularly monitor the food supply in these food stations. Deer feed is mainly composed of vegetation and finely mashed oats or wheat and so is inexpensive. Local residents could contribute grass trimmings and the like. Wheat or oats should cost approximately two thousand five hundred dollars a year, a hundredth of what it would cost to relocate the deer. This plan would allow us to keep the deer while eliminating the trouble they now cause.

Critics of this proposal might argue that the food stations would allow 7 the deer to prosper too much, perhaps even creating a population explosion. This seems unlikely since the canyon is also populated with such natural predators as coyotes. My proposal keeps the deer out of town without requiring any physical handling of them. It is humane and economically feasible. It solves the problem by removing its cause: the deer's need for food.

Questions for analysis

1. Chow begins with a dramatic anecdote. Why would an anecdote like this be an especially effective way to begin a proposal?

2. How much space does Chow need to define the problem for his readers? What assumptions does he seem to make about his readers' values and their knowledge of the problem? Cite evidence from the proposal in support of your answer.

3. How does Chow make himself sound credible and authoritative? Describe the voice you hear in this essay, pointing to specific parts of the text to illustrate your description.

4. Presumably the alternative solutions Chow rejects were proposed by actual people. Why do you think Chow decided not to name these people?

5. Do you think Chow's solution would really solve the problem? He makes the proposal seem easy to implement and inexpensive, but would it really be so simple or cheap? Can you think of counterarguments against Chow's proposal? How does he anticipate some of these counterarguments?

6. Have you ever thought to write a proposal to solve a problem in your community? Name one particular problem you could propose a solution to. How would you define the problem for your readers? Would you need to convince them the problem is really serious and in need of solving? How would you argue for your own proposed solution?

Like writers of other kinds of essays, proposal writers have to support their thesis with a reasoned argument. They have to give readers good reasons to accept their proposed solution and demonstrate that their proposal is better than other possible solutions to the problem. Notice that many of the reasons Chow gives for rejecting alternative solutions are the same reasons he gives for supporting his own solution. He criticizes the proposal to allow hunters to shoot deer on the grounds that it would be dangerous, inhumane, and would not really solve the problem. He argues that the proposal to relocate deer is more humane, but expensive, and if successful would ruin Moraga's natural ambiance. His own proposal, on the other hand, he says would be humane as well as economical, would solve the problem without harm to the ambiance.

Moreover, Chow does not just assert these reasons, but actually offers evidence in support. For instance, in arguing the relocation proposal is too expensive, he cites an estimated cost for the proposed solution, pointing out that the cost of this solution would be greater than the cost of the problem. Then, he estimates the cost of his own proposal and explains how it can be so low.

BASIC FEATURES OF PROPOSALS

Effective proposals typically include the following features: a well-defined problem, a proposed solution, a convincing argument, and a reasonable tone of voice.

A well-defined problem   Proposals are written to offer a solution to a problem. Before presenting the solution, a proposal writer must be sure that readers know what the problem is. Jeanette Germain spends the first nine paragraphs of her essay defining the problem, Carol Bly the first eight, Wendy Jo Niwa the first four.

They all begin by stating the problem. Germain simply asks why no one worries about the lack of a system for passing down the mother's family name to her children. Niwa describes a complex of problems: progress on the research is slow, tedious, and repetitive; mistakes and inconsistencies occur; student assistants are not learning what they hoped to.

Stating the problem is not enough, however: the writer must establish the fact that the problem actually exists and that it is serious enough to need solving. Sometimes a writer may assume that the reader will recognize the problem. Niwa, for example, describes in detail problems on the research project, but does not give examples or statistical evidence because she knows her reader will not deny the problem's existence. She does argue for the problem's seriousness, though, pointing out potentially negative consequences her reader would be sure to take seriously.

Other times a writer is addressing readers who may not already be aware of the problem under consideration. Germain, for instance, starts out by describing how her own family was completely unaware of the problem. She establishes the problem simply by declaring its seriousness to her personally and by suggesting how important it should be to anyone concerned about women giving up their family names when they marry.

Some writers dramatize the problem. Chow establishes both the existence and seriousness of the problem in his opening narrative. The anecdote he tells serves to remind readers of a situation they may have encountered personally or at least heard about from others.

In addition to stating the problem and establishing its existence and seriousness, a proposal writer must analyze the problem. It is necessary to examine the problem's causes and its consequences, its history and past efforts to deal with it. This information not only helps readers understand the problem, but it may also provide grounds for the proposed solution. When Chow explains that deer come into Moraga because their food supply runs low in the winter, he is setting the foundation for his proposal to supplement their food supply. In the same way, Niwa points out inconsistencies and delays that result from the lack of communication among researchers, laying the groundwork for her proposal to institute regular meetings.

A proposed solution   Once the problem is established, the writer presents and argues for a solution. As the writer's opinion on how the problem should be solved, this solution constitutes the thesis of the proposal. Chow states his thesis like this: "Before the cold season starts, we should stock about a hundred food stations in the woods, located in areas known to have high concentration of deer." Germain takes two sentences: "Daughters should have their mother's last name. Sons should have their father's."

A convincing argument   As an argument, the main purpose of a proposal is to convince readers that the writer's solution is the best way of solving the problem. Proposal writers argue for their solutions by demonstrating:

> that the proposed solution will solve the problem
> that it is a feasible way of solving the problem
> that it is better than other ways of solving the problem

Arguing that the proposed solution will solve the problem. Sometimes it is sufficient simply to propose a solution, but usually a writer will give reasons and evidence to show the proposed solution will indeed solve the problem. Germain seems to assume readers will immediately recognize how her proposed solution will solve the problem, asserting her solution with no discussion of how or why. Niwa and Chow, on the other hand, both go on to argue that their proposals would solve the problem by removing the cause (lack of communication in one case and lack of food in the other).

Arguing that the proposed solution is feasible. In arguing that the proposal is feasible, the writer must demonstrate how it can be implemented. The easier the proposed solution seems to implement, the more likely it is to win readers' support. Therefore, writers generally devote as much space as necessary to setting out the steps required to put the proposal into practice. This is especially important when the solution might seem difficult, time-consuming, or expensive to enact.

All the writers in this chapter offer specific suggestions for implementing their proposals. Niwa takes three paragraphs to discuss how her plan would be implemented. Chow explains how feeding areas would be identified, who would monitor the food supply, what the food would consist of, and how much it would cost. Even Germain, whose proposal seems easy to implement, devotes several paragraphs to explaining just how she suggests doing so. Bly offers a sample syllabus teachers could adopt for the course she proposes.

An important part of arguing that a proposal is feasible involves anticipating and refuting counterarguments. Counterarguments consist of any objections or reservations readers may have about the proposed solution. Chow anticipates the potential counterargument that his solution might make the problem worse by creating a deer population explosion and refutes it by arguing that natural predators will continue to keep the deer population under control. Niwa allows that her reader might be concerned that meetings would actually take time away from research but argues against this counterargument by asserting that efficiency would be greatly increased, thus making time at meetings well spent.

Considering and rejecting alternative solutions. Finally, the writer has to convince readers that his or her solution is preferable to other solutions. This is done by examining alternative ways of solving the problem. Germain and Chow consider several alternative solutions before proposing their own. Niwa brings up one alternative after stating her own. Bly is the only one who does not examine any alternatives, probably because her practical way of addressing the broader problem of greed is so unusual.

In offering reasons for rejecting alternative solutions, writers will often use these same reasons as support for their own solution. See how Chow considers two alternative solutions: to allow hunters to kill the deer and to relocate the deer. He rejects the first because it would be dangerous, inhumane, and not solve the problem and the second because it would be difficult to accomplish, cost too much, and ruin the natural ambiance of the town. Then he argues in favor of his own solution on the grounds that it would be less expensive than the relocation plan and more humane than the hunting plan, would not harm the ambiance of the town, and would actually solve the problem.

A reasonable tone of voice Regardless of the proposal or the argument made on its behalf, proposal writers must adopt a reasonable tone of voice. The trick is to advance an argument without "having" an argument. That is, writers must never take an adversarial or quarrelsome stance with their readers. The aim is to bridge any gap that may exist between writer and readers, not widen it.

Writers build such a bridge of shared concerns by showing respect for readers and treating their concerns seriously. They discuss counterarguments as an attempt to lay to rest any doubts readers may have. They consider alternative solutions as a way of showing they have explored every possibility in order to find the best possible solution.

Most important, they do not criticize those raising counterarguments or offering other solutions. Never do they question anyone's intelligence or good will. Attacking people personally is called *argumentum ad hominem* (Latin for "argument against the man") and is considered an error of reasoning.

GUIDE TO WRITING

THE WRITING TASK

Write an essay proposing a solution to a problem. It should be one you are familiar with or can research. Choose a problem faced by a group to which you belong, and address your proposal either to one or more members of the group or to an outsider who might help solve the problem.

INVENTION AND RESEARCH

As you prepare to write a proposal, you will need to choose a problem you can write about, find a tentative solution to it, test your choice of problem and solution, identify your prospective readers, develop reasons for adopting your proposal rather than an alternative, and research any necessary information.

Choosing a problem to write about

One problem may come to mind immediately, and you may already have a solution for it. If not, you may want to think about various problems in various groups before settling on a topic.

If you have already made a choice, briefly describe the problem, explaining why it is a problem for you and others in your group. If you are not yet sure what problem you want to solve, the following listing activity should prove helpful.

Listing problems. Divide a piece of paper into two columns. In the left-hand column list three or four communities, groups, or organizations to which you belong, and in the right-hand column list two or three problems or conflicts existing within each group. Here is an example:

college	poor advising
	insufficient library hours
	noisy dorms
	too many required courses

soccer team	poor attendance at games disorganized coaches player disagreements
job	high employee turnover unsafe working conditions inefficient procedures
religious group	not enough youth activities insufficient support from church

Choosing an important problem. Choose a problem on your chart which you consider especially important. It should be one that seems solvable and that would concern others in the group. You should of course select a problem you know enough about to explore in detail—and one you are willing to discuss in writing.

Analyzing the problem. Think about the problem you have chosen. Start to anayze the problem by writing out answers to the following questions.

☐ Does the problem really exist? How serious is it? Will other members of the group agree that it is indeed serious?

☐ What caused the problem? Is it a new problem or an old one? Can I identify any immediate causes as well as any deeper causes?

☐ What bad effects might the problem cause? How is it hurting group members? Is it endangering any long-range goals of the group?

☐ Is it an ethical or moral problem—whether or not it has any bad consequences?

☐ Are there any other similar problems?

☐ Does the problem affect everyone in the group equally?

Finding a tentative solution

Look at your analysis of the problem and think about your personal experience with it. Now take ten or fifteen minutes to write out a tentative solution.

You may want to start by considering solutions others have proposed. Or, you may want to approach the problem from your own perspective. Remember that problem solving demands creativity. Be imaginative: think of all the ways to solve your problem and thus to improve your situation.

Choosing the most promising solution. In a sentence or two state what you would consider the best possible way of solving the problem.

Listing specific steps. Write down each of the steps necessary to implement your solution.

Testing your choice   Now you should examine the problem and solution you have selected to see whether they will result in a strong proposal. For guidance, ask yourself the following questions:

- ☐ Is this a significant problem? Do other people in the group really care about it, or can they be persuaded to care?
- ☐ Is my solution feasible? Will it really solve the problem? Can it be implemented?

As you plan and draft your proposal, you will probably want to consider these questions again and again. If at any point you decide that you cannot answer them affirmatively and confidently, you may want to choose a different problem to write about or find another solution.

Identifying your readers   You must decide whom you wish to address—everyone in the group, a committee, an individual, someone outside the group. Write down a few sentences describing your readers and stating your reason for directing your proposal to them.

Profiling your readers. Take ten minutes to write about your readers. Use these questions to stimulate your writing:

- ☐ How informed are they likely to be about the problem? Have they shown any awareness of it?
- ☐ Why would this problem be important to them? Why would they care about solving it?
- ☐ Have they offered or supported any proposals to solve the problem? If so, what do their proposals have in common with my proposal?
- ☐ Do they ally themselves with any particular group or philosophy that might cause them to favor or reject my proposal? Do we all share any values or attitudes that I could use as a bridge to bring us together to solve the problem?
- ☐ How have they responded to other problems? Can I infer anything from their reactions in the past that would suggest how they may respond to my proposal?

Talking with a reader. Imagine one reader, someone who would question your assessment of the problem or your tentative solution. If you have someone particular in mind, name that person. Try to imagine how he or she would react to your proposal. Write out a dialogue between the two of you, setting it up as Wendy Jo Niwa does on page 200. Imagine there is some disagreement about your proposal—that is, assume you are forced to respond to questions or objections.

Take a minute to focus your thoughts. In two or three sentences, restate the problem and your proposed solution.

Defending your solution

Proposals have to be feasible—that is, they must be both reasonable and practical. Imagine that one of your readers opposes your proposed solution and confronts you with each of the following statements. Write several sentences refuting each one.

- ☐ It won't really solve the problem.
- ☐ We can't afford it.
- ☐ It will take too long.
- ☐ People won't do it.
- ☐ I don't even see how to get started on your solution.
- ☐ It's already been tried, with unsatisfactory results.
- ☐ You're making this proposal because it will benefit you personally.

Answering these questions now should help you to prepare responses to possible objections to your proposal. You may find that you need a better idea of how others are likely to feel about your proposal. You may want to talk to a few people involved. The more you know about your readers and their concerns, the better you will be able to anticipate any counterarguments they may offer or alternative solutions they might prefer.

Listing and developing reasons for adopting your proposal

To make a convincing case for your proposed solution you will need to offer your readers good reasons for adopting your proposal.

Listing reasons. Write down every plausible reason you could give that would persuade readers to accept your proposal. These reasons should be your answer to your readers' key question: "Why is this the best solution?" It might help to have a look at your writing in the preceding section, Defending your solution. You should of course try to think of other reasons.

Choosing the strongest reasons. Keeping your readers in mind, look over your list and put an asterisk next to the best reasons. If you do not consider two or three of your reasons strong, you may anticipate difficulty developing a strong proposal and should reconsider your topic.

Developing your strongest reasons. Now look at these strongest reasons. Make a list of these reasons, explaining briefly why you think each one will be effective with your particular readers. Then take around five minutes to write about each reason, developing your argument on its behalf.

Comparing your solution to alternative solutions

Even if your readers are likely to consider your proposal reasonable, they will probably want to compare your proposed solution with other possible solutions. List several alternative solutions that might be offered by other members of the group, and consider the advantages and disadvantages of each one next to your solution. You might find it helpful to put together a chart like this:

Possible Solutions	Advantages	Disadvantages
[My solution]		
[Alternative Solution 1]		
[Alternative Solution 2]		
etc.		

Researching your proposal

Thus far you have relied upon your own knowledge, experience, and instincts for solving the problem. You may now feel that you need to know more. We have already suggested that you talk to potential readers in order to anticipate their counterarguments or alternative proposals. You might also want to discuss your solution with someone in the group; their questions and objections can tell you a great deal.

You may also need to do some further research: to learn more about the causes of the problem, perhaps, or to find more technical information about implementing the solution. Now is a good time—before beginning to draft—to get any additional information you need. (See Chapter 20 for guidelines on library research.)

PLANNING AND DRAFTING

To help you plan your essay and begin drafting, review what you have discovered about your topic, prepare an outline, and set some specific goals for yourself.

Seeing what you have

Reread your invention writings now, asking yourself whether you have a good topic—an interesting problem with a feasible solution. If at this point you are doubtful about the significance of the problem or unsure about the potential success of your proposed solution, you might want to look for a new topic. If your invention sequence is still weak, you cannot really expect to be able to produce a rich, persuasive draft.

If your invention material seems thin but promising, you may be able to strengthen it with additional writing. Consider the following questions in trying to fill out your writing:

☐ Could I make a stronger case for the seriousness of the problem?

☐ Could I find more reasons for readers to support my solution?

☐ Are there any other ways of refuting attractive alternative solutions or troubling counterarguments?

Outlining the proposal The basic outline for a proposal is quite simple:

> the problem
> the solution
> the reasons for accepting the solution

This simple plan is nearly always complicated by other factors, however. In outlining your material you must take into consideration many other details: whether readers already recognize the problem, how much agreement exists on the need to solve the problem, how many alternative solutions are available, how much attention must be given to the other solutions, and how many counterarguments should be expected.

A possible outline for a proposal where readers may be unlikely to fully understand the problem and where other solutions have been proposed might look like this:

> presentation of the problem
> demonstration that the problem exists and is serious
>> causes of the problem
>> consequences of failing to solve the problem
> description of the proposed solution
> list of steps for implementing the solution
> discussion of reasons to support the solution
>> counterarguments
>> refutation of the counterarguments
> consideration of alternative solutions and statement of their disadvantages
> restatement of the proposed solution and its advantages

Your outline will of course reflect your own writing situation. As you work up an outline, think about what your readers know and feel. Concentrate on your own purpose and writing goals. Once you have a working outline, you should not hesitate to change it as necessary while writing. For instance, you might find it more effective to hold back on presenting your own solution until you have dismissed other possible solutions. Or you might find a better way to order the reasons for adopting your proposal as you draft. The purpose of an outline is to identify the basic features of your proposal, as the preceding example shows. Most of the information you will need to develop each feature can be found in your invention writing and research notes.

How much space you devote to each feature is determined by the topic, not the outline. Do not assume that each entry on your outline must be given one paragraph—in the preceding example, each of the reasons for supporting the solution may require a paragraph, but you might also discuss the reasons, counterarguments, and refutations all in one paragraph. The length of a proposal depends upon the topic. The important thing is that the proposal be coherently organized, and an outline helps you to do so.

Setting goals Before you actually begin your draft, you should think seriously about the overall goals of your proposal. Not only will the draft be easier to write once you have established clear goals, it is almost sure to be stronger and more convincing.

Following are goal-setting questions to consider now. You may find it useful to return to them while you are drafting, for they are designed to help you to focus on what exactly you want to accomplish with this proposal.

Your readers

- [ ] What do my readers already know about this problem?
- [ ] Are they likely to welcome my solution or resist it?
- [ ] Can I anticipate any specific reservations or objections they may have?
- [ ] How can I gain readers' enthusiastic support? How can I get them to help me implement the solution?
- [ ] What kind of voice would be most appropriate? How can I present myself so that I seem both reasonable and authoritative?

The beginning

- [ ] How can I begin so as to immediately engage my readers' interest? Shall I open with a personal anecdote, like Germain's, or a dramatic one, like Chow's? Shall I begin by stating something surprising, as Bly does? Or should I open my proposal as Niwa does, by commenting on something positive before announcing the problem?
- [ ] What information should I give first?

Defining the problem

☐ Is this a problem people know about, or is it relatively unknown?

☐ How much do I need to say about its causes or history?

☐ How can I establish the seriousness of the problem?

☐ Is it an urgent problem? How can I emphasize this?

☐ How much space should I devote to defining the problem?

Proposing a solution

☐ How should I state my thesis? When should I announce it explicitly?

☐ How can I make the solution seem easy to implement? Can I present the first step so that it looks easy to take?

☐ How can I present my solution so that it looks like the best way to proceed?

Rejecting alternative solutions

☐ How many alternative solutions should I mention? Which ones should I discuss?

☐ Should I indicate where these alternatives come from? Should I name those who proposed them?

☐ How can I reject these other solutions without seeming to criticize their proponents?

☐ What reasons should I give for rejecting the alternative solutions? Can I offer any evidence in support of my reasons?

Refuting counterarguments

☐ Should I mention every possible counterargument to my proposed solution? How might I choose among them?

☐ Has anyone already proposed these counterarguments? If so, should I name the person in my proposal?

☐ How can I refute the counterarguments without criticizing anyone?

☐ What specific reasons can I give for refuting each counterargument? How can I support these reasons?

Avoiding logical fallacies

☐ Will I be committing an *either/or* fallacy by presenting my solution as the only possible solution: either mine or nothing? Can I ignore any of the likely alternative solutions?

☐ Can I present other proposed solutions in such a way that they are easily rejected without being accused of building a *straw man*? (A straw man is easy to push over.)

☐ How can I show my readers that I have *accepted the burden of proof*? Can I make a comprehensive argument for my proposed solution? Will readers feel that it is one they should accept?

☐ If I discuss the causes of the problem, can I avoid the fallacy of *over-simplified cause*? Have I identified significant causes, or are some of them minor contributing causes? Have I accounted for all of the major causes?

☐ How can I argue reasonably against other possible solutions? Can I criticize other proposals without attacking the people involved and thus committing the *ad hominem* (Latin for "to the man") fallacy?

The ending

☐ How should the proposal end? Shall I end with a personal plan, as Germain does? Or should I simply end by summarizing my solution and restating the advantages?

☐ Is there something special about the problem itself I should remind readers of at the end?

☐ Should I end with an inspiring call to action or a scenario suggesting the dreaded consequences of our failure to solve the problem?

☐ Would a shift to humor or satire be an effective way to end?

Drafting the proposal   Before you consider the advice here about drafting a proposal, you might want to review the general advice on drafting in Chapter 1. Then review your outline. Let it help you write your proposal, but don't hesitate to change it if you find that drafting takes you in an unexpected direction. If you are really stuck, return to one of the invention activities to get yourself going again. You could explore the problem more fully, examine your readers once again, think about the advantages and disadvantages of your solution or reconsider alternate solutions, strengthen your defense against counterarguments, or try to come up with still more reasons for adopting your solution.

Ĉ As you draft, keep in mind the two main goals of proposal writing: (1) to establish that a problem exists that is serious enough to require a solution; and (2) to demonstrate that your proposed solution is feasible and is the best possible alternative.

READING A DRAFT WITH A CRITICAL EYE

A close reading has three steps: reading quickly for a general impression, pointing to strengths and weaknesses in the writing, and analyzing the effectiveness of the proposal. Whether you are reading your own draft or someone else's, the following guidelines can help you to do so with a critical eye.

First general impression Read the essay straight through to get a general impression. Put yourself in the position of a member of the group to whom the proposal is addressed. Try to assume the concerns of the group, and consider the proposal as if its suggestions were to affect you personally.

After this first reading, tell the writer whether the problem seems serious to you, and whether you would support the proposed solution.

Pointings As you read, highlight noteworthy features with *pointings,* a simple system of lines and brackets that is especially useful for revising a draft. Use this system as follows:

☐ Draw a straight line under any words or images that seem especially effective: strong verbs, specific details, memorable phrases, striking images.

☐ Draw a wavy line under any words or images that sound flat, stale, or vague. Also put the wavy line under any words or phrases that you consider unnecessary or repetitious.

☐ Look for pairs or groups of sentences that you think should be combined. Put brackets [ ] around these sentences.

☐ Look for sentences that are garbled, overloaded, or awkward. Put parentheses ( ) around these sentences. Parenthesize any sentence which seems even slightly questionable; don't worry now about whether or not it is actually incorrect. The writer needs to know that you, as one reader, had even the slightest hesitation about reading a sentence, even on first reading.

Analysis The following questions will help you analyze the parts of the proposal and evaluate their effectiveness.

1. Evaluate the definition of the problem. Has the writer given enough information about its causes and consequences? Tell the writer if there is anything more you wish to know about the problem.

2. Restate in your own words the proposed solution. Is it clear? Look at the reasons in support of this solution—are they sufficient? Which are

the most convincing reasons offered? Which are the least convincing ones? Why?

3. Look closely at the steps for implementing the proposal. Do they tell you everything you need to know? If not, ask specific questions to let the writer see what more a reader needs to know. Does the solution seem practical? If not, why not?

4. Consider the treatment of objections and counterarguments to the proposed solution. Point out any other counterarguments the writer may have missed. Cite the reasons and evidence against the counterarguments that you found the most convincing. Indicate also which was the least convincing, and why.

5. Does the writer discuss any alternative solutions? If not, should any be mentioned? If any are mentioned, does the writer argue against them effectively? What are the most convincing reasons given against these other solutions? Which are least convincing, and why?

6. Consider the balance. Are the key features treated adequately and fairly? Or is there too much of one thing and too little of another? Perhaps there is too much attention given to alternative solutions, too little to counterarguments. Point out any elements that need more or less emphasis, and explain why.

7. Evaluate the beginning. Is it at all engaging? Did it capture your attention? Does it forecast the main ideas and alert the reader to the plan of the proposal? Should it? See if you can suggest other ways to begin.

8. Evaluate the ending. Does it frame the proposal? If not, how might it do so? Can you suggest a stronger conclusion?

9. Describe the voice you hear in the proposal. Does it seem appropriate for its readers? Is it consistent from beginning to end? Point out any inconsistencies.

10. What final comments or suggestions can you offer to the writer? What is the strongest part of this proposal? What most needs additional work?

REVISING AND EDITING

Before considering this discussion of revising a proposal, you might want to review the general advice on revision in Chapter 1.

Revising a proposal   Consider any advice you may have from other readers as you reread your draft and make plans for revision. If you can, you might have someone else read the draft to help you solve any particularly difficult problems.

For example, if you are having trouble refuting one alternative solution, you might see if someone else can help.

Look now at the following tips on revising proposals.

Revising to strengthen the argument

☐ Reconsider your definition of the problem. Is it complete, or would it be stronger with more information? Should you add anything about its causes or potential dangers? Have you articulated its seriousness?

☐ Scrutinize your solution as closely as possible. Have you shown it to be both feasible and superior to all other possible solutions?

☐ Reread your argument with your readers in mind. Have you fully considered their experience and expectations, fears and biases? Think of all the factions within the group—does your argument appeal to them all? Should it?

☐ Look carefully at each part of your argument. Could you strengthen your proposal by rearranging these parts?

Revising for readability

☐ Are there any places where you tell readers more than they need to know? Less than they need to know?

☐ Reconsider your beginning. Would another beginning engage readers more quickly?

☐ Reconsider your ending. Does the proposal end gracefully and emphatically? Is the ending likely to appeal to your readers? Does it emphasize what you want it to?

☐ Look carefully at each sentence. Does it say what you want it to say? Does it repeat something said in the previous sentence? Does it state the obvious?

☐ Improve the flow of your writing by strengthening connections between sentences and paragraphs. See whether any sentences should be combined or separated into two sentences.

Editing and proofreading

As you revise a draft for the final time, you need to edit it closely. Though you probably corrected obvious errors in the drafting stage, usage and style were not your first priority. Now, however, you must find and correct any errors of mechanics, usage, punctuation, or style.

After you have edited the draft and produced the final copy, you must proofread carefully before turning in your essay.

LEARNING FROM YOUR OWN WRITING PROCESS

Take time now to look over all the work you have done on your proposal. Start with your invention materials—what was easiest? what was hardest? Did the readings influence your invention and drafting in any way? What difficulties did you encounter while you were drafting? How did you solve them?

Consider your final draft. What changes did you make from draft to revision? Did other readers' comments affect the final version? Look at specific changes you made, and explain why you made them.

What do you consider best about your proposal? What would you like to improve if you had still more time?

A WRITER AT WORK

ANALYZING THE READERS OF A PROPOSAL

One of the most important tasks facing all proposal writers is to analyze their prospective readers. Before beginning to write, they need to know who their readers will be, what they can be expected to know about the problem, and how they are likely to respond to the proposed solution. In this section we will look at how Wendy Jo Niwa went about analyzing her readers before drafting her proposal to improve a research project. Niwa's final draft is printed in this chapter on pages 177–180.

Niwa began by deciding who she wanted her readers to be. Initially she had considered addressing her proposal to the other students on the project, but she decided they already agreed with her and could not do anything about the problem anyway. She also considered sending it to the Psychology Department, but she thought that would merely cause trouble for the group leader. Finally she realized that the most obvious choice was the group leader himself, since he was the only one who would have reason or power to implement her proposal.

Once she had identified who her reader would be, Niwa was able to plan her proposal with the sure knowledge that he was aware of the problem. She was not sure, however, why he did nothing to try to solve it himself. In one of her invention activities, Niwa wrote, "I guess he's just too busy handling problems as they come up and taking care of other parts of the project. He's probably too involved to see what needs to be done. Or maybe he's lazy. I don't think he realizes how bored and frustrated we all are."

Niwa spent a good deal of time on one invention activity, Talking with a Reader. Constructing an imaginary dialogue with the group leader helped her to know what material to include in her proposal. She worked out a plan to implement the proposal, anticipated her reader's counter-arguments and figured out how to refute them, and found a way to bridge her own and her reader's concerns.

Because this invention activity was so productive for Niwa, we print it here in its entirety.

NIWA: I think we should all meet together in a group at least once a week on a set day at a set time. We need to discuss difficulties we may be having with the transcripts, share knowledge, check progress.

READER: How are we going to find a time which will accommodate everyone?

NIWA: All we have to do is write down our schedules and preferred times to meet. We can choose a day and time from these lists.

READER: But this will cut into the time usually used for work—this project needs to get done!

NIWA: If everyone agrees, we can meet outside of the 10 hours per week required of us on the project. However, I bet that a one-hour meeting as a group will take less time than we now spend discussing difficulties among ourselves. Our work would be much more efficient if we discussed and cleared up problems all at once. We could get through a lot more transcripts if we were clearer on what we were doing.

READER: If there are no problems with transcripts won't the time be wasted?

NIWA: No. We students are anxious to gain as much as possible from your experience. We could use the time to discuss topics of interest, research which is relevant to yours.

READER: What if no one has anything to discuss?

NIWA: We can make a schedule of tentative topics to discuss, and can take turns preparing brief presentations to guide discussion.

READER: What if the others are not willing to go along with your idea?

NIWA: If you make it a part of the requirement they will. Besides, many have already stated that they would be more than willing to put in extra effort and time.

READER: Why should I put in the extra time?

NIWA: I think you have an obligation to the students. Also it would be in your best interests. Correlations may be found which wouldn't have been had we not been consistent. Also your dissertation may be pushed along at a quicker pace.

READER: What type of organization are you talking about?

NIWA: Decide on whether each of us will be responsible for a different task or all working on the same task. A goal would make the work seem less tedious, morale would be lifted, and we'd all feel less frustration. By not staying on one task too long we'll all avoid getting burned out.

READER: What's wrong with the way it is now?

NIWA: Many students are frustrated, dissatisfied. The criteria is not well established. By trial and error, we end up spending twice as much time on a single task because we're always having to go back and redo it. We should establish the criteria clearly before we start work, not after.

Niwa concludes this section by restating the problem and her solution to it. Analyzing her reader helped her to clarify her goals in writing the proposal. She realized it was important not only to reduce boredom and frustration, but also to learn something from the group leader and from other students. Most of all, her imaginary conversation with the group leader made her appreciate how hard she would have to work to convince him.

Making Evaluations

In an article about the upcoming Rose Bowl game, a reporter for the *Los Angeles Times* evaluates the two competing Pacific Ten and Big Ten teams. She predicts victory for the Pacific Ten team, contending that it has a better-balanced offense as well as more depth and experience at each position. As support for her prediction, the reporter names several specific players and mentions some key plays from earlier games. To refute the likely counterargument that the Pacific Ten team won fewer games, she argues that it played a much tougher schedule than the Big Ten team.

The president of a large computer corporation writes a letter recommending one of his employees for an upper management position at another company. He praises her judgments, energy, and interpersonal skills, mentioning several incidents as support for his claims. For the most part, however, he concentrates on her contributions to several specific projects.

A *Skiing* reporter writes an article evaluating two popular slalom skis. He assumes his audience to be made up of experienced downhill skiers who may not have actually done any slalom racing. Using one technical criterion, design, he argues that one make of ski is superior to the other. He cites specific differences in waist width, sidecut radius, camber, and shovel stiffness as support for his judgment.

In a column syndicated to college newspapers, a writer reviews two newly revised paperback thesauri. Both are selling well in college bookstores. The reporter compares the two on the criteria of size, price, and usefulness. The criterion of usefulness leads to further comparisons of format and specific sample entries. She concludes by recommending one thesaurus over the other.

For her senior thesis, a political science major evaluates a state senator whom she dislikes and distrusts. After researching the senator's legislative activities and voting record, she decides that the best criteria for evaluating a senator are three: responsibility in carrying out his legislative duties, voting record in support of public programs, and willingness to educate the voters on important issues. These criteria provide adequate support for her negative judgment: the senator is often absent for important votes, he votes consistently against antipoverty bills, and he makes little effort to provide his constituents with news about important issues. She documents each of these reasons—and all the others in her paper—with specific evidence gathered in her research. At several points in the paper she contrasts the senator's activities and voting record with the records of other state senators.

7

□ A mid-term exam for a literature course includes two poems by John Updike that the students are not likely to have seen before. They are to decide which is the better poem and write an essay explaining why. Using criteria for evaluating poetry he learned in the class, one student argues that one poem is better because its rhythms are less predictable and more conversationlike and also because its imagery is more visual and hence more memorable. He provides several examples from the poems in support of each reason.

We all make evaluations many times each day. We do so spontaneously, in response to events, people, things. Rarely, however, do we think out a reasoned, detailed evaluation based on appropriate criteria. We constantly give reasons for our evaluations in a casual way, of course. Often we are called upon to justify our opinions to others, or we do so for ourselves, weighing the pros and cons of something.

In everyday conversation we often state opinions without thorough justification or development. Indeed, it would be impolite and unfriendly to insist that people justify their every opinion. By contrast, we expect opinions stated in writing to be authoritative and persuasive. We expect a planned, coherent, reasoned discussion. We assume the writer knows enough to use appropriate standards of evaluation, and we expect the reasons derived from these standards to be supported with evidence and examples.

The readings that follow will give you an idea of the specific strategies used by writers of evaluations.

READINGS

One of the most common forms of written evaluations is reviews—of movies, books, restaurants, vacation resorts, plays, concerts. Reviewers help us to decide where to go out for dinner, what movies to see, which novels to read.

This first essay is a review of a classic American movie, *The Treasure of the Sierra Madre*. Published in 1948, soon after the movie appeared, the review was written by James Agee. Agee was for many years a celebrated film critic for *The Nation;* in 1944 W. H. Auden called his reviews "the most remarkable regular event in American journalism today." He is best known for his novel *A Death in the Family,* for which he was posthumously awarded the Pulitzer Prize in 1958.

As you read his review, pay close attention to the way Agee argues for his judgment that *The Treasure of the Sierra Madre* is an outstanding movie.

**THE TREASURE OF THE
SIERRA MADRE**
JAMES AGEE

Several of the best people in Hollywood grew, noticeably, during their 1
years away at war; the man who grew most impressively, I thought, as an
artist, as a man, in intelligence, in intransigence, and in an ability to put
through fine work against difficult odds, was John Huston, whose *San Pietro*
and *Let There Be Light* were full of evidence of this many-sided growth. I
therefore looked forward with the greatest eagerness to the work he would
do after the war.

His first movie since the war has been a long time coming, but it was 2
certainly worth waiting for. *The Treasure of the Sierra Madre* is Huston's
adaptation of B. Traven's novel of the same title. It is not quite a completely
satisfying picture, but on the strength of it I have no doubt at all that Huston,
next only to Chaplin, is the most talented man working in American pictures,
and that this is one of the movie talents in the world which is most excitingly
capable of still further growth. *The Treasure* is one of very few movies made
since 1927 which I am sure will stand up in the memory and esteem of
qualified people alongside the best of the silent movies. And yet I doubt that
many people will fully realize, right away, what a sensational achievement,
or plexus of achievement, it is. You will seldom see a good artist insist less
on his artistry; Huston merely tells his story so straight and so well that one
tends to become absorbed purely in that; and the story itself—a beauty—is
not a kind which most educated people value nearly enough, today.

This story and Huston's whole handling of it are about as near to folk art 3
as a highly conscious artist can get; both also approach the global appeal,
to the most and least sophisticated members of an audience, which the best
poetic drama and nearly all the best movies have in common. Nominally an
adventure story, this is really an exploration of character as revealed in vivid
action; and character and action yield revelations of their own, political, met-
aphysical, moral, above all, poetic. The story unfolds so pleasurably on the
screen that I will tell as little as possible of it here. Three American bums of
the early 1920s (Walter Huston, Humphrey Bogart, Tim Holt) run into lottery
luck in Tampico and strike into the godforsaken mountains of Mexico in
search of gold. The rest of the story merely demonstrates the development
of their characters in relation to hardship and hard work, to the deeply primitive world these modern primitives are set against, to the gold they find, and
to each other. It is basically a tragic story and at times a sickeningly harsh
one; most of it is told as cheerfully brutal sardonic comedy.

This may be enough to suggest how rich the story is in themes, semi- 4
symbols, possible implications, and potentialities as a movie. Huston's most
wonderful single achievement is that he focuses all these elements as simply
as rays in a burning-glass: all you see, unless you look sharp, is a story told
so truly and masterfully that I suspect the picture's best audience is the kind
of men the picture is about, who will see it only by chance.

But this single achievement breaks down into many. I doubt we shall ever 5
see a film more masculine in style; or a truer movie understanding of char-

acter and of men; or as good a job on bumming, a bum's life, a city as a bum sees it; or a more beautiful job on a city; or a finer portrait of Mexico and Mexicans (compare it with all the previous fancy-filter stuff for a definitive distinction between poetry and poeticism); or a crueler communication of absolute desolateness in nature and its effect on men (except perhaps in *Greed*); or a much more vivid communication of hardship, labor, and exhaustion (though I wish these had been brutally and meticulously presented rather than skillfully sketched); or more intelligent handling of amateurs and semi-professionals (notably the amazing character who plays Gold-Hat, the bandit leader); or a finer selective eye for location or a richer understanding of how to use it; or scenes of violence or building toward violence more deeply authentic and communicative (above all in Huston's terrific use of listlessness); or smarter casting than that of Tim Holt as the youngest bum and that of Bruce Bennett as an intrusive Texan; or better acting than Walter Huston's beautiful performance; or subtler and more skillful collusions and variations of tempo (two hours have certainly never been better used in a movie); or a finer balance, in Ted McCord's perfect camera work, in every camera set-up, in every bit of editing, of unaffectedness, and sensitiveness. (As one fine example of that blend I recommend watching for the shot of Gold-Hat reflected in muddy water, which is so subtly photographed that in this noncolor film the hat seems to shed golden light.) There is not a shot-for-shot's sake in the picture, or one too prepared-looking, or dwelt on too long. The camera is always where it ought to be, never imposes on or exploits or over-dramatizes its subject, never for an instant shoves beauty or special meaning at you. This is one of the most visually alive and beautiful movies I have ever seen; there is a wonderful flow of fresh air, light, vigor, and liberty through every shot, and a fine athlete's litheness and absolute control and flexibility in every succession and series of shots. Huston shows that he is already capable of literally anything in movies except the profoundest kind of movie inventiveness, the most extreme kind of poetic concentration, artiness, soft or apathetic or sloppy or tasteless or excessive work, and rhetoric whether good or bad. His style is practically invisible as well as practically universal in its possible good uses; it is the most virile movie style I know of; and is the purest style in contemporary movies, here or abroad.

 I want to say a little more about Walter Huston; a few thousand words 6 would suit me better. Rightly or wrongly, one thing that adds to my confidence that the son, so accomplished already, will get better and better, is the fact that the father has done that, year after year. I can think of nothing more moving or happier than every instance in which an old man keeps right on learning, and working, and improving, as naturally and eagerly as a child learns the fundamentals of walking, talking, and everything else in sight until his parents and teachers destroy his appetite for learning. Huston has for a long time been one of the best actors in the world and he is easily the most likable; on both counts this performance crowns a lifetime. It is an all but incredible submergence in a role, and transformation; this man who has credibly played Lincoln looks small and stocky here, and is as gaily vivacious as a water bug. The character is beautifully conceived and written, but I think it is chiefly Walter Huston who gives it its almost Shakespearean wonderfulness, charm, and wisdom. In spite of the enormous amount of other talent at large in the picture, Huston carries the whole show as deftly and easily as he handles his comedy lines.

There are a few weaknesses in the picture, most of which concern me so 7 little I won't even bother to mention them. Traven's Teutonic or Melvillean excitability as a poet and metaphysician sometimes, I think, misleads him— and John Huston; magnificently as Walter Huston does it, and deeply as he anchors it in flesh and blood, the Vast Gale of Purifying Laughter with which he ends the picture strikes me as unreal, stuck-onto-the-character, close to arty; yet I feel tender toward this kind of cliché, if I'm right that it is one. One thing I do furiously resent is the intrusion of background-music. There is relatively little of it and some of it is better than average, but there shouldn't be any, and I only hope and assume that Huston fought the use of it. The only weakness which strikes me as fundamental, however, is deep in the story itself: it is the whole character of the man played by Bogart. This is, after all, about gold and its effects on those who seek it, and so it is also a fable about all human life in this world and about much of the essence of good and evil. Many of the possibilities implicit in this fable are finely worked out. But some of the most searching implications are missed. For the Bogart character is so fantastically undisciplined and troublesome that it is impossible to demonstrate or even to hint at the real depth of the problem, with him on hand. It is too easy to feel that if only a reasonably restrained and unsuspicious man were in his place, everything would be all right; we wouldn't even have wars. But virtually every human being carries sufficient of that character within him to cause a great deal of trouble, and the demonstration of that fact, and its effects, could have made a much greater tragicomedy— much more difficult, I must admit, to dramatize. Bogart does a wonderful job with this character as written (and on its own merits it is quite a character), miles ahead of the very good work he has done before. The only trouble is that one cannot quite forget that this is Bogart putting on an unbelievably good act. In all but a few movies one would thank God for that large favor. In this one it stands out, harmfully to some extent, for everything else about the picture is selfless.

It seems worth mentioning that the only thing which holds this movie 8 short of unarguable greatness is the failure of the story to develop some of the most important potentialities of the theme. In other words, "Hollywood," for once, is accountable only for some minor flaws. This is what it was possible to do in Hollywood, if you were talented enough, had standing enough, and were a good enough fighter, during the very hopeful period before the November Freeze. God knows what can be done now. But if anybody can hope to do anything, I count on Huston, who made *San Pietro* and *Let There Be Light* as an army officer and *The Treasure of the Sierra Madre* as a Hollywood writer-director.

Questions for analysis

1. Agee gives many reasons why he likes the movie. Some reasons he merely lists, but others he develops with specific illustrations from the movie. What are those reasons? Which are listed, and which are developed? Why do you suppose he chooses to develop the ones he does?

2. Film critics nearly always draw comparisons between movies. What comparisons does Agee make? Would further comparisons strengthen the review? If so, what kinds of comparisons would you like to see?

3. Agee wrote this review after the movie was released. Because readers of such reviews must be assumed to be unfamiliar with the movie, the writer must describe it before evaluating it, yet without telling any more than he has to. What does Agee choose to summarize from the movie? Where does he place this summary? How much space does he devote to it?

4. In paragraph 7, Agee points out some of the movie's weaknesses. Why do you think he mentions its weaknesses? How does paragraph 7 affect your response to the review?

5. How does Agee begin his review? How effective do you find this beginning? How else might Agee have begun?

6. How does Agee end his review? Is it an effective ending? Could you suggest any other way to conclude?

7. How would you state Agee's purpose in writing this review? How well do you think he achieves his purpose? What are some other possible purposes for a movie review?

8. What recent movie would you like to review in writing? How would you evaluate this movie? What reasons and evidence would you offer in support of your judgment?

Agee's review has all the features we expect of an evaluation: a firm judgment, reasons and evidence in support of the judgment, some description of the subject, and comparisons to similar things.

The thesis in an evaluation essay is simply the statement asserting the writer's judgment. Usually it is repeated in several ways throughout the essay. In paragraph 2, Agee states his thesis in an unmistakable way: he says the movie is "a sensational achievement" and predicts it will become a classic.

Evaluation essays have one special requirement: the writer must first decide on criteria, or standards, as a basis for judgment. The specific reasons and evidence supporting the writer's judgment derive from these criteria. Agee, for example, judges *The Treasure of the Sierra Madre* on the criteria of story line, theme, unity, cinematography, acting, and direction. The following table shows these criteria along with the specific reasons Agee gives to support his judgment:

Criteria: Reasons
story line: a masterfully told story
theme: a story rich in implications
unity: well-focused elements
cinematography: excellent camera work; skillful film editing
acting: excellent acting
direction: effective use of locations; director's style "invisible," "universal," and "virile"

Because Agee uses widely recognized criteria for evaluating movies, he does not have to define or justify his criteria because he knows they are shared by all moviegoers. In other situations, however, a writer might need to explain and justify criteria. For example, in an essay evaluating a teacher, a writer might first need to establish criteria for evaluating teachers. Whereas most people agree readily on appropriate criteria for evaluating movies, there exists no clear consensus about what makes a good teacher.

Often it is necessary to choose among many criteria; usually, writers will do so with their readers in mind. If Agee had reviewed the film for filmmakers, for example, rather than general moviegoers, he might have been concerned solely with cinematography, concentrating the whole review on camera work, editing and cutting, sound track, and quality of film stock.

The next essay evaluates the American civil rights movement of the early 1960s. When it appeared in *The American Scholar* in 1967, it was the first publication of a young black writer named Alice Walker. She has since published several collections of poetry and short stories as well as three novels, including *The Color Purple*, for which she was awarded the Pulitzer Prize in 1982.

How would a writer evaluate a social movement? What criteria would be appropriate? As you read, think about the criteria Walker uses for her evaluation.

THE CIVIL RIGHTS MOVEMENT: WHAT GOOD WAS IT?
ALICE WALKER

Someone said recently to an old black lady from Mississippi, whose legs had been badly mangled by local police who arrested her for "disturbing the peace," that the civil rights movement was dead, and asked, since it was dead, what she thought about it. The old lady replied, hobbling out of his presence on her cane, that the civil rights movement was like herself, "if it's dead, it shore ain't ready to lay down!" 1

This old lady is a legendary freedom fighter in her small town in the Delta. 2

She has been severely mistreated for insisting on her rights as an American citizen. She has been beaten for singing movement songs, placed in solitary confinement in prisons for talking about freedom, and placed on bread and water for praying aloud to God for her jailers' deliverance. For such a woman the civil rights movement will never be over as long as her skin is black. It also will never be over for twenty million others with the same "affliction," for whom the movement can never "lay down," no matter how it is killed by the press and made dead and buried by the white American public. As long as one black American survives, the struggle for equality with other Americans must also survive. This is a debt we owe to those blameless hostages we leave to the future, our children.

Perhaps it is naïve to be thankful that the movement "saved" a large 3 number of individuals and gave them something to live for, even if it did not provide them with everything they wanted. (Materially, it provided them with precious little that they wanted.) When a movement awakens people to the possibilities of life, it seems unfair to frustrate them by then denying what they had thought was offered. But what was offered? What was promised? What was it all about? What good did it do? Would it have been better, as some have suggested, to leave the Negro people as they were, unawakened, unallied with one another, unhopeful about what to expect for their children in some future world?

I do not think so. If knowledge of my condition is all the freedom I get 4 from a "freedom movement," it is better than unawareness, forgottenness and hopelessness, the existence that is like the existence of a beast. Man only truly lives by knowing, otherwise he simply performs, copying the daily habits of others, but conceiving nothing of his creative possibilities as a man, and accepting someone else's superiority and his own misery.

When we are children, growing up in our parents' care, we await the 5 spark from the outside world. Sometimes our parents provide it—if we are lucky—sometimes it comes from another source far from home. We sit, paralyzed, surrounded by our anxiety and dread, hoping we will not have to grow up into the narrow world and ways we see about us. We are hungry for a life that turns us on; we yearn for a knowledge of living that will save us from our innocuous lives that resemble death. We look for signs in every strange event; we search for heroes in every unknown face.

It was just six years ago that I began to be alive. I had, of course, been 6 living before—for I am now twenty-three—but I did not really know it. And I did not know it because nobody told me that I—a pensive, yearning, typical high-school senior, but Negro—existed in the minds of others as I existed in my own. Until that time my mind was locked apart from the outer contours and complexion of my body as if it and the body were strangers. The mind possessed both thought and spirit—I wanted to be an author or a scientist—which the color of the body denied. I had never seen myself and existed as a statistic exists, or as a phantom. In the white world I walked, less real to them than a shadow; and being young and well-hidden among the slums, among people who also did not exist—either in books or in films or in the government of their own lives—I waited to be called to life. And, by a miracle, I was called.

There was a commotion in our house that night in 1960. We had man- 7 aged to buy our first television set. It was battered and overpriced, but my mother had gotten used to watching the afternoon soap operas at the house where she worked as maid, and nothing could satisfy her on days when she did not work but a continuation of her "stories." So she pinched pennies and bought a set. . . . She placed herself in every scene she saw, with her braided hair turned blonde, her two hundred pounds compressed into a sleek size seven dress, her rough dark skin smooth and *white*. Her husband became dark and handsome, talented, witty, urbane, charming. And when she turned to look at my father sitting near her in his sweat shirt with his smelly feet raised on the bed to "air," there was always a tragic look of surprise on her face. Then she would sigh and go out to the kitchen looking lost and unsure of herself. My mother, a truly great woman—who raised eight children of her own and half a dozen of the neighbors' without a single complaint— was convinced that she did not exist compared to "them."

Six years ago, after half-heartedly watching my mother's soap operas and 8 wondering whether there wasn't something more to be asked of life, the civil rights movement came into my life. Like a good omen for the future, the face of Dr. Martin Luther King, Jr., was the first black face I saw on our new television screen. And, as in a fairy tale, my soul was stirred by the meaning for me of his mission—at the time he was being rather ignominiously dumped into a police van for having led a protest march in Alabama—and I fell in love with the sober and determined face of the movement. The singing of "We Shall Overcome"—that song betrayed by nonbelievers in it—rang for the first time in my ears. The influence that my mother's soap operas might have had on me became impossible. The life of Dr. King, seeming bigger and more miraculous than the man himself, because of all he had done and suffered, offered a pattern of strength and sincerity I felt I could trust. He had suffered much because of his simple belief in nonviolence, love and brotherhood. Perhaps the majority of men could not be reached through these beliefs, but because Dr. King kept trying to reach them in spite of danger to himself and his family, I saw in him the hero for whom I had waited so long.

What Dr. King promised was not a ranch-style house and an acre of 9 manicured lawn for every black man, but jail and finally freedom. He did not promise two cars for every family, but the courage one day for all families everywhere to walk without shame and unafraid on their own feet. He did not say that one day it will be us chasing prospective buyers out of our prosperous well-kept neighborhoods, or in other ways exhibiting our snobbery and ignorance as all other ethnic groups before us have done; what he said was that we had a right to live anywhere in this country we chose, and a right to a meaningful well-paying job to provide us with the upkeep of our homes. He did not say we had to become carbon copies of the white American middle-class; but he did say we had the right to become whatever we wanted to become.

Because of the movement, because of an awakened faith in the newness 10 and imagination of the human spirit, because of "black and white together"—for the first time in our history in some human relationship on and off TV—because of the beatings, the arrests, the hell of battle during the past years, I have fought harder for my life and for a chance to be myself, to be something more than a shadow or a number, than I have ever done before in my life. Before there had seemed to be no real reason for struggling beyond the effort for daily bread. Now there was a chance at that other that Jesus meant when He said we could not live by bread alone.

I have fought and kicked and fasted and prayed and cursed and cried 11 myself to the point of existing. It has been like being born again, literally. Just "knowing" has meant everything to me. Knowing has pushed me out into the world, into college, into places, into people.

Part of what existence means to me is knowing the difference between 12 what I am now and what I was then. It is being capable of looking after myself intellectually as well as financially. It is being able to tell when I am being wronged and by whom. It means being awake to protect myself and the ones I love. It means being a part of the world community, and being *alert* to which part it is that I have joined, and knowing how to change to another part if that part does not suit me. To know is to exist; to exist is to be involved, to move about, to see the world with my own eyes. This, at least, the movement has given me.

What good was the civil rights movement? If it had just given this country 13 Dr. King, a leader of conscience for once in our lifetime, it would have been enough. If it had just taken black eyes off white television stories, it would have been enough. If it had fed one starving child, it would have been enough.

If the civil rights movement is "dead," and if it gave us nothing else, it 14 gave us each other forever. It gave some of us bread, some of us shelter, some of us knowledge and pride, all of us comfort. It gave us our children, our husbands, our brothers, our fathers, as men reborn and with a purpose for living. It broke the pattern of black servitude in this country. It shattered the phony "promise" of white soap operas that sucked away so many pitiful lives. It gave us history and men far greater than Presidents. It gave us heroes, selfless men of courage and strength, for our little boys to follow. It gave us hope for tomorrow. It called us to life.

Because we live, it can never die. 15

Questions for analysis   1. For what purpose is Walker evaluating the civil rights movement? What readers does she seem to address?

2. How persuasive do you find Walker's evaluation? What parts of her essay are most convincing, what parts least convincing?

3. What reasons does Walker give in support of her evaluation? What criteria provide the basis for these reasons? Make a table listing her criteria along with the reasons given for each one.

4. What evidence does Walker offer to develop her argument? Given her purpose, what advantages and disadvantages does this kind of evidence have?

5. How does Walker anticipate and refute counterarguments to her evaluation? Does she do so successfully?

6. How does Walker begin her essay? What advantages or disadvantages does this beginning bring?

7. If you were asked to evaluate a social, political, or religious movement, which movement would you choose? What criteria would you use to judge it, and how would you develop your argument?

Walker's strategy is to argue for the value of the civil rights movement in terms of its results. Her claim is very clear: the movement is good because it produced beneficial results for blacks. Although Walker's piece is an impassioned personal statement, it is still a reasoned argument with evidence. It reminds us that evaluations can reflect strong personal preferences—like Agee's enthusiasm for *The Treasure of the Sierra Madre*—and still fulfill the requirements of argument: reasons and evidence based on critical analysis of the subject and awareness of readers' views.

In the next essay we see how a writer evaluates a person. The writer's goal is to persuade his readers to admire someone he admires.

The person is a sports figure of established reputation—Joe DiMaggio, who played for the New York Yankees in the 1940s and 1950s. The writer is himself a well-known sports reporter—Red Smith, a Pulitzer Prize-winning columnist for the *New York Times*. This piece was first published in 1947 in the sports section of the *Times*.

JOE DIMAGGIO
RED SMITH

After the Yankees chewed up the Dodgers in the second game of the World Series, Joe DiMaggio relaxed in the home club's gleaming tile boudoir and deposed at length in defense of Peter Reiser, the Brooklyn center fielder, who had narrowly escaped being smitten upon the isthmus rhombencephali that day by sundry fly balls. 1

The moving, mottled background of faces and shirt collars and orchids, Joe said, made a fly almost invisible until it had cleared the top deck. The tricky, slanting shadows of an October afternoon created a problem involving calculus, metaphysics, and social hygiene when it came to judging a line drive. The roar of the crowd disguised the crack of bat against ball. And so on. 2

Our Mr. Robert Cooke, listening respectfully as one should to the greatest 3 living authority on the subject, nevertheless stared curiously at DiMaggio. He was thinking that not only Reiser but also J. DiMaggio had played that same center field on that same afternoon, and there were no knots on Joe's slick coiffure.

"How about you, Joe?" Bob asked. "Do those same factors handicap you 4 out there?"

DiMaggio permitted himself one of his shy, toothy smiles. 5

"Don't start worrying about the old boy after all these years," he said. 6

He didn't say "the old master." That's a phrase for others to use. But it 7 would be difficult to define more aptly than Joe did the difference between this unmitigated pro and all the others, good, bad, and ordinary, who also play in major-league outfields.

There is a line that has been quoted so often the name of its originator 8 has been lost. But whoever said it first was merely reacting impulsively to a particular play and not trying to coin a mot when he ejaculated: "The son-ofagun! Ten years I've been watching him, and he hasn't had a hard chance yet!"

It may be that Joe is not, ranked on his defensive skill alone, the finest 9 center fielder of his time. Possibly Terry Moore was his equal playing the hitter, getting the jump on the ball, judging a fly, covering ground, and squeezing the ball once he touched it.

Joe himself has declared that his kid brother, Dominic, is a better fielder 10 than he. Which always recalls the occasion when the Red Sox were playing the Yanks and Dom fled across the county line to grab a drive by Joe that no one but a DiMaggio could have reached. And the late Sid Mercer, shading his thoughtful eyes under a hard straw hat, remarked to the press box at large: "Joe should sue his old man on that one."

Joe hasn't been the greatest hitter that baseball has known, either. He'll 11 not match Ty Cobb's lifetime average, he'll never threaten Babe Ruth's home-run record, nor will he ever grip the imagination of the crowds as the Babe did. Or even as Babe Herman did. That explains why the contract that he signed the other day calls for an estimated $65,000 instead of the $80,000 that Ruth got. If he were not such a matchless craftsman he might be a more spectacular player. And so, perhaps, more colorful. And so more highly re-warded.

But you don't rate a great ballplayer according to his separate, special 12 talents. You must rank him off the sum total of his component parts, and on this basis there has not been, during Joe's big-league existence, a rival close to him. None other in his time has combined such savvy and fielding and hitting and throwing—Tom Laird, who was writing sports in San Fran-cisco when Joe was growing up, always insisted that a sore arm "ruined" DiMaggio's throwing in his first season with the Yankees—and such tem-perament and such base running.

Because he does so many other things so well and makes no specialty of 13 stealing, DiMaggio rarely has received full credit for his work on the bases.

But travel with a second-division club in the league for a few seasons and count the times when DiMaggio, representing the tying or winning run, whips you by coming home on the unforeseen gamble and either beats the play or knocks the catcher into the dugout.

Ask American League catchers about him, or National Leaguers like Ernie 14 Lombardi. Big Lom will remember who it was who ran home from first base in the last game of the 1939 World Series while Ernie lay threshing in the dust behind the plate and Bucky Walters stood bemused on the mound.

These are the reasons why DiMaggio, excelled by Ted Williams in all 15 offensive statistics and reputedly Ted's inferior in crowd appeal and financial standing, still won the writers' accolade as the American League's most valuable in 1947.

It wasn't the first time Williams earned this award with his bat and lost 16 it with his disposition. As a matter of fact, if all other factors were equal save only the question of character, Joe never would lose out to any player. The guy who came out of San Francisco as a shy lone wolf, suspicious of Easterners and of Eastern writers, today is the top guy in any sports gathering in any town. The real champ.

Questions for analysis

1. Instead of announcing his judgment right away, how does Smith begin the essay? How else might he begin? What advantages or disadvantages does his beginning bring?

2. What reasons does Smith give to support his judgment?

3. What are the criteria underlying Smith's reasons? Do these seem like appropriate criteria for evaluating a baseball player?

4. Consider the order in which Smith presents his reasons. Why do you think he chose to order them as he did? Which reason seems most important to Smith's argument? Where does he place this reason, and how does he develop it? Can you suggest a better placement?

5. In paragraphs 9–11, Smith mentions several other extraordinary players as possible counterarguments. How does he refute these counterarguments? In your view, does including them weaken or strengthen his overall argument?

6. Smith uses some words not normally found on the sports pages— *boudoir* (a woman's private room), *deposed* (gave testimony), *smitten* (hit hard), *isthmus rhombencephali* (head), *mottled* (different shades of light and dark), *coiffure* (hairstyle), and *unmitigated* (unvarying in intensity and seriousness). What effect do such words have on his essay? How would the essay be different had he chosen language more expected in a sports column—*locker room* rather than *boudoir*, for example?

7. What outstanding person would you be interested in evaluating in writing? You might choose someone in sports, film, politics—or perhaps

a teacher or member of the clergy. What criteria would you use to evaluate this person? Would you need to convince your readers of the appropriateness of these criteria? What reasons would you use to support your argument?

Smith's essay illustrates the importance that comparison often holds in evaluations. He makes a point of comparing DiMaggio to several other talented baseball players, though he does not base his essay on comparison. Sometimes an evaluation can be developed as an elaborate, sustained comparison of two or more things. For example, Smith might have organized his column around a step-by-step comparison of Ted Williams and DiMaggio.

This essay also shows the effect that voice can have on an evaluation. Voice refers to the writer's attitude toward his or her subject and readers. We might describe the voice in Smith's piece here as playful admiration. James Agee's voice we might characterize as enthusiastic advocacy; Alice Walker's as impassioned moral judgment. These suggest the range of voices possible in evaluation essays. In many evaluative writing situations, including many college assignments, an impersonal voice is more appropriate.

Geoffrey Clemmons, a college freshman, wrote the next essay. It illustrates a very common type of evaluation: of a consumer product. Such evaluations are found in general consumer reports and in magazines devoted to particular products (cars, motorcycles, cameras). Clemmons, an enthusiastic scuba diver, evaluates a night-diving light, the UK 600.

He addresses his evaluation to other divers. With this in mind, notice the kind of evidence he presents to support his judgment.

THE UK 600
GEOFFREY CLEMMONS

Underwater Kinetics, a relatively new producer of sport scuba diving equipment, has quickly established itself as a leader in the industry. Already they produce a superior product at a competitive price. Their midrange-priced night-diving light, the UK 600, is a good example. For a compact light, the UK 600 is incredibly rugged. Its many technical innovations—in particular, its beveled reflector—put it in a league with bigger, more expensive models. Maintenance of the UK 600 is minimal and the cost of replacement parts is minuscule when compared with its closest competitors. The UK 600's best feature, though, is its low price. On the basis of price, performance, and durability, the UK 600 simply can't be beat. The average diver couldn't do better.

The UK 600 is smaller and lighter than most night-diving lights. It is 3.7 inches in diameter and 7 inches in length, and with its battery, it weighs only 43.5 ounces. It uses a six-volt heavy duty lantern battery which will burn for three to five hours. The battery is not rechargeable.

The UK 600 is virtually indestructible. The main part of the body is con- 3 structed entirely of ABS plastic, so that no metal parts are exposed to the corrosive salt water. The comfortable pistol grip (or optional lantern grip) mounts securely in a dovetail slot just behind the on/off switch, which allows the user to position the grip according to his or her preferred weight balance. Its lens, made of shatterproof Lexan plastic, is recessed beneath an outer bezel to protect it from scratching and bumping.

Several of its technical innovations are especially noteworthy. Chief among 4 them is the finely beveled reflecting surface. Instead of the smooth, concave, mirrored reflecting surface found in most flashlights, the UK 600 has a beveled reflecting surface. This focuses the light into a more uniform beam without the so-called "hot spots" and "cold spots" produced by conventional sealed beam lights. It uses a high temperature quartz bulb, which, in conjunction with the beveled reflector, produces a beam intensity of ten footcandles measured at ten feet, making the UK 600 one of the brightest sixvolt lights available. Another innovative feature is the use of a printed contact board in place of clip-on or screw-on battery contacts. The contact board virtually eliminates the problem of lamp failure due to loose contacts.

The simplicity of the UK 600's design makes maintenance simple and 5 inexpensive. The single O-ring seal, neatly situated behind the clear, screwon bezel, needs only periodic cleaning and regreasing. By contrast, sealedbeam models typically employ two seals: one in front of and one behind the reflector/lens combination. Their proximity to the heated bulb element causes them to dry out much more quickly. The UK 600's bulb is easily removable for replacement. Moreover, a replacement bulb costs just over three dollars, compared with twelve dollars or more, the cost of replacing an entire sealed beam. Service and warranty claims are handled through a vast network of dealers, saving consumers the costs involved with shipping the light back to the manufacturer.

There are bigger and brighter lights on the market, but the UK 600 should 6 satisfy the average diver's needs at a fraction of the cost of bigger lights. For the price, the UK 600 is the best nonrechargeable night diving light on the market today.

Questions for analysis

1. What would you say is the purpose of Clemmons' evaluation? Given that purpose, do his criteria and reasons seem appropriate? Does he slight or ignore any other important criteria?

2. Clemmons' beginning takes up about one-fourth the space in his essay. Why do you think he gave his opening such prominence? What is he attempting to do with it?

3. How does he use comparison and contrast?

4. How is the essay organized? Make a brief outline, indicating the purpose of each paragraph. How else might such an evaluation be organized? What advantages or disadvantages can you see in Clemmons' plan?

5. How would you describe the voice in this essay? How is it different from the voices in Agee, Walker, or Smith? Why do you think Clemmons used such a voice in this evaluation? Is it a voice you trust to evaluate the UK 600? If so, why? If not, why not?

6. What consumer product would you evaluate if asked to write such an evaluation? For whom would you write the evaluation? What criteria would you use in evaluating it?

Since Clemmons' essay is written for well-informed readers—other divers who can be assumed to follow developments in equipment quite closely—he is able to use certain technical terms without defining them. He talks about bezels, O-ring seals, ABS plastic, quartz bulbs, and sealed beam lights. If he were writing an evaluation for beginning divers, he would surely need to define many of these terms.

Whatever the experience of readers, however, writers evaluating consumer products must be experts on the product. Not only do they have to take more than a casual interest in it, they should have studied and used the product. They must know its advantages over competing products and they should know something about the history of the development of the product. Without this kind of expertise, it would be nearly impossible to write an authoritative evaluation.

Such expertise is required even to evaluate products for people who know very little about their technical or design features. An important purpose of consumer reports is to introduce consumers to the criteria necessary for judging products. For example, a driver considering buying a small car needs to know that piston speed is an important criterion of engine design on which to base an evaluation of large and small cars. The higher the piston speed (as measured by RPM's) at a certain road speed, the greater will be the engine wear. Hence, of two comparable cars, the one with the lower piston speed might in the long run be the better buy.

BASIC FEATURES OF EVALUATIONS

Presentation of the subject

Most evaluations include some description of the subject. For example, James Agee briefly summarizes *The Treasure of the Sierra Madre* (paragraph 3) and Alice Walker outlines the main principles of the civil rights movement (paragraphs 9, 10). Such descriptions are generally selective and written to a well-focused purpose—to support the writer's judgment.

An authoritative judgment

Evaluation essays are focused on a judgment—an assertion about the value of something. This judgment is the thesis, or main point, of the essay.

Such judgments assert that something is good or bad or that it is better or worse than something else. Usually this judgment is restated in various ways in the essay and repeated at the end. For example, in reviewing *The Treasure of the Sierra Madre,* Agee states his positive judgment of the movie in several ways:

> . . . I have no doubt at all that Huston [the director] . . . is the most talented man working in American pictures. . . .
>
> . . . [*Treasure*] will stand up in the memory and esteem of qualified people alongside the best of the silent movies.
>
> . . . a sensational achievement . . .
>
> . . . the story itself—a beauty . . .

Never are we in doubt about Agee's judgment.

In essays of evaluation we expect to hear an authoritative voice. Such a voice assures us that the writer has knowledge and self-confidence about the subject. James Agee seems to understand quite fully the movie he is reviewing (we might guess that he saw it more than once), and he clearly knows a lot about movies in general. Likewise, Red Smith's essay leaves no doubt that he had seen DiMaggio play in many baseball games and watched other good players over many decades of sports reporting. In the same way, Geoffrey Clemmons shows that he knows all about the UK 600 diving light—and something about other lights as well.

A convincing argument   To be convincing, the evaluation must be based on relevant criteria appropriate for the intended readers of the essay. For example, Agee's criteria—story line, theme, unity, cinematography, acting, direction—are relevant to movies (but not to baseball players) and appropriate for the average moviegoer who reads reviews in such magazines as *Rolling Stone, Time,* or the *New Yorker.*

The argument of the evaluation is developed with reasons and evidence. Writers say why they like or dislike something by giving us reasons, sometimes only one or two, other times many. These reasons are developed and supported with evidence from the subject of the evaluation. Most of the discussion in an evaluation essay is taken up with this evidence.

Clemmons says he likes the UK 600 diving light because it is inexpensive, durable, reliable, and easy to maintain. These are his reasons. He then supports these reasons with specific facts about the light—how much a new bulb costs, what materials are used, where to have it repaired. These facts are evidence.

For reasons and evidence to be persuasive, a writer must organize them into a convincing argument. The reasons must be arranged in some logical order with the most important reason either first or last. The most significant criterion is generally given the most weight (or space) in the essay. Also, the writer must be willing to acknowledge any weaknesses in something being praised (as Agee does in paragraph 7). Furthermore, he or she should be able to anticipate and refute any counterarguments; Smith, for example, acknowledges the reasons some people may rate other players higher than DiMaggio. Usually writers of evaluations restate their thesis at the end to provide an emphatic conclusion and a frame for the essay.

Comparison   Comparison and contrast is not a requirement in written evaluations, but it is nearly always used. Our minds turn naturally to comparisons when we are making judgments because judgments are relative: if we are evaluating a movie, we judge it relative to other movies; if we are evaluating a professional baseball player, we judge him relative to other baseball players. The criteria for our evaluations derive from characteristics of all movies or all baseball players.

All the evaluations in this chapter are positive. The writers all praise their subjects. For such evaluations, writers draw comparisons to similar things of less value. The purpose of the comparison, of course, is to increase the value of that which they are praising. Smith compares DiMaggio to several other baseball players he considers inferior: Terry Moore, Dominic DiMaggio, Ty Cobb, Babe Herman, Babe Ruth, and Ted Williams (paragraphs 9–11, 15, and 16).

Notice that although Walker does not compare the civil rights movement to other social movements, she does draw a contrast between her mother and herself. There is also an implied comparison of her mother and the old lady Walker calls a "legendary freedom fighter." Walker's life and the old lady's life have been transformed by the movement, their awareness of the possibilities for themselves and other black Americans completely changed. The mother, by contrast, continues to let television soap operas define her place in the world.

Strategies for presenting comparisons or contrasts in writing are analyzed and illustrated further in Chapter 17: Comparing and Contrasting.

GUIDE TO WRITING

THE WRITING TASK

Write an essay evaluating something you know about or can research. Carefully define your readers—are they familiar with the topic or is it perhaps new to them? Your evaluation cannot be merely subjective; it must be based on appropriate criteria and be supported by reasons and evidence.

INVENTION AND RESEARCH

Identifying a subject for evaluation

These writing activities will enable you to choose a subject, analyze it closely, and decide how you will argue to support your judgment. You may already have a good idea of what you would like to evaluate. Still, you may want to consider some other topics. This activity is designed to help you come up with some possibilities. If you are sure of your topic, however, skip now to Examining Your Knowledge of the Subject.

Listing possibilities. For each of the following categories list two or three things you might possibly evaluate.

- ☐ A poem, story, or novel
- ☐ A movie, play, or television series
- ☐ A musical recording or performance
- ☐ A noteworthy person—a professor, a political figure, an artist, an athlete
- ☐ An institution—a school, a library, an art collection
- ☐ A consumer product—a camera, a car, a computer
- ☐ A theory—supply-side economics, the big-bang theory, evolution
- ☐ A political position—gun control, nuclear arms freeze
- ☐ An essay or other work of nonfiction

Choosing a tentative topic. Once you have a list of possibilities, review the list looking for a tentative topic. Choose something you have encountered recently. Be sure it is something you have settled feelings about: you either like it or dislike it. Most important, select a subject you can evaluate with authority—you must know the proper criteria and have enough knowledge to give detailed examples. You might want to consider a topic you are now studying (a literary work, a scientific theory).

If you wish to evaluate a work of art—whether a story or a movie or a concert—you will be able to write a much stronger evaluation if you read it or see it now, even before you start writing about it.

You should write about a product only if you are very knowledgeable about it. A slight acquaintance with a product will never do: to write a convincing evaluation, you must have a great deal of experience using the product and be something of an expert about other models and types.

Examining your knowledge of the subject

Describe it. Describe your subject briefly in just a few sentences. What is it? How did you first encounter it?

Judge it. In a sentence or two state your judgment.

Explore it in writing. Write nonstop for around ten minutes, exploring your feelings and knowledge about the topic. The following questions can guide your writing here:

☐ How certain am I of my judgment? Do I have any doubts? Why do I feel the way I do?

☐ Do I like (or dislike) everything about my subject, or only certain parts of it?

☐ Are there any similar things I should consider (other products or movies, for example)?

☐ Is there anything I will need to do right away in order to evaluate this subject authoritatively? Will I need to do any research? Can I get the information I need?

Testing your choice   Now you should pause and test your choice. Before you invest any more time in this choice, consider the following questions:

☐ Do I know enough about this topic to describe it fully and to present detailed evidence to support an evaluation?

☐ Do I know (or can I find out) the appropriate criteria for evaluating such things?

☐ Do I have experience with other things of its type as a basis for comparison?

☐ Do I personally care enough about the topic and my judgment of it—positive or negative—to want to convince readers of the validity of my judgment?

You will want to keep these questions in mind and perhaps reconsider them as you invent and plan and later as you draft your essay. If you ever have trouble answering them affirmatively and confidently, you may want to choose something else to evaluate.

Identifying criteria   Criteria are standards for judging something. James Agee's criteria for evaluating a film, for instance, were story line, theme, unity, cinematography, acting, and direction. Because all rational judgments are based on criteria appropriate to the subject, it is advisable to take some time now to think of the criteria usually used to evaluate your subject.

Make a list of all the criteria you can think of for judging the topic you have chosen. From your analysis of the readings in this chapter, you may have some examples of criteria used for other topics. Here is a list of criteria you might make if you were evaluating a single lens reflex camera:

strength and reliability of construction

quality of optics

functions—balance of sophistication and ease of use

size of dealer network (for maintenance)

price

Your criteria should be impersonal (not based just on your personal tastes) and appropriate for the thing being evaluated. They should include nothing trivial, but instead should point to the most basic and important features.

Stop now to focus your thoughts. In one sentence restate the judgment you wish to make about your topic.

Analyzing your readers

You will be trying to convince particular readers to consider your evaluation seriously, perhaps even to take some action as a result, like seeing a certain movie, or buying a particular sailboat. Consequently, you must analyze these readers very carefully. You should do so now, so that you can next select reasons which might appeal to these readers.

Write for at least ten minutes exploring your readers' knowledge of the topic. These questions may stimulate your exploration:

☐ Do my readers have any knowledge of or experience with the topic? If not, how thoroughly will I have to describe it?

☐ Have they experienced anything similar?

☐ Are they familiar with the criteria for evaluating such things? Must readers have any special knowledge to understand my evaluation?

☐ Are my readers likely to disagree with my judgment? Why? Might they find my judgment controversial or surprising?

Generating reasons and evidence

Consider now the reasons for your judgment: why do you like or dislike the essay or senator or city or whatever you are evaluating? Then see what factual evidence you can offer to support those reasons. A good way to do this is to make a table containing criteria, reasons, and evidence. (See a sample table on pages 230–31.)

Listing reasons. Divide a piece of paper into three columns. In the left-hand column list all the criteria you identified as necessary and appropriate for evaluating your subject, skipping about five lines between each item. Then, in the middle column, list all the reasons, criterion-by-criterion, for your judgment. Select the reasons with your readers' sensibilities in mind. You may find more reasons for some criteria than for others; also, you may think of reasons that seem to fit with none of your criteria.

Finding evidence. When you have listed as many reasons as you can, move on to the right-hand column, and add any evidence you can think of to illustrate each reason—personal anecdotes, illustrations (quotations, paraphrases, summaries, descriptive details, etc.), statistics, or testimony (someone else's statement).

You will probably find that the amount of evidence you can find to support each reason will vary. Some reasons will have only one piece of evidence, while others may have several supporting facts.

Charting your criteria, reasons, and evidence in table form can be useful in identifying which reasons need additional evidence. It shows you at a glance how well each of your arguments is supported.

Reconsidering your criteria. Look at all the criteria you have identified so far. Can you see any ways to narrow or broaden certain criteria, or to combine two or more? Can you think of any additional criteria? Revise or extend your table of reasons, criteria, and evidence.

Elaborating on the most convincing reasons

By now you have had a chance to explore fully all the elements necessary to writing an evaluation essay: the subject itself, your judgment of it, the criteria of judgment on which your argument will be based, the reasons and evidence to support your judgment, and your readers. Next you should perform a critical analysis of each reason, the relations among all your reasons, their relation to your judgment, and their appropriateness for your readers.

Selecting the best reasons. For your particular readers, which of your reasons would be most convincing? Reconsider your table and select three to five of your strongest reasons. Put an asterisk by these.

Analyzing the reasons. Analyze each of your best reasons, guided by the questions that follow. Write a few sentences of analysis for each one of these reasons.

☐ How exactly does this reason directly support my judgment?
☐ Does the reason derive from an appropriate criterion?
☐ What is so important about this reason?
☐ Why did I choose this reason?
☐ Why will my readers find this reason convincing?
☐ What further evidence do I need to strengthen this reason?

Considering the set of reasons. Now analyze the reasons you selected as the best ones as an interrelated set. Guided by the following questions, write for at least five minutes on all of your best reasons:

☐ As a set, do my reasons slight an important criterion?

☐ Are any of the reasons similar? If so, might they be combined?

☐ Which reasons are the strongest? Why?

☐ Which ones are the weakest? Why?

☐ Should any reasons be dropped altogether?

☐ What would be the best sequence for presenting these reasons to my readers?

☐ Why would it be better than some other order?

Developing the reasons. To test how well you can integrate the evidence for a reason into a forceful argument, take your three most important reasons in turn and write quickly for at least five minutes on each one. These test writings may suggest that you need still further evidence to support a reason or that you have to figure out connections between bits of evidence.

PLANNING AND DRAFTING

Before you begin drafting, you will want to reflect on what you have discovered in your invention writings. You will also want to set goals to guide your drafting. This section helps you think about important goals of accommodating your readers, beginning and ending effectively, organizing for maximum effect, and avoiding logical fallacies.

Seeing what you have

You have by now done considerable thinking and writing about issues basic to all evaluative writing. You have chosen a subject and identified your readers, and you have charted the criteria, reasons, and evidence necessary to an evaluation. Reread it all thoughtfully to see what you have. Look for connections, patterns, surprises. Highlight anything promising by underscoring or making notes in the margin. Tinker with your criteria, reasons, and evidence to see that they all fit together. Try to decide what you need to research further.

If you are still not satisfied that you have enough material to develop a persuasive essay, you might want to select a different topic. Consider the questions under Testing Your Choice one last time.

Outlining the evaluation

Evaluations may be organized in various ways. The important thing is to include all essential parts: a presentation of the subject, a judgment of some kind, and reasons and evidence to support the judgment.

If your readers are already familiar with the topic, your outline might look like this:

presentation of the subject and your judgment
reason 1
   evidence
reason 2
   evidence
reason 3
   evidence, with a comparison
(etc.)
consideration of an opposing judgment
conclusion

If your readers are unfamiliar with the topic, however, you will need to begin with some description of your subject, including perhaps some background discussion and definition of terms. These are, of course, the most basic elements; there are many other possible organizations.

You will want to arrange your reasons in some logical order: from most obvious to least obvious, most general to most technical, least convincing to most convincing, from least important to most important.

Remember that an outline should serve only as a guide. It can help you to organize your invention materials and provide a sense of direction as you start drafting.

Setting goals   Before starting to draft, think about the important rhetorical goals for your essay. The following questions can help you to focus on particular decisions you will have to make as you plan and draft your essay.

Your readers

☐ What do my readers already know about my subject?

☐ How much experience and knowledge do they have with the general subject?

☐ If readers are unfamiliar with my subject, how can I describe it to them?

☐ What is the most appropriate voice for these readers? How can I present myself so as to make them trust my evaluation? Should I be witty? serious? casual? impersonal?

The beginning

☐ How should I begin? How can I capture my readers' attention? Should I open by stating my judgment? Should I quote some authority on the topic? Should I begin with an anecdote, as Walker and Smith do?

☐ What information should I give first? Should I provide some background, or simply state my judgment?

The criteria, reasons, and evidence

☐ Will people recognize and accept the criteria on which I am basing my evaluation? Do I need to define or justify my criteria?

☐ Will anyone question any of my reasons?

☐ Do I have evidence to support each of my reasons?

☐ Should I acknowledge any objections readers may have to my evaluation, as Smith does when he admits that some people consider other players better than DiMaggio?

☐ Should I acknowledge any weaknesses my subject may have, as Agee does about the film he reviews?

Avoiding logical fallacies

☐ Will I be able to base my argument on impersonal criteria and avoid considering my own *personal tastes?* (praising a movie because the main character reminds me of my favorite uncle, for example)

☐ Am I considering any *trivial criteria?* (condemning a movie because one of the characters wears a Save the Whales t-shirt, for example)

☐ Am I considering any *unimportant criteria?* (praising a movie because its outdoor scenes are filled with beautiful cumulus clouds, for example)

☐ Am I guilty of *hasty generalization?* (criticizing a movie because I disliked an earlier movie by the same director, or praising a movie because I have always admired its leading actress)

☐ Can I avoid making *weak comparisons?* (Should I acknowledge weaknesses in subjects I praise or strengths of those I criticize?)

☐ How can I show that I have *accepted the burden of proof?* Can I make a convincing argument for my evaluation, so that no one thinks I am exaggerating or overstating the case?

☐ Will I be committing an *either/or fallacy* if I claim that my subject is either all good or all bad?

☐ Can I compare my subject to something inferior without being accused of making a *straw man* argument? (A straw man is easily knocked down.)

The ending

☐ Shall I end by summarizing the reasons for my judgment?

☐ Should I restate my judgment?

☐ Do I want the ending to frame the essay by referring back to the opening?

Drafting the evaluation Before you begin to draft, you might want to look at the general advice about drafting in Chapter 1. Reread all your notes. If you are evaluating a published work (a poem, story, novel, etc.) reread it. If you are writing about a movie, go to see it again. Your subject must be completely fresh in your mind.

If you have trouble drafting, consider each element in your evaluation. Perhaps you should think of better reasons or add more evidence to support the reasons you give. You may need to take another look at your criteria. If you really get stuck, turn back to the invention activities to see if you can fill out your material.

READING A DRAFT WITH A CRITICAL EYE

Once you have completed your draft, read it over carefully. Adopt a critical viewpoint, looking to see what works and what needs improvement. Whether you are reading your own draft or one written by someone else, try to put yourself in the position of the intended readers.

First general impression Read the essay straight through to get a quick, general impression. Write down a few sentences stating your immediate reaction. If you are reading someone else's evaluation, let the writer know whether you agree or disagree, whether the essay convinced you or left you with questions.

Pointings It is important to maintain a critical focus as you read the essay now; one way to do this is by highlighting notable features of the writing with *pointings*. A simple system of marking a draft with underlining and brackets, these pointings are quick and easy to do and provide a lot of helpful information for revising the draft. Use pointings in the following way:

☐ Draw a straight line under any words or images that impress you as especially effective: strong verbs, precise descriptive details, memorable phrases, striking images.

☐ Draw a wavy line under any words or images that seem flat, stale, or vague. Also put a wavy line under any words or phrases that seem unnecessary or repetitious.

☐ Look for pairs or groups of sentences that you think should be combined. Put brackets [ ] around these sentences.

☐ Look for sentences that are garbled, overloaded, or awkward. Put parentheses ( ) around these sentences. Parenthesize any sentence that seems even slightly questionable; don't spend time worrying about whether it actually is incorrect. The writer needs to know that someone had even the slightest difficulty understanding a sentence.

Analysis   Consider the following points as you analyze an evaluation essay.

1. The writer's judgment should be clearly stated. Look to see that there is a firm judgment, rather than just a balance of good and bad points. Is it stated early enough in the essay?

2. If the criteria are not stated explicitly, what are they? Do any criteria need to be explained or justified? Have any important criteria been overlooked?

3. Study the reasons the writer gives for the judgment. Tell the writer whether these reasons seem relevant and convincing. Can you think of any other appropriate reasons?

4. Look closely at the way each reason is developed. What evidence does the writer provide? Not all reasons must be fully developed—some may only be listed—but all of them must be supported with evidence. Look then at the evidence—is it believable and authoritative?

5. Consider the order in which the reasons are given. Does one reason seem to lead logically to the next? Can you imagine a different order that might strengthen the argument?

6. Look at any comparisons in the draft. Is the basis for the comparison clear? Is it appropriate? Is it convincing? Can you think of any other comparisons that would help to support the evaluation?

7. Does the writer describe the subject adequately?

8. Describe the voice you hear in the essay. Is it consistent from start to finish? Does it seem appropriate for the intended readers?

9. Does the writer use any terms which may be unfamiliar to the intended readers? Are they defined adequately?

10. Consider the balance of the draft. Are the key features treated adequately? Is there too much description? Too little? Too many reasons? Not enough? Look to see if any such elements could use more or less emphasis, and advise the writer about specific changes.

11. Consider the effectiveness of the beginning. Does it engage your interest? If so, how? If not, how do you react? Can you suggest any alternative ways to open the essay?

12. Evaluate the ending. Is it graceful and satisfying? Can you suggest a different conclusion?

REVISING AND EDITING

Before you begin revising, you might want to look at the general advice on revising in Chapter 1. Then consider the following suggestions for revising evaluative essays.

Revising an evaluation Consider any advice you may have from other readers as you reread your draft. At this stage you should be most concerned with two things: the strength of your argument and the readability of your prose.

Revising to strengthen the argument

☐ Reconsider the criteria on which your evaluation is based. Are they clear, or do they need explaining? Are they all important, or are any trivial? Should you add any new criteria?

☐ Scrutinize your reasons. If you cannot improve a weak reason, drop it altogether.

☐ Examine all of your evidence. Have you provided enough evidence to support your reasons? Have you given too much evidence anywhere? Should you add any new facts or details?

☐ Consider the order of your reasons. Would some other order be more persuasive?

☐ Think about the presentation of your subject. Do you need to reduce or expand your description?

☐ Reread your evaluation with your readers in mind. Have you fully considered their experiences, prejudices, and expectations? How might they challenge your evaluation? Respond to counterarguments.

☐ Listen again to the voice in your paper. Should you modulate it to make it more authoritative, credible, trustworthy, consistent? Is it appropriate for your readers?

Revising for readability

☐ Consider your introduction. Is it engaging? Will it attract a reader's attention? Is it helpful? Does it forecast your plan? Should it?

☐ Look at all the cues and transitions you provide. Are they sufficient?

☐ Reconsider your conclusion. Is it sufficiently emphatic? Does it frame the essay? Do you want it to do so? Does it end your essay with a proper focus?

☐ Examine each sentence. Does it say what you want it to say? Does it state the obvious?

☐ Read to see how your writing flows. Do the sentences fit together gracefully? Should any sentences be broken up or be combined with another sentence?

Editing and proofreading As you revise a draft for the final time, you must sit down and edit it carefully. When you were drafting your essay, your main focus was on figuring out what you wished to say; usage and style were not your first priority. Now, however, you must take the time to find and correct any errors of mechanics, usage, punctuation, or style.

After editing the draft and typing or writing out your final copy, you must then proofread closely before submitting your essay to your instructor.

LEARNING FROM YOUR OWN WRITING PROCESS

Reflect now on the process you followed in writing this essay. Look over all your work—invention writing, draft, and revision. Think about the various problems you encountered choosing a subject or defining criteria or articulating reasons or finding evidence.

Study any changes you made between draft and revision and think about why you made them.

What are the strong points in your essay? What would you still like to improve?

A WRITER AT WORK

ANALYZING REASONS FOR AN EVALUATION

In planning an evaluation essay a writer must decide what reasons will be most convincing to readers. These reasons must be based on appropriate criteria, and at least some of them must be supported by factual evidence. In this section we will see how Geoffrey Clemmons analyzed the reasons he gives in his essay "The UK 600," printed earlier in this chapter on pages 215–16.

Following this chapter's Guide to Writing, Clemmons charted his criteria, reasons, and evidence in the form of a table as he was planning his essay evaluating the UK 600 night-diving light. Long before drafting, he analyzed this table in writing in order to see that his criteria were appropriate, his reasons sound, and his evidence sufficient. Here is his table.

CRITERIA	REASONS	EVIDENCE
Company reputation	The company is new but has a good reputation.	Just twelve years old. UK lights now outsell the former leaders.

CRITERIA	REASONS	EVIDENCE
		UK is a small company, very efficient. They concentrate on a limited number of products.
		They do good research on new products.
Price	UK 600 is competitively priced.	Prices for all brands are about the same. UK is better quality for that price—$39.95.
Design	Technical innovations such as beveled reflector and high-temp bulb add to performance at a low price.	Beveled reflectors and replaceable bulbs cut down on replacement costs for bulbs as opposed to sealed beams. Bevels distribute light more evenly. Better focus and intensity of light. Quartz bulb. Very bright for only 6 volts. Printed contact board. Light weight—43.5 ounces. Small and compact.
	The UK 600 is extremely durable.	ABS plastic body and Lexan lens are lighter than metal and resist corrosion. Lexan doesn't scratch much. Can't break it.
	Maintenance is minimal.	Replaceable bulbs cost about one-tenth as much as sealed beams. The only maintenance required is a rinse in fresh water and occasional silicon greasing. One seal, easy to get at.
Warranty	Extensive warranty coverage.	Dealer network handles warranty claims on the spot. All fragile parts are covered for up to one year. No mailing hassles.

After completing the table, Clemmons considered which reasons he should actually include in his essay. He decided that they were all good reasons backed by solid evidence and that they would be convincing to the readers he was addressing. After next analyzing each reason in writing, he considered all of the reasons together as a set. Together, these analyses helped him to test the appropriateness of each reason for his readers and the strength of the evidence supporting it, as well as the total effect of all the reasons.

Following is his written analysis.

Analyzing the reasons. Using the manufacturer's reputation as a rea- 1
son to support my judgment of the product is not essential but I consider it
important enough to warrant at least a brief mention. If I state at the beginning of the paper that the manufacturer has a good reputation, the reader
might be more inclined to believe the claims that I make about the product
later. I thought it was an appropriate part of the introduction instead of a main
reason.

Making a price comparison is almost always used in product reviews. Price 2
is probably the single most important factor for most people considering a
product. By comparing the UK 600 to other lights in the same price range, I
could show the reader that it stands out above the others. Maybe I should get
the exact prices of competing lights.

My descriptions of the UK 600's construction and technical innovations are 3
likely to be my most persuasive reasons. Since other lights in its class are
priced competitively, I will have to show that the light's construction sets it
above the others. I also have more first-hand experience with this reason than
with any of the others. Readers who are themselves divers will have to know
they can trust the light not to fail them. Is it reliable? Is it easy to carry? All
readers will want to know technical features.

Maintenance of the product is always one of the consumer's prime consid- 4
erations, so I think it deserves a few words. Maintenance of the UK 600 is simple and very inexpensive compared with other lights. At some time or another
the owner will have to replace a bulb or maybe a seal. Realizing this, Underwater Kinetics has made it a very easy and inexpensive process. This will be an
important reason because the light is expensive enough so that readers would
want to keep it a long time, rather than replace it like a cheap flashlight.

Considering the set of reasons. I think the set covers all the impor- 5
tant criteria: price, design, and the reputation of the company with its warranty and dealer network. Maintenance and warranty are closely related,
maybe not separate reasons, though I can see how they come from different
criteria. The strongest reasons are technical innovations, durability and safety,
and ease of maintenance. As reasons, they seem equal. But price is strong too.
Maybe price is not the same kind of reason as the others. If price is right, then
the others come into play. I'm not too sure about how to sequence the reasons—they all seem equally important. Maybe start with price and end with
maintenance. Evidence about company could come first, as part of introduction.

In both his draft and revision, Clemmons relied on his table of criteria,
reasons, and evidence and these analyses. The final revision shows us that
he did place the information about the reputation of the company and
price at the beginning of the essay. Notice how they provide a context
for his argument, which focuses on the criterion of design. Information
about the warranty is combined effectively with the discussion of maintenance.

Explaining Causes

☐ The national sales manager for the Vo-Tech Toy Company writes a report that attempts to explain the disappointing Christmas sales of the company's perennial best seller. For some unexplained reason, sales have declined after enjoying sharp increases over the previous five years. With limited time for research, the sales manager consults the business manager and then begins a telephone survey of company sales representatives and regional sales managers. Meanwhile, the business manager, an astute Texan, reads *The Wall Street Journal* and trade newsletters to see if there is an industry-wide trend to explain the decline. Their final report, which includes a graph showing the toy's sales history, attributes the decline to the immense popularity and increasing market share of two other toys: home computers and Cabbage Patch dolls. They flatly refuse to entertain the possibility that something is wrong with their toy, citing past sales as evidence of its acceptance in a cut-throat market.

☐ An American expert on international business writes a book about Japan's phenomenal postwar industrial success. She first argues that, despite what most Americans think, the Japanese do not enjoy an economic advantage of cheap labor. She also proves that aid from the Japanese government toward industrial reconstruction in the wake of the war cannot fully explain Japan's current success. Instead, she proposes that the continuing trend of Japan's achievement is best explained by the unusually efficient organization of businesses and by employee loyalty.

☐ In a midwestern city in the United States, a social worker writes a report that tries to explain the sudden rise in the number of pregnancies among unmarried teenagers. He does some research, interviewing teenagers, health-care professionals, and other social workers, and reads several recent articles on the same trend in other cities. His report dismisses several hypotheses, among them ignorance or fear of birth control on the part of the teenagers and desire to be on welfare. He argues instead for other causes, particularly the need of these women to have someone to care for and the fact that motherhood, for the majority, is a positive value in their community.

☐ A student in a communications course writes an essay outlining the reasons why people are spending more and more time in front of the TV. She considers three possible causes: the availability of cable TV, with its more elaborate and varied programming; prime-time mini-series and evening soap operas; and a downturn in the economy, which leads to people staying at home for relatively inexpensive entertainment. Based on her own TV-viewing experience and that of her family and friends (as well as an article in *TV Guide*), she attributes the trend mainly to the combination of cable TV and poor economic conditions. Because there has been no significant increase in either mini-series or evening soap operas, she eliminates this as a possible cause.

8

□ For his sociology class, a college student writes an essay explaining the increase in the number of divorces. To support his own analysis of the increase and to gather evidence, he reads several recent magazine articles and surveys classmates in order to see how many of their parents are divorced. The final paper first describes the trend briefly and then discusses three possible causes: the financial stresses of the late 1970s and early 1980s; the importance of the notion of "self-fulfillment" and its impact on marriage; and the post-1960s proclivity to question conventional values and norms. He concludes by noting that all these trends seem to have slowed in the mid-1980s but wonders whether this slowdown is only temporary.

We all quite naturally attempt to explain causes. Because we assume everything has a cause, we regularly ask "Why?" when we notice something new or unusual. Events or trends may catch us by surprise, but usually we can find a logical explanation.

Many things can be fully and satisfactorily explained. When children ask "Why is the sky blue in the day and black at night?" parents can attempt to provide definite answers. Science helps us answer questions like this. But there are other questions we can only answer tentatively: Why was Illinois defeated in the Rose Bowl? How did the United States become involved in Vietnam? Why is exercising increasingly popular? Events and trends such as these often have only possible explanations because we cannot design a scientific experiment to identify conclusively the actual cause. Declining SAT scores, for example, has been attributed to the rise in TV viewing among children. Though this is a plausible cause, we cannot know for certain that it is responsible for the drop in scores.

In this chapter you will write an essay arguing for the causes of a trend. A trend is a prevailing increase or decrease—in toy sales, divorce, whatever. You first need to show that the trend exists and then to propose some causes and argue for one or more as the best available explanation. You do not have to prove that your explanation is right, but you must convince readers that it is plausible.

READINGS

The readings that follow show several strategies writers use to establish the plausibility of their explanations. In the first selection, an explanation of the popularity of jogging, Carll Tucker considers several possible causes.

FEAR OF DEARTH
CARLL TUCKER

throdding

a place where something is kept in store

I hate jogging. Every dawn, as I thud around New York City's Central Park 1
reservoir, I am reminded of how much I hate it. It's so tedious. Some claim
jogging is thought conducive; others insist the scenery relieves the monotony.
For me, the pace is wrong for contemplation of either ideas or vistas. While
jogging, all I can think about is jogging—or nothing. One advantage of jogging around a reservoir is that there's no dry-shortcut home. *turning opposite direction*

to promote or assist

lack of interest
energy or spirit
languid (melancholy
attitude.

From the listless looks of some fellow trotters, I gather I am not alone in 2
my unenthusiasm: Bill-paying, it seems, would be about as diverting. Nonetheless, we continue to jog; more, we continue to *choose* to jog. From a
practically infinite array of opportunities, we select one that we don't enjoy
and can't wait to have done with. Why? *endless kind*

crutch to lean on or way
carrot - goal
slacken - loosen

For any trend, there are as many reasons as there are participants. This 3
person runs to lower his blood pressure. That person runs to escape the
telephone or a cranky spouse or a filthy household. Another person runs to
avoid doing anything else, to dodge a decision about how to lead his life or
a realization that his life is leading nowhere. Each of us has his carrot and
stick. In my case, the stick is my slackening physical condition, which keeps
me from beating opponents at tennis whom I overwhelmed two years ago.
My carrot is to win. *slow up; to make less active*

Beyond these disparate reasons, however, lies a deeper cause. It is no 4
accident that now, in the last third of the 20th century, personal fitness and
health have suddenly become a popular obsession. True, modern man likes
to feel good, but that hardly distinguishes him from his predecessors.

a narrow view of something

With zany myopia, economists like to claim that the deeper cause of 5
everything is economic. Delightfully, there seems no marketplace explanation
for jogging. True, jogging is cheap, but then not jogging is cheaper. And the
scant and skimpy equipment which jogging demands must make it a mar-
keter's least favored form of recreation.

Some scout-masterish philosophers argue that the appeal of jogging and 6
other body-maintenance programs is the discipline they afford. We live in a
world in which individuals have fewer and fewer obligations. The work week
has shrunk. Weekend worship is less compulsory. Technology gives us more
free time. Satisfactorily filling free time requires imagination and effort. Freedom is a wide and risky river; it can drown the person who does not know
how to swim across it. The more obligations one takes on, the more time
one occupies, the less threat freedom poses. Jogging can become an instant
obligation. For a portion of his day, the jogger is not his own man; he is
obedient to a regimen he has accepted.

Theologists may take the argument one step further. It is our modern 7
irreligion, our lack of confidence in any hereafter, that makes us anxious to
stretch our mortal stay as long as possible. We run, as the saying goes, for
our lives, hounded by the suspicion that these are the only lives we are likely
to enjoy.

a rising again into life, activity, or pro-minence

formal veneration WORSHIP. Religious beliefs & ritual;

All of these theorists seem to me more or less right. As the growth of cults and charismatic religions and the resurgence of enthusiasm for the military draft suggest, we do crave commitment. And who can doubt, watching so many middle-aged and older persons torturing themselves in the name of fitness, that we are unreconciled to death, more so perhaps than any generation in modern memory? 8

an inadequate supply. ——→ LACK

But I have a hunch there's a further explanation of our obsession with exercise. I suspect that what motivates us even more than a fear of death is a fear of dearth. Our era is the first to anticipate the eventual depletion of all natural resources. We see wilderness shrinking; rivers losing their capacity to sustain life; the air, even the stratosphere, being loaded with potentially deadly junk. We see the irreplaceable being squandered, and in the depths of our consciousness we are fearful that we are creating an uninhabitable world. We feel more or less helpless and yet, at the same time, desirous to protect what resources we can. We recycle soda bottles and restore old buildings and protect our nearest natural resource—our physical health—in the almost superstitious hope that such small gestures will help save an earth that we are blighting. Jogging becomes a sort of penance for our sins of gluttony, greed, and waste. Like a hairshirt or a bed of nails, the more one hates it, the more virtuous it makes one feel. 9

very high or highest region on a graded level

Something that's impaired or destroys

That is why *we* jog. Why *I* jog is to win at tennis. 10

Questions for analysis

1. If you find Tucker's explanation for the popularity of jogging convincing, how would you account for its effectiveness? If you find it unconvincing, how would you criticize it?

2. By opening the essay autobiographically, Tucker presents himself directly to his readers. Describe the impression you have of him. Does this beginning make his analysis more or less convincing? What is its effect on you as one particular reader?

3. Essays about trends usually begin by demonstrating that the trend exists. Why do you suppose Tucker does not bother to do this?

4. In paragraph 9, Tucker talks about our squandering of natural resources. How does he connect this discussion to his larger topic, jogging? How convincing do you find the causal connection he makes?

5. Tucker considers several possible causes for the popularity of jogging. Review each one, deciding whether he accepts it or rejects it. What does he gain by considering so many causes when he favors just one?

6. Why do you think Tucker orders the causes as he does? Consider whether a different order would be as effective or more effective.

7. Imagine you were asked to analyze the causes of a current trend in which you or your friends have a part. What would you choose to write about? What causes would you consider to explain the trend?

Tucker makes a point of distinguishing between "disparate" causes, those which explain an individual's decision to jog, and "deeper" causes, those which explain why many people decide to do so. Since a trend by definition indicates a general rather than an individual pattern, it is necessary to distinguish between individual, idiosyncratic causes and general, widespread, or underlying causes.

We might also think of this distinction in terms of apparent and hidden causes: by Tucker's analysis, people apparently run for diversion and for health, but actually they run out of guilt. Or we might think of it in terms of obvious causes and deep causes. In your own essay explaining a trend, you will want to consider hidden or deep causes as well as apparent or obvious ones.

Tucker discusses several possible general causes, including economic, philosophical, and theological ones. He refuses, however, to consider the possibility that the popular "obsession" with jogging has anything to do with concern for fitness and health. In rejecting this possibility, he points out that something that has not itself changed cannot be used to explain a change in something else. Since the desire for physical fitness, according to Tucker, has been with us constantly, it cannot explain this recent jogging fad. Simply put: a constant cannot cause a change. If Tucker were to offer the desire for fitness as a possible cause (and you might think he should), he would have to argue that it has intensified in recent times and that this intensification is expressed in the current jogging fad.

Tucker's thesis is stated in paragraph 9: jogging has increased because so many people feel guilty for destroying the planet and superstitiously believe that by improving their own health they might help save the planet. In an essay explaining trends, the thesis identifies both the trend and the main reason or reasons the writer offers as explanation. Usually these are brought together only at the end of the essay.

Tucker's analysis has a light—even humorous—tone. From the opening sentence it is clear that the essay will be neither dry nor impersonal. As we see him "thudding" around the reservoir, we get a definite comical impression of him and indeed of all joggers.

Whereas Tucker takes neither himself nor the trend he analyzes too seriously, the next two writers strike a very earnest note. Both are writing in a more academic context and although they are addressing the general reader, they make no special effort, as Tucker does, to amuse or even entertain their readers. Causal explanations, particularly those written for academic purposes, are typically fairly straightforward. The challenge is to make them interesting while convincing readers of your seriousness.

This next essay is from Robert Jastrow's book *Until the Sun Dies*. Jastrow is an astronomer who has taught at Columbia and at Dartmouth and now directs the Goddard Institute for Space Studies of the National Aeronautics and Space Administration.

MAN OF WISDOM
ROBERT JASTROW

Starting about one million years ago, the fossil record shows an accelerating growth of the human brain. It expanded at first at the rate of one cubic inch[1] of additional gray matter every hundred thousand years; then the growth rate doubled; it doubled again; and finally it doubled once more. Five hundred thousand years ago the rate of growth hit its peak. At that time the brain was expanding at a phenomenal rate of ten cubic inches every hundred thousand years. No other organ in the history of life is known to have grown as fast at this.[2]

What pressures generated the explosive growth of the human brain? A change of climate that set in about two million years ago may supply that part of the answer. At that time the world began its descent into a great Ice Age, the first to afflict the planet in hundreds of millions of years. The trend toward colder weather set in slowly at first, but after a million years patches of ice began to form in the north. The ice patches thickened into glaciers as more snow fell, and then the glaciers merged into great sheets of ice, as much as two miles thick. When the ice sheets reached their maximum extent, they covered two-thirds of the North American continent, all of Britain and a large part of Europe. Many mountain ranges were buried entirely. So much water was locked up on the land in the form of ice that the level of the earth's oceans dropped by three hundred feet.

These events coincided precisely with the period of most rapid expansion of the human brain. Is the coincidence significant, or is it happenstance?

The story of human migrations in the last million years provides a clue to the answer. At the beginning of the Ice Age Homo [man] lived near the equator, where the climate was mild and pleasant. Later he moved northward. From his birthplace in Africa[3] he migrated up across the Arabian peninsula and then turned to the north and west into Europe, as well as eastward into Asia.

When these early migrations took place, the ice was still confined to the lands in the far north; but eight hundred thousand years ago, when man was already established in the temperate latitudes, the ice moved southward until it covered large parts of Europe and Asia. Now, for the first time, men encountered the bone-chilling blasts of freezing winds that blew off the cakes of ice to the north. The climate in southern Europe had a Siberian harshness then, and summers were nearly as cold as European winters are today.

In those difficult times, the traits of resourcefulness and ingenuity must have been of premium value. Which individual first thought of stripping the pelt from the slaughtered beast to wrap around his shivering limbs? Only by such inventive flights of the imagination could the naked animal survive a harsh climate. In every generation, the individuals endowed with the attributes of strength, courage, and improvisation were the ones more likely to survive the rigors of the Ice Age; those who were less resourceful, and lacked the vision of their fellows, fell victims to the climate and their numbers were reduced.

The Ice Age winter was the most devastating challenge that Homo had ever faced. He was naked and defenseless against the cold, as the little mammals had been defenseless against the dinosaurs one hundred million years ago. Vulnerable to the pressures of a hostile world, both animals were forced to live by their wits; and both became, in their time, the brainiest animals of the day. 7

The tool-making industry of early man also stimulated the growth of the brain. The possession of a good brain had been one of the factors that enabled Homo to make tools at the start. But the use of tools became, in turn, a driving force toward the evolution of an even better brain. The characteristics of good memory, foresight, and innovativeness that were needed for tool-making varied in strength from one individual to another. Those who possessed them in the greatest degree were the practical heroes of their day; they were likely to survive and prosper, while the individuals who lacked them were more likely to succumb to the pressures of the environment. Again these circumstances pruned the human stock, expanding the centers of the brain in which past experiences were recorded, future actions were contemplated, and new ideas were conceived. As a result, from generation to generation the brain grew larger. 8

The evolution of speech may have been the most important factor of all. When early man mastered the loom of language, his progress accelerated dramatically. Through the spoken word a new invention in tool-making, for example, could be communicated to everyone; in this way the innovativeness of the individual enhanced the survival prospects of his fellows, and the creative strength of one became the strength of all. More important, through language the ideas of one generation could be passed on to the next, so that each generation inherited not only the genes of its ancestors but also their collective wisdom, transmitted through the magic of speech. 9

A million years ago, when this magic was not yet perfected, and language was a cruder art, those bands of men who possessed the new gift in the highest degree were strongly favored in the struggle for existence. But the fabric of speech is woven out of many threads. The physical attributes of a voice box, lips, and tongue were among the necessary traits; but a good brain was also essential, to frame an abstract thought or represent an object by a word. 10

Now the law of the survival of the fittest began to work on the population of early men. Steadily, the physical apparatus for speech improved. At the same time, the centers of the brain devoted to speech grew in size and complexity, and in the course of many generations the whole brain grew with them. Once more, as with the use of tools, reciprocal forces came into play in which speech stimulated better brains, and brains improved the art of speech, and the curve of brain growth spiraled upward. 11

Which factor played the most important role in the evolution of human 12 intelligence? Was it the pressure of the Ice-Age climate? Or tools? Or language? No one can tell; all worked together, through Darwin's law of natural selection, to produce the dramatic increase in the size of the brain that has been recorded in the fossil record in the last million years. The brain reached its present size about one hundred thousand years ago, and its growth ceased. Man's body had been shaped into its modern form several hundred thousand years before that. Now brain and body were complete. Together they made a new and marvelous creature, charged with power, intelligence, and creative energy. His wits had been honed by the fight against hunger, cold, and the natural enemy; his form had been molded in the crucible of adversity. In the annals of anthropology his arrival is celebrated by a change in name, from Homo erectus—the Man who stands erect—to Homo sapiens   the Man of wisdom.

Notes

[1] One cubic inch is a heaping tablespoonful. [Author's footnote.]
[2] If the brain had continued to expand at the same rate, men would be far brainier today than they actually are. But after several hundred thousand years of very rapid growth the expansion of the brain slowed down and in the last one hundred thousand years it has not changed in size at all. [Author's footnote.]
[3] Until recently, the consensus among anthropologists placed the origin of man in Africa. However, some recent evidence suggests that Asia may have been his birthplace. [Author's footnote.]

Questions for analysis

1. How convincing do you find Jastrow's argument? Consider your first impression and then evaluate the argument's plausibility.

2. How does Jastrow demonstrate that brain size has actually increased? What kinds of anthropological research does his evidence seem to be based on?

3. Jastrow argues for three possible causes of increasing brain size. What are these causes? Why do you think he presents them in the order he does?

4. Why do you suppose Jastrow does not consider any alternative causes or refute any counterarguments?

5. Which of the three causes are both causes *and* results of increasing brain size? How is this possible? What problems do you suppose writers of causal explanations face when they propose causes which are also results?

6. Narrative plays an important part in Jastrow's argument. Look for the various places where Jastrow uses narration. What role does each narrative play in the essay? Why is this an especially useful strategy in this essay?

7. In paragraphs 2, 3, 6, and 12, Jastrow asks questions. What function do these questions serve in the essay? How do they contribute to your understanding of the analysis?

8. Think of a completed prehistoric or historic trend to write about—evolutionary, social, political, economic, artistic, agricultural, recreational. It could be something from any century, a trend of many years or just a few years—the rise of nationalism, the decline of Federalism, Cubism. Name several plausible causes of this trend.

Jastrow's analysis is based on three kinds of causes: remote causes, immediate causes, and perpetuating causes. Man's move from his birthplace near the equator into the northern regions of the planet is a remote, or background, cause; the Ice Age is the immediate, or precipitating, cause; and man's invention of tools and use of language are both perpetuating causes.

The next selection is from a book by Victor Fuchs, *How We Live: An Economic Perspective on Americans from Birth to Death*. A professor of economics at Stanford, Fuchs has for many years been a research associate at the National Bureau of Economic Research. In recognition of his research and writing he has been elected Fellow of the American Academy of Arts and Sciences.

The tone of Fuchs's essay is even more serious than Jastrow's. He does not let his personality show. His essay is not only impersonal, it is drily factual; it seems to move slowly, but such slowness is actually a tribute to the rigor of Fuchs's careful reasoning and attention to detail.

As you read, pay attention to both the causes Fuchs rejects and the ones he proposes to explain the recent increase in suicides among young people.

SUICIDE AMONG YOUNG PEOPLE
VICTOR FUCHS

Although the vigor and vitality of most young people are the envy of their elders, a significant range of serious health problems are present at ages 15–24, including venereal disease, alcoholism, and drug abuse. Moreover, a large number of adolescents and youth are making themselves vulnerable to future health problems through cigarette smoking, poor diet, and inadequate exercise (Institute of Medicine 1978). One of the most disturbing trends is rising mortality among youth at a time when death rates at all other ages are declining rapidly. Male death rates at ages 15–19 and 20–24 were 12 percent *higher* in 1977 than in 1960, while mortality at other ages *declined* an average of 12 percent. A large differential in mortality trends by age is also evident for women. The deaths of young people take a tremendous emotional toll and are also particularly costly because these men and women are at the threshold of productive lives during which they and society could realize a return on the investment that has been made in them.

The principal reason for the <u>divergent</u> trends in mortality by age is the increase in self-destructive behavior by young men and women (see the tabulation below). <u>Among young men, suicide and motor vehicle accidents now</u> account for half of all deaths, <u>and among women for well over 40 percent</u>. More youth die from suicide alone than from cancer, cardiovascular disease, diabetes, pneumonia, and influenza combined. The rising death rate from homicide also contributes to the rising death rate among the young. Homicide rates have approximately doubled at most ages, but because it is a relatively more important cause of death among the young, this doubling has had more of an impact on their overall rate. <u>The high homicide rate among non-white men is particularly shocking, averaging about 50 per year per hundred thousand at ages 15–19 and over 100 per hundred thousand at ages 20–24</u>. These rates imply that almost one out of every 100 black youths who turn 15 becomes a homicide victim before the age of 25! Apart from violent deaths, the trends in mortality of young men and women have been as favorable as at older ages.

	Percent change in age-sex-specific death rates, 1960 to 1977	
	Ages 15–24	Ages 25 and over
Suicide	145	6
Motor vehicle accidents	25	−15
Homicide	113	83
All other causes	−22	−21

Why did suicide rates among young people increase so rapidly in the 1960s and 1970s? It is much easier to rule out answers to this question than to find ones that will withstand critical examination. For instance, it is highly unlikely that the trend is a result of differences in the reporting of suicides, although reporting practices do vary considerably over time and in different areas. Changes in reporting, however, would affect the suicide rate at all ages, and there was no comparable increase at other stages of life. The emotional trauma of the Vietnam War was felt more keenly by young people and this may have contributed to the increase in suicides, but there are two problems with this explanation. First, after the war ended the suicide rate among young people kept on rising, rather than falling back to prewar levels (see Figure 8.1). Second, suicide rates at ages 15–24 in Canada and Sweden have been rising as rapidly and are as high as in the United States. Neither country was much affected by the Vietnam War.

Suicides have been blamed on deteriorating economic conditions, but 4
Figure 8.1 shows that the rate has been rising in good times as well as bad;
the long-term trend is much stronger than any response to business cycle
fluctuations. Furthermore, the suicide level is slightly higher among white
than nonwhite youth and the rate of increase has been as rapid for whites
as for nonwhites, despite the large race differentials in youth employment.
One of the more mischievous arguments currently in vogue is that the problems of children and youth are the result of high unemployment and that
their solution lies in better macroeconomic policies. Of course low unemployment is better than high, and price stability is preferable to inflation, but
anyone who believes that the increases in suicides among youth, births to
unwed mothers, juvenile crime, and one-parent homes are primarily the result
of macroeconomic conditions is ignoring readily available evidence. All these
problems were increasing particularly rapidly during the second half of the

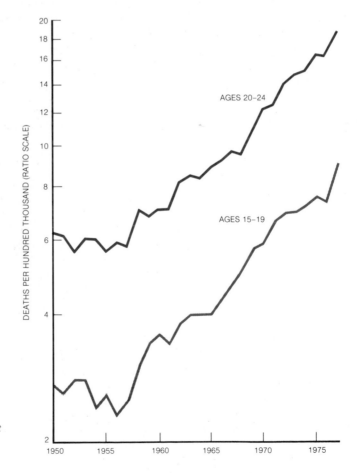

FIGURE 8.1.
Suicide rates among youth,
1950–1977
Sources: U.S. Bureau of the Cen-
sus, *Vital Statistics of the United
States,* 1950–1977; idem, *Current
Population Reports,* series P-25,
nos. 310, 519, 721, and 870.

1960s, when the unemployment rate averaged 3.8 percent and economic growth was extremely rapid.

Some mental health experts attribute the increases in suicides among the young to the rapid changes in the American family. A study at Bellevue Hospital in New York City of 102 teenagers who attempted suicide showed that only one-third of them lived with both parents (*Newsweek,* August 28, 1978, p. 74). Parents may be failing to provide enough structure and security for children either because they are not present or because they are preoccupied with their own lives and careers, or simply because they are too permissive. In a review of psychosocial literature on adolescence, Elder (1975) concludes: "Adolescents who fail to receive guidance, affection, and concern from parents—whether by parental inattention or absence—are likely to rely heavily on peers for emotional gratification, advice, and companionship, *to anticipate a relatively unrewarding future,* and to engage in antisocial activities" (italics added). On the other hand, some experts contend that too many demands and the setting of unrealistic standards by parents also predispose young people toward suicide.

Some evidence of a relation between family background and suicide appears in a long-term longitudinal study of fifty thousand male students of Harvard University and the University of Pennsylvania that compared the characteristics of 381 men who eventually committed suicide with a set of living control subjects randomly chosen from the same school and year as the suicides (Paffenbarger, King, and Wing 1969). One of the strongest results was a positive relation between suicide and loss of father. At the time of the original interview (average age 18) the future suicides were more likely than the controls to have a deceased father (12.4 percent versus 8.1 percent) or to have parents who had separated (12.6 percent versus 8.9 percent). The difference in paternal loss through death or separation was statistically significant at a high level of confidence. The future suicides also differed from the controls by having a larger percentage of fathers who were college-educated (69.1 percent versus 56.6 percent) and who were professionals (48.8 percent versus 38.4 percent). Loss of mother did not differ between the suicides and the controls.

It must be emphasized that the rapid increase in suicide rates among youth is unique to that age group—there is nothing comparable at other ages. By contrast, the doubling of death rates from homicide at young ages reflects a general increase in violent crime that has affected all age groups, although not in exactly equal degree.

For some problems, such as the sharp increase in suicides, no simple or even moderately complex public policy solution is in the offing. Young people may be succumbing to what Abraham Maslow (1959) forecast as the ultimate disease of our time—"valuelessness." The rise in suicides and other self-destructive behavior such as motor vehicle accidents and drug abuse may be the result of weakening family structures and the absence of fathers, as suggested by the study of Harvard University and University of Pennsylvania students. We can't be sure of the cause, but if it's along the lines suggested above, the challenge to public policy is staggering.

References

Elder, Glen H., Jr. 1975. Adolescence in the life cycle: An introduction. In *Adolescence in the life cycle: Psychological change and social context,* ed. Sigmund E. Dragastin and Glen H. Elder, Jr. New York: Halsted-Wiley.

Institute of Medicine. 1978. *Adolescent behavior and health.* Washington, D.C.: National Academy of Sciences.

Maslow, Abraham H. 1959. *New knowledge in human values.* New York: Harper and Brothers.

Paffenbarger, Ralph S. Jr.; Stanley H. King; and Alvin L. Wing. 1969. Characteristics in youth that predispose to suicide and accidental death in later life. *American Journal of Public Health* 59 (June): 900–908.

Questions for analysis

1. What causes does Fuchs propose to explain the increasing number of suicides among young people?

2. What kind of evidence does Fuchs offer for his proposed causes? How convincing do you find his argument?

3. In "ruling out answers" to his question at the beginning of paragraph 3, Fuchs rejects alternatives to his own proposed causes. List the alternative causes he rejects in paragraphs 3 and 4. Why do you think he devotes so much space to considering alternatives that he then rejects? Does this strategy influence your evaluation of his explanation? How?

4. How does Fuchs demonstrate that there is a trend of increased suicide among young people? What role do the table and figure play? Has he convinced you that the trend actually exists?

5. Fuchs uses published research both to demonstrate the trend and to argue for its causes. Review his references to such research and decide what contribution each reference makes to the essay.

6. In paragraph 7, Fuchs reiterates an alternative cause. Why do you think he does this? What effect does this strategy have on your evaluation of his argument?

7. How does Fuchs conclude his essay? Does he frame it by repeating some element of the beginning in the ending? How successful do you find his ending? Can you suggest a more effective conclusion?

8. Imagine you had the opportunity to write about some recent trend in "how we live" (to borrow the title of the book from which this essay was taken). What important trends have caught your attention? Choose one. How would you demonstrate that the trend really exists? What causes would you suggest?

Fuchs's essay is easy to read because it follows a simple plan:

beginning
    context for suicide trend
    demonstration of suicide trend
consideration and rejection of alternative causes
argument for proposed causes
    parental failure
    loss of father
reiteration of why the most likely alternative cause should be rejected
ending

Essays explaining trends nearly always begin by demonstrating the trend and then move on to the causes. The challenge in planning such an essay is in ordering the causes to make the most convincing argument. Another decision that must be made is where to take up alternative causes.

Fuchs's essay provides causal analysis typical of the social sciences. You will encounter such analysis often in the readings you will be required to do as a college student as well as in the social or political analysis found on the editorial pages of newspapers and magazines. You may very well be asked to write a causal analysis yourself, either as an essay exam or as a term paper.

Writing about trends involving people and groups usually demands the kind of careful arguments Fuchs presents. It is the sort of argumentative writing we rely on for help making personal and social-policy decisions when there is no unarguable scientific evidence to tell us what to do. Such analysis helps us to consider plausible arguments, decide which is the best one, and then decide what to do.

This next essay, written by college freshman Karen Selditz, analyzes the preponderance of radio/cassette headsets in public places. It is typical of the kind of trend essay you might write, discussing a very recent trend that can be demonstrated only from personal observation, without the benefit of library research.

Notice, however, how Selditz searches for the deeper causes that underlie the trend she analyzes.

HEADPHONES
KAREN SELDITZ

Every place I go and everywhere I look, I see people wearing headphones. 1
I see pocket-size high-fidelity radio and cassette headsets in libraries, lecture halls, airplanes, and grocery stores. "Modern and featherlight" headphones have become the height of fashion.

Take my sister Jane, for example. Always up on the latest innovation in 2 music, she was quick to purchase a miniature AM-FM/cassette headset. One time we were in the car on our way to go skiing, and she actually made us turn around because she had forgotten it. "I love listening to music while I ski," she confessed. "It gives me something to think about. And besides, I just wouldn't look as with it without headphones. My other sister, Molly, says she uses Jane's cassette player for the one-mile walk to junior high because she would be bored without it. At the suggestion of a friend, I decided to experiment with one while studying. At this very moment I sit working in the library, listening to Prince. My friend Brian says he wears his headset in self-defense, claiming it allows him to tune out the "teeny-bopper" music that he is otherwise subjected to at the beach. He doesn't have to ask people to turn down their music, he doesn't have to hear their music, and he isn't bothering anyone who might not like his music.

As I began examining all these reasons people give for listening to head- 3 sets in public places, one thing seemed clear: Jane would not wear hers on the ski slopes, Molly wouldn't wear hers on the way to school, Brian wouldn't wear his at the beach, others wouldn't wear theirs at home or at school, and I certainly wouldn't wear one in the library if it were not so stylish to do so. An interesting innovation catches people's attention. The price is right, and so most people can afford one. Soon everybody wants one. This is the way a fad is born, but it's also what sustains the early development of a lasting trend. Everyone likes new things, and all people want to be up on the newest trends. They embrace the latest styles because they don't want to seem old-fashioned, out-of-date, or not "with it."

As with any increase in the use of new gadgets, be they radio or cassette 4 headsets, video games, or word processors, we can point to technological innovations as a cause. But this seems too easy and too obvious. Certainly we wouldn't be seeing so many portable radio and cassette players now if someone hadn't designed the first one and someone else hadn't figured out how to put high fidelity into lightweight headphones. And those break-throughs wouldn't have been possible without the new electronics and the miniaturization of gadgets in general. And I might not even be aware of this trend if a lot of other important events hadn't taken place. For example, the need for electronics by the military and the space program greatly accelerated the development of miniaturized components for weapons and spacecraft. The need here was so great that mass production of such components im-mediately reduced their price. Competition from the Japanese and among such giant American companies as IBM and Apple Computer also pushed prices down. Prices went even lower as more and more American manufac-turers opened factories in Taiwan or Hong Kong or Singapore or the Philip-pines, where labor was cheaper. If all of this hadn't happened I wouldn't be listening all alone to my own music right now in a library full of people while I draft this essay. However, availability and affordability—the direct result of technological innovation and mass production—should not really be seen as the causes of a trend in the use of a new gadget, at least not as the main causes. They make the trend possible (and so are necessary causes) and they sustain it, but they don't really explain it. We have to look deeper to find the true causes of this particular trend. We especially have to think about what makes people buy new gadgets in the first place.

Even though I've argued that the increasing use of portable headsets can be explained by people's need to conform and be up-to-date, I think another possible cause is their desire to be anonymous and isolated in increasingly complicated and even dangerous social situations. These days people want to be left alone in public. They don't want to be approached or spoken to. With your headphones on, others leave you alone, and you wouldn't hear them even if they said something to you. If you are wearing headphones and reading a paperback novel, people don't expect you to say anything to them, even if you bump into them on a crowded sidewalk or stand alone with them in an elevator.

Still another possible explanation is that people want to numb themselves to experience and to life. They want to avoid reflecting on what's happening to them or thinking about what's going on in the world at large. They don't want to think. They may even be afraid of their own creative urges, thinking them weird or dangerous. They would rather not notice changes in their environment or pay attention to surprising events or to other people. With their headphones on and the volume on ten, they can move through the world in time with nothing but safely canned sounds reverberating between their ears.

These are the causes—a desire to be fashionable, a need for protection in public, and a fear of life experience—which can explain why people have fallen for radio or cassette headsets. Certainly everyone loves music—but all the time, every waking hour, at home and in public? It is reasonable to assume some saturation point for musical intake. Why, then, do so many people seem to be going beyond this point, pumping in the musical sounds while out and around in the world? Only, I think, for some of the deeper reasons I've proposed in this essay. There must be still other possible reasons. I'd love to talk about them with headset owners—that is, if they'll turn off the music long enough to talk.

Questions for analysis

1. Does Selditz succeed in demonstrating that the trend actually exists? If so, how does she make her case? If not, how might she have demonstrated it better?

2. What causes does Selditz propose to explain the trend? How convincing do you find her explanation?

3. What role does paragraph 4 play in the essay as a whole?

4. Write out a quick scratch outline of Selditz's essay. How effective do you find her plan? How might it be improved? (See Chapter 18: Invention and Inquiry for guidelines to making a scratch outline.)

5. How does the essay begin and end? Does the end frame the essay by referring back to the beginning? How effective do you find her beginning and ending?

6. Look at the transition sentences that begin each paragraph. How exactly does each one cue readers to a new topic?

7. What would you say Selditz's purpose is? What kind of readers do you think she is writing for? Describe the voice she chooses for addressing these readers—how would you characterize her attitude toward her readers and her topic?

8. What recent trend would you be interested in analyzing? How would you demonstrate that the trend exists? What causes would you suggest to explain the trend?

Selditz brings together the statement of the trend and its proposed causes in a thesis statement at the end of her essay. This thesis is presented concisely in the first sentence of paragraph 7.

Notice that Selditz makes an important distinction that you will have to make when choosing a topic for an essay explaining a trend: between a *fad* and a *trend*. A fad is more temporary and less significant than a trend, usually disappearing in just a few months. Changes in clothing and dancing styles are good examples of fads. Trends, by contrast, are continuing, steady changes over long periods of time, at least over a few years. Both portable headsets and jogging have lasted long enough to be considered trends, though at first they might have looked as if they would be short-lived fads. You can write about trends which are completed (such as an increase in brain size) or continuing (such as an increase in youth suicides).

Notice that Selditz considers both obvious and deeper causes of the trend she analyzes and bases her explanation on the deeper ones. She claims that the obvious cause of technological advancement is a necessary but not sufficient cause of the increasing use of Walkman-type devices. The trend could not have begun without technological innovation, but technology is an insufficient explanation for the trend. To be sufficient, an explanation for the popularity of any new gadget requires an analysis of people's motives for buying it.

The final essay, written by college freshman Kim Dartnell, looks at the plight of homeless American women. It illustrates how a writer can use library research to analyze a trend. In her essay Dartnell documents the trend and defines its special characteristics.

WHERE WILL THEY SLEEP TONIGHT?

KIM DARTNELL

On January 21, 1982, in New York City, Rebecca Smith died of hypo- 1 thermia, after living for five months in a cardboard box. Rebecca was one of a family of thirteen children from a rural town in Virginia. After graduating from high school and giving birth to a daughter, she spent ten years in mental institutions, where she underwent involuntary shock treatment for schizophrenia. It was when she was released to her sister's custody that Rebecca began wandering the streets of New York, living from day to day. Many New York City social workers tried unsuccessfully to persuade her to go into a city shelter. Rebecca died only a few hours before she was scheduled to be placed into protective custody. Rebecca Smith's story is all too typical. Rebecca herself, however, was anything but a typical homeless woman; not only did she graduate from high school, but she was the valedictorian of her class (Hombs and Snyder, 1982, p. 56).

Rebecca Smith is one of an increasing number of homeless women in 2 America. Vagrant men have always been a noticeable problem in American cities, and their numbers have increased in the 1980s. Vagrancy among women is a relatively new problem of any size, however. In 1979, New York City had one public shelter for homeless women. By 1983 it had four. Los Angeles has just recently increased the number of beds available to its skid-row homeless women (Stoner, 1983, p. 571). Even smaller communities have noticed an increase in homeless women. It is impossible to know the number of homeless women or the extent of their increase in the 1980s, but everyone who has studied the problem agrees that it is serious and that it is getting worse (Hombs and Snyder, 1982, p. 10; Stoner, 1984, p. 3).

Who are these women? Over half of all homeless women are under the 3 age of forty. Forty-four percent are black, forty percent white. The statistics for homeless men are about the same (Stoner, 1983, p. 570). There are several ways homeless women cope with their dangerous lifestyle. To avoid notice, especially by the police, some women will have one set of nice clothes that they wash often. They will shower in shelters or YWCA's and try to keep their hairstyle close to the latest fashions. An extreme is the small number of women who actually sleep on park benches, sitting up, to avoid wrinkling their clothes. On the other end of the spectrum is the more noticeable "bag lady," who will purposely maintain an offensive appearance and body odor to protect herself from rape or robbery. These women are almost always unemployed and poorly educated. "Homeless women do not choose their circumstances. They are victims of forces over which they have lost control" (Stoner, 1983, pp. 568, 569).

The question is, why has there been such an increase in the number of 4 vagrant American women? There are several causes of this trend. For one thing, more and more women are leaving their families because of abuse. It is unclear whether this increase is due to an actual increase of abuse in American families, or whether it results from the fact that it is easier and more socially acceptable for a woman to be on her own today. Once on her own, however, the woman all too often finds it difficult to support herself. A more substantial reason is the fact that social programs for battered women have been severely cut back, leaving victims of rape, incest, and other physical abuse nowhere else to go. To take one example, the Christian Housing Facility, a private organization in Orange County, California, that provides food, shelter, and counseling to abused families, sheltered 1,536 people in 1981, a 300-percent increase from the year before (Stoner, 1983, p. 573).

Evictions and illegal lockouts force some women onto the streets. Social welfare cutbacks, unemployment, and desertion all result in a loss of income. Once a woman cannot pay her rent, she is likely to be evicted, often without notice. 5

Another problem is a lack of inexpensive housing. Of today's homeless women, over fifty percent lived in single rooms before they became vagrants. Many of the buildings containing single-room dwellings or cheap apartments have been torn down to make way for land renovation. Hotels are being offered new tax incentives that make it economically unfeasible to maintain inexpensive single rooms. This is obviously a serious problem, one that sends many women out onto the streets every year. 6

Alcoholism has been cited as a major reason for the increase in the number of homeless women. I don't feel this is a major contributing factor, however. First, there hasn't been a significant general increase in alcoholism to parallel the rise in homeless women; second, alcoholism occurs at all levels of financial status, from the executive to the homeless. Rather, I would like to suggest that alcoholism is a result of homelessness, not the cause. 7

Probably the biggest single factor in the rising numbers of homeless women is the deinstitutionalization of the mentally ill. One study estimated that ninety percent of all vagrant women may be mentally ill (Stoner, 1983, p. 567), as was the case with Rebecca Smith. The last few years have seen an avalanche in the number of mental patients released. Between 1955 and 1980 the numbers of patients in mental institutions dropped by 75 percent, from about 560,000 to about 140,000. There are several reasons for this. New psychotonic drugs can now "cure" patients with mild disturbances. Expanded legal rights for patients lead to early release from asylums. Government-funded services such as Medicare allow some patients to be released into nursing or boarding homes. The problem is that many of these women have really not known any life outside the hospital and suddenly find themselves thrust out into an unreceptive world, simply because they present no threat to society, or are "unresponsive to treatment." Very few of them are ever referred to community mental health centers. Instead, many of them go straight out on the streets. They may live with family or in some other inexpensive housing, but sooner or later they are likely to end up in the streets. And once homeless, all funding stops, as someone without an address can't receive any benefits from the government. 8

Although deinstitutionalization seems to have been the biggest factor in the increase in vagrant women, there is some evidence that the main cause 9 is economic. In 1981, 3,500,000 Americans were living below the poverty line. Unemployment hit 10.1 percent in 1982, the highest it has been since 1940. Yet, that same year saw $2.35 billion cut from food-stamp programs. Reductions in Aid to Families with Dependent Children (AFDC) hit women particularly hard because four out of five AFDC families are headed by women, two thirds of whom have not graduated from high school. (All data are from Hombs and Snyder, 1982.) Coupled with inflation, recession, unemployment, and loss of other welfare benefits, these cuts have effectively forced many women into homelessness, and can be expected to continue to do so at a greater rate in the years to come.

The United States may be one of the world's most prosperous nations, but for Rebecca Smith and others like her, the American Dream is far from being fulfilled. 10

References

Stoner, M. R. (1983). The plight of homeless women. *Social Service Review, 57,* 565–581.

Stoner, M. R. (1984). An analysis of public and private sector provisions for homeless people. *The Urban and Social Change Review, 17.*

Hombs, M. E., and Snyder, M. (1982). *Homelessness in America.* Washington, D.C.: Community for Creative Non-Violence.

Questions for analysis

1. How convincing do you find Dartnell's explanation for the increasing numbers of homeless women? If you find it convincing, how would you explain its effectiveness?

2. What is her purpose in this essay? What does she seem to assume about her readers?

3. How does she demonstrate that the trend actually exists?

4. Write out a brief scratch outline of this essay. How does she order her proposed causes? What advantages or disadvantages do you see in this order? (See Chapter 18: Invention and Inquiry for discussion about making scratch outlines.)

5. How does she begin and end her essay? Can you suggest a different way to begin or end?

6. Think of a troubling social trend you might write about. How would you demonstrate its existence, and what causes would you propose to explain it?

Dartnell's essay illustrates how important a small amount of research can be for an essay explaining the causes of a social trend. She uses only three sources, all located on one visit to the library, which provide adequate documentation both for the trend and her proposed causes.

BASIC FEATURES OF ESSAYS EXPLAINING CAUSES

Essays that explain the causes of a trend typically include three basic features: a presentation of the trend, a convincing causal argument, and a reasonable, authoritative voice.

A presentation of the trend

In an essay about a trend a writer's first task is to demonstrate that the trend exists. Sometimes it will be obvious, as is the case with jogging and radio/cassette headsets. Even such obvious trends can be introduced engagingly, however, as Karen Selditz proves with the anecdotes she tells to open her essay. She uses these anecdotes as evidence of how widespread the trend is and how varied the motives are for participating in it.

With a trend that is less obvious, the writer must present an argument with evidence that it exists. Notice how Victor Fuchs very carefully documents the increase in youth suicides, presenting figures to show the sharp increase in suicides since 1960 as well as other statistics. In the same way, Kim Dartnell uses an anecdote and well-documented statistics to demonstrate that the number of homeless women is increasing. Because the situation she discusses is likely to be unfamiliar to some readers, she also describes some typical homeless women. These features—anecdotes and statistics—are discussed further in Chapter 16: Illustrating.

It is also necessary to provide some details—background, current status, likely direction. When did the trend start? Is it completed or continuing? Where did it take place? What did it look like? Are you sure this is a trend and not a mere fad? Is it *really* increasing or decreasing? Is this increase or decrease decelerating or accelerating? Where does your evidence come from? Is it authoritative? A thorough presentation of the trend will answer all these questions.

A convincing causal argument

At the heart of an essay that analyzes the causes of a trend is the causal argument itself—the presentation of the causes in an effective order, evidence in support of each cause, some anticipation of any counterarguments, and a refutation of alternative causes. In all the forms of writing, including fiction and nonfiction, there is nothing more elegant and satisfying than a convincing causal argument. With care and sustained critical thinking, any writer can compose a convincing causal argument.

If we could explain a trend scientifically by offering incontrovertible evidence for its causes, there would be no need for causal arguments. However, most trends—especially troubling social or political ones—cannot be explained definitively. Instead, they must be argued—as logically and plausibly as possible. Some of these arguments play a critical role in our lives—for example, in affecting the way money is spent for research or for social and educational programs. Ultimately, they help to determine judges' decisions and legislators' votes.

Since an explanation of a trend must be argued, rather than simply announced, writers need to be very sensitive to their readers. They must present their causes in a logical order that readers will be able to follow. Thus Kim Dartnell, writing for a somewhat uninformed readership, begins with immediate and personal causes (abuse) and concludes with background and perpetuating causes (economics). Robert Jastrow, on the other hand, moves from remote causes (migration) to precipitating ones (the Ice Age) to perpetuating ones (use of language and tools). To be convincing, writers should avoid any causes their readers would consider obvious or predictable.

Writers must marshal evidence for each cause they propose. They may use statistics, factual examples, and anecdotes. Fuchs gives statistics (paragraphs 5 and 6) to support his argument about the most likely cause of the increase in suicide among today's youth. Similarly, Dartnell offers statistical evidence of the economic forces behind female homelessness. Tucker and Selditz both use factual example (Tucker in paragraph 9, Selditz in paragraph 4) to support their arguments. The best example of anecdote is found in Dartnell's essay, which opens with a short anecdote about one particular homeless woman.

Most important, writers must anticipate readers' possible objections to the proposed causes, as well as showing they have considered (and accepted or rejected) any other possible causes. Tucker considers several explanations for the popularity of jogging, accepts them all, and then proposes one further explanation which he favors as the best one. Fuchs emphatically rejects several proposed causes before proposing his own explanation of the increase in youth suicides. Selditz is careful to consider—and then reject—technological innovation as an adequate explanation for the increased popularity of radio/cassette headsets. Dartnell anticipates the counterargument that many homeless women are alcoholics. Not only does she show evidence that alcoholism is not a cause of increased homelessness among women, but she goes on to suggest that it is actually an effect.

A reasonable, authoritative voice   Essays analyzing trends should be written in a voice readers can trust. It need not be a terribly serious voice; it can even be personal or playful. But it must be reasonable and authoritative. Readers will not take any other voice seriously. The voices in this chapter's readings range from informal (Selditz) to seriously academic (Fuchs). What they all have in common is authority and trustworthiness, a voice which emerges in the ways readers are addressed and the ways evidence is presented.

GUIDE TO WRITING

THE WRITING TASK

Explain why a trend has occurred. The trend may be one you have observed firsthand or one you learned about in the news or one you are learning about now in a course. Your essay should do two things: demonstrate the existence of the trend and analyze possible causes for it.

INVENTION AND RESEARCH

The following activities will help you find a topic, explore what you know about the topic, and do any necessary research about it.

Finding a trend

Listing trends. List all the trends you can think of. Make your list as long as possible, considering trends you have studied and can research as well as those you know firsthand. Try to think of trends you would like to understand better.

A trend is a noticeable change extending over many months or years. It can be identified by some sort of increase or decrease—a rise in the birth rate, a decline in test scores. It is an established, demonstrable change, as opposed to a fad, which is only a short-term, superficial change. For example, a new diet might become a fad if many overweight people try it out for a few months. But this would not make it a trend. It might, however, be considered part of a trend—a general increase in health-consciousness, for example. Be sure your topic is a trend, not a fad.

Be certain, as well, not to write about an event or a phenomenon. A plane crash would be an event, whereas increasingly crowded airspace or a decline in the quality of air-traffic control would be trends. Bird migration is a phenomenon, but any long-term change in bird-migration patterns might be a trend.

It is also possible to write about the results or effects of trends. This chapter is concerned only with causes—more particularly, with causal analysis, a basic strategy of argumentative writing.

Consider the following possibilities as you think about trends:

☐ Shifting patterns in education—back to basics, increased interest in science

☐ Changes in patterns of leisure or entertainment

☐ Changing patterns in the incidence of disease

- ☐ New themes in film
- ☐ New lifestyle patterns—marriage, divorce, parenthood
- ☐ Shifts in religious belief
- ☐ New patterns of political behavior
- ☐ Changing patterns in technology—telecommunications, energy, computers
- ☐ Societal changes—increases in the number of women working, unmarried teenagers having babies
- ☐ Changes in politics or world affairs—the growing opposition to nuclear arms
- ☐ Changes in economic conditions—the long-term rise or fall of interest rates
- ☐ Changing patterns in attitude or philosophy—the diminishing concern about world hunger, the growing concern for personal success
- ☐ Artistic movements—Romanticism, Impressionism, pop art
- ☐ Completed historical trends—free verse in the early twentieth century, electronic music in the sixties and seventies, female suffrage in the nineteenth century

Choosing a trend. Now pick one trend from your list to write about. You may or may not already have some ideas about why this trend occurred. As you analyze it in some detail, you will have the opportunity to weigh possible causes and to decide which ones are the most important.

Stop now to focus your thoughts. In one or two sentences, describe the trend you have decided to analyze.

Exploring what you know about your topic

Do some thinking now about the trend you have chosen to analyze. Consider it, probe it, discover what you know about it, figure out why you are interested in it, compare it to other trends, decide where you might find more information about it. Write for around ten minutes, noting down everything you seem to know about the trend itself.

Considering causes

Think now about what caused this trend. List all the causes you can think of and then analyze each one.

Listing causes. Write down all the things you can think of that might have caused this trend. There are several kinds of causes you should try to find, specifically:

- ☐ immediate, precipitating causes: those present just before the trend began

☐ remote, background causes: those from the more distant past

☐ perpetuating causes: those which may have helped the trend grow or keep going once it started

☐ obvious causes

☐ hidden causes

It might be helpful to list these causes in table form. Fold a piece of lined paper vertically to make two columns, the left-hand column narrower than the right-hand one. List the causes in the left-hand column, leaving five or six lines between each cause. (See the Writer at Work section at the end of this chapter for an example of such a table.)

Analyzing causes. In the right-hand column, next to each cause, explain why you think that potential cause is real and important. Consider each of the following questions as you analyze the causes.

☐ Is it a necessary cause? Without it, could the trend have occurred?

☐ Is it a sufficient cause? Could it alone have caused this trend?

☐ Would this cause affect everybody the same way?

☐ Would this cause always lead to trends like this?

☐ Is there any statistical evidence showing that this *cause* increases or decreases as the *trend* increases or decreases?

☐ Are there any particular incidents that demonstrate the cause's importance?

☐ Have any authorities suggested it is an important cause?

☐ Is it actually a result of the trend or a side effect of it rather than a cause?

☐ Is it a remote cause or an immediate cause?

☐ Is it a perpetuating cause?

☐ Is it an apparent cause or a hidden cause?

Testing your choice Look at your analysis of all the possible causes. Have you identified enough solid causes to support a strong explanation? If not, you could do some research to find other possible causes. If none of your causes seems likely, and you really have no idea why the trend occurred, you could return to your original list and choose a new trend to write about.

Researching the topic Thus far you have relied solely on your own knowledge of your topic. Now you need to decide whether you need to find further evidence. You might look for statements from authoritative sources or for definitive statistics. Doing research can be helpful in several ways: (1) to confirm your own hunches, (2) to suggest other causes, (3) to provide evidence in support of your proposed causes, and (4) to identify evidence against possible counterarguments.

Some trends can be explained fully and convincingly with your own knowledge and instincts. For new emerging trends you will be on your own to decide on the most plausible causes, for there may be no published explanations.

Library research may be required for other topics—completed historical trends, for instance. You might also find information or opinions on current trends. In doing research you should look for additional proof that the trend really exists or existed, proposed causes, and more evidence—to support your causes or to reject other ones. As you do research and further analysis, continue adding to your table of causes and analyses.

Considering your readers

Because you are trying not only to analyze the causes of a trend, but also to make a convincing case for some particular causes, you should know as much as possible about your prospective readers. Only after you have analyzed your readers can you confidently decide which causes will go into your essay. Take about ten minutes to answer the following questions:

- ☐ Whom do I expect to read this essay?
- ☐ Are they likely to be aware of the trend?
- ☐ If they are aware of the trend, what are they likely to know or think about it?
- ☐ What assumptions might my readers share about the causes of such a trend?

Making your explanation as convincing as possible

Once you have figured out your expectations of your readers, review the table of causes and analyses in order to select the causes that will be most appealing to these readers. List the causes in the order you think most effective.

Choose the two or three most important causes and write about each one for around five minutes, summing up all the evidence you have found. Develop your discussion with your readers in mind; remember that you must convince them that your causes are reasonable ones.

Anticipating and refuting counterarguments

You should expect readers to study your essay critically, considering your reasons and evidence carefully before accepting your explanation. It would be wise, therefore, to account for any possible objections they could raise. Consider the two most likely objections or counterarguments and figure out a way to refute them. Write out a few sentences to prepare your refutation.

Rejecting alternative explanations   As they read your essay, your readers may think of other causes. Try to think of two or three alternative causes now and write a few sentences about each one explaining why you are rejecting it. If you cannot think of alternative explanations, skip this activity.

PLANNING AND DRAFTING

You will now want to review what you have learned about your topic and start to plan your first draft.

Seeing what you have   Pause now to reflect on your notes. Reread everything carefully in order to decide whether you can really prove that the trend exists (or existed) and whether you can name causes to offer a convincing explanation of why it came about.

Outlining the essay   A causal analysis may contain as many as four basic features: (1) a description of the trend, (2) a presentation of proposed causes and reasons for them, (3) a refutation of counterarguments, and (4) the consideration and rejection of alternative causes.

If you wish to propose a single cause, you could begin with a statement about the trend, describing it and indicating its importance. Then state the cause and elaborate on the reasons it has contributed to the trend. In your conclusion you could then refer to—and explain—the absence of other explanations.

> introduction of the trend
> proposed cause
> reasons for cause
> conclusion

If you need to account for alternative causes, you could discuss them first and give your reasons for rejecting them before offering your own proposed cause. Many writers save their own cause for last, hoping to leave their readers with a clear picture of it. Both Tucker and Fuchs adopt this plan.

> introduction of the trend
> alternative causes and reasons for rejecting them
> proposed cause with reasons
> conclusion

Another option is to put your own cause first followed by alternatives.

This is a good way to show the relative advantage of your cause over each of the others. You might then end with a restatement of your cause.

> introduction of the trend
> proposed cause with reasons
> alternative causes compared to your cause
> concluding restatement of proposed cause

If you are offering several causes, you will have to present them in some logical order—by relative importance, perhaps. This approach could very well mention each proposed cause's shortcomings. The explanations themselves may be somewhat incomplete, becoming convincing only when viewed in combination. An outline of this plan might look like this:

> introduction of the trend
> explanation of each possible cause, mentioning reasons as well as short-comings
> conclusion

Jastrow follows a plan like this in his essay on the increase in brain size.

There are of course many other possible ways to organize a causal analysis, but these outlines should help you to start planning your own essay.

Setting goals   Before you begin your draft, you should consider some specific goals for your essay. Not only will the draft be easier to write once you have established clear rhetorical goals, but it is likely to be stronger and more convincing.

Following are goal-setting questions to consider now. You may find it useful to return to them while you are drafting, for they are designed to help you to focus on specific elements of an essay about a trend.

Your readers

☐ What are they likely to know about the topic?

☐ How much do I need to say about the trend in order to establish the fact that it exists?

☐ How can I make my readers interested in understanding why this trend occurred?

☐ How can I refute their potential counterarguments or reject their preferred explanations without unduly irritating them?

☐ How can I present myself to my readers so they will consider me reasonable, fair, and authoritative?

The beginning

☐ How can I make readers take this trend seriously and really want to think about what caused it? Should I personalize it, as Tucker and Selditz do? Should I begin with an anecdote, as Dartnell does? Should I cite statistics, as Jastrow and Fuchs do?

Special strategies for causal analysis

☐ How can I demonstrate conclusively that this trend really exists, that it is increasing or decreasing, and that it is truly a trend and not just a fad?

☐ How can I anticipate and refute readers' counterarguments to my proposed causes?

☐ How should I deal with alternative causes—by refuting them, or by accepting them as part of my argument?

Avoiding logical fallacies

☐ How can I avoid the fallacy of *oversimplified cause*? Have I assumed that a mere contributing cause is a sufficient one? Have I really identified a sufficient cause? Have I mentioned only one or two causes when I should be accounting for several?

☐ How can I avoid the *post hoc, ergo propter hoc* fallacy? (Latin for "after this, therefore because of this") Have I mistakenly assumed that something that occurred prior to the beginning of the trend was therefore a cause?

☐ How can I be sure not to *confuse causes with effects*? Sometimes effects can be sustaining causes of a trend (as in the Jastrow essay), but if that is so, I should acknowledge it as such. Are any of my causes also results? Are any of my causes actually results and not causes at all?

☐ How can I show readers that I have *accepted the burden of proof*? I must offer proof for all my assertions and not *shift the burden of proof* to my readers by assuming they will automatically understand certain assertions.

☐ How can I refute counterarguments without committing the *ad hominem* (Latin for "to the man") fallacy? Can I argue against them without ridiculing their proponents?

☐ How can I consider and reject alternative causes without committing the *straw man* fallacy? (A straw man is easy to push over.)

☐ Can I argue for one cause only without being accused of the *either/or fallacy*? Might readers find my argument more convincing if I acknowledge alternative causes?

The ending

☐ How should I end my essay? Should I frame it by referring back to the beginning? Do I need to summarize my causes, as Jastrow and Selditz do? Should I conclude with a conjecture about larger implications, as Fuchs does?

Drafting the essay   In addition to the general advice on drafting given in Chapter 1, consider the following tips on writing an essay of causal analysis:

☐ Remember that in writing about causes of trends you are dealing with probabilities rather than certainties; therefore, you should not try to claim you have the final conclusive answer but only that your explanation is plausible. Qualify your statements and acknowledge the worth of opposing views.

☐ Try to appeal to your readers' interests and concerns. Causal analysis is potentially rather dry. Make an effort to enliven your writing and involve your readers.

☐ Remember that your outline is just a plan. Writers often make major discoveries and reorganize as they draft. Be flexible. If you find your writing taking an interesting, unexpected turn, follow it to see where it leads. You will have an opportunity to look at it critically later.

☐ If you run into a problem or find you need more information as you draft, pause for a few minutes and see whether any of the invention activities will help. If, for instance, you are having difficulty making the trend seem important, you could analyze your readers further, find a way to personalize the trend with a quotation or an anecdote, or look for some attention-getting statistical evidence.

☐ If you are having difficulty refuting counterarguments, try composing a dialogue between yourself and an imaginary reader.

☐ If you find you need more information, you might want to interview an expert, survey a group, or do further library research.

READING A DRAFT WITH A CRITICAL EYE

Your instructor may ask you to critique another student's draft or just to reread your own. As you read, keep in mind the following key question: given the prospective readers, how would one strengthen the argument for the proposed causes?

First general impression   Read the essay straight through to get a general impression. Write just a few sentences stating your first reaction. Did the essay hold your interest? What surprised you most? What did you like best? Did you find the explanation convincing?

Pointings   As you read, highlight noteworthy features with *pointings,* a simple system of lines and brackets that is especially useful for revising a draft. Use this system as follows:

- ☐ Draw a straight line under any words or images that seem especially effective: strong verbs, specific details, memorable phrases, striking images.
- ☐ Draw a wavy line under any words or images that sound flat, stale, or vague. Also put the wavy line under any words or phrases that you consider unnecessary or repetitious.
- ☐ Look for pairs or groups of sentences that you think should be combined. Put brackets [ ] around these sentences.
- ☐ Look for sentences that are garbled, overloaded, or awkward. Put parentheses ( ) around these sentences. Parenthesize any sentence that seems even slightly questionable; don't worry now about whether or not it is actually incorrect. The writer needs to know that you, as one reader, had even the slightest hesitation about reading a sentence, even on first reading.

Analysis   Following are some suggestions for analyzing the parts of the essay.

1. Look at the presentation of the trend. Are you absolutely sure that it is a trend rather than a fad or a single event? Are you convinced that the trend exists (or existed)? Can you see a progression over time? What kind of evidence is offered to show this progression? Suggest specific ways to strengthen the presentation of the trend.

2. Focus on the proposed cause or causes. Are there too many? Too few? Can you recognize any sufficient cause? A necessary one? Are any of the suggested causes actually results? Can you think of any causes the writer has ignored? Is the total discussion of the causes convincing? Point out ways to improve the discussion about the causes.

3. Look for counterarguments. How does the writer anticipate and refute possible counterarguments? Which refutations do you find most convincing? Least convincing? Alert the writer to any other counterarguments.

4. Evaluate the treatment of alternative causes. Are they clearly presented? Is the argument against them convincing? Indicate any of these alternative causes that still seem plausible to you.

5. Consider the organization of the essay. Does the space devoted to the trend and its causes seem fair? Are the causes presented in an effective order? Try suggesting a better order.

6. Reread the beginning. Is it engaging? Does it make you want to read the essay? Try to suggest other ways to open the essay.

7. Study the ending. Does the essay conclude decisively? Try to suggest an alternative ending.

8. What final thoughts do you have about this draft? Does anything still need work? What is the strongest part of the draft? What is the single most encouraging comment you could make?

REVISING AND EDITING

Revising the essay Following are some guidelines for revising an essay that analyzes causes. General advice about revision can be found in Chapter 1.

Revising to strengthen the argument

☐ Should you qualify your argument?

☐ Have you presented the causes with more certainty than is actually the case?

☐ Have you oversimplified your case?

☐ Have you shown (or at least argued) that each of the causes actually *did* contribute to the trend?

☐ Have you placed too much importance on any one cause?

☐ Have you given too full an explanation, tracing causes too far back in time, arguing for the causes of causes, so that your argument loses some impact?

Revising for clarity and readability

☐ If the trend did not impress readers as important, think of ways to strengthen your presentation of it.

☐ Reconsider the opening. Would another beginning be more engaging? Does it supply adequate forecasting?

☐ Look at the ending. Does it frame the beginning? Should it? Is it sufficiently emphatic?

☐ Look carefully at each sentence. Does it say what you intend it to say? Does it repeat information given earlier? Does it explain the obvious?

☐ If readers had trouble following your argument, add or clarify transitions so as to make the parts of the essay cohere better.

Editing and proofreading

As you revise a draft for the final time, you need to edit it closely for any errors of mechanics, usage, punctuation, or style. These were not a priority in earlier stages, but they should be now. Proofread as carefully as possible before turning in your final essay.

LEARNING FROM YOUR OWN WRITING PROCESS

If your instructor asks you to analyze your own composing process, begin by rereading your draft and revision. Focus on the way you analyzed causes, mentioning uncertainties you may still have about your analysis. Point to some specific changes you made in your revision, and explain why you made them. Indicate what you like best about your revision, as well as what still seems to need work.

A WRITER AT WORK

ANALYZING CAUSES

For a writer planning an essay explaining the causes of a trend, the most important part of invention and research is analyzing the causes. The causes are the heart of the argument, and so it takes rigorous analysis of each cause during the invention stage to compose a convincing argument.

Here we will look at the table of causes and analyses that Kim Dartnell developed for her essay on homeless women. (The revised version of her essay is on pages 251–53.)

Dartnell began this invention activity intending to write about the trend of homelessness in general, without considering men and women separately. Only after she had started to do some research did she realize that not only was there an increasing number of homeless women but that there had been several recent reports on the subject.

She began her analysis before going to the library, entering the first four causes on her table and completing a partial analysis. After she decided to focus on women, she added the other causes and completed the analysis. Examine her table of causes and analyses now. As you study her analysis, remember the questions she was asking herself about each cause.

TABLE OF CAUSES AND ANALYSES

Causes	Analyses
1. unemployment	Necessary cause for this trend. Could be sufficient, would affect everybody the same way, causes loss of income. Precipitating cause that has grown in importance recently. Also an immediate cause of homelessness.
2. inflation	Relates to unemployment—as such, may be necessary but not sufficient by itself, especially affects unemployed and poor. Perpetuating, immediate, hidden cause.
3. alcoholism	Not necessary, not sufficient. Common conception is all homeless are drunks. Refute this cause since alcohol use hasn't risen in proportion to homelessness. Alcoholism is found at all levels of society, and so can't say that it causes homelessness. May be a result of unemployment or homelessness. No one really knows what causes alcoholism—or what it causes.
4. cutbacks in welfare	Necessary cause, could be sufficient. Affects women especially, causes loss of income, homelessness. Immediate cause—with no money, people forced to beg or move in with others.
5. abuse	There's always been abuse. Neither necessary nor sufficient. Affects women and children more. Research shows it's risen in proportion to homelessness (Stoner).
6. deinstitutionalization	Many women being released from mental institutions. Necessary, may be sufficient. Precipitating cause for the mentally ill. May be coupled with economic problems. Rebecca Smith is a good example. Evidence shows this is increasing as homelessness increases. Couldn't be a result. Perpetuates the trend. (Use Stoner, Hombs and Snyder data.)
7. evictions	Necessary and sufficient cause, due to economic reasons. Precipitating cause. Affects females more, but also affects men. As evictions increase, more homeless. Perpetuating cause.

8. lack of housing   Necessary and sufficient, but related to economic reasons. Cheap housing is harder to find due to redevelopment and gentrification. Renovation affects those already without housing more. Could mention Rebecca Smith. Perpetuating cause.

Once she had analyzed all these possible causes, Dartnell could decide how to use them to make the most convincing explanation. She had to decide which causes to emphasize, which ones to combine, which ones to omit entirely, and how to order them to produce the most effective argument. Also, she had to consider whether or not any of her causes should be refuted. Last, she had to try to find any potential objections to her arguments, which she would then have to answer. As it happened, she decided to use all of these causes in her argument except for alcoholism, which she would mention and refute.

She begins her essay with a discussion of abuse, thinking it was the one cause of homelessness that most affects women. She then discusses evictions and housing, treating each of these causes in a separate paragraph. Next she mentions—and refutes—alcoholism as a cause. Only then does she develop the cause for which she had the most evidence—deinstitutionalization. Finally, she combines several causes—unemployment, inflation, welfare cutbacks—into one paragraph on economic causes.

Certainly these causes might be presented in a different order—deinstitutionalization might be effectively placed either first or last, for example—but Dartnell's plan serves her topic well. By covering her topic so comprehensively and discussing it in a clear, logically organized manner, she presents a convincing argument.

Analyzing Literature

☐ For a history of science class, a student writes about the myth of the mad scientist in literature, focusing on two classic works: *Frankenstein* and *Dr. Jekyll and Mr. Hyde.* From her reading, she concludes that as a fictional figure, the mad scientist is socially isolated, obsessed with the desire for knowledge and power, and reckless of his own and others' safety. To demonstrate the accuracy of her analysis, the student quotes descriptions of the scientists in the two works and discusses their behavior.

☐ A journalist writing about the American newspaper publisher William Randolph Hearst (1863–1951) decides to model his article on the classic film about a Hearstlike character, *Citizen Kane.* He organizes his piece around a series of imagined interviews with people who knew and worked for Hearst. Throughout the article, he draws parallels between Hearst and his film counterpart to support the point that Hearst is finally as unknowable as Kane.

☐ In an introductory literature class, a student analyzes the structure and meaning of Edgar Allan Poe's poem "The Raven." As the thesis of her essay, she claims the poem's message of inescapable despair is conveyed by its repetition of words and sounds as well as by its monotonous rhythm. To underscore her conclusion, the student points to specific examples in the poem of repetition, alliteration, and rhythmic uniformity.

☐ A freshman in a composition course explores the relationship between setting and action in William Faulkner's story "Dry September." He argues that the setting can be viewed metaphorically, as a projection of the characters' emotions. To support his point, he draws parallels between descriptions of the setting and descriptions of the characters.

9

☐ After seeing Henrik Ibsen's *A Doll's House,* a student is so moved she decides to write about the play's feminist themes in her diary. She is disturbed by the decision of the play's protagonist, Nora, to leave her home and children. The student asks: if Nora felt she had never grown up or accepted responsibility, why was she leaving her children? To answer this question, she attempts to examine Nora's character in light of the expectations Nora's husband and society in general have of women.

Whether we are writing formal college essays about works of literature or chatting with friends about a film we just saw, we ask essentially the same central question: "What did you think of it?" Most people understand this question as a request for an evaluation ("Did you like it?"), but it can also be seen as a request for an interpretation ("What does it mean?").

Literature inspires interpretation because it exercises immense and mysterious power over us, a power we wish to understand. From earliest childhood, stories and nursery rhymes draw us irresistably into their web of words. Literary images, like images in our dreams, reverberate with meaning. They touch deep chords in us.

We may read a work of literature numerous times, and each time respond differently, finding something new in the work. We find so much potential meaning because language is indeterminate. That is, literary meaning is not fixed and finite, but shifts as contexts and perspectives shift. But neither is meaning arbitrary, since it remains tied to the words of the text. Meaning in literature is like ore waiting to be mined—or like a slab of granite waiting to be sculpted. As we analyze literary works, we interpret them and both find and create their meaning.

Analyzing literature involves engaging it with our feelings and values, our imaginations and intellects. Not only do we dissect a work of literature, examining its parts to see how they influence our understanding, but we also immerse ourselves in the work, letting it wash over us and exert its power. As we analyze a work of literature, we often see reflections of our own experience. But literature does not simply represent life. It invents life in the medium of language, creating its own verbal structure. As we share our interpretations with others, we explore our commonality of response as well as our individuality. We become members of what Stanley Fish has called an "interpretive community," forging shared understanding and human connections.

READINGS

This chapter focuses on writing interpretations of short fiction. In this section we will examine two essays on one literary work, Nathaniel Hawthorne's short story "Young Goodman Brown." This story is reprinted here for you to read before studying the essays analyzing it.

"Young Goodman Brown" is named for its main character, a young Puritan who lived in the New England colony of Salem. The author of the story, Nathaniel Hawthorne, was born in Salem in 1804, more than a century after the time the story takes place. Salem in 1692 was the site of the notorious witch trials, where John Hathorne, the author's ancestor, was one of the presiding judges. The action of the story is set a year or so before the Salem witch trials.

The story is annotated here with notes identifying the names of actual people involved in the trials, defining words no longer in use, and giving other information helpful for understanding the story fully. Hawthorne first published "Young Goodman Brown" in 1835. It was later collected with other Hawthorne stories in *Mosses from an Old Manse*.

YOUNG GOODMAN BROWN
NATHANIEL HAWTHORNE

Young Goodman[1] Brown came forth, at sunset, into the street of Salem 1 village, but put his head back, after crossing the threshold, to exchange a parting kiss with his young wife. And Faith, as the wife was aptly named, thrust her own pretty head into the street, letting the wind play with the pink ribbons of her cap, while she called to Goodman Brown.

"Dearest heart," whispered she, softly and rather sadly, when her lips 2 were close to his ear, "pr'y[2] thee, put off your journey until sunrise, and sleep in your own bed tonight. A lone woman is troubled with such dreams and such thoughts, that she's afeard of herself, sometimes. Pray, tarry with me this night, dear husband, of all nights in the year!"

"My love and my Faith," replied young Goodman Brown, "of all nights 3 in the year, this one night must I tarry away from thee. My journey, as thou callest it, forth and back again, must needs be done 'twixt now and sunrise. What, my sweet, pretty wife, dost thou doubt me already, and we but three months married!"

"Then, God bless you!" said Faith, with the pink ribbons, "and may you 4 find all well, when you come back."

"Amen!" cried Goodman Brown. "Say thy prayers, dear Faith, and go to 5 bed at dusk, no harm will come to thee."

So they parted; and the young man pursued his way, until, being about 6 to turn the corner by the meeting-house, he looked back, and saw the head of Faith still peeping after him, with a melancholy air, in spite of her pink ribbons.

"Poor little Faith!" thought he, for his heart smote him. "What a wretch 7 am I, to leave her on such an errand! She talks of dreams, too. Methought, as she spoke, there was trouble in her face, as if a dream had warned her what work is to be done tonight. But, no, no! 'twould kill her to think it. Well; she's a blessed angel on earth; and after this one night, I'll cling to her skirts and follow her to Heaven."

With this excellent resolve for the future, Goodman Brown felt himself 8 justified in making more haste on his present evil purpose. He had taken a dreary road, darkened by all the gloomiest trees of the forest, which barely stood aside to let the narrow path creep through, and closed immediately behind. It was all as lonely as could be; and there is this peculiarity in such a solitude, that the traveler knows not who may be concealed by the innumerable trunks and the thick boughs overhead; so that, with lonely footsteps, he may yet be passing through an unseen multitude.

"There may be a devilish Indian behind every tree," said Goodman Brown, 9 to himself; and he glanced fearfully behind him, as he added, "What if the devil himself should be at my very elbow!"

His head being turned back, he passed a crook of the road, and looking 10 forward again, beheld the figure of a man, in grave and decent attire, seated at the foot of an old tree. He arose, at Goodman Brown's approach, and walked onward, side by side with him.

"You are late, Goodman Brown," said he. "The clock of the Old South 11 was striking as I came through Boston; and that is full fifteen minutes agone."

"Faith kept me back awhile," replied the young man, with a tremor in 12 his voice, caused by the sudden appearance of his companion, though not wholly unexpected.

It was now deep dusk in the forest, and deepest in that part of it where 13 these two were journeying. As nearly as could be discerned, the second traveler was about fifty years old, apparently in the same rank of life as Goodman Brown, and bearing a considerable resemblance to him, though perhaps more in expression than features. Still, they might have been taken for father and son. And yet, though the elder person was as simply clad as the younger, and as simple in manner too, he had an indescribable air of one who knew the world, and would not have felt abashed at the governor's dinner table, or in King William's[3] court, were it possible that his affairs should call him thither. But the only thing about him, that could be fixed upon as remarkable, was his staff, which bore the likeness of a great black snake, so curiously wrought, that it might almost be seen to twist and wriggle itself, like a living serpent. This, of course, must have been an ocular deception, assisted by the uncertain light.

"Come, Goodman Brown!" cried his fellow-traveler, "this is a dull pace 14 for the beginning of a journey. Take my staff, if you are so soon weary."

"Friend," said the other, exchanging his slow pace for a full stop, "having 15 kept covenant by meeting thee here, it is my purpose now to return whence I came. I have scruples, touching the matter thou wot'st[4] of."

"Sayest thou so?" repled he of the serpent, smiling apart. "Let us walk 16 on, nevertheless, reasoning as we go, and if I convince thee not, thou shalt turn back. We are but a little way in the forest, yet."

"Too far, too far!" exclaimed the goodman, unconsciously resuming his 17 walk. "My father never went into the woods on such an errand, nor his father before him. We have been a race of honest men and good Christians, since the days of the martyrs.[5] And shall I be the first of the name of Brown, that ever took this path, and kept—"

"Such company, thou wouldst say," observed the elder person, inter- 18 preting his pause. "Well said, Goodman Brown! I have been as well ac- quainted with your family as with ever a one among the Puritans; and that's no trifle to say. I helped your grandfather,[6] the constable, when he lashed the Quaker[7] woman so smartly through the streets of Salem. And it was I that brought your father a pitch-pine knot, kindled at my own hearth, to set fire to an Indian village, in King Philip's war.[8] They were my good friends, both; and many a pleasant walk have we had along this path, and returned merrily after midnight. I would fain be friends with you, for their sake."

"If it be as thou sayest," replied Goodman Brown, "I marvel they never 19 spoke of these matters. Or, verily, I marvel not, seeing that the least rumor of the sort would have driven them from New England. We are a people of prayer, and good works, to boot, and abide no such wickedness."

"Wickedness or not," said the traveler with the twisted staff, "I have a 20 very general acquaintance here in New England. The deacons of many a church have drunk the communion wine with me; the selectmen, of divers towns, make me their chairman; and a majority of the Great and General Court[9] are firm supporters of my interest. The governor and I, too—but these are state secrets."

"Can this be so!" cried Goodman Brown, with a stare of amazement at 21 his undisturbed companion. "Howbeit, I have nothing to do with the gov- ernor and council; they have their own ways, and are no rule for a simple husbandman,[10] like me. But, were I to go on with thee, how should I meet the eye of that good old man, our minister, at Salem village? Oh, his voice would make me tremble, both Sabbath-day and lecture-day!"

Thus far, the elder traveler had listened with due gravity, but now burst 22 into a fit of irrepressible mirth, shaking himself so violently, that his snake- like staff actually seemed to wriggle in sympathy.

"Ha! ha! ha!" shouted he, again and again; then composing himself, 23 "Well, go on, Goodman Brown, go on; but pr'y thee, don't kill me with laughing!"

"Well, then, to end the matter at once," said Goodman Brown, consid- 24 erably nettled, "there is my wife, Faith. It would break her dear little heart; and I'd rather break my own!"

"Nay, if that be the case," answered the other, "e'en go thy ways, Good- 25
man Brown. I would not, for twenty old women like the one hobbling before
us, that Faith should come to any harm."

As he spoke, he pointed his staff at a female figure on the path, in whom 26
Goodman Brown recognized as a very pious and exemplary dame, who had
taught him his catechism,[11] in youth, and was still his moral and spiritual
adviser, jointly with the minister and Deacon Gookin.

"A marvel, truly, that Goody[12] Cloyse[13] should be so far in the wilderness, 27
at nightfall!" said he. "But, with your leave, friend, I shall take a cut through
the woods, until we have left this Christian woman behind. Being a stranger
to you, she might ask whom I was consorting with, and whither I was going."

"Be it so," said his fellow-traveler. "Betake you to the woods, and let me 28
keep the path."

Accordingly, the young man turned aside, but took care to watch his 29
companion, who advanced softly along the road, until he had come within
a staff's length of the old dame. She, meanwhile, was making the best of
her way, with singular speed for so aged a woman, and mumbling some
indistinct words, a prayer, doubtless, as she went. The traveler put forth his
staff, and touched her withered neck with what seemed the serpent's tail.

"The devil!" screamed the pious old lady. 30

"Then Goody Cloyse knows her old friend?" observed the traveler, con- 31
fronting her, and leaning on his writhing stick.

"Ah, forsooth, and is it your worship, indeed?" cried the good dame. 32
"Yea, truly is it, and in the very image of my old gossip, Goodman Brown,
the grandfather of the silly fellow that now is. But—would your worship
believe it?—my broomstick hath strangely disappeared, stolen, as I suspect,
by that unhanged witch, Goody Cory, and that, too, when I was all anointed
with the juice of smallage and cinque-foil and wolf's-bane—"[14]

"Mingled with fine wheat and the fat of a new-born babe," said the 33
shape of old Goodman Brown.

"Ah, your worship knows the recipe," cried the old lady, cackling aloud. 34
"So, as I was saying, being all ready for the meeting, and no horse to ride
on, I made up my mind to foot it; for they tell me, there is a nice young man
to be taken into communion[15] tonight. But now your good worship will lend
me your arm, and we shall be there in a twinkling."

"That can hardly be," answered her friend. "I may not spare you my arm, 35
Goody Cloyse, but here is my staff, if you will."

So saying, he threw it down at her feet, where, perhaps, it assumed life, 36
being one of the rods which its owner had formerly lent to the Egyptian
Magi.[16] Of this fact, however, Goodman Brown could not take cognizance.
He had cast up his eyes in astonishment, and looking down again, beheld
neither Goody Cloyse nor the serpentine staff, but his fellow-traveler alone,
who waited for him as calmly as if nothing had happened.

"That old woman taught me my catechism!" said the young man; and 37
there was a world of meaning in this simple comment.

They continued to walk onward, while the elder traveler exhorted his 38 companion to make good speed and persevere in the path, discoursing so aptly, that his arguments seemed rather to spring up in the bosom of his auditor, than to be suggested by himself. As they went, he plucked a branch of maple, to serve for a walking stick, and begin to strip it of the twigs and little boughs, which were wet with evening dew. The moment his fingers touched them, they became strangely withered and dried up, as with a week's sunshine. Thus the pair proceeded, at a good free pace, until suddenly, in a gloomy hollow of the road, Goodman Brown sat himself down on the stump of a tree, and refused to go any farther.

"Friend," said he, stubbornly, "my mind is made up. Not another step 39 will I budge on this errand. What if a wretched old woman do choose to go to the devil, when I thought she was going to Heaven! Is that any reason why I should quit my dear Faith, and go after her?"

"You will think better of this, by-and-by," said his acquaintance, com- 40 posedly. "Sit here and rest yourself awhile; and when you feel like moving again, there is my staff to help you along."

Without more words, he threw his companion the maple stick, and was 41 as speedily out of sight, as if he had vanished into the deepening gloom. The young man sat a few moments, by the roadside, applauding himself greatly, and thinking with how clear a conscience he should meet the minister, in his morning walk, nor shrink from the eye of good old Deacon Gookin. And what calm sleep would be his, that very night, which was to have been spent so wickedly, but purely and sweetly now, in the arms of Faith! Amidst these pleasant and praiseworthy meditations, Goodman Brown heard the tramp of horses along the road, and deemed it advisable to conceal himself within the verge of the forest, conscious of the guilty purpose that had brought him thither, though now so happily turned from it.

On came the hoof-tramps and the voices of the riders, two grave old 42 voices, conversing soberly as they drew near. These mingled sounds appeared to pass along the road, within a few yards of the young man's hiding-place; but owing, doubtless, to the depth of the gloom, at that particular spot, neither the travelers nor their steeds were visible. Though their figures brushed the small boughs by the wayside, it could not be seen that they intercepted, even for a moment, the faint gleam from the strip of bright sky, athwart which they must have passed. Goodman Brown alternately crouched and stood on tiptoe, pulling aside the branches, and thrusting forth his head as far as he durst, without discerning so much as a shadow. It vexed him the more, because he could have sworn, were such a thing possible, that he recognized the voices of the minister and Deacon Gookin, jogging along quietly, as they were wont to do, when bound to some ordination or ecclesiastical council. While yet within hearing, one of the riders stopped to pluck a switch.

"Of the two, reverend Sir," said the voice like the deacon's, "I had rather 43 miss an ordination-dinner[17] than tonight's meeting. They tell me that some of our community are to be here from Falmouth and beyond, and others from Connecticut and Rhode Island; besides several of the Indian powows,[18] who, after their fashion, know almost as much deviltry as the best of us. Moreover, there is a goodly young woman to be taken into communion.''

''Mighty well, Deacon Gookin!'' replied the solemn old tones of the min- 44 ister. ''Spur up, or we shall be late. Nothing can be done, you know, until I get on the ground.''

The hoofs clattered again, and the voices, talking so strangely in the empty 45 air, passed on through the forest, where no church had ever been gathered, nor solitary Christian prayed. Whither, then, could these holy men be journeying, so deep into the heathen wilderness? Young Goodman Brown caught hold of a tree, for support, being ready to sink down on the ground, faint and overburdened with the heavy sickness of his heart. He looked up to the sky, doubting whether there really was a Heaven above him. Yet there was the blue arch, and the stars brightening in it.

''With Heaven above, and Faith below, I will yet stand firm against the 46 devil!'' cried Goodman Brown.

While he still gazed upward, into the deep arch of the firmament, and 47 had lifted his hands to pray, a cloud, though no wind was stirring, hurried across the zenith, and hid the brightening stars. The blue sky was still visible, except directly overhead, where this black mass of cloud was sweeping swiftly northward. Aloft in the air, as if from the depths of the cloud, came a confused and doubtful sound of voices. Once, the listener fancied that he could distinguish the accents of townspeople of his own, men and women, both pious and ungodly, many of whom he had met at the communion-table, and had seen others rioting at the tavern. The next moment, so indistinct were the sounds, he doubted whether he had heard aught but the murmur of the old forest, whispering without a wind. Then came a stronger well of those familiar tones, heard daily in the sunshine, at Salem village, but never, until now, from a cloud of night. There was one voice, of a young woman, uttering lamentations, yet with an uncertain sorrow, and entreating for some favor, which, perhaps, it would grieve her to obtain. And all the unseen multitude, both saints and sinners, seemed to encourage her onward.

''Faith!'' shouted Goodman Brown, in a voice of agony and desperation; 48 and the echoes of the forest mocked him, crying—''Faith! Faith!'' as if bewildered wretches were seeking her, all through the wilderness.

The cry of grief, rage, and terror, was yet piercing the night, when the 49 unhappy husband held his breath for a response. There was a scream, drowned immediately in a louder murmur of voices, fading into far-off laughter, as the dark cloud swept away, leaving the clear and silent sky above Goodman Brown. But something fluttered lightly down through the air, and caught on a branch of a tree. The young man seized it, and beheld a pink ribbon.

''My Faith is gone!'' cried he, after one stupefied moment. ''There is no 50 good on earth; and sin is but a name. Come, devil! for to thee is this world given.''

And maddened with despair, so that he laughed loud and long, did Good- 51 man Brown grasp his staff and set forth again, at such a rate, that he seemed to fly along the forest path, rather than to walk or run. The road grew wilder and drearier, and more faintly traced, and vanished at length, leaving him in the heart of the dark wilderness, still rushing onward, with the instinct that guides mortal man to evil. The whole forest was peopled with frightful sounds; the creaking of the trees, the howling of wild beasts, and the yell of Indians; while, sometimes, the wind tolled like a distant church bell, and sometimes gave a broad roar around the traveler, as if all Nature were laughing him to scorn. But he was himself the chief horror of the scene, and shrank not from its other horrors.

"Ha! ha! ha!" roared Goodman Brown, when the wind laughed at him. 52 "Let us hear which will laugh loudest! Think not to frighten me with your deviltry! Come witch, come wizard, come Indian powow, come devil himself! and here comes Goodman Brown. You may as well fear him as he fear you!"

In truth, all through the haunted forest, there could be nothing more 53 frightful than the figure of Goodman Brown. On he flew, among the black pines, brandishing his staff with frenzied gestures, now giving vent to an inspiration of horrid blasphemy, and now shouting forth such laughter, as set all the echoes of the forest laughing like demons around him. The fiend in his own shape is less hideous, than when he rages in the breast of man. Thus sped the demoniac on his course, until, quivering among the trees, he saw a red light before him, as when the felled trunks and branches of a clearing have been set on fire, and throw up their lurid blaze against the sky, at the hour of midnight. He paused, in a lull of the tempest that had driven him onward, and heard the swell of what seemed a hymn, rolling solemnly from a distance, with the weight of many voices. He knew the tune; it was a familiar one in the choir of the village meeting-house. The verse died heavily away, and was lengthened by a chorus, not of human voices, but of all the sounds of the benighted wilderness, pealing in awful harmony together. Goodman Brown cried out; and his cry was lost to his own ear, by its unison with the cry of the desert.

In the interval of silence, he stole forward, until the light glared full upon 54 his eyes. At one extremity of an open space, hemmed in by the dark wall of the forest, arose a rock, bearing some rude, natural resemblance either to an altar or a pulpit, and surrounded by four blazing pines, their tops aflame, their stems untouched, like candles at an evening meeting. The mass of foliage, that had overgrown the summit of the rock, was all on fire, blazing high into the night, and fitfully illuminating the whole field. Each pendent twig and leaf festoon was in a blaze. As the red light arose and fell, a numerous congregation alternately shone forth, then disappeared in shadow, and again grew, as it were, out of the darkness, peopling the heart of the solitary woods at once.

"A grave and dark-clad company!" quoth Goodman Brown. 55

In truth, they were such. Among them, quivering to-and-fro, between 56
gloom and splendor, appeared faces that would be seen, next day, at the
council-board of the province, and others which, Sabbath after Sabbath,
looked devoutly heavenward, and benignantly over the crowded pews, from
the holiest pulpits in the land. Some affirm, that the lady of the governor
was there. At least, there were high dames well known to her, and wives of
honored husbands, and widows, a great multitude, and ancient maidens, all
of excellent repute, and fair young girls, who trembled, lest their mothers
should espy them. Either the sudden gleams of light, flashing over the obscure
field, bedazzled Goodman Brown, or he recognized a score of the church-
members of Salem village, famous for their especial sanctity. Good old Deacon Gookin had arrived, and waited at the skirts of that venerable saint, his
revered pastor. But, irreverently consorting with these grave, reputable, and
pious people, these elders of the church, these chaste dames and dewy vir-
gins, there were men of dissolute lives and women of spotted fame, wretches
given over to all mean and filthy vice, and suspected even of horrid crimes.
It was strange to see, that the good shrank not from the wicked, nor were
the sinners abashed by the saints. Scattered, also, among their pale-faced
enemies, were the Indian priests, or powows, who had often scared their
native forest with more hideous incantations than any known to English
witchcraft.

"But, where is Faith?" thought Goodman Brown; and, as hope came into 57
his heart, he trembled.

Another verse of the hymn arose, a slow and mournful strain, such as 58
the pious love, but joined to words which expressed all that our nature can
conceive of sin, and darkly hinted at far more. Unfathomable to mere mortals
is the lore of fiends. Verse after verse was sung, and still the chorus of the
desert swelled between, like the deepest tone of a mighty organ. And, with
the final peal of that dreadful anthem, there came a sound, as if the roaring
wind, the rushing streams, the howling beasts, and every other voice of the
unconverted wilderness, were mingling and according with the voice of guilty
man, in homage to the prince of all. The four blazing pines threw up a loftier
flame, and obscurely discovered shapes and visages of horror on the smoke-
wreaths, above the impious assembly. At the same moment, the fire on the
rock shot redly forth, and formed a glowing arch above its base, where now
appeared a figure. With reverence be it spoken, the figure bore no slight
similitude, both in garb and manner, to some grave divine of the New England
churches.

"Bring forth the converts!" cried a voice, that echoed through the field 59
and rolled into the forest.

At the word, Goodman Brown stepped forth from the shadow of the 60
trees, and approached the congregation, with whom he felt a loathful brotherhood, by the sympathy of all that was wicked in his heart. He could have
well nigh sworn, that the shape of his own dead father beckoned him to

advance, looking downward from a smokewreath, while a woman, with dim features of despair, threw out her hand to warn him back. Was it his mother? But he had no power to retreat one step, nor to resist, even in thought, when the minister and good old Deacon Gookin seized his arms, and led him to the blazing rock. Thither came also the slender form of a veiled female, led between Goody Cloyse, that pious teacher of the catechism, and Martha Carrier,[19] who had received the devil's promise to be queen of hell. A rampant hag was she! And there stood the proselytes, beneath the canopy of fire.

"Welcome, my children," said the dark figure, "to the communion of 61 your race! Ye have found, thus young, your nature and your destiny. My children, look behind you!"

They turned; and flashing forth, as it were, in a sheet of flame, the fiend- 62 worshippers were seen; the smile of welcome gleamed darkly on every visage.

"There," resumed the sable form, "are all whom ye have reverenced from 63 youth. Ye deemed them holier than yourselves, and shrank from your own sin, contrasting it with their lives of righteousness, and prayerful aspirations heavenward. Yet, here are they all, in my worshipping assembly! This night it shall be granted you to know their secret deeds; how hoary-bearded elders of the church have whispered wanton words to the young maids of their households; how many a woman, eager for widow's weeds, has given her husband a drink at bedtime, and let him sleep his last sleep in her bosom; how beardless youths have made haste to inherit their fathers' wealth; and how fair damsels—blush not, sweet ones!—have dug little graves in the garden, and bidden me, the sole guest, to an infant's funeral. By the sympathy of your human hearts for sin, ye shall scent out all the places—whether in church, bedchamber, street, field, or forest—where crime has been committed, and shall exult to behold the whole earth one stain of guilt, one mighty bloodspot. Far more than this! It shall be yours to penetrate, in every bosom, the deep mystery of sin, the fountain of all wicked arts, and which inexhaustibly supplies more evil impulses than human power—than my power, at its utmost!—can make manifest in deeds. And now, my children, look upon each other."

They did so; and, by the blaze of the hell-kindled torches, the wretched 64 man beheld his Faith, and the wife her husband, trembling before that unhallowed altar.

"Lo! there ye stand, my children," said the figure, in a deep and solemn 65 tone, almost sad, with its despairing awfulness, as if his once angelic nature could yet mourn for our miserable race. "Depending upon one another's hearts, ye had still hoped, that virtue were not all a dream. Now are ye undeceived! Evil is the nature of mankind. Evil must be your only happiness. Welcome, again, my children, to the communion of your race!"

"Welcome!" repeated the fiend-worshippers, in one cry of despair and 66 triumph.

And there they stood, the only pair, as it seemed, who were yet hesitating 67 on the verge of wickedness, in this dark world. A basin was hollowed, naturally, in the rock. Did it contain water, reddened by the lurid light? or was it blood? or, perchance, a liquid flame? Herein did the Shape of Evil dip his hand, and prepare to lay the mark of baptism upon their foreheads, that they might be partakers of the mystery of sin, more conscious of the secret guilt of others, both in deed and thought, than they could now be of their own. The husband cast one look at his pale wife, and Faith at him. What polluted wretches would the next glance shew them to each other, shuddering alike at what they disclosed and what they saw!

"Faith! Faith!" cried the husband. "Look up to Heaven, and resist the 68 Wicked One!"

Whether Faith obeyed, he knew not. Hardly had he spoken, when he 69 found himself amid calm night and solitude, listening to a roar of the wind, which died heavily away through the forest. He staggered against the rock and felt it chill and damp, while a hanging twig, that had been on fire, besprinkled his cheek with the coldest dew.

The next morning, young Goodman Brown came slowly into the street 70 of Salem village, staring around him like a bewildered man. The good old minister was taking a walk along the graveyard, to get an appetite for breakfast and meditate his sermon, and bestowed a blessing, as he passed, on Goodman Brown. He shrank from the venerable saint, as if to avoid an anathema. Old Deacon Gookin. was at domestic worship, and the holy words of his prayer were heard through the open window. "What God doth the wizard pray to?" quoth Goodman Brown. Goody Cloyse, that excellent old Christian, stood in the early sunshine, at her own lattice, catechizing a little girl, who had brought her a pint of morning's milk. Goodman Brown snatched away the child, as from the grasp of the fiend himself. Turning the corner by the meeting-house, he spied the head of Faith, with the pink ribbons, gazing anxiously forth, and bursting into such joy at sight of him, that she skipped along the street, and almost kissed her husband before the whole village. But, Goodman Brown looked sternly and sadly into her face, and passed on without a greeting.

Had Goodman Brown fallen asleep in the forest, and only dreamed a wild 71 dream of a witch-meeting?

Be it so, if you will. But, alas! it was a dream of evil omen for young 72 Goodman Brown. A stern, a sad, a darkly meditative, a distrustful, if not a desperate man, did he become, from the night of that fearful dream. On the Sabbath day, when the congregation were singing a holy psalm, he could not listen, because an anthem of sin rushed loudly upon his ear, and drowned all the blessed strain. When the minister spoke from the pulpit, with power and fervid eloquence, and, with his hand on the open Bible, of the sacred truths of our religion, and of saint-like lives and triumphant deaths, and of future bliss or misery unutterable, then did Goodman Brown turn pale, dreading, lest the roof should thunder down upon the gray blasphemer and his hearers. Often, awakening suddenly at midnight, he shrank from the bosom of Faith, and at morning or eventide, when the family knelt down at prayer, he scowled, and muttered to himself, and gazed sternly at his wife, and turned away. And when he had lived long, and was borne to his grave, a hoary corpse, followed by Faith, an aged woman, and children and grandchildren, a goodly procession, besides neighbors, not a few, they carved no hopeful verse upon his tombstone; for his dying hour was gloom.

NOTES

[1]A polite title for an ordinary man, used then as we use *mister* today.

[2]Short for *pray;* "pray thee," like *prithee* means "please."

[3]William III, the ruler of England from 1689–1702.

[4]Knows.

[5]The years 1553–58 during the reign of "Bloody Mary," the Catholic Queen of England who persecuted the Protestants.

[6]Reference to one of the author's ancestors, William Hathorne, who presided at the Salem witch trials in 1692.

[7]A religious group who were persecuted by the Puritans.

[8]King Philip, chief of the Wampanoag Indians, led a devastating war against the colonists in 1675–76.

[9]The legislature.

[10]Common man or farmer.

[11]A series of questions and answers summarizing Christian doctrine used to instruct children.

[12]Like *Goodman,* a polite title for a woman.

[13]The name of a woman tried as a witch in 1692.

[14]Plants associated with witchcraft.

[15]A religious ceremony to initiate new members.

[16]An allusion to the Bible, Exodus 7:9–12. To convince the Egyptian Pharaoh to free the Jews from slavery, the Lord has Aaron cast down his rod before the Pharaoh whereupon it turns into a serpent. The Pharaoh's magicians (Magi) perform the same miracle.

[17]Ceremony celebrating a newly ordained minister.

[18]Medicine men. *Powow* now means "gathering."

[19]The name of another woman tried as a witch in 1692.

The following essays will show two ways "Young Goodman Brown" can be interpreted. The writers of these essays—students in a freshman English course—began by reading the story analytically, thinking about its themes, characters, action, setting, and language, and then examining the way some of these components work together to create the story's literary effects and meaning.

The first essay, by Debbie Brawner, focuses on the main character, young Goodman Brown. Brawner analyzes Brown's character to show how he changed as a result of his experience in the forest. Notice how Brawner supports her analysis with evidence from the story.

A MESSAGE TO DECIPHER
DEBBIE BRAWNER

Nathaniel Hawthorne's ''Young Goodman Brown'' tells the story of a 1 spiritually weak man who is unable to overcome forces that threaten his faith. It is the story of Goodman Brown's journey into the self, a journey that proves tragic for him in the end. Brown's character undergoes many drastic changes during this journey: from a kind, loving, naive man able to see only good, he becomes nasty and guilty and able to see only evil, ending up finally sad and distrustful, unable to reconcile these two views of human nature. Given a simple mind that can perceive only in terms of black and white, he is unable to comprehend complexity or accept ambiguity.

At the beginning of the story, Goodman Brown is idealistic. Not only does 2 he believe totally in the goodness of human nature, but he seems oblivious to the sins of those he reveres. His family and ancestors he considers ''a race of honest men and good Christians . . . a people of prayer and good works'' (paragraphs 17 and 19); he sees Goody Cloyse, the minister, and Deacon Gookin as people untainted by sin; and he views his wife Faith as nothing less than ''a blessed angel on earth'' (paragraph 7). Brown himself has tried to live an exemplary life of Christian piety and faith, but he has failed and knows it. In fact, he has his whole life tried to repress his darker side, believing that good and evil cannot be present within the same personality. His unreasonable expectations of human nature have left him with feelings of guilt for his own failure to live up to the saintly standards by which he judges others. It is this guilt that leads Goodman Brown to confront the truths about his own nature, truths he had previously repressed.

His evening in the forest can thus be seen as a journey into the self (Gollin 3 123), a struggle between the two sides of Brown's character. The good side is represented by the persona Goodman Brown, the evil side by the devil (who even bears ''a considerable resemblance'' to Brown [paragraph 13]). The confrontation with the devil represents not only Brown's struggle with the repressed side of himself, but also his recognition of the presence of sin in the world. This journey forces him to face corruption, something he had hidden from himself by his ''own naive assertion of virtue in the world'' (Bell 78). While the devil tries to persuade him that virtue is a dream and ''evil the only reality,'' Brown clings to his belief in goodness (Martin 84). Of course each view is equally ridiculous. Human nature is neither all good nor absolutely evil: this is the lesson Brown should learn from his journey.

Instead, Goodman Brown is thrown into turmoil and confusion from the 4 moment he confronts the devil. The complexity of the truths that the devil reveals dulls Brown's vision. As it gets to be late in the evening and the light grows dimmer, he becomes more and more unsure about what he sees and hears. He is torn by conflicting desires—to flee the forest (the dark recesses of the self) or to pursue the new truths that confront him. When Goodman Brown fears he is going too far, stating that neither his father nor his grandfather ever went so deep into the forest, the devil insists that they had indeed been there with him many times. Though his good side defends his ancestors, saying his people would "abide no such wickedness" (paragraph 19), Brown's evil side wishes to believe in his ancestors' sinfulness in order to relieve his own guilt.

Ultimately, he is defenseless, as the devil presents evidence of evil in the most revered people. As each person's weaknesses are revealed, Brown's own belief falters. The sight of Goody Cloyce consorting with the devil causes him to waver, but when he sees the minister and Deacon Gookin doing the same, he doubts the very existence of heaven.

Even after these revelations, Goodman Brown's good side may have remained the dominant force in his character if he had not then seen that even Faith was on her way to the devil. This last "truth" causes him to snap. Without Faith, he is totally helpless against the forces of evil: in his own words, he needs "Heaven above and Faith below . . . [to] stand firm against the devil" (paragraph 46). The loss of Faith causes the turmoil within him to rage and the dark side of his character to become dominant. Though the forest grows wilder and more and more frightful, wild beasts roaring and wind tolling, it is Brown himself who is then "the chief horror of the scene" (paragraph 51). Led to believe the devil's assertion that evil dominates human nature, Brown gives himself to evil as he had to good—freely and zealously.

As Goodman Brown returns from the forest—or awakens from his dream— we see yet another shift in his character. Bewildered by what he has seen, he is now totally unsure how to interpret life. His attitude toward others has changed, however. When he passes the minister, he cowers; when Faith greets him, he looks "sternly and sadly into her face" and passes "without a greeting" (paragraph 70). He becomes "a stern, a sad, and darkly meditative, a distrustful, if not a desperate man" (paragraph 72).

Goodman Brown is ruined ultimately because of his inability to decipher the meaning of his experience. Instead of gaining understanding of the complexity of human nature and the conflicting sides within each person's character, he comes to distrust everyone. Never does he understand that with sincere faith in God, one can overcome evil. Though Brown continues to live with Faith until his death, he remains distant from her. Not surprisingly, "his dying hour [is] gloom" (paragraph 72). His vision limited and his character weak, young Goodman Brown is left with no hope of salvation.

LIST OF WORKS CITED

Bell, Michael Davitt. *Hawthorne and the Historical Romance of New England.* Princeton: Princeton University Press, 1971.

Gollin, Rita K. *Nathaniel Hawthorne and the Truth of Dreams.* Baton Rouge: Louisiana State University Press, 1979.

Martin, Terrence. *Nathaniel Hawthorne.* Boston: Twayne, 1981.

Questions for analysis   1. Brawner argues that Brown's experience in the forest causes his character to change. Describe in your own words the changes as Brawner interprets them.

2. How convincing is Brawner's argument? What do you find most convincing? Least convincing?

3. Brawner wrote this essay for readers (her instructor and classmates) who have already read "Young Goodman Brown." Hence, she does not have to describe the story. She does, however, have to show evidence from the text to support her thesis. What textual evidence does she give to support her statement (paragraph 2) that at first Brown sees only the good in human nature?

4. In paragraph 6 Brawner uses another kind of evidence from the story—she summarizes certain events and then explains what these events mean. Point out another place in the essay where Brawner summarizes and explains events from the story.

5. Brawner also offers a third kind of evidence: other critics' opinions. Where does she do this? Does quoting other critics help Brawner support her thesis in a way that she could not do herself? If so, how?

6. Brawner writes about a famous story by a highly esteemed writer. How would you describe the language she uses for this essay? Does it have an everyday quality, or does it seem special or formal in some way? Cite examples from her essay in your answer.

Readers of essays about literature generally look for two basic features: an idea about the work and proof that this idea is reasonable. Usually the main idea is given explicitly in a thesis statement, often early in the essay to let readers know exactly what interpretation the writer will be arguing for.

Brawner uses the opening paragraph of her essay both to state her thesis and to forecast the plan her essay will follow. The first two sentences describe what happens in the story. Notice, though, that this description does not simply summarize the action but rather gives some interpretation. Brawner considers Goodman Brown's experience in terms of spiritual faith, defining the journey he undertakes as a series of obstacles and judging the outcome as "tragic." In the third sentence, she explains how Brown's character changes as a result of his experience, identifying three specific stages in his character development. The last sentence of the paragraph explains why she considers the outcome tragic.

Brawner organizes the essay around these three stages in Brown's character development. Paragraph 2 presents the first stage by showing that before the journey Brown is a good man. In paragraphs 3–6, Brawner focuses on the second stage, Brown's struggle with his repressed, evil side. The last stage, Brown's inability to reconcile these two sides of his character, is discussed in paragraphs 7 and 8. Brawner makes the point that Brown's development is finally tragic by emphasizing his inability to accept the presence of both good and evil.

In addition to explicitly stating the essay's thesis and forecasting its organization, Brawner offers several kinds of evidence to support her thesis. Her primary source of evidence, of course, is the work itself. Trying to pin down the meaning of the work, Brawner quotes directly from it. Other evidence she uses includes summarizing events in the work and quoting published critics. Literary analysts use evidence much the way lawyers do. They build a case for their interpretation based on many different pieces of evidence, especially textual evidence. By referring specifically to the language of the literary work, they show readers how they arrived at their particular understanding—how the work conveys its meaning to them and how they create meaning as they read and analyze the work.

As lawyers base different arguments on the same body of evidence, so literary critics base different and often opposing interpretations on the same work. By focusing on the changes in Goodman Brown's character, Debbie Brawner is able to argue that the story is about the failure to accept moral ambiguity. The next writer, Sylvia Alfred, focuses on the story's symbolism. What does this focus lead her to say about the story?

THE SYMBOLISM IN "YOUNG GOODMAN BROWN"
SYLVIA ALFRED

"What if a young man who has seen only good in the world is confronted 1 with a vision of permeating evil?" Nathaniel Hawthorne seems to be asking this question in his story of Goodman Brown. In the story Hawthorne uses symbolism to explore the question of good and evil. Brown is an everyman who is also a good man. His wife, "aptly named" Faith, represents his faith in goodness. Brown departs from his faith on a symbolic journey to a Witches' Sabbath ceremony. There he weds himself to the knowledge of evil.

Hawthorne uses darkness and light as symbols for Brown's descent into 2 evil. The journey begins at sunset because it "must . . . be done twixt [sunset] and sunrise." It is "deep dusk" as he begins his walk with the devil, "deepening gloom" when he resolves to go back to Faith, and finally "the depth of the gloom" when he hears but cannot see the minister and deacon. The growing darkness symbolizes Brown's growing inability to see the truth. Light comes in meager amounts, "the faint gleam from the strip of bright sky," "the blue arch," and "the brightening stars." But after a cloud obscures the light, Brown does not see clearly until he sees by the infernal fire in the forest clearing. This firelight of hell reveals all the possible evil in the people of his world. When he returns to the village the next morning, even the natural light of the sun cannot lighten the burden of what he has seen in the darkness.

Hawthorne uses symbols of worship to show the witches' worship of evil 3 as the mirror image of the Christian worship of good. Brown approaches the "congregation" to the sound of a hymn, "a familiar one in the choir of the village meeting-house" but in "awful harmony." The flaming trees resemble candles about the "altar or pulpit." The call resounds for the "converts" to be brought forth and the dark ministerial figure welcomes them to the "communion," this unity with the "loathful brotherhood." A sermon is delivered offering penetration into "the deep mystery of sin." The converts are on the threshold of baptism by water, blood, and flame, all symbols of the Christian faith.

Only three months earlier, and in a Christian wedding ceremony, Good- 4 man Brown had wed himself to good by marrying Faith. Hawthorne's use of wedding symbolism suggests that Brown weds himself to evil at the Witches' Sabbath. Brown is led to the altar by the minister and Deacon Gookin as though they were groomsmen, just as Goody Cloyse and Martha Carrier bring forward a "veiled female" in the manner of bridal attendants. The pair stand "beneath the canopy of fire." At the point of recognition, they seem truly to know one another for the first time, seeing the evil in each other's hearts. This recognition of evil has overtones of Adam and Eve with the husband in this case the first, and perhaps the only, one to seek forbidden knowledge. The wedding symbolism ironically foreshadows the disunity in which Goodman Brown and his wife will live ever after.

The symbolism in "Young Goodman Brown" serves both to clarify and 5 to veil the meaning of the story. Brown travels a dark road, which has the quality of a journey into the depths of heart and mind. There is no literal description of how the road leads out of town, what direction it goes, where it terminates. It is pictured simply as "dreary," "narrow," and "lonely." The symbols of light and dark, sunshine and sunset, starlight and gloom, firelight and blackness reveal the polarization of good and evil. At the same time, there is an obscurity in the dusk and half light that keeps the reader wondering what is real and what exists only in Brown's inner vision. The use of Christian symbolism tells readers that the events are spiritually significant, yet they also lift the occurrences out of the realm of the ordinary into the supernatural.

These symbols are an excellent vehicle for Hawthorne's presentation of a 6 young man struggling with the reality of good and evil in his own life and in the lives of those in his community. Goodman Brown wants to see and to know, telling Faith as he sets off that he "must" tarry away from her. Yet he sees only the dark things of the forest, and he knows only evil. Back in the sunlit village, Brown can only see the minister as "anathema," Deacon Gookin as a wizard, and Goody Cloyse as a witch. Even Faith has become someone he shrinks from. In the end, she follows his corpse to its grave, symbolizing his having left faith behind; thus "no hopeful verse" *could* be carved upon his tombstone. In the forest, Brown exchanged faith and hope for doubt and despair. His story, which depends so strongly on symbolism, becomes itself a symbol for the possible choices of youth.

Questions for analysis   1. Alfred's thesis is about Hawthorne's use of symbolism in "Young Goodman Brown." State her thesis in your own words.

2. How does the opening paragraph forecast the essay's organization?

3. In paragraph 2, Alfred presents evidence for her claim that darkness and light are symbols in the story for "Brown's descent into evil." What kind of evidence does she offer? Does it come from one part of the story or from several parts? How does Alfred demonstrate that darkness and light symbolize Brown's descent into evil and not something else? What other evidence of darkness and light might she have included?

4. Alfred ends her essay with a two-paragraph conclusion. What exactly does she accomplish with such an extended conclusion?

5. Describe the voice you hear in this essay. How authoritative does it sound to you? Point to places in the essay where you think Alfred sounds most authoritative as well as to places where she sounds most tentative and unsure of herself.

6. Alfred assumes that "Young Goodman Brown" cannot be read literally but must be read metaphorically, yet she points out in paragraph 5 that the story's symbolism veils as well as clarifies meaning. What do you think her point is here? How does it affect her ability to interpret the story? What does it imply about all attempts to interpret literature?

Like Brawner, Alfred presents an orderly, coherent case for her interpretation. She makes her points explicit and clear so readers can follow her arguments. She uses the opening paragraph to orient readers, forecasting the key points she will develop to substantiate her thesis. Moreover, she opens each paragraph in her essay with a topic sentence, which directly states the main idea of the paragraph. In addition to keeping the main point clearly before the readers, topic sentences serve to establish the progression of points in the essay.

As evidence for her analysis of Hawthorne's use of symbol, Alfred quotes extensively from the story. She is selective, however: instead of mechanically citing every instance of light and dark symbolism, she selects several representative examples. Writers often use examples this way to support their generalizations. Of course, they have to be sure to choose examples that are typical rather than exceptional; otherwise, they could be accused of overgeneralizing about the entire work from a few carefully—and unfairly—selected examples.

Alfred also arranges her examples to illustrate patterns in the story. She does not list these examples randomly but groups them to develop her point. For instance, she shows how the light and dark symbolism is used to reveal stages in Brown's "descent into evil." Writers can make their case more convincing and coherent by carefully selecting and grouping evidence.

BASIC FEATURES OF LITERARY ANALYSIS

Writing about literature generally has only two key ingredients: an interpretation of the work and a convincing argument based on textual evidence for that interpretation.

The writer's interpretation At the center of a literary analysis lies the writer's interpretation of how the work achieves its particular effects and meaning. This is the point the writer is trying to communicate to readers; it provides the main focus for the essay. Without such a central point, the essay would be just an accumulation of ideas about the work rather than a coherent, reasoned analysis of the work.

In literary analysis, this main idea is usually given directly in a thesis statement. Something of a focal point, the thesis brings the parts of the essay into perspective, helping readers to understand how the subordinate ideas and details relate to one another as well as how they combine to illuminate the work.

For example, Sylvia Alfred announces her thesis at the beginning of the essay: "In the story Hawthorne uses symbolism to explore the question of good and evil." With this thesis, she can bring together various ideas she has about the work—that the forest grows increasingly dark until it is illuminated only by firelight, that the meeting in the forest is described in terms appropriate to a church service, that Brown and the figure he takes for Faith stand together before an altar as they did when they were married. By interpreting the work symbolically, Alfred is able not only to relate these ideas but to see them as expressions of the story's theme of the polarization of good and evil.

Although literary critics may want their analysis to account for subtleties in the work, they do not want their readers to have difficulty understanding their interpretation. No matter how complex their interpretation, they strive to make their writing direct and clear. Therefore, writers usually alert readers to the points they will be making, giving readers a context in which to understand their analysis of the work. Debbie Brawner, for example, provides a detailed forecast when she writes: "Brown's character undergoes many drastic changes during this journey: from a kind, loving, naive man able to see only good, he becomes nasty and guilty and able to see only evil, ending up finally sad and distrustful, unable to reconcile these two views of human nature." This forecasting statement enables readers to anticipate the organization of Brawner's essay and helps them to keep in focus the main idea that Brown's journey is tragic because he is never able to comprehend the complexity of human experience or accept its moral ambiguity.

A convincing argument   In addition to stating their interpretation of the literary work, writers need to present a convincing argument for their main points. They may sometimes assume that readers are familiar with the work, but never can they expect readers to see it as they do or automatically to understand—let alone accept—their interpretation.

Writers argue for their interpretation not so much to convince readers to adopt it but rather to convince them that it makes sense. They must demonstrate to readers how they "read" the work, pointing out specific details and explaining what they think these details mean.

The primary source of evidence for literary analysis, then, is the work itself. Writers quote the work, describe it, summarize it, and paraphrase it. They do more than just refer to a specific passage in the work, however: they explain the meaning of the passage in the light of their thesis. Since the language of literature is so suggestive, writers have to demonstrate to readers how they arrived at their understanding of the work by pointing to specific details in the work and explaining what these details mean to them. In the second paragraph of Brawner's essay, for example, she quotes from the story and summarizes a part of it, and then goes on to show how this textual evidence supports her interpretation.

It is also possible to find ideas and evidence in support of an interpretation from outside sources—other critics, biographical information about the author, historical facts. Not only can such evidence provide insight into the work, but also it may increase the writer's authority and lend the argument credibility. Brawner, for example, draws on the insights of three literary critics. She quotes these authorities to support her own interpretation of "Young Goodman Brown." Occasionally, writers refer to other critics in order to disagree with them; they build their own case not on, but in opposition to, other critics. Disagreements over interpretations are productive and healthy, leading to clearer insights and deeper understanding of the work.

GUIDE TO WRITING

THE WRITING TASK

Write an essay analyzing a work of short fiction to reveal how the work achieves its meaning. Your aim is not primarily to convince readers to adopt your view, but to convince them that your view is a reasonable one based on a thoughtful and imaginative reading of the work.

INVENTION AND RESEARCH

At this point you must choose a short story, analyze it carefully, develop a thesis, find evidence in the story for that thesis, and perhaps research other critics' analysis of the story.

Choosing a literary work

You may have been asked to write on a particular work or even to respond to a specific question on that work. If this is the case, turn now to the next section, Analyzing the Work.

If you need to choose a literary work on your own, you should consider—and read—several works before deciding on one to analyze. Choose a work which impresses you, one which excites your interest and imagination. You should not expect to understand the work completely on the first reading; just be sure to select one that you can study closely.

Analyzing the work

There are many routes to interpreting a literary work, but one that many students and teachers have found useful is a two-step process of annotating and inventorying. (Both these activities are discussed and illustrated in Chapter 18: Invention and Inquiry.) Annotating consists of noting down on the text your impressions, insights, hunches, and questions as you read and reread. Inventorying is a procedure for sorting through your annotations to find patterns and relationships.

Annotating. Before you begin annotating, look at the two examples in A Writer at Work at the end of this chapter. It is a good idea to annotate in two stages:

For your first reading, annotate only what strikes you most forcefully. Note down your first impressions and hunches, as well as anything you find surprising or confusing.

Then reread to annotate the text more fully, particularly those components of the work—character, language, setting, structure, point of view, theme—that suggest the story's meaning to you.

As you read and reread, your annotations will become more and more detailed; eventually, they will lead to your own interpretation of the work.

The following guide lists the basic components of a work of fiction and directs your attention to some of the aspects of those components that suggest meaning. Though they will not all apply to the story you are analyzing, some will lead to important discoveries. Your annotations may focus on only one or two components.

Any character

☐ The name the writer gives this character
☐ The character's thoughts, actions, and words
☐ The way the writer describes this character—a particular dominant trait or several characteristics
☐ How this character changes
☐ This character's values, motives, goals, beliefs
☐ How this character relates to other characters
☐ How this character compares with other characters
☐ Contradictions among his or her thoughts, words, and actions

Language

☐ Unusual words
☐ Words you need to define
☐ Words that suggest a particular feeling or mood
☐ Words that have multiple meanings
☐ Words that form patterns with other words in the text—repetitions, contradictions, tensions, echoes, connections of any kind at all
☐ Images and patterns of images (simile, metaphor, personification)
☐ Descriptions of visual details (shape, color, texture), sounds, smells
☐ Ironical statements—those that say one thing but may mean something else
☐ Symbols—objects or events having more than one level of meaning
☐ Paradoxical statements

Setting

☐ The place and time of the events
☐ Whether the setting changes
☐ The way the writer presents the setting
☐ The mood the setting creates
☐ Whether the setting causes, reflects, or contradicts the characters' actions, values, or moods
☐ How a different setting might alter the story's meaning

Structure

☐ The way the story begins
☐ Any foreshadowing of what will happen

☐ The plot

☐ Points of suspense or tension

☐ The conflict and the eventual climax

☐ Patterns in the work—repeated passages or sections, similar or opposite events

☐ The way the story ends—does it repeat anything from the beginning as a framing device? Are conflicts resolved? Do any uncertainties remain?

Point of view

☐ How we learn about the narrator—description, action, dialogue, statements that reveal attitudes and opinions, other characters' statements

☐ Whether the narrator is a character or just a disembodied voice

☐ Whether the narrator knows everything, including characters' thoughts and feelings, or has only limited knowledge

☐ Whether the narrator focuses on one character, restricting information to what that character knows, sees, thinks, and feels

☐ Whether the narrator can be trusted

☐ How the work would be changed with a different narrator

Themes

☐ Issues and problems raised in the story—philosophical, spiritual, moral, social, political, psychological, aesthetic

☐ Abstract ideas—nature, death, love, equality, alienation, utopia, science, money, heroism

☐ Conflicting forces—illusion vs. reality, death vs. rebirth, the individual vs. society, fate vs. free will, servitude vs. freedom, the city vs. the country

☐ Literary motifs—the quest, initiation rites, the double, self-discovery, the inescapability of death, the fall from innocence

Inventorying. After reading and rereading the work and annotating it heavily in different ways, make a detailed inventory of your annotations to discover what they can tell you about the story. As you were annotating, you almost certainly had many ideas about various meanings in the story; and these may be included in your annotations. Inventorying insures that you will not miss any insights and meanings that may become apparent from patterns, groupings, and connections in your annotations. Experiment with different ways of grouping your ideas and observations. Take risks. Expect to be surprised at the new meanings you may discover.

Finding a tentative thesis

Your aim now is to find a thesis you will be able to develop and support with specific evidence from the story. You may already have a tentative thesis in mind, but it is still advisable to consider several other possibilities.

Following is a list of questions that may lead to a thesis. This list is not exhaustive; it is intended only to give an idea of the kinds of questions you might profitably ask yourself about the story you are analyzing. Select one or more of these questions, and write for five to ten minutes on each one. It is a good idea to start out by trying to answer several questions.

☐ If the principal character undergoes some kind of change, how is this change significant?

☐ If the story seems to be about a relationship between characters, what makes this relationship significant?

☐ If the story calls particular attention to the characters' different values, motives, or beliefs, or if a single character embodies contradictory values, motives, or beliefs, what is the significance of these differences or contradictions?

☐ If you notice a pattern in the language of the story—images, symbols, metaphors, ironies, multiple meanings, paradoxes—what does this pattern suggest about the meaning of the story?

☐ If you detect a parallel between the setting and the characters' actions, values, or moods, how is this parallel significant?

☐ Is the narrative point of view significant? Is the story told from the point of view of a particular character? Does the narrator seem to be unreliable or a poor judge?

☐ If the story focuses on a particular theme, how is this theme conveyed in the plot and characterizations?

Briefly, in a sentence or two, state what you now think will be the thesis of your essay.

Finding textual evidence

Having settled on a tentative thesis, you now need to marshal evidence from the story to support that thesis.

Listing evidence. Search your annotated text and inventory for specific evidence. List everything you can find that seems relevant to your thesis—dialogue, events, descriptive details, key words, images. You may also find evidence that contradicts your thesis. Do not ignore this evidence. Let it lead you to clarify and revise your thesis.

Selecting the best evidence. Review the items in your list to see why you think each particular piece of evidence supports your thesis. Circle or star the evidence you think you will use in your essay.

Now pause for a moment to think about and clarify your thesis. Restate it and give your reasons for believing it to be true.

Researching other critics' analyses

Unless your instructor advises you against reading what other critics have written about this particular story, you might find it helpful to do some library research (see Chapter 20). Reading other critics may turn up alternative interpretations you will want to mention in your essay. It may help you anticipate objections to your interpretation. Or it may enable you to confirm your interpretation, as it did for Brawner. Keep careful notes of your research, noting direct quotations you may later use. Keep a record of your sources, including page numbers.

PLANNING AND DRAFTING

As you prepare to draft your essay, you will need to review your notes, make an outline, and set goals for drafting.

Seeing what you have

Review your notes. If you wish, reread the story. As you review what you have discovered about the story, ask yourself these questions:

- ☐ Can I express my thesis more clearly?
- ☐ What are my reasons for holding this thesis?
- ☐ Can my evidence be interpreted in some other way?
- ☐ Have I overlooked any important evidence?
- ☐ Have I glossed over or ignored any contradictions or problems?

Decide now whether or not you need to do further research. Postpone starting to draft if you find problems that still need to be worked out.

Outlining the essay

At this point you should try to develop a plan for your draft. You may compose a formal outline, a simple list of key points, or a clustering diagram. Each of these kinds of outlines is discussed in Chapter 18: Invention and Inquiry. Whichever method you choose, remember that an outline is only a tentative plan, something to chart your course. It need not be binding; if you have other thoughts along the way, try them out.

Setting goals

Before you start to draft, consider the special demands of literary analysis and of the story you are interpreting. Let the following questions guide you in setting goals.

Your readers

- ☐ Are my readers likely to know this story? If not, how much of the plot should I relate? If so, how can I lead them to see the story as I do?

☐ Might my readers be surprised by my interpretation? Will they disapprove? If so, what common ground can I establish to get them to accept my views?

The beginning

☐ Shall I begin by describing what the work is about, as Brawner does, or by identifying a central question, as Alfred does? Or should I begin in some other way?

☐ How shall I state my thesis? Should I put it in the first paragraph? Or should it go someplace later in the essay?

☐ Do I need to forecast my organization?

The argument

☐ How can I present myself as reasonable and authoritative?

☐ How can I fully explain and develop my ideas?

☐ How much evidence is needed to support each idea?

Avoiding logical fallacies of literary analysis

☐ Will I be committing an *either/or fallacy* by presenting my interpretation as the only possible interpretation?

☐ How can I show that I have accepted *the burden of proof*? Will my readers believe that I have taken responsibility for presenting a convincing argument for my interpretation?

☐ Can I avoid making a *straw man* of others' interpretations, oversimplifying or misrepresenting them to make my interpretation seem stronger? (Straw men are easier to push over than real men.)

☐ Can I avoid *hasty generalization* by offering adequate evidence for all the general statements I make about the work?

The ending

☐ Shall I end with an extended discussion, as Alfred does?

☐ Should I repeat key words from my essay, as Brawner does?

☐ Should I restate my thesis or summarize my main points?

☐ Should I end with a provocative question?

Drafting a literary analysis

Before going on to the following advice on drafting an essay of literary analysis, review the general advice on drafting in Chapter 1.

☐ Keep in mind the two goals of all literary analysis: presenting your interpretation and supporting that interpretation with textual evidence.

□ If some time has gone by since you last read the story, reread it quickly now. You should have the work fresh in your mind as you write.

□ As you draft, try to be as direct as you can. Explain your ideas fully. Make the relations between the thesis, the points you use to develop it, and the supporting evidence explicit for readers. Remember they will have different ways of reading and understanding the passages you quote or refer to. Show them how you are using specific evidence from the work to make your own point about the work.

READING A DRAFT WITH A CRITICAL EYE

As you read, remember the aim of literary analysis is *not* primarily to convince readers to adopt your idea, but to convince them that the idea is reasonable and based on imaginative, thoughtful analysis of the work.

First general impression   Read the essay straight through to get a quick, general impression. Write just a few sentences giving your first reaction. Did it make sense? Did it seem reasonable? Briefly paraphrase the essay's thesis. Make a note of any objections that might be raised.

Pointings   One good way to maintain a critical focus as you read the essay is to highlight noteworthy features of the writing with *pointings*. A simple system of lines and brackets, these pointings are quick and easy to do, and they can provide a lot of helpful information for revision. Use pointings in the following way:

□ Draw a straight line under words or images that impress you as especially effective: strong verbs, specific details, memorable phrases, striking images.

□ Draw a wavy line under any words or images that seem flat, stale, or vague. Also put the wavy line under any words or phrases that you consider unnecessary or repetitious.

□ Look for pairs or groups of sentences that you think should be combined. Put brackets [ ] around these sentences.

□ Look for sentences that are garbled, overloaded, or awkward. Put parentheses ( ) around these sentences. Put them around any sentence which seems even slightly questionable; don't worry now about whether or not you're certain about your judgment. The writer needs to know that you, as one reader, had even the slightest hesitation about understanding a sentence.

Analysis

1. To be convincing, literary analysis must be grounded in specific textual evidence. Point to any places where evidence must still be provided.

2. Textual evidence should be clearly related to a specific point. Alert the writer to any evidence that is not tied to an idea.

3. Ideas must not only be supported with textual evidence, but they must also be fully explained. Point to any ideas which need more clarification or development.

4. Point out any ideas that seem unrelated to the thesis, disconnected from the other ideas, or contradictory.

5. Literary analysis occasionally needs to relate details of the plot. Let the writer know, however, if too much space is devoted to plot summary and not enough to analysis.

6. If other critics are cited, decide whether they strengthen or weaken the essay's argument. Explain your views.

7. Evaluate the beginning. How does it prepare the reader for the essay? Suggest other ways to open.

8. Evaluate the ending. Is it too abrupt or mechanical? Does it oversimplify the argument or distort the thesis? Try to suggest an alternate ending.

9. What final comments or suggestions can you offer? Do you have any unanswered questions?

REVISING AND EDITING

Now you must revise your draft and edit your writing.

Revising Literary Analysis

You might want to review the general advice on revising in Chapter 1 before proceeding to the following specific advice for revising literary analysis.

Revising to strengthen the argument

☐ Reconsider your interpretation of the story. Can your thesis be refined? Should you add more evidence or explain more specifically how your evidence supports your thesis?

☐ Can you strengthen the logical connections among your ideas?

☐ If you cite other critics, could you make better use of their ideas?

☐ Reread your argument with your readers in mind. Have you fully considered the likelihood that they might interpret the story in some other way and that therefore you need to show them not only how you see it but why you see it as you do?

☐ Consider each of the main ideas. Are they now in the best possible order, or should they be presented in some other order?

Revising for readability

☐ Reconsider the beginning. Could you better prepare readers to follow your argument? Does the essay need a forecasting statement?

☐ Do you need to provide more explicit transitions between sentences and paragraphs?

☐ Do you sometimes give more details than you need to?

☐ Reconsider the ending. How can you improve it? Can you see any other point in the essay that would be a stronger place to end?

Editing and proofreading
As you revise a draft for the last time, you need to edit it closely. Though you no doubt corrected obvious errors of usage and style in the drafting stage, editing was not your first priority. Now, however, you must find and correct any errors of mechanics, usage, punctuation, or style.

When you have edited the draft and produced the final copy you must proofread it carefully for any careless mistakes.

LEARNING FROM YOUR OWN WRITING PROCESS

If your instructor asks you to write about what you learned from writing this essay, consider the following questions:

☐ How did my thesis evolve as I planned and drafted the essay?

☐ How did I go about analyzing the work?

☐ What problems, if any, did I have finding evidence to support the thesis?

☐ Why did I decide to organize the essay as I did?

☐ What specific revisions, if any, did I make in the draft and what were my reasons for making these changes?

A WRITER AT WORK

ANNOTATING A LITERARY WORK

This section demonstrates how writers annotate the literary works they are preparing to write about. Annotating is the most important invention activity in writing about literature, for it helps writers to read closely and analytically, to focus their reading, and to record their discoveries.

As they read, writers examine the work to see how it conveys its meaning and effects, writing their observations on the text and in the margins. They highlight language that seems important and also write down their reading responses—questions they have and their tentative answers, patterns they find, ideas and insights that occur to them as they read. Annotating helps writers figure out what they think about the work.

Usually writers read the work several times. They read initially to familiarize themselves with the work before deciding how to focus their analysis of it. They may read the work quickly the first time before they begin to annotate. Or they may begin annotating from the start, making general observations at first and more specific ones later, adding layer upon layer of annotation during each subsequent reading.

This section will show you two writers at work—Debbie Brawner and Sylvia Alfred, the two students whose essays on "Young Goodman Brown" appear earlier in this chapter. Even though both writers have a common view of "Young Goodman Brown"—both think the story is about Brown's struggle with good and evil—their annotated texts look quite different. This is partly because they have different styles of annotating and partly because they are attentive to different components of the work. Simply put, Alfred focuses on the story's symbolism, whereas Brawner is concerned primarily with character.

Brawner and Alfred both heavily annotate that part of the story in which Brown, "maddened with despair," traverses the woods until he comes to a clearing where a meeting is taking place. For Alfred, this part is interesting because she finds many symbolic correspondences between the forest meeting and a typical church meeting. For Brawner, it signifies important changes in Brown's character.

Let us first look at Alfred's annotations. In her essay, Alfred focuses on the story's symbolism, and you can see in her annotations how attentive she is to the language and imagery Hawthorne uses to present the scene. What follows is an excerpt of her annotated text, the result of several readings and stages of annotation.

stunned

Brown's faith in good/God gone

hopelessness

goes deeper into forest

wild sounds

church bell

medicine man

against God, sacrilege, curse

possessed by the devil

forest clearing, infernal fire
unnatural glow
hymn

meeting house = church

night, unenlightened
harmony

altar, candles
an evening meeting
Witches' Sabbath

"My Faith is gone!" cried he, after one (stupefied) moment. "There is no 1
good on earth; and sin is but a name. Come, devil! for to thee is this world
given."

And maddened with (despair,) so that he laughed loud and long, did Good- 2
man Brown grasp his staff and set forth again, at such a rate, that he seemed
to fly along the forest path, rather than to walk or run. The road grew <u>wilder</u>
and <u>drearier</u>, and more <u>faintly traced</u>, and vanished at length, leaving him in
the heart of the <u>dark</u> wilderness, still rushing onward, with the instinct that
guides mortal man to evil. The whole forest was peopled with <u>frightful sounds</u>;
the <u>creaking</u> of the trees, the <u>howling</u> of wild beasts, and the <u>yell</u> of Indians;
while, sometimes, the <u>wind tolled like a distant church bell</u>, and sometimes
gave a <u>broad roar</u> around the traveler, as if all Nature were laughing him to
scorn. But he was himself the chief horror of the scene, and shrank not from
its other horrors.

"Ha! ha! ha!" roared Goodman Brown, when the wind laughed at him. 3
"Let us hear which will laugh loudest! Think not to frighten me with your
<u>deviltry</u>! Come <u>witch</u>, come <u>wizard</u>, come Indian (powow) come <u>devil</u> himself!
and here comes Goodman Brown. You may as well fear him as he fear you!"

In truth, all through the <u>haunted</u> forest, there could be nothing more 4
frightful than the figure of Goodman Brown. On he flew, among the <u>black</u>
pines, brandishing his <u>staff with</u> frenzied gestures, now giving vent to an
inspiration of horrid (blasphemy,) and now shouting forth such laughter, as
set all the echoes of the forest laughing like <u>demons</u> around him. The <u>fiend</u>
in his own shape <u>is less</u> hideous than when he rages in the breast of man.
Thus sped the (demoniac) on his course, until, quivering among the trees, he
saw a <u>red light</u> before him, as when the felled trunks and branches of a
clearing have been set on <u>fire</u>, and throw up their (lurid) blaze against the sky,
at the hour of midnight. He paused, in a lull of the tempest that had driven
him onward, and heard the <u>swell of what seemed</u> a <u>hymn</u> rolling <u>solemnly</u>
from a distance, with the weight of many voices. <u>He knew the tune; it was
a familiar one in the choir of the village meeting-house</u>. The verse died heavily
away, and was <u>lengthened</u> by a <u>chorus</u>, not of human voices, but of all the
sounds of the (benighted) wilderness, pealing in <u>awful harmony</u> together.
Goodman Brown cried out; and his cry was lost to his own ear, by its (unison)
with the cry of the desert.

In the interval of silence, he stole forward, until the <u>light glared</u> full upon 5
his eyes. At one extremity of an open space, hemmed in by the <u>dark wall</u> of
the forest, arose a rock, bearing some rude, natural resemblance either to an
<u>altar</u> or a <u>pulpit</u>, and surrounded by <u>four blazing pines, their tops aflame,
their stems untouched, like candles at an evening meeting</u>. The mass of
foliage, that had overgrown the summit of the rock, was all on <u>fire, blazing</u>

hanging
foliage
assembly of worship

high into the night, and fitfully illuminating the whole field. Each (pendent) twig and leafy (festoon) was in a blaze. As the red light arose and fell, a numerous (congregation) alternately shone forth, then disappeared in shadow, and again grew, as it were, out of the darkness, peopling the heart of the solitary woods at once.

A glance will tell you that Alfred is interested in Hawthorne's choice of words. She circles many words she needs to define and writes their definitions in the margins. In addition, she underlines words that show patterns of symbolism. These patterns she often notes in marginal comments and with lines between synonyms and related words.

Alfred outlines the story by labeling plot elements (Brown "goes deeper into forest") and new scenes ("forest clearing"). Her comments tend to be short phrases, reminders of what she is seeing as she reads. This highlighting and commenting allows Alfred to identify what strikes her as most important about this part of the story. She refers to this scene extensively in her essay (pages 286–87, paragraphs 2-4).

Brawner also focuses on this part of the story, but she emphasizes Brown's behavior rather than the way the scene is described. She highlights everything Brown does and thinks, noting how he changes from one moment to the next. Descriptions of Brown attract her attention. Her marginal comments reveal this emphasis and illustrate a different style of annotating.

stupefied—dazed, stunned

Brown snaps at loss of Faith. Gives up belief in good. Believes world evil—the devil's. Goes mad. Picks up devil's staff.

Nature is wild, scornful.

Scene is frightening, but Brown is even more frightening—chief horror.

Brown challenges the devil, becomes one himself?

"My Faith is gone!" cried he, after one (stupefied) moment. "There is no 1 good on earth; and sin is but a name. Come, devil! for to thee is this world given."

And maddened with despair, so that he laughed loud and long, did Good- 2 man Brown grasp his staff and set forth again, at such a rate, that he seemed to fly along the forest path, rather than to walk or run. The road grew wilder and drearier, and more faintly traced, and vanished at length, leaving him in the heart of the dark wilderness, still rushing onward, with the instinct that guides mortal man to evil. The whole forest was peopled with frightful sounds; the creaking of the trees, the howling of wild beasts, and the yell of Indians; while, sometimes, the wind tolled [like] a distant church bell, and sometimes gave a broad roar around the traveler, [as if] all Nature were laughing him to scorn. But he was himself the chief horror of the scene, and shrank not from its other horrors.

"Ha! ha! ha!" roared Goodman Brown, when the wind laughed at him. 3 "Let us hear which will laugh loudest! Think not to frighten me with your deviltry! Come witch, come wizard, come Indian powow, come devil himself! [and] here comes Goodman Brown. You may as well fear him as he fear you!"

In truth, all through the haunted forest, there could be nothing more 4 frightful than the figure of Goodman Brown. On he flew, among the black pines, brandishing his staff with frenzied gestures, now giving vent to an inspiration of horrid blasphemy, and now shouting forth such laughter, as set all the echoes of the forest laughing [like] demons around him. The (fiend) in his own shape is less hideous than when he rages in the breast of man. Thus sped the (demoniac) on his course, until, quivering among the trees, he saw a red light before him, as when the felled trunks and branches of a clearing have been set on fire, and throw up their lurid blaze against the sky, at the hour of midnight. He paused, in a lull of the tempest that had driven him onward, and heard the swell of what [seemed] a hymn rolling solemnly from a distance, with the weight of many voices. He knew the tune; it was a familiar one in the choir of the village meeting-house. The verse died heavily away, and was lengthened by a chorus, not of human voices, but of all the sounds of the benighted wilderness, pealing in awful harmony together. Goodman Brown cried out; and his cry was lost to his own ear, by its (unison) with the cry of the desert.

In the interval of silence, he stole forward, until the light glared full upon 5 his eyes. At one extremity of an open space, hemmed in by the dark wall of the forest, arose a rock, bearing some rude, natural [resemblance] either to an altar or a pulpit, and surrounded by four blazing pines, their tops aflame, their stems untouched, [like] candles at an evening meeting. The mass of foliage, that had overgrown the summit of the rock, was all on fire, blazing high into the night, and (fitfully) illuminating the whole field. Each pendent twig and leafy festoon was in a blaze. As the red light arose and fell, a numerous congregation alternately shone forth, then disappeared in shadow, and again grew, as it were, out of the darkness, peopling the heart of the solitary woods at once.

Unlike Alfred, Brawner outlines the plot, paying special attention to Brown's actions. In annotating the description of the devil's meeting, she is interested less in symbolic correspondences than in analyzing Brown's perceptions in order to decide whether what he sees is real or imagined. She even puts brackets around words that suggest Brown may be imagining, rather than actually seeing, something.

In her essay, Brawner refers to this passage briefly (in paragraph 6, page 284). But she sees it as the story's climax, the turning point when Brown changes character by allowing his evil side to emerge.

Alfred's and Brawner's annotations are but two possible ways of reading "Young Goodman Brown." There is no single—or right—way to read and annotate a literary work.

Marginal annotations (left column):

Echoes of his laughing sound to him like demons' laughter.

fiend = evil spirit

Devil raging in his breast.

demoniac = raging, possessed

Thinks he hears a hymn.

Brown's cries join cries of other lost souls? Desert/wilderness

unison = harmony

Devil's meeting

Can't be sure what he sees—in and out of vision, things seem like other things.

fitfully = irregularly

Profiling People and Places

☐ A college student decides to profile a local radio station for the campus newspaper. In several visits to the station she observes its inner workings and interviews the manager, technicians, and disc jockeys. Her essay shows how the disc jockeys, who make a living by being outrageous, are nonetheless engaged in very routine day-to-day work.

☐ A journalist assigned to write about a Nobel prize-winning scientist decides to profile a day in her life. He spends a couple of days observing her at home and at work, and interviews colleagues, students, and family, as well as the scientist herself. Her daily life, he learns, is very much like that of other working mothers—a constant effort to balance the demands of her career against the needs of her family. He presents this theme in his essay by alternating details about the scientist's work career with those about her daily life.

☐ A student in an art history class writes a profile of a local artist recently commissioned to paint outdoor murals for the city. The student visits the artist's studio and talks with him about the process of painting murals. The artist invites the student to spend the following day as part of a team of local art students and neighborhood volunteers working on the mural under the artist's direction. This firsthand experience helps the student describe the process of mural painting almost from an insider's point of view.

☐ A student in a sociology class profiles a controversial urban renewal project. She discovers from newspaper reports the names of opponents and supporters of the project, and interviews several of them. Then she visits the site and takes a tour of it with the project manager. Her essay alternates description of the renovation with analysis of the controversy.

10

☐ For a writing workshop, a student profiles the library's rare book room. In the essay, he narrates his adventure into this previously uncharted territory. Expecting to find a sedate library with shelf after shelf of leather-bound first editions, he is surprised to find manuscript drafts, letters, diaries, and dog-eared annotated books (including some cheap paperback editions) from famous authors' libraries.

Magazines and newspapers are filled with profiles. Whereas traditional news stories report current events, profiles tell about the fascinating people, places, and activities in our community. Some profiles take us behind the scenes of familiar places, giving us a glimpse of their inner workings. Others introduce us to the exotic—peculiar hobbies, unusual professions, bizarre personalities. Still others probe the social, political, and moral significance of our institutions. At the heart of most profiles are vivid details and sharp contrasts that can capture readers' curiosity.

Writing a profile can be challenging and fun, taking you out into the community as well as into the library. By requiring you to sort through and organize information from a wide range of sources, it is an activity that will help you to develop your research and analytical skills as well as your creativity.

READINGS

The first selection, published in *Esquire* in 1983, profiles a team of brain surgeons as they perform a complicated operation. It provides an inside look at something very few of us are likely ever to see—the human brain.

David Noonan, a freelance journalist, started with a sure-fire subject, guaranteed to intrigue readers. He had to handle it with some delicacy, however, so as not to make readers uneasy with overly explicit description or uncomfortable with excessive amounts of technical terminology. Think about your own responses as you read this piece. Are you upset by any of the graphic detail or overwhelmed by the terminology?

INSIDE THE BRAIN
DAVID NOONAN

The patient lies naked and unconscious in the center of the cool, tiled 1
room. His head is shaved, his eyes and nose taped shut. His mouth bulges
with the respirator that is breathing for him. Clear plastic tubes carry anes-
thetic into him and urine out of him. Belly up under the bright lights he looks
large and helpless, exposed. He is not dreaming; he is too far under for that.
The depth of his obliviousness is accentuated by the urgent activity going on
all around him. Nurses and technicians move in and out of the room preparing
the instruments of surgery. At his head, two doctors are discussing the approach they will use in the operation. As they talk they trace possible incisions
across his scalp with their fingers.

It is a Monday morning. Directed by Dr. Stein, Abe Steinberger is going 2
after a large tumor compressing the brainstem, a case that he describes as
"a textbook beauty." It is a rare operation, a suboccipital craniectomy, su-
pracerebellar infratentorial approach. That is, into the back of the head and
over the cerebellum, under the tentorium to the brainstem and the tumor.
Stein has done the operation more than fifty times, more than any other
surgeon in the United States.

Many neurosurgeons consider brainstem tumors of this type inoperable 3
because of their location and treat them instead with radiation. "It's where
you live," says Steinberger. Breathing, heartbeat, and consciousness itself are
some of the functions connected with this primary part of the brain. Literally
and figuratively, it is the core of the organ, and operating on it is always very
risky. . . .

The human skull was not designed for easy opening. It takes drills and 4
saws and simple force to breach it. It is a formidable container, and its thickness testifies to the value of its contents. Opening the skull is one of the first
things apprentice brain surgeons get to do on their own. It is sometimes
called cabinet work, and on this case Steinberger is being assisted in the
opening by Bob Solomon.

The patient has been clamped into a sitting position. Before the first 5
incision is made he is rolled under the raised instrument table and he disappears beneath sterile green drapes and towels. The only part of him left
exposed is the back of his head, which is orange from the sterilizing agent
painted on it. Using a special marker, Steinberger draws the pattern of the
opening on the patient's head in blue. Then the first cut is made into the
scalp, and a thin line of bright-red blood appears.

The operation takes place within what is called the sterile field, a small 6
germfree zone created and vigilantly patrolled by the scrub nurses. The sterile
field extends out and around from the surgical opening and up over the
instrument table. Once robed and gloved, the doctors are considered sterile
from the neck to the waist and from the hands up the arms to just below
the shoulders. The time the doctors must spend scrubbing their hands has
been cut from ten minutes to five, but this obsessive routine is still the most
striking of the doctor's preparations. Leaning over the troughlike stainless-

steel sink with their masks in place and their arms lathered to the elbow, the surgeons carefully attend to each finger with the brush and work their way up each arm. It is the final pause, the last thing they do before they enter the operating room and go to work. Many at NI are markedly quiet while they scrub; they spend the familiar minutes running through the operation one more time. When they finish and their hands are too clean for anything but surgery they turn off the water with knee controls and back through the OR door, their dripping hands held high before them. They dry off with sterile towels, step into long-sleeved robes, and then plunge their hands down into their thin surgical gloves, which are held for them by the scrub nurse. The gloves snap as the nurse releases them around the doctors' wrists. Unnaturally smooth and defined, the gloved hands of the neurosurgeons are now ready; they can touch the living human brain.

"Drill the hell out of it," Steinberger says to Solomon. The scalp has been 7
retracted and the skull exposed. Solomon presses the large stainless-steel power drill against the bone and hits the trigger. The bit turns slowly, biting into the white skull. Shavings drop from the hole onto the drape and then to the floor. The drill stops automatically when it is through the bone. The hole is about a half inch in diameter. Solomon drills four holes in a diamond pattern. The skull at the back of the head is ridged and bumpy. There is a faint odor of burning bone.

The drilling is graphic and jarring. The drill and the head do not go to- 8
gether; they collide and shock the eye. The tool is too big; its scale and shape are inappropriate to the delicate idea of neurosurgery. It should be hanging on the wall of a garage. After the power drill, a hand drill is used to refine the holes in the skull. It is a sterilized stainless-steel version of a handyman's tool. It is called a perforator, and as Solomon calmly turns it, more shavings hit the floor. Then, using powerful plierlike tools called Leksell rongeurs, the doctors proceed to bite away at the skull, snapping and crunching bone to turn the four small holes into a single opening about three inches in diameter. This is a *craniectomy*; the hole in the skull will always be there, protected by the many layers of scalp muscle at the back of the head. In a *craniotomy* a flap of bone is preserved to cover the opening in the skull.

After the scalp and the skull, the next layer protecting the brain is the 9
dura. A thin, tough, leathery membrane that encases the brain, the dura (derived from the Latin for *hard*) is dark pink, almost red. It is rich with blood vessels and nerves (when you have a headache, it's the dura that aches), and now it can be seen stretching across the expanse of the opening, pulsing lightly. The outline of the cerebellum bulging against the dura is clear. With a crease in the middle, the dura-sheathed cerebellum looks oddly like a tiny pair of buttocks. The resemblance prompts a moment's joking. "Her firm young cerebellum," somebody says. . . .

The dura is carefully opened and sewn back out of the way. An hour and 10
fifteen minutes after the drilling began, the brain is exposed.

The brain exposed. It happens every day on the tenth floor, three, four, 11 and five times a day, day after day, week in and week out, month after month. The brain exposed. Light falls on its gleaming surface for the first time. It beats lightly, steadily. It is pink and gray, the brain, and the cerebellar cortex is covered with tiny blood vessels, in a web. In some openings you can see the curve of the brain, its roundness. It does not look strong, it looks very soft, soft enough to push your finger through. When you see it for the first time you almost expect sparks, tiny sparks arcing across the surface, blinking lights, the crackle of an idea. You stare down at it and it gives nothing back, reveals nothing, gives no hint of how it works. As soon as they see it the doctors begin the search for landmarks. They start talking to each other, describing what they both can see, narrating the anatomy.

In the operating room the eyes bear much of the burden of communi- 12
cation. With their surgical masks and caps in place, the doctors and nurses resort to exaggerated stares and squints and flying eyebrows to emphasize what they are saying. After more than two decades in the operating room, Dr. Stein has developed this talent for nonverbal punctuation to a fine art. His clear blue eyes narrow now in concentration as he listens to Abe explain what he wants to do next. They discuss how to go about retracting the cerebellum. "Okay, Abe," Stein says quietly. "Nice and easy now."

The cerebellum (the word means *little brain*) is one of the most compli- 13
cated parts of the brain. It is involved in the processing of sensory information of all kinds as well as balance and motor control, but in this case it is simply in the way. With the dura gone the cerebellum bulges out of the back of the head; it can be seen from across the room, protruding into space, striated and strange-looking.

When the cerebellum is retracted, the microscope is rolled into place and 14
the operation really begins. It is a two-man scope, with a cable running to a TV monitor and a videotape machine. Sitting side by side, looking through the scope into the head, Steinberger and Stein go looking for the tumor.

It is a long and tedious process, working your way into the center of the 15
human brain. The joke about the slip of the scalpel that wiped out fifteen years of piano lessons is no joke. Every seen and unseen piece of tissue does something, has some function, though it may well be a mystery to the surgeon. In order to spend hour after hour at the microscope, manipulating their instruments in an area no bigger than the inside of a juice can, neurosurgeons must develop an awesome capacity for sustained concentration.

After two hours of talking their way through the glowing red geography 16
of the inner brain, Stein and Steinberger come upon the tumor. "Holy Toledo, look at that," exclaims Steinberger. The tumor stands out from the tissue around it, purple and mean-looking. It is the end of order in a very small, orderly place. It does not belong. They pause a moment, and Abe gives a quick tour of the opening. "That's tumor, that's the brainstem, and that's the third ventricle," he says. "And that over there, that's memory."

A doctor from the pathology department shows up for a piece of the 17
tumor. It will be analyzed quickly while the operation is under way so the

surgeons will know what they are dealing with. The type of tumor plays an important part in decisions about how much to take out, what risks to take in the attempt to get it all. A more detailed tissue analysis will be made later.

It turns out to be a brainstem glioma, an invasive intrinsic tumor actually 18 growing up out of the brainstem. It is malignant. They get a lot of it but it will grow back. With radiation the patient could live fifteen years or even longer, and he will be told so. Abe Steinberger, in fact, will tell him. More than six hours after the first incision, the operation ends.

When the operation is over it is pointed out to Steinberger that he is the 19 same age as the patient. "Really?" he says. "It's funny, I always think of the patients as being older than me."

How they think of the patients is at the center of the residents' approach 20 to neurosurgery. It is a sensitive subject, and they have all given it a lot of thought. They know well the classic preconceived notion of the surgeon as a cold and arrogant technician. "You think like a surgeon" is a medical-school insult. Beyond that, the residents actually know a lot of surgeons, and though they say most of them don't fit the stereotype, they also say that there are some who really do bring it to life.

In many ways the mechanics of surgery itself create a distance between 21 the surgeon and the patient. A man with a tumor is a case, a collection of symptoms. He is transformed into a series of X rays, CAT scans, and angio-grams. He becomes his tumor, is even referred to by his affliction. "We've got a beautiful meningioma coming in tomorrow," a doctor will say. Once in the operating room the patient disappears beneath the drapes and is reduced to a small red hole. Though it is truly the ultimate intimacy, neuro-surgery can be starkly impersonal.

"The goal of surgery is to get as busy as you can doing good cases and 22 making people *better* by operating on them," says Phil Cogen. "That auto-matically cuts down the time you spend with patients." Though this frustrates Cogen, who has dreams and nightmares about his patients "all the time," he also knows there is a high emotional price to pay for getting too close. "One of the things you learn to do as a surgeon in any field is disassociate yourself from the person you're operating on. I never looked under the drapes at the patient until my third year in neurosurgery, when it was too late to back out."

While Cogen prides himself on not having a "surgical personality," Abe 23 Steinberger believes that his skills are best put to use in the operating room and doesn't worry too much about the problems of patient relations. "I sympathize with the patients," he says. "I feel very bad when they're sick and I feel great when they're better. But what I want to do is operate. I want to get in there and do it."

Questions for analysis   1. Did this profile arouse, and then satisfy, your curiosity? How? What did you find most interesting in it?

2. The closest Noonan comes to explicitly stating the theme of this essay is at the end of paragraph 21: "Though it is truly the ultimate intimacy, neurosurgery can be starkly impersonal." How does he demonstrate this incongruity?

3. Paragraph 2 contains some technical terms. How does Noonan make these words understandable to his readers? Why do you think he uses such specialized language? What else could he do?

4. Paragraphs 4–11 show the process of opening the skull. How does Noonan make this process especially vivid?

5. In paragraph 11 Noonan repeats the same sentence fragment twice: "The brain exposed." Why do you think he uses a sentence fragment here and even states it twice? How else could he have achieved the same effect?

6. The process of exposing the brain takes only an hour and fifteen minutes of the entire six-hour operation, yet Noonan uses eight paragraphs (4–11) telling about the procedure. The other four hours and forty-five minutes of the operation—including the retraction of the cerebellum (paragraph 13), the painstaking search for the tumor (paragraphs 14–16), and the removal of the tumor (paragraphs 17–18)—are described in six paragraphs. Examine these paragraphs closely. Compare the pace in paragraphs 4–11 with that in paragraphs 13–18.

7. Noonan quotes both Dr. Stein and Dr. Steinberger, letting us hear what they say during the operation (paragraphs 3, 7, 12, and 15). What do these quotations add to the essay? How might the essay have been different had Noonan paraphrased rather than quoted?

8. Look at paragraphs 1 and 2. Either one could well have opened the essay. What would have been gained and what would have been lost if Noonan had begun his essay with paragraph 2?

9. If you were asked to profile a highly skilled specialist at work, what specialty would you choose? What kind of information would you need to write such a profile?

Like all profile writers, Noonan had to research his subject thoroughly. Although most of his information obviously comes from observing and interviewing, he may also have done considerable background reading to familiarize himself with surgical terminology and procedures.

Just as important as the actual information a writer provides is the way he or she arranges and presents it. Information must be organized in a way appropriate to the audience as well as to the content itself. It must be both accessible to readers and focused on some main point or theme. Noonan focuses on the drama of the operation. He was clearly struck by the incongruity between the intimacy of probing a human brain and the impersonal way it was actually done. Profile writers often use an incongruity—a notable discrepancy or a surprising contradiction, for instance—as the theme of their profile.

Noonan uses narration to structure his profile. Instead of just telling us how brain surgery is done, he shows us the procedures firsthand. He presents us with an actual patient ("belly up under the bright lights"), and takes us through an actual operation—preparing the patient and the surgical instruments, drilling the skull to expose the brain, painstakingly searching through the brain for the tumor.

Narrating allows Noonan to re-create the drama of the operation. He gives his narrative immediacy by showing us the scene and much of the action in vivid, even startling detail. At the end of paragraph 5, for example, Noonan shows us the patient swathed in green draping, his scalp exposed and painted orange with sterilizing agent. We then witness as Dr. Steinberger outlines the incision in blue and as "a thin line of bright-red blood appears" along the line of the incision. Although he does not show us the surgeon cutting into the scalp, he shows us the results of this action—a thin line of blood.

One way Noonan creates tension and drama is by varying the pace of the narrative, slowing it here and quickening it there, closing in and moving back, telescoping or collapsing time as fits his purpose. Let us take a close look at the craniectomy (paragraphs 7–9) to see how Noonan varies the pace. He begins dramatically by quoting Dr. Solomon ("Drill the hell out of it"), then sets the stage by telling us that the scalp has already been retracted and the skull exposed. With a series of active present-tense verbs and present participles, Noonan re-creates the actual drilling for us. But he only shows us the drilling of one hole; he summarizes the drilling of the other three. He also interrupts the narrative to reflect on his own thoughts and feelings. When he returns to narrating, we see Dr. Solomon calmly turning the perforator as "more shavings hit the floor" and hear the snapping and crunching of bone as an opening is made between the holes.

Noonan not only paces his narrative, but he also paces the flow of information. He inserts bits of information into the narrative, as in paragraph 8 when he tells us that a hand drill called a perforator is used after the power drill and how a craniotomy differs from a craniectomy. Sometimes the information takes a minute, subordinated in a clause or a brief sentence. At other times, it takes longer and seems to suspend the narrative altogether, as when he explains the idea of a sterile field and describes the scrubbing-up process in paragraph 6.

By varying the duration of each narrative segment and controlling the amount of information he is presenting, Noonan maintains a brisk pace which keeps his readers informed as well as entertained.

The next writer, John McPhee, a master of this genre, regularly contributes profiles to the *New Yorker* and has published several collections of profiles.

"The Pinball Philosophy" is a profile of J. Anthony Lukas, a Pulitzer Prize-winning author who is also a pinball enthusiast. McPhee uses this incongruity as the focus of his profile, contrasting Lukas's staunch "respectability" with the "disreputable" game of pinball. As you read, consider how McPhee makes this incongruity the focal point of his essay.

THE PINBALL PHILOSOPHY
JOHN MCPHEE

New York City, March 1975

J. Anthony Lukas is a world-class pinball player who, between tilts, does some free-lance writing. In our city, he is No. ½. This is to say, he is one of two players who share pinball preeminence—two players whose special skills within the sport are so multiple and varied that they defy comparative analysis. The other star is Tom Buckley, of the *Times*. Pinball people tend to gravitate toward Lukas or Buckley. Lukas is a Lukasite. He respects Buckley, but he sees himself as the whole figure, the number "1." His machine is a Bally. Public pinball has been illegal in New York for many decades, but private ownership is permitted, and Lukas plays, for the most part, at home.

Lukas lives in an old mansion, a city landmark, on West Seventy-sixth Street. The machine is in his living room, under a high, elegant ceiling, near an archway to rooms beyond. Bally is the Rolls-Royce of pinball, he explains as he snaps a ball into action. It rockets into the ellipse at the top of the playfield. It ricochets four times before beginning its descent. Lukas likes a four-bounce hold in the ellipse—to set things up for a long ball. There is something faintly, and perhaps consciously, nefarious about Lukas, who is an aristocratic, olive-skinned, Andalusian sort of man, with deep eyes in dark wells. As the butts of his hands pound the corners of his machine, one can imagine him cheating at polo. "It's a wrist game," he says, tremoring the Bally, helping the steel ball to bounce six times off the top thumper-bumper and, each time, go back up a slot to the ellipse—an awesome economy of fresh beginnings. "Strong wrists are really all you want to use. The term for what I am doing is 'reinforcing.'" His voice, rich and dense, pours out like cigarette smoke filtered through a New England prep school. "There are certain basics to remember," he says. "Above all, don't flail with the flipper. You *carry* the ball in the direction you want it to go. You can almost cradle the ball on the flipper. And always hit the slingshot hard. That's the slingshot there—where the rubber is stretched between bumpers. Reinforce it hard. And never—never—drift toward the free-ball gate." Lukas reinforces the machine just as the ball hits the slingshot. The rebound comes off with blurring speed, striking bumpers, causing gongs to ring and lights to flash. Under his hands, the chrome on the frame has long since worn away.

Lukas points out that one of the beauties of his Bally is that it is asym- 3
metrical. Early pinball machines had symmetrical playfields—symmetrical
thumper-bumpers—but in time they became free-form, such as this one, with
its field laid out not just for structure but also for surprise. Lukas works in
this room—stacks of manuscript on shelves and tables. He has been working
for many months on a book that will weigh five pounds. It will be called
Nightmare: The Dark Side of the Nixon Years—a congenially chosen title,
implying that there was a bright side. The pinball machine is Lukas's collab-
orator. "When a paragraph just won't go," he says, "and I begin to say to
myself, 'I can't make this work,' I get up and play the machine. I score in a
high range. Then I go back to the typewriter a new man. I have beat the
machine. Therefore I can beat the paragraph." He once won a Pulitzer Prize.

The steel ball rolls into the "death channel"—Lukas's term for a long alley 4
down the left side—and drops out of sight off the low end of the playfield,
finished.

With another ball, he ignites an aurora on the scoreboard. During the 5
ball's complex, prolonged descent, he continues to set forth the pinball philosophy. "More seriously, the game does give you a sense of controlling
things in a way that in life you can't do. And there is risk in it, too. The ball
flies into the ellipse, into the playfield—full of opportunities. But there's always the death channel—the run-out slot. There are rewards, prizes, coming
off the thumper-bumper. The ball crazily bounces from danger to opportunity
and back to danger. You need reassurance in life that in taking risks you will
triumph, and pinball gives you that reaffirmation. Life is a risky game, but
you can beat it."

Unfortunately, Lukas has a sick flipper. At the low end of the playfield, 6
two flippers guard the run-out slot, but one waggles like a broken wing,
pathetic, unable to function, to fling the ball uphill for renewed rewards. The
ball, instead, slides by the crippled flipper and drops from view.

Lukas opens the machine. He lifts the entire playfield, which is hinged at 7
the back, and props it up on a steel arm, like the lid of a grand piano. Revealed
below is a neat, arresting world that includes spring-loaded hole kickers,
contact switches, target switches, slingshot assemblies, the score-motor unit,
the electric anti cheat, three thumper-bumper relays, the top rebound relay,
the key-gate assembly ("the key gate will keep you out of the death channel"), the free-ball-gate assembly, and—not least—the one-and-a-quarter-
amp slo-blo. To one side, something that resembles a plumb bob hangs
suspended within a metal ring. If the bob moves too far out of plumb, it
touches the ring. Tilt. The game is dead.

Lukas is not an electrician. All he can do is massage the flipper's switch 8
assembly, which does not respond—not even with a shock. He has about
had it with this machine. One cannot collaborate with a sick flipper. The
queasy truth comes over him: no pinball, no paragraphs. So he hurries down-
stairs and into a taxi, telling the driver to go to Tenth Avenue in the low
Forties—a pocket of the city known as Coin Row.

En route, Lukas reflects on his long history in the game—New York, 9
Cambridge, Paris—and his relationships with specific machines ("they're like
wives"). When he was the *Times'* man in the Congo, in the early sixties, the
post was considered a position of hardship, so he was periodically sent to
Paris for rest and rehabilitation, which he got playing pinball in a Left Bank
brasserie. He had perfected his style as an undergraduate at Harvard, sharing
a machine at the *Crimson* with David Halberstam ("Halberstam is aggressive
at everything he does, and he was very good"). Lukas's father was a Manhattan attorney. Lukas's mother died when he was eight. He grew up, for
the most part, in a New England community—Putney, Vermont—where he
went to pre-prep and prep school. Putney was "straitlaced," "very high-
minded," "a life away from the maelstrom"—potters' wheels, no pinball.
Lukas craved "liberation," and developed a yearning for what he imagined
as low life, and so did his schoolmate Christopher Lehmann-Haupt. Together,
one weekend, they dipped as low as they knew how. They went to New
York. And they went to two movies! They went to shooting galleries! They
went to a flea circus! They played every coin-operated machine they could
find—and they stayed up until after dawn! All this was pretty low, but not
low enough, for that was the spring of 1951, and still beyond reach—out
there past the fingertips of Tantalus—was pinball, the ban on which had
been emphatically reinforced a few years earlier by Fiorello H. LaGuardia, who
saw pinball as a gambling device corruptive of the city's youth. To Lukas,
pinball symbolized all the time-wasting and ne'er-do-welling that puritan Putney did not. In result, he mastered the game. He says, "It puts me in touch
with a world in which I never lived. I am attracted to pinball for its seediness,
its slightly disreputable reputation."

On Coin Row, Lukas knows just where he is going, and without a sidewise 10
glance passes storefronts bearing names like The World of Pinball Amusement
("SALES—REPAIR") and Manhattan Coin Machine ("PARTS—SUPPLIES"). He heads
directly for the Mike Munves Corporation, 577 Tenth Avenue, the New York
pinball exchange, oldest house (1912) on the row. Inside is Ralph Hotkins, in
double-breasted blazer—broker in pinball machines. . . .

Lukas greets Hotkins and then runs balls through a few selected machines. 11
Lukas attempts to deal with Hotkins, but Hotkins wants Lukas's machine and
a hundred and fifty dollars. Lukas would rather fix his flipper. . . .

Lukas starts for home but, crossing Forty-second Street, decides on pure 12
whim to have a look at Circus Circus, where he has never been. Circus Circus
is, after all, just four blocks away. The stroll is pleasant in the afternoon
sunlight, to and through Times Square, under the marquees of pornographic
movies *Valley of the Nymphs, The Danish Sandwich, The Organ Trail*. Circus
Circus ("GIRLS! GIRLS! GIRLS! Live exotic models") is close to Sixth Avenue and
consists, principally, of a front room and a back room. Prices are a quarter a
peep in the back room and a quarter to play (two games) in the front. The
game room is dim, and Lukas, entering, sees little at first but the flashing

scoreboards of five machines. Four of them—a Bally, a Williams, two Gott-liebs—flash slowly, reporting inexperienced play, but the fifth, the one in the middle, is exploding with light and sound. The player causing all this is hunched over, concentrating—in his arms and his hands a choreography of talent. Lukas's eyes adjust to the light. Then he reaches for his holster. The man on the hot machine, busy keeping statistics of his practice, is Tom Buckley.

"Tom." 13

"Tone." 14

"How is the machine?" 15

"Better than yours, Tone. You don't realize what a lemon you have." 16

"I love my Bally." 17

"The Bally is the Corvair of pinball machines. I don't even care for the art 18 on the back-glass. Williams and Gottlieb are the best. Bally is nowhere."

Buckley, slightly older than Lukas, has a spectacled and professional look. 19 He wears a double-breasted blazer, a buff turtleneck. He lives on York Avenue now. He came out of Beechhurst, Queens, and learned his pinball in the Army—in Wrightstown, New Jersey; in Kansas City. He was stationed in an office building in Kansas City, and he moved up through the pinball ranks from beginner to virtuoso on a machine in a Katz drugstore.

Lukas and Buckley begin to play. Best of five games. Five balls a game. 20 Alternate shots. The machine is a Williams FunFest, and Buckley points out that it is "classic," because it is symmetrical. Eack kick-out well and thumper-bumper is a mirror of another. The slingshots are dual. On this machine, a level of forty thousand points is where the sun sets and the stars come out. Buckley, describing his own style as "guts pinball," has a first-game score of forty-four thousand three hundred and ten. While Lukas plays his fifth ball, Buckley becomes avuncular. "Careful, Tony. You might think you're in an up-post position, but if you let it slide a little you're in a down-post position and you're finished." Buckley's advice is generous indeed. Lukas—forty-eight thousand eight hundred and seventy—wins the first game.

It is Buckley's manner to lean into the machine from three feet out. His 21 whole body, steeply inclined, tics as he reinforces. In the second game, he scores fifty thousand one hundred and sixty. Lukas's address is like a fencer's *en garde.* He stands close to the machine, with one foot projecting under it. His chin is high. Buckley tells him, "You're playing nice, average pinball, Tony." And Lukas's response is fifty-seven thousand nine hundred and fifty points. He leads Buckley, two games to none.

"I'm ashamed," Buckley confesses. And as he leans—palms pounding— 22 into the third game, he reminds himself, "Concentration, Tom. Concentration is everything."

Lukas notes aloud that Buckley is "full of empty rhetoric." But Lukas, in 23 Game 3, fires one ball straight into the death channel and can deliver only thirty-five thousand points. Buckley wins with forty. Perhaps Lukas feels rushed. He prefers to play a more deliberate, cogitative game. At home, between shots, in the middle of a game, he will go to the kitchen for a beer and return to study the situation. Buckley, for his part, seems anxious, and with good reason: one mistake now and it's all over. In the fourth game, Lukas lights up forty-three thousand and fifty points; but Buckley's fifth ball, just before it dies, hits forty-four thousand two hundred and sixty. Games are two all, with one to go. Buckley takes a deep breath, and says, "You're a competitor, Tony. Your flipper action is bad, but you're a real competitor."

Game 5 under way. They are pummelling the machine. They are heavy 24 on the corners but light on the flippers, and the scoreboard is reacting like a storm at sea. With three balls down, both are in the thirty-thousand range. Buckley, going unorthodox, plays his fourth ball with one foot off the floor, and raises his score to forty-five thousand points—more than he scored in winning the two previous games. He smiles. He is on his way in, flaring, with still another ball to play. Now Lukas snaps his fourth ball into the ellipse. It moves down and around the board, hitting slingshots and flippers and rising again and again to high ground to begin additional scoring runs. It hits sunburst caps and hole kickers, swinging targets and bonus gates. Minute upon minute, it stays in play. It will not die.

When the ball finally slips between flippers and off the playfield, Lukas 25 has registered eighty-three thousand two hundred points. And he still has one ball to go.

Buckley turns into a Lukasite. As Lukas plays his fifth ball, Buckley cheers. 26 "Atta way! Atta way, babes!" He goes on cheering until Lukas peaks out at ninety-four thousand one hundred and seventy.

"That was superb. And there's no luck in it," Buckley says. "It's as good 27 a score as I've seen."

Lukas takes a cool final look around Circus Circus. "Buckley has a way of 28 tracking down the secret joys of the city," he says, and then he is gone.

Still shaking his head in wonder, Buckley starts a last, solo game. His arms 29 move mechanically, groovedly, reinforcing. His flipper timing is offhandedly flawless. He scores a hundred thousand two hundred points. But Lukas is out of sight.

Questions for analysis

1. Why do you think McPhee chose to entitle his profile "The Pinball Philosophy"? (See paragraphs 3, 5, and 7 for presentation of that philosophy.)

2. McPhee frames the essay with two visual images, beginning with a scene in Lukas's home and concluding at the Circus Circus. Why is this such an appropriate "frame" for this essay?

3. Paragraph 2 describes Lukas's home, his pinball playing, and the man himself. The paragraph moves at a brisk pace—can you suggest how McPhee achieves this pace?

4. McPhee defines several words in paragraphs 2–6. What are those words, and why do you think he bothers to define them? Describe the strategies he uses to define them.

5. How does McPhee add drama to the showdown between Lukas and Buckley (paragraphs 12–29)?

6. What presence does McPhee himself have in this essay? How does he represent himself? What other roles could he have played?

7. Writers of profiles get much of their material from interviews. Some of this information they quote, while most of it they present in summary form. Skim this profile to see how much McPhee relies on quoting. Do any of the quotations contain information that you think could have been presented as effectively in summary? If so, which quotations? If not, what advantage does quoting seem to have over summarizing?

8. If you were asked to do a profile on someone who has an unusual job or hobby, whom would you choose? What questions would you ask the person?

Like David Noonan, McPhee uses narrative to organize his essay. As he shows Lukas playing pinball, he tells us all about Lukas, the game of pinball, and the mechanics of pinball machines. He shifts gracefully from telling about the playing process to describing the inner workings of the machine simply by having Lukas stop play to inspect a broken flipper. In the same way, he uses the cab ride to the repair shop as an occasion to tell us about Lukas's past and the banning of pinball.

The point of view McPhee adopts for this profile is interesting. Lukas acts as an interpreter, which enables McPhee to give an insider's knowledge while maintaining his own objective point of view. Another point of view profile writers can take is the first person. The advantage of the first-person point of view is that it allows writers to express their own insights and feelings about the subject.

This is the point of view Joan Didion takes in her profile of the California State Water Project. A prolific author of novels as well as essays, Didion writes often about her native California. Consider, as you read this piece, how she uses the first-person point of view to involve her readers and get them to share her interest in California's plumbing system, a subject not likely to be of great interest to most readers.

HOLY WATER
JOAN DIDION

Some of us who live in arid parts of the world think about water with a reverence others might find excessive. The water I will draw tomorrow from my tap in Malibu is today crossing the Mojave Desert from the Colorado River, and I like to think about exactly where that water is. The water I will drink tonight in a restaurant in Hollywood is by now well down the Los Angeles Aqueduct from the Owens River, and I also think about exactly where that water is: I particularly like to imagine it as it cascades down the 45-

degree stone steps that aerate Owens water after its airless passage through the mountain pipes and siphons. As it happens my own reverence for water has always taken the form of this constant meditation upon where the water is, of an obsessive interest not in the politics of water but in the waterworks themselves, in the movement of water through aqueducts and siphons and pumps and forebays and afterbays and weirs and drains, in plumbing on the grand scale.

Actually so much water is moved around California by so many different 2 agencies that maybe only the movers themselves know on any given day whose water is where, but to get a general picture it is necessary only to remember that Los Angeles moves some of it, San Francisco moves some of it, the Bureau of Reclamation's Central Valley Project moves some of it and the California State Water Project moves most of the rest of it, moves a vast amount of it, moves more water farther than has ever been moved anywhere. They collect this water up in the granite keeps of the Sierra Nevada and they store roughly a trillion gallons of it behind the Oroville Dam and every morning, down at the Project's headquarters in Sacramento, they decide how much of their water they want to move the next day. They make this morning decision according to supply and demand, which is simple in theory but rather more complicated in practice. In theory each of the Project's five field divisions—the Oroville, the Delta, the San Luis, the San Joaquin and the Southern divisions—places a call to headquarters before nine A.M. and tells the dispatchers how much water is needed by its local water contractors, who have in turn based their morning estimates on orders from growers and other big users. A schedule is made. The gates open and close according to schedule. The water flows south and the deliveries are made.

In practice this requires prodigious coordination, precision, and the best 3 efforts of several human minds and that of a Univac 418. In practice it might be necessary to hold large flows of water for power production, or to flush out encroaching salinity in the Sacramento-San Joaquin Delta, the most ecologically sensitive point on the system. In practice a sudden rain might obviate the need for a delivery when that delivery is already on its way. In practice what is being delivered here is an enormous volume of water, not quarts of milk or spools of thread, and it takes two days to move such a delivery down through Oroville into the Delta, which is the great pooling place for California water and has been for some years alive with electronic sensors and telemetering equipment and men blocking channels and diverting flows and shoveling fish away from the pumps. It takes perhaps another six days to move this same water down the California Aqueduct from the Delta to the Tehachapi and put it over the hill to Southern California. "Putting some over the hill" is what they say around the Project Operations Control Center when they want to indicate that they are pumping Aqueduct water from the floor of the San Joaquin Valley up and over the Tehachapi Mountains. "Pulling it down" is what they say when they want to indicate that they are lowering a water level somewhere in the system. They can put some over the hill by remote control from this room in Sacramento with its Univac and its big board and its flashing lights. They can pull down a pool in the San Joaquin by remote control from this room in Sacramento with its locked doors and its ringing alarms and its constant print-outs of data from sensors out there in the water itself. From this room in Sacramento the whole system takes on the aspect of a perfect three-billion-dollar hydraulic toy, and in certain ways it is. "LET'S START DRAINING QUAIL AT 12:00" was the 10:51 A.M. entry on the electronically recorded communications log the day I visited the Operations Control Center. "Quail" is a reservoir in Los Angeles County with a gross capacity of 1,636,018,000 gallons. "OK" was the response recorded in the log. I knew at that moment that I had missed the only vocation for which I had any instinctive affinity: I wanted to drain Quail myself. . . .

I have always wanted a swimming pool, and never had one. When it 4 became generally known a year or so ago that California was suffering severe drought, many people in water-rich parts of the country seemed obscurely gratified, and made frequent reference to Californians having to brick up their swimming pools. In fact a swimming pool requires, once it has been filled and the filter has begun its process of cleaning and recirculating the water, virtually no water, but the symbolic content of swimming pools has always been interesting: a pool is misapprehended as a trapping of affluence, real or pretended, and of a kind of hedonistic attention to the body. Actually a pool is, for many of us in the West, a symbol not of affluence but of order, of control over the uncontrollable. A pool is water, made available and useful, and is, as such, infinitely soothing to the western eye. . . .

"The West begins," Bernard DeVoto wrote, "where the average annual 5 rainfall drops below twenty inches." This is maybe the best definition of the West I have ever read, and it goes a long way toward explaining my own passion for seeing the water under control, but many people I know persist in looking for psychoanalytical implications in this passion. As a matter of fact I have explored, in an amateur way, the more obvious of these implications, and come up with nothing interesting. A certain external reality remains, and resists interpretation. The West begins where the average annual rainfall drops below twenty inches. Water is important to people who do not have it, and the same is true of control. Some fifteen years ago I tore a poem by Karl Shapiro from a magazine and pinned it on my kitchen wall. This fragment of paper is now on the wall of a sixth kitchen, and crumbles a little whenever I touch it, but I keep it there for the last stanza, which has for me the power of a prayer:

> It is raining in California, a straight rain
> Cleaning the heavy oranges on the bough,
> Filling the gardens till the gardens flow,
> Shining the olives, tiling the gleaming tile,
> Waxing the dark camellia leaves more green,
> Flooding the daylong valleys like the Nile.

I thought of those lines almost constantly on the morning in Sacramento 6
when I went to visit the California State Water Project Operations Control
Center. If I had wanted to drain Quail at 10:51 that morning, I wanted, by
early afternoon, to do a great deal more. I wanted to open and close the
Clifton Court Forebay intake gate. I wanted to produce some power down
at the San Luis Dam. I wanted to pick a pool at random on the Aqueduct
and pull it down and then refill it, watching for the hydraulic jump. I wanted
to put some water over the hill and I wanted to shut down all flow from the
Aqueduct into the Bureau of Reclamation's Cross Valley Canal, just to see
how long it would take somebody over at Reclamation to call up and com-
plain. I stayed as long as I could and watched the system work on the big
board with the lighted checkpoints. The Delta salinity report was coming in
on one of the teletypes behind me. The Delta tidal report was coming in on
another. The earthquake board, which has been desensitized to sound its
alarm (a beeping tone for Southern California, a high-pitched tone for the
north) only for those earthquakes which register at least 3.0 on the Richter
Scale, was silent. I had no further business in this room and yet I wanted to
stay the day. I wanted to be the one, that day, who was shining the olives,
filling the gardens, and flooding the daylong valleys like the Nile. I want it
still.

Questions for analysis

1. What do you learn about the water project from this essay? What
do you learn about Joan Didion? Which do you find more interesting—
the water project or Didion?

2. Toward the end of the essay, Didion quotes from a poem that she
thinks has "the power of prayer." Are you surprised to find a poem in an
essay about a water project? Why do you think she brings this poem into
her profile?

3. Each of the first four sentences of paragraph 3 begins with the
words "In practice." Why do you think Didion repeats herself this way?
What effect does this repetition have?

4. Paragraph 3 ends with a description of what Didion observed at
the Operations Control Center in Sacramento. Why do you think she
places this description here? Where else might she have put it?

5. Why do you think Didion mentions the attitudes of people in
"water-rich parts of the country" toward California swimming pools
(paragraph 4)?

6. The voice in Didion's essay inspires both positive and negative
reactions. Describe the voice as you hear it. Do you personally like it or
dislike it? Compare Didion's voice to the voice in either the Noonan or
the McPhee essay.

7. If you were asked to write a profile about something you felt strongly
about, what subject would you choose? How would you go about presenting the topic and also conveying your strong personal feelings?

Throughout her essay, Didion alternates information about the water project with reflections on what the system means for her personally and for society in general. Clearly, she is not fascinated with California's elaborate plumbing system simply because California is an agricultural state with a limited amount of water. To her, the water-delivery project has a larger, symbolic meaning. In suggesting that westerners have a psychic need for "control over the uncontrollable," she generalizes from her own particular experience. In this way, Didion becomes something of an interpreter for readers, helping us to gain a deeper understanding of the subject.

Didion cannot rely on narrative in this essay, since nothing very surprising or dramatic happens at the Control Center. Instead, she organizes her essay by juxtaposing information about the water project with reflections on the "holiness" of water control. In presenting information about the project, she uses a variety of writing strategies. She briefly describes the Univac computer in the Control Center with "its big board and its flashing lights." She narrates the process by which the water is moved through Oroville and into the Delta, down the California Aqueduct to Tehachapi and over the hill to Southern California. She classifies the project's field divisions and compares the different agencies responsible for moving water around the state. She defines specialized language like "putting some over the hill" and "pulling it down."

The last selection, written by college freshman Brian Cable, is a profile of a mortuary. Cable treats his subject with both seriousness and humor. Like Joan Didion, he lets readers know his feelings as he presents information about the mortuary and the people working there. Notice in particular the way Cable uses his visit to the mortuary as an occasion to reflect on death.

THE LAST STOP
BRIAN CABLE

Let us endeavor so to live that when we come to die even the undertaker will be sorry.   Mark Twain

Death is a subject largely ignored by the living. We don't discuss it much, 1 not as children (when Grandpa dies, he is said to be "going away"), not as adults, not even as senior citizens. Throughout our lives, death remains intensely private. The death of a loved one can be very painful, partly because of the sense of loss, but also because someone else's mortality reminds us all too vividly of our own.

Thus did I notice more than a few people avert their eyes as they walked 2 past the dusty-pink building that houses the Goodbody Mortuaries. It looked a bit like a church—tall, with gothic arches and stained glass—and somewhat like an apartment complex—low, with many windows stamped out of red brick.

It wasn't at all what I had expected. I thought it would be more like Forest 3
Lawn, serene with lush green lawns and meticulously groomed gardens, a
place set apart from the hustle of day-to-day life. Here instead was an odd
pink structure set in the middle of a business district. On top of the Goodbody
Mortuaries sign was a large electric clock. What the hell, I thought, mortuaries
are concerned with time too.

I was apprehensive as I climbed the stone steps to the entrance. I feared 4
rejection or, worse, an invitation to come and stay. The door was massive,
yet it swung open easily on well-oiled hinges. "Come in," said the sign.
"We're always open." Inside was a cool and quiet reception room. Curtains
were drawn against the outside glare, cutting the light down to a soft glow.

I found the funeral director in the main lobby, adjacent to the reception 5
room. Like most people, I had preconceptions about what an undertaker
looked like. Mr. Deaver fulfilled my expectations entirely. Tall and thin, he
even had beady eyes and a bony face. A low, slanted forehead gave way to
a beaked nose. His skin, scrubbed of all color, contrasted sharply with his jet
black hair. He was wearing a starched white shirt, grey pants, and black
shoes. Indeed, he looked like death on two legs.

He proved an amiable sort, however, and was easy to talk to. As funeral 6
director, Mr. Deaver ("call me Howard") was responsible for a wide range of
services. Goodbody Mortuaries, upon notification of someone's death, will
remove the remains from the hospital or home. They then prepare the body
for viewing, whereupon features distorted by illness or accident are restored
to their natural condition. The body is embalmed and then placed in a casket
selected by the family of the deceased. Services are held in one of three
chapels at the mortuary, and afterward the casket is placed in a "visitation
room," where family and friends can pay their last respects. Goodbody also
makes arrangements for the purchase of a burial site and transports the body
there for burial.

All this information Howard related in a well-practiced, professional man- 7
ner. It was obvious he was used to explaining the specifics of his profession.
We sat alone in the lobby. His desk was bone clean, no pencils or paper,
nothing—just a telephone. He did all his paperwork at home; as it turned
out, he and his wife lived right upstairs. The phone rang. As he listened, he
bit his lips and squeezed his adam's apple somewhat nervously.

"I think we'll be able to get him in by Friday. No, no, the family wants 8
him cremated."

His tone was that of a broker conferring on the Dow Jones. Directly behind 9
him was a sign announcing "Visa and Mastercharge Welcome Here." It was
tacked to the wall, right next to a crucifix.

"Some people have the idea that we are bereavement specialists, that 10
we can handle the emotional problems which follow a death. Only a trained
therapist can do that. We provide services for the dead, not counseling for
the living."

Physical comfort was the one thing they did provide for the living. The 11 lobby was modestly but comfortably furnished. There were several couches, in colors ranging from earth brown to pastel blue, and a coffee table in front of each one. On one table lay some magazines and a vase of flowers. Another supported an aquarium. Paintings of pastoral scenes hung on every wall. The lobby looked more or less like that of an old hotel. Nothing seemed to match, but it had a homey, lived-in look.

"The last time the Goodbodies decorated was in '59, I believe. It still 12 makes people feel welcome."

And so "Goodbody" was not a name made up to attract customers, but 13 the owners' family name. The Goodbody family started the business way back in 1915. Today, they do over five hundred services a year.

"We're in *Ripley's Believe It or Not*, along with another funeral home 14 whose owners' names are Baggit and Sackit," Howard told me, without cracking a smile.

I followed him through an arched doorway into a chapel which smelled 15 musty and old. The only illumination came from sunlight filtered through a stained glass ceiling. Ahead of us lay a casket. I could see that it contained a man dressed in a black suit. Wooden benches ran on either side of an aisle that led to the body. I got no closer. From the red roses across the dead man's chest, it was apparent that services had already been held.

"It was a large service," remarked Howard. "Look at that casket—a beau- 16 tiful work of craftsmanship."

I guess it was. Death may be the great leveler, but one's coffin quickly 17 reestablishes one's status.

We passed into a bright, fluorescent-lit "display room." Inside were thirty 18 coffins, lids open, patiently awaiting inspection. Like new cars on the show-room floor, they gleamed with high-glossy finishes.

"We have models for every price range." 19

Indeed, there was a wide variety. They came in all colors and various 20 materials. Some were little more than cloth-covered cardboard boxes, others were made of wood, and a few were made of steel, copper, or bronze. Prices started at $400 and averaged about $1,800. Howard motioned toward the center of the room: "The top of the line."

This was a solid bronze casket, its seams electronically welded to resist 21 corrosion. Moisture-proof and air-tight, it could be hermetically sealed off from all outside elements. Its handles were plated with 14kt. gold. The price: a cool $5,000.

A proper funeral remains a measure of respect for the deceased. But it is 22 expensive. In the United States the amount spent annually on funerals is about two billion dollars. Among ceremonial expenditures, funerals are second only to weddings. As a result, practices are changing. Howard has been in this business for forty years. He remembers a time when everyone was buried. Nowadays, with burials costing $2,000 a shot, people often opt instead for cremation—as Howard put it, "a cheap, quick, and easy means of disposal." In some areas of the country, the cremation rate is now over 60 percent.

Observing this trend, one might wonder whether burials are becoming obsolete. Do burials serve an important role in society?

For Tim, Goodbody's licensed mortician, the answer is very definitely yes. 23
Burials will remain in common practice, according to the slender embalmer
with the disarming smile, because they allow family and friends to view the
deceased. Painful as it may be, such an experience brings home the finality
of death. "Something deep within us demands a confrontation with death,"
Tim explained. "A last look assures us that the person we loved is, indeed,
gone forever."

Apparently, we also need to be assured that the body will be laid to rest 24
in comfort and peace. The average casket, with its inner-spring mattress and
pleated satin lining, is surprisingly roomy and luxurious. Perhaps such an air
of comfort makes it easier for the family to give up their loved one. In addition, the burial site fixes the deceased in the survivors' memory, like a new
address. Cremation provides none of these comforts.

Tim started out as a clerk in a funeral home, but then studied to become 25
a mortician. "It was a profession I could live with," he told me with a sly
grin. Mortuary science might be described as a cross between pre-med and
cosmetology, with courses in anatomy and embalming as well as in restorative
art.

Tim let me see the preparation, or embalming, room, a white-walled 26
chamber about the size of an operating room. Against the wall was a large
sink with elbow taps and a draining board. In the center of the room stood
a table with equipment for preparing the arterial embalming fluid, which
consists primarily of formaldehyde, a preservative, and phenol, a disinfectant.
This mixture sanitizes and also gives better color to the skin. Facial features
can then be "set" to achieve a restful expression. Missing eyes, ears, and
even noses can be replaced.

I asked Tim if his job ever depressed him. He bridled at the question: 27
"No, it doesn't depress me at all. I do what I can for people, and take
satisfaction in enabling relatives to see their loved ones as they were in life."
He said that he felt people were becoming more aware of the public service
his profession provides. Grade-school classes now visit funeral homes as often
as they do police stations and museums. The mortician is no longer regarded
as a minister of death.

Before leaving, I wanted to see a body up close. I thought I could be 28
indifferent after all I had seen and heard, but I wasn't sure. Cautiously, I
reached out and touched the skin. It felt cold and firm, not unlike clay. As I
walked out, I felt glad to have satisfied my curiosity about dead bodies, but
all too happy to let someone else handle them.

Questions for analysis   1. Why do you think Cable begins with the quotation by Mark Twain?
How does this particular epigraph shape your expectations of the profile?
What theme does it suggest?

2. At several points, Cable mentions his own preconceptions about mortuaries. Do you have any similar preconceptions? How does Cable appeal to such preconceptions to draw us into his essay?

3. Cable quotes Howard as saying "We provide services for the dead" (paragraph 10), but later in the essay Tim talks about the service funerals provide for the living (paragraph 24). How does Cable use this contradiction to bring out his theme?

4. Look again at paragraphs 18–21, where Cable describes the various caskets. What impression does this description give? How does it contrast with the preceding scene in the chapel (paragraph 15)?

5. Make a rough outline of this profile. How does Cable organize this profile? What seems to be his plan?

6. Look again at your outline. How much space would you estimate Cable devotes to describing the mortuary, explaining what goes on there, presenting Howard and Tim, reflecting on what he has seen and heard?

7. Look at the first and last paragraphs. How do they work to frame this profile?

8. Think of a place or activity about which you have strong preconceptions. Imagine writing a profile about it. What would you choose to tell about? What preconceptions do you hold? How might you use your preconceptions to capture readers' attention?

Cable uses humor in this profile as a way of distancing himself emotionally from a disturbing subject. Although profile writers are not autobiographers, they do often put themselves in their essays as a way of engaging their readers' interest. Cable's profile gives us an inside look at a subject we seldom allow ourselves to think about. By looking at a mortuary through his eyes, we can safely reflect upon our own attitudes toward death and the way society deals with it.

BASIC FEATURES OF PROFILES

Profiles include three essential ingredients. Their subjects are intriguing and well focused; they give vivid, detailed presentations of people, places, and activities; and they have an informative, entertaining pace.

An intriguing, well-focused subject

The subject of a profile is typically a specific person, place, or activity. In this chapter, John McPhee shows us J. Anthony Lukas, pinball player extraordinaire; Brian Cable describes a particular place, the Goodbody Mortuary; David Noonan and Joan Didion both present activities, brain surgery and water control. Although they focus on a person, place, or activity, these profiles contain all three elements: they examine certain people performing a special activity at a particular place.

Profiles resemble autobiographical writing in that they portray people, places, and events. Like autobiographies, profiles appeal to readers' natural curiosity about other people and the human condition in general. Their primary aim, however, is not self-disclosure. They seek instead to disclose some little-known or unusual aspect of their community. In this way, profile writers are closer to investigative reporters than to autobiographers. They take readers behind the scenes and inform them about strange personalities, peculiar places, and unfamiliar activities in their midst.

Although profile writers are reporters, some tend to be more impersonal and objective than others. John McPhee is the most impersonal writer represented in this chapter. Yet even he can not avoid interpreting his subject, as for instance when he describes Lukas as "faintly, and perhaps consciously nefarious" and suggests "one can imagine him cheating at polo." David Noonan does not even pretend to be objective. He uses his personal reactions to heighten the drama of his subject. To bring home to readers the disturbing image of a human skull being drilled, Noonan writes: "The drill and the head do not go together; they collide and shock the eye. The tool is too big. . . . It should be hanging on the wall of a garage." In what is perhaps the most subjective profile in this collection, Joan Didion uses her own preoccupation with water as a way of arousing readers' interest in a subject that is not inherently fascinating.

Indeed, few subjects are inherently fascinating. Profiles on celebrities might have instant appeal to some readers. Also subjects which could affect readers personally—like IRS audits and brain surgery—may readily arouse readers' curiosity. But most subjects must be made interesting.

Writers make even the most mundane subjects interesting by presenting them in a new light. They may simply take a close look at a subject usually taken for granted, as Cable does when he examines a mortuary. Or they might surprise us by revealing something we never expected to see, as McPhee does when he portrays his pinball enthusiasts as moral outlaws. Whatever they examine, profile writers bring attention to the uniqueness of the subject, showing what is special, definitive, or simply remarkable about it.

This special focus or theme nearly always reveals an incongruity in the subject or in the writer's response to it. Noonan, for instance, points to a discrepancy between the impersonality of neurosurgery and the extraordinary intimacy of such an operation. McPhee contrasts the seediness of pinball with the respectability of his two pinball players. Didion reveals, in the ordinary effort to circulate water around the state of California, the westerner's extraordinary reverence for water and impulse to play god.

Cable's thematic focus is his personal realization about how Americans seem to capitalize on death almost as a way of coping with it.

A vivid presentation

Profiles particularize their subjects—an actual operation, a real pinball-playing Pulitzer Prize-winning author, one state's water control project, the Goodbody Mortuary—rather than generalize about them. Profile writers are more interested in presenting individual cases than in making generalizations. Consequently, profiles present people, places, and activities vividly and in detail.

Successful profile writers master the writing strategies of describing, regularly using sensory imagery and figurative language. For example, the profiles in this chapter evoke the senses of sight (a "dusty-pink building" that "looked a bit like a church—tall, with gothic arches and stained glass—and somewhat like an apartment complex—low, with many windows stamped out of red brick"); touch ("a thin, tough, leathery membrane"); smell ("a faint odor of burning bone"); and hearing ("his voice, rich and dense, pours out like cigarette smoke filtered through a New England prep school"). Similes ("his voice . . . pours out like cigarette smoke") and metaphors ("Tenth Avenue in the low Forties—a pocket of the city known as Coin Row") also abound.

Profile writers often describe people in graphic detail ("an aristocratic, olive-skinned Andalusian sort of man, with deep eyes in dark wells"). They reveal personal habits and characteristic poses ("As he listened, he bit his lips and squeezed his adam's apple nervously"). They also use dialogue to suggest speakers' characters and their relationship:

"I love my Bally."

"The Bally is the Corvair of pinball machines. I don't even care for the art on the back-glass. Williams and Gottlieb are the best. Bally is nowhere."

Narrating may be even more important to profile writing than describing since narration is used by many writers to organize their essays. Some profiles read like stories. They create tension and suspense and build to a dramatic climax. McPhee, for instance, sets up his essay so that it will end in a dramatic showdown between the two best pinball players in New York City, Lukas and Buckley. Noonan's dramatization has two climaxes, first when the brain is exposed and second when the tumor is discovered. The climax of Cable's narrative of his visit to a mortuary occurs at the end when he touches a corpse. Each of these writers relies on pacing to develop and sustain tension and drama in their narratives.

An informative, entertaining pace

The primary purpose of a profile is to inform, but successful profile writers know that if you want to keep your readers' attention, you must entertain them as well. It is for this reason that they tell their stories dramatically and describe people and places vividly. They also carefully pace the flow of information. This kind of pacing is as important as narrative pacing.

Profiles present a great deal of factual detail about their subject, but this information is woven into the essay—conveyed in dialogue, interspersed throughout the narrative, given in the description. Noonan, for instance, tells us about the brain's parts (dura, cerebellum, brainstem), about surgical procedures (preparation of the patient and the surgeons, the difference between craniectomy and craniotomy), as well as about the attitudes of surgeons toward brain surgery. All of this information is given to us in bits and pieces rather than in one large chunk.

Parceling out information in this way increases the chances of comprehension because it allows readers to master one part of the information before going on to the next. Perhaps even more importantly, pacing the information injects a degree of surprise and thus makes readers anticipate what will come next. Profiles which vary the pacing of information may, in fact, actually keep readers reading.

GUIDE TO WRITING

THE WRITING TASK

Write an essay about an intriguing person, place, or activity in your community. Research your subject thoroughly, and then present what you have learned in a way that both informs and entertains readers.

INVENTION AND RESEARCH

Preparing to write a profile involves several activities: choosing a subject, exploring your preconceptions of it, researching it thoroughly, posing some preliminary questions, and finding a theme or focus for your profile.

Choosing a subject   When you choose a subject, you consider various possibilities, select a promising subject, and check that particular subject's accessibility.

Listing possibilities. You may already have chosen a subject for your profile. If so, turn now to Checking on Accessibility. But it might be advisable to take a few minutes now to consider some other possible subjects. The more possibilities you consider, the more confident you can be about your choice.

Following are several ideas you might use as a starting point for your own list of subjects. Try to extend your list to ten or twelve possibilities. Consider every subject you can think of, even the unlikeliest. Begin your list with subjects you are already familiar with but would like to know more about. Then add unfamiliar subjects—people or places or activities you find fascinating or bizarre or perhaps even forbidding. Take risks. People like to read about the unusual.

People

☐ Anyone with an unusual job or hobby—a private detective, chimneysweep, beekeeper, classic-car owner, dog trainer

☐ A homecoming queen candidate or weight-lifting contestant

☐ A TV celebrity, newspaper editor, radio disc jockey

☐ A popular local personality—parent of the year, a labor organizer, political activist, consumer advocate

☐ Campus president, ombudsman, fundraiser, distinguished teacher or researcher

Places

☐ A weight-reduction clinic, tanning salon, body-building gym

☐ Small claims court, Juvenile Hall, the consumer fraud office, the internal revenue service

☐ A used car lot, old movie house, used book store, antique shop, auction hall

☐ A hospital emergency room, hospice, birthing center, psychiatric unit, physical therapy center

☐ A place to eat—campus dining commons, a local diner, the oldest restaurant in town

☐ Campus radio station, computer center, agricultural research facility

Activities

☐ A citizens' volunteer program—voter registration, public TV auction, meals-on-wheels project

☐ An unusual sports event—a marathon, frisbee tournament, chess match, bicycle race

☐ Folk dancing, roller skating, rock climbing, poetry reading

Choosing a particular subject. Look over your list, and select a subject that you find personally fascinating, something you want to know more about. It should also be a subject you think you can make interesting to readers.

If you choose a subject with which you are familiar, it is a good idea to study it in an unfamiliar setting. Let us say you are a rock climber and decide to profile rock climbing. Do not rely on your own knowledge and authority. Seek out other rock-climbing enthusiasts and even some critics of the sport to get a more objective view of the subject. Then you would enjoy the advantage of knowing the questions to ask but not be so likely to predict the answers. When research is predictable for the writer, it is likely to lead to dull and uninspired writing.

Stop now to focus your thoughts. In a sentence or two, identify the subject you have chosen and explain why you think it is a good choice.

Checking on accessibility. Once you have chosen a subject, you need to make sure you will be able to research it. Begin by finding out who might be able to give you information. Make some preliminary phone calls and explain that you need information for a school research project. You will be surprised how helpful and informative people can be when they have the time. If you are unable to contact knowledgeable people or get access to the place you need to observe, you may not be able to write on this subject. Therefore, try to make initial contact now.

Exploring your preconceptions

Before you begin researching the subject, you should explore your initial thoughts and feelings about it. Write for around ten minutes, using the following questions as a guide:

☐ What do I already know about this subject?
How would I define or describe it?
What are its chief qualities or parts?
Do I associate anyone or anything with it?
What is its purpose or function?
How does it compare to other, similar subjects?

☐ What is my attitude toward this subject?
Why do I consider this subject intriguing?
Do I like it? respect it? understand it?
What about it interests me?

☐ What do I expect to discover as I research the subject?
What would surprise me about it?
Do I anticipate any troubling discoveries?
Might I find anything amusing in it?
Are there likely to be any notable incongruities—for example, between what the people are trying to do and what they are actually doing?

☐ How do my preconceptions about this subject compare with other people's?

What makes my point of view unique?

What attitudes and values relating to this subject do I share with other people?

Starting your research Gathering information about your subject may entail observing it several times, interviewing various people, and reading extensively on it.

Just as your reading will depend on the availability of materials, so the number of observational visits you make and interviews you conduct may depend on circumstances beyond your control. Still, you should try to plan some sort of research schedule now.

See Chapter 19: Field Research for advice on observation and interviews, Chapter 20: Library Research for advice on where to find documents and other information, and Chapter 21: The Research Paper for instructions on the proper way to cite sources.

Take time now to write out a tentative research schedule. Figure out first the amount of time you have to complete your essay, and then decide what visits you will need to make, whom you will need to interview, and what library work you will have to do. Estimate the time necessary for each.

You might put your plan on a chart like the following one:

Date	Time Needed	Purpose	Preparation
10/23	1 hour	observation	bring pad
10/25	1/2 hour	library	bring reference
10/26	45 minutes	interview	read brochure and write questions
10/30	2 hours	observe and interview	write questions

This plan will probably need to be modified once you actually begin work, but it is a good idea to keep some sort of schedule in writing.

Your first goal is to get your bearings. Some writers begin by observing the place or activity, while others start with an interview. Many read up on the subject before doing anything else.

It is probably best to read about the subject as soon as you can to get a sense of its main elements and concerns. Read also about other people, places, or activities that are similar to the one you have chosen to investigate.

Save your notes for use later when you draft your essay. Your instructor may also ask you to write a brief report of your observations and interviews. Chapter 19: Field Research gives some advice on writing up observation and interview notes.

Posing some preliminary questions

After making a preliminary survey of your subject, try writing some questions for which you would like to find answers. As you continue your research, you will find answers to many of these questions. Also, add questions to this list as they occur to you, and delete any that come to seem irrelevant.

Each subject invites its own special questions, and every writer has his or her own particular concerns. Here is an example of questions one student posed for a profile of a campus rape-crisis center:

☐ Is rape a special problem on college campuses? On this particular campus? Why?

☐ How much support does the center receive from the college administration? How much from students?

☐ How well qualified are the people working in the center? What do they actually do? Do they counsel women who have been raped? Advise women on avoiding rape? Teach women how to defend themselves?

☐ Do the police do anything to prevent rape on campus?

☐ Are most of the rapes on campus committed by known sex offenders? Or are they date rapes, committed by "friends"?

Finding a tentative focus

When you have completed your research, you must decide on a tentative theme for your profile. Do the following activities to help you review your research. Complete them both at one sitting, one right after the other.

Write a narrative of your research. Write nonstop for fifteen minutes, telling the story of your research—what you did first, what happened next, where you went, who you met. Do not consult your notes, but try to include everything you recall. Also, do not worry if details are omitted or events are out of order.

Write an analysis of your research. Do not bother to reread your narrative, but immediately begin writing an analysis of your research. Do not retell the story of your research. Try to answer as many of the following questions as you can:

☐ What was the most important thing I learned? Why does it seem so important?

☐ If I could find out the answer to one more question, what would be the question? Why is this question so crucial?

☐ Were there any incongruities, surprises, or contradictions? If so, what do they tell me about the subject?

☐ What is most memorable about the people I observed and talked to?

☐ What visual or other sensory impression is most memorable about the place I observed? What do I associate with this sensory impression?

☐ What is most striking about the activity I witnessed?

☐ What about this subject says something larger about our lives and times?

☐ What generalization or judgment do these personal reactions lead me to?

Stop and take a few moments to reflect on what you have discovered in doing these activities. Then, in a sentence or two, state what now seems to you to be a promising theme or focus for your profile. What do you want readers to see as they read your profile?

PLANNING AND DRAFTING

As preparation for drafting, you need to review your invention and research to see what you have, make a tentative outline, and set goals for yourself.

Seeing what you have You should now have a great deal of material from a variety of sources—notes from observational visits, interviews, and reading; some idea of your preconceptions; a list of questions, perhaps with some answers; and both a narrative and an analysis of your research. You should also have a tentative theme or focus for your profile.

Read it all over now to sort through your material. Some writers find it helpful to put promising ideas or key information on index cards so they can try out various combinations and arrangements. Others try arranging their material graphically, by clustering them around the central theme. However you prefer to sort and arrange your material, your aim now is to digest all the information you have gathered; to pick out the promising facts, details, anecdotes, and quotes; and to see how well your tentative theme focuses all the material you plan to include in the essay.

As you sort through your material, look at it in some of the following ways. They may help you find an even better theme or clarify the theme you already have.

☐ Contrast your preconceptions with your findings.

☐ Juxtapose your preliminary questions against the answers you have been able to find.

☐ Compare what different people say about the subject.

- ☐ Look for discrepancies between people's attitudes and values and their behavior.
- ☐ Compare your personal reactions to the reactions of the people directly involved.
- ☐ Contrast the place's appearance with the activity that occurs there.
- ☐ Juxtapose bits of information, looking for contrasts, incongruities, or dissonances.
- ☐ Look at the subject from the perspective of someone totally unfamiliar with it—a visitor from another country or even from another planet.
- ☐ Examine the subject as an anthropologist or archaeologist might, looking for artifacts that would explain what role the people, place, or activity had in the society at large.

Outlining the profile   Profile writers basically use two methods of organizing their material: they either arrange it chronologically in a narrative or analogically by putting related materials in juxtaposition.

If you plan to arrange your material chronologically by using narrative, you should construct a timeline of the key events. Star the event which you consider the high point or climax. If you decide to present any events out of chronological order, signal with an arrow where in the timeline you plan to place each event. Also, decide what point of view you will use and make a note of it. Indicate with a caret where you might insert particular information into the narrative.

If you plan to arrange your material by juxtaposing bits of information, you might use the clustering or outlining strategies described in Chapter 18: Invention and Inquiry to get a graphic view of the interconnections. Both these strategies involve dividing and grouping the information. After classifying your material, you might list the items in the order in which you plan to present them.

Setting goals   The following questions will help to establish particular goals for your first draft. Consider each one briefly now, and return to them as necessary as you draft.

Your readers

- ☐ Are my readers likely to be at all familiar with my topic? If not, what details do I need to provide to help them visualize it?
- ☐ If my readers are familiar with my subject, how can I present it to them in a new and engaging way? What information do I have that is likely to be new or entertaining to them?

☐ Is there anything I can say about this subject that will lead readers to reflect on their own lives and values?

The beginning

The opening plays an especially important role in profiles. Because readers are unlikely to have any particular reason to read a profile, the writer must work hard to arouse their curiosity and interest. The best beginnings are surprising and specific, the worst are abstract. Here are some strategies you might consider:

☐ Should I open with a striking image or vivid scene, as Noonan does?

☐ Should I begin with a statement of the central theme, as Didion and McPhee do?

☐ Should I start with an intriguing epigraph, as Cable does?

☐ Do I have an amazing fact that would catch readers' attention?

☐ Would it be best to begin by summarizing all the essential facts?

☐ Is there an anecdote that captures the essence of the subject?

☐ Should I open with a question, perhaps a rhetorical one then answered in the essay?

☐ Do I have any dialogue that would serve as a good beginning?

The general organization

If I organize my material chronologically:

☐ How can I make the narrative dramatic and intense?

☐ What information should I integrate into the narrative?

☐ What information will I need to suspend the narrative for? If I must suspend the narrative, how can I minimize the disruption and resume the dramatic pace?

☐ What information should I quote and what should I present in summary form?

☐ How can I set the scene vividly?

If I organize my material analogically:

☐ Which juxtapositions should I make abrupt? How can I make these contrasts dramatic or use them to lead readers to insights about the subject?

☐ Which juxtapositions should I make smooth with transitions?

☐ Where should I describe the place, people, or activity? How can I make any descriptions true and vivid?

The ending

☐ Should I try to frame the essay by repeating an image or phrase from the beginning or by completing an action?

☐ Would it be good to end by restating the theme?

☐ Should I end with a telling image, anecdote, or bit of dialogue?

Drafting a profile   Before actually beginning to write, you might look at the general advice on drafting in Chapter 1. By now, of course, you are not starting from scratch. If you have followed this guide, you will already have done a lot of invention and planning. Some of this material may even fit right into your draft with little alteration.

Be careful not to get stuck trying to write the perfect beginning. Start anywhere. Worry about perfecting your beginning at the revision stage.

Once you are actually writing, try not to be interrupted. Should you find you need to do some additional research, do it only after you have completed a first draft.

READING A DRAFT WITH A CRITICAL EYE

Now read over the draft. Ask yourself what works and what needs work. Whether you are reading your own draft or someone else's, your goal is the same: to suggest how the profile could be made better.

First general impression   Read quickly through the draft first to get an overall impression. Note down your immediate reaction. What do you consider most interesting in the essay? State the theme, and indicate whether or not it is well focused. Is the profile adequately informative? Can you see any holes or gaps? Did it hold your interest? You should not try to write a detailed critique now, but rather articulate the general impression the profile gives.

Pointings   One good way to maintain a critical focus as you read the essay is to highlight noteworthy features of the writing with *pointings*. A simple system of lines and brackets, these pointings are quick and easy to do, and they can provide a lot of helpful information for revision. Use pointings in the following way:

☐ Draw a straight line under any words or images that impress you as especially effective: strong verbs, specific details, memorable phrases, striking images.

☐ Draw a wavy line under any words or images that seem flat, stale, or vague. Also put the wavy line under any words or phrases that you consider unnecessary or repetitious.

☐ Look for pairs or groups of sentences that you think should be combined. Put brackets [] around these sentences.

☐ Look for sentences that are garbled, overloaded, or awkward. Put parentheses ( ) around these sentences. Put parentheses around any sentence that seems even slightly questionable; don't worry now about whether or not you're certain about your judgment. The writer needs to know that you, as one reader, had even the slightest hesitation about understanding a sentence.

Analysis Now read the draft more closely to analyze its strengths and failings. As you read, consider the following points.

1. Examine the pace of information. Point to any places where you felt bogged down or overwhelmed with information. These may be parts where there was too much new information or where the information was not clearly presented.

2. If narrative is used as an organizing strategy, see how well the narrative itself is paced. Point to any places where the narrative seemed to drag as well as where it seemed most dramatic and intense. Tell the writer what you think is the climax or high point of the narrative.

3. If the profile is organized analogically by juxtaposing material, indicate which contrasts are dramatic and what new insights they lead you to. Also, let the writer know if any of the juxtapositions seem too abrupt or confusing.

4. Look specifically at the description. Point out places where the description is vivid and specific. Also point to places where it is vague or blurred.

5. Evaluate any anecdotes. Indicate which seem to you to be pointless or boring.

6. Skim the essay for definitions. Indicate whether any definitions in the essay seem unnecessary. Also point out any terms that need defining.

7. Reread the beginning, and decide whether it is effective. Tell the writer whether it captured your attention. See whether there is any quotation, fact, or anecdote elsewhere in the draft that might make a better opening.

8. Look again at the ending. Let the writer know if it leaves you waiting for more, if it seems too abrupt, or if it oversimplifies the material. Suggest another ending, possibly by moving a passage or quotation from elsewhere in the essay.

REVISING AND EDITING

Revising a profile involves revising both to clarify the theme and to increase readability.

Revising a profile   A profile is frequently long and complex, and thus may well need more than one revision before you are satisfied. Before you begin revising, read the general advice on revising in Chapter 1. Then study the following specific suggestions for revising a profile.

Revising to clarify the theme

☐ Reconsider the focus. If your readers had difficulty describing the theme or suggested focusing on something different, you should either clarify or revise your theme. Clarifying your theme might involve making it more explicit or eliminating material that seems to contradict the point you are trying to make.

☐ Eliminate any dialogue, description, anecdote, or factual detail that does not contribute to the general theme.

Revising for pacing and readability

☐ Reconsider the pacing of information. If readers felt bogged down at any point, either reorganize the information or eliminate some of it.

☐ Reconsider the pacing of the narrative. If readers felt the narrative dragged at any point, liven it up.

☐ If readers were confused or felt juxtapositions were too abrupt, add appropriate transitions or revise sentences for smoother reading.

☐ If any descriptions seem vague, revise your language to be more precise and vivid.

☐ If any anecdotes seem boring or pointless, try speeding them up and sharpening their focus.

☐ Define any words that need explanation and eliminate any unnecessary definitions.

☐ If the opening fails to engage readers' attention, look back at the suggestions for beginning in Setting Goals.

Editing and proofreading   Once you revise a draft for the last time, you must edit it closely. As you were drafting, you surely corrected obvious errors of usage and style, but correctness probably was not your first priority. Now, though, you must look at your draft critically and objectively in order to find and correct any errors of mechanics, usage, punctuation, or style.

After you have edited the draft and produced your final copy, proofread your report to be certain that it contains no mistakes.

LEARNING FROM YOUR OWN WRITING PROCESS

If you are asked to write about your experience writing this essay, begin by reviewing your invention and planning materials. Note how you came to select your subject and how you then defined your theme. Point out any special problems you ran into when gathering information for this essay.

Then reread your draft. What direction were you following? Look over any critical reviews of your draft, and then reread your revision. What worked well in the first draft, and what needed reworking? How exactly did you go about reworking your draft? Where did you begin? What changes did you make, and how do you feel about them now? What other changes would you still like to make?

A WRITER AT WORK

THE INTERVIEW NOTES AND REPORT

When interviewing people for a profile, writers usually take notes. After the interview they may summarize their notes in a short report. In this section we will look at the interview notes and report Brian Cable prepared for his profile of a mortuary, printed on pages 321–24.

For his essay Cable first visited the mortuary and then conducted two interviews—with the funeral director and the mortician. Before each interview he divided some paper into two columns and then used the left-hand column for descriptive details and personal impressions, the right-hand column for questions he posed and information he found. Here we will see Cable's notes and report for his interview with the funeral director, Mr. Deaver.

Cable wrote out a few questions in advance of the interview and then took brief notes during the interview. He kept his attention fixed on Deaver, however, trying to keep the interview comfortable and conversational. He did not concern himself too much with note-taking during the actual interview because he planned to spend a half-hour directly afterward to complete his notes. During the interview, he noted down just enough to jog his memory, and to catch anything especially quotable. The typescript of Cable's interview notes follows.

The interview

<u>DESCRIPTIVE DETAILS &</u>
<u>PERSONAL IMPRESSIONS</u>

<u>QUESTIONS</u>

1. How do families of deceased view the mortuary business?
2. How is the concept of death approached?
3. How did you get into this business?

<u>INFORMATION</u>

weird looking
tall
long fingers
big ears
low sloping forehead
Like stereotype—skin
colorless

"Call me Howard"
How things work: Notification pick up body at home or hospital, prepare for viewing, restore distorted features—accident or illness, embalm, casket—family selects, chapel services (3 in bldg.), visitation room—pay respects, family & friends.

Can't answer questions about death—
"Not bereavement specialists. Don't handle emotional problems. Only a trained therapist can do that."
"We provide services for dead, not counseling for the living." (great quote)
Concept of death has changed in last 40 yrs (how long he's been in the business)
Funeral cost $500–600, now $2000

plays with lips
blinks
plays with adam's apple
desk empty—phone, no
paper or pen

angry
disdainful of the Neptune
Soc.

Phone call (interruption)
"I think we'll be able to get him in on Friday. No, no, the family wants him cremated."
*Ask about Neptune Society—cremation
Cremation "Cheap, quick, easy means of disposal."
Recent phenomenon. Neptune Society—erroneous claim to be only one. "We've offered them since the beginning. It's only now it's come into vogue."
Trend now back towards burial.
Cremation still popular in sophisticated areas
60% in Marin and Florida

Ask about paperwork—does it upstairs, lives there with wife Nancy

musty, old stained glass	Tour around (happy to show me around)
sunlight filtered	Chapel—Large service just done, Italian.
man in black suit	"Not a religious institution—A business."
roses	casket—"beautiful craftsmanship"—admires,
wooden benches	expensive
contrast brightness	Display room—caskets about 30 of them
flourescent lights	Loves to talk about caskets
plexiglass stands	"models in every price range"
	glossy (like cars in a showroom)
	cardboard box, steel, copper, bronze $400 up to
	$1800. Top of line: bronze, electronically welded,
	no corrosion—$5000

Cable's notes include many descriptive details of Deaver as well as of various rooms in the mortuary. Though most entries are short and sketchy, much of the language will find its way into the essay. In describing Deaver, for example, Cable notes the fact that he fits the stereotype. Cable will make much of this in his essay.

He puts quotation marks around Deaver's actual words. Some of the quotes are complete, whereas others are only fragmentary. We will see how he fills these quotes in when he writes up the interview. Cable caught many of Deaver's words and even several of his sentences. In only a few instances does he take down more than he can use. Even though profile writers want good quotes, they should not quote things they can better put in their own words. Direct quotation has a special, enlarged function in a profile—both to provide information and to capture the mood or character of the person speaking. Quoting is as much a means of characterization as of presenting information.

As you can see, Deaver was not able to answer any of Cable's questions. The gap between the questions and Deaver's responses led Cable to recognize some of his own misperceptions about mortuaries—namely, that they serve the living by helping them adjust to the death of their loved ones. This misperception becomes an important theme of his essay.

After filling in his notes following the interview, Cable took some time to reflect on what he had learned. Here are some of his thoughts:

> I was surprised how much Deaver looked like the undertakers in scary movies. Even though he couldn't answer any of my questions, he was friendly enough. It's obviously a business for him (he loves to talk about caskets and to point out all their features, like a car dealer kicking a tire). Best quote: "We offer services to the dead, not counseling to the living." I have to arrange an interview with Tim, the mortician.

Writing up an account of the interview a short time afterward helped Cable to fill in more details and to reflect further on what he had learned. His report shows him already beginning to organize the information he had gained from his interview with Deaver.

A report on the interview

I. His physical appearance

A. Tall, skinny with beady blue eyes embedded in his bony face. I was shocked to see him. He looked like the undertakers in scary movies. His skin was white and colorless, from lack of sunshine. He has a long nose and a low sloping forehead. He was wearing a clean white shirt. A most unusual man— have you ever seen those Ames Home Loan commercials? But he was friendly, and happy to talk to me. "Would I answer some questions? Sure."

II. What people want from a mortuary.

A. Well first of all, he couldn't answer any of the questions I had expected. As to how families cope with the loss of a loved one, he didn't know. "You'd have to talk to a psychologist about that," he said. He did tell me how the concept of death has changed over the last ten or so years.

B. He has been in the business for forty years. (forty years?!!?) One look at him and you'd be convinced he'd been there at least that long. He told me that in the old times *everyone* was buried. Embalmed, put in a casket, and paid final homage before being shipped underground forever and ever. Nowadays, many people choose to be cremated instead. Hence comes the success of the Neptune Society and those like it. They specialize in cremation. You can have your ashes dumped anywhere. "Not that we don't offer cremation services. We've offered them since the beginning," he added with a look of disdain. It's just that they've become so popular recently because they offer a "quick, easy, and efficient means of disposal." Cheap too—I think it is a reflection of a "no nonsense" society. The Neptune Society has become so successful because they claim to be the only ones to offer cremations as an alternative to expensive burial. "We've offered it all along. It's just only now come into vogue."

Sophisticated areas (I felt "progressive" would be more accurate) like Marin County have a cremation rate of over 60 percent. The phone rang. "Excuse me," he said. As he talked on the phone, I noticed how he played with his lips, pursing and squeezing them. He was blinking all the time too. Yet he wasn't a schitzo or anything like that. I meant to ask him how he got into this business, but I forgot. I did find out his name and title. Mr. Deaver, general manager of Goodbody Mortuaries (no kidding, that's the real name). He lived on the premises upstairs with his wife. I doubt if he ever left the place.

III. It's a business!

Some people have the idea that mortuaries offer counseling and peace of mind—a place where everyone is sympathetic and ready to offer advice. "In some mortuaries, this is true. But by and large this is a business. We offer services to the dead, not counseling to the living." I too had expected to feel an awestruck respect for the dead upon entering the building. I had also expected green lawns, ponds with ducks, fountains, flowers, peacefulness—you know, a "Forest Lawn" type deal. But it was only a tall, Catholic-looking building. "Mortuaries do not sell plots for burial," he was saying. "Cemeteries do that, after we embalm the body and select a casket. We're not a religious institution." He seemed hung up on caskets—though maybe he was just trying to impress upon me the differences between caskets. "Oh, they're very important. A good casket is a sign of respect. Sometimes if the family doesn't have enough money, we rent them a nice one. People pay for what they get just like any other business." I wonder when you have to return the casket you rent?

I wanted to take a look around. He was happy to give me a tour. We visited several chapels and visiting rooms—places where the deceased "lie in state" to be "visited" by family and friends. I saw an old lady in a "fairly decent casket," as Mr. Deaver called it. Again I was impressed by the simple businesslike nature of it all. Oh yes, the rooms were elaborately decorated, with lots of shrines and stained glass, but these things were for the customers' benefit. "Sometimes we have up to eight or nine corpses here at one time, sometimes none. We have to have enough rooms to accommodate." Simple enough, yet I never realized how much (trouble?) people were after they died. So much money, time, and effort go into their funerals.

As I prepared to leave, he gave me his card. He'd be happy to see me again, or maybe I could talk to someone else. I said I would arrange to call for an appointment with the mortician. I shook his hand. His fingers were long, and his skin was warm.

Writing up the interview thus helped Cable probe his subject more deeply. It also helped him to develop a witty voice for his essay. Although Cable's report is quite informal, some writers choose to make their reports as formal as published interviews.

PART TWO

Writing Strategies

Cueing the Reader

___

Writers provide readers with four basic kinds of cues or signals: (1) thesis and forecasting statements to orient readers to ideas and details; (2) paragraphing to group related ideas and details; (3) cohesive devices to make their writing cohere or "stick together" so that it makes sense; and (4) transitions to signal relationships or shifts in meaning. In this chapter, we will examine how to make each of these cueing strategies work.

___

ORIENTING STATEMENTS

To help readers find their way, especially in difficult and lengthy works, writers provide two kinds of orienting information: thesis statements to declare the main point and forecasting statements to identify the thesis and preview a text's plan.

Thesis statements   Although they may have a variety of forms and purposes, all essays are essentially assertive. That is, they assert or put forward the writer's point of view on a particular subject. We call this point of view the essay's thesis, or main idea.

To help readers understand what is being said about a subject, writers often provide a thesis statement early in the essay. The *thesis statement* is usually a single sentence that declares the essay's main idea. It operates as a cue by letting readers know which is the most important, overarching idea among the writer's many ideas and observations. The thesis statement, then, is like the focal point of a picture, directing the reader's attention to the one idea that brings all the other ideas and details into perspective. Here are some thesis statements from essays in Part I:

> It was a heavenly place for a boy, that farm of my uncle John's. Mark Twain, Chapter 4

> By any standards, the insect body must be reckoned the most successful of all the solutions to the problems of living on the surface of the earth. David Attenborough, Chapter 5

> I suspect that what motivates us even more than a fear of death is a fear of dearth.   Carll Tucker, Chapter 8

11

EXERCISE 11.1

Read one of the essays by Twain, Attenborough, or Tucker; then briefly explain how its thesis statement brings the ideas and details of the essay into perspective.

Each of the three preceding thesis statements is expressed directly in a single sentence. But sometimes writers need several sentences to state their thesis, and sometimes they imply the thesis rather than state it directly. For example, Alice Walker in "The Civil Rights Movement: What Good Was It?" (Chapter 7) states her thesis this way:

> Perhaps it is naive to be thankful that the movement "saved" a large number of individuals and gave them something to live for, even if it did not provide them with everything they wanted. . . . If knowledge of my condition is all the freedom I get from a "freedom movement," it is better than unawareness, forgottenness and hopelessness, the existence that is like the existence of a beast.   Alice Walker, *The American Scholar*

Walker presents her point in tentative terms, using conditional "perhaps" and "if . . . then" constructions. Rather than imposing her idea directly on her readers, she suggests it to them. She encourages her readers to evaluate the civil rights movement in human as well as political terms, in terms of what people learned as individuals from the very fact that there was a "freedom movement" as well as in terms of whether the movement achieved its political goals.

Personal and narrative writing often tends to have implied rather than explicit thesis statements. Readers usually must infer the general point. Kate Simon, in remembering Jimmy's death (Chapter 2), comes close to stating a thesis when she suggests at the end of the selection how children generally react to death:

> We were no longer interested in the family—the godlike child's gesture of quickly dissolving away anything that wasn't immediately attached to our ears, our eyes, our greeds, our envies. Our fears hung on for a while. No one mentioned Jimmy. His name was a black omen, a sign that children could die, and as fast as we could, we obliterated his name, too.
> Kate Simon, *Bronx Primitive*

EXERCISE 11.2

Read "A Hanging" by George Orwell or "Smooth and Easy" by Russell Baker, both in Chapter 2. What would you say is the thesis? If you cannot find an explicit statement of the thesis, express it in your own words. Then, briefly explain how the thesis brings the essay's ideas and details into focus for you.

Regardless of whether the thesis is explicitly stated or implied, readers by necessity look for something that will tell them the point of the essay. Readers need a context in which to understand the many diverse details and ideas they encounter as they read. If a thesis is not furnished for them, they naturally construct one themselves, or they try to.

The lack of a thesis statement makes reading more difficult. It complicates a relatively simple work and can make an intellectually challenging work virtually unreadable. Because expectations play such an important role in the way readers read, writers should keep in mind the audience they are addressing and what their readers' expectations are likely to be. One of the most important decisions a writer makes is whether to state explicitly or to imply the thesis. Another decision is where to place the thesis statement in the text.

The position of the thesis statement may influence how readers respond to an essay. Most readers expect to find some information early in the text that will give them a context for the essay. They expect essays to open with thesis statements, and they need such statements to orient them, particularly if they are reading about a new and difficult subject. A thesis statement placed at the beginning of an essay helps give readers a sense of control over the subject, enabling them to anticipate the content of the essay and more easily understand the relationship between its various ideas and details.

As the opening sentence of his essay, Attenborough's thesis statement announces the essay's main point and gives focus to the numerous details that follow. In a sense, the thesis statement functions as an umbrella; it is the most general statement that covers all the more specific information and ideas in the essay.

Forecasting statements   Actually a special kind of thesis statement, a *forecasting statement* not only identifies the thesis but also gives an overview of the way it will be developed. The opening paragraph of William Langer's essay on the plague (Chapter 5) illustrates the role of the forecasting statement:

> In the three years from 1348 through 1350 the pandemic of plague known as the Black Death, or, as the Germans called it, the Great Dying, killed at least a fourth of the population of Europe. It was undoubtedly

the worst disaster that has ever befallen mankind. Today we can have no real conception of the terror under which people lived in the shadow of the plague. For more than two centuries plague has not been a serious threat to mankind in the large, although it is still a grisly presence in parts of the Far East and Africa. Scholars continue to study the Great Dying, however, as a historical example of human behavior under the stress of universal catastrophe. In these days when the threat of plague has been replaced by the threat of mass human extermination by even more rapid means, there has been a sharp renewal of interest in the history of the 14th-century calamity. With new perspective, students are investigating its manifold effects: demographic, economic, psychological, moral and religious.   William Langer, "The Black Death"

This paragraph informs us that Langer's article is about the effects of the Black Death. His thesis, however, is not stated explicitly. It is implied by the forecasting statement that concludes the paragraph: "With new perspective, students are investigating its manifold effects: demographic, economic, psychological, moral and religious." With this sentence, Langer states that the study of the plague currently is focused on five particular categories. He then goes on to divide his essay into analyses of these five effects, taking them up in the order in which they appear in the forecasting statement.

EXERCISE 11.3
Look back at Debbie Brawner's essay, "A Message to Decipher," in Chapter 9. Find the forecasting statement in her essay, and then write a few sentences explaining how this forecasting sentence helps you anticipate the organization of the essay.

PARAGRAPHING

The indentation that signals the beginning of a new paragraph is a relatively modern printing convention. Old manuscripts show that paragraph divisions were not always marked. In order to make reading easier, scribes and printers began eventually to use the symbol ¶ to mark paragraph breaks. Indenting soon became common practice, but even that relatively modern custom seems to be changing today. Instead of indenting, some writers, particularly those in business, set paragraphs apart from the rest of the text by leaving an extra line of space above and below each paragraph.

The lack of paragraph cues makes reading extremely difficult. To illustrate, the paragraph indentions have been removed from the following introductory section of a chapter in Stephen Jay Gould's book *Ever Since Darwin*. Even with proper paragraphing, this selection might be difficult because it includes unfamiliar information and technical language. Without paragraphing, however, Gould's logic becomes hard to follow, and the mind and the eye long for a momentary rest. (Each of the thirty sentences in the selection is numbered at the beginning.)

(1) Since man created God in his own image, the doctrine of special creation has never failed to explain those adaptations that we understand intuitively. (2) How can we doubt that animals are exquisitely designed for their appointed roles when we watch a lioness hunt, a horse run, or a hippo wallow? (3) The theory of natural selection would never have replaced the doctrine of divine creation if evident, admirable design pervaded all organisms. (4) Charles Darwin understood this, and he focused on features that would be out of place in a world constructed by perfect wisdom. (5) Why, for example, should a sensible designer create only on Australia a suite of marsupials to fill the same roles that placental mammals occupy on all other continents? (6) Darwin even wrote an entire book on orchids to argue that the structures evolved to insure fertilization by insects are jerry-built of available parts used by ancestors for other purposes. (7) Orchids are Rube Goldberg machines; a perfect engineer would certainly have come up with something better. (8) This principle remains true today. (9) The best illustrations of adaptation by evolution are the ones that strike our intuition as peculiar or bizarre. (10) Science is not "organized common sense"; at its most exciting, it reformulates our view of the world by imposing powerful theories against the ancient, anthropocentric prejudices that we call intuition. (11) Consider, for example, the cecidomyian gall midges. (12) These tiny flies conduct their lives in a way that tends to evoke feelings of pain or disgust when we empathize with them by applying the inappropriate standards of our own social codes. (13) Cecidomyian gall midges can grow and develop along one of two pathways. (14) In some situations, they hatch from eggs, go through a normal sequence of larval and pupal molts, and emerge as ordinary, sexually reproducing flies. (15) But in other circumstances, females reproduce by parthenogenesis, bringing forth their young without any fertilization by males. (16) Parthenogenesis is common enough among animals, but the cecidomyians give it an interesting twist. (17) First of all, the parthenogenetic females stop at an early age of development. (18) They never become normal, adult flies, but reproduce while they are still larvae or pupae. (19) Secondly, these females do not lay eggs. (20) The offspring develop live within their mother's body—not supplied with nutrient and packaged away in a protected uterus but right inside the mother's tissues, eventually filling her entire body. (21) In order to grow, the

offspring devour the mother from the inside. (22) A few days later, they emerge, leaving a chitinous shell as the only remains of their only parent. (23) And within two days, their own developing children are beginning, literally, to eat them up. (24) *Micromalthus debilis,* an unrelated beetle, has evolved an almost identical system with a macabre variation. (25) Some parthenogenetic females give birth to a single male offspring. (26) This larva attaches itself to his mother's cuticle for about four or five days, then inserts his head into her genital aperture and devours her. (27) Greater love hath no woman. (28) Why has such a peculiar mode of reproduction evolved? (29) For it is unusual even among insects, and not only by the irrelevant standards of our own perceptions. (30) What is the adaptive significance of a mode of life that so strongly violates our intuitions about good design?   Stephen Jay Gould, *Ever Since Darwin*

A major difficulty in reading this selection is the need to hold the meaning of sentences "in suspension" as you read ahead. The meaning of an earlier sentence may be affected by the meaning of succeeding sentences. Without paragraphing, you are continually forced to remember and to anticipate close connections among sentences. For instance, the second sentence in the preceding Gould passage clarifies the meaning of the first sentence by giving specific examples. The third sentence restates the idea, while sentences 4 through 7 clarify and illustrate it.

EXERCISE 11.4

Here is the way the Gould selection divides into its six original paragraphs: sentences 1–7, 8–10, 11–12, 13–23, 24–27, 28–30. Put a paragraphing symbol ¶ in your own book immediately before the opening sentence of each paragraph. Later exercises will ask you to analyze some aspects of Gould's paragraphing.

Paragraphing helps readers by signaling when a sequence of related sentences begins and ends. The use of such paragraph signals tells you when you can stop holding meaning in suspension. The need for this kind of closure is a major consideration of writers. Gould, for example, begins a new paragraph with sentence 8 in order to draw a sharp distinction between the examples and the general principle. Similarly, he begins a new paragraph with sentence 24 to signal a shift from a description of the reproductive mode of the cecidomyian gall midge to that of the *Micromalthus debilis*. In this way, paragraphing keeps readers from being overloaded with information at the same time that it helps them follow the writer's train of thought.

Paragraphing also helps readers judge what is most important in what they are reading. With proper paragraphing, readers do not have to hunt for the most significant information or risk mistaking the writer's intentions. Writers typically emphasize important information by placing it at the two points where readers are most attentive—at the beginning and ending of a paragraph. Many writers position information to orient readers at the beginning of a paragraph, while they save the most important bit of information for last, as Gould does when he ends a paragraph with sentence 27.

Writers can give special emphasis to information by placing it in a paragraph of its own. Gould, for example, puts sentences 11 and 12 together in a separate paragraph. These two sentences could have been attached to either the preceding or following paragraphs. But Gould gives them a separate paragraph in order to emphasize the general point he is making. This paragraph serves as an important transition between the general discussion of how science explains things that go against intuition and the specific example of the bizarre adaptation of the cecidomyian gall midge.

Some writing situations call for fairly strict conventions for paragraphing. Readers may not be conscious of these conventions, but they would certainly notice if custom were not observed. For example, readers would be surprised if a newspaper did not have narrow columns and short paragraphs. This paragraphing convention is not accidental; it is designed to make newspaper reading easy and fast and to allow the reader to take in an entire paragraph at a glance. Journalists may use long, complex sentences, but their paragraphs are typically short and uncomplicated, as you can see in this example written by Jim Murray for the *Los Angeles Times*.

> When you talk of great sports upsets, there's Dempsey-Tunney, Schmeling-Louis I, the Miracle Braves of 1914, the Super Bowl Jets of 1969, the baseball Mets of the same year—and don't forget the first Ali-Liston fight.
>
> But I'm not at all sure the No. 1 shocker of all time didn't come in the snows of Sarajevo, Yugoslavia, last week when a kid from the Alpine fastnesses of Van Nuys, a young man who never loosed a yodel in his life, a boy who stole hubcaps with the rest of the car attached, became, of all things, the world's greatest downhill racer. It's a great part for Leo (Spit) Gorcey.
>
> Bill Johnson is as unlikely an American hero as, well, Joe Namath, to pull a name out of a hat. He doesn't fit the mold of the great Alpinists of our day, for some reason. He looks like a kid who made a wrong turn on his way to the surf at Santa Monica or the drag strips of Orange County.
>
> Downhill skiers are usually born in quaint little chalets on mountaintops in Europe and they answer to Fritz or Franz or Jean-Claude, and the view out their back window is the Matterhorn, not Catalina. They wear hats with brooms in them and they learned to ski before they learned to walk and they're as at home in the snow as a penguin.   Jim Murray, *Los Angeles Times*

Business writing also tends to adhere to the convention of short paragraphs. Memo readers frequently do not want an excess of details or qualifications. Instead, they prefer a concise overview, a capsule that is easy to swallow. College instructors, on the other hand, want students to qualify their ideas and support them with specifics. They care less about how long it takes to read a paragraph than about how well developed the writing is. Therefore, paragraphs in college essays usually have several sentences. In fact, it is not unusual to find quite long paragraphs, as this example from an undergraduate history essay on the status of women in Victorian England illustrates:

> A genteel woman was absolutely dependent upon the two men in her life: first her father, and then her husband. From them came her economic and social status; they were the center of her thoughts and the objects of any ambitions she might have. The ideal woman did not live for herself; she barely had a self, because her entire existence was vicarious. Legally, a woman had almost no existence at all. Until her marriage, a daughter was completely in the power of her father; upon her marriage, she was legally absorbed by her husband. Any money she had became his, as did all of her property, including her clothes and even those things that had been given her as personal gifts before her marriage. Any earnings she might make by working belonged to her husband. A woman could not be sued for debt separately from her husband because legally they were the same person. She could not sign a lease or sue someone in court without having her husband be the complainant, even in cases of long separation. In cases of a husband's enmity, she had almost no legal protection from him. Under English law, divorces could be obtained, in practice, only by men. A man could divorce his wife on the grounds of adultery, but the reverse was not the case.

If any rule for paragraphing is truly universal, it is this: paragraphs should be focused, unified, and coherent. That is, the sentences in a paragraph should be meaningfully related to one another, and the relationships among the sentences should be clear. The sentences that follow may look like a paragraph, but they do not work because they lack focus, unity, and coherence.

> Maturity and attitude go together because both determine why you want to become a model. I went to the university for two years, not because I wanted to but because I was pushed into it. I used to think models were thought of as dumb blondes, but after being here at the university I realized that people still have respect for modeling and know all the hard work put in it.

Even though each of these sentences mentions either modeling or the university or both, the two topics are not connected. With each sentence, the focus shifts. There is no unity because there is no single idea controlling the sentences. The various elements of the writing do not "stick together" to form a coherent meaning, and the reader may well become disoriented.

EXERCISE 11.5
Look at the Gould passage earlier in this chapter. Analyze how Gould's paragraphing helps you follow his meaning. Would you have paragraphed this passage differently? Explain how and why.

Topic-sentence strategies   A *topic sentence* lets readers know the focus of a paragraph in simple and direct terms. It is a cueing strategy to the paragraph much as a thesis or forecasting statement is to the whole essay. Because paragraphing usually signals a shift in focus, readers expect some kind of reorientation in the opening sentence. They need to know whether the new paragraph is going to introduce another aspect of the topic or develop one already introduced. This need is especially strong when readers are under pressure to read quickly and efficiently.

Announcing the topic. Some topic sentences simply announce the topic. Here are a few examples taken from Carl Sagan's book *Dragons of Eden:*

Many examples of a connection between "right" and "straight" can be found.

From experiments such as those with squirrel monkeys, MacLean has developed a captivating model of brain structure and evolution that he calls the triune brain.

My fundamental premise about the brain is that its workings—what we sometimes call "mind"—are a consequence of its anatomy and physiology, and nothing more.

There are reasons to think that the beginnings of altruistic behavior are in the limbic system.

The seeming fact that mammals and birds both dream while their common ancestor, the reptiles, do not is surely noteworthy.

These topic sentences do more than merely identify the topic; they also indicate how the topic will be developed in subsequent sentences—by citing examples, describing experiments or behavior, presenting reasons and evidence, telling anecdotes, classifying, defining, comparing, or contrasting. Paragraphs may be developed in any one of these ways or by a combination of strategies. (See Chapters 12 through 17.)

Following is one of Sagan's paragraphs that shows how the topic in the first sentence is developed:

> <u>Many examples of a connection between "right" and "straight" can be found</u>. In Mexican Spanish you indicate straight (ahead) by saying "right right"; in Black American English, "right on" is an expression of approval, often for a sentiment eloquently or deftly phrased. "Straight" meaning conventional, correct or proper is a commonplace in colloquial English today. In Russian, right is *"prava,"* a cognate of *"pravda,"* which means "true." And in many languages "true" has the additional meaning of "straight" or "accurate," as in "his aim was true."
> Carl Sagan, *Dragons of Eden*

EXERCISE 11.6

Read "The Kitchen," the autobiographical selection by Alfred Kazin in Chapter 4. Indicate which paragraphs begin with topic sentences and briefly explain how these topic sentences help you anticipate the paragraph's topic and suggest its method of development.

Forecasting subtopics. Other topic sentences do more than simply announce the topic and indicate how it will be developed. They actually give readers a detailed overview or forecast of subtopics that will be developed. The following paragraph shows the relationship between the subtopics mentioned in the opening sentence and their appearance later in the paragraph. The subtopics are <u>underscored</u> in the first sentence and then connected by lines to the point in the paragraph where they subsequently appear.

> <u>Oppressed groups are denied education, economic independence, the power of office, representation, an image of dignity and self-respect, equality of status, and recognition as human beings</u>. Throughout history women have been consistently denied all of these, and their denial today, while attenuated and partial, is nevertheless consistent. The <u>education</u> allowed them is deliberately designed to be inferior, and they are systematically programmed out of and excluded from the knowledge where power lies today—e.g., in science and technology. They are confined to conditions of <u>economic dependence</u> based on the sale of their sexuality in marriage, or a variety of prostitutions. Work on a basis of economic independence allows them only a subsistence level of life—often not even that. They do not hold <u>office</u>, are <u>represented</u> in no positions of power, and authority is forbidden them. The <u>image</u> of woman fostered by cultural media, high and low, then and now, is a marginal and demeaning existence, and one outside the human condition—which is defined as the prerogative of man, the male.   Kate Millett, *Sexual Politics*

Notice that the subtopics are taken up in the same order they are presented in the opening sentence: education first, followed by economic independence, power of office, and so on. This correlation between topic sentence and paragraph organization makes the paragraph easy to follow. Even so, such a structure is not necessarily mechanical in its execution. One subtopic may be developed in a sentence while another requires two or more sentences. The last two subtopics in Millett's piece—equality of status and recognition as human beings—are not directly brought up but are implied in the last sentence.

Asking a question about the topic. Writers occasionally put their topic sentences in a question-answer format, posing a rhetorical question in one sentence which is then answered in the next sentence. Here is a paragraph illustrating this strategy.

> What about motion that is too slow to be seen by the human eye? That problem has been solved by the use of the time-lapse camera. In this one, the shutter is geared to take only one shot per second, or one per minute, or even one per hour—depending upon the kind of movement that is being photographed. When the time-lapse film is projected at the normal speed of twenty-four pictures per second, it is possible to see a bean sprout growing up out of the ground. Time-lapse films are useful in the study of many types of motion too slow to be observed by the unaided human eye.   James C. Rettie, "But a Watch in the Night"

EXERCISE 11.7
Look at the selection by Jeanette Germain in Chapter 6, or the essay by Robert Jastrow in Chapter 8. Where does the writer use the rhetorical question as a topic-sentence strategy? Analyze how the rhetorical question is answered.

Question-answer topic sentences do not always appear at the beginning of a paragraph. On occasion, a question at the end of one paragraph may combine with the first sentence of the following paragraph. For an example, see paragraphs 3 and 4 in the selection by Alice Walker in Chapter 7.

Making a transition. Not all topic sentences simply point forward to what will follow. Some also refer back to earlier sentences. Such sentences work both as topic sentences, stating the main point of the paragraph, and as transitions, linking that paragraph to the previous one. Here are a few topic sentences from *Aristotle for Everybody* by Mortimer J. Adler which use specific transitional terms (underscored) to tie the sentence to a previous statement:

<u>Nevertheless</u> there is something permanent in this special kind of change.

<u>Like</u> sensations, ideas are neither true nor false.

<u>On the other hand</u>, a piece of music—a song that is sung over and over again—does not exist just at one place and at one time.

<u>So, too</u>, are teachers.

There is one <u>further</u> difference between a song or a story and a painting or a statue.

<u>Not only</u> must these basic biological needs be satisfied beyond the level of the barest minimum required to sustain life but, in addition, many other human needs must be satisfied in order to approach the fulfillment of all our capacities and tendencies.

Sometimes the first sentence of a paragraph serves as a transition, while a subsequent sentence—in this case the last—states the topic. The underscored sentences illustrate this strategy in the following example:

> . . . Splayed, monstrous, and mud-smeared, it haunts the future. That it is the footprint of some wandering reptilian beast of the coal swamps may be granted, but it is also a vertebrate. Its very body forecasts the times to come.
>
>   <u>It would be erroneous, however, to conceive of reptiles as being the major preoccupation of our geological prophets</u>. They scanned the anatomy of fishes, birds, and salamanders, seeking in their skeletons anticipations of the more perfect structure of man. If they found footprints of fossil bipeds it was a "sign" foretelling man. All things led in his direction. Prior to his entrance the stage was merely under preparation. In this way the blow to the human ego has been softened. The past was only the prologue to the Great Play. <u>Man was at the heart of things after all</u>.
> Loren Eiseley, *The Immense Journey*

Occasionally, particularly in long essays, whole paragraphs serve as transitions, linking one sequence of paragraphs with those that follow. Even though we have taken the next transition paragraph out of its context, you can see that it summarizes what went before (evidence of contrast) and sets up what will follow (evidence of similarity):

> Yet it was not all contrast, after all. Different as they were—in background, in personality, in underlying aspiration—these two great soldiers had much in common. Under everything else, they were marvelous fighters. Furthermore, their fighting qualities were really very much alike.
> Bruce Catton, "Grant and Lee: A Study in Contrasts"

Positioning the topic sentence. Although topic sentences may go anywhere in a paragraph, stating the topic in the first sentence has the advantage of giving readers a sense of where the writing is likely to go.

Nearly all the topic sentences shown thus far have appeared at the beginning of the paragraph, the favored position for the topic sentence that orients the reader.

A topic sentence that does not open a paragraph is most likely to appear at the end. When placed in the concluding position, topic sentences usually summarize or generalize preceding information. In the following example, the topic is not stated explicitly until the last sentence.

> Every moment of the day the world bombards the human speaker with information and experiences. It clamors for his attention, claws his senses, intrudes into his thoughts. Only a very small portion of this total experience is language—yet the speaker must use this small portion to report on all the experiences that exist or ever existed in the totality of the world since time began. Try to think about the stars, a grasshopper, love or hate, pain, anything at all—and it must be done in terms of language. There is no other way; thinking is language spoken to oneself. <u>Until language has made sense of experience, that experience is meaningless.</u>
> Peter Farb, *Word Play*

When a topic sentence is used in a narrative, it will often appear as the last sentence. This concluding topic sentence often evaluates or reflects on events, as is evident in the following paragraph from Russell Baker's autobiography:

> I hadn't known she could play the piano. She wasn't playing very well, I guess, because she stopped occasionally and had to start over again. She concentrated intensely on the music, and the others in the room sat absolutely silently. My mother was facing me but didn't seem to see me. She seemed to be staring beyond me toward something that wasn't there. All the happy excitement died in me at that moment. <u>Looking at my mother, so isolated from us all, I saw her for the first time as a person utterly alone.</u>   Russell Baker, *Growing Up*

EXERCISE 11.8

Look back at "Smooth and Easy," the selection by Baker in Chapter 2. Pick out the paragraphs that have their topic sentences at the end.

In rare cases, the topic sentence for one paragraph will appear at the end of the preceding paragraph, as in this example:

> . . . <u>And apart from being new, psychoanalysis was particularly threatening</u>.
>
> French psychiatrists tended to look at the sufferings of their patients either as the result of organic lesions or moral degeneration. In either case, the boundary between the "healthy" doctor and the "sick" patient was clear. Freud's theory makes it hard to draw such lines by insisting

that if the psychiatrist knew himself better, he would find more points in common with the patient than he might have thought. . . . Sherry Turkle, *Psychoanalytic Politics*

In some cases, the topic sentence for a paragraph appears at the beginning of the preceding paragraph. Following is an example of a two-paragraph sequence in which the topic sentence opens the first paragraph:

<u>Almost without exception all human languages have built into them a polarity, a veer to the right</u>. "Right" is associated with legality, correct behavior, high moral principles, firmness, and masculinity; "left," with weakness, cowardice, diffuseness of purpose, evil, and femininity. In English, for example, we have "rectitude," "rectify," "righteous," "right-hand man," "dexterity," "adroit" (from the French "*à droite*"), "rights," as in "the rights of man," and the phrase "in his right mind." Even "ambidextrous" means, ultimately, two right hands.

On the other side (literally), we have "sinister" (almost exactly the Latin word for "left"), "gauche" (precisely the French word for "left"), "gawky," "gawk," and "left-handed compliment." The Russian "*nalevo*" for "left" also means "surreptitious." The Italian "*mancino*" for "left" signifies "deceitful." There is no "Bill of Lefts."   Carl Sagan, *Dragons of Eden*

EXERCISE 11.9
Now that you have seen several topic-sentence strategies, look again at the Gould passage earlier in this chapter and identify the strategies he uses. Then evaluate how well his topic sentences work to orient you as a reader.

COHESIVE DEVICES

In addition to thesis and forecasting statements, paragraphing, and topic sentences, writers also use certain cohesive devices to cue the reader. Cohesive devices help readers follow a writer's train of thought by connecting key words and phrases throughout a passage. Among such devices are pronoun reference, same-word repetition, synonym repetition, sentence-structure repetition, and collocation.

Pronoun reference   One common cohesive device is pronoun reference. As noun substitutes, pronouns refer or point to nouns that either precede or follow them, and thus serve to connect phrases or sentences. The nouns that come before the pronouns are called antecedents. In the following paragraph, the pronouns (all *it*) form a chain of connection with their antecedent, *George Washington Bridge*.

In New York from dawn to dusk to dawn, day after day, you can hear the steady rumble of tires against the concrete span of the <u>George Washington Bridge</u>. The bridge is never completely still. <u>It</u> trembles with traffic. <u>It</u> moves in the wind. <u>Its</u> great veins of steel swell when hot and contract when cold; <u>its</u> span often is ten feet closer to the Hudson River in summer than in winter.   Gay Talese, "New York"

In the preceding example, there is only one pronoun-antecedent chain, and the antecedent comes first so all the pronouns refer back to it. When there are multiple pronoun-antecedent chains with references forward as well as back, writers have to make certain that readers will not mistake one pronoun's antecedent for another's.

Same-word repetition   To avoid confusion, a writer will often use a second cohesive device: the repetition of words and phrases. This device is used especially if a pronoun might confuse readers:

The basic problem of communicating across interstellar distances would certainly be removed if we could send bursts of <u>tachyons</u>—instead of sluggish electromagnetic radiation, moving merely at the speed of light—from a "transmitter" to a "receiver." If <u>tachyons</u> really do exist—and the balance of evidence now is in their favor—it is only a matter of time before such a possibility becomes first a probability and then a reality. John Gribbin, *Time Warps*

The next example illustrates how a writer utilizes several overlapping chains of word repetition to avoid confusion and make the selection clear for the reader.

<u>Natural selection</u> is the central concept of Darwinian theory—the <u>fittest</u> <u>survive</u> and spread their favored traits through populations. <u>Natural selection</u> is defined by Spencer's phrase "<u>survival</u> of the <u>fittest</u>," but what does this famous bit of jargon really mean? Who are the <u>fittest</u>? And how is "<u>fitness</u>" defined? We often read that <u>fitness</u> involves no more than "differential reproductive success"—the production of more <u>surviving</u> offspring than other competing members of the population. Whoa! cries Bethell, as many others have before him. This formulation defines <u>fitness</u> in terms of <u>survival</u> only. The crucial phrase of <u>natural selection</u> means no more than "the <u>survival</u> of those who <u>survive</u>"—a vacuous <u>tautology</u>. (A <u>tautology</u> is a phrase—like "my father is a man"—containing no information in the predicate ["a man"] not inherent in the subject ["my father"]. <u>Tautologies</u> are fine as definitions, but not as testable scientific statements—there can be nothing to test in a statement true by definition.) Stephen Jay Gould, *Ever Since Darwin*

Notice that Gould uses repetition to keep readers focused on the key concepts of "natural selection," "survival of the fittest," and "tautology." These key terms may vary in form—*fittest* becomes *fitness* and *survival* changes to *surviving* and *survive*—but they continue to serve as links in the chain of meaning.

Synonym repetition

In addition to repeating the same word, writers also use synonyms, words with identical or very similar meanings, to connect important ideas. In the following example, the author sets up a complex chain of synonym and same-word repetitions:

> There is an underlying <u>force that</u> <u>drives together</u> the several creatures comprising myxotricha, and then <u>drives the assemblage into union</u> with the termite. If we could understand this <u>tendency</u>, we would catch a glimpse of the <u>process</u> that <u>brought single cells together</u> for the construction of metazoans, culminating in the invention of roses, dolphins, and, of course, ourselves. It might turn out that the same <u>tendency</u> underlies the <u>joining of organisms</u> into <u>communities</u>, <u>communities</u> into <u>ecosystems</u>, and <u>ecosystems</u> into the <u>biosphere</u>.   Lewis Thomas, *The Lives of a Cell*

The "force that drives together" is represented as both a "tendency" and a "process." The result of this force is that single cells are brought "together," made an "assemblage" or "union" of increasing size and complexity—from "organisms" to "communities," to "ecosystems," finally forming "the biosphere."

Sentence-structure repetition

Writers occasionally repeat the same sentence structure in order to emphasize the connections among their ideas. Following is an example from Isaac Asimov:

> But the life forms are as much part of the structure of the Earth as any inanimate portion is. It is all an inseparable part of a whole. <u>If</u> any animal is isolated totally from other forms of life, <u>then</u> death by starvation will surely follow. <u>If</u> isolated from water, death by dehydration will follow even faster. <u>If</u> isolated from air, whether free or dissolved in water, death by asphyxiation will follow still faster. <u>If</u> isolated from the Sun, animals will survive for a time, but plants would die, and <u>if</u> all plants died, all animals would starve.   Isaac Asimov, "The Case Against Man"

From the third sentence to the last, Asimov repeats the "If this . . . then that" sentence structure to emphasize the various points he is making.

Collocation

Words collocate when they occur together in expected ways around a particular topic. For example, in a paragraph on tugboats operating out of the port of New York, a reader might expect to encounter words such as *deckhand, engineer, tramp freighter, dock, pilot, Sandy Hook,* or *hawser.* Collocations occur quite naturally to a writer, and they usually form a recognizable network of meaning for readers.

In the paragraph that follows, five collocation chains are used:

1. housewife—cooking—neighbor—home
2. clocks—calculated cooking times—progression—precise
3. obstinacy—vagaries—problem
4. sun—clear days—cloudy ones—sundial—cast its light—angle—seasons—sun—weather
5. cooking—fire—matches—hot coals—smoldering—ashes—go out—bed-warming

The seventeenth-century housewife not only had to make do without thermometers, she also had to make do without clocks, which were scarce and dear throughout the sixteen hundreds. She calculated cooking times by the progression of the sun; her cooking must have been more precise on clear days than on cloudy ones. Marks were sometimes painted on the floor, providing her with a rough sundial, but she still had to make allowance for the obstinacy of the sun in refusing to cast its light at the same angle as the seasons changed; but she was used to allowing for the vagaries of sun and weather. She also had a problem starting her fire in the morning; there were no matches. If she had allowed the hot coals smoldering under the ashes to go out, she had to borrow some from a neighbor, carrying them home with care, perhaps in a bed-warming pan. Waverly Root and Richard de Rouchement, *Eating in America*

EXERCISE 11.10
The preceding section illustrates the following cohesive devices: pronoun reference, same-word repetition, synonym repetition, sentence-structure repetition, and collocation. Look again at the Gould passage on adaptation earlier in the chapter, and identify the cohesive devices you find in it. How do these cohesive devices help you to read the essay and make sense of it?

TRANSITIONS

The final type of cueing discussed in this chapter is the transition. A *transition,* sometimes called a connective, serves as a bridge, connecting one paragraph, sentence, clause, or word with another. Not only does a transition signal a connection, it also identifies the kind of connection by indicating to readers how the item preceding the transition relates to that which follows it. Transitions help readers anticipate how the next paragraph or sentence will affect the meaning of what they have just read. Following is a discussion of three basic groups of transitions, based on the relationships they indicate: logical, temporal, and spatial.

Logical relationships   Transitions help readers follow the logic of an argument. How such transitions work is illustrated in this tightly— and passionately—reasoned paragraph by James Baldwin:

> The black man insists, by whatever means he finds at his disposal, that the white man cease to regard him as an exotic rarity <u>and</u> recognize him as a human being. This is a very charged and difficult moment, <u>for</u> there is a great deal of will power involved in the white man's naivete. Most people are not naturally malicious, <u>and</u> the white man prefers to keep the black man at a certain human remove <u>because</u> it is easier for him <u>thus</u> to preserve his simplicity <u>and</u> to avoid being called to account for crimes committed by his forefathers, <u>or</u> his neighbors. He is inescapably aware, <u>nevertheless</u>, that he is in a better position in the world <u>than</u> black men are, <u>nor</u> can he quite put to death the suspicion that he is hated by black men <u>therefore</u>. He does not wish to be hated, <u>neither</u> does he wish to change places, <u>and</u> at this point in his uneasiness he can scarcely avoid having recourse to those legends which white men have created about black men, the most unusual effect of which is that the white man finds himself enmeshed, so to speak, in his own language which describes hell, <u>as well as</u> the attributes which lead one to hell, <u>as being</u> black as night.
> James Baldwin, "Stranger in the Village"

Following is a partial list of transitions showing logical relations:

To introduce another item in a series: first, second; in the second place; for one thing . . . for another; next; then; furthermore; moreover; in addition; finally; last; also; similarly; besides; and; as well as.

To introduce an illustration or other specification: in particular; specifically; for instance; for example; that is; namely.

To introduce a result or a cause: consequently; as a result; hence; accordingly; thus; so; therefore; then; because; since; for.

To introduce a restatement: that is; in other words; in simpler terms; to put it differently.

To introduce a conclusion or summary: in conclusion; finally; all in all; evidently; clearly; actually; to sum up; altogether; of course.

To introduce an opposing point: but; however; yet; nevertheless; on the contrary; on the other hand; in contrast; conversely; still; neither . . . nor.

To introduce a concession to an opposing view: certainly; naturally; of course; it is true; to be sure; granted.

To resume the original line of reasoning after a concession: nonetheless; all the same; even though; still; nevertheless.

Temporal relationships   In addition to showing logical connections, transitions indicate sequence or progression in time (temporal relationships), as this example illustrates:

> Well, a few weeks later at the front I had trouble with one of the men in my section. By this time I was a "cabo," or corporal, in command of twelve men. It was static warfare, horribly cold, and the chief job was getting sentries to stay awake and at their posts. One day a man suddenly refused to go to a certain post, which he said quite truly was exposed to enemy fire. He was a feeble creature, and I seized hold of him and began to drag him towards his post. This roused the feelings of the others against me, for Spaniards, I think, resent being touched more than we do. Instantly, I was surrounded by a ring of shouting men: "Fascist! Fascist! Let that man go! This isn't a bourgeois army. Fascist!" etc., etc. . . .
> George Orwell, "Looking Back on the Spanish War"

Following is a partial list of temporal transitions:

To indicate frequency: frequently; hourly; often; occasionally; now and then; day after day; again and again.

To indicate duration: during; briefly; for a long time; minute by minute; for many years.

To indicate a particular time: then; at that time; in those days; last Sunday; next Christmas; in 1988; at the beginning of August; at six o'clock; first thing in the morning; two months ago; when this first started.

To indicate the beginning: at first; in the beginning; before then; in the preceding weeks.

To indicate the middle: in the meantime; while this was going on; meanwhile; as it was happening; at that moment; at the same time; simultaneously; next; then.

To indicate the end and beyond: eventually; finally; at last; in the end; subsequently; later; afterwards.

Spatial relationships   Spatial transitions orient readers to the objects in a scene, as illustrated in this paragraph:

> On Georgia 155, I crossed Troublesome Creek, then went through groves of pecan trees aligned one with the next like fenceposts. The pastures

grew a green almost blue, and syrupy water the color of a dusty sunset filled the ponds. <u>Around</u> the farmhouses, <u>from</u> wires strung high <u>above</u> the ground, swayed gourds hollowed out for purple martins.

The land rose <u>again on the other side</u> of the Chattahoochee River, and Highway 34 went to the ridgetops where long views <u>over</u> the hills opened <u>in all directions.</u> <u>Here</u> was the tail of the Appalachian backbone, its gradual descent <u>to</u> the Gulf. <u>Near</u> the Alabama stateline stood a couple of LAST CHANCE! bars. . . .   William Least Heat Moon, *Blue Highways*

Following is a partial list of transitions showing spatial relationships:

To indicate closeness: close to; near; next to; alongside; adjacent to; facing; here.

To indicate distance: in the distance; far; beyond; away; on the far side; there.

To indicate direction: up or down; forward(s) or backward(s); sideways; along; across; at an angle; to the right or left; in front of or behind; above or below; inside or outside.

EXERCISE 11.11

Return to the Gould passage on adaptation earlier in this chapter, and underline the logical, temporal, and spatial transitions he uses. How do they help you to relate different kinds of details and ideas?

Describing

Writers share their perceptions and understanding by drawing pictures with words. These word-pictures give readers the impression of direct, firsthand experience. Describing, the process of drawing word-pictures, re-creates the world as the writer knows it.

To describe, writers must notice what their senses tell them. Noticing is only half of describing, however; the other half is finding the language to record the fine discriminations their senses make. To do this, writers develop a vocabulary that is rich, subtle, and specific enough to allow them to describe what they observe with particularity and precision.

For scientific, engineering, and other technical purposes, writers try to describe things as objectively and impersonally as possible. For many purposes, however, writers want their descriptions not only to reflect accurately the objects they observe but to be suggestive as well. They want to suggest or evoke subjective associations and feelings about what they are describing.

Here are two pieces of description, one more objective than the other. The first, part of an essay on Lake Mead, was written by a geology student:

> Lake Mead was formed when the Colorado River was impounded by Hoover Dam in the Black Canyon, approximately 420 miles upstream from the river's mouth in the Gulf of California. The present morphology of the Lake Mead area consists of a series of steep, narrow canyons separating wide sloping basins. The river cut through the softer material to form these deep, narrow valleys and thus left the wide sloping basins. The major reaches of the reservoir from the upper end to Hoover Dam are Pierce, Iceberg, and Gregg basins, Virgin Canyon, Virgin and Boulder basins, and the Overton arm extending northward from Virgin basin. When filled to its maximum operating level (1,229 feet above mean sea level), Lake Mead has a depth of up to 589 feet above the original stream bed, a shoreline of 550 miles, and a surface area of 225 square miles; it extends upstream 115 miles. The weight of the total impounded water has been estimated at 40×10^{19} tons, of which approximately 60% is located in the Virgin and Boulder basins. An additional 4×10^6 acre-feet of interstitial water are located in the subsurface sedimentary formations surrounding the lake.

The writing in this passage is highly objective and technical. The writer describes the lake by giving its history (formation), describing its shape

12

(morphology), naming its divisions (major reaches), and citing its vital statistics—depth, shoreline and upstream dimensions, surface area, weight, and water volume. This description is full of detail—factual, mostly quantifiable information. The writer does not refer to her sensory impressions of the lake: the sound of the dam, the appearance of the lake and the surrounding landscape, the smell or the feel of the breeze off the lake. Nor does she place herself in the scene by indicating her vantage point. In fact, nothing in her language suggests that she has ever observed the lake firsthand.

In the next selection, Vladimir Nabokov recalls the room belonging to his governess (whom he calls Mademoiselle). Nabokov's description is very personal, revolving around his own sensory impressions and feelings as a child. Although he points out many items, he gives no quantifiable information, no vital statistics. He is more interested in re-creating the atmosphere and evoking the mood of the place than in citing facts about it.

> Mademoiselle's room, both in the country and in town, was a weird place to me—a kind of hothouse sheltering a thick-leaved plant imbued with a heavy, enuretic odor. Although next to ours, when we were small, it did not seem to belong to our pleasant, well-aired home. In that sickening mist, reeking, among other woolier effluvia, of the brown smell of oxidized apple peel, the lamp burned low, and strange objects glimmered upon the writing desk: a lacquered box with licorice sticks, black segments of which she would hack off with her penknife and put to melt under her tongue; a picture postcard of a lake and a castle with mother-of-pearl spangles for windows; a bumpy ball of tightly rolled bits of silver paper that came from all those chocolates she used to consume at night; photographs of the nephew who had died, of his mother who had signed her picture *Mater Dolorosa*, and of a certain Monsieur de Marante who had been forced by his family to marry a rich widow.
> Vladimir Nabokov, *Speak, Memory*

Nabokov's subjective description is as true as the geology student's objective description, although Nabokov's is true to his personal experience and the student's is true to the verifiable facts. Descriptive writing ranges between these extremes of objectivity and subjectivity, as the descriptions you will read in this chapter illustrate. A writer decides how objective or subjective to make a description based on the purpose for writing and the readers' needs and expectations.

Regardless of whether a description is to be more or less objective, describing involves three basic strategies: naming, detailing, and comparing.

NAMING

To describe, writers point to and name objects or features of their subjects. In the following passage, for example, Annie Dillard identifies the face, chin, fur, underside, and eyes of a weasel she once encountered in the woods:

> He was ten inches long, thin as a curve, a muscled ribbon, brown as fruitwood, soft-furred, alert. His <u>face</u> was fierce, small and pointed as a lizard's; he would have made a good arrowhead. There was just a dot of <u>chin</u>, maybe two brown hairs' worth, and then the pure white <u>fur</u> began that spread down his <u>underside</u>. He had two black <u>eyes</u> I didn't see, any more than you see a window.   Annie Dillard, *Teaching a Stone to Talk*

The underscored nouns name the parts of the weasel on which Dillard focuses her attention. The nouns she uses are concrete: they refer to actual, tangible parts of the animal. They are also fairly specific: they identify parts of one particular animal, the weasel she saw.

In looking for the right word to name something, writers can usually choose from a variety of words. Some words may be concrete (referring to tangible objects or actual instances), while others are abstract (referring to ideas or qualities). *Nose, tooth,* and *foot* are concrete words, whereas *love, faith,* and *justice* are abstract.

Some words may be specific (referring to a particular instance or individual), while others are general (referring to a class which includes many particular instances). *Specific* and *general* are relative terms. That is, the specificity of a word cannot be measured absolutely but only by contrasting it with other words that could be substituted for it. For example, *vegetable* is more specific than *food* but more general than *carrot*.

If you compare the following description to Dillard's, you will see how each writer has made particular word choices:

> The expression of this snake's <u>face</u> was hideous and fierce; the <u>pupils</u> consisted of a vertical slit in a mottled and coppery <u>iris</u>; the <u>jaws</u> were broad at the base, and the <u>nose</u> terminated in a triangular projection.
> Charles Darwin, *The Voyage of the Beagle*

Like Dillard, Darwin uses the word *face*, though he specifies the expression on the snake's face. He could have used *eyes*, as Dillard does, but he uses the more specific *pupils* and *iris* instead. *Chin*, however, would not substitute for *jaws* because *jaws* refers to the bone structure of the lower face, while *chin* refers to something different—the prominence of the lower jaw. Darwin could have used the technical terms *maxilla* and *mandible*, the names of the upper and lower jaw bones. He chose not to use these words, even though they are more specific than *jaws*, possibly because they might be unfamiliar to readers or more specific than necessary. As a rule of thumb, writers prefer more specific nouns for naming, but they adjust the degree of specificity to the particular needs of their readers.

EXERCISE 12.1

This is an exercise in close observation and naming. Go to a place where you can sit for a while and observe the scene. It might be a landscape or a cityscape, indoors or outdoors, crowded or solitary. Write for five minutes, listing everything in the scene that you can name.

Then, for each noun on your list, try to think of two or three other nouns you could use in its place. Write these other names down.

Finally, write a paragraph describing the scene. Use the nouns you think go together best, assuming your readers are unfamiliar with the scene.

In addition to naming perceivable objects and features, writers name sensations (<u>stink</u> and <u>plunk</u>) and qualities (the <u>sweetness</u> of the lumber):

> When the sun fell across the great white pile of the new Telephone Company building, you could smell the stucco burning as you passed; then some liquid <u>sweetness</u> that came to me from deep in the rings of the freshly cut lumber stacked in the yards, and the fresh plaster and paint on the brand-new storefronts. <u>Rawness</u>, sunshiny <u>rawness</u> down the end streets of the city, as I thought of them then—the hot ash-laden <u>stink</u> of the refuse dumps in my nostrils and the only sound at noon the resonant metal <u>plunk</u> of a tin can I kicked ahead of me as I went my way. Alfred Kazin, *A Walker in the City*

EXERCISE 12.2

Read "Uncle John's Farm," the Mark Twain piece printed in Chapter 4, and notice how much naming he uses in his description. Then, write a few sentences explaining why you think Twain uses so much naming in this passage. What impression does all this naming make on you? How specific is his naming? How subjective or objective is it?

DETAILING

Although nouns can be quite specific, detailing is a way of adding more specificity to them, thus making description even more particular and precise. Naming answers the questions "What is it?" and "What are its parts or features?" Detailing answers questions like these:

- ☐ What size is it?
- ☐ How many are there?
- ☐ What is it made of?
- ☐ Where is it located?
- ☐ What is its condition?
- ☐ What is its use?
- ☐ Where does it come from?
- ☐ What is its effect?
- ☐ What is its value?

To add details to names, writers add modifiers—adjectives and adverbs, phrases and clauses. Modifiers make nouns more specific by supplying additional information about them.

Notice, in this passage about a weasel, how many modifying details Annie Dillard provides. She indicates size, shape, color, texture, value, and amount.

He was <u>ten</u> <u>inches</u> <u>long</u>, <u>thin</u> as a curve, a <u>muscled</u> ribbon, <u>brown</u> as fruitwood, <u>soft-furred</u>, <u>alert</u>. His face was <u>fierce</u>, <u>small</u> and <u>pointed</u> as a lizard's; he would have made a <u>good</u> arrowhead. There was just a <u>dot</u> of chin, maybe <u>two</u> <u>brown</u> <u>hairs'</u> worth, and then the <u>pure</u> <u>white</u> fur began that spread down his underside. He had <u>two</u> <u>black</u> eyes I didn't see, any more than you see a window.   Annie Dillard, *Teaching a Stone to Talk*

Like names, details can be more or less specific. For example, because "ten inches long" is a measurable quantity, it is more precise than the relative term *small*. Other detailing words like *good* and *pure* are also relative. Even *brown*, although it is more precise than the general word *color*, could be specified further, as Dillard does, by comparing it to the color of fruitwood.

Following is an example of detailing and naming by a science writer. Notice how many of his detailing words are specific yet also relative:

You are doubtless aware that the common nettle owes its <u>stinging</u> property to the <u>innumerable stiff</u> and <u>needle-like</u>, though <u>exquisitely delicate</u>, hairs which cover its surface. Each stinging-needle tapers from a <u>broad</u> base to a <u>slender</u> summit, which, though <u>rounded</u> at the end, is of such microscopic fineness that it readily penetrates, and breaks off in, the skin. Thomas Henry Huxley, "On the Physical Basis of Life"

EXERCISE 12.3
Choose a common household item like a clock, vacuum cleaner, television set, or toaster which you can examine closely. Study this object for at least ten minutes. Then describe it for someone who has never seen it, using as many specific naming and detailing words as you can.

Modifiers are also used to identify a person's character traits, as the following passage about Maya Angelou's mother illustrates:

> By no amount of agile exercising of a wishful imagination could my mother have been called lenient. Generous she was; indulgent, never. Kind, yes; permissive, never.   Maya Angelou, *Gather Together In My Name*

EXERCISE 12.4
Look at Lillian Hellman's description of Dashiell Hammett in Chapter 3. What modifiers does she use to describe Hammett's character? How does this detailing contribute to the overall impression the selection gives you of Hammett?

COMPARING

Whereas naming and detailing call on the power of observation, comparing brings the imagination into play. Comparison makes language even more precise and description more evocative. Look again at Annie Dillard's description of a weasel to see how she uses comparison:

> He was ten inches long, thin as a curve, a muscled ribbon, brown as fruitwood, soft-furred, alert. His face was fierce, small and pointed as a lizard's; he would have made a good arrowhead. There was just a dot of chin, maybe two brown hairs' worth, and then the pure white fur began that spread down his underside. He had two black eyes I didn't see, any more than you see a window.   Annie Dillard, *Teaching a Stone to Talk*

This passage illustrates two kinds of comparison: simile and metaphor. Both figures of speech compare things that are essentially dissimilar. A *simile* directly expresses a similarity by using the word *like* or *as* to announce the comparison. Dillard uses a simile when she writes that the weasel was "thin as a curve." A *metaphor*, on the other hand, is an implicit comparison by which one thing is described as though it were the other. Dillard uses a metaphor when she describes the weasel as "a muscled ribbon."

Here are more examples of comparison used to describe:

Sometimes I rambled to pine groves, <u>standing like temples</u>, or <u>like fleets at sea</u>, full-rigged, with wavy boughs, and rippling with light. . . .   Henry David Thoreau, *Walden*

Just below the path, <u>raising their heads</u> above the endless white crosses of a soldier's cemetery, were strange red flowers.   Alfred Kazin, *A Walker in the City*

Comparing enhances a description by showing readers the thing being described in a surprising new way that can be suggestive and revealing. Although this strategy is called comparing, it includes both comparing and contrasting because differences can be as illuminating as likenesses. Once two things are connected, put into context with one another through comparing, they play off each other in unexpected ways.

EXERCISE 12.5

Compare the following description of a country store to paragraph 4 of Maya Angelou's description of her grandmother's store in Chapter 4. Point out examples of naming and detailing in both descriptions. Then point out where Angelou adds comparing to the other two strategies. How does this addition enrich her description?

The old store, lighted only by three fifty-watt bulbs, smelled of coal oil and baking bread. In the middle of the rectangular room, where the oak floor sagged a little, stood an iron stove. To the right was a wooden table with an unfinished game of checkers and a stool made from an apple-tree stump. On shelves around the walls sat earthen jugs with corncob stoppers, a few canned goods, and some of the two thousand old clocks and clockworks Thurmond Watts owned.   William Least Heat Moon, *Blue Highways*

EXERCISE 12.6

Most writers use comparison only occasionally to achieve particular effects. Notice that Kate Simon, in "Jimmy and Death" in Chapter 2, uses simile (in paragraph 1) and metaphor (in paragraph 4) to characterize Jimmy's mother. What exactly do these figures of speech add to Simon's portrayal of Mrs. Petrides and to the effect of the selection as a whole?

Useful as comparison is, there are a few pitfalls to avoid with this strategy. Be sure that the connection between the two things being compared is clear and appropriate to your description. Avoid using clichéd expressions, comparisons which are so overused that they have become predictable and consequently do not reveal anything new. Following are some examples of comparisons that have been worn out and thus do not enrich a description:

The kiss was as sweet as honey.

I am as busy as a bee.

That picture stands out like a sore thumb.

EXERCISE 12.7

Take five minutes to list as many clichés as you can think of. Then, pair up with another student, and discuss your lists to decide whether the entries are all clichés. When you are done, figure out what turns a comparison into a cliché for you, and together write a sentence defining a cliché.

EXERCISE 12.8

In Chapter 3 Mary McCarthy describes her paternal grandmother. Look at McCarthy's description of the way Grandmother McCarthy regarded her home (paragraph 3) and analyze her description in terms of naming, detailing, and comparing. What impression of Grandmother McCarthy does the language of this description give you? How does this brief description reinforce the overall impression you get of her grandmother in this selection from Mary McCarthy's memoirs?

USING SENSORY DESCRIPTION

Writers use three basic strategies in describing—naming, detailing, and comparing—but they have many language resources, and some limitations, for reporting their sense impressions. These resources help convey sights, sounds, smells, touches, and tastes.

In describing, the sense of sight seems to have primacy over the other senses. Just think of the words commonly used to define describing: re-presenting observations, making verbal images or word-pictures. *Describere,* the Latin root for describe, even means "to sketch or copy." Perhaps people rely more on the sense of sight than on the other senses. Certainly our vocabulary for reporting what we see is larger and more varied than our vocabulary for reporting any other sense impression.

For the other senses, quite a few nouns and verbs designate sounds; a smaller number of nouns, but few verbs, describe smells; and very few nouns or verbs convey touch and taste. Furthermore, these nonvisual sensations do not invite as much naming as sights do because they are not readily divided into constituent features. For example, we have many names to describe the visible features of a car, but few to describe the sounds a car makes. Nevertheless, writers detail the qualities and attributes of nonvisual sensations—the loudness or tinniness or rumble of an engine, for instance.

The sense of sight When people describe what they see, they identify the objects in their field of vision. As the following passages illustrate, these objects may include animate as well as inanimate things and their features. Details may range from words delineating appearance to those evaluating it.

The first selection, by Henry David Thoreau, depicts a nature scene with a lot of activity; the second passage, by Ernest Hemingway, describes F. Scott Fitzgerald's face.

> As I sit at my window this summer afternoon, hawks are circling about my clearing; the tantivy of wild pigeons, flying by twos and threes athwart my view, or perching restless on the white pine boughs behind my house, gives a voice to the air; a fish hawk dimples the glassy surface of the pond and brings up a fish; a mink steals out of the marsh before my door and seizes a frog by the shore; the sedge is bending under the weight of the reed-birds flitting hither and thither. . . .   Henry David Thoreau, *Walden*

> Scott was a man then who looked like a boy with a face between handsome and pretty. He had very fair wavy hair, a high forehead, excited and friendly eyes and a delicate long-lipped Irish mouth that, on a girl, would have been the mouth of a beauty. His chin was well built and he had good ears and a handsome, almost beautiful, unmarked nose.   Ernest Hemingway, *A Moveable Feast*

EXERCISE 12.9

Using Hemingway's description of Fitzgerald's face as a model, write a few sentences describing someone's face. Do not rely on memory for this exercise: describe someone who is before you as you write. You can even look in the mirror and describe your own face.

When you are done, read what you have written and assess the impression it gives of the person. If you feel it gives a weak or contradictory impression, revise your description. Then, in a sentence or two, explain what impression it gives and why you think it gives this impression rather than another.

The sense of hearing In reporting auditory impressions, writers seldom name the objects from which the sounds come without also naming the sensations: the murmur of a voice, the rustle of the wind, the squeak of a hinge, the sputter of an engine. *Onomatopoeia* is the term for names of sounds that echo the sounds themselves: *squeak, murmur, hiss, boom, tinkle, twang, jangle, rasp.* Sometimes writers make up words like *plink, chirr, sweesh-crack-boom,* and *ca-ra-wong* to imitate sounds they wish to describe. Qualitative words like *powerful* and *rich* as well as relative terms like *loud* and *low* often specify sounds further. Detailing sounds sometimes involves the technique called *synesthesia,* applying words commonly used to describe one sense to another, such as describing sounds as *sharp* and *soft.*

To write about the sound of Yosemite Falls, John Muir uses all these naming and describing techniques. He also uses comparison when he refers metaphorically to the water's powerful "voice":

> This noble fall has far the richest, as well as the most powerful, voice of all the falls of the Valley, its tones varying from the sharp hiss and rustle of the wind in the glossy leaves of the live oaks and the soft, sifting, hushing tones of the pines, to the loudest rush and roar of storm winds and thunder among the crags of the summit peaks. The low bass, booming, reverberating tones, heard under favorable circumstances five or six miles away, are formed by the dashing and exploding of heavy masses mixed with air upon two projecting ledges on the face of the cliff, the one on which we are standing and another about 200 feet above it. The torrent of massive comets is continuous at time of high water, while the explosive, booming notes are wildly intermittent, because, unless influenced by the wind, most of the heavier masses shoot out from the face of the precipice, and pass the ledges upon which at other times they are exploded.   John Muir, *The Story of My Boyhood and Youth*

The following passage describes the Doppler effect, the rise and fall of sound as something loud passes quickly by. The author uses a few distinct nouns to name and discriminate kinds of sound and also uses modifiers to detail gradations in sound. But his most interesting technique here is the way he suddenly shifts senses—from hearing to touch—when the car passes by.

> At first a faint sighing, like wind in the tops of distant trees. Then the birth of another sound within the sigh, a sharper sound, very faint but growing steadily, a kind of whine, first heard as a pinpoint in the higher registers, building rapidly to a full hum across the spectrum, growing louder and louder, and then (at the very instant a shock wave of air slammed softly across my shoulders) overtaking the sigh, reversing itself, and plunging down the scale of a steady hum. I watched the black car racing away ahead of me.   Frank Conroy, *Stop-time*

EXERCISE 12.10

Find a noisy spot—a restaurant, a football game, a nursery school, a dorm—where you can perch for a half hour or so. Listen attentively to the sounds of the place and make notes about what you hear. Then, write a paragraph describing the place through its sounds.

When you are done, read your description. In a sentence or two, sum up what impression it gives and why you think it gives this particular impression. If it does not give a strong impression, you may want to revise your paragraph before writing your analysis.

EXERCISE 12.11

George Orwell identifies various sounds in "A Hanging," printed in Chapter 2. Read the essay quickly, looking for each time he names a sound. Notice the contrast between the moments of noise and the moments of silence. How do the sounds contribute to the impact this story has on you?

The sense of smell   The English language has a meager stock of words to express the sense of smell. In addition to the word *smell*, only about ten commonly used nouns describe this sensation: *odor, scent, vapor, aroma, fragrance, perfume, bouquet, stench, stink*. Although there are other, rarer words like *fetor* and *effluvium*, writers tend not to use them, probably for fear their readers will not know them. Few verbs describe receiving or sending odors— *smell, sniff, waft*—but a fair number of detailing adjectives are available: *redolent, pungent, aromatic, perfumed, stinking, musty, rancid, putrid, rank, foul, noisome, acrid, sweet*, and *cloying*.

In the next passage, Conroy uses comparing in addition to naming and detailing. Notice how he describes the effect the odor has on him:

> The perfume of the flowers rushed into my brain. A lush aroma, thick with sweetness, thick as blood, and spiced with the clear acid of tropical greenery. My heart pounded like a drowning swimmer's as the perfume took me over, pouring into my lungs like ambrosial soup.
> Frank Conroy, *Stop-time*

In reporting smells, naming the objects from which they come can be very suggestive:

> It is the smells of the school that I remember best: the sour smell of the oil they rubbed the desks with; the classroom smell of chalk dust and old pulled-down maps; the smell of fuller's earth scattered in wide arcs along the corridors, ahead of the pushbrooms that formed fat kittens out of the dirt tracked daily in by some 300 pairs of feet; the smell of a master's unlighted pipe; the smell that would periodically drift through the school late in the morning to tell us that we were going to have corned beef and cabbage for lunch; the steamy, chlorinated smell of the indoor pool; the smell of the gym, which was a mixture of wintergreen oil and sneakers.   Stephen Birmingham, "New England Prep School"

EXERCISE 12.12

Go someplace with strong smells where you can stay for ten or fifteen minutes. You may choose an eating place (a cafeteria, a donut shop, a cafe), a place where something is being manufactured (a saw mill, a bakery, a canning plant), or some other place that has distinctive odors (a zoo, a perfume counter, a locker room). Take notes while you are there on what you smell, and then write a paragraph describing the place through its smells.

EXERCISE 12.13

Look at Alfred Kazin's description of his family's kitchen in Chapter 4. Read through the passage, looking for particular smells he associates with the place. Then, briefly explain how the smells he describes contribute to your understanding of the significance this place has for him.

EXERCISE 12.14

Think of a smell you remember vividly from your own childhood. What smell is it? What do you associate with this particular smell? Write a paragraph describing this smell; try to do so in a way that lets readers understand what associations this smell has for you.

The sense of touch Writers describing the sense of touch tend not to name the sensation directly or even to report the act of feeling. Probably this omission occurs because so few nouns and verbs describe tactile sensations besides words like *touch, feeling, tickle, itch,* and *tingle.* Nevertheless, a large stock of words describe temperature (*hot, warm, mild, tepid, cold, arctic*), moisture content (*wet, dry, sticky, oily, greasy, moist, parched*), texture (*gritty, silky, smooth, crinkled, coarse, rough, soft, sharp*), and weight (*heavy, light, ponderous, buoyant, feathery*). Read the following passages with an eye for descriptions of touch.

> The midmorning sun was deceitfully mild and the wind had no weight on my skin. Arkansas summer mornings have a feathering effect on stone reality.   Maya Angelou, *Gather Together In My Name*

> It was an ordeal for me to walk the hills in the dead of summer for then they were parched and dry and offered no shade from the hot sun and no springs or creeks where thirst could be quenched.   William O. Douglas, *Go East, Young Man*

EXERCISE 12.15

Briefly describe the feel of the sun, a cold wind, a shower first thing in the morning, a kiss, bare feet on hot sand, or any other tactile sensation you might think of. Then explain what impression your description makes and why you think it makes this particular impression.

The sense of taste Other than *taste, savor,* and *flavor,* few words name the gustatory sensations directly. Certain words do distinguish among the four types of taste—*sweet* (*saccharine, sugary, cloying*); *sour* (*acidic, tart*); *bitter* (*acrid, biting*); *salty* (*briny, brackish*), while several other words describe specific tastes (*piquant, spicy, pungent, peppery, savory,* and *toothsome*).

In addition to these words, the names of objects tasted and other details may indicate the intensity and quality of a taste. Notice Hemingway's descriptive technique in the following selection.

> As I ate the oysters with their strong taste of the sea and their faint metallic taste that the cold wine washed away, leaving only the sea taste and the succulent texture, and as I drank their cold liquid from each shell and washed it down with the crispy taste of the wine, I lost the empty feeling and began to be happy and to make plans.   Ernest Hemingway, *A Moveable Feast*

Possibly more than any other sense, taste is closely associated with other senses. In the next passage James Agee provides a rich context of sense impressions to describe a meal served in a poor, rural home:

> The biscuits are large and shapeless, not cut round, and are pale, not tanned, and are dusty with flour. They taste of flour and soda and damp salt and fill the mouth stickily. They are better with butter, and still better with butter and jam. The butter is pallid, soft, and unsalted, about the texture of coldcream; it seems to taste delicately of wood and wet cloth, and it tastes "weak." The jam is loose, of little berries, full of light raspings of the tongue; it tastes a deep sweet purple tepidly watered, with a very faint sheen of a sourness as of iron. Field peas are olive-brown, the shape of lentils, about twice the size. Their taste is a cross between lentils and boiled beans; their broth is bright with seasoning of pork, and of this also they taste. The broth is soaked up in bread. The meat is a bacon, granular with salt, soaked in the grease of its frying: there is very little lean meat in it. What there is is nearly as tough as rind; the rest is pure salted stringy fat. The eggs taste of pork too. They are fried in it on both sides until none of the broken yolk runs, are heavily salted and peppered while they fry, so that they come to table nearly black, very heavy, rinded with crispness, nearly as dense as steaks. Of milk I hardly know how to say; it is skimmed, blue-lighted; to a city palate its warmth and odor are somehow dirty and at the same time vital, a little as if one were drinking blood. There is even in so clean a household as this an odor of pork, of sweat, so subtle it seems to get into the very metal of the cooking-pans beyond any removal of scrubbing . . . and it seems to be this odor, and a sort of wateriness and discouraged tepidity, which combine to make the food seem unclean, sticky, and sallow with some invisible sort of disease.   James Agee, *Let Us Now Praise Famous Men*

EXERCISE 12.16

Describe the taste of your favorite food or meal as Agee does in the preceding passage. Then explain what impression your description makes and why you think it makes this particular impression.

EXERCISE 12.17

Look at the Angelou and Twain selections in Chapter 4, noting the descriptions of food in both. Compare the ways these two writers describe food. Why do you suppose food plays such a prominent role in writing about remembered places?

CREATING A DOMINANT IMPRESSION

Description impresses a scene, object, or person upon the reader's mind. The most effective description creates a dominant impression, a mood or atmosphere that reinforces the writer's purpose. Naming, detailing, and comparing—all the choices about what to include and what to call things— come together to create this effect, as the following passage by Mary McCarthy illustrates. Notice that McCarthy directly states the idea she is trying to convey in the last sentence, the paragraph's topic sentence.

> Whenever we children came to stay at my grandmother's house, we were put to sleep in the sewing room, a bleak, shabby, utilitarian rectangle, more office than bedroom, more attic than office, that played to the hierarchy of chambers the role of a poor relation. It was a room seldom entered by the other members of the family, seldom swept by the maid, a room without pride; the old sewing machine, some cast-off chairs, a shadeless lamp, rolls of wrapping paper, piles of pins, and remnants of material united with the iron folding cots put out for our use and the bare floor boards to give an impression of intense and ruthless temporality. Thin, white spreads, of the kind used in hospitals and charity institutions, and naked blinds at the windows reminded us of our orphaned condition and of the ephemeral character of our visit; there was nothing here to encourage us to consider this our home.   Mary McCarthy, *Memories of a Catholic Girlhood*

Everything in the room made McCarthy and her brothers feel unwanted, discarded, orphaned. The room itself is described in terms applicable to the children. (Like them it "played to the hierarchy of chambers the role of a poor relation.") The objects she names, together with their distinguishing details—"cast-off chairs," "shadeless lamp," "iron folding cots," "bare floor boards," "naked blinds"—contribute to this overall impression, thus enabling McCarthy to convey her purpose to her readers.

Writers sometimes comment directly during their descriptions. McCarthy, for instance, states that the sewing room gave "an impression of intense and ruthless temporality," everything serving to remind the children that they were orphans and did not live there. Often, however, writers want description to speak for itself. They *show* rather than tell, letting the descriptive language evoke the impression by itself. Such is the case in the following description of an English country house from a novel by Charles Dickens:

> The waters are out in Lincolnshire. An arch of the bridge in the park has been sapped and sopped away. The adjacent low-lying ground, for half a mile in breadth, is a stagnant river, with melancholy trees for islands in it, and a surface punctured all over, all day long, with falling rain. My Lady Dedlock's "place" has been extremely dreary. The weather, for many a day and night, has been so wet that the trees seem wet through, and the soft loppings and prunings of the woodsman's axe can make no crack or crackle as they fall. The deer, looking soaked, leave quagmires where they pass. The shot of a rifle loses its sharpness in the moist air, and its smoke moves in a tardy little cloud towards the green rise, coppice-topped, that makes a background for the falling rain. The view from my Lady Dedlock's own windows is alternately a lead-coloured view, and a view in Indian ink. The vases on the stone terrace in the foreground catch the rain all day; and the heavy drops fall, drip, drip, drip, upon the broad flagged pavement, called, from old time, the Ghost's Walk, all night. On Sundays, the little church in the park is mouldy; the oaken pulpit breaks out into a cold sweat; and there is a general smell and taste as of the ancient Dedlocks in their graves.   Charles Dickens, *Bleak House*

EXERCISE 12.18

Write a paragraph or two describing your bedroom or some other room where you have spent a lot of time. Describe the room in a way that conveys a strong mood or atmosphere. Then write a few sentences describing the dominant impression you want your description to make, explaining your purpose in describing the room this way and the techniques you used.

EXERCISE 12.19

Look at Orwell's account of a hanging in Chapter 2. Read the piece quickly, noting how Orwell describes the scene. What dominant impression does his description give? How does the scene reinforce the story?

ASSUMING A VANTAGE POINT

Writing effectively about a scene requires taking a vantage point—that is, selecting the point or position from which to describe the scene. By presenting the objects and features there from a particular vantage point, the writer puts the scene into perspective for readers.

A stationary vantage point   A writer who stays still takes on a fixed or stationary vantage point. In the following passage, the author takes a position in a subway station and describes what he sees without moving around the station:

> Standing in a subway station, I began to appreciate the place—almost to enjoy it. First of all, I looked at the lighting: a row of meager electric bulbs, unscreened, yellow, and coated with filth, stretched toward the black mouth of the tunnel, as though it were a bolt hole in an abandoned coal mine. Then I lingered, with zest, on the walls and ceiling: lavatory tiles which had been white about fifty years ago, and were now encrusted with soot, coated with the remains of a dirty liquid which might be either atmospheric humidity mingled with smog or the result of a perfunctory attempt to clean them with cold water; and, above them, gloomy vaulting from which dingy paint was peeling off like scabs from an old wound, sick black paint leaving a leprous white subsurface. Beneath my feet, the floor was a nauseating dark brown with black stains upon it which might be stale oil or dry chewing gum or some worse defilement; it looked like the hallway of a condemned slum building. Then my eye traveled to the tracks, where two lines of glittering steel—the only positively clean objects in the whole place—ran out of darkness into darkness above an unspeakable mass of congealed oil, puddles of dubious liquid, and a mishmash of old cigarette packets, mutilated and filthy newspapers, and the debris that filtered down from the street above through a barred grating in the roof. As I looked up toward the sunlight, I could see more debris sifting slowly downward, and making an abominable pattern in the slanting beam of dirt-laden sunlight. I was going on to relish more features of this unique scene: such as the advertisement posters on the walls—here a text from the Bible, there a half-naked girl, here a woman wearing a hat consisting of a hen sitting on a nest full of eggs, and there a pair of girl's legs walking up the keys of a cash register—all scribbled over with unknown names and well-known obscenities in black crayon and red lipstick; but then my train came in at last. . . .   Gilbert Highet, "The Subway Station"

Although Highet stays still, his eyes move. He uses these eye movements to order the description of what he sees, looking first at the lights, then at the walls and ceilings, at the floor, at the tracks, toward the sunlight, and finally at the posters on the wall. Although Highet seems to describe objects as they catch his attention, writers sometimes give details in a more orderly pattern—for example, from left to right, top to bottom, big to small.

A moving point of view   Instead of remaining fixed in one spot, a writer may move through a scene. Such is the case with the next author, who describes what he sees as he drives down the highway:

The highway, without warning, rolled off the plateau of green pastures and entered a wooded and rocky gorge; down, down, precipitously down to the Kentucky River. Along the north slope, man-high columns of ice clung to the limestone. The road dropped deeper until it crossed the river at Brooklyn Bridge. The gorge, hidden in the tableland and wholly un-expected, was the Palisades. At the bottom lay only enough ground for the river and a narrow strip of willow-rimmed.

Houses on stilts and a few doublewides rose from the damp flats like toadstools. Next to one mobile home was a partly built steel boat longer than the trailer.   William Least Heat Moon, *Blue Highways*

Notice how the author uses spatial transitions like *down, along, from,* and *next* to orient his readers to his movements. An extended discussion of transitions and a list of transitions commonly used to indicate spatial relations are in Chapter 11: Cueing the Reader.

Combined vantage points   Writers sometimes use more than one stationary vantage point or combine stationary and moving vantage points. In these cases, the important thing is to orient the readers to any change in position.

In the next selection, Willie Morris begins with a moving vantage point and then uses several stationary points.

One walked up the three flights through several padlocked doors, often past the garbage which the landlords had neglected to remove for two or three days. Once inside our place, things were not bad at all. There was a big front room with an old floor, a little alcove for a study, and to the back a short corridor opening up into a tiny bedroom for my son and a larger bedroom in the back. The kitchen was in the back bedroom. I had not been able to find a view of an extensive body of water at popular prices, but from the back window, about forty-yards out, there *was* a vista of a big tank, part of some manufacturing installation in the building under it, and the tank constanty bubbled with some unidentified greenish substance. From this window one could also see the tarred rooftops of the surrounding buildings, and off to the right a quiet stretch of God's earth, this being the parking lot next door.

From the front room the view of the street was more animated. Across the street there was a large bar which seemed to remain open twenty-four hours a day, and in front of this, on the corner, one could look down at any hour and see the little circles of people, just standing, watching the mad traffic on lower Madison.   Willie Morris, *North Toward Home*

EXERCISE 12.20

Look back at the paragraph you wrote for Exercise 12.1. What vantage point did you take in that description? Is your vantage point always clear? If you can improve it, revise the paragraph.

EXERCISE 12.21

Look at Mark Twain's piece about his uncle's farm in Chapter 4. What vantage point or points does he use in this essay?

USING FUNCTIONAL DESCRIPTION

Functional description is a specialized kind of highly objective description used primarily by scientists, engineers, and technical writers to present the physical specifications of an object or mechanism so that readers will know how it functions. Functional description emphasizes how the parts work together.

Here are two examples. The first describes the structure of DNA, deoxyribose nucleic acid. It was written by James Watson and Francis Crick, the Nobel Prize-winning scientists who discovered DNA's structure.

> We wish to put forward a radically different structure for the salt of deoxyribose nucleic acid. This structure has two helical chains each coiled round the same axis (see diagram). We have made the usual chemical assumptions, namely, that each chain consists of phosphate diester groups joining β-D-deoxyribofuranose residues with 3′,5′ linkages. The two chains (but not their bases) are related by a dyad perpendicular to the fibre axis.

This figure is purely diagrammatic. The two ribbons symbolize the two phosphate-sugar chains, and the horizontal rods the pairs of bases holding the chains together. The vertical line marks the fibre axis.

Both chains follow right-handed helices, but owing to the dyad the sequences of the atoms in the two chains run in opposite directions. Each chain loosely resembles Furberg's model No. 1; that is, the bases are on the inside of the helix and the phosphates on the outside. The configuration of the sugar and the atoms near it is close to Furberg's "standard configuration," the sugar being roughly perpendicular to the attached base. . . .   James Watson and Francis Crick, "Molecular Structure of Nucleic Acids"

The first thing to notice in the preceding passage is that, in addition to the written description or word-picture, Watson and Crick diagram DNA's "two helical chains each coiled round the same axis." Second, their language is specific but also technical; many readers will have difficulty understanding them. Third, they quantify and characterize, but they do not use sensory images.

In this second example of functional description, an anonymous writer for a construction company describes the photoelectric smoke detectors the company has installed in its newly built houses.

The photoelectric smoke detector is similar to a ceiling light fixture. It is attractively housed in a white plastic case 5 inches in diameter and 3 inches deep. Like a light fixture, it is directly connected to a conventional 120 circuit for continuous power. A schematic of the photoelectric smoke detector is shown in Figure 1. Connected to the power supply is a constant light-emitting source housed in a compartment with a convex lens. Across

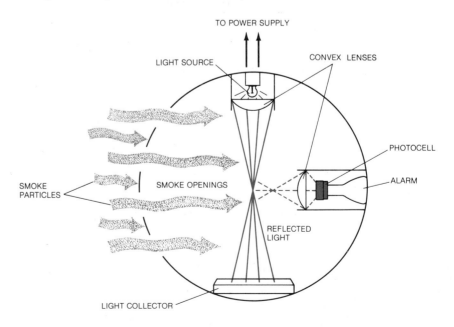

FIGURE 1.
Schematic of Photoelectric Smoke Detector Smoke Chamber

from the light source is a light collector. On one side of the detector are the smoke openings, through which any smoke will pass. Opposite the window, in another compartment, is a second convex lens with a photocell electrically connected to the alarm.

These components of the photoelectric smoke detector interact either spatially or electrically. There are no moving parts. The light-emitting source is continuously powered by the house current. The light beams are refracted through the convex lens, focused through a point opposite the photocell, and then absorbed by the light collector. When smoke floats into the chamber through the smoke openings, however, the smoke particles reflect and scatter the light beams. Because all of the light beams are focused in front of the photocell, some of the reflected light will enter the second convex lens and be refracted into the photocell. This activates the solid-state circuitry in the cell, which then triggers the alarm. The alarm immediately emits a continuous signal with a strength of 85 decibels at 10 ft.

Like the DNA description, this one uses a diagram or "schematic," as it is called. In the first paragraph, the writer names and details the components of the smoke detector and compares it to a light fixture. The second paragraph tells about the process by which the smoke alarm is set off. (See Chapter 13: Narrating, for more about process narrative.)

EXERCISE 12.22

Look at the essay by David Attenborough in Chapter 5. The opening sentence of paragraph 3 is a brief functional description. What do you think makes it a functional description? How is it like the descriptions of DNA structure and the smoke alarm?

EXERCISE 12.23

Write a functional description of some simple mechanical object—a can opener, corkscrew, mechanical pencil, or bicycle, for example. As you write, decide how technical your description should be if your readers are to understand it.

Narrating

Narration is a basic writing strategy for presenting action. Writers use narration for a variety of purposes: they illustrate and support their ideas with anecdotes, entertain readers with suspenseful stories, predict what will happen with scenarios, and explain how something should happen with process narrative. This chapter focuses on how writers make their narratives work—how they sequence narrative action, shape narrative structure, and present the narrative from various points of view. Finally, it looks at one special use of narrative: to present a process.

SEQUENCING NARRATIVE ACTION

One of the most important elements writers must consider in presenting action is sequencing. One way writers sequence action is by presenting it along a narrative time line. Simple chronological sequencing can be best illustrated with process narrative. Because these narratives present instructions for readers to follow, each action must be carefully identified and set out in a clear, straightforward order. How this simple sequencing works is illustrated in the following selection from a piece by Jim Villas on making fried chicken:

> Placing whole chicken in center of cutting board (breast-side up, neck toward you), grab leg on left firmly, pull outward and down toward board, and begin slashing down through skin toward thigh joint, keeping knife close to thigh. Crack back thigh joint as far as possible, find joint with fingers, then cut straight through to remove (taking care not to pull skin from breast). Turn bird around and repeat procedure on other thigh. Jim Villas, "Fried Chicken"

Such play-by-play narrating takes place occasionally in fiction as well. Here is an example from "Big Two-Hearted River: Part II," a story by Ernest Hemingway. This excerpt shows the actions Nick takes while fishing with grasshoppers as bait.

> Holding the rod in his right hand he let out line against the pull of the grasshopper in the current. He stripped off line from the reel with his left hand and let it run free. He could see the hopper in the little waves of the current. It went out of sight.

13

There was a tug on the line. Nick pulled against the taut line. It was his first strike. Holding the now living rod across the current, he brought in the line with his left hand.   Ernest Hemingway, *In Our Time*

EXERCISE 13.1

Look at George Orwell's essay "A Hanging" in Chapter 2. Read it carefully, making a time line of the events in the story. Compare your time line to those of others in your class. Did you all include the same events? Did you put the events in the same order? How do you account for any differences among time lines?

EXERCISE 13.2

Think of something memorable you did that you could narrate in some detail. You might recall a race you ran in, a school play you performed in, an unusual activity you participated in, or an adventure in a strange place. Reflect on what you did, making a time line of the events in the order in which they occurred. Then, write a narrative following the chronological sequence set out in your time line.

On occasion, writers complicate the narrative sequence by referring to something that occurred earlier, with a *flashback,* or that will occur later, with a *flashforward.* Film and modern fiction have made flashbacks familiar to us as methods of presenting past events dramatically or contrasting the past with the present. One way to introduce a flashback is in the form of a vivid memory which intrudes on the character's thoughts.

Flashbacks   Here is an example of a flashback from a narrative by Annie Dillard. Dillard has been telling how she spent a day observing praying mantis egg cases hatch. In the following excerpt she interrupts the forward movement of her narrative to tell about an experience she had years before.

Night is rising in the valley; the creek has been extinguished for an hour. . . . The scene that was in the back of my brain all afternoon, obscurely, is beginning to rise from night's lagoons. It really has nothing to do with praying mantises. But this afternoon I threw tiny string lashings and hitches with frozen hands, gingerly, fearing to touch the egg cases for a minute because I remembered the Polyphemus moth. . . .
   Once, when I was ten or eleven years old. . .   Annie Dillard, *Pilgrim at Tinker Creek*

Flashforwards   Not only do writers flash back to actions in the distant past, they also flash forward to actions occurring some time after the main action they are presenting. Another passage by Dillard offers an example of this kind of complex action:

> It was before dawn when we found a highway out of town and drove into the unfamiliar countryside. By the growing light we could see a band of cirrostratus clouds in the sky. <u>Later the rising sun would clear these clouds before the eclipse began.</u>   Annie Dillard, *Teaching a Stone to Talk*

Narratives usually move in chronological sequence from past to present, with occasional flashbacks or flashforwards for variety. But, as the next passage shows, a narrative can also move from the present to the recent past and then to the more distant past:

> The crowd was excited to see Caudill and Guidugli spill their blood, yes, but if the truth be told, <u>they had been even happier several minutes earlier, when</u> Stanton Long, a machine operator, had staggered to the side of the ring and, in great pain, vomited the entire contents of his stomach onto the concrete floor below. And <u>they had laughed mightily when</u> Raymond Morris, a forty-five-year-old bartender, had convulsed on the mat after taking a beating from a man twenty-two years his junior. . . .
>   <u>Three weeks earlier</u>, the posters had gone up in the bars and factories around Dayton. HOW TOUGH ARE YOU? read the headline that stood next to a large drawing of a man's fist.   Bob Greene, ''That's Entertainment''

EXERCISE 13.3

Look back at the narrative time line and the narrative you developed for Exercise 13.2. Pick an event from your time line that you could use in a flashback or, if none is appropriate, think of another event that is. Rewrite your narrative inserting this event in a flashback.

Then do the same for a flashforward, either picking an event from your time line or thinking of a new event. Revise your original chronological narrative by inserting the flashforward.

Now read all three versions, and think about how the changes in sequencing change the overall effect of your story. Which version of the story is the most dramatic or suspenseful? Do the changes introduce a revealing contrast?

Narrative time signals   Writers use three methods to signal shifts in narrative time: clock time, temporal transitions, and verb tense. You can see all three at work in the following passage from "Death of a Pig," an essay by E. B. White. The essay is about what happened when the pig White was raising to be butchered became ill and died. The pages that follow refer back to this passage often to illustrate the three methods of signaling time shifts. For now, just read the passage:

It was about four o'clock in the afternoon when I first noticed that there was something wrong with the pig. He failed to appear at the trough for his supper, and when a pig (or a child) refuses supper a chill wave of fear runs through any household, or ice-household. After examining my pig, who was stretched out in the sawdust inside the building, I went to the phone and cranked it four times. Mr. Dameron answered. "What's good for a sick pig?" I asked. (There is never any identification needed on a country phone; the person on the other end knows who is talking by the sound of the voice and by the character of the question.)

"I don't know, I never had a sick pig," said Mr. Dameron, "but I can find out quick enough. You hang up and I'll call Henry."

Mr. Dameron was back on the line again in five minutes. "Henry says roll him over on his back and give him two ounces of castor oil or sweet oil, and if that doesn't do the trick give him an injection of soapy water. He says he's almost sure the pig's plugged up, and even if he's wrong, it can't do any harm."

I thanked Mr. Dameron. I didn't go right down to the pig, though. I sank into a chair and sat still for a few minutes to think about my troubles, and then I got up and went to the barn, catching up on some odds and ends that needed tending to. Unconsciously I held off, for an hour, the deed by which I would officially recognize the collapse of the performance of raising a pig; I wanted no interruption in the regularity of feeding, the steadiness of growth, the even succession of days. I wanted no interruption, wanted no oil, no deviation. I just wanted to keep on raising a pig, full meal after full meal, spring into summer into fall. I didn't even know whether there were two ounces of castor oil on the place.

Shortly after five o'clock I remembered that we had been invited out to dinner that night and realized that if I were to dose a pig there was no time to lose. The dinner date seemed a familiar conflict: I move in a desultory society and often a week or two will roll by without my going to anybody's house to dinner or anyone's coming to mine, but when an occasion does arise, and I am summoned, something usually turns up (an hour or two in advance) to make all human intercourse seem vastly inappropriate. I have come to believe that there is in hostesses a special power of divination, and that they deliberately arrange dinners to coincide with pig failure or some other sort of failure. At any rate, it was after five o'clock and I knew I could put off no longer the evil hour.

When my son and I arrived at the pigyard, armed with a small bottle of castor oil and a length of clothesline, the pig had emerged from his house and was standing in the middle of his yard, listlessly. He gave us a slim greeting. I could see that he felt uncomfortable and uncertain. I had brought the clothesline thinking I'd have to tie him (the pig weighed more than a hundred pounds) but we never used it. My son reached down, grabbed both front legs, upset him quickly, and when he opened his mouth to scream I turned the oil into his throat—a pink, corrugated area I had never seen before. I had just time to read the label while the neck of the bottle was in his mouth. It said Puretest. The screams, slightly muffled by oil, were pitched in the hysterically high range of pig-sound, as though torture were being carried out, but they didn't last long: it was all over rather suddenly, and, his legs released, the pig righted himself. E. B. White, "Death of a Pig"

Clock time. White uses clock time to orient readers and to give a sense of duration. He tells us that the action lasted a little over an hour, beginning at about four o'clock and ending a little after five. Moreover, he indicates that he called Mr. Dameron as soon as he had assessed the situation and then had to wait five minutes for him to call back. He makes clear that once he learned what to do, he spent most of the hour avoiding the task.

In the following brief example by George Simpson, clock time serves the writer's purpose by making readers aware of the speed with which actions were taken:

9:05 P.M. An ambulance backs into the receiving bay, its red and yellow lights flashing in and out of the lobby. A split second later, the glass doors burst open as a nurse and an attendant roll a mobile stretcher into the lobby. When the nurse screams, "Emergent!" the lobby explodes with activity as the way is cleared to the trauma room. Doctors appear from nowhere and transfer the bloodied body of a black man to the treatment table. Within seconds his clothes are stripped away.   George Simpson, "The War Room at Bellevue"

EXERCISE 13.4

Look at David Noonan's essay about the brain in Chapter 10. Read the essay quickly, noting the use of clock time. What do you think is the writer's purpose for using clock time in this essay? What effect does it have on you?

Temporal transitions. Another means of showing time passing is with temporal transitions, words and phrases that locate a point in time or relate one point to another. Some familiar ones include *then, when, at that time, before, after, while, next, later, first,* and *second;* see Chapter 11: Cueing the Reader for a more detailed discussion of these time markers. Look back at the first paragraph of the White passage from "Death of a Pig." White uses several temporal transitions in the paragraph: *when* (twice), *first,* and *after.*

Process narrative uses many temporal transitions, as you can see in this passage from an essay about wasps and spiders:

> <u>When</u> the grave is finished, the wasp returns to the tarantula to complete her ghastly enterprise. <u>First</u>, she feels it all over <u>once more</u> with her antennae. <u>Then</u> her behavior becomes more aggressive. She bends her abdomen, protruding her sting, and searches for the soft membrane at the point where the spider's legs join its body—the only spot where she can penetrate the horny skeleton. <u>From time to time</u>, as the exasperated spider slowly shifts ground, the wasp turns on her back and slides with the aid of her wings, trying to get under the tarantula for a shot at the vital spot. <u>During</u> all this maneuvering, which can last <u>for several minutes</u>, the tarantula makes no move to save itself. <u>Finally</u> the wasp corners it against some obstruction and grasps one of its legs in her powerful jaws. <u>Now at last</u> the harassed spider tries a desperate but vain defense. The two contestants roll over and over on the ground. It is a terrifying sight and the outcome is always the same.   Alexander Petrunkevitch, "The Spider and the Wasp"

EXERCISE 13.5

Look back at the narratives you wrote for Exercises 13.2 and 13.3. Did you use temporal transitions in your own writing? If you did, try to explain why. If you did not, would your writing be improved if you added temporal transitions? Which ones would you add, and where? Explain why you would add these particular transitions at these places.

Verb tense. Verb tense also plays an important role in presenting time in narrative. It indicates when the actions occur and whether they are complete or in progress. White, for example, sets most of his narrative in the simple past tense, complicating his narrative only when he reports actions occurring simultaneously: "When my son and I arrived at the pigyard, . . . the pig had emerged from his house and was standing in the middle of his yard. . . ." To convey the time relations among these actions, he uses three past tenses in one sentence:

> simple past to indicate a completed action: "my son and I arrived"
>
> past perfect to indicate the action occurred before another action: "the pig had emerged"
>
> past progressive to indicate an ongoing action that had been in progress for some time: the pig "was standing"

EXERCISE 13.6

Look now at Fred Wolf's essay on Galileo in Chapter 5. Examine the verb tenses the writer uses in the anecdotes (paragraphs 3, 6, and 7–8).

Compare the tenses he uses in each anecdote. Are they the same? If not, how do they differ? Why might a writer use different tenses in the same essay?

Both verb tense and temporal transitions can distinguish actions that occurred repeatedly from those that occurred only once. In the following passage, for example, Willie Morris uses the tense marker *would* along with the time marker *many times* to indicate recurring actions. When he moves from action which occurred repeatedly to action which occurred only once, he shifts to the simple past tense, signaling this shift with the phrase *on one occasion*.

> <u>Many times</u>, walking home from work, I <u>would see</u> some unknowing soul venture across that intersection against the light and <u>then</u> freeze in horror when he saw the cars ripping out of the tunnel toward him. <u>For a brief instant</u> the immobile human <u>would stand</u> there, transfixed by the vehicle bearing down upon him, the contrast of desperate vulnerable flesh and hard chrome never failing to send a horrible tremor through an onlooker's being. <u>Then</u>, suddenly, the human reflex <u>would take</u> over, and the pedestrian <u>would jackknife</u> <u>first</u> one way, <u>then</u> another, arms flaying the empty air, and <u>often</u> the car would literally *skim* the man, brushing by him so close it <u>would touch</u> his coat or his tie. If another car coming behind did not nail him <u>then</u>, much the way a linebacker moves in for the kill after the tackle or end merely slows down a ball-carrier, the pedestrian <u>would stand</u> there <u>briefly</u>, all the blood drained from his face, oblivious to the curses from the driver of the car which had just missed him. If there was a cop on the corner he <u>would wait while</u> the man staggered in his shock to the sidewalk beyond, there to accost him: "Ya crazy, hah? Ya stupid? Walkin' against the light! Hah! Ya almost got killed, ya know it? Ya *know* it?" I saw this ritual several times; <u>on one occasion</u>, feeling sorry for the person who had brushed against the speeding car, I <u>hurried</u> across the intersection after him to cheer him up a little. Catching up with him down by 32nd I <u>said</u>, "That was good legwork, sir. Excellent moves for a big man!" but the man <u>looked</u> at me with an empty expression in his eyes, and <u>then moved</u> away mechanically and trancelike, heading for the nearest bar.　Willie Morris, *North Toward Home*

SHAPING NARRATIVE STRUCTURE

Conflict　Sequencing is not the only way to structure a narrative. Another device writers use to turn a sequence of actions into a story is conflict. Conflict adds the question "So what?" to "What happened next?" It provides motivation and purpose for the actions of characters. In this way, conflict gives narrative its dramatic structure.

The conflict in most narrative takes the form of a struggle between the main character and an opposing force. This force may take many forms—another person, nature, society's rules and values, elements within the character such as conflicting values or desires.

In this excerpt from Orwell's "A Hanging" (reprinted in full in Chapter 2), the conflict is between the narrator's sense of the sanctity of life and his duty to perform his role in the execution. As the dog tries to turn the death march into a game, the conflict between the forces that celebrate life and those that take it away is brought into the open.

> We set out for the gallows. Two warders marched on either side of the prisoner, with their rifles at the slope; two others marched close against him, gripping him by arm and shoulder, as though at once pushing and supporting him. The rest of us, magistrates and the like, followed behind. Suddenly, when we had gone ten yards, the procession stopped short without any order or warning. A dreadful thing had happened—a dog, come goodness knows whence, had appeared in the yard. It came bounding among us with a loud volley of barks, and leapt round us wagging its whole body, wild with glee at finding so many human beings together. It was a large woolly dog, half Airedale, half pariah. For a moment it pranced round us, and then, before anyone could stop it, it had made a dash for the prisoner, jumping up tried to lick his face. Everyone stood aghast, too taken aback even to grab at the dog.   George Orwell, "A Hanging".

EXERCISE 13.7

What is the conflict in the narratives you wrote for Exercises 13.2 and 13.3? Write a few sentences, stating what you see as the central conflict of your narratives.

EXERCISE 13.8

Look at "Inside the Brain" by David Noonan in Chapter 10. What do you think is the central conflict in this essay? Write a few sentences describing this conflict.

Tension Conflict gives narrative its creative tension, and this tension makes readers want to read on to find out what will happen. Tension in narrative does not refer to hostility or anxiety, but to tautness. This sense of tension comes from its Latin root, *tendere,* meaning "to stretch." Tension keeps a narrative stretched taut and makes it suspenseful. By setting up an unresolved conflict, a writer can make readers care about the action and ultimate resolution of the conflict.

Conflict also imposes structure on narrative action in another way: by focusing the action toward some purpose. That is, instead of the simple "and then-and then-and then" structure which a time line gives, conflict provides a one-thing-leads-to-another structure. Each part of the action then plays an instrumental role in the narrative. In this way, it can help to support the theme of the narrative.

EXERCISE 13.9

Look at Russell Baker's essay in Chapter 2. Although this narrative has a fairly simple "and then" structure, it also has a lot of tension. Read the story quickly, paying special attention to your response to it. At what points do you feel excited? When do you have a sense of anticipation or suspense? How do these feelings affect your enjoyment of the story?

Pacing Although writers may place actions in the context of clock time, they do not really try to reproduce time as it is measured by clocks. Clock time moves at a uniform rate. Five minutes always takes the same time no matter what is happening during that period. Imagine writing about an action that took five minutes and using the same number of words (or syllables) to present what happened in each minute. No minute would have more space than another; none would have more emphasis. If everything were emphasized equally, readers would be unable to distinguish among the actions. Such a narrative would be monotonous and unnatural.

Narrative time is more like psychological time than clock time. People experience time subjectively according to their feelings, not objectively according to a mechanical measurement. Sometimes, time seems to drag; at other times, it passes rapidly, especially when people are intensely involved in what they are doing.

Pacing refers to the techniques writers use to create the sense of duration in narrative time. They pace narratives by emphasizing more important actions and deemphasizing less important ones. To emphasize a sequence of action, a writer heightens the drama, thus making the action last longer or seem more intense. Two common techniques for doing this are using sentences with momentum and presenting the action through dialogue.

Momentum. The writer George Plimpton participated in the Detroit Lions football training camp in order to write a book about professional football. In this passage from his book, Plimpton tells what happened when he had his big chance in a practice scrimmage.

> Since in the two preceding plays the concentration of the play had been elsewhere, I had felt alone with the flanker. Now, the whole heave of the play was toward me, flooding the zone not only with confused motion but noise—the quick stomp of feet, the creak of football gear, the strained

grunts of effort, the faint *ah-ah-ah,* of piston-stroke regularity, and the stiff calls of instruction, like exhalations. "Inside, inside! Take him inside!" someone shouted, tearing by me, his cleats thumping in the grass. A call—a parrot squawk—may have erupted from me. My feet splayed in hopeless confusion as Barr came directly toward me, feinting in one direction, and then stopping suddenly, drawing me toward him for the possibility of a buttonhook pass, and as I leaned almost off balance toward him, he turned and came on again, downfield, moving past me at high speed, leaving me poised on one leg, reaching for him, trying to grab at him despite the illegality, anything to keep him from getting by. But he was gone, and by the time I had turned to set out after him, he had ten yards on me, drawing away fast with his sprinter's run, his legs pinwheeling, the row of cleats flicking up a faint wake of dust behind.
George Plimpton, *Paper Lion*

Although the action lasted only a few moments, Plimpton gives a close-up of it. But his narrative is not slowed down by all the details because he uses active verbs and verb phrases. Here is the way one sentence works, one which incidentally includes a bit of dialogue:

"Inside, inside! Take him inside!" someone <u>shouted</u>, (verb) <u>tearing</u> by me, (participial phrase) <u>his cleats thumping</u> in the grass. (absolute phrase)

Sequences of short sentences and phrases also create momentum. You can see how this works in an example from Russell Baker's piece on flying in Chapter 2—particularly in the way Baker sets up the climax of the crucial flight test. Look back at paragraph 16 to see how the pace quickens until it reaches an apex in the dramatic last sentence:

First, a shallow dive to gain velocity, then push the stick slowly, firmly, all the way over against the thigh, simultaneously putting in hard rudder, and there we are, hanging upside down over the earth and now—keep it rolling, don't let the nose drop—reverse the controls and feel it roll all the way through until—coming back to straight-and-level now—catch it, wings level with the horizon, and touch the throttle to maintain altitude precisely at 5,000 feet.   Russell Baker, *Growing Up*

EXERCISE 13.10
When you wrote about the Baker selection for Exercise 13.9, did you select the preceding passage as an exciting or suspenseful part? Look back at the context of this paragraph, particularly the events leading up to it. What role do you think these events play in making this passage dramatic?

Dialogue. Another way of dramatizing narrative action is dialogue. Writers use it to reveal conflict directly, without the narrator's intruding commentary. Dialogues are not mere recordings of conversation, but pointed representations of conversation. Through dialogue, readers gain insight into the personality and motives of the characters.

By using dialogue, Richard Wright shows what happened when a white man confronted a black delivery boy. Notice that the dialogue does not have the free give-and-take of conversation. Instead, it is a series of questions which get evasive answers: "he said" . . . "I lied" . . . "he asked me" . . . "I lied." The dialogue is tense, revealing the extent of the boy's fear and defensiveness.

> I was hungry and he knew it; but he was a white man and I felt that if I told him I was hungry I would have been revealing something shameful.
>
> "Boy, I can see hunger in your face and eyes," he said.
>
> "I get enough to eat," I lied.
>
> "Then why do you keep so thin?" he asked me.
>
> "Well, I suppose I'm just that way, naturally," I lied.
>
> "You're just scared, boy," he said.
>
> "Oh, no, sir," I lied again.
>
> I could not look at him. I wanted to leave the counter, yet he was a white man and I had learned not to walk abruptly away from a white man when he was talking to me. I stood, my eyes looking away. He ran his hand into his pocket and pulled out a dollar bill.
>
> "Here, take this dollar and buy yourself some food," he said.
>
> "No, sir," I said.
>
> "Don't be a fool," he said. "You're ashamed to take it. God, boy, don't let a thing like that stop you from taking a dollar and eating."
>
> The more he talked the more it became impossible for me to take the dollar. I wanted it, but I could not look at it. I wanted to speak, but I could not move my tongue. I wanted him to leave me alone. He frightened me.
>
> "Say something," he said.   Richard Wright, *Black Boy*

Wright does not try to communicate everything through dialogue. He intersperses information which supports the dialogue—description, reports of the boy's thoughts and feelings, as well as some movement—in order to help readers understand the unfolding drama.

Writers also use dialogue to reveal a person's character and show the dynamics of interpersonal relationships. Notice, for instance, the way Lillian Hellman uses dialogue to write about Dashiell Hammett (Chapter 3), particularly at the end of paragraph 10:

> . . . Hammett laughed as I struggled to get back the sail. I don't know why, but I yelled angrily, "So you're a Dostoevsky sinner-saint. So you are." The laughter stopped, and when I finally came in to the dock we didn't speak as we carried up the packages and didn't speak through dinner.

> Later that night, he said, "What did you say that for? What does it mean?"
> I said I didn't know why I said it and I didn't know what it meant.
> Lillian Hellman, *An Unfinished Woman*

This dialogue is quite realistic. It shows the way people talk to one another and their silences. The reference to Dostoevsky, a Russian novelist, is not unexpected in a conversation between writers. But the dialogue does something more: it gives readers real insight into the way Hellman and Hammett were with each other. Such dialogue allows readers to overhear private conversations.

EXERCISE 13.11

Look at the complete Hellman selection in Chapter 3. Read it quickly, noting the way dialogue helps you understand the relationship between Hellman and Hammett. Other than the example just cited, what are the important dialogues in this essay? What do they reveal? How do they compare to the preceding dialogue? Do they have the same tone of annoyance? Do they use silence as much as conversation?

The preceding Hellman passage also exemplifies two methods of presenting dialogue: quoting and summarizing. In summarizing, writers choose their own words instead of quoting actual words used; this allows them to condense dialogue as well as to emphasize what they wish. When Hellman writes "I said I didn't know why I said it," she is summarizing her own words.

EXERCISE 13.12

Red Smith uses dialogue in his essay on Joe DiMaggio in Chapter 7. Read the piece, focusing on paragraphs 1–6; how does the dialogue in these paragraphs reveal DiMaggio's character to you? Describe the impression the dialogue gives you of DiMaggio, analyzing how you think the dialogue creates its particular effect.

EXERCISE 13.13

Write several paragraphs of narrative, including some dialogue. Write about an incident that occurred between you and someone you consider a close friend or associate—a friend, a relative, an enemy, a boss. Try to compose a dialogue that conveys the closeness of your relationship.

Read over your dialogue, and reflect on the impression it gives. In a sentence or two, state what you think the dialogue reveals about your relationship with this person.

Besides techniques to quicken the pace of narrative, writers also have techniques to do the reverse. Two techniques to slow the pace include reporting feelings and thoughts, and summarizing action.

Reporting feelings and thoughts. Look at Piri Thomas's account of a fight he once had with a street gang. Notice how he changes the pace of the action when he reports his thoughts during the fight. Every time he mentions his thoughts (in italics), the action pauses:

> Big-mouth came at me and we grabbed each other and pushed and pulled and shoved. *Poppa,* I thought, *I ain't gonna cop out. I'm a fighter, too.* I pulled away from Tony and blew my fist into his belly. He puffed and butted my nose with his head. I sniffed back. *Poppa, I didn't put my hands to my nose.* I hit Tony again in that same weak spot. He bent over in the middle and went down to his knees.   Piri Thomas, *Down These Mean Streets*

Summarizing action. The next selection, about a soccer game in Central America, uses summary to slow the pace of the narrative. In this passage, the author tells us what happened when the ball repeatedly went into the stands. He tells about the first time (paragraphs 1–6) in great detail, using sentences with a lot of momentum and dialogue to dramatize the action. In telling about the second time, he slows the pace by presenting fewer details and no dialogue, simply stating that the announcer made a threat. In effect, he summarizes what happened the second time, giving this action much less space (only one paragraph rather than the six before).

> Some minutes later the ball was kicked into the Shades section. It was thrown back onto the field, and the game was resumed. Then it was kicked into the Suns section. The Suns fought for it. One man gained possession, but he was pounced upon and the ball shot up and ten Suns went tumbling after it. A Sun tried to run down the steps with it. He was caught and the ball wrestled from him. A fight began, and now there were scores of Suns punching their way to the ball. The Suns higher up in the section threw bottles and cans and wadded paper on the Suns who were fighting, and the shower of objects—meat pies, bananas, hankies—continued to fall. The Shades, the Balconies, the Anthill, watched this struggle.
>
> And the players watched, too. The game had stopped. The Mexican players kicked the turf, the Salvadorean team shouted at the Suns.
>
> *Please return the ball.* It was the announcer. He was hoarse. *If the ball is not returned, the game will not continue.*
>
> This brought a greater shower of objects from the upper seats—cups, cushions, more bottles. The bottles broke with a splashing sound on the concrete seats. The Suns lower down began throwing things back at their persecutors, and it was impossible to say where the ball had gone.
>
> The ball was not returned. The announcer repeated his threat.

The players sat down on the field and did limbering-up exercises until, ten minutes after the ball had disappeared from the field, a new ball was thrown in. The spectators cheered but, just as quickly, fell silent. Mexico had scored another goal.

Soon, a bad kick landed the ball into the Shades. This ball was fought for and not thrown back, and one could see the ball progressing through the section. The ball was seldom visible, but one could tell from the free-for-alls now here, now there—where it was. The Balconies poured water on the Shades, but the ball was not surrendered. And now it was the Suns' turn to see the slightly better-off Salvadoreans in the Shades section behaving like swine. The announcer made his threat: the game would not resume until the ball was thrown back. The threat was ignored, and after a long time the ref walked onto the field with a new ball.   Paul Theroux, *Old Patagonian Express*

EXERCISE 13.14

Look back at "Jimmy and Death," the piece by Kate Simon in Chapter 2. Read it quickly, paying special attention to paragraphs 2 and 3. How does Simon pace the narrative in these two paragraphs? Look particularly for places where she uses the momentum of her sentences and dialogue to quicken the pace and where she uses reports of feelings and summaries to slow down the pace. Write a brief analysis of your response to the way Simon paces her narrative.

TAKING A POINT OF VIEW

In narrative writing, point of view refers to the narrator's relation to the action at hand. Basically, writers use two points of view: first person and third person. First person is used to narrate action in which the writer participated. For instance, when Piri Thomas writes, "Big-mouth came at me and we grabbed each other and pushed and pulled and shoved," he is using a first-person point of view. Third person, on the other hand, is used to narrate action in which people other than the narrator were involved. When Paul Theroux writes, "The Suns fought for it. One man gained possession, but he was pounced upon and the ball shot up and ten Suns went tumbling after it," he is using a third-person point of view.

First person Because they are telling about their own experiences, autobiographers typically write first-person narrative, using the first-person pronoun *I*. Notice the point of view in the following excerpt from Robert Lowell's autobiographical essay "91 Revere Street."

One day when the saucer magnolias were in bloom, I bloodied Bull-dog Binney's nose against the pedestal of George Washington's statue in full view of Commonwealth Avenue; then I bloodied Dopey Dan Parker's nose; then I stood in the center of the sundial tulip bed and pelted a little enemy ring of third-graders with wet fertilizer.   Robert Lowell, *Life Studies*

When, in the same essay, Lowell writes about experiences he shared with his family, he uses the first-person plural pronouns *we* and *our:*

New England winters are long. Sunday mornings are long. Ours were often made tedious by preparations for dinner guests. Mother would start airing at nine. Whenever the air grew so that it hurt, she closed the den windows; then we were attacked by sour kitchen odors winding up a clumsily rebuilt dumb-waiter shaft. The windows were thrown again open. We sat in an atmosphere of glacial purity and sacrifice. Our breath puffed whitely.   Robert Lowell, *Life Studies*

Third person When writers tell another person's story, as in biography, they use the third-person pronouns *he, she,* and *they* instead of the first-person *I* or *we*. In this next passage, Maxine Hong Kingston tells about what happened one day to her great grandfather when he was working in Hawaii.

The other great grandfather, Bak Sook Goong, did not spend much of his time with the men. One day off, when following a stream, he heard the voices and laughter of women, and from behind bushes, saw them in a pool at the foot of a waterfall. Some naked women were bathing. Nude women sitting on the rocks were weaving flowers and leaves into crowns for their drying hair. They were singing, and laughed at the end of lines, so he knew it had to be a lascivious song. And one of them was looking at him, into his eyes. Instead of covering herself, she held his gaze and washed herself here and there. Then she said something, and the women tugged him out of hiding. They made him bathe with them. Maxine Hong Kingston, *China Men*

EXERCISE 13.15

Look at all the readings in Chapter 2. Do the writers use the first-person or the third-person point of view? Could you imagine any of these essays being written in another point of view? Take a paragraph from one of them, and rewrite it in another point of view.

EXERCISE 13.16

Think of a brief incident involving you and one other person. Write about the incident from your own, first-person, point of view. Then write about the incident from the third-person point of view, as though the other person is telling it. What impact does a change in point of view have on your story?

PRESENTING A PROCESS

Process narrative typically explains how something is done or how to do it. For example, in *Oranges,* a book about the Florida citrus industry, John McPhee tells how the technical operation of bud grafting is done. He is not writing directions for readers to follow. If he were, his narrative would be much more detailed and precise. Instead, he tells us as much as he thinks nonspecialists need or want to know.

> One of Adams' men was putting Hamlin buds on Rough Lemon stock the day I was there. He began by slicing a bud from a twig that had come from a registered budwood tree of which there are forty-five thousand in groves around Florida, each certified under a state program to be free from serious virus disease and to be a true strain of whatever type of orange, grapefruit, or tangerine it happens to be. Each bud he removed was about an inch long and looked like a little submarine, the conning tower being the eye of the bud, out of which would come the shoot that would develop into the upper trunk and branches of the ultimate tree. A few inches above the ground, he cut a short vertical slit in the bark of a Rough Lemon liner; then he cut a transverse slit at the base of the vertical one, and, lifting the flaps of the wound, set the bud inside. The area was bandaged with plastic tape. In a couple of weeks, Adams said, the new shoot would be starting out of the bud and the tape would be taken off. To force the growth of the new shoot, a large area of the bark of the Rough Lemon would be shaved off above the bud union. Two months after that, the upper trunk, branches, and leaves of the young Rough Lemon tree would be cut off altogether, leaving only a three-inch stub coming out of the earth, thick as a cigar, with a small shoot and a leaf or two of the Hamlin flippantly protruding near the top.   John McPhee, *Oranges*

EXERCISE 13.17

Look at the selection by Robert Jastrow in Chapter 8. Read it carefully, noting the way the author tells about the process of the ice age and of people's response to it. Why do you think Jastrow includes this process narrative in his essay? Write a few sentences explaining Jastrow's purpose.

In contrast to the McPhee example, here is a process narrative that provides both information and directions. This selection comes from an article written for the *American Journal of Physiology.* Notice all the precise detail, technical terminology, and careful, step-by-step narrating. Because objectivity is important to such writing, the writers use the passive voice.

> Ten 20- to 25-kg male baboons (*Papio anubis*) were tranquilized with ketamine, 10 mg/kg, intubated, mechanically ventilated, and anesthetized

with halothane, 1.5 vol%. Instrumentation was implanted through a thoracotomy in the fifth left intercostal space. A miniature pressure transducer (Konigsberg P22, Konigsberg Instruments, Pasadena, CA) was implanted in the left ventricle through a stab wound in the apex, and a pair of ultrasonic transducers was implanted on opposing endocardial surfaces of the left ventricle. Tygon catheters were implanted in the left atrium and aorta. The transducer wires and catheters were run subcutaneously and buried in the interscapular area.   Stephen F. Vatner and Michael Zimpfer, "Bainbridge Reflex in Conscious, Unrestrained, and Tranquilized Baboons"

EXERCISE 13.18

Proposal writers generally uses process narrative to explain how readers could implement a proposed solution to a problem. In Chapter 6, look at paragraphs 20–21 and 23 of Jeanette Germain's essay, paragraphs 5–7 of Wendy Jo Niwa's essay, and paragraph 6 of Jim Chow's essay. After reading these process narratives, decide whether the proposed solutions appear to you to be implementable. If you think any of the solutions is not implementable, indicate what is wrong with it.

Like the Vatner and Zimpfer passage, our final selection is also an example of scientific writing, but it is much less technical because it is written for nonspecialists. Written by a biologist for a college textbook, it explains the process by which viruses were discovered. Process narratives of this kind are fairly common in science writing. They tend to be quite entertaining and to satisfy their readers' curiosity about the process of scientific discovery.

The discovery of viruses. By the latter part of the nineteenth century the idea had become firmly established that many diseases are caused by microorganisms. Pioneer bacteriologists such as Louis Pasteur and Robert Koch had isolated the pathogens for a number of diseases that afflict human beings and their domestic animals. But for some diseases, notably smallpox, biologists, try as they might, could find no causal microorganism. As early as 1796 it had been known that smallpox could be induced in a healthy person by something in the pus from a smallpox victim, and Edward Jenner had demonstrated that a person vaccinated with material from cowpox lesions developed an immunity to smallpox. Yet no bacterial agent could be found.

A crucial experiment was performed in 1892 by a Russian biologist, Dmitri Iwanowsky, who was studying a disease of tobacco plants called tobacco mosaic. The leaves of plants with this disease become mottled and wrinkled. If juice is extracted from an infected plant and rubbed on the leaves of a healthy one, the latter soon develops tobacco mosaic disease. If, however, the juice is heated nearly to boiling before it is rubbed on the healthy leaves, no disease develops. Concluding that the disease must be caused by bacteria in the plant juice, Iwanowsky passed juice from an infected tobacco plant through a very fine porcelain filter in order to remove the bacteria; he then rubbed the filtered juice on the leaves of healthy plants. Contrary to his expectation, the plants developed mosaic disease. What could the explanation be?

Iwanowsky suggested two possibilities. Either bacteria in the infected plants secrete toxins, and it is these rather than the bacterial cells themselves that are present in infectious juice. Or the bacteria that cause this disease are much smaller than other known bacteria and can pass unharmed through a fine porcelain filter. When it was later demonstrated that the infectious material in filtered juice could reproduce in a new host, Iwanowsky abandoned his first explanation in favor of the second—that some type of extremely small bacterium was the causal agent of the disease. During the next several decades many other diseases of both plants and animals were found to be caused by infectious agents so small that they could pass through porcelain filters and could not be seen with even the best light microscopes. These microbial agents of disease came to be called filterable viruses, or simply viruses. They were still assumed to be very small bacteria.

There were, however, a few hints that viruses might be something quite different from bacteria. First, all attempts to culture them on media customarily used for bacteria failed. Second, the virus material, unlike bacteria, could be precipitated from an alcoholic suspension without losing its infectious power. But not until 1935 was it conclusively demonstrated that viruses and bacteria are two very different things. In that year W. M. Stanley of the Rockefeller Institute isolated and crystallized tobacco mosaic virus. If the crystals were injected into tobacco plants, they again became active, multiplied, and caused disease symptoms in the plants. That viruses could be crystallized showed that they were not cells but must be much simpler chemical entities.   William Keeton, *Biological Science*

EXERCISE 13.19

Write a simple process narrative, explaining how to do something— make a sandwich, build a doghouse, write a poem, perform a scientific experiment, fly a kite. Address your narrative to someone who knows nothing about performing the task you are telling about.

Defining

Defining is an essential strategy for all kinds of writing. Just as all writers depend on dictionary definitions, so they need to use sentence definitions and extended definitions. Historical and stipulative definitions are also useful in certain writing situations.

Autobiographers must occasionally define objects, events, and activities for readers from other generations, cultures, or locales. The following examples (with definitions underlined) are from Chapter 2.

> Big, clumsy Mrs. Kaplan, the loudest behemoth of the house, took her length of *kishka* (stuffed intestine), her specialty . . .   Kate Simon, *Bronx Primitive*

> Even some instructors had trouble doing a falling leaf. The plane had to be brought precisely to its stalling point, then dropped in a series of sickening sideways skids, first to one side, then to the other, like a leaf falling in a breeze, by delicate simultaneous manipulations of stick, rudder pedals, and throttle.   Russell Baker, *Growing Up*

Writers sharing information or explaining how to do something must very often define important terms for readers who are unfamiliar with the subject. These examples come from readings in Chapter 5.

> The plague epidemics were frequently accompanied by severe outbreaks of typhus, syphilis and "English sweat"—apparently a deadly form of influenza . . .   William Langer, "The Black Death"

> All three sections [of an insect's body] are enclosed within an external skeleton made, primarily, of chitin. This brown fibrous material was first developed over 550 million years ago by the early segmented creatures, the trilobites and crustaceans. Chemically, it is similar to cellulose and in its pure form it is flexible and permeable.   David Attenborough, *Life on Earth*

To convince readers of an evaluation, interpretation, or explanation or to move readers to take action on a proposal, a writer must define concepts important to an argument. These examples come from Chapter 8.

> I suspect that what motivates us even more than a fear of death is a fear of dearth. Our era is the first to anticipate the eventual depletion of all natural resources. . . . We see the irreplaceable being squandered. . . . Carll Tucker, "Fear of Dearth"

14

Once more, as with the use of tools, reciprocal forces came into play <u>in which speech stimulated better brains, and brains improved the art of speech, and the curve of brain growth spiraled upward.</u>
Robert Jastrow, *Until the Sun Dies*

As these examples illustrate, there are many kinds of definitions and many forms that they take. This chapter will illustrate the major kinds and forms of definitions, beginning with dictionaries as sources of definitions. After dictionary definitions come various forms of sentence definition. This type of definition, the most common basic form in writing, relies on different sentence patterns to provide concise definitions. Following this are various illustrations of multi-sentence extended definitions, including definition by etymology, or word history, and by stipulation.

DICTIONARY DEFINITIONS

The most familiar source of definitions is the dictionary, where words are defined briefly with other words. In a short space, dictionaries tell us a lot about words: how they are pronounced, what forms they take as they function differently in sentences, what they mean, how they look in context in a sample phrase or clause, and where they originated. Here is an example from *The American Heritage Dictionary:*

definition ——
part of speech ——
syllabification ——

pronunciation ——

illustrative use ——

etymology ——

other forms ——

in-trep-id (ĭn-trĕp′ĭd) *adj.* Marked by resolute courage; fearless and bold: *an intrepid mountaineer.* [Fr. *intrépule* < Lat. *intrepidus* : *in-*, not + *trepidus*, alarmed.] —in′tre-pid′i-ty (-trə-pĭd′ĭ-tē), in-trep′id-ness *n.* —in-trep′id-ly *adv.*

405

Other dictionary entries may include still more information. For example, if a word has more than one meaning, all of its meanings will be presented. From the context in which you read or hear the word, you can nearly always tell which meaning applies.

A good dictionary is an essential part of your equipment as a college student. It should always be within reach when you are reading so that you can look up unfamiliar words in order to understand what you read and to expand your vocabulary. When you are writing, you can use a dictionary to check spellings and the correct forms of words. You can also check the meanings of words about which you are unsure.

A good current dictionary like *The American Heritage Dictionary* or *Webster's New Collegiate Dictionary* is well worth the money. You may want to ask your instructor for advice about which dictionary to buy in your college bookstore. Though a hardback dictionary like the *American Heritage* will cost two or three times more than a paperback, it will be a sound and relatively inexpensive investment (about fifteen dollars). Hardback dictionaries usually have the advantages of more entries, fuller entries, larger type, and a thumb index.

To present a great deal of information in a small space, dictionaries have to rely on many abbreviations, codes, and symbols. These differ somewhat from one dictionary to the next, but you can learn the system of abbreviations in your dictionary by reading the front matter carefully. You will also find a range of interesting topics and lists in the front and end matter in some dictionaries: articles on usage and language history, reviews of punctuation rules, biographical entries, geographical entries, and lists of colleges and universities.

Any dictionary you would buy for desk use would be an *abridged* dictionary, which does not include many technical or obsolete words. An *unabridged* dictionary contains every known current and obsolete word in the language. Two unabridged dictionaries are preeminent: *Oxford English Dictionary* and *Webster's Third New International Dictionary,* the latter the standard reference for American English. Libraries have these impressive dictionaries.

A special dictionary called a thesaurus can be useful for a writer, but only if it is used judiciously. It is a dictionary of synonyms, words with identical or very similar meanings. The motive for searching out synonyms should be to use just the right word, not to impress readers. Straining to impress readers with unusual words will more often than not lead to embarrassment from a word used in the wrong context.

Here is an example from *Roget's II, The New Thesaurus*. It offers alternatives to *brave,* used as an adjective. Among the synonyms for *brave* is *intrepid,* noted in the dictionary definition above.

brave *adjective*
Having or showing courage: *a brave effort to rescue the drowning child.* **Syns:** audacious, bold, courageous, dauntless, doughty, fearless, fortitudinous, gallant, game, gutsy (*Informal*), gutty, heroic, intrepid, mettlesome, plucky, stout, stouthearted, unafraid, undaunted, valiant, valorous.

Some thesauri also offer antonyms, words opposite in meaning to the word of interest. (An antonym of *brave,* for example, would be *cowardly.*)

The great limitation of a thesaurus is that it does not tell you which synonym would be most appropriate for a particular writing situation. *Brave* and *intrepid* are not simply interchangeable. Which word you might use would depend on your readers, your purpose, and the exact meaning you hoped to convey with the sentence in which the word appears. In the preceding list, the only clue to appropriateness is the information that *gutsy* is informal. Checking each word in a good dictionary would be necessary to select the most appropriate word from a set like the preceding one. Because of this troublesome limitation, a thesaurus is most useful in reminding you of a synonym you have temporarily forgotten but which has shades of meaning you know well.

A solution to the limitations of a thesaurus is a dictionary of synonyms with words in a set like the preceding one but with each synonym defined, contrasted, and illustrated with quotations. An excellent choice is *Webster's New Dictionary of Synonyms,* which provides enough information to let you make an appropriate choice. Your college bookstore will have this book for about the cost of a hardback dictionary. This volume's entry for *brave* notes eleven common synonyms for *brave* as an adjective, ranging from *courageous* to *audacious.* Each synonym is defined and then quoted in context from a respected source, as this portion of the entry shows:

brave *adj* **Brave, courageous, unafraid, fearless, intrepid, valiant, valorous, dauntless, undaunted, doughty, bold, audacious** are comparable when they mean having or showing no fear when faced with something dangerous, difficult, or unknown. **Brave** usually indicates lack of fear in alarming or difficult circumstances rather than a temperamental liking for danger ⟨the *brave* soldier goes to meet Death, and meets him without a shudder—*Trollope*⟩ ⟨he would send an explosion ship into the harbor . . . a *brave* crew would take her in at night, right up against the city, would light the fuses, and try to escape—*Forester*⟩ **Courageous** implies stouthearted resolution in contemplating or facing danger and may suggest a temperamental readiness to meet dangers or difficulties ⟨I am afraid . . . because I do not wish to die. But my spirit masters the trembling flesh and the qualms of the mind. I am more than brave, I am *courageous*—*London*⟩ ⟨a man is *courageous* when he does things which others might fail to do owing to fear—*Russell*⟩ **Unafraid** simply indicates lack of fright or fear whether because of a courageous nature or because no cause for fear is present ⟨enjoy their homes *unafraid* of violent intrusion—*MacArthur*⟩ ⟨a young, daring, and creative people—a people *unafraid* of change—*MacLeish*⟩ **Fearless** may indicate lack of fear, or it may be more positive and suggest undismayed resolution ⟨joyous we too launch out on trackless seas, *fearless* for unknown shores—*Whitman*⟩ ⟨he gives always the impression of *fearless* sincerity . . . one always feels that he is ready to say bluntly what every one else is afraid to say—*T. S. Eliot*⟩ **Intrepid** suggests either daring in meeting danger or fortitude in enduring it ⟨with the *intrepid* woman who was his wife, and a few natives, he landed there, and set about building a house and clearing the scrub—*Maugham*⟩ ⟨the *intrepid* guardians of the place, hourly exposed to death, with famine worn, and suffering under many a perilous wound—*Wordsworth*⟩

This entry shows that *brave* and *intrepid* are very close in meaning, but that *intrepid* would be the better choice if you wanted to suggest "daring in meeting danger" rather than "lack of fear" in facing danger when it comes. You might call a U.S. Navy pilot flying off an aircraft carrier an *intrepid pilot,* but you would probably describe your letter carrier, who only occasionally faces a barking dog, as *brave.*

To summarize our advice about dictionaries: buy a respected hardback dictionary for looking up the meanings of new words you encounter and for checking spellings and correct usage. Buy an inexpensive paperback thesaurus for a quick look at sets of synonyms. Buy a respected hardback dictionary of synonyms in order to discriminate among synonyms and pick the most appropriate word. These resources will enable you to write essays with correct spellings and verb forms and with just the right words.

SENTENCE DEFINITIONS

All fields of study and all institutions and activities have their own unique concepts and definitions. Coming to a new area for the first time, a participant or a reader is often baffled by the particular way of naming things. In college, a basic course in a field often seems like an entire course in definitions of new terms. In the same way, a sport like sailing requires newcomers to learn many definitions. In such cases, writers of textbooks and sailing manuals rely on brief sentence definitions. For these definitions they use a variety of sentence strategies to define the special terms of their subjects.

Following are some sentence strategies from one widely used introductory college biology text, Sylvia Mader's *Inquiry into Life.* These examples illustrate some of the sentence strategies an author may use to name and define terms for readers. Because all these examples come from one book, they show how a particular writer relies again and again on each of these strategies. The names of the strategies come either from key words, characteristic punctuation, or grammatical function.

The most obvious sentence strategies simply announce a definition. (In each of the following examples the word being defined is in italics, while the definition is underlined.)

Strategy A: *means*

Homo habilis means <u>handyman</u>.

Strategy B: *which means that*

These patterns are *ritualized,* which means that <u>the behavior which is</u>
<u>stereotyped, exaggerated, and rigid is always performed in the same way</u>
<u>so that its social significance is clear.</u>

Strategy C: *insert with parentheses.* Either the definition or the word
to be defined can be inserted:

<u>Viral infections can spread from the nasal cavities to the sinuses</u> (*sinusitis*),
<u>to the middle ears</u> (*otitis media*), <u>to the larynx</u> (*laryngitis*), <u>and to the</u>
<u>bronchi</u> (*bronchitis*).

Thus an ecosystem contains both a *biotic* (<u>living</u>) and *abiotic* (<u>nonliving</u>)
environment.

Strategy D: *insert with dashes*

The human blastula, termed the blastocyst, consists of a hollow ball with
<u>a mass of cells</u>—*the inner cell mass*—at one end.

Strategy E: *is/are*

<u>An environmental factor that increases the chances of a mutation</u> is a
mutagen.

Somatic mutations are <u>mutations that affect the individual's body cells.</u>

Strategy F: *called/termed*

<u>At the time of ejaculation, sperm leaves the penis in a fluid</u> called *seminal*
fluid.

Strategy G: *refers to*

Morphogenesis refers to <u>the shaping of the embryo and is first evident</u>
<u>when certain cells are seen to move, or migrate, in relation to other cells.</u>

Strategy H: *or*

In humans the *gestation period,* <u>or length of pregnancy,</u> is approximately
nine months.

EXERCISE 14.1

This is the first of three exercises on sentence strategies for brief definitions. The exercises become steadily more difficult in that you will be writing structurally more complex sentences. Nevertheless, most of the sentences will be manageable, even easy. If you do all of them, including the easy ones, you will have a quick, comprehensive survey of most of the possibilities open to you when you need to define a term concisely in a sentence.

All three exercises include words you may not know, so you will have the challenge of working an unfamiliar dictionary definition into a particular sentence form, a form that you might actually use in your own writing. Though you will have to use the dictionary to complete nearly all of the sentences, these are not exercises in the use of the dictionary, nor are they designed to increase your vocabulary. They are writing exercises of a special kind—practice with many of the sentence forms writers use to define unfamiliar terms.

Write out each of the following sentences, filling in the blanks with definitions in a current dictionary. As an alternative to this exercise, make up your own sentences in these same patterns, using new terms either from a course you are now taking or from a sport or hobby you know well. (Each particular strategy is identified by letter after each exercise item.)

1. A *clinometer* is _____ . (E)

2. *Ecumenism* refers to _____ . (G)

3. The report said the thieves resorted to a *subterfuge,* which means that they _____ . (B)

4. _____ is called an *ectomorph.* (F)

5. They danced the *habana*— _____ —and the *samba*— _____ . (D)

6. Instead of a *eulogy* (_____), he delivered a *harangue* (_____). (C)

7. That fall marked the return of the *tabard,* or _____ , to fashion news. (H)

8. To a fencer, a *riposte* means _____ . (A)

The sentence strategies so far all declare in a straightforward way that the writer is defining a term. Other strategies, signaled by certain sentence relationships, are less direct but still quite apparent. They can be identified by the word introducing the subordinate sentence part that contains the definition.

Strategy I: *which/that/where*

Fraternal twins, which originate when two different eggs are fertilized by two different sperm, do not have identical chromosomes.

The grasslands of all continents support populations of *grazers* that feed on grasses and *browsers* that feed on shrubs and trees.

The region of the inguinal *canal,* where the spermatic cord passes into the abdomen, remains a weak point in the abdominal wall.

Strategy J: *because*

Hemophilia is called the bleeders disease because the afflicted person's blood is unable to clot.

Strategy K: *when*

When a mutagen leads to an increase in the incidence of cancer it is called a *carcinogen.*

Strategy L: *if*

If the thyroid fails to develop properly, a condition called *cretinism* results.

These sentence parts—all of them subordinate clauses—play an important role in sentences by adding details, expressing time and cause, and indicating conditions or tentativeness. In all these examples from *Inquiry into Life,* however, the clauses have a specific defining role to play in the sections of the text where they appear. In this specialized way, they are part of a writer's repertoire for sentence definitions.

EXERCISE 14.2

To try out these kinds of clauses as defining strategies, write out the following sentences, using your dictionary for the definitions required in the blank spaces. As an alternative, you may create your own sentences in these patterns from specialized subject matter in a course you are now taking or from the special terms in a sport or hobby.

1. *Bureaucratese,* talk and writing which _____ , is the curse of the land. (I)

2. It was considered a *buyer's market* because _____ . (J)

3. Because _____ , the poem could be classified as a *Shakespearean sonnet.* (J)

4. When someone _____ , it is called *plagiarism.* (K)

5. When _____ , you have *senile dementia.* (K)

6. If _____ , *edema* results. (L)

Still other defining strategies are available to writers. One of the most common strategies is the appositive phrase. In it, one noun defines another noun in a brief inserted phrase called an appositive. Sometimes the appositive contains the definition; other times it contains the word to be defined. Because this is such an important defining strategy, here are illustrations of several variations.

Strategy M: *appositive*

The nasal cavities open into the *cranial sinuses*, air-filled spaces in the skull, and finally empty into the *nasopharynx*, a chamber just beyond the soft palate.

Sperm are produced in the testes, but they mature in the *epididymus*, a tightly coiled tubule about twenty feet in length that lies just outside each testis.

A viscous and gelatinous material, the *vitreous humor*, fills the large cavity behind the lens.

Breathing consists of taking air in, *inspiration*, and forcing air out, *expiration*.

Certain phrases can also point out words to be defined and thus indirectly introduce definitions.

Strategy N: *in the case of*

In the case of *hyperthyroidism* (too much thyroxin), the thyroid gland is enlarged and overactive, causing a goiter to form and the eyes to curiously protrude.

Strategy O: *according to*

According to the *Malthusian view*, the depletion curve tells us that there are limits to growth and that we are rapidly approaching those limits. . . .

Sometimes a writer can assume that readers will recall the meaning of the Latin or Greek roots of a word. In this case the writer may just point to these definitions.

Strategy P: *as the name implies*

As their name implies *monosaccharides* are simple sugars with only one unit.

In a comparative definition, two or more terms are defined in part by comparison or contrast with each other. For these multiple definitions, writers rely on a great variety of syntactic and stylistic strategies including these two: (1) phrases in a series following either the main verb or a colon and (2) contrast sentences beginning with words or phrases like *even though*, *in spite of*, or *whereas*. The various parts of the comparison are always grammatically parallel, that is, similar in form.

Strategy Q: *comparative*

The special senses include the *chemoreceptors* for taste and smell, the *light receptors* for sight, and the *mechanoreceptors* for hearing and balance.

Lakes and ponds can be divided into three life zones: the *littoral zone* is closest to the shore, the *limnetic zone* forms the sunlit body of the lake, and the *profundal zone* is below the level of light penetration.

Whereas a *miscarriage* is the unexpected loss of an embryo or fetus, an *abortion* is the purposeful removal of an embryo or fetus from the womb.

EXERCISE 14.3

With the aid of a dictionary, write out the following sentences. Alternatively, you may compose sentences in these patterns from information in courses you are taking or from the special terms in a sport or hobby.

1. According to the *Calvinists*, _____ . (O)

2. In the case of *caricature*, _____ . (N)

3. *Aerobics*, as the name implies, _____ . (P)

4. To remember large numbers of facts for an exam, some students rely on a *mnemonic*, _____ . (M)

5. Human hormones include *testosterone*, which _____ , and *estrogen*, which _____ . (Q)

6. In the human eye, the *rod cells* _____ whereas the *cone cells* _____ . (Q)

7. Major components of the human eye are the *cornea*, _____ ; the *iris*, _____ ; the *pupil*, _____ ; the *lens*, _____ ; and the *retina*, _____ . (Q)

EXERCISE 14.4

Turn to the essay by David Noonan in Chapter 10, and analyze the sentence definitions in paragraphs 2, 6, 9, 13, and 18. (Some of these paragraphs contain more than one sentence definition.) Classify each definition as one of the preceding sentence types. What is the purpose of all these definitions in the selection as a whole?

EXTENDED DEFINITIONS

In many writing situations, a writer may need to provide readers with a definition much fuller than the brief sentence definition, one extending over several sentences. Here is how Mark Twain defines a word he learned on a trip to New Orleans.

> We picked up one excellent word—a word worth traveling to New Orleans to get; a nice limber, expressive, handy word—"lagniappe." They pronounce it lanny-*yap*. It is Spanish—so they said. We discovered it at the head of a column of odds and ends in the Picayune, the first day; heard twenty people use it the second; inquired what it meant the third; adopted it and got facility in swinging it the fourth. It has a restricted meaning, but I think the people spread it out a little when they choose. It is the equivalent of the thirteenth roll in a "baker's dozen." It is something thrown in, gratis, for good measure. The custom originated in the Spanish quarter of the city. When a child or a servant buys something in a shop—or even the mayor or the governor, for aught I know—he finishes the operation by saying—
>
> "Give me something for lagniappe."
>
> The shopman always responds; gives the child a bit of licorice root, gives the servant a cheap cigar or a spool of thread, gives the governor—I don't know what he gives the governor; support, likely.
>
> When you are invited to drink—and this does occur now and then in New Orleans—and you say, "What, again?—no, I've had enough"; the other party says, "But just this one more time—this is for lagniappe." When the beau perceives that he is stacking his compliments a trifle too high, and sees by the young lady's countenance that the edifice would have been better with the top compliment left off, he puts his "I beg pardon—no harm intended," into the briefer form of "Oh, that's for lagniappe." If the waiter in the restaurant stumbles and spills a gill of coffee down the back of your neck, he says, "For lagniappe, sah," and gets you another cup without extra charge.   Mark Twain, *Life on the Mississippi*

This extended definition relies on a variety of strategies—word history, personal experience, many examples, and even dialogue.

In a less playful, though equally imaginative, approach to definition, Joan Didion defines a special feature of the weather in Los Angeles.

> The Santa Ana, which is named for one of the canyons it rushes through, is a *foehn* wind, like the *foehn* of Austria and Switzerland and the *hamsin* of Israel. There are a number of persistent malevolent winds, perhaps the best known of which are the mistral of France and the Mediterranean sirocco, but a *foehn* wind has distinct characteristics: it occurs on the

leeward slope of a mountain range and, although the air begins as a cold mass, it is warmed as it comes down the mountain and appears finally as a hot dry wind. Whenever and wherever a *foehn* blows, doctors hear about headaches and nausea and allergies, about "nervousness," about "depression." In Los Angeles some teachers do not attempt to conduct formal classes during a Santa Ana, because the children become unmanageable. In Switzerland the suicide rate goes up during the *foehn,* and in the courts of some Swiss cantons the wind is considered a mitigating circumstance for crime. Surgeons are said to watch the wind, because blood does not clot normally during a *foehn.* A few years ago an Israeli physicist discovered that not only during such winds, but for the ten or twelve hours which precede them, the air carries an unusually high ratio of positive to negative ions. No one seems to know exactly why that should be; some talk about friction and others suggest solar disturbances. In any case the positive ions are there, and what an excess of positive ions does, in the simplest terms, is make people unhappy.   Joan Didion, *Slouching Towards Bethlehem*

In order to define Santa Ana, or *foehn,* winds, Didion concentrates on their results, giving several examples of their ill effects on people. She also compares the results in different countries.

A science text provides another example of the way certain important concepts require extended definition. This definition comes from the expanding field of ecology.

Demes A deme is a small local population, such as all the deer mice or all the red oaks in a certain woodland or all the perch in a given pond. Although no two individuals in a deme are exactly alike, the members of a deme do usually resemble one another more closely than they resemble the members of other demes, for at least two reasons: (1) They are more closely related genetically, because pairings occur more frequently between members of the same deme than between members of different demes; and (2) they are exposed to more similar environmental influences and hence to more nearly the same selection pressures.

It must be emphasized that demes are not clear-cut permanent units of population. Although the deer mice in one woodlot are more likely to mate among themselves than with deer mice in the next woodlot down the road, there will almost certainly be occasional matings between mice from different woodlots. Similarly, although the female parts of a particular red oak tree are more likely to receive pollen from another red oak tree in the same woodlot, there is an appreciable chance that they will sometimes receive pollen from a tree in another nearby woodlot. And the woodlots themselves are not permanent ecological features. They have only a transient existence as separate and distinct ecological units; neighboring woodlots may fuse after a few years, or a single large woodlot

may become divided into two or more separate smaller ones. Such changes in ecological features will produce corresponding changes in the demes of deer mice and red oak trees. Demes, then, are usually temporary units of population that intergrade with other similar units.
William T. Keeton, *Biological Science*

As a writer drafting an essay, your choice of appropriate definition strategies will be guided by your awareness of what you want to accomplish and by your knowledge of who your readers will be. You need not even be consciously aware of particular choices while you are writing a first draft. Later, though, when you are revising this first draft, you will have a special advantage if you can look critically at the way you defined key terms. If your repertoire of defining strategies includes all the variations illustrated so far in this chapter, you will be able to revise with much more confidence and power.

Sometimes you may need only a brief sentence definition. At other times, you may need an extended definition that includes brief anecdotes and examples as in the extended definitions by Twain, Didion, and Keeton. Though it happens very rarely, some published essays and reports are concerned solely with the definition of an important or problematic concept. Usually, however, definition is only a part of an essay. A long piece of writing, like a term paper or a textbook or a research report, may include many kinds of brief and extended definitions, all of them integrated with other writing strategies.

EXERCISE 14.5
Choose one term of central importance in an activity or subject you know well. Choose a word with a well-established definition, one agreed on by everyone knowledgeable about the topic.

Write an extended definition of several sentences for this important term. Write for readers your own age who will be encountering the term for the first time when they read your definition.

EXERCISE 14.6
Read "To Unteach Greed," Carol Bly's essay in Chapter 6, and analyze her extended definition of *technique* in paragraph 9. How does she define this term? What purpose does the definition have within the whole selection?

HISTORICAL DEFINITIONS

Writers will occasionally trace the history of a word—from its first use, to its adoption into other languages, to its shifting meanings over the centuries. Such a strategy can be a rich addition to an essay, bringing to the definition of an important concept a surprising depth and resonance. An historical definition usually begins with the roots of a word, but it extends well beyond that to trace the word's history over a long period of time. Such a history always serves a writer's larger purpose, as the two examples here show.

The first is from John McPhee's remarkable book on oranges.

> The word "orange" evolved from Sanskrit. The Chinese word for orange, in ancient as well as modern Chinese, is *jyu,* but it did not migrate with the fruit. India was the first major stop in the westward travels of citrus, and the first mention of oranges in Sanskrit literature is found in a medical book called the *Charaka-Samhita,* which was compiled approximately two thousand years ago. The Hindus called an orange a *naranga,* the first syllable of which, according to Tolkowsky, was a prefix meaning fragrance. This became the Persian *naranj,* a word the Muslims carried through the Mediterranean. In Byzantium, an orange was an *nerantzion.* This, in Neo-Latin, became variously styled as *arangium, arantium,* and *aurantium*—eventually producing *naranja* in Spain, *laranja* in Portugal, *arancia* in Italy, and *orange* in France.   John McPhee, *Oranges*

McPhee wants us to understand oranges in a special way, as more than a fruit which gets processed for a juice concentrate. His word history lets him tell us how long the orange has been around and in what exotic places it has thrived.

In this second example, from a book discussing the recent rise of witchcraft and paganism in America, the writer uses an historical definition of the word *pagan* as background to her own definition and also as a way of instructing us in how we should feel about the new pagans.

> *Pagan* comes from the Latin *paganus,* which means a country dweller, and is itself derived from *pagus,* the Latin word for village or rural district. Similarly, *heathen* originally meant a person who lived on the heaths. Negative associations with these words are the end result of centuries of political struggles during which the major prophetic religions, notably Christianity, won a victory over the older polytheistic religions. In the West, often the last people to be converted to Christianity lived on the outskirts of populated areas and kept to the old ways. These were the Pagans and heathens—the word Pagan was a term of insult, meaning "hick."
>
> Pagan had become a derogatory term in Rome by the third century. Later, after the death of Julian, the last Pagan emperor, in 362 A.D. the word Pagan came to refer to intellectual Pagans like Julian. Gore Vidal, in his extraordinary novel *Julian,* wrote a fictional description of this event in which the Pagan orator Libanius, after attending the funeral of a Christian notable, writes in his journal: "There was a certain amount of good-humored comment about 'pagans' (a new word of contempt for us Hellenists) attending Christian services. . . ." Julian, by the way, has long been

one of Neo-Paganism's heroes, and an early Neo-Pagan journal was called *The Julian Review*. Centuries later the word *Pagan* still suffers the consequences of political and religious struggles, and dictionaries still define it to mean a godless person or an unbeliever, instead of, simply, a member of a different kind of religion.

Pagan is also often associated with hedonism. This makes some sense, since many ancient Pagan religions incorporated sexuality into ecstatic religious practice. One scholar, writing on the use of mystical experience by young people in the 1960s, observed that a characteristic of many groups was "the idea of paganism—the body is a temple in which there is nothing unclean, a shrine to be adorned for the ritual of love." New attitudes toward sexuality play a part in some, but not all, Neo-Pagan groups, and the old Pagan religions had their share of ascetics, but generally, Neo-Pagans seem to have healthy attitudes toward sex.

I use *Pagan* to mean a member of a polytheistic nature religion, such as the ancient Greek, Roman, or Egyptian religions, or, in anthropological terms, a member of one of the indigenous folk and tribal religions all over the world. People who have studied the classics or have been deeply involved with natural or aboriginal peoples are comparatively free of the negative and generally racist attitudes that surround the word *Pagan*. Margot Adler, *Drawing Down the Moon*

EXERCISE 14.7

Though any good dictionary tells the origins of words, historical, or etymological, dictionaries give much more information, enough to trace changes in use of a word over long periods of time. The preeminent historical dictionary of our language is the *Oxford English Dictionary*. Less imposing is *A Dictionary of American English,* and even less imposing is *A Dictionary of Americanisms*.

Look up the historical definition of any one of the following words in *A Dictionary of Americanisms,* and write several sentences on its roots and development. As an alternative, you may choose any word with a complex history from one of the above dictionaries.

basketball	eye-opener
bazooka	filibuster
bedrock	gerrymander
blizzard	jazz
bogus	pep
bonanza	picayune
bushwhack	podunk
canyon	rubberneck
carpetbag	sashay
dugout	two bits

STIPULATIVE DEFINITIONS

The historical definition of pagans in the preceding section concludes with a stipulative definition: "I use *Pagan* to mean a member of a polytheistic nature religion. . . ." *To stipulate* means to seek or assert agreement on something. A stipulative definition is one in which the writer declares a certain meaning, generally not one found in the dictionary.

Stipulative definitions have a variety of important functions, several of which are illustrated here. In the next example, a prominent historian of science proposes a stipulative definition of the word *ecology*.

> Ernst Haeckel, the great popularizer of evolutionary theory in Germany, loved to coin words. The vast majority of his creations died with him a half-century ago, but among the survivors are "ontogeny," "phylogeny," and "ecology." The last is now facing an opposite fate—loss of meaning by extension and vastly inflated currency. Common usage now threatens to make "ecology" a label for anything good that happens far from cities or anything that does not have synthetic chemicals in it. In its more restricted and technical sense, ecology is the study of organic diversity. It focuses on the interactions of organisms and their environments in order to address what may be the most fundamental question in evolutionary biology: "Why are there so many kinds of living things?"   Stephen Jay Gould, *Ever Since Darwin*

Important concepts in specialties like biology may gradually take on fuzzy or overly broad popular definitions. The specialists may then have to rescue a concept by redefining it, as Gould does here. He is asking his readers to agree with him that *ecology* means "the study of organic diversity." He stipulates a redefinition and asks us to use the word only as he defines it, at least for the duration of his book.

Another use of stipulative definition is to sort through alternative definitions of a problematic concept—*pure breed of cats* in the next example—in order to reject these alternative definitions and argue for another definition the writer favors.

> What is a pure breed of cats, and what constitutes a pure-bred animal? These terms can have a number of meanings. One of the simplest is merely to regard as pure-bred a cat that has been properly registered with a responsible body (such as the Governing Council of the Cat Fancy [GCCF] in Britain, or the Cat Fanciers' Association [CFA] or one of the other similar associations in the United States). Such a cat will have a pedigree of similarly registered parents, grandparents and so on for a given number of generations—normally at least four. This ensures that the cat has "respectable" parentage and is likely to be a representative specimen of the breed—though it says nothing about its quality.

However, the process of registration and the writing of pedigrees is, in a sense (and without meaning to be derogatory), merely window dressing. They simply set a seal upon a more fundamental definition of pure breeds of cats. This relates to the characteristics of the individuals constituting a recognized breed and how these may differ from those of other cats: from alley cats and from other recognized breeds. In one sense, a breed is a group of animals that sufficient people are mutually agreed to recognize as such. This is not enough in itself, however; the group must have coherent distinguishing features that set them apart from all other cats, and hence distinctive underlying genetic characteristics.   Michael Wright and Sally Walters, *The Book of the Cat*

EXERCISE 14.8
Write several sentences of a stipulative definition for one of the following alternatives.

1. Define in your own way TV game shows, soap operas, police dramas, or horror movies. Try for a stipulative definition of what these (or some other form of TV or movie entertainment) are generally like. In effect, you will be saying to your readers, other students in your class who are familiar with these forms of entertainment, "Let's agree for now to define X this way."

2. Do the same for some hard-to-define concept—like *loyalty, love, bravery, fame, shyness, sportsmanship, male chauvinism,* or *worthwhile courses.*

3. Think of a new development or phenomenon in contemporary romance, music, TV, leisure, fashion, or eating habits. Invent a name for it, and write a stipulative definition for it.

Classifying

In much writing, the first thing a writer must do is find some way to combine scattered observations or facts and then to label these new combinations. This writing strategy is called *classifying*.

This is a strategy used to organize everything from short sections of an essay to entire books. In either case, classification is very often used together with other writing strategies—definition, illustration, contrast, or any other. With long or short works, classification generally provides only the framework; other strategies are then necessary to develop the piece fully.

In reports and textbooks, classification is quite common. In fact, you can find it on just about any page of most college textbooks. In the following example from a recent book on the computer revolution, the three-part division of information is announced in the first sentence, and the parts are labeled. Each part is then defined and discussed in a separate paragraph in the order forecast by the opening sentence.

> There are essentially three categories of machine: simple machines, programmable machines and robots.
>
> Simple machines, to all intents and purposes, are nothing more than powerful mechanical muscles; they are either controlled by a human being, or have been designed and constructed to perform an endless series of repetitive acts. Hydraulic excavators, steam engines and motor cars all fall into this category.
>
> Programmable machines are more sophisticated. They are devices which can be programmed to do any of a number of different tasks or, in the more ambitious cases, a sequence of tasks. The program is set into the device by the human who controls it. They have only become widely used in recent years, though some of the very earliest versions were invented at around the same time as the first simple machines. Jacquard's loom was a programmable machine—and it was also one of the first true machines.
>
> The robot is different, and in an important way. It, too, is capable of performing a variety of tasks, or a sequence of tasks, but the choice of tasks at any particular moment is determined not only by a pre-set program, but also by some information *fed into it from the outside world which is relevant to the task it is performing.* The information it absorbs is fed into it through sensing devices attached to its own structure, and

not by command signals from a human. A simple machine, or even a programmed one, is capable of performing quite a complex task, but it will go on doing it indefinitely in really blockheaded fashion until something intervenes to stop it; a robot, on the other hand, will take account of change in its environment and adjust its behavior accordingly.
Christopher Evans, *The Micro Millennium*

The next example shows how classification is used by writers other than textbook authors. See how Ernest Hemingway uses the strategy to open a chapter in *Death in the Afternoon,* his classic book on bullfighting in Spain. To help us understand how a bullfight develops, Hemingway divides it into three acts. He names each act after the major action: the trial of the lances, the banderillas, and the death. The third act he divides further into three parts (or scenes, to continue his analogy between a bullfight and a play).

There are three acts to the fighting of each bull and they are called in Spanish los tres tercios de la lidia, or the three thirds of the combat. The first act, where the bull charges the picadors, is the suerte de varas, or the trial of the lances. Suerte is an important word in Spanish. It means, according to the dictionary: Suerte, f., chance, hazard, lots, fortune, luck, good luck, haphazard; state, condition, fate, doom, destiny, kind, sort; species, manner, mode, way, skillful manœuvre; trick, feat, juggle, and piece of ground separated by landmark. So the translation of trial or manœuvre is quite arbitrary, as any translation must be from the Spanish.

The action of the picadors in the ring and the work of the matadors who are charged with protecting them with their capes when they are dismounted make up the first act of the bullfight. When the president signals for the end of this act and the bugle blows the picadors leave the ring and the second act begins. There are no horses in the ring after the first act except the dead horses which are covered with canvas. Act one is the act of the capes, the pics and the horses. In it the bull has the greatest opportunity to display his bravery or cowardice.

Act two is that of the banderillas. These are pairs of sticks about a yard long, seventy centimetres to be exact, with a harpoon-shaped steel point four centimetres long at one end. They are supposed to be placed, two at a time, in the humped muscle at the top of the bull's neck as he charges the man who holds them. They are designed to complete the work of slowing up the bull and regulating the carriage of his head which has been begun by the picadors: so that his attack will be slower, but surer and better directed. Four pair of banderillas are usually put in. If they are placed by the banderilleros or peones they must be placed, above all other considerations, quickly and in the proper position. If the matador himself places them he may indulge in a preparation which is usually accompanied by music. This is the most picturesque part of the bullfight and the part most spectators care for the most when first seeing fights. The mission of the banderilleros is not only to force the bull by hooking to tire his neck muscles and carry his head lower but also, by placing them at one side or another, to correct a tendency to hook to that side. The entire act of the banderillas should not take more than five minutes. If it is prolonged the bull becomes discomposed and the fight loses the tempo it must keep, and if the bull is an uncertain and dangerous one he has too many opportunities to see and charge men unarmed with any lure, and so develops a tendency to search for the man, the bundle, as the Spanish call him, behind the cloth when the matador comes out for the last act with the sword and muleta.

The president changes the act after three or at most four pairs of banderillas have been placed and the third and final division is the death. It is made up of three parts. First the brindis or salutation of the president and dedication or toasting of the death of the bull, either to him or to some other person by the matador, followed by the work of the matador with the muleta. This is a scarlet serge cloth which is folded over a stick which has a sharp spike at one end and a handle at the other. The spike goes through the cloth which is fastened to the other end of the handle with a thumb screw so that it hangs in folds along the length of the stick. Muleta means literally crutch, but in bullfighting it refers to the scarlet-serge-draped stick with which the matador is supposed to master the bull, prepare him for killing and finally hold in his left hand to lower the bull's head and keep it lowered while he kills the animal by a sword thrust high up between his shoulder blades.

These are the three acts in the tragedy of the bullfight, and it is the first one, the horse part, which indicates what the others will be and, in fact, makes the rest possible. It is in the first act that the bull comes out in full possession of all of his faculties, confident, fast, vicious and con-quering. All his victories are in the first act. At the end of the first act he has apparently won. He has cleared the ring of mounted men and is alone. In the second act he is baffled completely by an unarmed man and very cruelly punished by the banderillas so that his confidence and his blind general rage goes and he concentrates his hatred on an individual object. In the third act he is faced by only one man who must, alone, dominate him by a piece of cloth placed over a stick, and kill him from in front, going in over the bull's right horn to kill him with a sword thrust between the arch of his shoulder blades.   Ernest Hemingway, *Death in the Afternoon*

The way a topic is divided can be illustrated with a diagram showing the relations among the parts and subparts of the division. Here is such a diagram of Hemingway's piece:

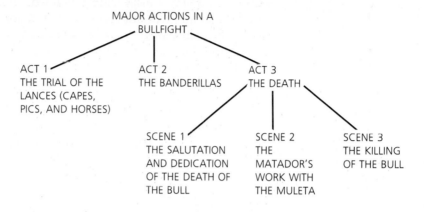

PRINCIPLES OF DIVISION

Each division and subdivision of a topic must meet certain requirements: significance, consistency, exclusiveness, and completeness. These may be defined as follows:

Significance   The division must be appropriate to the writer's purpose.

Consistency   The parts resulting from the division must all be based on the same principle of division.

Exclusiveness   The parts resulting from the division should not overlap.

Completeness   No important parts should be omitted in the division.

The Hemingway piece illustrates these principles of division. The point, or *significance,* of Hemingway's division seems to be to reveal the dramatic sequence of activities in a bullfight. Hemingway's division of the bullfight into acts that follow each other in time is of course rather obvious, but his point in this division is to highlight the contribution the key action of each act makes to the defeat of the bull. This division is *consistent* in that the parts, or acts—the trial of the lances, the banderillas, and the death—are all formed on the same principle. Each one is a major action in the drama. The division is *exclusive* because there is no overlap: actions in one act do not usually occur again in other acts. It is *complete* because Hemingway's acts include all the actions responsible for the defeat of the bull. The subdivision of his third act into the major activities of the matador also fulfills these same principles.

Such division results from a writer's analysis of a topic and of the information he or she has gathered on it plus any ideas or insights about the topic. For example, if you were in Tucson trying to tell a friend about the trees on your Chicago street, you would have some particular reason for mentioning trees and a specific point to make. It is unlikely your point would be that some trees are big and others small, or some evergreen and others deciduous. In relentlessly sunny, relatively treeless Tucson, you might be thinking about the variations in leaf colors or in the shade-giving characteristics of Chicago trees. The point you want to make determines the principle of division. Following are two ways you might divide the topic to organize your explanation.

DECIDUOUS TREES OF CHICAGO

EXERCISE 15.1

Diagram the division in the first example in this chapter, the selection from *The Micro Millennium* by Christopher Evans. Then decide whether the division is consistent, exclusive, and complete. What would you say is the significance or point of the division?

EXERCISE 15.2

Pick at least two of the following topics, and divide them in two or three different ways. Diagram each division, and then state its significance, or point. Be sure that, for the point it makes, each division is consistent, exclusive, and complete.

teachers	crimes
dreams	poets
lies	popular music groups
restaurants	tools for writing
bars	ways of avoiding writing
cars	football offenses
movies	field hockey defenses
students	

Biologist Sylvia Mader's *Inquiry into Life,* featured in Chapter 14: Defining, also illustrates a typical use of division. In the following example from a section of that book identifying the parts of the human ear, Mader offers a straightforward three-part division. She announces it immediately, names the parts of the division, and then presents the information appropriate to each part.

Like Hemingway's division of a bullfight into three acts, Mader's division of the parts of the ear follows a simple plan. To suit their different purposes, Hemingway's division results in a *temporal* plan while Mader's results in a *spatial* plan, moving from outside to inside. In the text where this selection appears, several drawings illustrate the division of the ear Mader describes. There is also a chart, included here, which diagrams the division and lists all the main anatomical terms within each division.

The ear has three divisions: outer, middle, and inner. The **outer ear** consists of the **pinna** (external flap) and **auditory canal.** The opening of the auditory canal is lined with fine hairs and sweat glands. In the upper wall are modified sweat glands that secrete earwax to help guard the ear against the entrance of foreign materials such as air pollutants.

The **middle ear** begins at the **tympanic membrane** (eardrum) and ends at a bony wall in which are found two small openings covered by membranes. These openings are called the **oval** and **round windows.** The posterior wall of the middle ear leads to many air spaces within the **mastoid process.**

Three small bones are found between the tympanic membrane and the oval window. Collectively called the **ossicles,** individually they are the **hammer** (malleus), **anvil** (incus), and **stirrup** (stapes) because their shapes resemble these objects. The hammer adheres to the tympanic membrane, while the stirrup touches the oval window.

The eustachian tube extends from the middle ear to the nasopharynx and permits equalization of air pressure. Chewing gum, yawning, and swallowing in elevators and airplanes helps move air through the eustachian tubes upon ascent and descent.

Whereas the outer ear and middle ear contain air, the inner ear is filled with fluid. The **inner ear,** anatomically speaking, has three areas: the first two, called the vestibule and semicircular canals, are concerned with balance; and the third, the cochlea, is concerned with hearing.

The **semicircular canals** are arranged so that there is one in each dimension of space. The base of each canal, called the **ampulla,** is slightly enlarged. Within the ampullae are little hair cells.

The **vestibule** is a chamber that lies between the semicircular canals and the cochlea. It contains two small sacs called the **utricle** and **saccule.** Within both of these are little hair cells surrounded by a gelatinous material containing calcium carbonate granules, or **otoliths.**

The **cochlea** resembles the shell of a snail because it spirals. Within the tubular cochlea are three canals: the vestibular canal, the **cochlear**

canal, and the tympanic canal. Along the length of the basilar membrane, which forms the lower wall of the cochlear canal, are little hair cells, and just above them is another membrane, called the **tectorial membrane.** The hair cells plus the tectorial membrane are called the **organ of Corti.** When this organ sends nerve impulses to the cerebral cortex, it is interpreted as sound.   Sylvia Mader, *Inquiry into Life*

The Ear

	Outer Ear	Middle Ear	Inner Ear Cochlea	*Sacs plus semicircular canals*
Function	Directs sound waves to tympanic membrane	Picks up and amplifies sound waves	Hearing	Maintains equilibrium
Anatomy	Pinna Auditory canal	Tympanic membrane Hammer (malleus) Anvil (incus) Stirrup (stapes)	Vestibular canal Tympanic canal Cochlear canal Contains organ of Corti Auditory nerve starts here	Saccule and utricle (contain otoliths and hair cells) Semicircular canals (contain hair cells in ampullae)
Media	Air	Air (eustachian tube)	Fluid	Fluid

Path of vibration: Sound waves—vibration of tympanic membrane—vibration of hammer, anvil, and stirrup—vibration of oval window—fluid pressure waves of fluids in canals of inner ear lead to stimulation of hair cells—bulging of round window.

The point of this division is clear: to identify the parts of the ear. In the larger context of the chapter in which it appears, however, its purpose is to name the parts so that the reader will be able to follow a discussion of the function of the ear, its physiology rather than its anatomy. The chart, you will notice, includes the function of each division of the ear.

STRATEGIES FOR COHERENCE

Writers must take care in presenting a division of information so readers can follow it easily. In the Mader example, the initial statement of the division forecasts the plan of the presentation. Mader names the parts in the order they will appear: outer, middle, inner ear. Each part is introduced in a new paragraph and always with the same syntax at the beginning of a sentence: "The outer ear. . . . The middle ear. . . . The inner ear. . . ."

Such strategies of coherence (discussed more fully in Chapter 11: Cueing the Reader), are important methods of helping a reader understand and follow a division.

EXERCISE 15.3

Look again at the first selection in this chapter (from *The Micro Millennium* by Christopher Evans) to examine the strategies the writer uses to present a coherent division of information. Does the initial statement of the division name all the groups and forecast the order in which they will be discussed? What other writing strategies does the writer use to steer the reader through the presentation?

USING DIVISION WITH OTHER WRITING STRATEGIES

The last example of division comes from a book that attempts to explain the new physics to nonphysicists.

There are two kinds of mass, which means that there are two ways of talking about it. The first is gravitational mass. The gravitational mass of an object, roughly speaking, is the weight of the object as measured on a balance scale. Something that weighs three times more than another object has three times more mass. Gravitational mass is the measure of how much force the gravity of the earth exerts on an object. Newton's laws describe the effects of this force, which vary with the distance of the mass from the earth. Although Newton's laws describe the effects of this force, they do not define it. This is the mystery of action-at-a-distance. . . .

The second type of mass is inertial mass. Inertial mass is the measure of the resistance of an object to acceleration (or deceleration, which is negative acceleration). For example, it takes three times more force to move three railroad cars from a standstill to twenty miles per hour (positive acceleration) than it takes to move one railroad car from a standstill to twenty miles per hour. . . . Similarly, once they are moving, it takes three times more force to stop three cars than it takes to stop the single car. This is because the inertial mass of the three railroad cars is three times more than the inertial mass of the single railroad car.

Inertial mass and gravitational mass are equal. This explains why a feather and a cannonball fall with equal velocity in a vacuum. The cannonball has hundreds of times more gravitational mass than the feather (it weighs more) but it also has hundreds of times more resistance to motion than the feather (its inertial mass). Its attraction to the earth is hundreds of times stronger than that of the feather, but then so is its inclination not to move. The result is that it accelerates downward at the same rate as the feather, although it seems that it should fall much faster.

The fact that inertial mass and gravitational mass are equal was known three hundred years ago, but physicists considered it a coincidence. No significance was attached to it until Einstein published his general theory of relativity.   Gary Zukav, *The Dancing Wu Li Masters: An Overview of the New Physics*

This example illustrates the relation of division to other essential writing strategies. Zukav divides his topic into two kinds of mass: gravitational and inertial. Then he defines each one. In the first paragraph, to define gravitational mass, he relies in part on the illustration of an ordinary balance scale. In the second paragraph, to define inertial mass, he contrasts the action of three railroad cars with that of one railroad car. These two paragraphs show how naturally dividing and naming lead to definition, illustration, and contrast.

The point of Zukav's division is the principle he states at the beginning of the third paragraph. Once he has roughly and quickly identified the two kinds of mass, he considers how they are related—namely, that they are equal. And then he illustrates this principle by contrasting a feather with a cannonball.

EXERCISE 15.4

Analyze each of the following classifications. First, within the context of the whole selection, decide the point or significance of the division. Then decide whether the division is consistent, exclusive, and complete. To focus your analysis, you might want to make a diagram of the division. Here are the classifications, each from a selection in Part I of this book:

Chapter 4 "Uncle John's Farm," Mark Twain, paragraph 10

Chapter 5 "The External Skeleton of the Insect," David Attenborough, paragraph 3

Chapter 5 "The Black Death," William Langer, entire piece

Chapter 6 "A Proposal to Strengthen the Language Acquisition Project," Wendy Jo Niwa, paragraphs 5–7

Chapter 8 "Fear of Dearth," Carll Tucker, paragraphs 5–7

Chapter 8 "Suicide among Young People," Victor Fuchs, paragraph 2 and table

EXERCISE 15.5

Choose one of the following writing activities. Each one asks for some division; be sure that your analysis observes the principles of a good division: significance, consistency, exclusiveness, and completeness. Include in your writing appropriate strategies of coherence, such as forecasting, paragraphing (optional in a brief piece), and repeated sentence patterns.

1. Write several sentences in which you identify the major periods in your life. Label and briefly define each period.

2. Describe a familiar activity (running, sleeping, eating Chinese food) in a new way by dividing it into stages. Label and define each stage.

3. Develop in writing one of the divisions you created in Exercise 15.2.

Illustrating

This chapter looks closely at five forms of illustration: developed examples, lists, evidence, anecdotes, and scenarios. Each can help make your writing more persuasive, more specific and concrete, and more memorable.

DEVELOPED EXAMPLES

A developed example is the basic form of illustration. Essentially it consists of a general statement with a few sentences of more detailed explanation and elaboration. Sometimes the example is specifically signaled by the phrase *for example* or *for instance*.

Here are the opening paragraphs of a chapter on lenses from one of Annie Dillard's books:

> You get used to looking through lenses; it is an acquired skill. When you first look through binoculars, for instance, you can't see a thing. You look at the inside of the barrel; you blink and watch your eyelashes; you play with the focus knob till one eye is purblind.
>
> The microscope is even worse. You are supposed to keep both eyes open as you look through its single eyepiece. I spent my childhood in Pittsburgh trying to master this trick: seeing through one eye, with both eyes open. The microscope also teaches you to move your hands wrong, to shove the glass slide to the right if you are following a creature who is swimming off to the left—as if you were operating a tiller, or backing a trailer, or performing any other of those paradoxical maneuvers which require either sure instincts or a grasp of elementary physics, neither of which I possess.   Annie Dillard, *Teaching a Stone to Talk*

The first sentence (a topic sentence) introduces the two examples that follow. Dillard develops the topic by inviting readers to remember what it was like to use binoculars and microscopes for the first time. She concentrates on the actions of viewers—blinking, playing with the knob, keeping both eyes open, moving the glass slide.

This second sample of illustration by developed example is from Mark Twain. There are two developed examples here, each demonstrating one way that the Mississippi River keeps shifting its location. Twain's strategy is to use the consequences of each type of shift to develop the example.

16

The Mississippi is remarkable in still another way—its disposition to make prodigious jumps by cutting through narrow necks of land, and thus straightening and shortening itself. More than once it has shortened itself thirty miles at a single jump! These cutoffs have had curious effects: they have thrown several river towns out into the rural districts, and built up sand bars and forests in front of them. The town of Delta used to be three miles below Vicksburg: a recent cutoff has radically changed the position, and Delta is now *two miles above* Vicksburg.

Both of these river towns have been retired to the country by that cutoff. A cutoff plays havoc with boundary lines and jurisdictions: for instance, a man is living in the State of Mississippi today, a cutoff occurs tonight, and tomorrow the man finds himself and his land over on the other side of the river, within the boundaries and subject to the laws of the State of Louisiana! Such a thing, happening in the upper river in the old times, could have transferred a slave from Missouri to Illinois and made a free man of him.

The Mississippi does not alter its locality by cutoffs alone: it is always changing its habitat *bodily*—is always moving bodily *sidewise*. At Hard Times, La., the river is two miles west of the region it used to occupy. As a result, the original *site* of that settlement is not now in Louisiana at all, but on the other side of the river, in the State of Mississippi. *Nearly the whole of that one thousand three hundred miles of old Mississippi River which La Salle floated down in his canoes, two hundred years ago, is good solid dry ground now.* The river lies to the right of it, in places, and to the left of it in other places.

Although the Mississippi's mud builds land but slowly, down at the mouth, where the Gulf's billows interfere with its work, it builds fast enough in better protected regions higher up: for instance, Prophet's Island contained one thousand five hundred acres of land thirty years ago; since then the river has added seven hundred acres to it.

But enough of these examples of the mighty stream's eccentricities for the present—I will give a few more of them further along in the book. Mark Twain, *Life on the Mississippi*

Like Dillard, Twain develops a single topic with two examples. A new paragraph clearly signals the beginning of the second example in both selections. Both Dillard and Twain rely on definition and division as the basis for illustration. Dillard divides her topic into binoculars and microscopes, but she does not define anything because she assumes readers know what binoculars and microscopes are. Twain divides his topic into cutoffs and sidewise shifts, and he also defines each of these river maneuvers for us. But both writers move well beyond division and definition to provide engaging developed examples.

In the next example the political columnist George Will uses an amusing variation of the developed example. He makes up an example from music lyrics he heard at a country music concert:

> If [country] music does indeed answer the question about how ''country'' folks are getting on, the answer is: Poorly. This music speaks feelingly of lives in which one thing has led to another, which in turn has led to much more, all of it dismal. I have pieced together from many lyrics this picture of the misfortunes that attend typical ''country'' lives:
>
> *You wore my high-school ring and letter sweater before bright neon lights made you up and walk away from standing by your man/ leaving the crops in the field and me jamming gears with nothing to do but keep on trucking in my eighteen-wheeler/ listening to the windshield wipers when I'm not drinking Falstaff and Wild Turkey and putting the last dime from my faded jeans into a jukebox to help me make it through the night/ wishing I could make the alimony payments and visit little Billie and Betsy Sue.*
>
> *So in the Elko, Nevada, Greyhound depot I shot the man, my best friend, who took you and even my pickup truck/ and I wound up here on Death Row listening to the lonesome whistle of the night train rolling south through the cotton fields from Nashville to that little bit of Heaven, Biloxi/ where we were dirt-poor, eating beans and gravy, and didn't even have a gun rack for the pickup/ but we were happy until you became a good-timing woman and left me with nothing to look at but four walls of the cheap hotel room/ where I drink black coffee and read the Good Book, just like my daddy, a preacher man, and Mom, a widower sharecropper's daughter, back in the dusty one-room shack where/ we didn't have much and wouldn't take welfare and loved this great country in spite of gun control.* relating to heardsmen / shepards
>
> Well, now. If such lyrics are an accurate survey of bucolic life, that life hurts like the dickens, and we might as well admit that civilization has come a cropper and the fabric of society is unraveling, even in the country. But there is this to be said for the forthright sorrowfulness of country music: it is a timely assertion of an endangered right—the right to be unhappy.   George Will, *The Pursuit of Virtue and Other Tory Notions*

Some developed examples are not quite so tidy as these pieces from Dillard, Twain, and Will. Here is a much less symmetrical example from John McPhee:

Soft miry land that shakes or yields under the foot.

image/ presents

to secure tightly

Among outdoor-equipment suppliers in the United States, Bean's is more or less the source pond—a business begun in 1912, when the Maine Hunting Shoe was developed by a noted woodsman, Leon Leonwood Bean. Boots with leather tops and rubber bottoms, they are of considerable utility in the quagmires of the north woods, and Bean's still sells them—eighty-eight thousand pairs a year. Bean's-boots simulacra are in the mail-order catalogues of nearly all the other outdoor suppliers in the country. Adding item after item over the years, Bean, who died in 1967, built a national reputation. In recent times, the company has further expanded, somewhat disturbingly, to become a kind of balsam-scented department store, but, for all its Japanese pot holders and Seventh Avenue jumpers, it still has truly serviceable woods equipment in sufficient variety to hold position in the field. If you travel in bush Alaska, you find Bean's catalogues in cabin after cabin there, and Bean's boots and garments on the people. Most transactions are by mail, but the home store, in Freeport, in Cumberland County, is open twenty-four hours a day seven days a week. I know people who have gone shopping at Bean's at four o'clock in the morning and have reported themselves to have been by no means the only customers there. The store is a rampant mutation of New England connective architecture—an awkward, naïve building, seeming to consist of many wooden boxes stacked atop one another and held together by steel exterior trusses. There is nothing naïve about the cash register. Sometimes it is necessary to go off to the woods for indefinite periods to recover from a visit to Bean's. John Kauffmann and I have stopped there at nine in the morning, fanned out for boots, mink oil, monoculars, folding scissors, Sven saws, fishing gear, wool shirts, met at noon by the windproof-match bin, gone out to lunch (lobsters—four—on the wharf at South Freeport), and returned to Bean's for a good part of the afternoon. Saltonstall, in his travels, makes regular visits to Bean's and, among trusted friends, is not too shy to admit it.   John McPhee, *Giving Good Weight*

This section works by a strategy that could be called *additional comment*. Though it includes many examples, they are anything but parallel. They are organized under a topic sentence—L. L. Bean's outdoor equipment business is the best known in the country—but some examples are developed more fully than others. The examples shift rapidly across quite varied topics: history of the business, initial products, comparison to department stores, catalogues in Alaska, store operation, its architecture, a typical shopping trip there. And yet, despite all this rapid shifting, the selection is coherent. A reader follows it easily even though there are no consistent clues in the sentence beginnings to signal new examples.

The preceding four selections illustrate very well how flexible this writing strategy is. Watch how writers vary the strategy of illustration by developed examples. Experiment with it yourself. Be guided by your readers' needs: readers respond with interest to a dense pattern of detailed examples, but they can become confused and lose interest if the examples are not clustered and related.

EXERCISE 16.1

Write a one- or two-sentence general statement based on one of the following topics. Then illustrate the statement with one or two developed examples. Avoid the temptation to keep restating the general statement. Go immediately to your first example. Direct your illustration to an audience of other students in your class.

a change in your hometown

a popular trend (music, movies, TV)

the image of a particular group of people projected by advertising

a basic academic principle

a useless modern invention

EXERCISE 16.2

Analyze the following paragraphs from selections in Part I. For each paragraph, describe how the writer develops the example. Also identify the purpose of the example within the selection as a whole. What does it contribute?

Chapter 3 "Nana," Amiri Baraka, paragraphs 5 and 6

Chapter 5 "Galileo: The First Active Observer," Fred Wolf, paragraph 5

Chapter 5 "The External Skeleton of the Insect," David Attenborough, paragraph 4

Chapter 7 "The Treasure of the Sierra Madre," James Agee, paragraph 5

Chapter 7 "The Civil Rights Movement: What Good Was It?" Alice Walker, paragraph 9

Chapter 10 "Inside the Brain," David Noonan, paragraphs 4 and 21

LISTS

Listing, a special form of illustration, is a writing strategy used in all types of writing. Poets, novelists, reporters, and scientists all use it to good effect. It is simply the quick accumulation of specific examples without taking time to develop any of them. It looks easy, but choosing the items for the list can be tricky. They need to suggest the range and variety of the scene or topic, and they need to create a single dominant impression.

One of John McPhee's recent pieces, "Giving Good Weight," reports what he learned about fresh fruit and vegetable markets in New York City. As part of his research he visited farms, and he also worked at the markets, weighing and selling vegetables. Very early in this long profile are two pages filled with lists. Here is the first of them.

This is the Brooklyn market, in appearance the most cornucopian of all. The trucks are drawn up in a close but ample square and spill into its center the colors of the country. Greengage plums. Ruby Red onions. Yellow crookneck squash. Sweet white Spanish onions. Starking Delicious plums.

Fall pippins ("Green as grass and curl your teeth"). McIntoshes, Cortlands, Paulareds. ("Paulareds are new and are lovely apples. I'll bet they'll be in the stores in the next few years.")

Pinkish-yellow Gravensteins. Gold Star cantaloupes. Patty Pan squash. Burpless cucumbers.

Cranberry beans.

Silver Queen corn. Sweet Sue bicolor corn, with its concise tight kernels, its well-filled tips and butts. Boston salad lettuce. Parris Island romaine lettuce. Ithaca iceberg crunchy pale lettuce. Orange tomatoes.

Cherry Bell tomatoes.

Moreton Hybrid, Jet Star, Setmore, Supersonic, Roma, Saladette tomatoes.

Campbell 38s.

Campbell 1327s.

Big Boy, Big Girl, Redpak, Ramapo, Rutgers London-broil thick-slice tomatoes.

Clean-shouldered, supple-globed Fantastic tomatoes. Celery (Imperial 44).

Hot Portugal peppers. Four-lobed Lady Bell glossy green peppers. Aconcagua frying peppers.

Parsley, carrots, collard greens.

Stuttgarter onions, mustard greens.

Dandelions.   John McPhee, *Giving Good Weight*

[handwritten margin note: red or green apples]

This list is cornucopian itself. It spills out onto the page like fruits and vegetables sprawling from a horn of plenty. It specifies colors, types of produce, and even varieties, especially of tomatoes, which get named sixteen times. Why would McPhee bother to name sixteen different tomatoes? Apparently he likes the sounds of the names. But he also wants to present the amazing variety of vegetables at a farmer's market (perhaps as opposed to a supermarket).

This next list immediately follows the preceding one.

> The people, in their throngs, are the most varied we see—or that anyone is likely to see in one place west of Suez. This intersection is the hub if not the heart of Brooklyn, where numerous streets converge, and where Fourth Avenue comes plowing into the Flatbush-Atlantic plane. It is also a nexus of the race. "Weigh these, please." "Will you please weigh these?" Greeks. Italians. Russians. Finns. Haitians. Puerto Ricans. Nubians. Muslim women in veils of shocking pink. Sunnis in total black. Women in hiking shorts, with babies in their backpacks. Young Connecticut-looking pants-suit women. Their hair hangs long and as soft as cornsilk. There are country Jamaicans, in loose dresses, bandannas tight around their heads. "Fifty cents? Yes, dahling. Come on a sweetheart, mon." There are Jews by the minyan, Jews of all persuasions—white-bearded, black-bearded, split-bearded Jews. Down off Park Slope and Cobble Hill come the neo-bohemians, out of the money and into the arts. "Will you weigh this tomato, please?" And meantime let us discuss theatre, books, environmental impacts. Maybe half the crowd are men—men in cool Haspel cords and regimental ties, men in lipstick, men with blue eyelids. Corporate-echelon pinstripe men. Their silvered hair is perfect in coif; it appears to have been audited. Easygoing old neighborhood men with their shirts hanging open in the summer heat are walking galleries of abdominal and thoracic scars—Brooklyn Jewish Hospital's bastings and tackings. (They do good work there.)   John McPhee, *Giving Good Weight*

a number/ list

Notice how this engaging list illustrates the opening general statement. Perhaps better than any other piece so far in this chapter, this selection shows how general statements relate to specific illustrative details in strong writing. To state the relationship as a working rule for writers: use many details and very few general statements. McPhee might have described the market as follows:

> The people are the most varied we see. They come from a great many different places in the city. In their accents and dress we get a sense of their different origins. Some dress informally, and some dress formally. They are all ages.

In other words, he might have given all general statements. Instead, he gives us authentic details. In fact, it is much harder for a writer to string generalities together effectively than to give one generality and then some illustrations of it. As you can see from McPhee's example, listing is a powerful illustrator of generalities.

And finally, here is an example of a list in a college biology textbook. Typical of topic statements in textbooks, the first sentence here is not really a thesis or an assertion, but only a general organizing statement for what follows.

Only a few of the many anatomical changes that occurred in the course of evolution from ape ancestor to modern humans can be mentioned here: (1) The jaw became shorter (making the muzzle shorter), and the teeth became smaller. (2) The point of attachment of the skull to the vertebral column shifted from the rear of the braincase to a position under the braincase, the skull thus becoming balanced more on top of the vertebral column. (3) The braincase became much larger, and, as it did, a prominent vertical forehead developed. (4) The eyebrow ridges and other keels on the skull were reduced as the muscles that once attached to them became smaller. (5) The nose became more prominent, with a distinct bridge and tip. (6) The arms (though probably never as long as in the modern apes) became shorter. (7) The feet became flattened, and then an arch developed. (8) The big toe moved back into line with the other toes and ceased being apposable. The various fossil humans are intermediate in these characteristics.　　William T. Keeton, *Biological Science*

Here the list provides a great deal of information in a hurry, each item a conclusion from decades of anthropological research. This passage might appear to be a division, but since it does not organize the next large section of the chapter, it is simply illustration by listing. It is a very brisk and businesslike way to lay out concisely the "anatomical changes that occurred in the course of evolution."

EXERCISE 16.3
Choose some busy activity you can observe conveniently. Make a general statement about the activity, and then illustrate it with a list of visual details you see at the scene of the activity. Select and present the list so that it conveys a dominant impression of the activity.

EXERCISE 16.4
Analyze the lists in the following selections from Part I. For each list, consider these questions: How long is the list? What kinds of items does it include? What dominant impression does it give? What is the purpose of the list within the whole selection?

Chapter 4 "Uncle John's Farm," Mark Twain, paragraph 1
Chapter 4 "The Kitchen," Alfred Kazin, last half of paragraph 2 beginning with the sentence "A large electric bulb . . ."
Chapter 8 "Fear of Dearth," Carll Tucker, paragraph 3
Chapter 10 "The Pinball Philosophy," John McPhee, paragraph 7
Chapter 10 "Holy Water," Joan Didion, the last sentence in paragraph 1

EVIDENCE

Writers of reports and arguments often use evidence to illustrate their general statements and claims. Selectively paraphrasing and quoting published sources is one way to provide evidence. This strategy is illustrated in Chapter 21: Using and Acknowledging Sources, which discusses how to integrate evidence from other sources into your essays and reports. Two other ways to supply evidence are through statistics and authorities.

Statistics   Statistics are numbers. If they come from a reliable source, and if readers believe you are presenting them fairly, statistics can be especially effective illustrations.

In this first example, a newspaper columnist presents statistics on pornography in America. His column advances the ironic argument that the nation should preserve the birthplaces of all its great industries—oil, airplanes, department stores, and pornography. In spite of his deliberate irony (saying one thing and meaning another), Will must demonstrate that pornography is, indeed, a major industry if his argument is to work.

> The California Department of Justice estimates that U.S. pornographers do $4 billion of business annually. That is as much as the "conventional" movie and record industries, combined. And the sum may be more than twice that high. The 10 leading "skin" magazines alone have a combined monthly circulation of 16 million and will have revenues of about $475 million this year, almost $400 million of it from circulation.
>
> About 2 million people a week pay an average of $3.50 at the 780 "adult" cinemas that will gross more than $365 million this year. The movie *Deep Throat* cost $25,000 and has grossed $50 million so far. The average pornographic film returns about 200 percent on investment in eighteen months.   George Will, *The Pursuit of Virtue and Other Tory Notions*

Will selects statistics which demonstrate the huge size of the pornography industry, specifically magazines and movies. He also wants to show the magnitude of profits being made in pornography. Beginning with the estimated total revenues from pornography, he then estimates the revenues from magazines and films, concluding with a particular film example.

This next illustration, from Ken Auletta's book on America's underclass, presents statistics on violent crime, especially murder. In order to develop his argument that a permanent urban underclass is a growing threat to the social order, the writer uses statistics in two ways: to show the increase in crime and to demonstrate that we have much more violent crime than other countries.

For the average person, the most worrisome group are the violent criminals. Crime in America is now both more violent and more random. Crime
statistics tell part of the story. In 1970, there were about 1,500 murders
in the entire state of California. Nine years later, there were 1,975 murders
in Los Angeles County alone. St. Louis, Missouri, which ranked as the
murder capital of the nation, had 230 reported murders in 1978. In 1979,
its murder rate jumped 24 percent. Eighty-four percent of the victims
were black. Killings in Atlanta rose from 141 in 1978 to 231 in 1979; in
Houston, from 462 to 632. Nationally, according to the FBI, violent crimes
have risen in eleven of the past twelve years.

In 1979 and 1980, violent crime jumped 11 percent. In 1980, New
York City averaged five homicides a day (1,814)—more than triple the
murder rate in all of Canada and ten times the declining murder rate in
Tokyo, which has 40 percent more people. That same year New York had
3,711 rapes, 43,476 assaults, 210,703 burglaries and 249,421 cases of
theft. There were an estimated 23,044 murders in the United States in
1980; in all of England and Wales in 1979, there were but 629.
Ken Auletta, *The Underclass*

Here, the author selected statistics to show the size of the problem and
some of its results. The American numbers alone seem huge and worrisome. The contrast with the much smaller numbers in other countries
makes the American numbers seem even bigger.

In both of the two preceding examples, the writers selected and arranged statistics to support a particular point of view on a social problem.
Each one first makes an assertion and then offers statistics as proof.

Writers are ethically responsible for their use of statistics. Not only
must they take them from reliable, authoritative sources, but they have to
select particular statistics carefully so as to avoid misrepresenting or mis-
using the information. Chapter 20: Library Research describes strategies
to help you locate statistics. Whenever possible, use sources in which
statistics first appeared rather than summaries or digests of others' statistics. For example, you would want to get medical statistics from a reputable and authoritative professional periodical like the *New England Journal of Medicine* rather than from a popular news weekly. If you are uncertain
about the most authoritative sources, ask a reference librarian or a professor who is a specialist on your topic.

EXERCISE 16.5
Analyze the use of statistics in the following selections in Part I of this
book. The first shows how statistics are used by an historian; the second,
by an economist.

Chapter 5 "The Black Death," William Langer, paragraphs 8 and 9
Chapter 8 "Suicide among Young People," Victor Fuchs

Identify the sources of the statistics in each of the selections. Do they seem to be the original sources? How might you find out whether the sources are authoritative and reputable?

How does each writer integrate the statistics into the text of the selection? By direct quotation from the source? By paraphrase or summary? In tables or figures?

What part do the statistics play in each selection? Do you find the statistics convincing?

Authorities   To support their generalizations and arguments, writers do not hesitate to cite authorities. They refer to them and quote them. Quoting a respected authority on a topic generally adds weight to an argument.

From Loretta Schwartz-Nobel's book on starvation in America comes a typical example. The writer cites an authority, a researcher at a well-known oceanographic institute, to support her argument.

> Dr. John Ryther, a highly respected and well-known marine biologist at the Woods Hole (Massachusetts) Oceanographic Institution, points out that there are about one billion acres of coastal wetlands in the world. If only one-tenth of these wetlands were used to raise fish, the potential yield of fish using improved methods of production would be one hundred million tons a year. This is the equivalent of the yield from the entire world's commercial fisheries.
>
> Dr. Ryther has also devised a complex continuous culture system which produces oysters, seaweed, worms, flounder, and abalone. It ultimately becomes a biological sewage treatment plant returning clean water to the sea.
>
> If this kind of system were implemented on a large scale it could produce a million pounds of shellfish a year from each one-acre production facility. By using advanced culture techniques like those developed at Woods Hole, Dr. Ryther estimates that the yield could well be multiplied tenfold within the next three decades.   Loretta Schwartz-Nobel, *Starving in the Shadow of Plenty*

The writer could simply have mentioned a system for wetland culture, but instead she emphasizes that it comes from a respected expert—thereby adding to her own authority and to the credibility of her material. (After all, she is not an expert on all the technical aspects of her topic.) Instead of quoting him directly, she paraphrases the information from him.

EXERCISE 16.6

Analyze the way authorities are used in the following selections from Part I of this book. For each selection decide whether or not you find the use of authorities convincing. How might you find out exactly how highly respected the authorities are?

How does the writer integrate the authority's words or opinions into the text of the selection? By direct quotation? By paraphrase or summary in the writer's own language? What role does the authority have in the piece as a whole?

Chapter 5 "The Black Death," William Langer, paragraphs 24 and 27

Chapter 6 "What to Name the Children When He's Kept His Name and You've Kept Yours," Jeanette Germain, paragraph 18

Chapter 8 "Fear of Dearth," Carll Tucker, paragraphs 5–7

Chapter 8 "Suicide among Young People," Victor Fuchs, paragraph 8

Chapter 9 "A Message to Decipher," Debbie Brawner, paragraph 3

Chapter 10 "The Pinball Philosophy," John McPhee, the entire piece

Chapter 10 "Holy Water," Joan Didion, paragraph 5

ANECDOTES

Anecdotes are short narratives that serve a particular purpose in a larger piece of writing. Their specificity helps to clarify general ideas. In the following example, William Ashworth knows that his readers will go to sleep if he deals only with abstractions and statistics. On the other hand, he knows he can engage his readers in the human side of a problem by showing what happens when one person performs a familiar act in one apartment. Consequently, he opens a chapter of his book on the water shortage with the following anecdote. The anecdote directly supports Ashworth's central arguments about the complex interconnectedness of big-city water systems and the heavy demands made on them. This narrative is not mere diversion. Diverting it is, but it also serves a purpose.

> I have a friend who lives in a small walk-up apartment in New York City's Greenwich Village. It is a comfortable apartment, loaded with books and paintings and good music, but it is not a particularly fancy one: a single room plus kitchen and bath, simply furnished, the plaster falling in places, the steam heat loud and largely uncontrollable. All the little things which demonstrate that the resident, whatever his other good qualities might be, is not a wealthy man.
>
> Despite its lack of ostentation, however, there is one thing that my friend's apartment has in common with the most elegant penthouses up on Fifth Avenue. It has, in the kitchen and the bath, a total of four sets of controls to the largest and most intricate machine in Eastern North America. The controls are called faucets. The machine is the New York City water system.

When my friend turns his tap to draw a glass of water, he sets in motion a chain of events that will be felt as far away as the upper Delaware River, 120 miles and more to the northwest. In the walls of his building, water moves in pipes; beneath the street, water gurgles in mains. Deep in the stony roots of Manhattan, masses of water in two large tunnels move ever so slightly. The reservoirs that feed the tunnels ripple and draw down a fraction of a centimeter; the aqueducts that feed the reservoirs fill them back up. The machine sighs into a new equilibrium—until one of the seven million New Yorkers who hold the controls disturbs it once again.   William Ashworth, *Nor Any Drop to Drink*

The narrative turns out to be a story about the water, not about Ashworth or his friend. But the friend and his small apartment are essential context for the narrative. The friend seems to be an ordinary person who, wealthy or not, can set in motion an entire water system. A reader can identify with this friend and, through his story, view the water system in a new way.

EXERCISE 16.7

Analyze the anecdotes in the following selections from Part I of this book. How long is each anecdote in relation to the length of the whole piece? Does the anecdote simply narrate events, or does it describe a scene (as the Ashworth anecdote does) or people in the scene? Does the writer comment on the significance of the anecdote or leave it to the reader to infer its importance? What role does the anecdote play in the piece as a whole? Do you find it informative or convincing?

Chapter 3 "Nana," Amiri Baraka, paragraph 1 (second half)

Chapter 4 "Uncle John's Farm," Mark Twain, paragraphs 4–8

Chapter 5 "Galileo: The First Active Observer," Fred Wolf, paragraphs 3–4, 6, and 7–8

Chapter 6 "What to Name the Children When He's Kept His Name and You've Kept Yours," Jeanette Germain, paragraphs 4–9

Chapter 6 "To Unteach Greed," Carol Bly, paragraphs 5–6

Chapter 7 "The Civil Rights Movement: What Good Was It?" Alice Walker, paragraphs 7 and 8

EXERCISE 16.8

Write an anecdote to support or contradict one of the following generalizations:

1. Crime does not pay.
2. The early bird catches the worm.

3. Don't put off till tomorrow what you can do today.
4. If at first you don't succeed, try, try again.
5. Don't get mad, get even.

SCENARIOS

Whereas an anecdote tells about something that happened, a scenario is a narrative that tells about what might happen. Writers create scenarios to make their arguments and explanations more vivid and convincing. Scenarios raise and answer the question "What if?"

Look at the following example. To support her opinion about the wastefulness of beef-raising methods in America, Loretta Schwartz-Nobel creates a restaurant scenario:

> America's beef raising methods waste more than food. They use eight times as much water as growing vegetables and grains. It takes at least ten thousand pounds of water to produce every pound of grain-fed beef. An acre of land used to raise steer produces about one pound of protein. That same acre could provide seventeen pounds of protein if it were planted with soybeans.
>
> To imagine what this means in practical, everyday terms, picture yourself at a restaurant in front of an eight-ounce steak and then imagine the room filled with forty-five to fifty people with empty bowls in front of them. For the feed costs of your steak, each of their bowls could be filled with a cup of soybeans or cooked grain.   Loretta Schwartz-Nobel, *Starving in the Shadow of Plenty*

The writer wants us to imagine ourselves at a table in this restaurant. Because we are familiar with restaurants, we can easily imagine the scene she sets and picture those fifty people with empty bowls staring at us accusingly.

The next example comes from an essay on the threat of nuclear war. Like analogies, scenarios use the familiar to define or illustrate the unknown. If you know Chicago, you will readily appreciate the devastation represented in this scenario of the effects of a nuclear bomb dropped on that city:

> On the freeways radiating from the Loop, automobiles, trucks, and buses were simultaneously evaporated and blown away, their particles sucked up into the fireball to become components of the radioactive cloud.
>
> Along the Stevenson Expressway, some seven or eight miles from Ground Zero, scores of oil storage tanks exploded—ruptured by the shock wave and then ignited from the grass and shrubbery burning around them.

At this range, too, aluminum siding on homes evaporated and some concrete surfaces exploded under thermal stress. The few buildings still standing were in danger of imminent collapse—and all were engulfed by flames. Highway spans caved in. Asphalt blistered and melted.

Clothing caught fire, and people were charred by intense light and heat. Their charcoal limbs would, in some instances, render their shapes recognizably human.

With greater distance from Ground Zero, the effects diminished. About ten miles from the Loop, in the area around the Brookfield Zoo, the fireball was merely brighter than a thousand suns. Glass did not melt, but shattered window fragments flew through the air at about 135 miles per hour. All trees were burning even before the shock wave uprooted most of them.

Railroad bridges collapsed, and railroad cars were blown from their tracks. Automobiles were smashed and twisted into grotesque shapes. One- and two-story wood frame homes, already burning, were demolished by the shock wave, which also knocked down cinderblock walls and brick apartment buildings.

Those who had taken shelter underground—or, more probably, just happened to be there—survived for fifteen minutes or a half hour longer than those who were exposed. They suffocated as oxygen was drawn away by the firestorm that soon raged overhead.

At O'Hare Airport, the world's busiest, aircraft engaged in landing or takeoff crashed and burned. Planes on the ground were buffeted into each other and adjacent hangars, their fuselages bent and partially crushed by the shock wave. Some thirty seconds before the shock wave struck, aluminum surfaces facing the fireball had melted and the aircraft interiors had been set aflame.   Erwin Kroll and Theodore Pastol, "The Day the Bomb Went Off"

EXERCISE 16.9

Writers often use scenarios to discuss the possible effects of trends or events. Choose one of the following trends, and write a scenario illustrating the possible effects.

1. The effects of cable TV's popularity on commercial and public TV

2. The effects of the widespread popularity of aerobic dancing and exercise on Americans

3. The effects of increasing tuition costs on college students

4. The effects on American society if colleges were available only to the very wealthy

5. The effects on American culture if the United States ran out of gasoline

EXERCISE 16.10

Scenarios predict positive or negative outcomes of trends, events, or actions. They are especially useful to proposal writers who want to make conjectures about the results of accepting a solution—or an alternative solution—to a problem.

In Chapter 6, Jeanette Germain describes a scenario in paragraph 14 of her essay "What to Name the Children When He's Kept His Name and You've Kept Yours." Read this brief scenario and identify its purpose in Germain's essay.

Comparing and Contrasting

Writers use comparison to analyze and evaluate two or more things. We might compare two people we know well, three motorcycles we are considering buying for a cross-country tour, four Humphrey Bogart movies, three lemon trees that are growing at different rates against the white stucco wall near the pool, or two theories about the causes of inflation and unemployment. But as soon as comparison begins, contrast edges its way in, for rarely are two things totally alike. The contrasts, or differences, between the four Bogart movies may be more enlightening than the similarities. *Comparison*, then, brings similar things together for examination, to see how they are alike. *Contrast* is a form of comparison that emphasizes their differences.

Comparison and contrast is more than a writing strategy, of course. It is a basic way of thinking and learning. We compare objects, events, and ideas as readily as we evaluate them. A basic principle of learning theory says that we acquire new concepts most readily if we can see how they are similar to or different from concepts we already know.

Professional writers say that comparison and contrast is a basic strategy they would not want to be without. For some writing situations (like the ones above) it has no substitute. Indeed, some writing is essentially extended comparison. But for all lengths and kinds of writing, comparison and contrast regularly alternates with other writing strategies in presenting information.

Chances are good that you will confront many test questions and essay assignments asking you to compare and contrast some things—two poems, three presidents, four procedures for surveying public opinion. This is a popular format with instructors in all academic disciplines, because it requires critical, analytical thinking and writing. They see it as one of the best ways to challenge students intellectually.

TWO WAYS OF COMPARING AND CONTRASTING

There are two ways to organize comparison and contrast in writing: in chunks and in sequence. In *chunking*, each item of the comparison is presented separately; in *sequencing*, the items are compared point by point.

17

For example, a chunked comparison of two motorcycles would present all points about the Pirsig 241X first and then consider all points about the Kawazuki 500S, whereas a sequenced comparison would consider the Pirsig and the Kawazuki point by point. In a chunked comparison discussion is organized around each separate item being compared. In a sequenced comparison it is organized around each common feature of the items being compared.

Look now at an example of chunked comparison, one that contrasts the effects westward migration had on American men in the nineteenth century with its effects on women:

> The westward move for many men was the physical expression of a break with the past and a setting out for a new life. The journey occurred when the rhythms of maturity were primed for a change. The determination to go West was either the initial separation from a man's parental family or the second major move, the move "upward" in the search for economic mobility and success. The adventure took on the color of some "dramatic rite of passage to mastery and adulthood" in the life cycle of frontier men.
>
> <u>But</u> the journey could have no natural place in the life cycle of the women. The journey was a violation of life's natural rhythms for women of childbearing years. There was simply no way that the rigorous exertions of the overland journey could be considered "normal" for a pregnant woman. And yet a woman's pregnancy mattered very little to emigrant families; certainly it was not sufficient cause to defer the trip.
>
> Even with the best of care, childbirth was a precarious business in the nineteenth century. It was even more risky on the open road, followed by immediate travel in a wagon with no springs and with very little access to water for drinking or for bathing. Any complications of delivery proved critical. And frailty in the newborn was life-threatening. The prospect of childbirth on the Trail must have meant months of heightened anxiety to women.   Lillian Schlissel, *Women's Diaries of the Westward Journey*

The two parts of the comparison—men and women—are discussed separately, first one and then the other. The shift from the first discussion to the contrasting one is signaled by the word *but* and by a new paragraph. Each discussion begins with a general statement which is then developed by examples.

A biology text provides another example of a chunked comparison. This selection, from a chapter on evolution, contrasts Lamarckian and modern views of evolutionary change. (Have you ever wondered how giraffes got their long necks?) Here the shift to the second half of the discussion occurs at the beginning of the last paragraph. The writer signals the contrast with an unmistakable transitional expression: *on the other hand*.

> The theory of *evolution by natural selection* proposed by Darwin and Wallace had an influential rival during the nineteenth century in the concept of *evolution by the inheritance of acquired characteristics*—an old and widely held idea often identified with Jean Baptiste de Lamarck (1744–1829), who was one of its more prominent supporters in the early 1800s.
>
> The Lamarckian hypothesis was that somatic characteristics acquired by an individual during its lifetime could be transmitted to its offspring. Thus the characteristics of each generation would be determined, in part at least, by all that happened to the members of the preceding generations—by all the modifications that occurred in them, including those caused by experience, use and disuse of body parts, and accidents. Evolutionary change would be the gradual accumulation of such acquired modifications over many generations. The classic example (though by now rather hackneyed) is the evolution of the long necks of giraffes.
>
> According to the Lamarckian view, ancestral giraffes with short necks tended to stretch their necks as much as they could to reach the tree foliage that served as a major part of their food. This frequent neck stretching caused their offspring to have slightly longer necks. Since these also stretched their necks, the next generation had still longer necks. And so, as a result of neck stretching to reach higher and higher foliage, each generation had slightly longer necks than the preceding generation.
>
> The modern theory of natural selection, <u>on the other hand,</u> proposes that ancestral giraffes probably had short necks, but that the precise length of the neck varied from individual to individual because of their different genotypes. If the supply of food was somewhat limited, then individuals with longer necks had a better chance of surviving and leaving progeny than those with shorter necks. This means, not that all the individuals with shorter necks perished or that all with longer necks survived to reproduce, but simply that a slightly higher proportion of those with longer necks survived and left offspring. As a result, the proportion of individuals with genes for longer necks increased slightly with each succeeding generation.   William T. Keeton, *Biological Science*

Schematically, a chunked comparison looks simple enough. As the two preceding examples show, it is easy to block off such a discussion in a text and then point to the various parts. And yet it can in fact be more complicated for a writer to plan than a sequenced comparison. Sequenced comparison may be closer to the way people perceive and think about similarities or differences in things. For example, if you noticed that two surfboards were different, this awareness would probably come all at once. Yet you would identify the specific differences one at a time. A sequenced comparison would point to the differences in just this way—one at a time—whereas a chunked comparison would present all the features of one surfboard and then do the same for the second. Thus the chunked strategy requires that a writer organize all the points of comparison before starting to write. With sequencing, however, it is possible to take up each point of comparison as it comes to mind.

In the next example, John McPhee uses sequencing to contrast Florida and California oranges:

> An orange grown in Florida usually has a thin and tightly fitting skin, and it is also heavy with juice. Californians say that if you want to eat a Florida orange you have to get into a bathtub first. California oranges are light in weight and have thick skins that break easily and come off in hunks. The flesh inside is marvelously sweet, and the segments almost separate themselves. In Florida, it is said that you can run over a California orange with a ten-ton truck and not even wet the pavement. The differences from which these hyperboles arise will prevail in the two states even if the type of orange is the same. In arid climates, like California's, oranges develop a thick albedo, which is the white part of the skin. Florida is one of the two or three most rained-upon states in the United States. California uses the Colorado River and similarly impressive sources to irrigate its oranges, but of course irrigation can only do so much. The annual difference in rainfall between the Florida and California orange-growing areas is one million one hundred and forty thousand gallons per acre. For years, California was the leading orange state, but Florida surpassed California in 1942, and grows three times as many oranges now. California oranges, for their part, can safely be called three times as beautiful.
> John McPhee, *Oranges*

The points of contrast between Florida and California oranges are taken up in sequence: thickness of skin, juiciness, rainfall differences that account for the skin and juiciness, production, beauty. Notice that the sequence is not perfectly symmetrical: McPhee devotes more sentences to some contrasts than to others.

In the next example, from David Attenborough's natural history of the earth, sequencing is used to draw an elegant contrast between bird wings and airplane wings:

> Bird wings have a much more complex job to do than the wings of an aeroplane, for in addition to supporting the bird they must act as its engine, rowing it through the air. Even so the wing outline of a bird conforms to the same aerodynamic principles as those eventually discov-

<u>ered by man when designing his aeroplanes,</u> and if you know how different kinds of aircraft perform, you can predict the flight capabilities of similarly shaped birds.

Short stubby wings enable a tanager and other forest-living birds to swerve and dodge at speed through the undergrowth just as they helped the fighter planes of the Second World War to make tight turns and aerobatic manoeuvres in a dog-fight. More modern fighters achieve greater speeds by sweeping back their wings while in flight, just as peregrines do when they go into a 130 kph dive, stooping to a kill. Championship gliders have long thin wings so that, having gained height in a thermal up-current they can soar gently down for hours and an albatross, the largest of flying birds, with a similar wing shape and a span of 3 metres, can patrol the ocean for hours in the same way without a single wing beat. Vultures and hawks circle at very slow speeds supported by a thermal and they have the broad rectangular wings that very slow flying aircraft have. Man has not been able to adapt wings to provide hovering flight. He has only achieved that with the whirling horizontal blades of a helicopter or the downward-pointing engines of a vertical landing jet. Hummingbirds have paralleled even this. They tilt their bodies so that they are almost upright and then beat their wings as fast as 80 times a second producing a similar down-draught of air. So the hummingbird can hover and even fly backwards. David Attenborough, *Life on Earth*

The important thing to note about this example is the limited, focused basis for the comparison: the shape of wings. Attenborough specifies this basis in the second sentence of the passage (underscored here). Though birds and planes both fly, there is almost nothing else they have in common. They are so obviously different that it would even seem silly to compare them in writing. But Attenborough finds a valid—and surprising—basis for comparison and develops it in a way that is both informative and entertaining. A successful comparison always has these qualities: a valid basis for comparison, a limited focus, and information that will catch a reader's attention.

EXERCISE 17.1

Pick any one of the following subjects and write several sentences comparing and contrasting. Be careful to limit the basis for your comparison, and underline the sentence that states the *basis* for the comparison.

two sports

two explanations or theories

two ways of achieving the same goal (travel by bus or subway, using flattery or persuasion to get what you want) two things that seem to be unlikely subjects for comparison (a child and a puppy, soccer and ballet)

EXERCISE 17.2

Analyze the specified comparisons in the following selections from Part I. How is each comparison organized? (It may or may not be neatly chunked or sequenced.) Why do you think the writer organizes the comparison in that way? What is the role of the comparison in the whole piece? How effective do you consider the comparison?

Chapter 5 "The Black Death," William Langer, paragraphs 13–16 and 19–22

Chapter 7 "The Treasure of the Sierra Madre," James Agee, paragraph 2

Chapter 7 "The Civil Rights Movement: What Good Was It?" Alice Walker, paragraphs 7 and 8

Chapter 7 "Joe DiMaggio," Red Smith, paragraphs 1–7

Chapter 8 "Suicide among Young People," Victor Fuchs, paragraph 2

Chapter 10 "Holy Water," Joan Didion, paragraph 4

EXERCISE 17.3

Some of the selections in Part I are organized around comparisons. Identify and evaluate the comparisons in each of the following pieces. (Remember that the comparison may be stated or implied.)

Chapter 2 "Smooth and Easy," Russell Baker

Chapter 3 "Dashiell Hammett," Lillian Hellman

Chapter 6 "What to Name the Children When He's Kept His Name and You've Kept Yours," Jeanette Germain

Chapter 7 "Joe DiMaggio," Red Smith

Chapter 10 "The Pinball Philosophy," John McPhee

ANALOGY

One special form of comparison is the *analogy,* in which one part of the comparison is used simply to explain the other. See how John McPhee uses two different analogies—the twelve-month calendar and the distance along two widespread arms—to explain the duration of geologic time.

In like manner, geologists will sometimes use the calendar year as a unit to represent the time scale, and in such terms the Precambrian runs from New Year's Day until well after Halloween. Dinosaurs appear in the middle of December and are gone the day after Christmas. The last ice sheet melts on December 31st at one minute before midnight, and the Roman Empire lasts five seconds. With your arms spread wide again to represent all time on earth, look at one hand with its line of life. The Cambrian begins in the wrist, and the Permian Extinction is at the outer end of the palm. All of the Cenozoic is in a fingerprint, and in a single stroke with a medium-grained nail file you could eradicate human history. Geologists live with the geologic scale. Individually, they may or may not be alarmed by the rate of exploitation of the things they discover, but, like the environmentalists, they use these repetitive analogies to place the human record in perspective—to see the Age of Reflection, the last few thousand years, as a small bright sparkle at the end of time.   John McPhee, *Basin and Range*

You may have seen other analogies to geologic time. Because it takes a great imaginative leap to comprehend this concept, writers consistently rely on analogy to explain it.

Scientists have always made good use of analogy—in both their thinking and their writing. Modern physics, in particular, is full of concepts that strain the comprehension and imagination of the nonscientist. One such concept is the uncertainty principle, a concept that is very difficult for anybody but a physicist to define. In the following excerpt, Gary Zukav does so with an analogy—likening the uncertainty principle to a movie projector that is always slightly out of focus.

The uncertainty principle reveals that as we penetrate deeper and deeper into the subatomic realm, we reach a certain point at which one part or another of our picture of nature becomes blurred, and there is no way to reclarify that part without blurring another part of the picture! It is as though we are adjusting a moving picture that is slightly out of focus. As we make the final adjustments, we are astonished to discover that when the right side of the picture clears, the left side of the picture becomes completely unfocused and nothing in it is recognizable. When we try to focus the left side of the picture, the right side starts to blur and soon the situation is reversed. If we try to strike a balance between these two extremes, both sides of the picture return to a recognizable condition, but in no way can we remove the original fuzziness from them.

The right side of the picture, in the original formulation of the uncertainty principle, corresponds to the position in space of a moving particle. The left side of the picture corresponds to its momentum. According to the uncertainty principle, we cannot measure accurately, at the same time, both the position *and* the momentum of a moving particle. The more precisely we determine one of these properties, the less we know about the other. If we precisely determine the position of the particle, then, strange as it sounds, there is *nothing* that we can know about its momentum. If we precisely determine the momentum of the particle, there is no way to determine its position.   Gary Zukav, *The Dancing Wu Li Masters: An Overview of the New Physics*

Notice what a strong visual image Zukav's analogy produces—it is very easy to imagine alternating sides of the movie screen going in and out of focus. Explanatory analogies almost always use very familiar objects for comparison, probably because they are trying to explain something very unfamiliar.

Here is a sports analogy from a sociological study of Hamilton, Ohio. It comes from a chapter describing a hearing held to examine a school board's decision to fire one teacher, Sam Shie. The writer uses analogy to describe the three lawyers, comparing them to an aggressive basketball team.

> The cross-examination of Dr. Helms was conducted by Randy Rogers, the young associate of Holbrock's. Rogers was tall and strongly built, lacking by only a couple of inches the height of a professional basketball player who weakens the opposition by fouling often and drawing fouls in return. This was close to the function Rogers performed for the defense. With Hugh Holbrock, Robert Dunlevey, and Randy Rogers all ranged against Carl Morgenstern, it was sometimes hard to tell just who the underdog was at the hearings. Sam Shie, to be sure, was a lone teacher up against a community's educational establishment which was trying to purge him. But at the hearings themselves, almost all the spectators were on Shie's side; he was being supported by the Ohio Education Association, and he had three articulate, variously styled lawyers who disputed virtually everything Carl Morgenstern or one of his witnesses said. Each came at Morgenstern from a different angle with a new tactic, trying to wear him down the way a basketball team will use a full-court press, a fast break, the setting of a pick or screen, the switching of defensive assignments to bewilder an opponent. Hugh Holbrock made long, arcing, oratorical shots from outside the key, Robert Dunlevey dribbled spectacularly around any position Morgenstern took, and Randy Rogers would try to provoke Morgenstern into exchanges of anger and procedural wrangles. Rogers was surly to Morgenstern, who would respond by being loftily sardonic. A few times Morgenstern slipped and got mad at Rogers, who was polite to witnesses but steeled himself to a single pitch of fury when he was addressing Morgenstern. The rest of the time Rogers sat moodily at the defense table—in effect on the bench—while Holbrock and Dunlevey performed their own specialties.   Peter Davis, *Hometown*

Analogies are tricky. They may at first seem useful, but actually it is a rare analogy that is consistently useful at all the major points of comparison. Some analogies break down early; others are downright misleading.

To be successful, a writer must carry out a conceptual analysis to be sure the analogy really holds.

Thus, most writers exercise caution with analogy, using it less often than definition, classification, or illustration, for instance. Nevertheless, you will run across analogies regularly; indeed, it would be hard to find a book without one. For certain very abstract information and some writing situations, analogy is the writing strategy of choice.

EXERCISE 17.4

Choose a principle or process that you know well. You might select a basic principle from the natural or social sciences; or you could consider a complex bodily movement, a physiological process, or a process of social change.

Write an analogy of several sentences that explains this principle or process to a reader who is unfamiliar with it. Look for something very familiar to compare it with that will help the reader understand the principle or process without a technical explanation. You may find yourself making some false starts, where your analogy holds up for only a few sentences. Writing out the analogy lets you discover whether it is plausible, consistent, and truly explanatory.

EXERCISE 17.5

In Chapter 10 John McPhee uses an analogy in his presentation of the pinball game between Lukas and Buckley (paragraphs 12–29). What is this analogy? What advantages or disadvantages do you see in this analogy? Why do you think McPhee chose it? Evaluate its effectiveness within the essay as a whole.

PART THREE

Research Strategies

Invention and Inquiry

This chapter presents a catalogue of strategies writers use to explore their subjects and to find out what they have to say about them. Writers are like scientists: they ask questions, inquiring about how things work, what they are, where they occur, and how more information can be learned about them. Writers are also like artists: they use what they know and have learned to create something new and imaginative, inventing meaning and form.

These invention and inquiry strategies are not mysterious or magical. They are tricks of the trade available to everyone and should appeal to your common sense and experience in solving problems. Developed by writers, psychologists, and linguists, they represent the ways writers, engineers, scientists, composers—in fact, all of us—creatively solve problems.

Once these general strategies become familiar, they will help you tackle any writing situation you encounter in college or on the job. The best way to learn these strategies is to use them as you write an actual essay. Part I, Chapters 2–10, shows you when these general strategies can be most helpful and how to make the most efficient use of them. The guides to invention and research in these chapters offer easy-to-use adaptations of the general strategies, adaptations designed to satisfy the special requirements of the essay you are writing.

The general strategies for invention and inquiry in this chapter are grouped into three categories:

Mapping: a condensed visual representation of your thinking or planning

Writing: the composition of phrases or sentences to discover information and ideas and to find relationships among ideas

Reading: a systematic use of reading to understand and to explore information for its possibilities in your own writing

Within each category the individual strategies are arranged alphabetically.

The invention and inquiry activities give you a powerful advantage in thinking and planning for writing. They enable you to explore and research a topic fully before you begin drafting, and they also help you solve problems as you are drafting and before you revise.

18

MAPPING

Mapping involves making a visual record of invention and inquiry. Writers use mapping strategies to help them think about a topic. In making maps, they usually use key words and phrases—their private shorthand or code—to record material they want to remember, questions they need to answer, and even new sources of information they want to check. The maps they create show the ideas, details, and facts they are examining. They also show possible ways materials can be connected and focused. Maps might be informal graphic displays with words and phrases circled and connected by lines to show relationships, or they might be formal sentence outlines. Mapping can be especially useful because it gives you an immediate visual representation of your thinking and planning. Mapping strategies include clustering, listing, and outlining.

Clustering   Clustering is an invention activity which reveals possible relations among facts and ideas. Unlike listing (the next mapping strategy), clustering requires a brief period of initial planning. You must first come up with a tentative division of the topic into subparts or main ideas. Clustering works as follows:

1. In a word or phrase, write your topic in the center of a piece of paper. Circle it.

2. Also in a word or phrase, write down the main parts or central ideas of your topic. Circle these, and connect them to the topic in the center.

3. The next step is to generate facts, details, examples, or ideas related in any way to these main parts of the topic. Cluster these around the main parts.

Clustering can be useful for any kind of writing. Writers use it in the early stages of planning an essay in order to find subtopics in a topic or to organize information. They may try and discard several clusters before finding one that is promising. Writers also use clustering to plan brief sections of an essay as they are drafting.

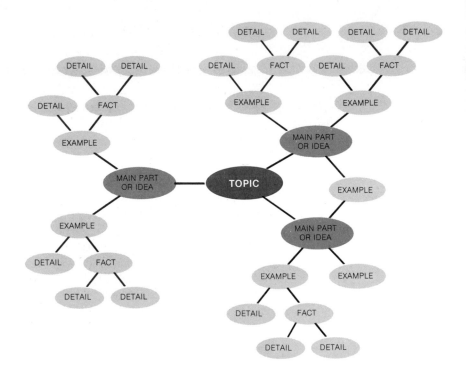

Listing   Listing is a familiar activity. We make shopping lists and lists of errands to do or people to call. A list of things to accomplish can reassure us when we are behind in our work or facing deadlines.

Listing can also be a great help in planning an essay. It enables you to recall what you already know about a topic and suggests what more you may need to find out. It is an easy way to get started doing something productive, instead of just worrying about what you will write. A list has an interesting way of riding along on its own momentum. The first item in the list leads easily to the next.

Listing has always been a basic activity for writers. It can be especially useful for those who have little time for planning—for example, reporters facing deadlines or college students taking essay exams. Listing lets you put your ideas in order quickly. It can also help as a first step in discovering possible writing topics.

Listing is a solitary form of brainstorming, a popular technique of problem solving in groups. If you were working with a group to generate ideas for a cooperative writing project, then you would be engaged in true brainstorming.

Here is how listing works best as an invention activity:

1. Give your list a title.

2. Write as fast as you can, relying on short phrases.

3. Include anything that seems at all useful. Do not try to be judgmental at this point.

4. After you have finished, or even as you write, reflect on the list and organize it in the following way. This is a very important step, for it may lead you to further discoveries about your topic.

> put an asterisk by the most promising items
>
> number key items in order of importance
>
> put items in related groups
>
> cross out items that do not seem promising
>
> add new items

Outlining   Outlining is both a way of planning and a means of inventing. Any outline may provide the plan for an essay; but, as soon as you start making an outline, you will begin to see new possibilities in your subject. You may discover new ways of dividing or grouping information. You can estimate whether you have adequate information to develop each major point. You will know whether there is a plan for the information which will be appropriate for your tentative thesis. If not, you may decide to revise your thesis.

There are three main forms of outlining: scratch, topic, and sentence. (Keep in mind that clustering and treeing are also ways of outlining.)

A scratch outline is an informal outline, really only a rough list of the main points (and sometimes subpoints as well) of an essay. You have no doubt made scratch outlines many times—both to clarify difficult reading and to plan essays or essay exams. As an example, here is a scratch outline for Victor Fuchs's essay in Chapter 8.

SUICIDE AMONG YOUNG PEOPLE

death rate rising for 15–24 year olds

mainly more murders and suicides

why more suicides?—not a result of new ways of reporting suicides or of Vietnam War or of bad economy

causes probably in family—divorce, no discipline, loss of father

increase in suicide really is unique to this age group

no simple solution possible

We can imagine Fuchs making such a scratch outline before he began drafting his essay. (A different scratch outline emphasizing strategies of causal analysis rather than content follows Fuchs's essay.)

Scratch outlines can help you organize information while you are still gathering it. The Guide to Writing for each chapter in Part I offers possibilities for outlining the kind of writing you are working on in that chapter. Before you begin a first draft, organize your invention and research notes in a scratch outline. As you draft, you may need to change this scratch outline. Once you have had advice on your draft and a chance to consider revising it, you may need a new scratch outline for a differently organized revision.

Items in an outline do not necessarily coincide with paragraphs, although they may. Sometimes two or more items may be developed in the same paragraph. At other times one item may represent two or more paragraphs. Whether items in an outline represent paragraphs or not, they usually do not indicate the extent to which that item is developed in the essay.

Topic and sentence outlines are more formal than scratch outlines. They follow a conventional format of numbered and lettered headings and subheadings. Some instructors require topic or sentence outlines with essays or research papers. Following is a *topic* outline of Fuchs's essay:

SUICIDE AMONG YOUNG PEOPLE

I. Increasing death rate in the 15–24 age group
II. Increase explained by self-destructive behavior
   A. Homicide
   B. Suicide
III. Unacceptable causes of the increase
   A. Change in reporting of suicides
   B. Attitudes towards Vietnam War
   C. Unemployment and weak economy
IV. Probable causes of the increase
   A. Divorce or lack of discipline
   B. Loss of father
V. Increase in suicides unique to 15–24 age group
VI. Challenge of this problem for public policy

Notice that a period follows the Roman numerals and capital letters. The items in the outline are words or brief phrases, not sentences. Each item is not followed by a period, and the first word is capitalized. It is customary in a topic outline for items at the same level of indentation to be grammatically parallel. Under Item IV, for instance, the A and B items both begin with nouns:

A. *Divorce* or lack of discipline
B. *Loss* of father

The items would not be grammatically parallel if B began with an infinitive phrase (*to* plus a verb), like this:

A. *Divorce* or lack of discipline
B. *To lose* a father

Following is a *sentence* outline of Fuchs's essay. The items are complete sentences, with the first word capitalized and the last word followed by a period.

SUICIDE AMONG YOUNG PEOPLE

I. The death rate is rising only for Americans in the age group 15–24.
II. This increase is a result of self-destructive behavior.
    A. The homicide rate is rising in the 15–24 age group, especially among blacks.
    B. The suicide rate is also increasing.
III. Many explanations have been offered for the increasing suicide rate.
    A. The trend is not the result of a change in ways of reporting suicides.
    B. The trend cannot be explained by attitudes toward the Vietnam War.
    C. The trend cannot be explained by unemployment or a bad economy.
IV. The causes of the trend can most probably be located in family situations.
    A. Children in families where little guidance is provided or where parents are divorced are more likely to commit suicide.
    B. Children who have lost a father are more likely to commit suicide.
V. The increase in suicide rates is unique to the 15–24 age group.
VI. Whatever the cause of the increasing suicide rate among young people, since there is no apparent solution, it creates a serious challenge to public policy.

Sentence outlines can be considerably more detailed than this one, to the point of containing most of the information in the essay; but for an essay the length of Fuchs's they are usually about as detailed as this one. Should you want to make a more detailed outline, you would probably need more levels of information than the preceding two outlines contain; and you would follow this convention for identifying levels:

    I. (Main topic)
        A. (Subtopic of I)
        B.
            1. (Subtopic of I.B)
            2.
                a. (Subtopic of I.B.2)
                b.
                    (1) (Subtopic of I.B.2.b.)
                    (2)
                        (a) (Subtopic of I.B.2.b.(1))
                        (b)

Any division of a topic at one level must result in at least two items in the level beneath it.

WRITING

Not surprisingly, writers rely heavily on writing to find out what they know about a topic. Writing itself is a powerful tool for thinking. By writing, you can recall details of scenes or people, remember facts and ideas, find connections in new information you have collected.

Unlike most mapping strategies, the strategy of writing invites you to produce complete sentences. The sentence gives this strategy much of its generative power. Because sentences are complete statements, they take you further than listing or clustering. They enable you to explore ideas and define relationships, to bring ideas together or show how they differ, to identify causes and effects. Sentences can follow one another naturally and develop a chain of thought.

This section presents several invention and inquiry strategies which invite you to formulate complete sentences and thus produce brief exploratory pieces of writing. Some are guided, systematic strategies, while others are more flexible. Even though they call for complete sentences that are related to one another, they do not require planning or polishing. They may be associational or fragmentary, playful or serious.

The writing strategies for invention and inquiry include cubing, dialogues, diaries, dramatizing, drafting, dictating, journals, looping, and questioning.

Cubing Cubing is useful for a quick exploration of a writing topic. It lets you probe the topic from six different perspectives. The activity is known as cubing because a cube has six sides. Following are the six perspectives in cubing:

Describing What does your subject look like? What size is it? Color? Shape? Texture? Name its parts.

Comparing What is your subject similar to? Different from?

Associating What does it make you think of? What connections does it have to anything else in your experience? Be creative here. Include any connection you can think of.

Analyzing How is it made? Where did it come from? Where is it going? How are its parts related?

Applying What can you do with it? What uses does it have?

Arguing What arguments can you make for it? Against it?

Following are some rules that will help you to use cubing productively:

1. Select a topic or subject or even part of a subject. This can be a person, a scene, an event, an object, a problem, an idea, or an issue. Hold it in focus.

2. Write about the subject from *all six* of the cubing perspectives.

3. Limit yourself to three to five minutes for each perspective. The whole activity will then take no more than a half hour.

4. Keep going until you have written about your subject from all six perspectives. Remember that the special advantage of cubing is the quick *multiple* perspectives it provides.

5. As you write from each perspective, begin with what you know about your subject. However, do not limit yourself to your present knowledge. Indicate what else you need to know about your subject, and suggest where you might find that information.

6. Reread what you have written. Look for bright spots, surprises. Recall the part that was easiest for you to write. Recall the part where you felt a special momentum and pleasure in the writing. Look for an angle or an unexpected insight. These special parts may suggest a focus or a topic within a larger subject, or they may provide specific details to include in a draft.

Dialogues A dialogue is a conversation between two or more people. You can use dialogue to search for topics, find a focus, explore ideas, or consider opposing viewpoints. As an invention activity, writing a dialogue requires you to make up all parts of the conversation. Imagine two particular people talking, or hold a conversation yourself with some imagined person, or pretend that you are talking out loud to yourself. Follow these steps:

1. Write a conversation between two speakers. Label the speakers "1" and "2," or make up names for them.

2. If you get stuck, you might have one of the speakers ask the other a question.

3. Write brief responses in order to keep the conversation moving fast. Do not spend much time planning or rehearsing responses. Write what first occurs to you—just as in a real conversation, where people take quick turns to prevent any awkward silences.

You can find an example of a dialogue in the Writer at Work section at the end of Chapter 2: Remembering Events. In that dialogue a college writer is re-creating a conversation with someone in an event she plans to write about.

Dialogues can be especially useful with personal experience essays about events, people, and places. For these kinds of writing, dialogues help you remember relationships and rehearse conversations you might want to include in a draft. Dialogues can also help you recall conversations with significant people in an activity or a place you are profiling or anticipate counterarguments to any of your points in a proposal, an evaluation, or a causal explanation.

Diaries   Many people keep a private diary at some point in their lives. For some it serves only as a log of daily events, but for others it is a form of serious analysis of problems, crises, relations with other people. In these ways writing in a diary is not a preparation for other writing, for it serves an immediate, practical purpose.

Most professional writers, especially poets, novelists, and screenwriters, would make no distinction between their private diaries and their public journals. All of their experience is potentially public in that any of it may end up in some form in their creative writing. Even though you might never base later writings on your diary, it still can contribute in important ways to your writing development. For that reason we suggest briefly kinds of writing you can include in your diary that go beyond mere summary and comment on events.

☐ Make lists of things that upset you, frighten you, interest you, make you skeptical.

☐ Write about your fantasies and dreams.

☐ Write about yourself objectively as "he" or "she."

☐ Write letters you would never send.

☐ Write dialogues.

Dramatizing   Dramatizing is an invention activity based on the idea that people behave very much like actors in a play. It was developed by the philosopher Kenneth Burke as a way of thinking about how people interact in real life and as a way of analyzing literature and the arts.

Thinking about human behavior in dramatic terms can be very productive for writers. Drama has action, actors, setting, motives, and methods. Since stars and acting go together, you can use a five-pointed star to remember these five points of dramatizing:

Each point provides a different perspective on human behavior. We can think of each point independently and in various combinations. Let us begin by looking at each point in order to see how it helps us analyze people and their interactions.

Action. An action is anything that happens, has happened, will happen, or could happen. Action includes events that are physical (running a marathon or eating a meal), mental (discovering a cure for cancer or thinking about a book you have read), and emotional (falling in love or feeling depressed). This category also refers to the results of activity (a term paper or a sweater).

Actor. The actor is involved in the action. He or she may be responsible for it or simply be affected by it. The actor does not have to be a person. It can be a force, something that causes an action. For example, if the action is a rise in the price of roller skates, the actor could be increased demand or short supply. Dramatizing may also include a number of co-actors working together or at odds with one another.

Setting. The setting is the situation, the background of the action. We usually think of setting as the place and time an event occurs, but it can also refer to the historical background of an event or the childhood of a person.

Motive. The motive is the purpose or reason for an action. It refers to the intention actors may have or the end an action serves.

Method. Method is the way an action occurs, the techniques an actor uses. It refers to whatever makes things happen. Each of these points suggests a simple invention question:

Action = What?
Actor = Who?
Setting = When and where?
Motive = Why?
Method = How?

This list looks like the familiar newspaper reporter's invention activity for remembering to include all the essential details in a report of an event. But dramatizing goes further, in that it enables us to consider a much fuller set of invention questions generated by considering relations or interactions between the five elements of a dramatic situation. We can think about actors' motives, the effect of the setting on the actors, the relations between actors, and so on.

We have adapted Burke's invention activity for use in exploring human motivations and relationships in particular events or situations, fictional or real. Hence, you could use this activity to learn more about yourself in an event you were going to narrate, about other people you wanted to write about, or about significant people in a place you were going to write about. You could use it, as well, to explore characters in stories or movies you were analyzing or evaluating. You could also use it to analyze readers who might resist your solution to a problem.

To use this activity, imagine the person you want to write about (yourself, another person, a fictional character) in a particular situation or event or series of events. Holding this image in focus, write answers to any questions in the following list that apply. You may draw a blank on some questions. You may have little to say to some and a lot to say to others. Be exploratory and playful. Write quickly, following digressions; relying on words, lists, phrases, even drawings; composing sentences.

☐ What did the person do?
☐ How did the person come to be involved in this situation or event?
☐ Why does the person do what he or she does?
☐ What goals is the person trying to accomplish?
☐ How is the person trying to accomplish these goals?
☐ To what extent do other people in the event recognize what the person is trying to accomplish?

☐ What might prevent this person from carrying out these goals?

☐ What might the person do that he or she is not doing?

☐ What do the person's actions reveal about the person?

☐ What does the person's language reveal about the person?

☐ How does the event's setting influence the person's actions?

☐ How does the time of the event influence what the person does?

☐ Where did this person come from?

☐ How is this person different from what he or she used to be?

☐ What might this person become?

☐ How is this person like others in the event?

☐ How is this person different from others in the event?

Drafting   Sometimes writers know approximately what they want to say. Sometimes, too, writers have time for only one draft and possibly a quick revision. Even in these situations, listing or clustering can be useful. Still, there are occasions when the appropriate thing to do is to write or dictate a complete draft, attempting to come as close as possible to the finished version you imagine. For example, an experienced newspaper reporter may type or dictate over the phone a brief news report that requires little revision at the copy editor's desk. After many years on the job, the head of a National Weather Bureau station can confidently draft the brief hourly weather forecast that is broadcast locally. Once the research data are organized and interpreted, a medical researcher who has published dozens of reports in specialized journals can quickly draft a new report that conforms closely to the format required by those journals. A college senior who has just won a national prize for a collection of her photographs can readily explain what was new in that work in a letter to the high school art teacher who introduced her to photography.

These expert writers and talkers would probably concede that with more time for invention their writing would be even stronger. Nevertheless, in some writing situations an immediate attempt at a complete draft is a good strategy, and in such situations the goal is to come as close as possible to your best prose on the first attempt. There are two ways in which even this strategy is an invention activity, however: (1) all composing is a discovery of what you want to say and how to say it, and (2) some revisions are nonetheless required in nearly all attempts.

There are no special rules for immediate drafting and dictating. You will want to bypass one of the other invention strategies in this chapter and immediately attempt a full draft only under these conditions:

☐ You consider yourself unusually knowledgeable about the topic.

☐ You feel certain you already know essentially what you want to say. You have a focus, a thesis, a rough plan, even a vision of where it will all come out.

☐ You have written about the topic many times.

Even if you are desperately short of time, you cannot produce good writing unless you can meet these conditions.

As you write an immediate draft, you may get stuck. The clock is ticking. Your instructor or your colleagues expect a draft early tomorrow. You feel a twinge of panic. Under such conditions, make a diversion to listing, clustering, even a brief looping exercise (discussed later in this chapter) to get yourself unstuck.

Dictating   Dictating is still used in the business world for letters, memos, and brief reports. The person dictating attempts to construct written discourse orally. With experience, many people become surprisingly adept at this activity.

A few professional writers, including some novelists, dictate early versions of their books. Here, they use dictation less as a shortcut to finished text than as a tentative, exploratory invention activity. These dictations nearly always require extensive revisions and sometimes are discarded as mere warmups.

The major limitation to dictation is that taped material must then be typed or written out. Since thirty minutes of dictation produces many pages of typescript, transcription can be time consuming and costly. For those who can employ it, however, dictation and transcription can be a productive writing strategy, both for immediate drafts and for inventive explorations.

The technology of dictation is now available to everyone in the form of inexpensive portable tape recorders. The only barrier to its widespread use in composing remains the cost of transcription. However, this cost may not be a barrier for long. Researchers are close to solving the technical problems of converting talk instantaneously into print on a word processor, thus allowing writers to see immediately what they have said.

Journals   Professional writers often use journals to keep notes, and so might you. It is quite easy to start a writer's journal. Buy a special spiral or bound notebook, and start writing. Here are some possibilities:

☐ Keep a list of new words you encounter. Always include the full sentence in which you found the word.

☐ Write about concepts you learn in courses you take. These entries will help you clarify new concepts and remember them. You could also write about the progress and direction of your learning in particular courses—the experience of being in the course, your feelings about what is happening and what you are learning. For this journal activity—and others concerned with writing to clarify and elaborate new learning—write experimentally and playfully. You may sometimes want to start writing immediately, without planning or rehearsing, just to see what the act of writing itself will lead you to. Try different styles and voices. Do not worry too much about spelling or punctuation.

☐ Respond to your reading, assigned and personal. Write about your personal associations to the reading, your reflections, reactions, evaluations. Try to explain new concepts. Paraphrase difficult passages. Summarize important passages. Copy memorable sentences and short passages and comment on them. (This last activity—copying and commenting—has been practiced by students and writers for centuries under the name *commonplace book*. In a commonplace book writers copied notable passages from books and then commented on them.)

☐ Write to prepare for particular class meetings. If you know the topic of the lecture or discussion, write about the main ideas you have learned from assigned readings. Write about the relation of these new ideas to other ideas in the course or to information you have picked up elsewhere. List questions you have about the topic. After class, write to summarize what you have learned. List questions you have about the ideas presented or discussed in class.

Writing in this way to prepare for classes, or to summarize them, is quite different from the writing that you will collect in your class notebook, where you will record a portion of the content of the lecture or discussion. Recording on the spot the information being passed along by others is an important part of being a student, but it does not involve reflecting, evaluating, interpreting, synthesizing, summarizing—the kinds of thinking and writing we recommend for your learner's journal. Writing to learn and remember is active, engaged writing. It requires judgment and critical thinking. By contrast, notetaking during a lecture, though it requires you to make choices, is relatively passive.

☐ Record observations and overheard conversations.

☐ Write for ten or fifteen minutes every day about whatever is on your mind in connection with recent observations and learning. Focus these meditative writings outwardly on your new experiences and your understandings, interpretations, and reflections on them. Write only what you would be willing to share with others. Writing about deeply personal matters and about your own emotional development is private and so would be better put in a diary.

☐ Write sketches of people—friends or strangers who catch your attention.

☐ Organize a day or a week. You could write about your goals and priorities. You could list specific things to accomplish.

☐ Keep a log over several days or weeks about a particular event unfolding in the news—a sensational trial, an environmental disaster, a political campaign, a campus controversy, the fortunes of a sports team.

If you begin to keep a journal, you will think of still other ways to use it. There are many possibilities. All of the writing in your journal has immediate value for learning, observing experience closely, and organizing your life. It may also end up in other writing—essay tests, essays, reports, letters.

Some writers organize their logs into well-defined sections, one section for new words, one for continuing events, one for entries about a particular course, and so on.

Looping   Looping—the strategy of writing quickly but *returning* to your topic—is especially useful for the first stages of exploring a topic. From almost any starting point, no matter how general or unfocused, looping enables you to find a center of interest and eventually a thesis. The rules are simple:

1. Write down your area of interest. You may know only that you have to write about another person or a movie you have seen or a cultural trend that has caught your attention. Or, you may be searching for a topic in a broad historical period or one related to a major political event.

Although you may wander from this topic as you write, you will want to keep coming back to it. Your purpose is to find a focus for writing, or a thesis.

2. Write nonstop for ten minutes. Start with the first thing that comes to mind. Write rapidly, without looking back to reread or to correct anything. *Do not stop writing. Keep your pencil moving.* That is the key to looping. If you cannot think of anything new to write for a moment, rewrite the last sentence. Trust the act of writing to lead you to new insights. Follow diversions and digressions, but keep returning to your topic.

3. At the end of ten minutes, pause to reread what you have written. Decide what is most important—a single insight, a pattern of ideas, an emerging theme, a visual detail, anything at all that stands out. Some writers call this a "center of gravity" or a "hot spot." To complete the first loop, express this center in a single sentence.

4. Begin with this summary sentence and write nonstop again for ten minutes.

5. Summarize in one sentence again to complete the second loop.

6. Keep looping until one of your summary sentences produces what seems to be a focus or thesis. You may need only two or three loops; you may need more.

Questioning   Asking questions about a problem or topic is a way to learn about it and decide what to do or say. However, when we first encounter a problem, our questions may be scattered. Also, we are not likely to think right away of all the important questions we ought to ask. The advantage of a basic list of questions for invention, like the ones for cubing and dramatizing discussed earlier in this chapter, is that it reminds you of all of the ways of viewing a subject and hence of important questions to ask. It is a useful and systematic approach to exploring a problem.

The questions immediately following come from classical rhetoric (what the Greek philosopher Aristotle called "topics") and a modern approach to invention called *tagmemics*. Tagmemics, based on the work of American linguist Kenneth Pike, provides questions about all the ways we make sense of the world, all the ways we sort and classify experience and come to understand it.

Here are the steps in using questions for invention: (1) Think about your subject. (By "subject," we mean any event, person, problem, project, idea, or issue. In other words, anything you might write about.) (2) Start with the first question, and move right through the list. Try to answer each question at least briefly with a word or phrase. Some questions may invite several sentences, or even a page or more of writing. You may draw a blank on a few questions. Skip them. Later, with more experience with questions for invention, you can start anywhere in the list. (3) Write your responses quickly, without much planning. Follow digressions or associations. Do not screen anything out. Be playful.

What is your subject?

- ☐ What is your subject's name?
- ☐ What other names has it had?
- ☐ What other names do people use for your subject now?
- ☐ Why do people call it something you do not call it?
- ☐ Imagine a photograph of your subject. What would it look like?
- ☐ What word, besides its name, best summarizes it?
- ☐ What would you put into a time capsule to stand for your subject?
- ☐ Where did it come from?
- ☐ What caused it?
- ☐ Why does it exist?
- ☐ What are its results?

☐ How would your subject look from different vantage points or perspectives?

☐ What particular experiences have you had with the subject? Do these experiences remind you of problems you have had with the subject? Do these experiences remind you of what you know about the subject?

What parts does your subject have and how are they related?

Think about your subject as having several different parts or characteristics:

☐ Name the parts.

☐ Describe each part using some of the questions in the preceding subject list.

☐ How is each part related to the other parts?

How is your subject similar to and different from other subjects?

☐ What is your subject similar to?

☐ In what ways is it similar?

☐ What is your subject different from?

☐ In what ways is it different?

☐ Of all the things in the world, what seems to you most unlike your subject? In what ways are they unlike each other? Now, just for fun, note how they are alike.

How much can your subject change and still remain the same?

☐ How has your subject changed from what it once was?

☐ How is it changing now? From moment to moment, day to day, year to year?

☐ How much can it change and still remain the same?

☐ What are some different forms your subject takes?

☐ How does the subject change each time you see it or think about it?

☐ What does it become when it is no longer itself?

Where does it fit in the world?

☐ When and where did your subject originate?

☐ Has your subject always existed?

☐ Can you imagine a time in the future when your subject will not exist?

☐ When and where do you experience it?

☐ Is this subject part of something larger?

☐ Is the subject an important part of this larger thing?

☐ Does the subject cause this larger thing or result from it?

☐ Is the subject always separate from this larger thing of which it is a part, or does it sometimes blend into it?

☐ What do other people think of your subject?

READING

In many situations, writers must rely on information in books, films, maps, photographs, documents, archives, or museums. Their invention and inquiry in these situations involves gathering, analyzing, selecting, and organizing information from such sources.

Most of the writing you will do in college or on the job will be based at least in part on printed texts. This section presents several strategies for invention and inquiry that will enable you to write about ideas and information you acquire in your reading. The strategies include annotating, inventorying, outlining, paraphrasing, and summarizing. They will help you write about your reading in the following ways:

to gather and organize new information from your reading

to understand the new information

to connect information from different sources

to relate information to what you already know, believe, and feel

to condense and record information so that you can use it when writing exams, research papers, and arguments about issues and policies.

Annotating   Annotations are the notes we make in margins of books we own. Annotations can be exclamations of outrage or of insight, questions, brief summaries, sequential labeling of arguments or main points, even doodles—anything at all that records succinctly what the reader is learning and feeling. Some readers do it consistently, even obsessively, filling margins with notes. Others rarely do it. Most writers also underline important sentences or passages, or they may highlight them with special colored markers.

Annotations and underlining serve two purposes: (1) to record reactions, questions, and understandings, and (2) to organize the text for reviewing, studying, or writing about it. As a preliminary to writing, annotations can be a very important invention activity; crucial details, examples, quotations, and main points that would be required in a summary, essay, or research report, are marked.

Annotating involves a number of specific activities:

☐ Writing words, phrases, or sentences: these writings can comment, question, evaluate, define, relate, challenge

☐ Underlining or highlighting words or phrases

☐ Circling or boxing words or phrases

☐ Connecting related items with lines

☐ Numbering a sequence of related items: arguments, examples, names

☐ Bracketing a part of the text, either within the text itself or with a line in the margin.

Annotating can be light or heavy, depending on the difficulty of the material and your plans for writing about it. For a literary text you plan to analyze and interpret, your annotations may be heavy and quite varied. You will make some annotations the first time you read it and more when you reread it. Here is the way one reader annotated the first section of Nathaniel Hawthorne's story "Young Goodman Brown." The complete story appears in Chapter 9: Analyzing Literature.

odd name—main character?

Young Goodman Brown came forth, at sunset, into the street of Salem village, but put his head back, after crossing the threshold, to exchange a parting kiss with his young

is she faithful or unfaithful?

wife. And Faith, as the wife was (aptly) named, thrust her own pretty head into the street, letting the wind play with the pink ribbons of her cap, while she called to Goodman Brown.

lips, whispers, "dearest"—romantic

"Dearest heart," whispered she, softly and rather sadly, when her lips were close to his ear, "pr'y thee put off your journey until sunrise, and sleep in your own bed to-night. A lone woman is troubled with such dreams and such thoughts, that she's afeard of herself, sometimes. Pray, (tarry) with me this night, dear husband, of all nights in the year!"

why so frightened?

"My love and my Faith," replied young Goodman Brown, "of all nights in the year, this one night must I tarry away from thee. My journey, as thou callest it, forth and back again, must needs be done (twixt) now and sunrise. What,

between?

my sweet, pretty wife, (dost thou) doubt me already, and we but three months married!"

"Then, God bless you!" said Faith, with the pink ribbons

seems to give in easily

"and may you find all well, when you come back."

"Amen!" cried Goodman Brown. "Say thy prayers, dear Faith, and go to bed at dusk, and no harm will come to thee."

So they parted; and the young man pursued his way, until, being about to turn the corner by the meeting-house, *why so much attention to these pink ribbons? seems to contrast with darkness and fear*

he looked back, and saw the head of Faith still peeping after him, with a melancholy air, in spite of her pink ribbons.

"Poor little Faith!" thought he, for his heart smote him. "What a wretch am I, to leave her on such an errand! She talks of dreams, too. Methought, as she spoke, there was trouble in her face as if a dream had warned her what work is to be done tonight. But, no, no! 'twould kill her to think it. Well; she's a blessed angel on earth; and after this one night, I'll cling to her skirts and follow her to Heaven."

what work?

sadness, loneliness, regret, evil, darkness—something dreadful is about to occur

With this excellent resolve for the future, Goodman Brown felt himself justified in making more haste on his present evil purpose. He had taken a dreary road, darkened by all the gloomiest trees of the forest, which barely stood aside to let the narrow path creep through, and closed immediately behind. It was all as lonely as could be; and there is this peculiarity in such a solitude, that the traveler knows not who may be concealed by the innumerable trunks and the thick boughs overhead; so that, with lonely footsteps, he may yet be passing through an unseen multitude.

narrator sees and knows all

ghosts?

At a glance you can see how many different annotating activities this writer found useful: writing comments and questions, connecting related items, circling unusual or unknown words, underlining certain words, and bracketing part of the text in the margin. The written comments indicate that the reader actively sought to understand the story.

Annotating an informational text is different from annotating a story or a poem. You are not so much probing an art form as you are organizing and clarifying information. Consequently, in annotating an informational text, you might want to concentrate on underlining main ideas, deciding how the information is organized, and marking the most important facts. Here is the way one student annotated a paragraph in an essay on Native American writing systems.

certain characteristics—social organization, literacy functions (letters, religious services, records)

The Native American groups which, despite all obstacles, have developed traditions of literacy in their own languages seem to share certain characteristics. All of them, of course, have preserved some sort of social organization, at least at the local community level. It would seem that such groups have also found one or more functions for their own literacy. Thus the spread of Fox, Winnebago, Cherokee, and Mahican literacy occurred at the same time that these several tribes were divided by migrations. In all four cases it seems reasonable to suppose that the first individuals to become literate were motivated by a desire to communicate with relatives who had departed for the west or, as the case

what kinds of obstacles?

forcibly removed or broken by whom?

may be, had lingered behind in the east. The Aleuts and Yupiks were never forcibly "removed" or broken into separate reservation communities; but their dispersed settlements and frequent hunting and fishing expeditions made the ability to read and write letters a useful skill. Motivation for literacy is not always based on the need to correspond with absent friends and relatives, however. The Cherokee syllabary, for example, has long been used in the context of <u>religious services</u> and religious instruction where those to whom messages are read are all present in the same room with those who are reading. Likewise, the Cherokee medical practitioners who <u>record</u> curing formulas in the syllabary do so primarily for their own reference, not for unspecified readers at some remote place and time. <u>The factors that tend to perpetuate native literacy, then, need not include a felt need to communicate with distant members of a tightly knit society; but they do seem to include the perception of literacy as a useful skill which enables the literate to achieve some worthwhile objective.</u>

seven different tribes mentioned—strong evidence

main point

Inventorying

Inventorying is a useful activity for understanding, analyzing, and interpreting reading. It is a natural follow-up to annotating. When you annotate you try to identify significant information. Inventorying helps you find relationships and patterns in this information, which in turn helps you to decide how you might interpret or evaluate it. Once you have a thesis, inventorying enables you to review the reading for evidence to support your thesis.

An early inventory to find patterns in a text involves making several lists of related items. Consider the following possibilities:

- ☐ Recurring images (similes, metaphors)
- ☐ Noticeable stylistic features
- ☐ Repeated descriptions
- ☐ Consistent ways of characterizing people or events and of defining terms
- ☐ Repeated words and phrases
- ☐ Repeated subjects or topics
- ☐ Repeated examples or illustrations
- ☐ Reliance on particular writing strategies

What patterns you discover depend on the kind of reading you are analyzing. Here is an inventory a student made from the annotations of the first section of the Hawthorne story:

Suggestions of danger

troubled

afeard

no harm

melancholy

heart smote him

wretch

trouble

kill her

evil purpose

Setting for an "evil purpose"

dreary road

darkened road

gloomiest trees

closed

lonely

solitude

concealed

Characterizing Brown's wife

faith

pretty head

pink ribbons

affectionate

intimate

sweet, pretty wife

yielding

blessed angel

In inventorying a long work, you might want to include page numbers of items in your lists. You may want to inventory your annotations of a literary work before you write about it. You may also want to inventory the reading you do for a report, for demonstrating that a trend exists, or for background on an activity you are profiling. For much of the writing you do as a college student, you will find inventorying (and annotating) not just helpful but essential.

Outlining   Outlining an essay or a chapter in a book can help you understand and remember the material. An outline displays the main features or main ideas in an essay. It presents only the framework and hence is quite general, even abstract. Some inventories move toward outlines when they involve comprehensive lists of the parts of a story or an essay.

An outline may be an informal list of phrases or a formal numbered and indented set of sentences. It may be presented as a visual cluster, a possibility illustrated earlier in this chapter.

Paraphrasing   In many of the writing activities in this book and in much of the writing you do in college, you will use information from printed sources. The three basic ways of integrating this information into your own writing are by means of quotation, paraphrase, and summary. One of the most important writing decisions you will have to make again and again is which one of these to use.

A quotation is an exact reproduction of the language in the source. (Strategies for integrating quoted material smoothly into your writing are demonstrated in Chapter 21: The Research Paper.)

A paraphrase is a presentation in your own words of *all* the information in a brief passage. Paraphrase alternates with quotations and with your own analysis or commentary. When you summarize, you present in your own words just the main ideas in a passage.

Here is a student's paraphrase of the first five sentences of a paragraph from the article on Native American writing systems printed earlier in this chapter.

Original

The Native American groups which, despite all obstacles, have developed traditions of literacy in their own languages seem to share certain characteristics. All of them, of course, have preserved some sort of social organization, at least at the local community level. It would seem that such groups have also found one or more functions for their own literacy. Thus the spread of Fox, Winnebago, Cherokee, and Mahican literacy occurred at the same time that these several tribes were divided by migrations. In all four cases it seems reasonable to suppose that the first individuals to become literate were motivated by a desire to communicate with relatives who had departed for the west or, as the case may be, had lingered behind in the east.

Paraphrase

Native American groups had to overcome many obstacles in order to develop writing systems in their own languages. The groups that did develop writing are alike in several ways: they maintained their social structure, and they were able to put writing to good use. For example, writing became more common in the Fox, Winnebago, Cherokee, and Mahican tribes after they were separated through migration. Tribal members probably wanted to write to relatives they could no longer see regularly.

The first thing to note about the paraphrase is that it contains *all* the information in the original. It is not just a summary. It is a complete reproduction in the student's own words. Although it has the same number of sentences as the original, the information is grouped into sentences in somewhat different ways. In using this information in an essay, the writer might quote the original; but, unless it contains crucial evidence or memorable language, it probably should be paraphrased.

Without changing the information in any way, paraphrase aims to clarify and simplify the original. It may explain difficult material, or it may restate a complicated argument.

Just as you must indicate the source of quotations, you must also indicate the source of paraphrased material. (Chapter 21 illustrates ways to document your sources.)

Paraphrase is also useful as a strategy of inquiry. It is a way of understanding difficult material by restating it in your own words. It is very time-consuming, though, and should only be used with short passages.

Summarizing   A summary is a selection of main ideas. All talking and writing involves some degree of summary. If we tell someone what our day was like, we summarize. When we write, we summarize our experience or knowledge.

As you write, you occasionally summarize your own writing, especially in longer essays or reports: you pause to remind the reader what you have said so far and forecast what is to come next. Some endings to essays are summaries. Summaries, an important writing strategy, are mentioned prominently in Chapter 5.

As a writer, you also summarize information from other writers. In informative and argumentative essays, essay exams and research reports, you interweave your own analysis and commentary with quotations, paraphrases, and summaries from other writers.

Here is one student's summary of the paragraph from the essay on Native American writing systems that appeared earlier in this chapter. Read the complete paragraph, and then examine the student's summary.

Summary

Native Americans developed their own writing systems in order to write letters and keep records.

The preceding sentence is one possible summary of the main idea of the paragraph. It does not leave out any important part of the main idea, nor does it include any of the examples or illustrations. It is stated in the student's own language, not the language of the original, though, of course, certain key terms must be repeated.

To summarize a longer selection, you would read and reread it carefully, annotating as you go. You could then inventory or outline the selection in order to be certain you have identified all the main ideas. You would then be able to write a coherent summary.

Field Research

In universities, government agencies, and the business world, field research can be as important as library research or experimental research. In specialties such as sociology, political science, anthropology, polling, advertising, and news reporting, field research is the basic means of gathering information.

This chapter is a brief introduction to three of the major kinds of field research: observations, interviews, and questionnaires. The writing activities involved are central to several academic specialties. If you major in education, journalism, or one of the social sciences, you probably will be asked to do writing based on observations, interviews, and questionnaire results. You will also read large amounts of information based on these ways of learning about people, groups, and institutions.

For writing activities in this book, observations and interviews are essential for the profile essay in Chapter 10: Profiling People and Places. Interviewing could be helpful, as well, in documenting a trend and exploring its causes (Chapter 8: Explaining Causes), in case you wanted to consult a campus or community expert on the trend. In proposing a solution to a problem (Chapter 6: Making Proposals), you might want to interview someone who could help you outline the steps in a somewhat technical or complicated solution; or, you might want to consult with people who are concerned about the problem or whom you must persuade to take action on your proposed solution. If many people are affected, you might want to find out what they know with a questionnaire. In writing a report on an academic subject (Chapter 5: Reporting Information), you might want to interview a faculty member who is a specialist on that subject, or you might want to plan a questionnaire study as a basis for a report. Although you probably will not wish to interview the person you write about in Chapter 3: Remembering People, interviewing often plays a major role in family and group histories. There is renewed interest in this kind of writing, sparked in part by Alex Haley's *Roots* and the television series based on it in the late 1970s.

OBSERVATIONS

This section offers guidelines for planning an observational visit, taking notes on your observations, and later writing them up. Some kinds of

19

writing are based on observations from single visits—travel writing, restaurant reviews, social workers' case reports, insurance investigators' accident reports—but most observational writing is based on several visits. An anthropologist or sociologist studying an unfamiliar group or activity might observe it for months, filling several notebooks with notes. If you are writing about a place (Chapter 10: Profiling People and Places), you almost certainly will want to make two or three (or more) observational visits, some of them perhaps combined with interviews.

Second and third visits to observe further and to take more notes are important because as you learn more about a place from observations, interviews, or reading, you will discover new ways to look at it. Gradually you will have more and more questions of different kinds which can only be answered by follow-up visits.

Planning the observational visit To ensure that your observational visits are worthwhile, you must plan them carefully.

Getting access. If the place you propose to visit is public, you probably will have easy access to it. If everything you need to see is within view of anyone passing by or using the place, you can make your observations without any special arrangements. Indeed, you may not even be noticed.

Most observational visits that are part of special inquiries—reports for a sociology or education class, the profile in Chapter 10—require special access. Hence, you will need to arrange your visit, calling ahead or making a get-acquainted visit, in order to introduce yourself and state your purpose. Find out the times you may visit, and be certain you can get to it easily.

Announcing your intentions. State your intentions directly and fully. Say who you are, where you are from, and what you hope to do. You may be surprised at how receptive people can be to a student on assignment from a college course. Not every place you wish to visit will welcome you, however. A variety of constraints on outside visitors exist in private businesses as well as public institutions. But generally, if people know your intentions, they may be able to tell you about aspects of a place or activity you would not have thought to observe.

Taking your tools. Take a notebook with a firm back so that you will have a steady writing surface, perhaps a small stenographer's notebook with a spiral binding across the top. Using this notebook, you can flip a page full of notes over and under and out of the way. Remember also to take a writing instrument.

Some observers dictate their observations into portable tape recorders. You might want to experiment with this method. We recommend, though, that for your first observations you record in writing. Your instructor or other students in your class may want to see your written notes.

Observing and taking notes

Following are some brief guidelines for observing and taking notes.

Observing. Some activities invite multiple vantage points, whereas others seem to limit the observer to a single perspective. Take advantage of every perspective available to you. Come in close, take a middle position, and stand back. Study the scene from a stationary position and also try to move around it. The more varied your perspectives, the more you are likely to observe.

Your purpose in observing is both to describe the activity and to analyze it. You will want to look closely at the activity itself, but you will also want to think about what makes this activity special, what seems to be the point of it.

Try to be an innocent observer: pretend you have never seen anything like this activity before. Look for typical features of the activity as well as unusual features. Look at it from the perspective of your readers. Ask what details of the activity would surprise and inform and interest them.

Taking notes. You undoubtedly will find your own style of note-taking, but here are a few pointers.

Write only on one side of the page. Later, when you organize your notes, you may want to cut up the pages and file notes under different headings.

Take notes in words, phrases, or sentences. Draw diagrams or sketches, if they help you see and understand the place.

Note any ideas or questions that occur to you.

Use quotation marks around any overheard conversation you take down.

Since you can later reorganize your notes quite easily, you do not need to take notes in any planned or systematic way. You might, however, want to cover these possibilities:

The setting. The easiest way to begin is to name objects you see. Just start by listing objects. Then record details of some of these objects—color, shape, size, texture, function, relation to similar or dissimilar objects. Although your notes probably will contain mainly visual details, you might also want to record sounds and smells. Be sure to include some notes about the shape, dimensions, and layout of the place. How big is it? How is it organized?

The people. Record the number of people, their activities, their movements and behavior. Describe their appearance or dress. Record parts of overheard conversations. Note whether you see more men than women, more of one racial group rather than of another, more older than younger people. Most important, note anything surprising and unusual about people in the scene.

Your personal reactions. Include in your notes any feelings you have about what you observe. Also record, as they occur to you, any hunches or ideas or insights you have.

Reflecting on your observation Immediately after your observational visit (within just a few minutes, if possible), find a quiet place to reflect on what you saw, review your notes, and add to your notes. Give yourself at least a half hour for quiet thought.

What you have in your notes and what you recall on reflection will suggest many more images and details from your observations. Add these to your notes.

Finally, review all of your notes, and write a few sentences about your main impressions of the place. What did you learn? How did this visit change your preconceptions about the place? What surprised you most? What is the dominant impression you get from your notes?

Writing up your notes Your instructor may ask you to write up your notes as a report on the observational visit. If so, review your notes, looking for patterns and vivid details. You might find inventorying or clustering (Chapter 18: Invention and Inquiry) useful for discovering patterns and relationships in your notes.

Decide on the main impression you want readers to have of the place. Use this as the focus for your report.

Now draft a brief description of the place. Your purpose is to present a general impression of the place through a selection of the details in your notes. Assume your readers have never been to the place, and try to present a vivid impression of it. (See Chapter 12: Describing for a full discussion of strategies for descriptive writing.)

Follow-up visits   Rather than repeat yourself in follow-up visits, try to build on what you have already discovered. You should probably do some interviewing and reading before another observational visit so that you will have a greater understanding of the subject when you observe it again. It is also important to develop a plan for your follow-up: questions to be answered, hypotheses to be tested, types of information you would like to discover.

INTERVIEWS

Like making observations, interviewing tends to involve four basic steps: (1) planning and setting up the interview, (2) notetaking, (3) reflecting on the interview, and (4) writing up your notes.

Planning and setting   The first step in interviewing involves choosing an interview subject and
up the interview   then arranging and planning the interview.

Choosing an interview subject. The first step is to decide whom to interview. If you are writing about something in which several people are involved, choose subjects representing a variety of perspectives—a range of different roles, for example. If you are profiling a single person, most, if not all, of your interviews will be with that person.

You should be flexible because you may be unable to speak to the person you targeted and may wind up with someone else—the person's assistant, perhaps. Do not assume this interview subject will be worthless. You might even learn more from the assistant than you would from the person in charge.

Arranging an interview. You may be nervous about calling up a busy person and asking for some of his or her time. Indeed, you may get turned down. But if so, it is possible that you will be referred to someone who will see you, someone whose job it is to talk to the public.

Do not feel that just because you are a student you do not have the right to ask for people's time. You will be surprised how delighted people are to be asked about themselves, particularly if you get them when they are not feeling harried. You would probably be flattered if someone requested an interview with you. People love to talk—about anything! Usually, the problem is that no one will listen to them. And, since you are a student on assignment, some people may feel that they are doing a form of public service to talk with you.

A note about presenting yourself. When introducing yourself to arrange the interview, give a short and simple description of your project. If you talk too much, you could prejudice or limit the person's response. But it is a good idea to exhibit some enthusiasm for your project. If you lack enthusiasm, the person probably might not feel like talking to you.

Keep in mind that the person you are interviewing is donating time to you. Be certain that you call ahead to arrange a specific time for the interview. Be on time. Bring all the materials you need, and express your thanks when the interview is over.

Planning for the interview. The planned interview is the one that tends to go best. It will help if you have made an observational visit and done some background reading before the interview. In preparation for the interview, you should do two things: consider your objectives and prepare some questions.

Think about your main objectives. Do you want an orientation to the place (the "big picture") from this interview? Do you want this interview to lead you to interviews with other key people? Do you want mainly facts or information? Do you need clarification of something you have heard in another interview or observed or read? Do you want to learn more about the person, or learn about the place through the person, or both? Should you trust or distrust this person?

The key to good interviewing is flexibility. You may be looking for facts, but your interview subject may not have any to offer. In that case, you should be able to shift gears and go after whatever your subject has to discuss.

Prepare some questions in advance. Take care in composing these questions; they can be the key to a successful interview. Bad questions rarely yield useful answers.

What is a bad question? Any question that places unfair limits on respondents is a bad question. Two specific types to avoid are forced-choice questions and leading questions.

Forced-choice questions are bad because they impose your terms on your respondents. Consider this example: "Do you think rape is an expression of sexual passion or of aggression?" A person may think that neither sexual passion nor aggression satisfactorily explains rape. A better way to phrase the question would be to ask, "People often fall into two camps on the issue of rape. Some think it is an expression of sexual passion, while others argue it is really not sexual but aggressive. Do you think it is either of these? If not, what is your opinion?" This form of questioning allows you to get a reaction to what others have said at the same time it gives the person freedom to set the terms.

Leading questions are bad because they assume too much. An example of this kind of question is this: "Do you think the increase in the occurrence of rape is due to the fact that women are perceived as competitors in a severely depressed economy?" This question assumes that there is an increase in the occurrence of rape, that women are perceived (apparently by rapists) as competitors, and that the economy is severely depressed. A better way of asking the question might be to make the assumptions more explicit by dividing the question into its parts: "Do you think there is an increase in the occurrence of rape? What could have caused it? I've heard some people argue that the economy has something to do with it. Do you think so? Do you think rapists perceive women as competitors for jobs? Could the current economic situation have made this competition more severe?"

Good questions come in many different forms. One way of considering them is to divide them into two types: open and closed. *Open questions* give the respondent range and flexibility. They also generate anecdotes, personal revelations, and expressions of attitudes. Following are examples of open questions:

☐ I wonder if you would take a few minutes to tell me something about your early days in the business. I'd be interested to hear about how it got started, what your hopes and aspirations were, what problems you faced and how you dealt with them.

☐ Tell me about a time you were (name an emotion).

☐ What did you think of (name a person or event)?

☐ What did you do when (name an event) happened?

The best questions are those that allow the subject to talk freely but to the point. If the answer strays too far from the point, a follow-up question may be necessary to refocus the talk. Another tack you may want to try is to rephrase the subject's answer, to say something like: "Let me see if I have this right," or "Am I correct in saying that you feel. . . ." Often, a person will take the opportunity to amplify the original response by adding just the anecdote or quotation you've been looking for.

Closed questions usually request specific information. For example:

☐ How do you do (name a process)?

☐ What does (name a word) mean?

☐ What does (a person, object, or place) look like?

☐ How was it made?

Taking your tools   As for an observational visit, you will need a notebook with a firm back so that you can write on it easily without the benefit of a table or desk. We recommend a full-size ($8\frac{1}{2} \times 11$) spiral or ring notebook.

In this notebook, divide several pages into two columns with a line drawn about one third of the width of the page from the left margin. Use the lefthand column to note details about the scene, the person, the mood of the interview, other impressions. Head this column DETAILS AND IMPRESSIONS. At the top of the righthand column, write several questions. You may not use them, but they will jog your memory. This column should be titled INFORMATION. In this column you will record what you learn from answers to your questions. (See Chapter 10 for an example.)

Taking notes during the interview

Because you are not taking a verbatim transcript of the interview (if you wanted a literal account, you would use a tape recorder or shorthand), your goals are to gather information and to record a few good quotations and anecdotes. In addition, because the people you interview may be unused to giving interviews and so will need to know you are listening, it is probably a good idea to do more listening than notetaking. You may not have much confidence in your memory, but, if you pay close attention, you are likely to recall a good deal of the conversation afterward. During the interview, you should take some notes: a few quotations; key words and phrases to jog your memory; along with observational jottings about the scene, the person, and the mood of the interview. Remember that *how* something is said is as important as *what* is said. Pick up material that will give the interview write-up texture—gesture, physical appearance, verbal inflection, facial expression, dress, hair, style, body language, anything that makes the person an individual.

Reflecting on the interview

As soon as you finish the interview, find a quiet place to reflect on it, and review your notes. This reflection is essential because so much happens in an interview that you cannot record at the time. You need to spend at least a half hour, maybe longer, adding to your notes and thinking about what you learned.

At the end of this time, write a few sentences about your main impressions from the interview. What did you learn? What surprised you most? How did the interview change your attitude or understanding about the person or place? How would you summarize your main impressions of the person? How did this interview influence your plans to interview others or to reinterview this person? What do you want to learn from these next interviews?

Writing up your notes

Your instructor may ask you to write up your notes as a report on the interview. If so, review your notes, looking for useful details and information. Decide what main impression you want to give of this person. Choose details that will contribute to this impression. Select quotations and paraphrases of information you learned from the person. Your task is to integrate this material into an essay presenting the person and what you learned about the subject.

To find a focus for your interview write-up, you might use looping. Clustering might give you suggestions for organizing the interview. Invention questions and dramatizing will help you consider the person from different perspectives. (All of these strategies are discussed in Chapter 18: Invention and Inquiry.)

QUESTIONNAIRES

Questionnaires let you survey the attitudes or knowledge of large numbers of people. You could carry out many face-to-face or phone interviews to get the same information, but questionnaires have the advantages of economy and efficiency. Some questionnaires, such as ones you filled out in applying to college, just collect demographic information: your name, age, sex, home town, religious preference, intended major. Others, such as the Gallup and Harris polls, collect opinions on a wide range of issues. At election times we are reminded of these kinds of polls. Still other kinds of questionnaires, ones used in academic research, are designed to help answer important questions about personal and societal problems.

This section will briefly outline procedures you can follow to carry out an informal questionnaire survey of people's opinions or knowledge, and then to write up the results. (For formal studies using questionnaires, you would need considerable technical information about designing the study, sampling the population of interest, and analyzing the data. This information is available from many sources, some of which are listed at the end of this chapter.)

Focusing your study   A questionnaire study usually has a limited focus. You might need to interview a few people in order to find this focus.

Let us assume that you went to the Student Health Clinic (SHC) and had to wait over an hour to see a nurse. Sitting there with many other students, you decide this is a problem that needs to be studied. Furthermore, it seems an ideal topic for a proposal essay (Chapter 6: Making Proposals) you have been assigned in your writing class. It is a problem you can study in order to propose a solution.

To study this problem, you do not have to explore the entire operation of SHC. You are not interested in how nurses and doctors are hired or how efficient their system of ordering supplies is. You have a particular concern: how successful is SHC in scheduling appointments and organizing its resources to meet student needs? More specifically: do students often have to wait too long to see a nurse or doctor? You might also want to know *why* this is the case, if it is; but you can only seek an answer to that question by interviewing SHC staff. Your primary interest is in how long students usually wait for appointments, what times are most convenient for students to schedule appointments, whether SHC resources are concentrated at those times, and so on. Now you have a limited focus, and you can collect valuable information with a fairly brief questionnaire.

To be certain about your focus, however, you should talk informally to several students to find out whether they think there is a problem. You might also want to talk to people at SHC, explaining your plans and asking for their views on the problem.

Whatever your interest, be sure to limit the scope of your study. Try to focus on one or two important questions. With a limited focus, your questionnaire can be brief, and people will be more willing to fill it out. Based on a limited amount of information, your study will be easier to organize and report.

Writing questions   Two basic forms of questions—closed and open—were introduced earlier in this chapter. In the following section are additional illustrations of how these types of questions may be used in the context of a questionnaire.

Closed questions. Following are examples of some forms of closed questions. You probably will use more than one form in a questionnaire, because you will have several kinds of information to collect.

Checklists

With your present work and class schedule, when are you able to visit the SHC? (Check as many boxes as necessary.)

☐ 8–10 A.M.
☐ 10–12 A.M.
☐ noon hour
☐ 1–3 P.M.
☐ 3–5 P.M.

Which services do you expect to use at the SHC this year?

☐ allergy desensitization
☐ immunization
☐ optometry
☐ dental care
☐ birth control
☐ illness or infection
☐ counseling
☐ health education

Two-way questions

Have you made an appointment this year at SHC?

____ yes

____ no

Have you ever had to wait more than 30 minutes at SHC for a scheduled appointment?

____ yes

____ no

If you could, would you schedule appointments at the SHC after 7:00 P.M.?

____ yes

____ no

____ uncertain

Multiple-choice questions

How frequently have you had to wait at the SHC for a scheduled appointment?

____ always

____ usually

____ occasionally

____ never

From your experience so far with SHC, how would you rate its services?

____ inadequate

____ barely adequate

____ adequate

____ better than adequate

____ outstanding

Ranking scales

With your present work and class schedule, which times during the day (Monday through Friday) would be most convenient for you to schedule appointments at SHC? Put a 1 by the most convenient time, a 2 by the next most convenient time, until you have ranked all the choices.

____ mornings

____ afternoons before 5 P.M.

____ 5–7 P.M.

____ 7–10 P.M.

Open questions. Open questions ask the respondent to write a brief answer.

What services do you expect to need at SHC this year?

_____

_____

_____

From your experiences with appointments at SHC, what advice would you give students about making appointments?

_____

_____

_____

What do you believe would most improve services at SHC?

_____

_____

_____

You may want to use a combination of closed and open questions for your questionnaire. Both offer advantages: closed questions will give you definite answers, but open questions can give information you may not have expected as well as providing lively quotations for your report.

Trying out the questions. As soon as you have a collection of possible questions, try them out on a few typical readers. You need to know which questions are unclear, which seem to duplicate others, which seem most interesting. These tryouts will enable you to assess which questions will give you the information you need. Readers also can help you come up with additional questions.

Designing the questionnaire

Write a brief, clear introduction stating the purpose of the questionnaire and explaining how you intend to use the results. Give advice on answering the questions, and estimate the amount of time needed to complete the questionnaire. If you are going to give the questionnaire to groups of people in person, you can give this information orally.

Select your most promising questions, and decide on an order. Any logical order is appropriate. You might want to begin with the least complicated questions or the most general ones. You may find it necessary or helpful to group the questions by subject matter or form. Certain questions may lead to others. You might want to place open questions at the end.

Design the questionnaire so that it looks attractive and readable. Make it look easy to complete. Do not crowd questions together to save paper. Provide plenty of space for readers to answer open questions, and remind them to use the back of the page if they need more space.

Testing the questionnaire

Make a few copies of your first design, and ask at least two or three readers to complete the questionnaire. Find out how much time they needed to complete it. Talk to them about any confusions or problems they experienced. Review their responses with them to be certain each question is doing what you want it to do. From what you learn, reconsider your design, and revise particular questions.

Administering the questionnaire

Decide who will fill out your questionnaire and how you can arrange for them to do it. The more readers you have, the better; but constraints of time and expense almost certainly will limit the number. You can mail questionnaires or distribute them to dormitories or workplace mailboxes, but the return will be low. It is unusual for even half the people receiving mail questionnaires to return them. If you do mail the questionnaire, be sure to mention the deadline for returning it. Give directions for returning the questionnaire, and include a stamped, addressed envelope for off-campus mail.

You might want to arrange to distribute the questionnaire yourself to some groups in class, at dormitory meetings, or at work.

If you were doing a formal questionnaire, you would need a truly representative group of readers (a random or stratified random sample). For an informal study, try to get a reasonably representative group. For example, to study satisfaction with the appointments schedule at SHC, you would want to have readers who had been to SHC. You might even want to find seniors rather than freshman readers because after four years seniors would have made more visits to SHC. If many students commute, you would want to be sure to have commuters among your readers.

Your report will be much more convincing if you can demonstrate that your readers represent the group whose opinions or knowledge you claim to be studying. As few as 25 or 30 readers could be adequate for an informal study.

Writing up the results

Now that you have the completed questionnaires, what do you do with them?

Summarizing the results. Begin by tallying the results from the closed questions. Take an unused questionnaire, and tally next to each choice. Suppose you had 25 readers. Here is how the tally might look for the first checklist question.

With your present work and class schedule, when are you able to visit the SHC? (Check as many boxes as necessary.)

☐ 8–10 A.M. ⅃⅃⅃ ⅃⅃⅃ ⅃⅃⅃ Ⅲ (18)

☐ 10–12 A.M. IIII II (7)
☐ noon hour IIII IIII III (13)
☐ 1–3 P.M. III (3)
☐ 3–5 P.M. IIII IIII (9)

Each tally mark represents one response to that item. The totals add up to more than 25 because readers were asked to check *all* the times they could make appointments.

Next consider the open questions. Read all 25 answers to each question separately to see the kind and variety of response to each. Then decide whether you want to code any of the open questions so that you can summarize results from them quantitatively, as you would with closed questions. For example, you might want to classify the types of advice given as responses to an open question proposed earlier: "From your experiences with appointments at SHC, what advice would you give students about making appointments?" You could then report the numbers of readers (of your 25) who gave each type of advice. For an opinion question ("How would you evaluate the most recent appointment you had at SHC?"), you might simply code the answers as positive, neutral, and negative and then tally the results accordingly for each kind of response. However, responses to open questions are perhaps most often used as a source of quotations for your report.

You can report results from the closed questions as percentages, either within the text of your report or in tables. (See the Fuchs essay in Chapter 8 for one possible format for a table. You can find other formats in social science texts you may be using or even in magazines or newspapers. Conventional formats for tables in social science reports are illustrated in *Publication Manual of the American Psychological Association,* 3rd edition, Washington, D.C.: American Psychological Association, 1983). You can make tables of results either for individual questions or for groups of questions with identical forms.

You can quote responses to the open questions within your text. You can weave them into your discussion like quoted material from books (see Chapter 21: The Research Paper for strategies for integrating quoted material), or you can organize several responses into lists and then comment on them. Since readers' interests can be engaged more easily with quotations than with percentages, plan to use many open responses in your report.

There are computer programs which will produce quantitative results from closed questions and will even print out tables you can insert into your report. For a small informal study, however, such programs probably would not save you much time.

Organizing and writing the report. If you planned your questionnaire to collect information about a trend (Chapter 8: Explaining Causes) or a problem needing a solution (Chapter 6: Making Proposals), then your results would be only a small part of a larger essay. If you are writing a proposal, the Guide to Writing in Chapter 6 will help you explore the results and present them effectively.

In organizing the report of your results, you might want to consider a plan which usually is followed for research reports in the social sciences:

Statement of the Problem
> Context for your study
> Your question
> Need for your study
> Brief preview of your study and forecast of the plan of your report

Review of Other Related Studies (if you know of any)
Procedures
> Designing the questionnaire
> Selecting the readers
> Administering the questionnaire
> Summarizing the results

Results: presentation of what you learned, with little if any commentary or interpretation
Summary and Discussion: brief summary of your results, and discussion of their significance (commenting, interpreting, exploring implications, and comparing to other related studies)

SOURCES OF FURTHER INFORMATION ON FIELD RESEARCH

Babbie, Earl. (1973). *Survey research methods*. Belmont, California: Wadsworth.

Banaka, William H. (1971). *Training in depth interviewing*. New York: Harper & Row.

Brady, James. (1977). *The craft of interviewing*. New York: Vintage.

Brandt, Richard M. (1972). *Studying behavior in natural settings*. New York: Holt, Rinehart and Winston. (Chapters 4, 5, 6)

Fowler, Floyd J. (1984). *Survey research methods*. Beverly Hills: Sage.

Oppenheim, A. N. (1966). *Questionnaire design and attitude measurement*. New York: Basic Books.

Williamson, John B., Karp, David A., and Dalphin, John R. (1977). *The research craft: An introduction to social science methods*. Boston: Little, Brown. (Chapters 6, 7, 8)

Library Research

For many students, doing research in a library involves a variety of diverse activities: checking the card catalog, browsing in the stacks, possibly consulting the *Readers' Guide to Periodical Literature,* and asking the reference librarian for help. Although librarians are there to help in time of need, all college students should nevertheless learn basic library research skills. This chapter presents the search strategy, a systematic and efficient way of doing library research.

The search strategy was developed by librarians to make library research manageable and productive. Although specific search strategies will vary to fit the needs of individual research problems, the general process will be demonstrated here: how to get started; where to find sources; what types of sources are available and what sorts of information they provide; how to evaluate these sources; and, most important, how to go about this process of finding and evaluating sources *systematically.*

Before you begin doing research for a paper, you should familiarize yourself with your college library. College libraries differ from public libraries and high school libraries in that they are oriented more toward research.

OVERVIEW OF A SEARCH STRATEGY

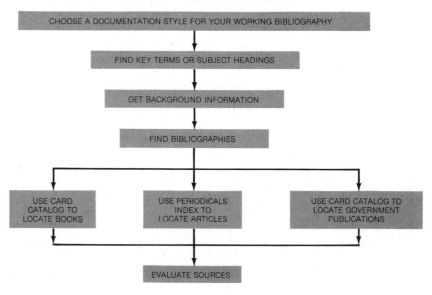

CHOOSE A DOCUMENTATION STYLE FOR YOUR WORKING BIBLIOGRAPHY

FIND KEY TERMS OR SUBJECT HEADINGS

GET BACKGROUND INFORMATION

FIND BIBLIOGRAPHIES

USE CARD CATALOG TO LOCATE BOOKS

USE PERIODICALS INDEX TO LOCATE ARTICLES

USE CARD CATALOG TO LOCATE GOVERNMENT PUBLICATIONS

EVALUATE SOURCES

20

Library research can be useful at various stages of the writing process. How you use the library depends on the kind of essay you are writing and the special needs of your subject, as the writing guides in Part I indicate. You may, for example, need to do research immediately to choose a subject. Or you may choose a topic without the benefit of research but then use the library to find specific information to support your thesis. But no matter when you use library research, you will need to have a search strategy. This search strategy will guide you in setting up a working bibliography and a documentation style, in searching for key words or subject headings, in seeking background information, in finding bibliographies, and in using the card catalog and specialty indexes. Finally, it will help you evaluate the sources that you will use in your writing.

A WORKING BIBLIOGRAPHY

A working bibliography is a preliminary, ongoing record of books, articles, pamphlets—all the sources of information you discover as you research your subject. (A final bibliography, on the other hand, lists only sources actually used in your paper.) Some of the sources in your working bibliography may turn out to be irrelevant, while others simply will be unavailable. In addition, you can use your working bibliography as a means of keeping track of any encyclopedias, bibliographies, and indexes you consult, even though you may not list these resources in your final bibliography.

Because you probably will have to cite many different sources, you must decide on a documentation style before you write. Chapter 21 presents the documentation styles sponsored by the Modern Language Association (MLA) and the American Psychological Association (APA). Other disciplines often have their own preferred styles of documentation, which your instructor may wish you to use. Decide on a style to use at the beginning, when you are constructing a working bibliography, as well as later, when you compile a final bibliography.

Practiced researchers keep their working bibliography either in a notebook or on index cards. They make a point of keeping bibliographical information separate from notes they take on the sources listed in their bibliography. (At the end of this chapter is a brief discussion of taking notes from your reading.)

NOTEBOOK FORM

AUTHOR ——————

CALL NUMBER ——————

FULL TITLE ——————

PUBLISHING IMPRINT ——————

BIBLIOGRAPHICAL SOURCE ——————

AUTHOR ——————

FULL TITLE BUT NO PUBLISHING IMPRINT ——————

BIBLIOGRAPHY IN BACK OF BOOK ——————

> *Anorexia Nervosa*
>
> RC 628
> B72
>
> *Bruch, Hilde. Eating Disorders: Obesity, Anorexia Nervosa, and the Person Within.*
>
> *New York: Basic Books, 1973.*
>
> Bibliographic Index
>
> *Sours, John A. Starving to Death in a Sea of Objects: The Anorexia Nervosa Syndrome.*
>
> *Bibliography pp. 388–431.*

INDEX CARD FORM

CALL NUMBER ——————

AUTHOR ——————

FULL TITLE ——————

PUBLISHING IMPRINT ——————

> RC 628
> B72
>
> *Bruch, Hilde. Eating Disorders: Obesity, Anorexia Nervosa, and the Person Within.*
>
> *New York: Basic Books, 1973.*

Many researchers find index cards more convenient because they are so easily alphabetized. Others find them too easy to lose and prefer, instead, to keep everything—working bibliography, notes, and drafts—in one notebook. Whether you use cards or a notebook, the important thing is to make your entries accurate and complete. If the call number is incomplete or inaccurate, you will not be able to find the book in the stacks. If the volume number for a periodical is incorrect, you may not be able to locate the article. If the author's name is misspelled, you may have trouble finding the book in the card catalog.

KEY SUBJECT HEADINGS

To research a subject, you need to know how it is classified, what key words are used as subject headings in encyclopedias, bibliographies, and the card catalog. As you learn more about your subject, you will discover how other writers refer to it, how it usually is subdivided, and also what subjects are related to it. To begin your search, you should consult the *Library of Congress Subject Headings*. This reference book lists the standard subject headings used in card catalogs and in many encyclopedias and bibliographies. It usually can be found near the card catalog.

Sometimes, the words you think would be used for subject headings are not the ones actually used. For example, if you look up "World War I," you will find a cross reference to "European War, 1914–1918." But, if you look up "bulimia," you will find neither a heading nor a cross reference. Since many people call bulimia an "eating disorder," you might try that heading. But again you would draw a blank. If you tried "appetite," however, you would be referred to "anorexia," a related disorder. Here is the entry for "appetite":

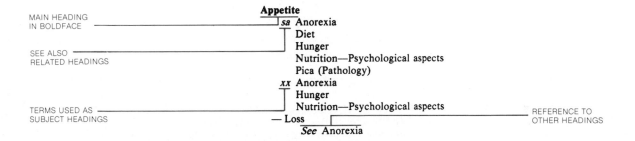

MAIN HEADING IN BOLDFACE

SEE ALSO RELATED HEADINGS

TERMS USED AS SUBJECT HEADINGS

Appetite
   sa Anorexia
      Diet
      Hunger
      Nutrition—Psychological aspects
      Pica (Pathology)
  xx Anorexia
      Hunger
      Nutrition—Psychological aspects
 — Loss
    See Anorexia

REFERENCE TO OTHER HEADINGS

If you then look up "anorexia," you still will not find "bulimia," but you can expect some of the publications on anorexia to deal also with bulimia. In this process of trying possible headings and following up cross references, you also will find related headings such as "nutrition," "obesity," and "psychological."

BACKGROUND INFORMATION

Once you have decided on the form and style of a working bibliography and have found promising subject headings, your search strategy will lead you to the gathering of background sources of information. Such sources will give you a general understanding of the nature and scope of your research subject. They may also provide a historical perspective on the subject, helping you grasp its basic principles and ideas, suggesting what its major divisions or aspects might be, and identifying important people associated with it.

Encyclopedias are the best sources of background information. You have no doubt heard of the *Encyclopaedia Britannica,* probably the best-known general encyclopedia. But there are many specialized encyclopedias. To use encyclopedias effectively, you need to know what subject headings you are looking for. Check each encyclopedia's subject index to locate your subject.

General encyclopedias General encyclopedias are usually multivolume works that contain articles on all areas of knowledge. Written by experts, the articles frequently conclude with a list of important works and bibliographies. Most encyclopedias arrange their subjects alphabetically. Following are the standard general encyclopedias:

> *Encyclopaedia Britannica*
> *Encyclopedia Americana*
> *Collier's Encyclopedia*
> *World Book Encyclopedia*
> *New Columbia Encyclopedia*
> *Dictionary of the History of Ideas*
> *Harper's Dictionary of Modern Thought*

Here is the *Encyclopedia Americana* entry for "Anorexia Nervosa."

ANOREXIA NERVOSA, an-ə-rek′sē-ə nər-vō′sə, a psychosomatic illness in which self-inflicted starvation leads to a devastating loss of weight. It occurs chiefly among well-to-do high school and college girls, affecting about one out of every 200 girls in that group. Girls affected with this disorder have a pathological fear of being fat, which leads to a relentless pursuit of excessive slimness coupled with an intense interest in food. Severe personality problems are common. The typical patient is overcompliant in childhood, and thus inadequately prepared for adolescence and independence. Excessive control over weight —to the point of starvation—represents an effort to establish a sense of selfhood and autonomy. Starvation, in turn, creates its own physiological and psychological symptoms and complications.
Anorexics characteristically see themselves unrealistically and experience their bodies as something separate from, not part of, their true selves. Abstinence from food may alternate with eating binges, which are followed by efforts to remove

the unwanted food through self-induced vomiting, laxatives, and diuretics. These practices may result in serious disturbances in the electrolyte balance, at times with a fatal outcome. Though anorexics give a first impression of being active and vigorous, they suffer from a paralyzing sense of ineffectiveness. They gain a sense of accomplishment from controlling their weight, and they experience deep feelings of depression and self-hatred when they regain any weight.

Anorexia nervosa has a tendency to be self-perpetuating, leading to chronic invalidism or even to death. These tragic outcomes are avoidable when proper treatment is started before the condition becomes firmly established. Early warning signs include fanaticism about losing weight, a frantic increase in activities, social isolation, and sleep deprivation. Treatment involves restitution of normal nutrition, resolution of the patient's overintense involvement with her family, and clarification of the underlying personality problems. Weight gain alone, without resolution of the psychological problems, is not sufficient.

HILDA BRUCH, M. D., *Author of "The Golden Cage: The Enigma of Anorexis Nervosa" and "Eating Disorders: Obesity, Anorexia Nervosa, and the Person Within"*

Specialized encyclopedias Specialized encyclopedias focus on a single area of knowledge. To find specialized encyclopedias, look in the subject card catalog under the appropriate subject heading. Encyclopedias usually are catalogued under the subheading "Dictionaries" and are kept in the reference section of the library. Here is a partial list of specialized encyclopedias:

> *Encyclopedia of Education*
> *Encyclopedia of Philosophy*
> *Grove's Dictionary of Music and Musicians*
> *International Encyclopedia of the Social Sciences*
> *Harvard Encyclopedia of American Ethnic Groups*
> *McGraw-Hill Dictionary of Art*
> *McGraw-Hill Encyclopedia of Science and Technology*
> *Oxford Classical Dictionary*
> *Oxford Companion to American History*

BIBLIOGRAPHIES

A bibliography is simply a list of publications on a given subject. Whereas an encyclopedia gives you background information on your subject, a bibliography gives you an overview of what has been published on the subject. Its scope may be broad or narrow. Some bibliographers try to be exhaustive, including every title they can find, while most are selective. To discover how selections were made, check the bibliography's preface or introduction. Occasionally, bibliographies are annnotated: that is, they provide brief summaries of the entries and, sometimes, also evaluate them. Bibliographies may be found in a variety of places: in encyclopedias, in the card catalog, and in secondary sources. To be efficient, however, the best way to locate a comprehensive, up-to-date bibliography on your subject is to use the *Bibliographic Index*.

The *Bibliographic Index* is a master list of bibliographies with fifty or more titles. It includes bibliographies from articles, books, and government publications. Here is a sample entry:

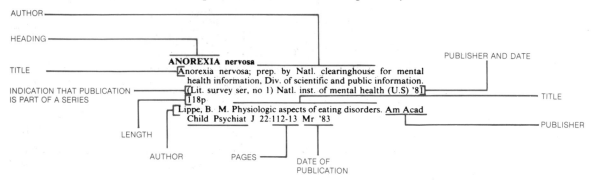

The first reference is to a bibliography put out by the National Institute of Mental Health—a government publication. The second is a bibliography included in a book.

A new volume of *Bibliographic Index* is published every year. Because this index is not cumulative, you should check back over several years, beginning with the most current volume.

THE CARD CATALOG

The card catalog in your library contains cards with the names of authors, subjects, and titles. Author, subject, and title cards all give the same basic information.

1. The *call number*—always in the upper lefthand corner, indicates the numerical code under which the book is filed in the library. Books will be filed in the library by their call numbers, which are assigned according to subject. Most college research libraries use the Library of Congress

subject headings and numbering system. Call numbers have at least two rows of numbers. The top row indicates the general subject classification, whereas the second row places the book within this classification. Subsequent rows identify the copyright and publication date for multiple editions.

2. The *author*—appears last name first, followed by birth and death dates. If there are multiple authors, there is an author card under each author's name.

3. The *title*—exactly as it appears on the title page of the book, except here only the first word is capitalized.

4. The *author* again—this time just as it appears on the title page. If there are multiple authors, all authors are listed here.

5. The *imprint*—includes the place of publication (usually just the city), publisher, and year of publication. If the book was published simultaneously in the U. S. and abroad, both places of publication and both publishers are included.

6. *Collation*—descriptive information about book's length and size. Roman numeral indicates the number of pages used for front matter (preface, contents, and acknowledgments).

7. *Notes*—indicate any special features (for example, a bibliography or an index).

8. *Subject headings*—indicate how the book is listed in the Subject Catalog. These suggest headings you can use to find other books related to your subject.

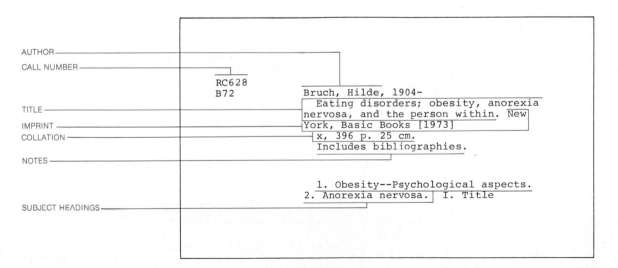

AUTHOR

CALL NUMBER

RC628
B72

Bruch, Hilde, 1904-
   Eating disorders; obesity, anorexia nervosa, and the person within. New York, Basic Books [1973]

TITLE

IMPRINT

COLLATION

x, 396 p. 25 cm.
Includes bibliographies.

NOTES

1. Obesity--Psychological aspects.
2. Anorexia nervosa. I. Title

SUBJECT HEADINGS

The same basic card is used also for title and subject cards, but the latter have headings printed at the top. The title card has the title above the author's name:

TITLE

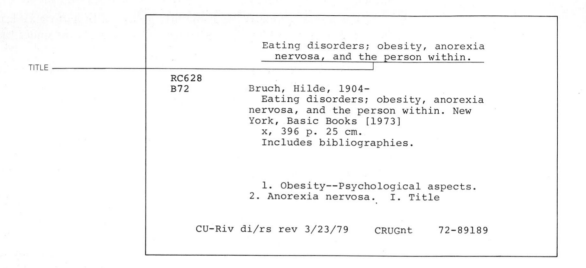

The subject card has the subject above the author's name. Notice that the two subject cards that follow correspond to the subject headings at the bottom of the author and title cards.

PRIMARY
SUBJECT
HEADING

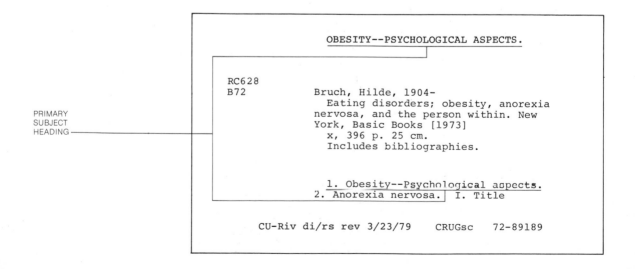

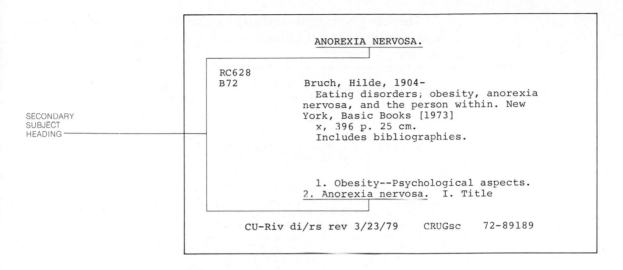

SECONDARY SUBJECT HEADING ───────────

ANOREXIA NERVOSA.

RC628
B72   Bruch, Hilde, 1904-
              Eating disorders; obesity, anorexia
          nervosa, and the person within. New
          York, Basic Books [1973]
              x, 396 p. 25 cm.
              Includes bibliographies.

              1. Obesity--Psychological aspects.
          2. Anorexia nervosa.   I. Title

          CU-Riv di/rs rev 3/23/79   CRUGsc   72-89189

Remember: an "author" may be a person, a corporation, an association, a city, or a bureau. As such, author cards are filed alphabetically by an author's last name or by the first word in a group name (*International* for International Business Machines, for example). Title cards are filed alphabetically by the first word of the title, except if the first word is an article: a title beginning with *a, an,* or *the* is filed under its second word.

PERIODICALS INDEXES AND ABSTRACTS

The most up-to-date information on a subject usually is not found in books, but in recently published articles that appear in journals and serials, or periodicals, as they often are called. Periodicals appear daily, weekly, quarterly, or annually (hence the name *periodical*). Articles in such publications usually are not listed in the card catalog; to find them, you must instead use periodicals indexes and abstracts. Indexes will only list articles, whereas abstracts summarize as well as list them.

Following is an example from an index you may be familiar with already—the *Readers' Guide to Periodical Literature:*

SUBJECT HEADING ─────── **Anorexia nervosa**
Anorexia nervosa. D. K. Mano. *Natl Rev* 35:1626-8 D ─────── PERIODICAL
TITLE ─────── 23 '83
Anorexia nervosa: a hormonal link [abnormal levels of
  vasopressin] *Newsweek* 101:69 My 23 '83
VOLUME AND PAGE ─────── A brother remembers [K. Carpenter] R. Carpenter. il ─────── DATE
  pors *People Wkly* 20:152-3+ N 21 '83
Can an athlete take fitness too far? [M. Wazeter's suicide
  attempt linked to athletic competition] N. Amdur. il
  pors *Seventeen* 42:24+ Jl '83

The following example is from a less familiar, more specialized reference work: *Psychological Abstracts*.

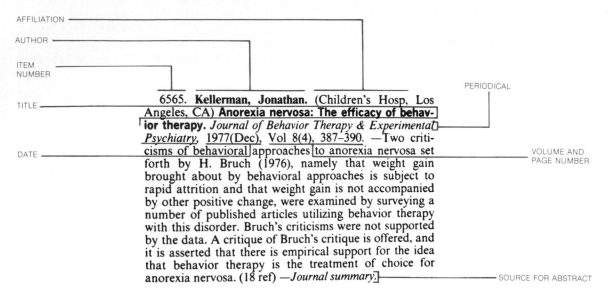

AFFILIATION
AUTHOR
ITEM NUMBER
PERIODICAL
TITLE
DATE
VOLUME AND PAGE NUMBER
SOURCE FOR ABSTRACT

6565. **Kellerman, Jonathan.** (Children's Hosp, Los Angeles, CA) **Anorexia nervosa: The efficacy of behavior therapy.** *Journal of Behavior Therapy & Experimental Psychiatry,* 1977(Dec), Vol 8(4), 387–390. —Two criticisms of behavioral approaches to anorexia nervosa set forth by H. Bruch (1976), namely that weight gain brought about by behavioral approaches is subject to rapid attrition and that weight gain is not accompanied by other positive change, were examined by surveying a number of published articles utilizing behavior therapy with this disorder. Bruch's criticisms were not supported by the data. A critique of Bruch's critique is offered, and it is asserted that there is empirical support for the idea that behavior therapy is the treatment of choice for anorexia nervosa. (18 ref) —*Journal summary.*

Many periodicals indexes use the Library of Congress subject headings, but some have their own systems. *Psychological Abstracts,* for example, has a separate volume for subject headings. Following is an excerpt from that volume:

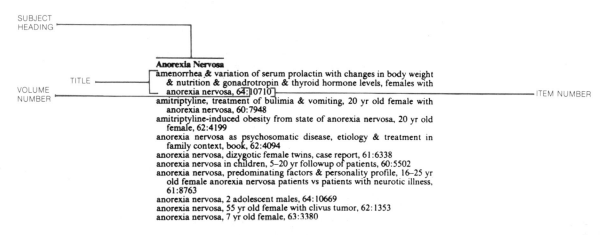

SUBJECT HEADING
TITLE
VOLUME NUMBER
ITEM NUMBER

Anorexia Nervosa
amenorrhea & variation of serum prolactin with changes in body weight & nutrition & gonadrotropin & thyroid hormone levels, females with anorexia nervosa, 64:10710
amitriptyline, treatment of bulimia & vomiting, 20 yr old female with anorexia nervosa, 60:7948
amitriptyline-induced obesity from state of anorexia nervosa, 20 yr old female, 62:4199
anorexia nervosa as psychosomatic disease, etiology & treatment in family context, book, 62:4094
anorexia nervosa, dizygotic female twins, case report, 61:6338
anorexia nervosa in children, 5–20 yr followup of patients, 60:5502
anorexia nervosa, predominating factors & personality profile, 16–25 yr old female anorexia nervosa patients vs patients with neurotic illness, 61:8763
anorexia nervosa, 2 adolescent males, 64:10669
anorexia nervosa, 55 yr old female with clivus tumor, 62:1353
anorexia nervosa, 7 yr old female, 63:3380

Check the opening pages of the index you are using to see how it classifies its subjects.

Like encyclopedias, periodicals indexes and abstracts exist in both general and specialized forms.

General indexes

General indexes list articles in nontechnical, general interest publications. They cover a broad range of subjects. Most have separate author and subject listings as well as a list of book reviews. Following are some general indexes:

> *Readers' Guide to Periodical Literature* (1905–present) covers more than 180 popular periodicals.
>
> *Humanities Index* (1974–present) covers archaeology, history, classics, literature, performing arts, philosophy, and religion.
>
> *Social Sciences Index* (1974–present) covers economics, geography, law, political science, psychology, public administration, and sociology.
>
> *Public Affairs Information Service Bulletin* [PAIS] (1915–present) covers articles and other publications by public and private agencies on economic and social conditions, international relations, and public administration. Subject listing only.

Specialized indexes

Specialized indexes list articles in periodicals devoted to technical or scholarly research reports. Following is a list of some specialized indexes:

> *Accountant's Index* (1944–present)
>
> *Almanac of American Politics* (1972–present)
>
> *American Statistics Index* (1973–present)
>
> *Applied Science and Technology Index* (1958–present)
>
> *Biological and Agricultural Index* (1964–present)
>
> *Congressional Digest* (1921–present)
>
> *Congressional Quarterly Weekly Reports* (1956–present)
>
> *Education Index* (1929–present)
>
> *Engineering Index* (1920–present)
>
> *Historical Abstracts* (1955–present)
>
> *Index Medicus* (1961–present)
>
> *MLA International Bibliography of Books and Articles in the Modern Languages and Literature* (1921–present)
>
> *Philosopher's Index* (1967–present)
>
> *Psychology Abstracts* (1927–present)
>
> *Statistical Abstracts of the United States* (annual)
>
> *Statistical Yearbook* (1949–present)

Newspaper indexes   Newspapers often provide information unavailable elsewhere, especially accounts of current events, analyses of recent trends, texts of important speeches by public officials, obituaries, and film and book reviews. Libraries usually miniaturize newspapers and store them on microfilm (reels) or microfiche (cards), which must be placed in viewing machines in order to be read. Following are some general and specialized newspaper indexes:

General news indexes

Facts on File (1941–present)
Keesing's Contemporary Archives (1931–present)

Indexes to particular newspapers

Christian Science Monitor Index (1960–present)
(London) *Times Index* (1785–present)
New York Times Index (1851–present)
Wall Street Journal Index (1972–present)

Computerized newspaper and periodical indexes

The *National Newspaper Index*—lists items in the *New York Times, Wall Street Journal,* and *Christian Science Monitor.*
Magazine Index—lists articles in nearly 400 general periodicals.

GOVERNMENT PUBLICATIONS

The countless documents published by agencies of the United States government and by state governments and United Nations organizations may be an additional source of useful information. Most college research libraries have a government publications collection, usually catalogued and housed separately. The collection should include agency publications, statistics, research reports, and public service pamphlets. Following are some indexes of government publications.

The *Monthly Index to the United States Government Publications* (1895–present)—separate cumulative index is published annually.
CIS Index and *CIS Abstracts* (1970–present)—Congressional Committee documents.
Public Affairs Information Service Bulletin [PAIS] (1915–present)—PAIS indexes government documents as well as books on political and social issues.

International Bibliography, Information, Documentation (1973–present)—indexes selected documents published by the United Nations and other international organizations.

United Nations Documents Index (1950–present)—comprehensive index to documents published by the United Nations.

EVALUATING SOURCES

The final phase of a search strategy involves evaluating the sources in your working bibliography to determine which to use in your essay. Obviously, you must decide which sources provide information relevant to the topic. But you also must decide how credible or trustworthy your sources are. Just because a book is published or an essay appears in print does not necessarily mean the information in it is reliable.

Begin the evaluation of your sources by narrowing your working bibliography to the most relevant sources. Then determine how reliable these sources are.

Scope. To decide how relevant a particular source is, you need to examine it in depth. Do not depend on title alone, for it may be misleading. If the source is a book, check its table of contents and index to see how many pages are devoted to the aspect of the subject you are exploring. You most likely will want an in-depth, not a superficial, treatment of the major aspects of your topic. Read the preface to discover the author's bias or special way of looking at the subject. The introduction to a book or opening paragraphs of an article should alert you to the author's basic approach to the subject. Abstracts, printed with many scholarly articles, give you a quick idea of the scope and approach of the selection.

Date of publication. The date of publication may be an important clue. If you are addressing a current trend or problem, then you want the most up-to-date sources available. Similarly, if you are writing about a scientific or technological subject that is undergoing rapid change, only the most recent information will be useful. However, older sources often establish the principles, theories, and data upon which later work rests. Since many older works are considered classics, you may want to be familiar with them. To determine which sources are classics, note which are cited most often in encyclopedia articles, bibliographies, and recent works on the subject.

Variety. You will also want your sources to represent a variety of viewpoints on the subject. Just as you would not depend on a single author for all of your information, so you do not want to use authors who all belong to the same school of thought. To determine which school each author belongs to, look at the preface and introduction and the sources the author used.

Bibliographies. Selective bibliographies, particularly those with annotations, can also help you gauge the reliability of sources on your list. Check the bibliography's preface or introduction to discover the principle of selection. You may also want to check other bibliographies, particularly more recent ones and those included in respected books on the subject.

Book reviews. Book reviews can be very helpful in establishing the reliability of a source, but sometimes a reviewer's approach to the subject differs so radically from the author's that a *review* in and of itself is not a reliable gauge of a book's value. There are several indexes you can use to find book reviews, but you will need the book's author, title, and date of publication. If you are missing anything, you can consult the card catalog, the *National Union Catalog,* or *Books in Print.* Most book reviews appear within a year after a book's publication, but scholarly books tend to be reviewed later, if at all. Remember: not all books are reviewed.

Many indexes not only indicate where you can find reviews; they also summarize some of them. Here is an example from *Book Digest:*

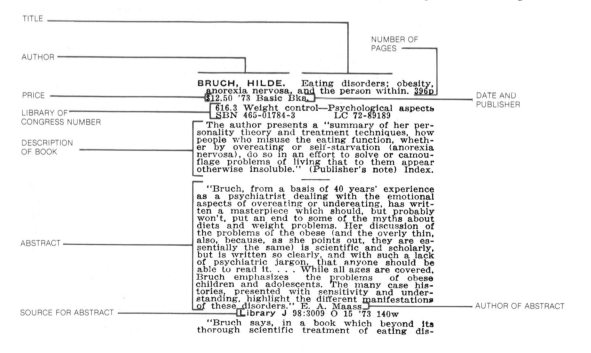

TITLE

NUMBER OF PAGES

AUTHOR

PRICE

DATE AND PUBLISHER

LIBRARY OF CONGRESS NUMBER

DESCRIPTION OF BOOK

ABSTRACT

SOURCE FOR ABSTRACT

AUTHOR OF ABSTRACT

BRUCH, HILDE. Eating disorders; obesity, anorexia nervosa, and the person within. 396p $12.50 '73 Basic Bks

616.3 Weight control—Psychological aspects

SBN 465-01784-3   LC 72-89189

The author presents a "summary of her personality theory and treatment techniques, how people who misuse the eating function, whether by overeating or self-starvation (anorexia nervosa), do so in an effort to solve or camouflage problems of living that to them appear otherwise insoluble." (Publisher's note) Index.

"Bruch, from a basis of 40 years' experience as a psychiatrist dealing with the emotional aspects of overeating or undereating, has written a masterpiece which should, but probably won't, put an end to some of the myths about diets and weight problems. Her discussion of the problems of the obese (and the overly thin, also, because, as she points out, they are essentially the same) is scientific and scholarly, but is written so clearly, and with such a lack of psychiatric jargon, that anyone should be able to read it. . . . While all ages are covered, Bruch emphasizes the problems of obese children and adolescents. The many case histories, presented with sensitivity and understanding, highlight the different manifestations of these disorders." E. A. Maass

Library J 98:3009 O 15 '73 140w

"Bruch says, in a book which beyond its thorough scientific treatment of eating dis-

orders, is characterised by an enormous fund of good sense, [that] such disorders are merely the visible result of underlying physiological and psychological mechanisms. . . . The whole problem of body imagery is a fascinating one, and Dr Bruch has made an invaluable contribution to it. As a psychiatrist she has properly concentrated on the psychological aspects of her problem but throughout she has shown herself fully aware of the sociological factors, in particular the pressure of social ideals."
Peter Riviére
New Statesman 87:296 Mr 1 '74 550w

"[It is because Bruch's book avoids the unjustified dogma of 'popular' dieting books] that it is outstanding. . . . On the other hand, two words of caution are necessary. The first is that Professor Bruch is a psychiatrist and . . . patients she sees tend to be either those who have gross psychological, or indeed psychotic, features, or those who have failed to respond to all other forms of therapy. . . . Secondly [the] book is based entirely on experience in the United States. . . . Generally, however, [she] presents a commendably balanced picture. She may overstress the psychiatric aspect, but not unduly; indeed, this may almost be a commendation in view of the unbalanced stress laid on the physical aspect by so many other writers on the subject."
TLS p296 Mr 22 '74 480w

Following is a list of some indexes of book reviews:

Book Review Digest (1905–present) covers about 70 British and American periodicals with a cumulative author and title index for 1905–1974.

Book Review Index (1965–present) covers 255 English language periodicals.

Current Retrospective Index to Book Reviews in Scholarly Journals (1886–1974) covers 500 social science periodicals. Volumes 1–11 list reviews and Volumes 12–15 list titles of books reviewed.

Index to Book Reviews in the Humanities (1960–present) covers many scholarly journals not covered elsewhere.

Richard A. Gray's *Guide to Book Review Citations: A Bibliography of Sources* lists specialized indexes.

TAKING NOTES

Having found your sources, you will need to take notes as you read. If you own the work or have a photocopy of the relevant parts, you may want to annotate to help you read analytically. You should know how to paraphrase, summarize, and outline. All of these reading skills are discussed and illustrated in Chapter 18: Invention and Inquiry. You will also want to write down quotations you might use in your essay. Conventions for quoting are covered in the next chapter, The Research Paper: Using and Acknowledging Sources.

You may already have a method of notetaking you prefer. Some people like to use index cards for notes as well as for their working bibliography.

They use small 3 × 5 inch index cards for their bibliography and larger ones (4 × 6 or 5 × 7) for notes. Some even use a different color index card for each of their sources. Other people prefer to keep their notes in a notebook. Still others enter their notes into a computer. It really does not matter what method you use as long as you keep accurate notes.

Accuracy in notetaking is of paramount importance in order to minimize the risk of copying facts incorrectly or of misquoting. Another common error in notetaking is to use the author's words without enclosing them in quotation marks. This error could lead easily to plagiarism, the unacknowledged use of another's words or ideas. Double check all your notes and try to be as accurate as you can.

The Research Paper: Using and Acknowledging Sources

Much of the writing you will do in college requires you to use outside sources in combination with your own firsthand observation and reflection. When you get information and ideas from reading, lectures, and interviews, you are using sources.

Using sources is not only acceptable, it is expected in college. Educated people very often are original thinkers, but they nearly always base their original thought on the work of others. In fact, most of your college education is devoted to teaching you two things: (1) what Matthew Arnold called "the best that has been thought and said," and (2) the way to analyze the thoughts and words of others, integrate them into your own thinking, and effectively convey your thinking to others.

Writers—students and professionals alike—occasionally misuse sources by failing to acknowledge them properly. The word *plagiarism,* which derives from the Latin word for "kidnapping," refers to the unacknowledged use of another's words, ideas, or information. Some people plagiarize simply because they do not know the conventions for using and acknowledging sources. This chapter will make clear how to incorporate sources into your writing and how to acknowledge your use of those sources.

Others plagiarize because they keep sloppy notes and thus fail to distinguish between what is their own and what is their source's. Either they neglect to enclose their source's words in quotation marks or do not indicate when they are paraphrasing or summmarizing a source's ideas and information. If you keep a working bibliography and careful notes, as described in Chapter 20: Library Research, you will not make this mistake.

There is still another reason some people plagiarize: They feel unable to write the paper by themselves. They feel overwhelmed by the writing task or by the deadline or by their own and others' expectations of them. This sense of inadequacy is not experienced by students alone. In a recent *Los Angeles Times* article on the subject, a journalist who had plagiarized explained why he had done it. He said that when he read a column by another journalist on a subject he was preparing to write about, he felt that the other writer "said what I wanted to say and he said it better." If you experience this same nervousness about your work, speak to your instructor. Most colleges have writing centers or other facilities to help students gain the skills and confidence to write papers.

USING SOURCES

Writers commonly use sources by quoting them, but they may also paraphrase or summarize information and ideas. Be selective in using quotation to support your ideas. As a general rule, quote only when your source's language is particularly vivid, memorable, or well known, or when your source is so respected by your readers that quoting would lend authority to your writing. If the phrasing does not matter, it is preferable to paraphrase or summarize (see Chapter 18: Invention and Inquiry) rather than quote.

Quoting   Quotations should duplicate the source exactly. If the source has an error, copy it and add the Latin word *sic* in brackets immediately after the error to indicate that it is not yours but your source's:

> According to a recent newspaper article, "Plagirism [*sic*] is a problem among journalists and scholars as well as students."

However, you can change quotations (1) to emphasize particular words by underlining or italicizing them, (2) to omit irrelevant information or to make the quotation conform grammatically to your sentence by using ellipses, and (3) to make the quotation conform grammatically or to insert information by using brackets.

Underlining or italicizing for emphasis. Underline or italicize the words you want to emphasize, and add the phrase (*emphasis added*) or (*italics added*) at the end of the sentence. In his essay on youth suicide in Chapter 8, Victor Fuchs emphasizes that part of the quotation that refers specifically to suicide:

In a review of psychosocial literature on adolescence, Elder (1975) concludes: "Adolescents who fail to receive guidance, affection, and concern from parents—whether by parental inattention or absence—are likely to rely heavily on peers for emotional gratification, advice, and companionship, *to anticipate a relatively unrewarding future,* and to engage in antisocial activities" (italics added).

Using ellipses for omissions. Ellipsis marks of three periods with spaces before and after (. . .) should be used to indicate an omission. If the omission occurs at the end of a sentence, place a sentence period directly after the last word, followed by the three spaced periods. If the omission is followed by a parenthetical citation, use three spaced periods before the parentheses and a sentence period directly after them.

Here are two examples from Chapter 5. The first is from William Langer's essay on the plague, and the second is from Scott Sumner's piece on the composer John Cage:

> Everywhere, wrote chroniclers of the epidemics in London then and later, there was "drinking, roaring and surfeiting. . . . In one house you might hear them roaring under the pangs of death, in the next tippling, whoring and belching out blasphemies against God."

> Cage delights in seeing ". . . the performer . . . and the listener too . . . *discovering* the nature of the structure . . ." (Cage and Reynolds 582).

When you quote a small part of a sentence, you need not use ellipses; instead, you may integrate a single word or phrase into your sentence simply by enclosing it in quotation marks, as Debbie Brawner does in her essay on "Young Goodman Brown" from Chapter 9:

> The devil tries to persuade Brown that virtue is a dream and "evil the only reality," while Brown clings to the belief that virtue is the only reality.

Using brackets for insertions or changes. You may also use brackets to make a quotation conform grammatically to your sentence. In this example from Chapter 9, Brawner adapts Hawthorne's phrase "his dying hour was gloom" to fit the tense of her sentence:

> Because of this doubt, "his dying hour [is] gloom."

Sumner (Chapter 5) uses brackets and ellipses to make a quotation fit into his sentence:

> Virgil Thompson, who was music critic at the *Herald Tribune,* wrote: "Mr. Cage has . . . develop[ed] the rhythmic element of composition . . . to a point of sophistication unmatched in the technique of any living composer."

You may also use brackets to add or substitute explanatory material in a quotation. In her essay in Chapter 6, Carol Bly uses brackets to identify a character in the novel *Anna Karenina:*

> The sentence about technique had sent a pang through Mihailov's [the painter's] heart, and looking angrily at Vronsky he suddenly scowled.

Several kinds of changes necessary to make a quotation conform grammatically to another sentence may be made without any signal to readers: (1) the first letter of the first word in a quotation may be changed from capital to lower case, (2) the punctuation mark at the end of a quotation may be changed, and (3) double quotation marks (enclosing the entire quotation) may be changed to single quotation marks (enclosing a quotation within the larger quotation).

Placing quotations   A quotation may either be incorporated into the text by enclosing it in quotation marks or set off from the text in a block without quotation marks.

In-text quotations. Incorporate brief quotations (no more than four typed lines of prose or three lines of poetry) into your text. When you quote poetry, use a slash with spaces before and after (/) to signal the end of each line of verse:

> Alluding to St. Augustine's distinction between City of God and Earthly City, Lowell writes that "much against my will / I left the City of God where it belongs."   Steven Gould Axelrod, *Robert Lowell: Life and Art*

You may identify the source at either the beginning or the end of a quotation, or you may interrupt the quotation to do so:

> Morton Feldman (an associate of Cage) explains the importance of Cage: "You have to remember how straight-laced everything had always been in music. Just to change one thing in music was a life's work. But John changed everything." (Scott Sumner, Chapter 5)

> "We're in *Ripley's Believe It or Not,* along with another funeral home whose owners' names are Baggit and Sackit," Howard told me, without cracking a smile. (Brian Cable, Chapter 10)

> "The West begins," Bernard DeVoto wrote, "where the average annual rainfall drops below twenty inches." (Joan Didion, Chapter 10)

Block quotations. Put in block form, *without quotation marks,* five or more typed lines of prose or four or more lines of poetry. This example comes from Joan Didion's essay in Chapter 10:

> This fragment of paper is now on the wall of a sixth kitchen, and crumbles

a little whenever I touch it, but I keep it there for the last stanza, which has for me the power of a prayer:

> It is raining in California, a straight rain
> Cleaning the heavy oranges on the bough,
> Filling in the gardens till the gardens flow,
> Shining the olives, tiling the gleaming tile,
> Waxing the dark camellia leaves more green,
> Flooding the daylong valleys like the Nile.

Punctuating introductory statements

Statements that introduce quotations take a range of punctuation marks. Here are several examples of ways writers in Part I introduce quotations:

Introducing a statement with a colon

But whoever said it first was merely reacting impulsively to a particular play and not trying to coin a mot when he ejaculated: "The sonofagun! Ten years I've been watching him, and he hasn't had a hard chance yet!" (Red Smith, Chapter 7)

Introducing a statement with a comma

As Boccaccio wrote, "the reverend authority of the laws, both human and divine, was all in a manner dissolved and fallen into decay, for lack of the ministers and executors thereof." (William Langer, Chapter 5)

Introducing a statement using *that*

By inserting bolts, rubber, wood, glass, and other materials between the piano strings, Cage made a piano <u>that</u> was in effect "a percussion orchestra under the control of a single player."

Introducing a statement using "what . . . as"

Young people may be succumbing to <u>what Abraham Maslow (1959) forecast as</u> the ultimate disease of our time—"valuelessness." (Victor Fuchs, Chapter 8)

Avoiding grammatical tangles

When you incorporate quotations into your writing and especially when you omit or change words, you run the risk of creating ungrammatical sentences. Here are three common errors you should make an effort to avoid: verb incompatibility, ungrammatical omissions, and sentence fragments.

Verb incompatibility. When this error occurs, the verb form in the introductory statement is grammatically incompatible with the verb form in the quotation. When your quotation has a verb form that does not fit in with your text, it is usually possible to use just part of the quotation, thus avoiding verb incompatibility. In the following example, *suggests* and *bearing* do not fit together as the sentence is written; see how the revised sentence is restructured to make them compatible.

NOT   The narrator suggests that Brown and the Devil are related in this way, ". . . [the Devil] bearing a considerable resemblance to him. . . ."

BUT   The narrator suggests that Brown and the Devil are related <u>when he describes the Devil as</u> ". . . bearing a considerable resemblance to him. . . ."

An awkward omission. Sometimes the omission of text from the quotation results in an ungrammatical sentence. In the following example, the quotation was awkwardly and ungrammatically excerpted. The revised sentences show two ways of correcting the grammar: first, by adapting the quotation (with brackets) so that its two parts fit together grammatically; second, by using only one part of the quotation.

NOT   Hawthorne's language implies that Brown may have imagined the Devil's arguments: "They continued to walk onward, while the elder traveler . . . his arguments seemed rather to spring up in the bosom of his auditor, than to be suggested by himself."

BUT   Hawthorne's language implies that Brown may have imagined the Devil's arguments: "They continued to walk onward, while the elder traveler[<u>'s</u>] . . . arguments seemed rather to spring up in the bosom of his auditor, than to be suggested by himself."

OR   Hawthorne's language implies that Brown may have imagined the Devil's arguments; <u>he writes that the</u> ". . . arguments seemed rather to spring up in the bosom of his auditor, than to be suggested by himself."

An incomplete introductory sentence. Sometimes when a quotation is a complete sentence, writers will carelessly neglect the introductory sentence—often, for example, forgetting to include a verb. Even though the quotation is a complete sentence, the total statement is then a sentence fragment.

NOT   Brown, who relies on his wife Faith for his own steadfastness: "With Heaven above, and Faith below, I will stand firm against the Devil!"

BUT   Brown, who relies on his wife Faith for his own steadfastness, <u>proclaims:</u> "With Heaven above, and Faith below, I will stand firm against the Devil!"

Paraphrasing and summarizing In addition to quoting their sources, writers have the option of summarizing them. This method allows them to use the source's information, but to present it in their own words.

The following examples show how writers summarize statistics and facts as well as thoughts and ideas:

> A study at Bellevue Hospital in New York City of 102 teenagers who attempted suicide showed that only one third of them lived with both parents (*Newsweek,* August 28, 1978, p. 74). (Victor Fuchs, Chapter 8)

> Some 70 years ago the English Catholic prelate and historian (later cardinal) Francis Gasquet, in a study entitled *The Great Pestilence,* tried to demonstrate that the Black Death set the stage for the Protestant Reformation by killing off the clergy and upsetting the entire religious life of Europe. (William Langer, Chapter 5)

Notice in the preceding examples that each writer acknowledges his source by name. Even when you use your own words to present someone else's information, you generally must acknowledge the fact that you borrowed the information. The only information that does not require acknowledgment is common knowledge (John F. Kennedy was assassinated in Dallas), familiar sayings ("haste makes waste"), and well-known quotations ("Give me liberty or give me death!").

ACKNOWLEDGING SOURCES

Although there is no universally agreed-upon system for acknowledging sources, there is agreement on both the need for documentation and the items which should be included. Writers should acknowledge sources for two reasons: to give credit to those sources, and to enable readers to consult the sources for further information. This information should be included when documenting sources: (1) name of author, (2) title of publication, and (3) publication source, date, and page.

Most documentation styles combine some kind of citation in the text with a separate list of references keyed to the textual citations. There are basically two ways of acknowledging sources: (1) parenthetical citations keyed to a works-cited list, and (2) footnotes (or endnotes) plus a bibliography. The Modern Language Association (MLA), a professional organization of English instructors, has until very recently endorsed the footnote style of documentation. But, with the 1984 revision of the *MLA Handbook,* the MLA has gone over to the simpler parenthetical citation method. The new MLA style is similar to the style endorsed by the American Psychological Association (APA)—the style used by many social and natural science instructors.

In Part I of this book, you can find examples of the new MLA style (Scott Sumner in Chapter 5 and Debbie Brawner in Chapter 9) and the APA style (Victor Fuchs and Kim Dartnell in Chapter 8). This chapter presents the basic features of the new MLA and the APA styles.

If you have any questions, consult the *MLA Handbook for Writers of Research Papers,* Second Edition (1984), or the *Publication Manual of the American Psychological Association,* Third Edition (1983). The *MLA Handbook* includes both the new and old MLA styles.

Parenthetical citation in text   The MLA and APA styles both advocate parenthetical citations in the text keyed to a works-cited list at the end of the paper. However, they differ on what should be included in the parenthetical citation. Whereas the MLA uses an author-page citation, the APA uses an author-year-page citation.

MLA   Dr. James is described as a "not-too-skeletal Ichabod Crane" (Simon 68).

APA   Dr. James is described as a "not-too-skeletal Ichabod Crane" (Simon, 1982, p. 68).

Notice that the APA style uses a comma between author, year, and page as well as "p." for page (Simon, 1982, p. 68), whereas the MLA puts nothing but space between author and page (Simon 68). For a block quotation, put the citation after the final period; otherwise, put the citation before the final period.

If the author's name is used in the text, put the page reference in parentheses as close as possible to the borrowed material, but without disrupting the flow of the sentence. For the APA style, cite the year in parentheses directly following the author's name, and place the page reference in parentheses before the final sentence period. In the case of block quotations for both MLA and APA, put the page reference in parentheses two spaces after the final sentence period.

MLA   Simon describes Dr. James as a "not-too-skeletal Ichabod Crane" (68).

APA   Simon (1982) describes Dr. James as a "not-too-skeletal Ichabod Crane" (p. 68).

To cite a source by two or more authors, the MLA uses all the authors' last names, unless the entry in the works-cited list gives the first author's name followed by "et al." The APA uses all the authors' last names the first time the reference occurs and the last name of the first author followed by "et al.," subsequently.

MLA   Dyal, Corning, and Willows identify several types of students, including the "Authority-Rebel" (4).

APA Dyal, Corning, and Willows (1975) identify several types of students, including the "Authority-Rebel" (p. 4).

MLA The Authority-Rebel "tends to see himself as superior to other students in the class" (Dyal, Corning, and Willows 4).

APA The Authority-Rebel "tends to see himself as superior to other students in the class" (Dyal et al., 1975, p. 4).

To cite one of two or more works by the same author(s), the MLA uses the author's last name, a shortened version of the title, and the page. The APA uses the author's last name plus the year and page.

MLA When old paint becomes transparent, it sometimes shows the artist's original plans: "a tree will show through a woman's dress" (Hellman, Pentimento 1).

APA When old paint becomes transparent, it sometimes shows the artist's original plans: "a tree will show through a woman's dress" (Hellman, 1973, p. 1).

To cite a work listed only by its title, both the MLA and the APA use a shortened version of the title.

MLA Lillian Hellman calls Dashiell Hammett: "my closest, my most beloved friend" (*Woman* 224).

APA Lillian Hellman (1969) calls Dashiell Hammett: "my closest, my most beloved friend" (*Woman* p. 224).

To quote material taken not from the original but from a secondary source that quotes the original, both the MLA and the APA give the secondary source in the works-cited list, and cite both the original and secondary sources in the text.

MLA E. M. Forster says "the collapse of all civilization, so realistic for us, sounded in [Matthew Arnold's] ears like a distant and harmonious cataract" (qtd. in Trilling 11).

APA E. M. Forster says "the collapse of all civilization, so realistic for us, sounded in [Matthew Arnold's] ears like a distant and harmonious cataract" (cited in Trilling, 1955, p. 11).

List of works cited Keyed to the parenthetical citations in the text, the list of works cited identifies all the sources the writer uses. Every source cited in the text must refer to an entry in the works-cited list. And, conversely, every entry in the works-cited list must correspond to at least one parenthetical citation in the text.

Whereas the MLA style manual uses the title "Works Cited," the APA prefers "References." Both alphabetize the entries according to the first author's last name. When several works by an author are listed, the APA recommends these rules for arranging the list:

☐ Same name single-author entries precede multiple-author entries:

> Aaron, P. (1985).
>
> Aaron, P., & Zorn, C. R. (1982).

☐ Entries with the same first author and different second author should be alphabetized according to the second author's last name:

> Aaron, P., & Charleston, W. (1979).
>
> Aaron, P., & Zorn, C. R. (1982).

☐ Entries by the same authors should be arranged by year of publication, in chronological order:

> Aaron, P., & Charleston, W. (1979).
>
> Aaron, P., & Charleston, W. (1984).

☐ Entries by the same author(s) with the same publication year should be arranged alphabetically by title (excluding *A*, *An*, *The*), and low-ercase letters (*a*, *b*, *c*, and so on) should follow the year in parentheses:

> Aaron, P. (1985a). Basic . . . .
>
> Aaron, P. (1985b). Elements . . . .

The essential difference between the MLA and APA styles of listing sources is the order in which the information is presented. The MLA follows this order: author's name; title; publication source, year, and page. The APA puts the year after the author's name. The examples that follow indicate other minor differences in capitalization and arrangement between the two documentation styles.

BOOKS

A book by a single author

MLA Simon, Kate. Bronx Primitive. New York: Harper, 1982.

APA Simon, Kate. (1982). Bronx primitive. New York: Harper and Row.

A book by an agency or corporation

MLA Association for Research in Nervous and Mental Disease. The Circulation of the Brain and Spinal Cord: A Symposium on Blood Supply. New York: Hafner, 1966.

APA Association for Research in Nervous and Mental Disease. (1966). The circulation of the brain and spinal cord: A symposium on blood supply. New York: Hafner Publishing Co.

A book by two authors

MLA   Strunk, W., Jr., and E. B. White. <u>The Elements of Style</u>. 4th ed. New York: Macmillan, 1983.

APA   Strunk, W., Jr., & White, E. B. (1983). <u>The elements of style</u>. (4th ed.). New York: Macmillan.

A book by three or more authors

MLA   Dyal, James A., William C. Corning, and Dale M. Willows. <u>Readings in Psychology: The Search for Alternatives.</u> 3rd ed. New York: McGraw-Hill, 1975.

OR   Dyal, James A., et al. <u>Readings in Psychology: The Search for Alternatives</u>. 3rd ed. New York: McGraw-Hill, 1975.

APA   Dyal, James A., Corning, William C., & Willows, Dale M. (1975). <u>Readings in psychology: The search for alternatives</u>. (3rd ed.). New York: McGraw-Hill.

A book by an unknown author

Use title in place of author.

MLA   <u>College Bound Seniors</u>. Princeton, NJ: College Board Publications, 1979.

APA   <u>College bound seniors</u>. (1979). Princeton, NJ: College Board Publications.

An edition prepared by a named editor

APA   Arnold, Matthew. <u>Culture and anarchy</u>. (J. Dover Wilson, Ed.). Cambridge: Cambridge University Press, 1966. (Originally published, 1869.)

If you refer to the text itself, begin with the author:

MLA   Arnold, Matthew. <u>Culture and Anarchy</u>. Ed. J. Dover Wilson. Cambridge: Cambridge UP, 1966.

If you cite the editor in your text, begin with the editor:

MLA   Wilson, J. Dover, ed. <u>Culture and Anarchy</u>. By Matthew Arnold. Cambridge: Cambridge UP, 1966.

An anthology

MLA   Dertouzos, Michael L., and Joel Moses, eds. <u>The Computer Age: A Twenty-Year View</u>. Cambridge, MA: MIT, 1979.

APA   Dertouzos, Michael L., & Moses, Joel. (Eds.). (1979). <u>The computer age: A twenty-year view</u>. Cambridge, MA: MIT Press.

A translation

APA   Tolstoy, Leo. (1972). <u>War and Peace</u>. (Constance Garnett, Trans.). London: Pan Books. (Originally published 1868–1869).

If you are referring to the work itself, begin with the author:

MLA   Tolstoy, Leo. <u>War and Peace</u>. Trans. Constance Garnett. London: Pan, 1972.

If you cite the translator in your text, begin the entry with the translator's name:

MLA   Garnett, Constance, trans. <u>War and Peace</u>. By Leo Tolstoy. London: Pan, 1972.

A work in an anthology

MLA   Faulkner, William. ''Dry September.'' <u>Literature: The Human Experience</u>. Ed. Richard Abcarian and Marvin Klotz. New York: St. Martin's, 1983. 549–557.

OR   Bell, Daniel. ''The Social Framework of the Information Society.'' In <u>The Computer Age: A Twenty-Year View</u>. Ed. Michael L. Dertouzos and Joel Moses. Cambridge, MA: MIT, 1979. 163–211.

APA   Bell, Daniel. (1979). The social framework of the information society. In Michael L. Dertouzos and Joel Moses (Eds.), <u>The computer age: A twenty-year view</u> (pp. 163–211). Cambridge, MA: MIT.

An essay in an anthology by the same author

MLA   Weaver, Richard. ''The Rhetoric of Social Science.'' In his <u>Ethics of Rhetoric</u>. South Bend, Indiana: Gateway, 1953, 186–210.

APA   Weaver, Richard. (1953). The rhetoric of social science. In Weaver, Richard, <u>Ethics of rhetoric</u> (pp. 186–210). South Bend, Indiana: Gateway Editions.

ARTICLES

An article in a journal with continuous annual pagination

MLA   Dworkin, Ronald. ''Law as Interpretation.'' <u>Critical Inquiry</u> 9 (1982): 179–200.

APA   Dworkin, Ronald. (1982). Law as interpretation. <u>Critical Inquiry</u>, <u>9</u>, 179–200.

An article in a journal that paginates each issue separately

MLA   Festinger, Leon. ''Cognitive Dissonance.'' <u>Scientific American</u> 2 (Oct. 1962): 93–102.

APA   Festinger, Leon. (1962, October). Cognitive dissonance. <u>Scientific American</u>, <u>2</u>, 93–102.

An article from a daily newspaper

MLA Lubin, J. S. "On Idle: The Unemployed Shun Much Mundane Work, at Least for a While." <u>The Wall Street Journal</u> 5 December 1980: 1, 25.

APA Lubin, J. S. (1980, December 5). On idle: The unemployed shun much mundane work, at least for a while. <u>The Wall Street Journal</u>, pp. 1, 25.

OTHER SOURCES

Computer software

MLA Hogue, Bill. <u>Miner 2049er</u>. Computer Software. Big Five Software.

OR <u>Microsoft Word</u>. Computer Software. Microsoft, 1984.

APA Hogue, Bill. (1982). <u>Miner 2049er</u>. [Computer program.]. Van Nuys, CA: Big Five Software.

OR <u>Microsoft Word</u>. (1984). [Computer program.]. Bellevue, WA: Microsoft.

Records and tapes

MLA Beethoven, Ludwig van. <u>Violin Concerto in D Major, op. 61</u>. Cond. Alexander Gauk. U. S. S. R. State Orchestra. David Oistrakh, violinist. Allegro, ACS 8044, 1980.

OR Springsteen, Bruce. "Dancing in the Dark." <u>Born in the U. S. A.</u> Columbia, QC 38653, 1984.

APA Beethoven, Ludwig van. (Composer). (1980). <u>Violin Concerto in D Major, op. 61.</u> (Cassette Recording No. ACS 8044). New York: Allegro.

OR Springsteen, Bruce. (Singer and Composer). (1984). "Dancing in the Dark." <u>Born in the U. S. A.</u> (Record No. QC 38653). New York: Columbia.

Interviews

MLA Lowell, Robert. "Robert Lowell." With Frederick Seidel. <u>Paris Review</u> 25 (Winter–Spring): 56–95.

OR Franklin, Anna. Personal Interview. 3 September 1983.

APA Lowell, Robert. [Interview with Frederick Seidel.]. <u>Paris Review</u>, <u>25</u>, (Winter–Spring), pp. 56–95.

OR Franklin, Anna. [Personal Interview.]. 3 September 1983.

A SAMPLE RESEARCH PAPER

Here is a student research paper on the effects of television viewing. To support the thesis that "television leaves the imprint of [its] distorted world on our consciousness, so much so that it becomes the world that we experience as real," the author cites seven different sources—books, articles, and a television program. He uses the new MLA documentation style and format.

AUTHOR IDENTIFICATION

Bruce Coughran

English 1

Ms. Brown

December 10, 1984

TITLE

Through the Eyes of Television:
A Look at Some Effects of Television Watching

2 DOUBLE SPACES

COMMON KNOWLEDGE

5-SPACE INDENTATION

Our modern society changes so rapidly that it is hard to imagine what life was like only a few generations ago. It is easy to forget that many of the things that we take so much for granted in our daily lives did not exist when some of our grandparents were born. Telephones, automobiles, airplanes, home electricity, radio and petroleum products all have come into popular use only in the last 75 years. These technological innovations have had a tremendous influence on our lives. In the last 25 years, scarcely one generation, a new technological marvel has grown into the very fabric of our society and has become its eyes, ears, heart and voice.

That technology is television. It reaches throughout our society at almost every level and forms a shared experience that almost becomes a social conscience. Television has become our main storyteller. We learn from it about our history and our present. It forms the basis for social norms, what is accepted and what is not. It increasingly is our marketplace, our social meeting ground, and even the place where our political battles are won or lost. It has become our link with the "outside

Coughran 2

world." We can sometimes forget that it is not a true reflection of our world, but one that is distorted by the race for ratings and advertising dollars. And yet, television leaves the imprint of this distorted world on our consciousness, so much so that it becomes the world that we experience as real.

Television occupies a place in our society that could scarcely be imagined 35 years ago when the first sets began to trickle into American homes. Television sets are found in 98% of American households, and the amount of time involved in TV viewing eclipses that of all other leisure activities except sleeping (Swerdlow 86). The average American home has a television set turned on for six hours every day, and it has been reported that a child, by age 15, will have spent more hours watching television than he will spend in the classroom (Swerdlow 88).

SOURCE OF STATISTIC CITED

What happens during all those hours in front of the set? We are bombarded with a constant stream of images, stories, characters and situations that create, in effect, a self-contained world. Although there appears to be a wide variety of programs, this world varies little from a few broad, widely held stereotypes (Comstock et al. 19). The world of TV consists of similar stories, situations and characters primarily because of the financial pressure on the modern television industry. Television's life blood is advertising revenue, and revenue is dependent on ratings. The television networks are increasingly unwilling to take any chances. They rely on proven formulas and material, and this leads to a total uniformity of the messages that television puts out.

SOURCE OF IDEA CITED

Despite the fact that the bulk of research on television has focused on its effects on children (particularly with respect to the influence of televised violence on antisocial behavior), a much broader aspect is less studied. This is the effect of television on the broad social consciousness. This aspect of television's impact has been called the "most pervasive

Coughran 3

SOURCE OF QUOTATION
CITED

and least well documented" (Swerdlow 96). The creation of concepts of
social reality, that is, the perception of "the way the world is," is heavily
influenced by television. As an example, most of us have definite ideas
about the process of law enforcement, what private detectives, doctors,
and lawyers do in their day-to-day lives. This is true in spite of the fact
that few of us have direct exposure to these situations. For many people,
these conceptions come increasingly from the situations that we encounter through the television tube.

These images come across as a total impression, the trappings of
an artificial environment where we live a portion of our daily lives.
They are not "learned" per se, as one would learn from educational
material (when one is consciously learning). These images and broad
concepts about the world seep into our consciousness, unfiltered by our
discrimination. Viewing, for almost all programs, is a passive activity,
in which thought or judgement is rarely exercised. In addition, most
television watching is habitual, and is done by the clock, not by the
program (Hawkins and Pingree 292), so that the effect is one of a constantly reinforced image of society that trickles into our minds, hour
after hour, year after year.

SOURCE OF INFORMATION
CITED

Not only is this image of society pervasive and easy to accept, it
is also very different from reality. Television is dominated by white
males in their "prime years," with the young and the old both under
represented in proportion to their percentage in the population (Comstock et al. 3). The same is true for blacks and other ethnic minorities
(Comstock et al. 3). In television's world, women tend to be under 35,
and men tend to be over 35. As women get older on television, they
become less successful, whereas men become more successful as they
age ("Television" 7).

The distribution of occupations is also radically different in the world of television. Prime time TV shows contain about ten times as many doctors and lawyers, twenty five times as many judges and policemen, and fifty times as many private investigators as occur in the general population. Blue collar workers are greatly under represented, making up 9.9% of the characters on prime time shows and 49.7% of the general population (Swerdlow 93).

Violence has been a hotbed of research and the evidence is irrefutable that television portrays a much more violent world than one would otherwise conclude from statistics or everyday experiences. Violence occupies a central place in many television shows, from crime dramas to children's Saturday morning cartoons. Violence is often committed by the "heroes" of television dramas. The use of violent, socially disapproved or even illegal methods in order to achieve socially approved ends is a common theme (Comstock et al. 4). The average rate of violent acts is between six and ten per hour (Gerbner et al. 184). This creates an aggregate pattern of violence that is perceived as an integral part of society. Fully 64% of the main characters on prime time TV (and 30% of all characters) are involved in some type of violent act as either a perpetrator or a victim, or both (Gerbner et al. 194). This is in sharp contrast to the actual census data indicating a rate of violent crimes of .32 per 100 persons (a third of one percent) (Gerbner et al. 194).

It is easy to dismiss the wide discrepancies between television portrayals and real life as an inherent quality of fiction, which may make it more interesting. There is, however, at least some evidence that many of the aspects of the television world are accepted as accurate by a significant number of people. Studies have shown that children tend to believe that television is an accurate representation of reality, and many teenagers believe that television shows life "the way it really is"

Coughran 5

(Swerdlow 97). One study even indicated that real life experience failed to change the perceived reality of television; in other words, television seemed "truer" than personal experience (Swerdlow 97).

In addition, it has been suggested that TV trivializes violence, making it more likely that people will accept violence and violent behavior ("Television" 8). Television shows frequently portray extremely violent situations: fights, beatings, rape and murder. These are situations that arouse powerful emotions in us. Just when these emotions are starting to rise, it is time for a commercial. The viewer's attention goes from the horror of rape or murder in one moment to "BAN underarm deodorant" in the next. This has the effect of defusing our most powerful emotional responses to these violent acts. Studies have shown that although television can be a powerful teacher of how activities are performed ("mechanics"), it is a very weak teacher of the emotional responses that accompany those actions (McGinley and Murray 257–58). We learn about violence from the TV, but without the strong emotional responses that accompany the actual experience of violence.

There are even some indications that the role models portrayed on television are emulated by society (Swerdlow 97). George Gerbner, who has studied the effects of television on society for some fifteen years at the University of Pennsylvania, says: "Increasingly, media cultivated facts and values have become standards by which we judge even personal experiences and family and community behavior" (193). Many people report that life is not as exciting as it is "supposed to be" (Swerdlow 98). Physicians and medical schools speak about the "Marcus Welby" syndrome. Many people have an idyllic view of doctors. As patients, they expect quick, easy cures at little cost or inconvenience. As prospective medical students, they expect to find easy answers, never make mistakes, and have lower levels of stress than is possible in most medical careers. A recent study shows that many police detectives follow procedures similar to those shown on television, not in order to catch criminals, but to satisfy the public image of how they "should" behave (Swerdlow 97).

There has been relatively little attention paid to TV's "culturization" effects (i.e., how television is shaping the individual's self image, social image, and the culture in which he lives). This is partly due to the lack of recognition that such a process is taking place, but it is also due to the inherent experimental problems involved. Experiments are most easily performed on isolated subjects, short time scales, and easily measured effects. The types of effects we are talking about occur over years and are difficult to detect.

Perhaps the most serious problem is the lack of a scientific "control" group. Since virtually all members of society are exposed to at least some television on a regular basis, it is impossible to compare "non-viewers" with "viewers." Non-viewers are, almost by definition, abnormal. It is necessary to resort to comparing light viewers with heavy viewers (according to the number of hours per day of television exposure). This can present an inherent problem since heavy television viewing can be correlated with other factors such as race, education, age, and employment status (Hughes 291). These factors must be taken into account, and it is difficult to know if there are others that have not been identified.

There is also the problem of eliminating the possibility of "reverse causation." For example, if heavy television viewers are more violent, is it because heavy TV viewing makes one more prone to violence, or that those who are more prone to violence tend to watch more television? Also, how can more subtle effects be detected?

There is a technique that was developed by Dr. George Gerbner of

Coughran 7

the University of Pennsylvania to try to measure the socialization effects. Gerbner formulated questions that dealt with aspects of society that are skewed on TV relative to the real world. He asked people questions about the world and about their television watching habits. His findings show that those who watch more television tend to adopt TV's warped picture of the world, i.e., they tend to give the "television answers" to questions about the real world.

Gerbner surveyed thousands of people during the last fifteen years as to their viewing habits and asked them questions about their world. In apparent accord with the distortions of the world projected by television, heavy viewers were more prone to overestimate the number of people involved in law enforcement, and the number of times police use violence in their work (Gerbner et al. 195). They were also more prone to overestimate the number of people who are involved with crimes, and the proportion of crimes that are violent ("Television" 7).

Coinciding with the under representation of older people, heavy viewers were more likely to believe that the population of elderly persons is declining (Swerdlow 93), (it is not), and were more likely to view the elderly in an unfavorable light ("Television" 7).

Moreover, the surveys showed that the people who watched large amounts of television experienced more fear of victimization, and thought of the world as being a more violent place than those who watched less television. Heavy viewers tended to overestimate their chances of being involved in violence (Gerbner et al. 195). They were also more likely to say that they were afraid to walk alone at night, and were more likely to buy guns, locks, and dogs for protection (Gerbner et al. 196–99). In addition, heavy viewers were more likely to approve of violence as a means of solving problems than were light viewers (Gerbner et al. 196).

Heavy television watchers also tended to score higher on tests of suspicion and mistrust. They were more likely to say that most people only look out for themselves, take advantage of others, and cannot be trusted (Gerbner et al. 195). More heavy viewers than light viewers tended to say that "you can't be too careful" when dealing with people.

Gerbner presents strong evidence that people who watch large amounts of television do seem to live in a world that is more violent, where people are less trustworthy, and where crime is more to be feared, than their neighbors who watch less television. It seems reasonable, even probable, that other more subtle aspects of our perceived world are also heavily influenced by our exposure to television's distorted images.

Television pervades our entire society. Our children will learn more about the way the world is from the television than they will from any other source, their parents included. We must increasingly become aware of the effects of this new guest in our homes, and seek to counteract some of its effects. We must strive to regain a sense of community and family, to regain that experience that we call reality.

Television will not go away. If anything, its influence will increase in the next decade as new technologies such as cable and satellite reception become commonplace. But what is needed is an understanding and an appreciation of the effects of television on one's experience of the wider world, and the knowledge that television is not always to be believed. We must retain our sense of reality apart from the world of TV, and this will only come with the recognition of the detrimental effects of habitual heavy TV viewing. Just as was the case with cigarette smoking, a widespread awareness of TV's detrimental effects will not eliminate this habitual (it has even been called addictive) behavior. However, without the widespread knowledge that television viewing in

Coughran 9

large amounts *has* harmful effects, its beneficial potentialities cannot
begin to be exploited.

Works Cited

Comstock, George, et al. Television and Human Behavior. New York:
    Columbia UP, 1978.

Gerbner, George, et al. "Cultural Indicators: Violence Profile No. 9." Journal
    of Communication (Summer 1978): 176–207.

Hawkins, Robert and Suzanne Pingree. "Uniform Messages and Habitual
    Viewing: Unnecessary Assumptions in Social Reality Effects." Human Communication Research 7 (1981): 291–301.

Hughes, Michael. "The Fruits of Cultivation Analysis: A Reexamination
    of Some Effects of Television Watching." Public Opinion Quarterly
    44 (1980): 287–302.

McGinley, Hugh and Robert Murray. "Paired-Associate and Emotional
    Learning Through Television Modeling." Journal of General Psychology 100 (1979): 251–58.

"The Television Explosion." Nova. Transcript. PBS. WGBH, Boston. 14
    Feb. 1982.

Swerdlow, Joel. "A Question of Impact." Wilson Quarterly (Winter 1981):
    86–99.

5-SPACE INDENTATION

2 SPACES

PART FOUR

Writing under Pressure

Essay Examinations

Even though the machine-scorable multiple-choice test has sharply reduced the number of essay exams administered in schools and colleges, you can be certain that essay exams will continue to play a significant role in the education of liberal arts students. Many instructors—especially in the humanities and social sciences—still believe an exam that requires you to write is the best way to find out what you have learned and, more important, how you can use what you have learned. Instructors who give essay exams want to be sure you can sort through the large body of information covered in a course, identify what is important or significant, and explain your decision. They want to see whether you understand the concepts that provide the basis for a course and whether you can use those concepts to interpret specific materials, to make connections on your own, to see relationships, to draw comparisons and contrasts, to synthesize diverse information in support of an original assertion. They may even be interested in your ability to justify your own evaluations based on appropriate criteria and to argue your own opinions with convincing evidence. Your instructors hope they are encouraging you to think more critically and analytically about a subject; they feel a written exam best allows you to demonstrate that you are doing so.

As a college student, then, you will be faced with a variety of essay exams, from short-answer essays of a few sentences to take-home exams which may require hours of planning and writing. You will find that the writing activities and strategies discussed in Parts I and II of this book—particularly explaining, arguing, defining, comparing and contrasting, and illustrating—as well as the mapping strategies in Chapter 18—clustering, listing, and outlining—describe the skills that will help you do well on all sorts of these exams. This chapter proposes some more specific guidelines for you to follow in preparing for and writing essay exams, and analyzes a group of typical exam questions to help you determine which strategies will be most useful. But you can also learn a great deal from your experiences with essay exams in the past, the embarrassment and frustration of doing poorly on one and the great pleasure and pride of doing well. Do you recall the very best exam you ever wrote? Do you remember how you wrote it and why you were able to do so well? How can you be certain to approach such writing tasks confidently and to complete them successfully? Keep these questions in mind as you consider the following guidelines.

PREPARING FOR AN EXAM

First of all, essay exams require a comprehensive understanding of large amounts of information. Since exam questions can reach so far and wide into the course materials—and in such unpredictable ways—you cannot hope to do well on them if you are not keeping up with readings and assignments from the beginning of the course. Do the reading, go to lectures, take careful notes, participate in discussion sections, organize small study groups with classmates to explore and review course materials throughout the semester. Trying to cram weeks of information into a single night of study will never allow you to do your best.

Then, as an exam approaches, find out what you can about the form it will take. There is little that is more irritating to instructors than the pestering inquiry, "Do we need to know this for the exam?"; but it is generally legitimate to ask whether the questions will require short or long answers, how many questions there will be, whether you may choose which questions to answer, and what kinds of thinking and writing will be required of you. Some instructors may hand out study guides for exams, or even lists of potential questions. However, beyond a sense of how the exam will be structured, you will often be on your own in determining how best to go about studying.

Try to avoid simply memorizing information aimlessly. As you study, you should be clarifying the important issues of the course and using these issues to focus your understanding of specific facts and particular readings. If the course is a historical survey, distinguish the primary periods and try to see relations among the periods and the works or events that define them. If the course is thematically unified, determine how the particular materials you have been reading express those themes. If the course is a broad introduction to a general topic, concentrate on the central concerns of each study unit and see what connections you can discover among the various units. Try to place all you have learned into perspective, into a meaningful context. How do the pieces fit together? What fundamental ideas have the readings, the lectures, and the discussions seemed to emphasize? How can those ideas help you digest the information the course has covered?

One good way to prepare yourself for an exam is by making up questions you think the instructor might give and then planning answers to them with classmates. Returning to your notes and to assigned readings with specific questions in mind can help enormously in your process of understanding. The important thing to remember is that an essay exam tests more than your memory of specific information; it requires you to use specific information to demonstrate a comprehensive grasp of the topics covered in the course.

READING THE EXAM CAREFULLY

Before you answer a single question, read the entire exam and apportion your time realistically. Pay particular attention to how many points you may earn in different parts of the exam; notice any directions that suggest how long an answer should be or how much space it should take up. As you are doing so, you may wish to make tentative choices of the questions you will answer and decide on the order in which you will answer them. If you have immediate ideas about how you would organize any of your answers, you might also jot down partial scratch outlines. But before you start to complete any answers, write down the actual clock time you expect to be working on each question or set of questions. Careful time management is crucial to your success on essay exams; giving some time to each question is always better than using up your time on only a few and never getting to others.

You will next need to analyze each question carefully before beginning to write your answer. Decide what you are being asked to do. It can be easy at this point to become flustered, to lose concentration, even to go blank, if your immediate impulse is to cast about for ideas indiscriminately. But if you first look closely at what the question is directing you to do and try to understand the sort of writing that will be required, you can begin to recognize the structure your answer will need to take. This tentative structure will help focus your attention on the particular information that will be pertinent to your answer.

Consider this question from a sociology final:

Drawing from lectures on the contradictory aspects of American values, discussions of the "bureaucratic personality" and the type of behavior associated with social mobility, discuss the problems of bettering one-self in a relatively "open" complex, industrial society such as the United States.

Such a question can cause momentary panic, but nearly always you can define the writing task you face. Look first at the words that give you directions: *draw from* and *discuss*. The term *discuss* is fairly vague, of course, but here it probably invites you to list and explain the problems of bettering oneself. The problems are already identified in the opening phrases: contradictory values, bureaucratic personality, certain behavior. Therefore, you would plan to begin with an assertion (or thesis) which included the key words in the final clause (open, complex, industrial society) and then take up each problem—and maybe still other problems you can think of—in separate paragraphs.

This question essentially calls for recall, organization, and clear presentation of facts from lectures and readings. Though it looks confusing at first, once it is sorted out, it contains the key terms for the answer's thesis, as well as its main points of development. In the next section are some further examples of the kinds of questions often found on essay exams. Pay particular attention to how the directions and the key words in each case can help you define the writing task involved.

SOME TYPICAL ESSAY EXAM QUESTIONS

Following are nine categories of exam questions, divided according to the sort of writing task involved and illustrated by examples. You will notice that, although the wording of the examples in a category may differ, the essential directions are very much the same.

All of the examples are unedited and were written by instructors in six different departments in the humanities and social sciences at two different state universities. Drawn from short quizzes, mid-terms, and final exams for a variety of freshman and sophomore courses, these questions demonstrate the range of essays you may be expected to write.

Define or identify Some questions require you to write a few sentences defining or identifying material from readings or lectures. Almost always such questions allow you only a very few minutes to complete your answer.

You may be asked for a brief overview of a large topic, as in Question 22.1. This question, from a twenty-minute quiz in a literature course, could have earned as much as 15 of the 100 points possible on the quiz:

Question 22.1

Name and describe the three stages of African literature.

Answering this question would simply involve following the specific directions. A student would probably *name* the periods in historical order and then *describe* each period in a separate sentence or two.

Other questions, like 22.2, will supply a list of more specific items to identify. This example comes from a final exam in a communications course, and the answer to each part was worth as much as 4 points on a 120-point exam.

Question 22.2

Define and state some important facts concerning each of the following:
  A. Demographics
  B. Instrumental model
  C. RCA
  D. Telephone booth of the air
  E. Penny Press

With no more than three or four minutes for each part, students taking this exam would offer a concise definition (probably in a sentence). Then that definition would be expanded with facts relevant to the main topics in the course.

Sometimes the list of items to be identified can be quite complicated, including quotes, concepts, and specialized terms; it may also be worth a significant number of points. The next example illustrates the first five items in a list of fifteen that opened a literature final. Each item was worth 3 points, for a total of 45 out of a possible 130 points.

Question 22.3

Identify each of the following items:
  1. projection
  2. "In this vast landscape he had loved so much, he was alone."
  3. Balducci
  4. *pied noir*
  5. the Massif Central

Although the directions do not say so specifically, it is crucial here not only to identify each item but to explain its significance in terms of the overall subject, as well. In composing a definition or identification, always ask yourself a simple question: Why is this item important enough to appear on the exam?

Recall details of a specific source   Sometimes instructors will ask for a straightforward summary or paraphrase of a specific source—a report, for example, or a book or film. Such questions hold the student to recounting details directly from the source and do not encourage interpretation or evaluation. In this example from a mid-term exam in a sociology course, students were allowed about ten minutes and required to complete the answer on one lined page provided with the exam.

Question 22.4

In his article, "Is There a Culture of Poverty?", Oscar Lewis addresses a popular question in the social sciences. What is "the culture of poverty?" How is it able to come into being, according to Lewis? That is, under what conditions does it exist? When does he say a person is no longer a part of the culture of poverty? What does Lewis say is the future of the culture of poverty?

The phrasing here invites a fairly clearcut structure. Each of the five specific questions can be turned into an assertion and illustrated with evidence from Lewis's book. For example, the first two questions could become assertions like these: "Lewis defines the culture of poverty as _____ ," and "According to Lewis the culture of poverty comes into being through _____ ." The important thing in this case is to stick closely to an accurate summary of what the writer said and not waste time evaluating or criticizing his ideas.

Explain the importance or significance

Another kind of essay exam question asks students to explain the importance or significance of something covered in the course. Such questions require you to use specific examples as the basis for a more general discussion of what has been studied. This will often involve interpreting a literary work by concentrating on a particular aspect of it, as in Question 22.5. This question was worth 10 out of 100 points and was to be answered in 75 to 100 words:

Question 22.5

In the last scene in *The Paths of Glory*, the owner of a cafe brings a young German girl onto a small stage in his cafe to sing for the French troops, while Colonel Dax looks on from outside the cafe. Briefly explain the significance of this scene in relation to the movie as a whole.

In answering this question, a student's first task would be to reconsider the whole movie, looking for ways this one small scene illuminates or explains larger issues or themes. Then, in a paragraph or two, the student would summarize these themes and point out how each element of the specific scene fits into the overall context.

You may also be asked to interpret specific information to show that you understand the fundamental concepts of a course. The following example from a communications mid-term was worth a possible 10 of 100 points and was allotted twenty minutes of exam time.

Question 22.6

Chukovsky gives many examples of cute expressions and statements uttered by small children. Give an example or two of the kind of statements that he finds interesting. Then state their implications for understanding the nature of language in particular and communications more generally.

Here, the student must start by choosing examples of children's utterances from Chukovsky's book. These examples would then provide the basis for demonstrating one's grasp of the larger subject.

Questions like these are usually more challenging than definition and summary questions because you must decide for yourself the significance or importance or implications of the information. You must also consider how best to organize your answer so that the general ideas you need to communicate are clearly developed.

Apply concepts to works   Very often courses in the humanities and social sciences emphasize significant themes, ideologies, or concepts. A common essay exam question asks students to apply the concepts to works studied in the course. Rather than setting up specific information to be interpreted more generally, such questions will provide you with a general idea and require you to illustrate it with specific examples from your reading.

On a final exam in a literature course, an instructor posed this writing task. It was worth 50 points out of 100, and students had about an hour to complete it.

Question 22.7

Many American writers have portrayed their characters or their poetic speaker as being engaged in a quest. The quest may be explicit or implicit, external or psychological, and it may end in failure or success. Analyze the quest motif as it appears in the work of four of the following writers: Edwards, Franklin, Hawthorne, Thoreau, Douglass, Whitman, Dickinson, James, Twain.

On another literature final, the following question was worth 45 of 130 points. Students had about forty-five minutes to answer it.

Question 22.8

Several of the works studied in this course depict scapegoat figures. Select two written works and two films and discuss how their authors or directors present and analyze the social conflicts that lead to the creation of scapegoats.

Question 22.7 instructs students to *analyze,* Question 22.8 to *discuss;* yet the answers for each would be structured very similarly. An introductory paragraph would define the concept—the *quest* or a *scapegoat*—and refer to the works to be discussed. Then a paragraph or two would be devoted to each of the four separate works, developing specific evidence to illustrate the concept. A concluding paragraph would probably attempt to bring the concept into clearer focus, which is, after all, the point of answering these questions.

Comment on a quotation

On essay exams, instructors will often ask students to comment on quotations they are seeing for the first time. Usually such quotations will express some surprising or controversial opinion that complements or challenges basic principles or ideas in the course. Sometimes the writer being quoted is identified, sometimes not. In fact, it is not unusual for instructors to write the quotation themselves.

A student choosing to answer the following question from a literature final would have risked half the exam—in points and time—on the outcome.

Question 22.9

Argue for or against this thesis: "In *A Clockwork Orange,* both the heightened, poetic language and the almost academic concern with moral and political theories deprive the story of most of its relevance to real life."

The directions here clearly ask for an argument. A student would need to set up a thesis indicating that the novel either is or is not relevant to real life, and then point out how its language and its theoretical concerns can be viewed in light of this thesis.

The next example comes from a mid-term exam in a history course. Students had forty minutes to write their answers, which could earn as much as 70 points on a 100-point exam.

Question 22.10

"Some historians believe that economic hardship and oppression breed social revolt; but the experience of the United States and Mexico between 1900 and 1920 suggests that people may rebel also during times of prosperity."

Comment on this statement. Why did large numbers of Americans and Mexicans wish to change conditions in their countries during the years from 1900 to 1920? How successful were their efforts? Who benefited from the changes that took place?

Although here students are instructed to "comment," the three questions suggest evidence to be used in constructing an argument. Just as in Question 22.9, a successful answer will require a clear thesis stating a position on the views expressed in the quotation, specific reasons to support that thesis, and evidence from readings and lectures to argue for the reasons. In general, whether you agree or disagree with the quotation is not as important as whether you can argue your case reasonably and convincingly, demonstrating a firm grasp of the subject matter.

Compare and contrast   It could well be that instructors' most favored essay exam question is one which requires a comparison or contrast of two or three principles, ideas, works, activities, or phenomena. This kind of question requires you to explore fully the relations between things of importance in the course, to analyze each thing separately and then search out specific points of likeness or difference. Students must, thus, show a thorough knowledge of the things being compared, as well as a clear understanding of the basic issues on which comparisons and contrasts can be made.

Often, as in Question 22.11, the basis of comparison will be limited to a particular focus; here, for example, two works are to be compared in terms of their views of colonialism.

Question 22.11

Compare and analyze the views of colonialism presented in Memmi's *The Colonizer and the Colonized* and Pontecorvo's *The Battle of Algiers*. Are there significant differences between these two views?

Sometimes, however, instructors will simply identify what is to be compared, leaving students the task of choosing the basis of the comparison, as in the next three examples from a communications exam, a history exam, and a literature exam.

Question 22.12

In what way is the stage of electronic media fundamentally different from all the major stages that preceded it?

Question 22.13

What was the role of the United States in Cuban affairs from 1898 until 1959? How did our role there compare with our role in the rest of Spanish America during the same period?

Question 22.14

Write an essay on one of the following topics:
1. Squire Western and Mr. Knightley
2. Dr. Primrose and Mr. Elton

Whether the point of comparison is stated in the question or left for you to define for yourself, it is important that your answer be limited to those aspects of likeness or difference that are most relevant to the general concepts or themes covered in the course. (A thorough discussion of this writing strategy is in Chapter 17: Comparing and Contrasting.)

Synthesize information from various sources

In a course with several assigned readings, an instructor may give students an essay exam question which requires them to pull together (to synthesize) information from all the readings.

The following example was one of four required questions on a final exam in a course in Third World studies. Students had about thirty minutes to complete their answer.

Question 22.15

On the basis of the articles read on El Salvador, Nicaragua, Peru, Chile, Argentina, and Mexico, what would you say are the major problems confronting Latin America today? Discuss the major types of problems with references to particular countries as examples.

This question asks students to do a lot in thirty minutes. They must first decide which major problems to discuss, which countries to include in each discussion, and how to use evidence from many readings to develop their answers. A carefully developed forecasting statement will be essential to developing a coherent essay.

Summarize and explain causes or results

In humanities and social science courses much of what students study concerns the causes or results of trends, actions, and events. Hence, it is not too surprising to find questions about causes and results on essay exams. Sometimes the instructor expects students to recall causes or results from readings and lectures. At other times, the instructor may not have in mind any particular causes or results and wants to find out what students are able to propose.

These examples come from mid-term and final exams in literature, communications, and sociology courses:

Question 22.16

Why do Maurice and Jean not succumb to the intolerable conditions of the prison camp (the Camp of Hell) as most of the others do?

Question 22.17

Given that we occupy several positions in the course of our lives and given that each position has a specific role attached to it, what kinds of problems or dilemmas arise from those multiple roles and how are they handled?

Question 22.18

Explain briefly the relationship between the institution of slavery and the emergence of the blues as a new Afro-American musical expression.

Question 22.19

Analyze the way in which an uncritical promotion of the new information technology (computers, satellites, etc.) may support, unintentionally, the maintenance of the status quo.

These questions are presented in several ways ("why," "what kind of problem," "explain the relationship," "analyze the way"), but they all require a list of causes or results in the answer. The causes or results would be organized under a thesis statement, and each cause or result would be argued and supported with evidence from lectures or readings.

If you write the essays assigned in Chapter 6: Making Proposals and Chapter 8: Explaining Causes, you will be learning writing strategies for answering essay exam questions about causes or results.

Criticize or evaluate   Occasionally instructors will invite students to evaluate a concept or work. Nearly always they want more than opinion: they expect a reasoned, documented judgment based on appropriate criteria. Such questions not only test students' ability to recall and synthesize pertinent information; they also allow instructors to find out whether students can apply criteria taught in the course, whether they understand the standards of judgment that are basic to the subject matter.

On a final examination in a literature course a student might have chosen either one of the following questions about novels read in the course. Each would have been worth half the total points, with about an hour to answer it:

Question 22.20

Which has the more effective plot: *The Secret Agent* or *A Passage to India*?

Question 22.21

A Clockwork Orange and *The Comfort of Strangers* both attempt to examine the nature of modern decadence. Which does so more successfully?

To answer these questions successfully, students would obviously have to be very familiar with the novels under discussion. They would also have to establish criteria appropriate to evaluating an effective plot or a successful examination of modern decadence. Students would have to make a judgment favoring one novel over the other, give reasons for this judgment, and argue each reason with evidence from the novels. Since these questions require contrasts of one novel with another, they would also involve the writing strategies mentioned in the earlier section on comparing and contrasting.

This next question was worth 10 of 85 points in a communications course mid-term exam. Students were asked to answer the question "in two paragraphs."

Question 22.22

Eisenstein and Mukerji both argue that moveable print was important to the rise of Protestantism. Cole extends this argument to say that print set off a chain of events that was important to the history of the United States. Summarize this argument, and criticize any part of it if you choose.

Here students are asked to criticize or evaluate an argument in a course reading. The instructor wants to know what students think of this argument and also, even though he does not say so, why they judge it as they do. Answering this unwritten "why" part of the question is the challenge: students must come up with reasons appropriate to evaluating the arguments and with evidence to support their reasons.

Evaluative questions like these involve the same sorts of writing strategies as those discussed in Chapter 7: Making Evaluations.

PLANNING YOUR ANSWER

The amount of planning you do for a question will depend on how much time it is allotted and how many points it is worth. For short-answer definitions and identifications, a few seconds of thought will probably be sufficient. (Be careful not to puzzle too long over individual items like these. Skip over any you cannot recognize fairly quickly; often, answering other questions will help jog your memory.) For answers that require a paragraph or two, you may want to jot down several important ideas or specific examples to help focus your thoughts and give you a basis for organizing your information.

For longer answers, though, you will need to develop a much more definite strategy of organization. You have time for only one draft, so allow a reasonable period—as much as a quarter of the time allotted the question—for making notes, determining a thesis, and developing an outline. Jotting down pertinent ideas is a good way to begin; then you can plan your organization with a scratch outline (just a listing of points or facts) or a cluster (both of these are illustrated in Chapter 18: Invention and Inquiry).

For questions with several parts (different requests or directions, a sequence of questions) make a list of the parts so that you do not miss or minimize one part. For questions presented as questions (rather than directives) you might want to rephrase each question as a writing topic. These topics will often suggest how you should outline the answer.

You may have to try two or three outlines or clusters before you hit on a workable plan. But be realistic as you outline—you want a plan you can develop within the limited time allotted for your answer. Hence, your outline will have to be selective—not everything you know on the topic, but what you know that can be developed clearly within the time available.

WRITING YOUR ANSWER

As with planning, your strategy for writing depends on the length of your answer. For short identifications and definitions, it is usually best to start with a general identifying statement and then move on to describe specific applications or explanations. Two sentences will almost always suffice, but make sure you write complete sentences.

For longer answers, begin by stating your point (or thesis) clearly and explicitly. An essay exam is not an occasion for indirectness: you want to strive for focus, simplicity, and clarity. In stating your point and developing your answer use key terms from the question; it may look as though you are avoiding the question unless you use key terms (the same key terms) throughout your essay. If the question does not supply any key terms, you will find that you have provided your own by stating your main point. Use these key terms throughout the answer.

If you have devised a promising outline for your answer, then you will be able to forecast your overall plan and its sub-points in your opening sentences. Forecasting always impresses readers and has the very practical advantage of making your answer easier to read. You might also want to use briefer paragraphs than you ordinarily do and signal clear relations between paragraphs with transition phrases or sentences. Such strategies are illustrated fully in Chapter 5: Reporting Information and Chapter 11: Cueing the Reader.

As you begin writing your answer, freely strike out words or even sentences you want to change by drawing through them neatly with a single line. Do not stop to erase. Do not strike out with elaborate messy scratchings. Instructors do not expect flawless writing, but they are put off by unnecessary messiness.

As you move ahead with the writing, you will certainly think of new subpoints and new ideas or facts to include later in the paper. Stop briefly to make a note of these on your original outline. If you find that you want to add a sentence or two to sections you have already completed, write them sideways in the margin or at the top of the page, with a neat arrowed line to show where they fit in your answer.

Do not pad your answer with irrelevancies and repetitions just to fill up space. You may have had one instructor who did not seem to pay much attention to what you wrote, but most instructors read exams carefully and are not impressed by the length of an answer alone. Within the time available, write a comprehensive, specific answer without padding.

Watch the clock carefully to ensure that you do not spend too much time on one answer. You must be realistic about the time constraints of an essay exam, especially if you know the material well and are prepared to write a lot. If you write one dazzling answer on an exam with three required questions, you earn only 33 points, not enough to pass at most colleges. This may seem unfair, but keep in mind that instructors plan exams to be reasonably comprehensive. They want you to write about the course materials in two or three or more ways, not just one way.

If you run out of time when you are writing an answer, jot down the remaining main ideas from your outline, just to show that you know the material and with more time could have continued your exposition.

Write legibly and proofread. Remember that your instructor will likely be reading a large pile of exams. Careless scrawls, misspellings, omitted words, and missing punctuation (especially missing periods needed to mark the ends of sentences) will only make that reading difficult, even exasperating. A few seconds of careful proofreading can improve your grade.

MODEL ANSWERS TO SOME TYPICAL ESSAY EXAM QUESTIONS

Here we will analyze several successful answers and give you an opportunity to analyze one for yourself. These analyses, along with the information we have provided elsewhere in this chapter, should greatly improve your chances of writing successful answers.

Short answers   A literature mid-term exam opened with ten items to identify, each worth 3 points. Students had only about two minutes to identify each item. Here are three of freshman Brenda Gossett's identifications, each one earning her the full 3 points.

> *Rauffenstein:* He was the German general who was in charge of the castle where Boeldieu, Marical, and Rosenthal were finally sent in *The Grand Illusion*. He along with Boeldieu represented the aristocracy, which was slowly fading out at that time.

> *Iges Peninsula:* This peninsula is created by the Meuse River in France. It is there that the Camp of Hell was created in *The Debacle*. The Camp of Hell is where the French army was interned after the Germans defeated them in the Franco-Prussian War.

Pache: He was the "religious peasant" in the novel *The Debacle*. It was he who inevitably became a scapegoat when he was murdered by Loubet, LaPoulle, and Chouteau because he wouldn't share his bread with them.

The instructor said only "identify the following" but clearly wanted both identification and significance of the item to the work in which it appeared. Gossett gives him both and gets full credit. She mentions particular works, characters, and events. Though she is very rushed, she answers in complete sentences. She does not misspell any words or leave out any commas or periods. Her answers are complete and correct.

Paragraph-length answers　One question on a weekly literature quiz was worth 20 points of the total of 100. With only a few minutes to answer the question, students were instructed to "answer in a few sentences." Here is the question and Camille Prestera's answer:

In *Things Fall Apart,* how did Okonkwo's relationship with his father affect his attitude toward his son?

Okonkwo despised his father, who was lazy, cowardly, and in debt. Okonkwo tried to be everything his father wasn't. He was hard-working, wealthy, and a great warrior and wrestler. Okonkwo treated his son harshly because he was afraid he saw the same weaknesses in Nwoye that he despised in his father. The result of this harsh treatment was that Nwoye left home.

Prestera begins by describing Okonkwo and his father, contrasting the two sharply. Then she explains Okonkwo's relationship with his son Nwoye. Her answer is coherent and straightforward.

Long answers　On final exams, at least one question requiring an essay-length answer is not uncommon. John Pixley had an hour to plan and write this essay for a final exam in a literature course.

Question

Many American writers have portrayed their characters or their poetic speaker as being engaged in a quest. The quest may be explicit or implicit, external or psychological, and it may end in failure or success. Analyze the quest motif as it appears in the work of four of the following writers: Edwards, Franklin, Hawthorne, Thoreau, Douglass, Whitman, Dickinson, James, Twain.

John Pixley's Answer

Americans pride themselves on being ambitious and on being able to strive for goals and to tap their potentials. Some say that this is what the "American Dream" is all about. It is important for one to do and be all that one is capable of. This entails a quest or search for identify, experience, and happiness. Hence,

Key term (*quest*) is mentioned in introduction.

First writer is identified immediately.

Edwards's work and the details of his quest are presented.

Transition sentence identifies second writer. Key term is repeated.

Contrast with Edwards adds coherence to essay.

Another key term (*external*) from the question is included.

Franklin's particular kind of quest is described.

Transition sentence identifies third writer. Key term is repeated.

Comparison of Whitman to Edwards and Franklin sustains coherence of essay.

Whitman's quest is defined.

the idea of the quest is a vital one in America, and it can be seen as a theme throughout American literature.

In eighteenth-century Colonial America, Jonathan Edwards dealt with this theme in his autobiographical and personal writings. Unlike his fiery and hard-nosed sermons, these autobiographical writings present a sensitive, vulnerable man trying to find himself and his proper, satisfying place in the world. He is concerned with his spiritual growth, in being free to find and explore religious experience and happiness. For example, in *Personal Narrative*, he very carefully traces the stages of religious beliefs. He tells about periods of abandoned ecstasy, doubts, and rational revelations. He also notes that his best insights and growth came at times when he was alone in the wilderness, in nature. Edwards' efforts to find himself in relation to the world can also be seen in his "Observations of the Natural World," in which he relates various meticulously observed and described natural phenomena to religious precepts and occurrences. Here, he is trying to give the world and life, in which he is a part, some sense of meaning and purpose.

Although he was a contemporary of Edwards, Benjamin Franklin, who was very involved in the founding of the U.S. as a nation, had a different conception of the quest in his writings. He sees the quest as being one for practical accomplishment, success, and wealth. In his *Autobiography,* he stresses that happiness involves working hard to accomplish things, getting along with others, and establishing a good reputation. Unlike Edwards', his quest is external and bound up with society. He is concerned with his morals and behavior, but, as seen in Part 2 of the *Autobiography*, he deals with them in an objective, pragmatic, even statistical way, rather than in sensitive pondering. It is also evident in this work that Franklin, unlike Edwards, believes so much in himself and his quest that he is able to laugh at himself. His concern in this society can be seen in *Poor Richard's Almanac,* in which he gives practical advice on how to find success and happiness in the world, how to "be healthy, wealthy, and wise."

Still another vision of the quest can be seen in the poetry of Walt Whitman in the mid-nineteenth century. The quest that he portrays blends elements of those of Edwards and Franklin. In "Song of Myself," which clearly is autobiographical, the speaker emphasizes the importance of finding, knowing, and enjoying oneself as part of nature and the human community. He says that one should come to realize that one is lovable, just as are all other people and all of nature and life. This is a quest for sensitivity and awareness, as Edwards advocates, and for great self-confidence, as Franklin advocates. Along with Edwards, Whitman sees that peaceful isolation in nature is important; but he also sees the importance of interacting with people, as Franklin does. Being optimistic and feeling good—both in the literal and figurative sense—is the object of this quest. Unfortunately, personal disappointment and national crisis (i.e., the Civil War) shattered Whitman's sense of confidence, and he lost the impetus of this quest in his own life.

This theme of the quest can be seen in prose fiction as well as in poetry   5
and autobiography. One interesting example is "The Beast in the Jungle," a
short story written by Henry James around 1903. It is interesting in that the
principal character, John Marcher, not only fails in his life-long quest, but his
failure comes about in a most subtle and frustrating way. Marcher believes that
something momentous is going to happen in his future. He talks about his belief to only one person, a woman named May. May decides to befriend him for
life and watch with him for the momentous occurrence to come about, for "the
beast in the jungle" to "pounce." As time passes, May seems to know what this
occurrence is and eventually even says that it has happened; but John is still
in the dark. It is only long after May's death that the beast pounces on him in
his recognition that the "beast" was his failure to truly love May, the one
woman of his life, even though she gave him all the encouragement that she
possibly, decently could. Marcher never defined the terms of his quest until it
was too late. By just waiting and watching, he failed to find feeling and passion.
This tragic realization, as someone like Whitman would view it, brings John
Marcher's ruin.

As seen in these few examples, the theme of the quest is a significant one   6
in American literature. Also obvious is the fact that there are a variety of approaches to, methods used in, and outcomes of the quest. This is an appropriate
theme for American literature since Americans cherish the right to "the pursuit of happiness."

This is a strong answer for two reasons: (1) Pixley has the information
he needs, and (2) he has organized it carefully and presented it coherently
and correctly.

EXERCISE 22.1

The following essay was written by Don Hepler. He is answering the
same essay exam question as his classmate John Pixley. Analyze Hepler's
essay to discover whether it meets the criteria of a good essay exam answer.
Review the criteria earlier in this chapter under "Writing Your Answer"
and in the commentary on John Pixley's answer.

Try to identify the features of Hepler's essay which contribute to its
success.

Don Hepler's Answer

The quest motif is certainly important in American literature. By consider-   1
ing Franklin, Thoreau, Douglass, and Twain, we can see that the quest may be
explicit or implicit, external or psychological, a failure or a success. Tracing the
quest motif through these four authors seems to show a developing concern in
American literature with transcending materialism to address deeper issues. It
also reveals a drift toward ambiguity and pessimism.

Benjamin Franklin's quest, as revealed by his *Autobiography*, is for mate-   2 rial comfort and outward success. His quest may be considered an explicit one, because he announces clearly what he is trying to do: perfect a systematic approach for living long and happily. The whole *Autobiography* is a road map intended for other people to use as a guide; Franklin apparently meant rather literally for people to imitate his methods. He wrote with the assumption that his success was reproducible. He is possibly the most optimistic author in American literature, because he enjoys life, knows exactly *why* he enjoys life, and believes that anyone else willing to follow his formula may enjoy life as well.

By Franklin's standards, his quest is clearly a success. But his *Autobiography* portrays only an external, not a psychological success. This is not to suggest that Franklin was a psychological failure. Indeed, we have every reason to believe the contrary. But the fact remains that Franklin *wrote* only about external success; he never indicated how he really felt, emotionally. Possibly it was part of Franklin's over-riding optimism to assume that material comfort leads naturally to emotional fulfillment. 3

Henry David Thoreau presents a more multi-faceted quest. His *Walden* is, on the simplest level, the chronicle of Thoreau's physical journey out of town and into the woods. But the moving itself is not the focus of *Walden*. It is really more of a metaphor for some kind of spiritual quest going on within Thoreau's mind. Most of the action in *Walden* is mental, as Thoreau contemplates and philosophizes, always using the lake, the woods, and his own daily actions as symbols of higher, more eternal truths. This spiritual quest is a success, in that Thoreau is able to appreciate the beauty of nature, and to see through much of the sham and false assumptions of town life and blind materialism. 4

Thoreau does not leave us with nearly as explicit a "blueprint" for success as does Franklin. Even Franklin's plan is limited to people of high intelligence, personal discipline, and sound character; Franklin sometimes seems to forget that many human beings are in fact weak and evil, and so would stand little chance of success similar to his own. But at least Franklin's quest could be duplicated by another Franklin. Thoreau's quest is more problematic, for even as great a mystic and naturalist as Thoreau himself could not remain in the woods indefinitely. This points toward the idea that the real quest is all internal and psychological; Thoreau seems to have gone to the woods to develop a spiritual strength that he could keep and take elsewhere on subsequent dealings with the "real world." 5

The quest of Frederick Douglass was explicit, in that he needed physically to get north and escape slavery, but it was also implicit because he sought to discover and re-define himself through his quest, as did Thoreau. Douglass's motives were more sharply focused than either Franklin's or Thoreau's; his very humanness was at stake, as well as his physical well-being and possibly even his life. But Douglass also makes it clear that the most horrible part of slavery was the mental anguish of having no hope of freedom. His learning to read, and his maintenance of this skill, seems to have been as important as the 6 maintenance of his material comforts, of which he had very few. In a sense, Douglass's quest is the most psychological and abstract so far, because it is for the very essences of freedom and humanity, both of which were mostly taken for granted by Franklin and Thoreau. Also, Douglass's quest is the most pessimistic of the three; Douglass concludes that physical violence is the only way out, as he finds with the Covey incident.

Finally, Mark Twain's *Huckleberry Finn* is an example of the full range of   7 meaning that the quest motif may assume. Geographically, Huck's quest is very large. But again, there is a quest defined implicitly as well as one defined explicitly, as Huck (without consciously realizing it) searches for morality, truth, and freedom. Twain's use of the quest is ambiguous, even more so than the previous writers, because while he suggests success superficially (i.e., the "happily-ever-after" scene in the last chapter), he really hints at some sort of ultimate hopelessness inherent in society. Not even Douglass questions the good or evil of American society as deeply as does Twain; for Douglass, everything will be fine when slavery is abolished; but for Twain, the only solution is to "light out for the territories" altogether—and when Twain wrote, he knew that the territories were no more.

Twain's implicit sense of spiritual failure stands in marked contrast to   8 Franklin's buoyant confidence in material success. The guiding image of the quest, however, is central to American values and, consequently, a theme that these writers and others have adapted to suit their own vision.

EXERCISE 22.2

Analyze the following essay exam questions in order to decide what kind of writing task they present. What is being asked of the student as a learner in the course and as a writer? Given the time constraints of the exam in which this question appeared, what plan would you propose for writing the answer?

Following each question is the number of points it is worth and the amount of time allotted to answer it.

1. Cortazar is a producer of fantastic literature. Discuss first what fantastic literature is. Then choose four stories by Cortazar (any four) as examples and discuss the fantastic elements in these stories. Refer to the structure, techniques and narrative styles that he uses in these four stories. If you like, you may refer to more than four, of course. (Points: 30 of 100. Time: 40 of 150 minutes.)

2. During the course of the twentieth century, the United States has experienced three significant periods of social reform—the progressive era, the age of the Great Depression, and the decade of the 1960s. What were the sources of reform in each period? What were the most significant reform achievements of each period as well as the largest failings? (Points: 35 of 100. Time: 75 of 180 minutes.)

3. Since literature is both an artistic and ideological product, each writer comments on his material context through his writing.

a. What is Rulto's perspective of his Mexican reality and how is it portrayed through his stories?

b. What particular themes does he deal with, especially in these stories: "The Burning Plain," "Luvina," "They gave us the land," "Paso del Norte," and "Tell them not to kill me."

c. What literary techniques and structures does he use to convey his perspective? Refer to a specific story as an example.

(Points: 30 of 100. Time: 20 of 50 minutes.)

4. Why is there a special reason to be concerned about the influence of TV watching on kids? In your answer include a statement of:

a. Your own understanding of the *general communication principles* involved for any TV watcher.

b. What's special about TV and kids?

c. How advertisers and producers use this information. (You should draw from the relevant readings as well as lectures.)

(Points: 20 of 90. Time: 25 of 90 minutes.)

5. Analyze the autobiographical tradition in American literature, focusing on differences and similarities among authors and, if appropriate, changes over time. Discuss four authors in all. In adddition to the conscious autobiographers—Edwards, Franklin, Thoreau, Douglass—you may choose one or two figures from among the following fictional or poetic quasi-autobiographers: Hawthorne, Whitman, Dickinson, Twain. (Points: 50 of 120. Time: 60 of 180 minutes.)

6. How does the system of (media) sponsorship work and what, if any, ideological control do sponsors exert? Be specific and illustrative! (Points: 33 of 100. Time: 60 of 180 minutes.)

7. Several of the works studied in this course analyze the tension between myth and reality. Select two written works and two films and analyze how their authors or directors present the conflict between myth and reality and how they resolve it—if they resolve it. (Points: 45 of 130. Time: 60 of 180 minutes.)

8. *Man's Hope* is a novel about the Spanish Civil War written while the war was still going on. *La Guerre est Finie* is a film about Spanish revolutionaries depicting their activities nearly thirty years after the Civil War. Discuss how the temporal relationship of each of these works to the Civil War is reflected in the character of the works themselves and in the differences between them. (Points: 58 of 100. Time: 30 of 50 minutes.)

9. Write an essay on one of these topics: The role of the narrator in *Tom Jones* and *Pride and Prejudice* or Uncle Toby and Miss Bates (characters in two eighteenth-century novels). (Points: 33 of 100. Time: 60 of 180 minutes.)

Sonia Pitt-Rivers. Reprinted by permission of Harcourt Brace Jovanovich, Inc. and by permission of the estate of the late Sonia Brownell Orwell and Martin Secker & Warburg Ltd.

Simon, Kate. Excerpted from BRONX PRIMITIVE. Copyright © 1982 by Kate Simon. Reprinted by permission of Viking Penguin Inc.

Smith, Red. "Joe DiMaggio." From THE RED SMITH READER, by Red Smith, edited by Dave Anderson. Copyright © 1947 by The New York Herald Tribune, Inc. Reprinted by permission of Random House, Inc.

Tucker, Carll. "Fear of Dearth." © 1979 Saturday Review Magazine. Reprinted by permission.

Twain, Mark. Specified selections (approximately 1600 words) abridged from Chapters 2–4 of THE AUTOBIOGRAPHY OF MARK TWAIN edited by Charles Neider. Copyright © 1959 by The Mark Twain Company. Copyright © 1959 by Charles Neider. Reprinted by permission of Harper & Row, Publishers, Inc.

Twain, Mark. Excerpts from LIFE ON THE MISSISSIPPI by Mark Twain. Harper & Row, Publishers, Inc.

Walker, Alice. "The Civil Rights Movement: What Good Was It?" Copyright 1967 by Alice Walker. Reprinted from her volume IN SEARCH OF OUR MOTHERS' GARDENS by permission of Harcourt Brace Jovanovich, Inc.

White, E. B. "Death of a Pig." Specified selection from ESSAYS OF E. B. WHITE. Copyright 1947, © 1975 by E. B. White. Reprinted by permission of Harper & Row, Publishers, Inc.

Wolf, Fred A. "Galileo the First Active Observer." Slight abridgement from TAKING THE QUANTAM LEAP: THE NEW PHYSICS FOR NONSCIENTISTS by Fred Alan Wolf. Copyright © 1981 by Fred Alan Wolf. Reprinted by permission of Harper & Row, Publishers, Inc.

Author and Title Index

Subject Index